Sale and Hire Purchase

Sale and Hire Purchase

by

J. K. MACLEOD, LL.B., Ph.D.
Lecturer in Law at the University of Nottingham

LONDON

BUTTERWORTHS

1971

ENGLAND: BUTTERWORTH & CO. (PUBLISHERS) LTD.
                LONDON: 88 KINGSWAY, WC2B 6AB

AUSTRALIA: BUTTERWORTH & CO. (AUSTRALIA) LTD.
                SYDNEY: 586 PACIFIC HIGHWAY, NSW 2067
                MELBOURNE: 343 LITTLE COLLINS STREET, 3000
                BRISBANE: 240 QUEEN STREET, 4000

CANADA: BUTTERWORTH & CO. (CANADA) LTD.
                TORONTO: 14 CURITY AVENUE, 374

NEW ZEALAND: BUTTERWORTH & CO. (NEW ZEALAND) LTD.
                WELLINGTON: 26/28 WARING TAYLOR STREET, 1
                AUCKLAND: 35 HIGH STREET, 1

SOUTH AFRICA: BUTTERWORTH & CO. (SOUTH AFRICA) (PTY.) LTD.
                DURBAN: 152/154 GALE STREET

ISBN—Casebound: 0 406 62119 5
Limp: 0 406 62120 9

*Printed in Great Britain by Butler & Tanner Ltd.,
Frome and London*

Preface

In offering a work which does not appear to fit neatly into any of the existing subject "pigeon-holes", I should perhaps explain that it developed from a number of conclusions which I have drawn from teaching the law of sale to undergraduates over the last eight years. These conclusions are as follows—

1. Any course is of more interest to the students if it has a topical theme and can be related to its modern applications. It seems to me that today the two most important spheres of application of the law relating to sales of goods are (a) international sales and (b) the complex of transactions leading normally to a sale to a consumer; and that it might be that a more effective text-book could be produced by concentrating on one of these. I have chosen to concentrate primarily on the latter. (For comparative discussion of this subject, see Goode & Ziegel, *Hire Purchase and Conditional Sale*; and *Instalment Credit* (Ed. Diamond), especially Ch. 4.)

2. For the exposition to be meaningful, consumer sales must be set in their context—that is, in a discussion of the different ways in which consumers obtain the enjoyment of goods. This will necessarily cut across traditional subject boundaries, involving primarily sale and hire purchase, but including some other parts of contract, personal property and tort.

3. Sale and hire purchase virtually have the same economic end in view and should be seen together. Treatment in parallel, instead of the more normal discussion in series, should better display the similarities and distinctions that exist between the two forms of transaction and the statutory treatment of them.

4. Some authors try to isolate sale and hire purchase from their personal property background; but I have found it more satisfactory to set the subject in that context. At the same time, "personal property" seems to me too large and too fragmented to be able to form a good single academic course and the concept is so negative—being derived from contrast with "real property"—that it lacks cohesion and any unified principles which a student can grasp. I thought that it might be better to introduce students to personal property law *via* a theme.

5. It is a bad thing for students to be allowed to separate contract and tort from one another and from all else. Hence, I have not hesitated to pose problems which more properly belong to a traditional contract or tort course, and to indicate where those subjects overlap one another

(e.g. misrepresentations, or the chain of distribution from producer to consumer or remedies).

6. It should not be the function of a student's text-book to seek to provide all the answers. Hence, I have deliberately asked questions without always seeking to provide an answer. Further, I have referred extensively to other works in an attempt to familiarise students with these, whilst choosing for himself how far he will pursue discussions away from the basic theme. To those many works cited I readily acknowledge my debt.

Whilst the foregoing conclusions are my own, I would not have had the temerity to embark on the writing of this work without the encouragement of Professor Brian Hogan. Looking back over the five years during which it has been written, I am very conscious of the debt I owe to the many students who have persisted in asking awkward questions, and to my colleagues on the staff of the Nottingham University Law Department who have patiently answered my many enquiries and freely given of their ideas. My thanks are especially due to Professor J. C. Smith and Mr. P. J. Clarke, both of whom have stalwartly read the whole of the original typescript and have between them tactfully saved me from many inaccuracies of law and infelicities of style; and also to Mr. G. K. Morse who has kindly read the page-proofs. Naturally, I am wholly responsible for such errors of law and defects of style as remain.

In the quotations cited, any alterations which I have made have been indicated by the use of square brackets. I have endeavoured to state the law as on 1st January, 1971, but have found it possible to incorporate some material which became available to me after that date. However, it should be noted that, at the time of writing, the Report of the Crowther Committee on Consumer Credit has not yet been published; and that the reversal by the House of Lords of the decision of the Court of Appeal in *Christopher Hill, Ltd.* v. *Ashington Piggeries, Ltd.* (1971), *Times*, 24 February, has come too late for inclusion in the text. (The House of Lords reversed the decision of the Court of Appeal on both the s. 14 (1) claims, but rejected the claims on the bases of ss. 13 and 14 (2).)

February, 1971   J. K. MACLEOD

Table of Contents

	PAGE
Preface	v
Table of Statutes	xvii
Tables of Cases	xxv
Bibliography	lv

PART I

THE NATURE OF THE CONTRACT

CHAPTER I INTRODUCTION ... 3

1. The scope of the enquiry ... 3
   1. The categories of the Law ... 3
   2. The interpretation of the Acts ... 4
2. Definition of a contract of sale ... 5
   1. A contract ... 6
   2. A contract of sale ... 6
   3. A contract for the sale of goods ... 8
   4. A transfer of property from seller to buyer ... 8
   5. A price ... 8
3. Definition of a contract of hire purchase ... 9
   1. Development of the common law form ... 9
     (a) Preserving the security against the "buyer" and his creditors ... 9
     (b) Defeating the bona fide transferee for value ... 12
     (c) Maintenance of the security ... 13
   2. The statutory definition of h.p. ... 14
   3. Difficulties arising from the legal form ... 16

CHAPTER 2 SUBJECT-MATTER OF THE CONTRACT ... 18

1. The meaning of "goods" ... 18
   1. Chattels personal other than things in action and money ... 18
   2. Emblements and industrial growing crops ... 18
   3. Things attached to or forming part of the land ... 18
2. Different types of goods ... 19
   1. "Existing goods" ... 19
   2. "Future goods' ... 19
   3. "A chance" ... 20

3. The price 21
  1. Gifts 22
  2. Sales of skill and labour 23
  3. Barter or exchange 23
4. Financing sales 24
  1. Direct financing 25
  2. Indirect financing 25
5. Consumer protection 26
  1. Contracts of purchase 26
  2. Instalment credit contracts 28

CHAPTER 3   FORMALITIES AND FORMATION 32

1. Formalities of the agreement 32
  1. Sales 32
  2. Consumer sales 33
2. Formation of the agreement 34
  1. The pre-contract stage 34
  2. The general principles of formation 35
    (1) Offer and acceptance 35
    (2) Mistake 37
    (3) Invalidity 37
  3. Statutory provisions 39
    (1) Agency for the purposes of receiving notices 39
    (2) Copies of the agreement 40
    (3) Cancellation of the agreement 42
  4. The terms controls 45

PART 2

THE CONTENTS OF THE CONTRACT

CHAPTER 4   CONTRACTUAL TERMS 49

1. Representations and terms 49
2. The nature of terms 50
3. Express and implied terms 52

CHAPTER 5   UNDERTAKINGS AS TO TITLE 55

1. Introduction 55
2. The implied condition as to title 56
  (1) The "right to sell" 57
  (2) Breach of the undertaking 58
3. The implied warranties as to title 64

CHAPTER 6   UNDERTAKINGS AS TO DESCRIPTION AND
QUANTITY   67

1. Introduction   67
2. Sales by description   67
3. Undertakings as to description   70
4. Undertakings as to quantity   76

CHAPTER 7   UNDERTAKINGS AS TO FITNESS AND
MERCHANTABILITY   80

1. Introduction   80
2. Undertakings as to fitness   83
   1. The undertakings   83
   2. The content of the undertakings   84
   3. The qualification of the undertakings   86
      (1) Sales by a dealer   86
      (2) Knowledge of particular purpose   87
      (3) Reliance   90
   4. Exclusion of the undertakings   93
3. Undertakings as to merchantability   94
   1. The undertakings   94
   2. The content of the undertakings   95
   3. The qualifications of the undertakings   101
      (1) Sales by description   101
      (2) Sales by a dealer   101
      (3) Examination by transferee   102
   4. Exclusion of the undertakings   104

CHAPTER 8   THE SIGNIFICANCE OF SAMPLES   106

1. Contracts by sample   106
2. Undertakings in contracts by sample   107
      (1) Title   107
      (2) Correspondence with sample   107
      (3) Opportunity for inspection   109
      (4) Merchantability and fitness   111

CHAPTER 9   OTHER IMPLIED TERMS AND OBLIGATIONS   112

1. Terms and obligations derived from statute   112
      (1) The S.G.A.   112
      (2) The H.P.A.   112
      (3) Other statutes   114
2. Terms and obligations derived from common law   114
      (1) In sale   115
      (2) In hire purchase   115

CHAPTER 10   PRODUCT LIABILITY   118

1. Within the contractual nexus   118
  (1) A contractual promise   118
    (1) A single contract   118
    (2) A chain of contracts   119
    (3) A collateral contract   120
  (2) Other remedies   121
    (1) Misrepresentation   122
    (2) Illegality and unenforceability   122
    (3) Mistake   122
2. Outside the contractual nexus   124
  (1) Liability for acts or omissions   124
  (2) Liability for statements   128
3. The future   131

CHAPTER 11   AVOIDANCE AND WAIVER OF TERMS   132

1. Provisions rendered void by statute   132
  (1) The H.P.A.   133
  (2) The Misrepresentation Act 1967   134
  (3) The proposals of the Law Commission   135
2. Provisions rendered void at common law   136
  (1) The nature and effect of exclusion clauses   136
  (2) Incorporation of the exclusion clause in the transaction   137
  (3) The attitude of the courts to exclusion clauses   138
3. Variation and waiver   145
  (1) Variation of liability by contract   145
  (2) The doctrine of waiver   146

PART 3

THE CONVEYANCE

CHAPTER 12   THE EFFECTS OF THE CONTRACT   153

1. Contract and conveyance   153
2. Property and title   153

CHAPTER 13   THE PASSING OF PROPERTY   157

1. Introduction   157
2. The passing of property in specific goods   161
  1. Unconditional contracts   162
  2. Conditional contracts   164

3. The passing of property in unascertained goods   167
   1. The rule   167
   2. Appropriation   169
   3. The importance of assent   175
4. "Sale or return" transactions   176
   1. The passing of property   177
   2. The property/title borderline   180
5. The reservation of a right of disposal   181

CHAPTER 14   THE TRANSFER OF TITLE   183

1. *Nemo dat quod non habet*   183
   1. The rule   183
   2. Exceptions to the *nemo dat* rule   184
      (1) Agency   184
      (2) Consent of the owner   185
2. Estoppel   189
   1. Introduction   189
   2. The common law doctrine of estoppel   191
✳3. Voidable title   198
4. Mercantile agency   202
   1. A mercantile agent   204
   2. Possession of goods or documents of title   206
      (a) Possession   206
      (b) Goods and documents of title   207
   3. The consent of the owner   209
      (1) Consent   209
      (2) Owner   210
   4. Dispositions by a m.a. in the ordinary course of business   211
      (a) The disposition   211
      (b) By a mercantile agent   211
      (c) The ordinary course of business   211
   5. The transferee must take *bona fide* and without notice   214
   6. The effect of the exception   215
✳5. Sellers in possession   215
   1. Seller in possession   216
   2. Delivery and disposition to a *bona fide* transferee   218
   3. Effect of the exception   219
✳6. Buyers in possession   220
   1. Buyer in possession   221
   2. The seller's consent to the buyer's possession   223
   3. Delivery and disposition to a *bona fide* transferee   225
   4. Effect of the exception   226

7. Sales of motor vehicles   230
   1. Dispositions to private purchasers   232
   2. Dispositions to trade or finance purchasers   234
8. Sales in market overt   236
   1. The law   236
   2. Proposals for reform   238
9. Miscellaneous powers of sale   238
   1. Common law powers   238
   2. Statutory powers   239
   3. Court orders   240

CHAPTER 15 RISK AND IMPOSSIBILITY   241

1. Risk   241
   1. Delay in delivery   242
   2. Transit   244
   3. Bailment   248
2. Impossibility   249
   1. Initial impossibility   250
   2. Subsequent impossibility   254
      (a) When may a contract be frustrated?   254
      (b) What is the effect of frustration?   257

PART 4

THE PRICE

CHAPTER 16 DELIVERY AND PAYMENT   263

1. Delivery   263
   1. The meaning and rules of delivery   263
   2. The duty of delivery   265
      (a) Tender of delivery   266
      (b) Acceptance of delivery   267
2. Payment   271
3. The time of delivery and payment   272
   1. Where delivery and payment are concurrent terms   273
   2. Where delivery and payment are not concurrent terms 276
4. Performance by instalments   276
   1. Delivery by instalments   276
   2. Payment by instalments   279

CHAPTER 17 FINANCING THE PRICE   282

1. Introduction   282
   1. The relationship between dealer and customer   282

2. The relationship between finance company and
customer 284
(1) The deposit 286
(2) Misrepresentations by the dealer 288
3. The relationship between finance company and
dealer 289
(1) Stocking Plans 289
(2) Dealer Recourse 290
2. Direct financing 291
1. Chattel mortgaging 291
(a) Circular transactions 293
(b) Open-ended transactions 297
2. Moneylending 300
3. Indirect financing 305
1. The different types of transfer 306
(a) Absolute transfers 306
(b) Non-absolute transfers 308
2. The form of indirect financing 310

CHAPTER 18 SECURITY FOR THE PRICE 313

1. Security through possession 313
1. The unpaid seller 313
2. The unpaid seller's rights against the goods 314
3. The unpaid seller's lien 318
(a) The nature of the lien 318
(b) The conditions under which it is exercisable 319
(c) Termination of the lien 321
4. The unpaid seller's right of stoppage in transit 325
2. Security without possession 329
1. Agreements outside the H.P.A. 330
(a) Repossession through self-help 330
(b) Repossession through court action 332
2. Agreements within the H.P.A. 334
(a) Notice of default 334
(b) Repossession 336
(c) Death of the hirer or buyer 342
3. The personal security provided by a surety 344
(a) Sureties at common law 346
(b) Sureties under the H.P.A. 347

PART 5

DISCHARGE AND REMEDIES

CHAPTER 19   DISCHARGE OF CONTRACTUAL OBLIGATIONS   351

1. Discharge in accordance with the contract   351
    1. Discharge by performance   351
    2. Discharge by stipulated event   353
        (a) Termination by the transferee   353
        (b) Termination by other stipulated event   355
2. Other types of discharge   357
    1. Discharge by rescission   357
        (a) Rescission for misrepresentation   357
        (b) Rescission for breach of contract   360
    2. Discharge by subsequent act or event   362

CHAPTER 20   REMEDIES OF THE OWNER OR SELLER   364

1. Remedies of the owner or seller against the goods   365
    1. Remedies of a seller   365
        (a) The original contract of sale   365
        (b) The title to the goods   368
    2. Real remedies of an owner letting goods on h.p.   370
2. Personal remedies of the owner or seller   370
    1. Action for the price or rent   370
        (a) Action for the price of goods sold   370
        (b) Action for arrears of rentals   374
    2. Action for damages   376
        (a) Quantification of damages   378
        (b) Common law and statutory restrictions   386

CHAPTER 21   REMEDIES OF THE HIRER OR BUYER   396

1. Rescission   396
    1. Rescission for breach of contract   396
        (a) Rescission by the buyer   397
        (b) Rescission by the hirer   402
    2. Rescission for misrepresentation   403
2. Restitution in quasi-contract   404
    1. The relationship to rescission   405
    2. The failure of consideration must be total   406
3. An action for damages   408
    1. Damages for non-delivery   409
        (a) Sale   409
            Prima facie rule   410
            Consequential loss   412
        (b) Hire purchase   414

2. Damages for other breaches of contract   415
   (a) Actions in respect of a defective title   416
   (b) Actions in respect of a late delivery   417
      Prima facie rule   417
      Consequential loss   420
   (c) Actions in respect of a defect in quality   214
      Prima facie rule   214
      Consequential loss   254
4. Specific performance   428

INDEX   431

Table of Statutes

References to "*Stats.*" are to Halsbury's Statutes of England (3rd Edn.) showing the volume and page at which the annotated text of the Act will be found.

PAGE

Administration of Justice
    Act 1965 (7 *Stats.*
    744)—
  s. 22   239
Administration of Justice
    Act 1970   ..   .. 345, 364
  s. 13 (5)   345
    14 (3)   345
    17 (2)   239
    40   ..   38, 330, 331, 364
      (1), (2)   331
      (3) 331, 332
Advertisements   (Hire
    Purchase) Act 1967
         27, 29, 31, 38
Anchors and Chain Cables
    Act 1899—
  s. 2   114
Auctions (Bidding Agree-
    ments) Act 1927 (2
    Stats. 501)   37
  s. 2   37
Auctions (Bidding Agree-
    ments) Act 1969   ..   37
Bankruptcy Act 1914 (3
    Stats. 33)   10
  s. 38 (1)   310
      (2) 10, 307
    40   239
      (3)   240
    41   240
    43 ..   ..   .. 299, 307
    44   307
Bankruptcy and Deeds of
    Arrangement   Act
    1913 (3 *Stats.* 18)—
  s. 15   240

PAGE

Bills of Exchange Act
    1882 (3 *Stats.* 188)   345
  s. 56   345
    62   362
    69, 70   272
Bills of Lading Act 1855   182
  s. 1–3   249
Bills of Sale Act 1878 (3
    Stats. 245) ..   33, 238, 308
  s. 4 ..   ..   10, 207, 307
    8   307
Bills of Sale Act (1878)
    Amendment   Act
    1882 (3 *Stats.* 261) 7, 10, 33,
         217, 221, 292, 308
  s. 3   10
    9   292
    15   307
    17   292
  Sch.   53
Companies Act 1948 (5
    Stats. 110)—
  s. 95 ..   292, 296, 297, 298,
           308, 309, 310
      (1)   292
      (2) 292, 297, 308, 309, 310
    320 (1)   307
Companies Act 1967 (22
    Stats. 725)—
  s. 123 (1) 304, 305
      (2), (3)   305
Companies Consolidation
    Act 1908—
  s. 93   298
Consumer Protection Act
    1961   ..   4, 27, 38, 114
Conveyancing Act 1881—
  s. 7   55

	PAGE
County Courts Act 1959 (7 *Stats.* 302)—	
s. 99	342
Criminal Law Act 1967 (8 *Stats.* 552)—	
Sch. 3, Pt. III	236
Decimal Currency Act 1967 (6 *Stats.* 855)..	271
Decimal Currency Act 1969	271
s. 10	113
Disposal of Uncollected Goods Act 1952 (2 *Stats.* 715)	185, 239
Emergency Laws (Re-enactments and Re-peals) Act 1964)—	
s. 1	45
Emergency Powers (De-fence) Act 1939 ..	45
Fabrics (Misdescription) Act 1913—	
s. 3	114
Factors Act 1889 (1 *Stats.* 94) ..	182, 187, 203, 264, 290
s. 1	204
(1)	204, 205, 211, 212
(2)	206, 216
(3), (4)	207
(5)	7, 211
2 ..	189, 209, 210, 219, 223, 224, 228, 290
(1)	203, 207, 208, 209, 210, 211, 212, 215, 216, 218, 227, 229, 232
(2) ..	210, 224, 228
(3)	224
(4)	210, 224
3	219, 224, 290
4–6	211, 219, 224
7	215, 219, 224
8 ..	215, 218, 219, 228
9 ..	12, 216, 219, 220, 221, 223, 224, 225, 226, 227, 228, 229, 230, 323

	PAGE
Factors Act 1889—*contd.*	
s. 10	220, 225, 226, 227, 229, 323
11	182, 225
12 (1)	203
(2) ..	203, 229
(3)	203
13	203
Factors (Scotland) Act 1890	224
Fertilisers and Feeding Stuffs Act 1926 (1 *Stats.* 596)—	
s. 2	114
Food and Drugs Act 1955 (14 *Stats.* 15; 21 *Stats.* 478)	27, 114
Gaming Act 1845 (14 *Stats.* 523)	20
Hire Purchase Act 1938	4, 14, 15, 28, 33, 39, 40, 140, 286, 287, 334, 336
s. 2, 4	29
5 ..	29, 123, 286, 287
7	29
8	29, 133
(3)	93
11–18	29
21 (1)	343
Hire Purchase Act 1954 ..	29
Hire Purchase Act 1964 ..	29, 39, 40, 42, 187, 223, 230, 238, 334, 336
s. 16, 23	133
27 ..	231, 232, 233, 234, 235, 236
(1) ..	230, 231
(2) ..	232, 233
(3) ..	234, 235
(4)	235
(5)	231
(6) ..	234, 235
28	233, 235
(1) ..	235, 236
(2), (3)	235
(4)	236

	PAGE
Hire Purchase Act 1964—*contd.*	
s. 28 (5)	235
29 (1) ..	231, 232, 233
(2)	232
(3) ..	.. 232, 233
(4)	231
(5) ..	.. 233, 234
34 (3)	30
Hire Purchase Act 1965..	4, 30,
	31, 40, 223, 231,
	286, 329, 334, 336,
	363, 395
s. 1	14, 18, 231
(1)	57
(2)	14
2 (2), (3)	30
4	30
5	31, 33, 46,
	113, 114, 146
(1)	31, 33
(2)	33
6	.. 33, 348
7	.. 33, 348
(1)	34
(2)	30, 34
8	30, 41, 348
(2)–(4)	41
9	30, 31, 348
(2)–(5)	42
(6)	41
10	.. 33, 348
(1)–(3)	42
11	31, 42, 43
(1)	42
(2)	42, 43
(3), (4)	44
(5) ..	40, 41, 43
12 ..	31, 42, 43, 44, 336
(3) ..	31, 39, 43, 286
13	31, 42, 43, 45
(1)–(9)	45
14	31, 42, 43, 375
(1) ..	.. 44, 348
(2) ..	.. 44, 45
(3), (4)	44
15	.. 42, 43
(1), (2)	44

	PAGE
Hire Purchase Act 1965—*contd.*	
s. 15 (3)	45
(4)–(6)	44
16	286, 288, 289
(1) ..	.. 288, 289
(2)–(4)	288
17 ..	31, 64, 94, 97, 107
(1) ..	54, 56, 58
(2) ..	.. 94, 97, 101, 105
(3) ..	.. 95, 102
(4) ..	83, 86, 87, 90,
	91, 93, 111, 286
(5)	58
18 ..	.. 31, 83, 95, 105
(1)	105
(2) ..	.. 104, 105
(3) ..	55, 105, 133
(4) ..	.. 84, 93
19 ..	31, 76, 106, 108, 111
(1) ..	.. 107, 109
(2) ..	70, 71, 108
20 (1) ..	.. 60, 397
(2)	397
(3)	55
(4)	397
21 (1) ..	.. 113, 343
(2) ..	.. 113, 348
(3), (4)	113
22	31, 114, 348
(1)–(3)	348
23	.. 31, 348
24	113
25	31, 334, 335
(1) ..	.. 334, 335
(2)	334
(3)	335
(4) ..	.. 335, 348
(5)	335
26	.. 31, 336
(2)	344
27 ..	.. 355, 364, 384,
	394, 395
(1)	354
(2), (3)	355
(4)	354
28 ..	.. 351, 354, 387,
	394, 395

PAGE

Hire Purchase Act 1965—*contd.*

s. 28 (1), (2)	..	..	394, 395
(3)	..	..	112, 394
(4)	..	337, 354, 394
(5)	..	..	394
29	..	31, 53, 133, 286, 336
(2)	..	39, 133, 336, 337, 354, 394, 395
(3)	..	40, 43, 44, 76, 108, 110, 133, 289
(4)	..	34, 36, 42, 133, 146, 295
(5)	..	..	133
30	..	..	31, 343, 344
(1)	343, 344, 348, 394
(2), (3)	..	..	344
(4)	..	..	133, 344
31	..	..	39, 40, 286
(1)	..	..	40
(2)	..	..	40, 354
(3)	..	..	40, 354
(4)	..	..	40
32	..	..	34
33 (1)	..	..	336
34	..	..	114, 339, 369
(1)	..	..	337, 338
(2)	113, 338, 339, 348, 370, 375
35	..	339, 341, 375, 395
(1), (2)	..	..	339
(3)	..	..	340
(4)	..	333, 340, 355, 376
(5)	..	..	340
36	..	..	339
(1)–(3)	..	..	340
37	..	..	339, 376
(1), (2)	..	..	340
38	..	..	339, 341
(1)	..	..	341
(2)	..	..	341, 376
(3)	..	..	341
(4), (5)	..	..	342
39	..	..	339
(1)–(3)	..	..	341
(4)	..	..	341, 342

Hire Purchase Act 1965—*contd.*

s. 39 (5)	..	..	341
(8)	..	..	342
40	..	..	339, 340
(1)	..	..	340
(3)	..	..	338
41	..	339, 341, 375, 395
42	..	..	339, 340, 342
(1), (5), (6)	..	342
43	..	..	339, 395
(3)	..	..	341, 395
44	..	..	339, 341, 376
45	..	..	..	339
46	..	..	..	344
47	..	..	..	337
48	..	..	..	339
(1), (2)	..	..	339
(3), (4)	..	..	376
49 (1)	..	..	337, 339
(2)–(4)	..	..	337
50	..	..	337, 376
51	..	..	112, 271, 337
52	..	..	339, 377
53	..	..	..	11
54	..	..	..	223
55 (1)	..	..	22, 337
56	..	..	113, 337, 394
58	..	..	..	41
(1)	..	22, 40, 113, 263, 289, 339, 343, 347, 348
(2)	..	22, 271, 337
(3)	..	..	40, 289
(4)	..	..	40
(5)	..	40, 90, 289
(6)	..	..	14
Sch. 1, 2	..	..	34
3	..	..	344
5	..	..	230

Hop (Prevention of Frauds) Act 1866 (1 *Stats.* **441)**—

s. 18	..	..	..	114

Infants Relief Act 1874 (17 *Stats.* **412)**—

s. 1	..	..	..	114
Larceny Act 1916, s. 45		238

PAGE

Law of Distress Amend-
ment Act 1908 (9
Stats. 537) 11
s. 4 .. .. .. 11, 12
(1) 11
Law of Property Act
1925—
s. 40 .. .. .. 32, 114
(1) 19
53 (1) 309
136 307
Law Reform (Contribu-
tory Negligence) Act
1945 (23 *Stats.* 789) 136
s. 1 (1) 386
4 386
Law Reform (Enforce-
ment of Contracts)
Act 1954 (7 *Stats.*
14)—
s. 1 .. .. .. 32, 145
Law Reform (Frustrated
Contracts) Act 1943
(7 *Stats.* 9) 23, 255,
257, 407
s. 1 (1) 257
(2) 258, 259
(3) 259
2 (5) .. 23, 257, 258
Law Reform (Married
Women and Tort-
feasors) Act 1935 (17
Stats. 128) 126
s. 6 62
Law Reform (Miscel-
laneous Provisions)
Act 1934 (13 *Stats.*
115; 25 *Stats.* 752)—
s. 1 (1) 342
3 (1) 379
Laws in Wales Act 1542
(6 *Stats.* 460)—
s. 47 236
Matrimonial Proceedings
and Property Act
1970—
s. 41 185

PAGE

Mercantile Law Amend-
ment Act 1856 (7
(*Stats.* 8)—
s. 5 347
Merchandise Marks Act
1862 .. .. 4, 27
Merchant Shipping Act
1894— 32
s. 24 32
Misrepresentation Act
1967 (22 *Stats.* 675) 50, 121,
133, 138, 162, 408
s. 1 .. 122, 359, 361, 403,
404
2 378
(1) .. 75, 121, 122
(2) .. 122, 358, 359
(3) 122
3 .. .. .. 134, 135
4 (1) 167, 398
(2) 399, 401
Mock Auctions Act 1961
(2 *Stats.* 503) .. 37
Money-lenders Act 1900
(22 *Stats.* 693) .. 300, 305
s. 6 301
Moneylenders Act 1927
(22 *Stats.* 700) .. 300, 305
Plant Varieties and Seeds
Act 1964 (1 *Stats.*
630)—
s. 13, 17, 28 114
Post Office Act 1953 (25
Stats. 413)—
s. 58 325
Post Office Act 1969 (25
Stats. 463)—
s. 29 325
Rag Flock Material Act
1951—
s. 10 114
Resale Prices Act 1964 .. 24
Restrictive Trade Prac-
tices Act 1956 .. 24
Restrictive Trade Prac-
tices Act 1968 .. 24

	PAGE			PAGE
Road Traffic Act 1960 ..	27	Sale of Goods Act 1893—*contd.*		
s. 68	38	s. 14 (1)	96, 97, 99, 102,	
Road Traffic Act 1963—			111, 284, 389	
s. 68	114	(2)	67, 68, 72, 73, 82,	
Sale of Goods Act 1893..	3		86, 88, 94, 95,	
s. 1 .. .. .. 5, 21, 51			96, 97, 98, 100,	
(1) .. 6, 8, 23, 56, 57			101, 102, 103,	
(2) .. 6, 7, 56, 222			104, 111,	
(3) 8, 157			125	
(4) .. 9, 153, 157		(3)	112	
3 32		(4)	115	
4 .. .. .. 6, 145		15 ..	51, 67, 97, 100, 107,	
5 .. .. .. 19, 20			111, 135	
(1) 19		(1)	106	
(2) 20, 56		(2)	72, 94, 101, 102,	
(3) .. 20, 171, 173			103, 104, 107, 109,	
6 .. 22, 250, 251, 252,			111, 269	
	253, 255, 258	16 .. .. 154, 157, 167		
7 .. 253, 255, 257, 258		17 ..	111, 153, 154, 160,	
8 21			163, 167	
(1), (2) 21		(1)	158	
9 21		(2) 111, 158		
(1) 21, 22		18 ..	74, 154, 158, 159,	
(2) 21			161, 163, 167, 168,	
10 (1) 273, 274, 275, 279,			181, 401	
	314, 366, 370	(1)	158, 160, 161, 162,	
11 .. .. .. 50, 51			165, 168, 173, 263,	
(1) 51, 60, 74, 147, 162,			295	
	167, 397, 398, 399,	(2), (3) ..	161, 164, 165,	
	400		166, 167, 168	
(3) 250		(4)	176, 177, 178, 179,	
12 .. 51, 55, 56, 64, 65,			180, 181, 206	
	107	(5)	165, 167, 168, 170,	
(1) .. 56, 59, 65,			175, 263	
	66, 95	19 ..	154, 181, 182,	
(2) 65			246, 369	
13 .. 51, 67, 69, 70, 71,		(1) 181, 182		
	72, 73, 74, 76,	(2)	182	
	77, 78, 79, 101,	(3) 182, 227		
	106, 108, 109,	20 ..	154, 241, 242, 245,	
	135		246, 248	
14 .. 51, 53, 67, 70, 81,		21	231	
	88, 115, 135,	(1)	183, 184, 185, 189,	
	282		190, 191, 196, 218	
(1) 67, 72, 73, 82, 83,		(2) .. 203, 215, 238		
	84, 85, 86, 87,	22	238	
	88, 90, 91, 93,	(1), (2)	236	

PAGE

Sale of Goods Act 1893—*contd.*

s. 23	..	.. ..	199
24	..	.. ..	238
25	..	.. 207, 223, 228	
(1)	189, 215, 216, 217,		
	218, 219		
(2)	7, 163, 187, 209,		
	219, 220, 221, 222,		
	223, 224, 225, 226,		
	227, 228, 229, 230,		
	232, 323		
(3)	.. ..	215	
26	..	.. ..	9
(1)	.. ..	239, 240	
27	..	263, 267, 271, 397	
28	..	269, 273, 275, 276,	
	314, 320, 321		
29	..	.. 264, 265	
(1)	.. ..	244, 264	
(2)	.. ..	274	
(3)	.. ..	224, 264	
(4)	.. ..	273, 281	
(5)	.. ..	265	
30	..	76, 77, 79, 253,	
	276, 399		
(1)	77, 78, 79, 167,		
	353, 398		
(2)	.. 78, 79, 398		
(3)	74, 78, 79, 398,		
	399		
(4)	.. ..	77	
31 (1)	.. ..	276, 279	
(2)	.. ..	278	
32	..	.. ..	246
(1)	246, 247, 264, 326		
(2), (3)	.. ..	246, 247	
33	..	.. 82, 244, 245	
34	..	110, 269, 273, 397,	
	400, 402		
35	..	120, 399, 400, 401	
36	..	.. 268, 401	
37	..	265, 267, 268, 319	
38	..	.. ..	319
(1)	.. 314, 321, 323		
(2)	.. ..	313	
39	..	276, 314, 315, 317,	
	325		

PAGE

Sale of Goods Act 1893—*contd.*

s. 39 (1)	314, 315, 316, 317,		
	318, 323, 325		
(2)	226, 316, 317, 322		
41	..	.. ..	315
(1)	276, 318, 319, 320,		
	321, 323		
(2)	.. .. 264, 321		
42	..	.. .. 315, 318	
43	..	.. .. 315, 322	
(1)	186, 318, 321, 322,		
	323		
(2)	.. .. 321, 323		
44	..	.. 315, 324, 325	
45	..	315, 325, 326, 327	
(1)	.. 264, 325, 327		
(2)	.. ..	327	
(3)	.. .. 326, 327		
(4)	.. ..	327	
(5)	.. ..	326	
(6)	.. ..	327	
(7)	.. .. 318, 328		
46	..	.. 315, 325, 328	
(2)	.. ..	329	
47	..	185, 186, 187, 220,	
	225, 226, 227, 229,		
	323, 324, 325		
48	..	.. ..	317
(1)	.. .. 324, 365		
(2)	.. ..	369	
(3)	275, 317, 365, 368		
(4)	317, 353, 365, 368		
49	..	.. ..	372
(1)	.. ..	370	
(2)	276, 370, 371, 372		
50	..	.. ..	409
(2)	.. 388, 409, 415		
(3)	382, 383, 384, 410		
51	..	.. ..	409
(1)	.. .. 276, 409		
(2)	.. .. 409, 415		
(3)	382, 383, 410, 411		
52	..	.. .. 173, 429	
53	..	.. ..	415
(1)	.. ..	415	
(2)	.. ..	416	
(3)	.. ..	421	

	PAGE
Sale of Goods Act 1893—*contd.*	
s. 53 (4)	415
54 .. 388, 404, 410	416, 421
55 .. 56, 79, 115, 132,	252, 315, 323
56 .. 180, 265, 268, 366,	401
57	328
58 (1)	18, 164
(2)	162
(3)	37, 38
61 (1)	156
(2) 3, 5, 37, 185, 236,	317, 319
(3)	7, 32
(4)	3, 7, 33
62	159
(1) 6, 7, 18, 19, 20, 21,	23, 50, 95, 153, 154, 159, 242, 258, 264, 313, 397
(2)	199
(3)	320
(4)	165

	PAGE
Statute of Forcible Entry	
1381	330
Statute of Frauds (1677)	
(7 *Stats.* 6) .. 5, 128, 145	
s. 4	346
Statute of Frauds Amend-	
ment Act 1828 (7	
Stats. 7)	130
s. 6	128
Theft Act 1968 (8 *Stats.*	
782)—	
s. 28	238
31 (2)	238
Trade Descriptions Act	
1968 .. 4, 27, 29, 38,	114
s. 35	38
Trading Stamps Act 1964	18
Uniform Law on Inter-	
national Sales Act	
1967	83
Weights and Measures	
Act 1963	27
s. 22	114

Table of Cases

the following Table references are given where applicable to the English and Empire Digest where a digest of the cases will be found.

A

	PAGE
B.D. (Metals and Waste), Ltd. v. Anglo Chemical Co, [1955] 2 Lloyd's Rep. 456	410
ingdon Finance Co. v. Champion, [1961] C.L.Y. 3931	330
ingdon R.D.C. v. O'Gorman, [1968] 2 Q.B. 811; [1968] 3 All E.R. 79; [1968] 3 W.L.R. 240; 112 Sol. Jo. 584; 19 P. & C.R. 725, C.A.; Digest Supp.	12
ram Steamship Co. v. Westville Steamship Co., [1923] A.C. 773; [1923] All E.R. Rep. 645; 93 L.J.P.C. 38; 130 L.T. 67, H.L.; 35 Digest (Repl.) 71	357
am v. Newbigging. See Newbigging v. Adam	
dis v. Gramophone, Ltd., [1909] A.C. 488; [1908–10] All E.R. Rep. 1; 78 L.J.K.B. 1122; 101 L.T. 466; H.L.; 17 Digest (Repl.) 75	378
bermarle Supply Co., Ltd. v. Hind, [1928] 1 K.B. 307; [1927] All E.R. Rep. 401; 97 L.J.K.B. 25; 138, L.T. 102; 43 T.L.R. 783; 71 Sol. Jo. 777, C.A.; 32 Digest (Repl.) 288	13
lerslade v. Hendon Laundry, Ltd., [1945] K.B. 189; [1945] 1 All E.R. 244; 114 L.J.K.B. 196; 172 L.T. 153; 61 T.L.R. 216; 89 Sol. Jo. 164, C.A.; 3 Digest (Repl.) 102	140
lridge v. Johnson (1857), 7 E. & B. 885; 26 L.J.Q.B. 296; 3 Jur. N.S. 913; S.W.R. 703; 39 Digest (Repl.) 607 .. .. 23, 168, 169, 170, 171, 172, 175	
exander v. Glenbroome, Ltd., [1957] 1 Lloyd's Rep. 157	176
lan (J. M.) (Merchandising), Ltd. v. Cloke, [1963] 2 Q.B. 340; [1963] 2 All E.R. 258; [1963] 2 W.L.R. 899; 107 Sol. Jo. 213; 61 L.G.R. 304, C.A.; Digest Cont. Vol. A 285	38
lester (David), Ltd., Re, [1922] 2 Ch. 211; [1922] All E.R. Rep. 589; 127 L.T. 434; 38 T.L.R. 611; 66 Sol. Jo. 486; [1922] B & C.R. 190; 3 Digest (Repl.) 311 ..	310
chor Line, (Henderson Brothers), Ltd., Re, [1937] 1 Ch. 1; [1936] 2 All E.R. 941; 105 L.J. Ch. 330; 155 L.T. 100; 80 Sol. Jo. 572; 55 H.L.R. 251, C.A.; 39 Digest (Repl.) 448 .. .. 158, 163	
cona v. Rogers (1876), 1 Ex. D. 285; [1874–80] All E.R. Rep. 369; 46 L.J.Q.B. 121; 35 L.T. 115; 24 W.R. 1000, C.A.; 7 Digest (Repl.) 117	307
derson v. Ryan, [1967] I.R. 34 .. .. 184, 198	
derson (W. B.) & Sons, Ltd. v. Rhodes (Liverpool), Ltd., [1967] 2 All E.R. 850; Digest Supp.	130
drews v. Hopkinson, [1957] 1 Q.B. 229; [1956] 3 All E.R. 422; [1956] 3 W.L.R. 732; 100 Sol. Jo. 768; 26 Digest (Repl.) 666 .. 52, 125, 126, 283, 428	
drews Brothers (Bournemouth), Ltd. v. Singer & Co., Ltd., [1934] 1 K.B. 17; [1933] All E.R. Rep. 479; 103 L.J.K.B. 90; 150 L.T. 172; 50 T.L.R. 33, C.A.; 39 Digest (Repl.) 573 .. .. 70, 71, 139	
glo-Auto Finance, Ltd. v. James, [1963] 3 All E.R. 566; [1963] 1 W.L.R. 1042; 107 Sol. Jo. 534, C.A.; Digest Cont Vol. A 470 .. .. 385, 394	
on (1596). See Market-Overt Case	
t. Jurgens Margarinefabrieken v. Louis Dreyfus & Co., [1914] 3 K.B. 40; 83 L.J.K.B. 1344; 111 L.T. 248; 19 Com. Cas. 333; 39 Digest (Repl.) 747 .. .. 157, 225	
pleby v. Sleep, [1968] 2 All E.R. 265; [1968] 1 W.L.R. 948; 112 Sol. Jo. 380; 66 L.G.R. 555; Digest Supp.	8
chbolds, Ltd. v. Spanglett, Ltd., [1961] 1 Q.B. 374; [1961] 1 All E.R. 417; [1961] 2 W.L.R. 170; 105 Sol. Jo. 149, C.A.; Digest Cont. Vol. A 285	38
cos, Ltd. v. Ronaasen & Son, Ltd., [1933] A.C. 470; [1933] All E.R. Rep. 646; 102 L.J.K.B. 346; 149 L.T. 98; 49 T.L.R. 231; 77 Sol. Jo. 99; 38 Com. Cas. 166; 45 Ll.L. Rep. 33, H.L.; 39 Digest (Repl.) 719 .. .. 71, 72, 73, 76, 352	

PA

Argentino, The (1888), L.R. 13 P.D. 191; 58 L.J.P. 1; 59 L.T. 914; 37 W.R. 210; 6 Asp. M.L.C. 348, H.L.; affd. *sub nom.* Gracie (Owners) *v.* Argentino (Owners), The Argentino (1889), 14 App. Cas. 519, H.L.; 17 Digest (Repl.) 80 3

Arpad, The, [1934] P. 189; [1934] All E.R. Rep. 326; 103 L.J.P. 129; 152 L.T. 521; 50 T.L.R. 505; 78 Sol. Jo. 534; 18 Asp. M.L.C. 510; 40 Com. Cas. 16, C.A.; 41 Digest (Repl.) 461   411, 412, 4

Aruna Mills, Ltd. *v.* Dhanrajmal Gobindram, [1968] 1 Q.B. 655;]1968] 1 All E.R. 113; [1968] 2 W.L.R. 101; 111 Sol. Jo. 924; [1968] 1 Lloyd's Rep. 304; Digest Supp.   4

Aryeh *v.* Lawrence Kostiris & Son, Ltd., [1967] 1 Lloyd's Rep. 63, C.A.   4

Ascherson *v.* Tredegar Dry Dock and Wharf Co., Ltd., [1909] 2 Ch. 401; [1908–10] All E.R. Rep. 510; 78 L.J. Ch. 697; 101 L.T. 519; 16 Mans 318; 26 Digest (Repl.) 130

Asfar & Co. *v.* Blundell, [1896] 1 Q.B. 123; 65 L.J.Q.B. 138; 73 L.T. 648; 44 W.R. 130; 12 T.L.R. 29; 40 Sol. Jo. 66; 8 Asp. M.L.C. 106; 1 Com. Cas. 185, C.A.; 41 Digest (Repl.) 572   ..   ..   99, 2

Ashby *v.* Tolhurst, [1937] 2 K.B. 242; [1937] 2 All E.R. 837; 106 L.J.K.B. 783; 156 L.T. 518; 53 T.L.R. 770; 81 Sol. Jo. 419, C.A.; 3 Digest (Repl.) 56   3

Ashdown *v.* Samuel Williams & Sons, Ltd., [1957] 1 Q.B. 409; [1957] 1 All E.R. 35; [1956] 3 W.L.R. 1104; 100 Sol. Jo. 945, C.A.; Digest Cont. Vol. A 1158   ..   1

Ashford Shire Council *v.* Dependable Motors, Ltd., (1961) A.C. 336; [1961] 1 All E.R. 96 [1960] 3 W.L.R. 999; 104 Sol. Jo. 1055, P.C.; 39 Digest (Repl.) 548   ..

Ashworth *v.* Wells (1898), 78 L.T. 136; 14 T.L.R. 227, C.A.; 39 Digest (Repl.) 591..   4

Associated Distributors, Ltd. *v.* Hall, [1938] 2 K.B. 83; [1938] 1 All E.R. 511; 107 L.J.K.B. 701; 158 L.T. 236; 54 T.L.R. 433; 82 Sol. Jo. 136, C.A.; 26 Digest (Repl.) 667   3

Astley Industrial Trust, Ltd. *v.* Grimley, [1963] 2 All E.R. 33; [1963] 1 W.L.R. 584; 107 Sol. Jo. 474, C.A.; Digest Cont. Vol. A 646   ..   ..   93, 142, 283, 284, 4

Astley Industrial Trust, Ltd. *v.* Grimston Electric Tools, Ltd. (1965), 109 Sol. Jo. 149   3

Astley Industrial Trust, Ltd. *v.* Miller, [1968] 2 All E.R. 36; Digest Supp.   204, 207, 2
                                                                              213, 333, 377, 3

Attryde's Case. *See* Farnworth Finance Facilities, Ltd. *v.* Attryde

Australian Knitting Mills, Ltd. *v.* Grant (1933), 50 C.L.R. 387   ..   ..   ..

Automobile and General Finance Corporation, Ltd. *v.* Morris (1929), 73 Sol. Jo. 451; 26 Digest (Repl.) 660   ..   ..   299, 301, 3

Avery *v.* Bowden (1855), 5 E. & B. 714; 25 L.J.Q.B. 49; affd. (1856), 6 E. & B. 953; 26 L.J.Q.B. 3; 28 L.T.O.S. 145; 3 Jur. N.S. 238; 5 W.R. 41; 41 Digest (Repl.) 322..   3

Azemar *v.* Casella (1867), L.R. 2 C.P. 677; 36 L.J.C.P. 263; 16 L.T. 571; 15 W.R. 998; 39 Digest (Repl.) 534   1

B

B. and P. Wholesale Distributors *v.* Marko, [1953] C.L.Y. 3266..   2

Babcock *v.* Lawson (1880), 5 Q.B.D. 284; 49 L.J.Q.B. 408; 42 L.T. 289; 28 W.R. 591, C.A.; 39 Digest (Repl.) 655   1

Badham *v.* Lambs, Ltd., [1946] K.B. 45; [1945] 2 All E.R. 295; 115 L.J.K.B. 180; 173 L.T. 139; 61 T.L.R. 569; 89 Sol. Jo. 381; 45 Digest (Repl.) 77   ..   ..

Badische Co., Ltd., *Re*, [1921] 2 Ch. 331; 91 L.J. Ch. 133; 126 L.T. 466; 12 Digest (Repl.) 450   ..   ..

Badische Anilin und Soda Fabrik *v.* Basle Chemical Works, Bindschedler, [1898] A.C. 200; 67 L.J. Ch. 141; 77 L.T. 573; 46 W.R. 255; 14 T.L.R. 82, H.L.; 39 Digest (Repl.) 609   1

Baker *v.* Market Harborough Industrial Co-operative Society, Ltd., [1953] 1 W.L.R. 1472; 97 Sol. Jo. 861, C.A.; Digest Cont. Vol. A 1179   ..   ..   127, 1

Baker *v.* Monk (1864), 4 De G. J. & Sm. 388; 10 L.T. 86; 10 Jur. N.S. 691; 12 W.R. 779; 25 Digest (Repl.) 275   ..   ..

Baldry *v.* Marshall, [1925] 1 K.B. 260; [1924] All E.R. Rep. 155; 94 L.J.K.B. 208; 132 L.T. 326, C.A.; 39 Digest (Repl.) 552   ..   ..   84, 90, 1

Ballantine & Co. *v.* Cramp and Bosman (1923), 129 L.T. 502   ..   ..

Bank of England *v.* Vagliano Brothers, [1891] A.C. 107; 60 L.J.Q.B. 145; 64 L.T. 353; 39 W.R. 657; 7 T.L.R. 333, H.L.; 3 Digest (Repl.) 179   ..   ..   ..

PAGE

ᴋer (William) Junior) & Co., Ltd. v. Ed. T. Agius, Ltd. (1927), 43 T.L.R. 751; 33
Com. Cas. 120; 39 Digest (Repl.) 576 .. .. 78, 397, 398

ᴋnett v. H. and J. Packer & Co., Ltd., [1940] 3 All E.R. 575; 36 Digest (Repl.) 88 125

ᴄrow v. Arnaud (1846), 8 Q.B. 604; 6 L.T.O.S. 453; 10 Jur. 319; 17 Digest (Repl.) 124 382

ᴄrow, Lane and Ballard, Ltd. v. Phillip Phillips & Co., Ltd. [1929] 1 K.B. 574; [1928]
All E.R. Rep. 74; 98 L.J.K.B. 193; 140 L.T. 670; 45 T.L.R. 133; 72 Sol. Jo. 874;
34 Com. Cas. 119; 39 Digest (Repl.) 495 .. .. 77, 167, 252, 253, 254, 259, 401

ᴋtlett v. Sidney Marcus, Ltd., [1965] 2 All E.R. 753; [1965] 1 W.L.R. 1013; 109 Sol.
Jo. 451, C.A.; Digest Cont. Vol. B 630 .. .. 93, 99, 104

ᴋton Thompson & Co., Ltd. v. Stapling Machine Co., [1966] Ch. 499; [1966] 2 All E.R.
222; [1966] 2 W.L.R. 1429; 110 Sol. Jo. 313; Digest Cont. Vol. B 480 374

ᴀle v. Taylor, [1967] 3 All E.R. 253; [1967] 1 W.L.R. 1193; 111 Sol. Jo. 668, C.A.;
Digest Supp. 69

ᴀudesert Shire Council v. Smith (1966), 40 A.L.J.R. 211 124

ᴄkett v. Tower Assets, Co., Ltd., [1891] 1 Q.B. 638; 60 L.J.Q.B. 493; 64 L.T. 497;
55 J.P. 438; 39 W.R. 438; 7 T.L.R. 400, C.A.; 7 Digest (Repl.) 19 294

ᴇr v. Walker (1877), 46 L.J.Q.B. 677; 37 L.T. 278; 41 J.P. 728; 25 W.R. 880; 39 Digest
(Repl.) 541 82

ᴀnke v. Bede Shipbuilding Co., Ltd., [1927] 1 K.B. 649; [1927] All E.R. Rep. 689; 96
L.J.K.B. 325; 136 L.T. 667; 43 T.L.R. 170; 71 Sol. Jo. 105; 17 Asp. M.L.C. 222;
32 Com. Cas. 134; 39 Digest (Repl.) 449 429

ᴀrend & Co. v. Produce Brokers, Co., [1920] 3 K.B. 530, [1920] All E.R. Rep. 125;
90 L.J.K.B. 143; 124 L.T. 281; 36 T.L.R. 775; 15 Asp. M.L.C. 139; 25 Con. Cas.
286; 39 Digest (Repl.) 722 .. .. 77, 408

ᴅl v. Lever Brothers, Ltd., [1932] A.C. 161; [1931] All E.R. Rep. 1; 101 L.J.K.B. 129;
146 L.T. 258; 48 T.L.R. 133; 76 Sol. Jo. 50; 37 Com. Cas. 98, H.L.; 35 Digest
(Repl.) 23 .. .. 123, 405

ᴅsize Motor Supply Co. v. Cox, [1914] 1 K.B. 244; [1911–13] All E.R. Rep. 1084; 83
L.J.K.B. 261; 110 L.T. 151; 26 Digest (Repl.) 660 .. .. .. 374, 380

ᴅvoir Finance Co., Ltd. v. Harold Cole & Co., Ltd., [1969] 2 All E.R. 904, [1969] 1
W.L.R. 1877; Digest Supp. 39, 204, 209

ᴅvoir Finance Co., Ltd., v. Stapleton, [1970] 3 All E.R. 664; [1970] 3 W.L.R. 530;
114 Sol. Jo. 719, C.A. 38, 39, 380

ᴀnett v. Griffin Finance, [1967] 2 Q.B. 46; [1967] 1 All E.R. 515; [1967] 2 W.L.R. 561;
112 Sol. Jo. 150, C.A.; Digest Supp. 296

ᴀtinck, Ltd. v. Cromwell Engineering Co., [1971] 1 All E.R. 33; [1971] 3 W.L.R.
1113; 114 Sol. Jo. 823 337

ᴀtley Brothers v Metcalfe & Co., [1906] 2 K.B. 548; 75 L.J.K.B. 891; 95 L.T. 596;
22 T.L.R. 676 C.A.; 39 Digest (Repl.) 543 86

ᴀtley (Dick), Ltd., v. Harold Smith (Motors), Ltd., [1965] 2 All E.R. 65; [1965] 1
W.L.R. 623; 109 Sol. Jo. 329, C.A.; Digest Cont. Vol. B 630 49

ᴀtworth Finance, Ltd. v. Lubert, [1968] 1 Q.B. 680; [1967] 2 All E.R. 810; [1967]
3 W.L.R. 378; 111 Sol. Jo. 272, C.A.; Digest Supp. 116, 346

ᴀtworth Finance, Ltd. v. White (1962), L.J. 140, Cty. Ct. 286

ᴄg v. Sadler and Moore, [1937] 2 K.B. 158; [1937] 1 All E.R. 637; 106 L.J.K.B. 593;
156 L.T. 334; 53 T.L.R. 430; 81 Sol. Jo. 158; 42 Com. Cas. 228, C.A.; 39 Digest
(Repl.) 802 39

ᴄrill v. Road Haulage Executive, [1952] 2 Lloyd's Rep. 490 381

ᴄry & Son v. Star Brush Co. (1915), 31 T.L.R. 603; 60 Sol. Jo. 11, C.A.; 39 Digest
(Repl.) 628 177

ᴄge v. Parkinson (1862), 7 H. & N. 955; 31 L.J. Ex. 301; 8 Jur. N.S. 1014; 10 W.R.
349; sub nom. Smith v. Parkinson, 7 L.T. 92; 39 Digest (Repl.) 574 115

ᴄgin & Co., Ltd. v. Permanite, Ltd., [1951] 1 K.B. 422; on appeal, [1951] 2 K.B. 314;
[1951] 2 All E.R. 191; [1951] 2 T.L.R. 159; 95 Sol. Jo. 414, C.A.; 17 Digest (Repl.)
130 .. .. 426, 427

ᴄgs v. Evans, [1894] 1 Q.B. 88; 69 L.T. 723; 58 J.P. 84; 10 T.L.R. 59; 1 Digest (Repl.)
386 213

ᴀopsgate Motor Finance Corporation, Ltd. v. Transport Brakes, Ltd., [1949] 1 K.B.
322; [1949] 1 All E.R. 37; [1949] L.J.R. 741; 65 T.L.R. 66; 93 Sol. Jo. 71, C.A.;
33 Digest (Repl.) 489 .. .. 208, 237

PA

Blackburn Bobbin Co., Ltd. *v.* T. W. Allen & Sons, [1918] 1 K.B. 540; affd., [1918] 2 K.B. 467; 87 L.J.K.B. 1085; 119 L.T. 215; 34 T.L.R. 508, C.A.; 12 Digest (Repl.) 452 2

Blades *v.* Higgs (1861), 10 C.B.N.S. 713; 30 L.J.C.P. 347; 4 L.T. 551; 25 J.P. 743; 7 Jur. N.S. 1289; *subsequent proceedings* (1862), 12 C.B.N.S. 501; (1863) 13 C.B.N.S. 844; (1865), 11 H.L. Cas. 621, H.L.; 15 Digest (Repl.) 996 3

Blakey *v.* Pendlebury Property Trustees, [1931] 2 Ch. 255; [1931] All E.R. Rep. 270; 10 L.J. Ch. 399; 145 L.T. 524; 47 T.L.R. 503; [1931] B. & C.R. 29, C.A.; 5 Digest (Repl.) 860 .. .. 307, 3

Bloxam *v.* Sanders (1825), 4 B. & C. 941; 7 Dow & Ry. K.B. 396; 39 Digest (Repl.) 777   2
3

Blythe Shipbuilding Co. and Dry Docks Co., Ltd., *Re.* Forster *v.* Blythe Shipbuilding and Dry Docks Co., Ltd., [1926] Ch. 494; [1926] All E.R. Rep. 373; 95 L.J. Ch. 350; 134 L.T. 643, C.A.; 39 Digest (Repl.) 614 I

Boks & Co. *v.* J. H. Rayner & Co. (1921), 37 T.L.R. 800, C.A.; 39 Digest (Repl.) 717   2

Bolt and Nut Co. (Tipton), Ltd. *v.* Rowlands, Nicolls & Co., Ltd., [1964] 2 Q.B. 10; [1964] 1 All E.R. 137; [1964] 2 W.L.R. 98; 107 Sol. Jo. 909, C.A.; Digest Cont. Vol. B 143 2

Booth Steamship Co., Ltd. *v.* Cargo Fleet Iron Co., Ltd., [1916] 2 K.B. 570; [1916–17] All E.R. Rep. 938; 85 L.J.K.B. 1577; 115 L.T. 199; 32 T.L.R. 535; 13 Asp. M.L.C. 451; 22 Com. Cas. 8, C.A.; 39 Digest (Repl.) 774 3

Borries *v.* Hutchinson (1865), 18 C.B.N.S. 445; 5 New Rep. 281; 34 L.J.C.P. 169; 11 L.T. 771; 11 Jur. N.S. 267; 13 W.R. 386; 39 Digest (Repl.) 815 4

Borthwick (Thomas) (Glasgow), Ltd. *v.* Bunge & Co., Ltd., [1969] 1 Lloyds Rep. 17   2

Bostock & Co., Ltd., *v.* Nicholson & Sons, Ltd., [1904] 1 K.B. 725; 73 L.J.K.B. 524; 91 L.T. 626; 53 W.R. 155; 20 T.L.R. 342; 9 Com. Cas. 200; 39 Digest (Repl.) 589   4
427, 4

Bow McLachlan & Co. *v.* Ship Camosun, [1909] A.C. 597; [1908–10] All E.R. Rep. 931; 79 L.J.P.C. 17; 101 L.T. 167; 25 T.L.R. 833, P.C.; 16 Digest (Repl.) 200   4

Bowes *v.* Shand (1877), 2 App. Cas. 455; [1874–80] All E.R. Rep. 174; 46 L.J.Q.B. 561; 36 L.T. 857; 25 W.R. 730; 5 Asp. M.L.C. 461, H.L.; 39 Digest (Repl.) 520   2

Bowmakers, Ltd. *v.* Barnett Instruments, Ltd., [1945] K.B. 65; [1944] 2 All E.R. 579; 114 L.J.K.B. 41; 172 L.T. 1; 61 T.L.R. 62; 89 Sol. Jo. 22, C.A.; 12 Digest (Repl.) 310 2

Bowmaker (Commercial), Ltd. *v.* Day, [1965] 2 All E.R. 856, n.; [1965] 1 W.L.R. 1396; 109 Sol. Jo. 853; Digest Cont. Vol. B 334 .. .. 60, 4

Bowmaker (Commercial), Ltd. *v.* Smith, [1965] 2 All E.R. 304; [1965] 1 W.L.R. 855; 109 Sol. Jo. 329, C.A.; Digest Cont. Vol. B 327 2

Bowmaker, Ltd, *v.* Wycombe Motors, Ltd., [1946] K.B. 505; [1946] 2 All E.R. 113; 115 L.J.K.B. 411; 175 L.T. 133; 62 T.L.R. 437; 90 Sol. Jo. 407; 32 Digest (Repl.) 288 2

Bradford Advance Co., Ltd. *v.* Ayres, [1924] W.N. 152; 7 Digest (Repl.) 57 .. 2

Bradford Old Bank *v.* Sutcliffe, [1918] 2 K.B. 833; 88 L.J.K.B. 85; 119 L.T. 727; 34 T.L.R. 619; 62 Sol. Jo. 753; Com. Cas. 27, C.A.; 26 Digest (Repl.) 69.. .. 2

Bradley *v.* (H.) Newsom Sons & Co., [1919] A.C. 16; [1918–19] All E.R. Rep. 625; 88 L.J.K.B. 35; 119 L.T. 239; 34 T.L.R. 613; 14 Asp. M.L.C. 340; 24 Com. Cas. 1, H.L.; 12 Digest (Repl.) 384 2

Bradley and Cohn, Ltd. *v.* Ramsey & Co. (1912), 106 L.T. 771; 28 T.L.R. 388, C.A.; 39 Digest (Repl.) 628 I

Brady *v.* St. Margaret's Trust, Ltd., [1963] 2 Q.B. 494; [1963] 2 All E.R. 275; [1963] 2 W.L.R. 1162, C.A.; Digest (Repl.) 651 .. .. 380, 3

Bragg *v.* Villanova (1923), 40 T.L.R. 154; 39 Digest (Repl.) 717 2

Braithwaite *v.* Foreign Hardwood Co., [1905] 2 K.B. 543; 74 L.J.K.B. 688; 92 L.T. 637; 21 T.L.R. 413; 10 Asp. M.L.C. 52; 10 Com. Cas. 189, C.A.; 39 Digest (Repl.) 509 I
2

Branwhite *v.* Worcester Works Finance, Ltd., [1969] 1 A.C. 552; [1968] 3 All E.R. 104; [1968] 3 W.L.R. 760; 112 Sol. Jo. 758, H.L.; Digest Supp.   285, 287, 405, 4

Braude (London), Ltd. *v.* Porter, [1959] 2 Lloyd's Rep. 161 4

Bray *v.* Palmer, [1953] 2 All E.R. 1449; [1953] 1 W.L.R. 1455; 97 Sol. Jo. 830, C.A.; 51 Digest (Repl.) 857 2

PAGE

dge *v.* Campbell Discount Co., Ltd., [1962] A.C. 600; [1962] 1 All E.R. 385; [1962] 2 W.L.R. 439; 106 Sol. Jo. 94, H.L.; Digest Cont. Vol. A 648 .. 392, 393, 394

dge *v.* Wain (1816), 1 Stark 504; 39 Digest (Repl.) 591 224

ght *v.* Rogers, [1917] 1 K.B. 917; 86 L.J.K.B. 804; 117 L.T. 61; 61 Sol. Jo. 370; 39 Digest (Repl.) 585 415

ghty *v.* Norman (1862), 3 B. & S. 305; 1 New Rep. 93; 32 L.J.Q.B. 38; 7 L.T. 422; 9 Jur. N.S. 495; 11 W.R. 167; 7 Digest (Repl.) 138 274

nsmead *v.* Harrison (1872), L.R. 7 C.P. 547; 41 L.J.C.P. 190; 27 L.T. 99; 20 W.R. 784; 46 Digest (Repl.) 525 333

stol and West of England Bank *v.* Midland Rail Co., [1891] 2 Q.B. 653; 61 L.J.Q.B. 115; 65 L.T. 234; 40 W.R. 148; 7 T.L.R. 627; 7 Asp. M.L.C. 69, C.A.; 1 Digest (Repl.) 72 248

stol Tramways Carriage Co., Ltd. *v.* Fiat Motors, Ltd., [1910] 2 K.B. 831; [1908–10] All E.R. Rep. 113; 79 L.J.K.B. 1107; 103 L.T. 443; 26 T.L.R. 629, C.A.; 39 Digest (Repl.) 511 .. .. 90, 91, 97

ain *v.* Rossiter (1879), 11 Q.B.D. 123; 48 L.J.Q.B. 362; 40 L.T. 240; 43 J.P. 332; 27 W.R. 482, C.A.; 40 Digest (Repl.) 39 352

annia Hygienic Laundry, Ltd. *v.* Thornycroft, Ltd. (1925), 94 L.J.K.B. 858; 41 T.L.R. 667; on appeal, 95 L.J.K.B. 237; 135 L.T. 83; 42 T.L.R. 198; 17 Digest (Repl.) 141 428

tish and Benningtons, Ltd. *v.* North Western Cachar Tea Co., Ltd., [1923] A.C. 48; [1922] All E.R. Rep. 224; 92 L.J.K.B. 62; 128 L.T. 422; 28 Com. Cas. 265; 13 Ll. L.R. 67, H.L.; 39 Digest (Repl.) 664 .. .. 149, 266, 267, 352

tish Berna Motor Lorries, Ltd. *v.* Inter-Transport Co., Ltd. (1915), 31 T.L.R. 200; 26 Digest (Repl.) 667 258

tish Oil and Cake Co., Ltd. *v.* Burstall & Co. (1923), 39 T.L.R. 406; 67 Sol. Jo. 577; 39 Digest (Repl.) 828 426

tish Westinghouse Electric and Manufacturing Co., Ltd. *v.* Underground Electric Rail. Co. of London, Ltd., [1912] A.C. 673; [1911–13] All E.R. Rep. 63; 81 L.J.K.B. 1132; 107 L.T. 325; 56 Sol. Jo. 734, H.L.; 39 Digest (Repl.) 592

oks *v.* Beirnstein, [1909] 1 K.B. 98; 78 L.J.K.B. 243; 99 L.T. 970; 39 Digest (Repl.) 780 .. .. 379, 390, 391, 418

wn *v.* Muller (1872), L.R. 7 Exch. 319; 41 L.J. Ex. 214; 27 L.T. 272; 21 W.R. 18; 39 Digest (Repl.) 818 374

wn *v.* Sheen and Richmond Car Sales, Ltd., [1950] 1 All E.R. 1102; 26 Digest (Repl.) 666 411

wn & Co. *v.* Bedford Pantechnicon Co., Ltd. (1889), 5 T.L.R. 449, C.A.; 1 Digest (Repl.) 385 .. .. 25, 283, 423

wn (B. S.) & Sons, Ltd. *v.* Craiks, Ltd., [1970] 1 All E.R. 823; [1970] 1 W.L.R. 752; 114 Sol. Jo. 282; 1970 S.L.T. 141, H.L. 205

lberg *v.* Jerwood and Ward (1935), 51 T.L.R. 99, 78 Sol. Jo. 878; 1 Digest (Repl.) 387 .. .. 89, 98, 99, 100

lding and Civil Engineering Holidays Scheme Management *v.* Post Office, [1966] 1 Q.B. 247; [1965] 1 All E.R. 163; [1965] 2 W.L.R. 72; 108 Sol. Jo. 939, C.A.; Digest Cont. Vol. B 213 205

l *v.* Robinson (1854), 10 Exch. 342; 2 C.L.R. 1276; 24 L.J.Q.B. 677; 37 L.T. 278; 41 J.P. 728; 25 W.R. 880; 39 Digest (Repl.) 712 18

rfitt *v.* Kille, [1939] 2 K.B. 743; [1939] 2 All E.R. 372; 108 L.J.K.B. 669; 160 L.T. 481; 55 T.L.R. 645; 83 Sol. Jo. 419; 37 L.G.R. 304; 45 Digest (Repl.) 390 .. 245

tterworth *v.* Kingsway Motors, Ltd., [1954] 2 All E.R. 694; [1954] 1 W.L.R. 1286; 98 Sol. Jo. 717; 26 Digest (Repl.) 671 .. 59, 60, 62, 63, 64, 126, 402, 406, 408, 427

C

char Tea Case. *See* British and Benningtons, Ltd. *v.* North Western Cachar Tea Co., Ltd.

n *v.* Pockett's Bristol Channel Steam Packet Co., Ltd., [1899] 1 Q.B. 643; 68 L.J.Q.B. 515; 80 L.T. 269; 47 W.R. 422; 15 T.L.R. 247; 43 Sol. Jo. 331; 8 Asp. M.L.C. 517; 4 Com. Cas. 168, C.A.; 39 Digest (Repl.) 636 .. 182, 224, 226, 225, 227

dwell's Case. *See* Car and Universal Finance Co., Ltd. *v.* Caldwell

Cammell Laird, Ltd. *v.* Manganese Bronze and Brass, Ltd., [1934] A.C. 402; [1934] All
  E.R. Rep. 1; 103 L.J.K.B. 289; 151 L.T. 142; 50 T.L.R. 350; 39 Com. Cas. 194,
  H.L.; 39 Digest (Repl.) 544 .. .. 91, 92,
Campbell Discount Co., Ltd. *v.* Gall, [1961] 1 Q.B. 431; [1961] 2 All E.R. 104; [1961]
  2 W.L.R. 514; 105 Sol. Jo. 232, C.A.; Digest Cont. Vol. A 644   30, 189, 196, 2
                                                                    287, 288, 296, 3
Campbell Mostyn (Provisions), Ltd. *v.* Barnett Trading Co., [1954] 1 Lloyd's Rep. 65   3
Canada Export Co. *v.* Eilers (1929), 35 Com. Cas. 90
Capital Finance, Ltd. *v.* Bray, [1964] 1 All E.R. 603; [1964] 1 W.L.R. 323; 108 Sol. Jo.
  95, C.A.; 46 Digest (Repl.) 481 .. .. 117, 332,
Car and Universal Finance Co., Ltd. *v.* Caldwell, [1965] 1 Q.B. 525; [1964] 1 All E.R.
  290; [1964] 2 W.L.R. at p. 606; 108 Sol. Jo. 15, C.A.; Digest Cont. Vol. B 634   199, 2
                                                                              202, 230, 2
Carlos Federspiel & Co. *v.* Charles Twigg & Co., Ltd., [1957] 1 Lloyd's Rep. 240   1
                                                                   169, 170, 171, 175, 2
Carr *v.* James Broderick, Ltd., [1942] 2 K.B. 275; [1942] 2 All E.R. 441; 111 L.J.K.B.
  667; 167 L.T. 335; 58 T.L.R. 373; 26 Digest (Repl.) 673   3
Carr *v.* London and North Western Rail. Co. (1875), L.R. 10 C.P. 307; [1874–80] All
  E.R. Rep. 418; 44 L.J.C.P. 109; 31 L.T. 785; 39 J.P. 279; 23 W.R. 747; 46 Digest
  (Repl.) 462 3
Case of Market Overt. *See* Market Overt Case
Central Meat Products, Ltd. *v.* McDaniel, Ltd., [1952] 1 Lloyd's Rep. 562 4
Central Newbury Car Auctions, Ltd. *v.* Unity Finance, Mercury Motors, [1957] 1 Q.B.
  371; [1956] 3 All E.R. 905; [1956] 3 W.L.R. 1068; 100 Sol. Jo. 927, C.A.; 21 Digest
  (Repl.) 485 1
Champanhac & Co., Ltd. *v.* Waller & Co., Ltd., [1948] 2 All E.R. 724; 39 Digest (Repl.)
  558 1
Chandler *v.* Webster, [1904] 1 K.B. 493; 73 L.J.K.B. 401; 90 L.T. 217; 52 W.R. 290;
  20 T.L.R. 222; 48 Sol. Jo. 245, C.A.; 12 Digest (Repl.) 464
Chanter *v.* Hopkins (1838), 4 M. & W. 399; 1 Horn & H. 377; 8 L.J. Ex. 14; 3 Jur. 58; 39
  Digest (Repl.) 551
Chao (Trading as Zung Fu Co.) *v.* British Traders and Shippers, Ltd. *See* Kwei Tek
  Chao (Trading as Zung Fu Co.) *v.* British Traders and Shippers, Ltd.
Chapman *v.* Michaelson, [1909] 1 Ch. 238; 78 L.J. Ch. 272; 100 L.T. 109; 25 T.L.R.
  101, C.A.; 35 Digest (Repl.) 240
Charles Rickards, Ltd. *v.* Oppenaim. *See* Rickards (Charles), Ltd. *v.* Oppenaim.
Charter *v.* Sullivan, [1957] 2 Q.B. 117; [1957] 1 All E.R. 809; [1957] 2 W.L.R. 528; 101
  Sol. Jo. 265, C.A.; 39 Digest (Repl.) 795 .. .. .. 382, 383, 384,
Charterhouse Credit, Ltd. *v.* Tolly, [1963] 2 Q.B. 683; [1963] 2 All E.R. 432; [1963] 2
  W.L.R. 1168; 107 Sol. Jo. 234, C.A.; Digest Cont. Vol. A 649   142, 143, 374, 3
                                                                    423, 424,
Chatterton *v.* Maclean, [1951] 1 All E.R. 761; 26 Digest (Repl.) 169   308,
Cheetham & Co., Ltd. *v.* Thornham Spinning Co., Ltd., [1964] 2 Lloyd's Rep. 17
Chess (Oscar), Ltd. *v.* Williams, [1957] 1 All E.R. 325; [1957] 1 W.L.R. 370; 101 Sol. Jo.
  186, C.A.; 39 Digest (Repl.) 514 .. ..
Chetwynd's Estate, *Re*, Dunn's Trust, Ltd. *v.* Brown, [1938] Ch. 13; [1937] 3 All E.R.
  530; 106 L.J. Ch. 330; 157 L.T. 125; 53 T.L.R. 917; 81 Sol. Jo. 626, C.A.; 12
  Digest (Repl.) 599 .. ..
Chillingworth *v.* Esche, [1924] 1 Ch. 97; 93 L.J. Ch. 129; 129 L.T. 808; 40 T.L.R. 23;
  68 Sol. Jo. 80, C.A.; 12 Digest (Repl.) 98 .. ..
Chinery *v.* Viall (1860), 5 H. & N. 288; 29 L.J. Ex. 180; 2 L.T. 466; 8 W.R. 629; 3 Digest
  (Repl.) 120 .. .. 276, 325, 380,
Christopher Hill, Ltd. *v.* Ashington Piggeries, Ltd. *See* Hill (Christopher), Ltd. *v.*
  Ashington Piggeries, Ltd.
Churchill (Lord), Manisty *v.* Churchill (1888), 39 Ch.D. 174; 58 L.J. Ch. 136; 59 L.T.
  597; 36 W.R. 805; 23 Digest (Repl.) 351 .. ..
City Fur Manufacturing Co., Ltd. *v.* Fureenbond (Brokers), London, Ltd., [1937] 1 All
  E.R. 799; 81 Sol. Jo. 218; 39 Digest (Repl.)
Clare *v.* Maynard (1835), 6 Ad. & El. 519; 1 Nev. & P.K.B. 701; Will. Woll. & Dav.
  274; 6 L.J.K.B. 138; 2 Digest (Repl.) 360 422,

PAGE

rke v. Army and Navy Co-operative Society, [1903] 1 K.B. 155; 72 L.J.K.B. 153; 88 L.T. 1; 19 T.L.R. 80, C.A.; 39 Digest (Repl.) 563 126

rke v. Bates, [1913] L.J.C.C.R. 63; Affd., [1913] L.J.C.C.R. 114 .. .. 254, 258

rke v. Reilly (1962), 96 I.L.T.R. 96 163

y v. Crump. Ltd., [1964] 1 Q.B. 533; [1963] 3 All E.R. 687; [1963] 3 W.L.R. 866; 107 Sol. Jo. 664, C.A.; Digest Cont. Vol. A 76 126

yton v. Le Roy, [1911] 2 K.B. 1031; 81 L.J.K.B. 49; 104 L.T. 419; 75 J.P. 229; 27 T.L.R. 206; reversed, [1911] 2 K.B. 1046; [1911–13] All E.R. Rep. 284; 81 L.J.K.B. 58; 105 L.T. 430; 27 T.L.R. 479; 75 J.P. 521, C.A.; 33 Digest (Repl.) 491 .. 237

pins Oil Co., Ltd. v. Edinburgh and District Water Trustees, [1907] A.C. 291; 76 L.J.P.C. 79, H.L.; 17 Digest (Repl.) 179 391

ugh v. London and North Western Rail. Co. (1871), L.R. 7 Exch. 26; [1861–73] All E.R. Rep. 646; 41 L.J. Ex. 17; 25 L.T. 708; 20 W.R. 189; 39 Digest (Repl.) 653 358

debank Engineering and Shipbuilding Co. v. Don Jose Ramos Yzquierdo-y-Castaneda, [1905] A.C. 6; [1904–7] All E.R. Rep. 251; 74 L.J.P.C. 1; 91 L.T. 666; 21 T.L.R. 58, H.L.; 12 Digest (Repl.) 492 .. .. 391, 392

k, Re ex parte Rosevear China Clay Co. (1879), 11 Ch. D. 560; on appeal, 11 Ch. D. 560; 48 L.J. Bcy. 100; 40 L.T. 730; 27 W.R. 591; 4 Asp. M.L.C. 144, C.A.; 39 Digest (Repl.) 685 326

en v. Roche, [1927] 1 K.B. 169; 95 L.J.K.B. 945; 136 L.T. 219; 42 T.L.R. 674; 70 Sol. Jo. 942; 39 Digest (Repl.) 482 .. .. 333, 414

ntat v. Myhan & Son (1914), 84 L.J.K.B. 2253; 110 L.T. 749; 78 J.P. 193; 30 C.L.R. 282; 12 L.G.R. 274, C.A.; 39 Digest (Repl.) 574 132

e v. North-Western Bank (1875), L.R. 10 C.P. 354; [1874–80] All E.R. Rep. 486; 44 L.J.C.P. 233; 32 L.T. 733; 1 Digest (Repl.) 385 204

ley v. Overseas Exporters, [1921] 3 K.B. 302; [1921] All E.R. Rep. 596; 90 L.J.K.B. 1301; 126 L.T. 58; 37 T.L.R. 797; 26 Com. Cas. 325; 39 Digest (Repl.) 671 .. 371

mission Car Sales (Hastings), Ltd. v. Saul, [1957] N.Z.L.R. 144 269, 317, 368, 369

mmonwealth Trust, Ltd. v. Akotey, [1926] A.C. 72; [1925] All E.R. Rep. 270; 94 L.J.P.C. 167; 134 L.T. 33; 41 T.L.R. 641, P.C.; 39 Digest (Repl.) 773 .. 188

mptoir D'Achat et de Vente du Boerenbond Belge S/A v. Luis de Ridder, Limitada, [1949] A.C. 293; [1949] 1 All E.R. 269; [1949] L.J.R. 513; 65 T.L.R. 126; 93 Sol. Jo. 101, H.L.; 39 Digest (Repl.) 640 .. .. .. 244, 248, 409

nsolidated Co. v. Curtis & Son, [1892] 1 Q.B. 495; 61 L.J.Q.B. 325; 56 J.P. 565; 40 W.R. 426; 8 T.L.R. 403; 36 Sol. Jo. 328; 3 Digest (Repl.) 50 369

oden Engineering, Ltd. v. Stamford, [1953] 1 Q.B. 86; [1952] 2 All E.R. 915; [1952] 2 T.L.R. 822; 96 Sol. Jo. 802, C.A.; 17 Digest (Repl.) 155 .. .. 393, 394

k v. Lewis, [1952] 1 D.L.R. 1; [1951] S.C.R. 830; 36 Digest (Repl.) 142 .. 128

per, Re ex parte Trustee of Property of Bankrupt v. Registrar and High Bailiff of Peterborough and Huntingdon County Courts, [1958] Ch. 922; [1958] 3 All E.R. 97; [1958] 3 W.L.R. 468; 102 Sol. Jo. 635 239

y (William) & Son v. I.R. Comrs., [1964] 3 All E.R. 66; [1964] 1 W.L.R. 1332; 108 Sol. Jo. 579; [1964] 2 Lloyd's Rep. 43; on appeal, [1966] A.C. 1088; [1965] 1 All E.R. 917; [1965] 2 W.L.R. 924; 109 Sol. Jo. 254, [1965] 1 Lloyd's Rep. 313; [1965] T.R. 77; 44 A.T.C. 61, H.L.; Digest Cont. Vol. B. 99 16

turier v. Hastie (1856), 5 H.L. Cas. 673; 25 L.J. Ex. 253; 28 L.T.O.S. 240; 2 Jur. N.S. 1241; 12 Digest (Repl.) 414 .. .. 246, 250, 252, 253

entry v. Great Eastern Rail. Co. (1883), 11 Q.B.D. 776; 52 L.J.Q.B. 604; 49 L.T. 641, C.A.; 21 Digest (Repl.) 485 194

mer v. Giles (1883), 1 Cab. & El. 151; Affd. (1884), Times, May 4th; 26 Digest (Repl.) 672 .. .. 330, 372

ssfield v. Such (1852), 8 Exch. 159; 22 L.J. Ex. 65, subsequent proceedings (1853), 8 Ex Ch. 825; I.C.L.R. 668; 22 L.J. Ex. 325; 21 L.T.O.S. 187; 1 W.R. 470; 51 Digest (Repl.) 578 332

inane v. British "Rema" Manufacturing Co., Ltd., [1954] 1 Q.B. 292; [1953] 2 All E.R. 1257; [1953] 3 W.L.R. 923; 97 Sol. Jo. 811, C.A.; 39 Digest (Repl.) 593 426

dy v. Lindsay (1878), 3 App. Cas. 459; 38 L.T. 573; 42 J.P. 483; 26 W.R. 406; 14 Cox C.C. 93; sub nom. Lindsay & Co. v. Cundy, 47 L.J.Q.B. 481, H.L.; 39 Digest (Repl.) 654 .. .. 183, 199

Cunliffe v. Harrison (1851), 6 Exch. 903; 20 L.J. Ex. 325; 17 L.T.O.S. 189; 39 Digest (Repl.) 608 .. ..
Curtis v. Chemical Cleaning and Dyeing Co., Ltd., [1951] 1 K.B. 805; [1951] 1 All E.R. 631; [1951] 1 T.L.R. 452; 92 Sol. Jo. 253, C.A.; 3 Digest (Repl.) 103 ..
Curtis v. Maloney, [1950] 2 All E.R. 201; 66 (pt. 2) 147; 94 Sol. Jo. 437; affd., [1951] 1 K.B. 736; [1950] 2 All E.R. 982; 66 (pt. 2) T.L.R. 869; 94 Sol. Jo. 761, C.A.; 21 Digest (Repl.) 609 .. ..
Cutter v. Powell (1795), 6 Term Rep. 320; 42 Digest (Repl.) 706 .. ..

D

D. and C. Builders, Ltd. v. Rees, [1966] 2 Q.B. 617; [1965] 3 All E.R. 837; [1966] 2 W.L.R. 288; 109 Sol. Jo. 971, C.A.; Digest Cont. Vol. B. 142 145,
Daniels and Daniels v. White & Sons, Ltd. and Tanbard, [1938] 4 All E.R. 258; 160 L.T. 128; 82 Sol. Jo. 912; 39 Digest (Repl.) 541 .. .. 90, 98, 125,
Darlington (Peter), Ltd. v. Gosho, Ltd., [1964] 1 Lloyd's Rep. 149 71,
David Allester, Ltd., Re. See Allester (David) Ltd., Re.
Davies v. Burnett, [1902] 1 K.B. 666; 71 L.J.K.B. 355; 86 L.T. 565; 66 J.P. 406; 50 W.R. 391; 18 T.L.R. 354; 46 Sol. Jo. 300; 20 Cox, C.C. 193; 8 Digest (Repl.) 672
Davis v. Oswell (1837), 7 C. & P. 804; 46 Digest (Repl.) 514 .. ..
Davis & Co., Re, ex parte Rawlings (1888), 22 Q.B.D. 193; 37 W.R. 203; 5 T.L.R. 119, C.A.; 18 Digest (Repl.) 271 .. ..
Dawson, (G. F.) (Clapham), Ltd. v. Dutfield, [1936] 2 All E.R. 232; 39 Digest (Repl.) 784
Daywood, Ltd. v. Heath, [1961] 2 Lloyd's Rep. 512 .. ..
De Freville v. Dill (1927), 96 L.J.K.B. 1056; [1927] All E.R. Rep. 205; 138 L.T. 83; 43 T.L.R. 702; 33 Digest (Repl.) 709 .. ..
De Gorter v. Attenborough (1904), 21 T.L.R. 19; 1 Digest (Repl.) 392 .. .. ..
De la Bere v. Pearson, Ltd., [1908] 1 K.B. 280; 77 L.J.K.B. 380; 98 L.T. 71; 24 T.L.R. 120, C.A.; 36 Digest (Repl.) 44 .. ..
Delaney v. Wallis & Sons (1884), 14 L.R. It. 31 .. ..
Demby Hamilton, Ltd. v. Barden, [1949] 1 All E.R. 435; 39 Digest (Repl.) 647 ..
De Medina v. Norman (1842), 9 M. & W. 820; 11 L.J. Ex. 320; 30 Digest (Repl.) 419
Dennant v. Skinner, [1948] 2 K.B. 164; [1948] 2 All E.R. 29; [1948] L.J.R. 1576; 39 Digest (Repl.) 651 .. ..
Denny v. Skelton (1916), 86 L.J.K.B. 280; 115 L.T. 305; 13 Asp. M.L.C. 437; 39 Digest (Repl.) 604 .. ..
Derry v. Peek (1889), 14 App. Cas. 337; [1886-90] All E.R. Rep. 1; 58 L.J. Ch. 864; 61 L.T. 265; 54 J.P. 148; 38 W.R. 33; 5 T.L.R. 625; 1 Meg. 292, H.L.; 9 Digest (Repl.) 127 .. ..
Dexters, Ltd. v. Hill Crest Oil Co., (Bradford), Ltd., [1926] 1 K.B. 348; [1925] All E.R. Rep. 273; 95 L.J.K.B. 386; 134 L.T. 494; 42 T.L.R. 212; 31 Com. Cas. 161, C.A.; 39 Digest (Repl.) 828 .. ..
Dick Bentley, Ltd. v. Harold Smith (Motors), Ltd. See Bentley (Dick), Ltd. v. Harold Smith (Motors), Ltd.
Dies v. British and International Mining and Finance Corporation, Ltd., [1939] 1 K.B. 724; 108 L.J.K.B. 398; 160 L.T. 563; 39 Digest (Repl.) 826 373,
Doak v. Bedford, [1964] 2 Q.B. 587; [1964] 1 All E.R. 311; [1964] 2 W.L.R. 545; 128 J.P. 230; 108 Sol. Jo. 76; 62 L.G.R. 249; Digest Cont. Vol. B. 465 .. ..
Dobell (G. C.) & Co., Ltd. v. Barber and Garratt, [1931] 1 K.B. 219; 100 L.J.K.B. 65; 144 L.T. 266; 47 T.L.R. 66; 74 Sol. Jo. 836; 36 Com. Cas. 87, C.A.; 2 Digest (Repl.) 159 .. ..
Docker v. Hyams, [1969] 3 All E.R. 808; [1969] 1 W.L.R. 1060; 113 Sol. Jo. 381; [1969] 1 Lloyd's Rep. 487, C.A.; Digest Supp. .. ..
Domestic Electric Rentals, v. Dawson, [1943] L.J.C.C.R. 31 .. ..
Donoghue (or McAlister) v. Stevenson, [1932] A.C. 562; [1932] All E.R. Rep. 1; 101 L.J.P.C. 119; 147 L.T. 281; 48 T.L.R. 494; 76 Sol. Jo. 396; 37 Con. Cas. 350, H.L.; 36 Digest (Repl.) 85 125,
Doobay v. Mohabeer, [1967] 2 A.C. 278; [1967] 2 All E.R. 760; [1967] 2 W.L.R. 1395; 111 Sol. Jo. 234, P.C.; Digest Supp. 424,
Doyle v. Olby (Ironmongers), Ltd., [1969] 2 Q.B. 158; [1969] 2 All E.R. 119; [1969] 2 W.L.R. 673; 113 Sol. Jo. 128, C.A.; Digest Supp. .. ..

PAGE

ummond v. Van Ingen (1887), 12 Asp. Cas. 284; 56 L.J.Q.B. 563; 57 L.T. 1; 36
   W.R. 20; 3 T.L.R. 541, H.L.; 39 Digest (Repl.)   560 .. .. 104, 106, 111
ury v. Victor Buckland, Ltd., [1941] 1 All E.R. 269; 85 Sol. Jo. 117, C.A.; 26 Digest
   (Repl.) 659 .. .. 25, 282, 284
Jardin v. Beadman Brothers, Ltd., [1952] 2 Q.B. 712; [1952] 2 All E.R. 160; [1952]
   1 T.L.R. 1601; 96 Sol. Jo. 414; 1 Digest (Repl.) 392 223
imenil (Peter) & Co., Ltd. v. Ruddin, Ltd., [1953] 2 All E.R. 294; [1953] 1 W.L.R.
   815, 97 Sol. Jo. 437; [1953] 2 Lloyd's Rep. 4, C.A.; Digest Cont. Vol. A. 290 .. 278
nkirk Colliery Co. v. Lever (1878), 9 Ch. D. 20; 39 L.T. 239; 26 W.R. 841, C.A.;
   51 Digest (Repl.) 695 383
nlop Pneumatic Tyre Co., Ltd. v. New Garage and Motor Co., Ltd., [1915] A.C. 79;
   [1914–15] All E.R. Rep. 739; 83 L.J.K.B. 1574; 111 L.T. 862; 30 T.L.R. 625,
   H.L.; 17 Digest (Repl.) 149 .. .. 391, 394
nlop Pneumatic Tyre Co., Ltd. v. Selfridge & Co., Ltd., [1915] A.C. 847; [1914–15]
   All E.R. Rep. 333; 84 L.J.K.B. 1680; 113 L.T. 386; 31 T.L.R. 399; 59 Sol. Jo.
   439, H.L.; 39 Digest (Repl.) 645 .. .. 139, 184
er v. Munday, [1895] 1 Q.B. 742; [1895–9] All E.R. Rep. 1022; 64 L.J.Q.B. 448;
   72 L.T. 448; 59 J.P. 276; 43 W.R. 440; 11 T.L.R. 282; 14 R. 306, C.A.; 1 Digest
   (Repl.) 701 330

E

stern Distributors, Ltd. v. Goldring, [1957] 2 Q.B. 600; [1957] 2 All E.R. 525;
   [1957] 3 W.L.R. 237; 101 Sol. Jo. 553, C.A.; 26 Digest (Repl.) 675   33, 189, 190, 191,
                                                    193, 194, 196, 197, 198, 217, 218, 339
wards, Re, ex parte Chalmers (1873), L.R. 8 Ch. App. 289; 42 L.J. Bcy. 37; 28 L.T.
   325; 21 W.R. 349; 5 Digest (Repl.) 999 .. .. 316, 318
wards (P.) Ltd. v. Vaughan (1910), 26 T.L.R. 545, C.A.; 39 Digest (Repl.)   624, 176, 181
inger Aktiengesellschaft v. Armstrong (1874), L.R. 9 Q.B. 473; 43 L.J.Q.B. 211;
   30 L.T. 871; 38 J.P. 774; 23 W.R. 127; 39 Digest (Repl.) 810 421
ion (Lord) v. Hedley Brothers, [1935] 2 K.B. 1; 104 L.J.K.B. 334; 152 L.T. 507; 51
   T.L.R. 313; 79 Sol. Jo. 270, C.A.; 2 Digest (Repl.) 37 158
esmere (Earl) v. Wallace, [1929] 2 Ch. 1, 98 L.J. Ch. 177; 140 L.T. 628; 45 T.L.R.
   238; 73 Sol. Jo. 143, C.A., 25 Digest (Repl.) 418 20
is v. John Stenning & Son, [1932] 2 Ch. 81; [1932] All E.R. Rep. 597; 101 L.J. Ch.
   401; 147 L.T. 449; 76 Sol. Jo. 232; 46 Digest (Repl.) 525 363
is v. Rowbotham, [1900] 1 Q.B. 740; [1900–3] All E.R. Rep. 299; 69 L.J.Q.B. 379;
   82 L.T. 191; 48 W.R. 423; 16 T.L.R. 258, C.A.; 31 Digest (Repl.) 286 375
phick v. Barnes (1880), 5 C.P.D. 321; 49 L.J.Q.B. 698; 44 J.P. 651; 29 W.R. 139; 39
   Digest (Repl.) 496 176
cy, Ltd. v. Hyde (1926), unreported 393
ipire Cream Co. v. Quinn (1928), 154 N.Y. App. Div. 302 99
nis Case. See United Dominions Trust (Commercial), Ltd. v. Ennis.
mail (Trading as H. M. H. Esmail & Sons) v. J. Rosenthal & Sons, Ltd. (1964), 108
   Sol. Jo. 839; [1964] 2 Lloyd's Rep. 447, C.A.; on appeal sub nom. Rosenthal (J.)
   & Sons), v. Esmail (Trading as H. M. H. Esmail & Sons), [1965] 2 All E.R. 860;
   [1965] 1 W.L.R. 1117; 109 Sol. Jo. 553, H.L.; Digest Cont. Vol. B 632   266, 270, 277,
                                                         398, 399, 400
iblissements Chainbaux v. Harbormaster, Ltd., [1955] 1 Lloyd's Rep. 303 .. 148
ans v. Triplex, Ltd., [1936] 1 All E.R. 283; 36 Digest (Repl.) 86 .. .. 125, 127
ans v. Truman (1831), 2 B. & Ad. 886; 1 Mood. & R. 10; 1 Digest (Repl.) 393 .. 226

F

C. Finance, Ltd. v. Francis (1970), 114 Sol. Jo. 568, C.A. 337
rnworth Finance Facilities, Ltd. v. Attryde, [1970] 2 All E.R. 774; [1970] 1 W.L.R.
   1053; 114 Sol. Jo. 354, C.A. 91, 142, 143, 144, 414
rquharson Brothers & Co. v. King & Co., (1902) A.C. 325; [1900–3] All E.R. Rep.
   120; 71 L.J.K.B. 667; 86 L.T. 810; 51 W.R. 94; 18 T.L.R. 665; 46 Sol. Jo. 584,
   H.L.; 1 Digest (Repl.) 432 .. ..192, 193, 194

Fastnedge, *Re, ex parte* Kemp (1874), 9 Ch. App. 383; 43 L.J. Bcy. 50; 30 L.T. 109;
  22 W.R. 462; 5 Digest (Repl.) 860 .. ..
Fawcett *v.* Star Car Sales, Ltd. [1960] N.Z.L.R. 406 .. ..
Felston Tile Co., Ltd. *v.* Winget, Ltd., [1936] 3 All E.R. 473, C.A.; 26 Digest (Repl.)
  660 .. ..
Ferrier, *Re, ex parte* Trustee *v.* Donald, [1944] Ch. 295; 114 L.J. Ch. 15; 60 T.L.R.
  295; 88 Sol. Jo. 171; 39 Digest (Repl.) 624 .. ..
Fibrosa Spolka Akcyjna *v.* Fairburn Lawson Combe Barbour, Ltd., [1942] 1 K.B. 12;
  [1941] 2 All E.R. 300; 165 L.T. 73; 57 T.L.R. 547, 46 Con. Cas. 229, C.A.;
  affd., [1943] A.C. 32; [1942] 2 All E.R. 122; 111 L.J.K.B. 433; 167 L.T. 101;
  58 T.L.R. 308; 86 Sol. Jo. 232, 233, H.L.; 39 Digest (Repl.) 672 .. .. 147, 405,
Finance Houses Association, Ltd.'s Agreement, *Re*, [1965] 3 All E.R. 509; L.R. 5 R.P.
  366; [1965] 1 W.L.R. 1419; 109 Sol. Jo. 813; Digest Cont. Vol. B. 708 ..
Financings Ltd. *v.* Baldock, [1963] 2 Q.B. 104; [1963] 1 All E.R. 443; [1963] 2 W.L.R.
  359; 107 Sol. Jo. 15, C.A.; Digest Cont. Vol. A 650 .. .. 385, 393,
Financings, Ltd. *v.* Stimson, [1962] 3 All E.R. 386; [1962] 1 W.L.R. 1184, C.A.;
  Digest Cont. Vol. A. 644 .. .. 35, 114, 116, 285,
Finlay (James) & Co., Ltd. *v.* N. V. Kwik Hoo Tong, [1929] 1 K.B. 400; [1928] All
  E.R. Rep. 110; 98 L.J.K.B. 251; 140 L.T. 389; 45 T.L.R. 149; 34 Com. Cas. 143;
  17 Asp. M.L.C. 566; 32 Ll.L.R. 245, C.A.; 39 Digest (Repl.) 707 390, 419, 422,
Fisher *v.* Harrods, Ltd., [1966] 1 Lloyd's Rep. 500; 110 Sol. Jo. 133; Digest Cont. Vol.
  B. 560 .. ..
Fisher, Ltd. *v.* Eastwoods, Ltd., [1936] 1 All E.R. 421; 12 Digest (Repl.) 395 ..
Fisher, Reeves & Co. *v.* Armour & Co., [1920] 3 K.B. 614; 90 L.J.K.B. 172, 124 L.T.
  122; 36 T.L.R. 800; 64 Sol. Jo. 698; 15 Asp. M.L.C. 91; 26 Com. Cas. 46, C.A.;
  39 Digest (Repl.) 535 .. ..
French *v.* Hoggett, [1967] 3 All E.R. 1042, [1968] 1 W.L.R. 94; 132 J.P. 91; 111 Sol.
  Jo. 906; 66 L.G.R. 383; Digest Supp. .. ..
Fitt *v.* Cassanet (1842), 4 Man. & G. 898; 5 Scott, N.R. 902; 12 L.J.C.P. 70; 6 Jur.
  1125; 39 Digest (Repl.) 826 .. ..
Foley *v.* Classique Coaches, Ltd., [1934] 2 K.B.1; [1934] All E.R. Rep. 88; 103 J.L.K.B.
  550; 151 L.T. 242, C.A.; 39 Digest (Repl.) 502 .. ..
Folkes *v.* King, [1923] 1 K.B. 282; [1922] All E.R. Rep. 658; 92 L.J.K.B. 125; 128 L.T.
  405; 39 T.L.R. 77; 67 Sol. Jo. 227; 28 Com. Cas. 110; 86 J.P. Jo. 552, C.A.;
  1 Digest (Repl.) 390 .. .. 208, 209,
Ford Motor Co. (England), Ltd. *v.* Armstrong (1915), 31 T.L.R. 267; 59 Sol. Jo. 362,
  C.A.; 17 Digest (Repl.) 159 .. ..
Forman & Co. Pty., Ltd. *v.* The Liddesdale, [1900] A.C. 190; 69 L.J.P.C. 44; 82 L.T.
  331; 9 Asp. M.L.C. 45, P.C.; 1 Digest (Repl.) 473 352,
France *v.* Gaudet (1871), L.R. 6 Q.B. 199; 40 L.J.Q.B. 121; 19 W.R. 622; 39 Digest
  (Repl.) 824 411,
Frank H. Wright, Ltd. *v.* Frodsor, Ltd. *See* Wright (Frank H.), Ltd. *v.* Frodsor.
Freeman *v.* Cooke (1848), 2 Ex 654; [1843–60] All E.R. Rep. 185; 6 Dow. & L. 187; 18
  L.J. Ex. 114; 12 L.T.O.S. 66; 12 Jur. 777; 5 Digest (Repl.) 1061 .. ..
Freeth *v.* Burr (1874), L.R. 9 C.P. 208; [1874–80] All E.R. Rep. 751; 43 L.J.C.P. 91;
  29 L.T. 773; 22 W.R. 370; 12 Digest (Repl.) 379 278,
Frost *v.* Aylebury Dairy Co., [1905] 1 K.B. 608; [1904–07] All E.R. Rep. 132; 74
  L.J.K.B. 386; 92 L.T. 527; 53 W.R. 354; 21 T.L.R. 300; 49 Sol. Jo. 312, C.A.;
  39 Digest (Repl.) 546 .. .. 84, 85, 87,

G

Gainsford *v.* Carroll (1824), 2 B. & C. 624; 4 Dow. & Ry. K.B. 161; 2 L.J.O.S.K.B. 112;
  39 Digest (Repl.) 816 .. ..
Galbraith *v.* Mitchenall Estates, Ltd., [1965] 2 Q.B. 473; [1964] 2 All E.R. 653; [1964]
  3 W.L.R. 454; 108 Sol. Jo. 749; Digest Cont. Vol. B. 242 15,
Galbraith and Grant, Ltd. *v.* Block, [1922] 2 K.B. 155; [1922] All E.R. Rep. 443; 91
  L.J.K.B. 649; 127 L.T. 521; 38 T.L.R. 669; 66 Sol. Jo. 596; 39 Digest (Repl.) 666
Gall's Case. *See* Campbell Discount Co., Ltd. *v.* Gall.
Gallagher *v.* Shilcock, [1949] 2 K.B. 765; [1949] 1 All E.R. 921; [1949] L.J.R. 1721;
  65 T.L.R. 496; 93 Sol. Jo. 302; 39 Digest (Repl.) 776 .. .. 317, 366, 367,

PAGE

llie *v.* Lee. *See* Saunders *v.* Anglia Building Society.

rdiner *v.* Gray (1815), 4 Camp. 144; 39 Digest (Repl.) 556 95

rnac Grain Co., Inc. *v.* H.M.F. Faure and Fairclough, Ltd. and Bunge Corporation,
[1968] A.C. 1130, n.; [1967] 2 All E.R. 353; [1967] 3 W.L.R. 143, n.; 111 Sol. Jo.
434; [1967] 1 Lloyd's Rep. 495, H.L.; Digest Supp... 200

ddling *v.* Marsh, [1920] 1 K.B. 668; [1920] All E.R. Rep. 631; 89 L.J.K.B. 526; 122
L.T. 775; 36 T.L.R. 337; 39 Digest (Repl.) 543 .. .. 81, 125, 428

neral and Finance Facilities, Ltd. *v.* Cook Cars (Romford), Ltd., [1963] 2 All E.R.
314; [1963] 1 W.L.R. 644; 107 Sol. Jo. 294, C.A.; 46 Digest (Repl.) 524 .. 333, 381

nn *v.* Winkel (1912), 107 L.T. 434; [1911–13] All E.R. Rep. 910; 107 L.T. 434; 28
T.L.R. 483; 56 Sol. Jo. 612; 17 Com. Cas. 323, C.A.; 39 Digest (Repl.) 629 177, 178

orge Inglefield, Ltd., *Re, See* Inglefield (George) Ltd. *Re.*

baud *v.* Great Eastern Rail. Co., [1921] 2 K.B. 426; [1921] All E.R. Rep. 35; 90
L.J.K.B. 535; 125 L.T. 76; 37 T.L.R. 422; 65 Sol. Jo. 454; C.A.; 8 Digest (Repl.)
141 140

les *v.* Edwards (1797), 7 Terms Rep. 181; 12 Digest (Repl.) 257 408

llard *v.* Brittan (1841), 8 M. & W. 575; 1 Dowl. N.S. 424; 11 L.J. Ex. 133; 39 Digest
(Repl.) 780 415

ynn *v.* Margetson & Co., [1893] A.C. 351; [1891–4] All E.R. Rep. 693; 62 L.J.Q.B.
466; 69 L.T. 1; 9 T.L.R. 437; 7 Asp. M.L.C. 366; I.R. 193, H.L.; 41 Digest
(Repl.) 164 140

dley *v.* Perry, [1960] 1 All E.R. 36; [1960] 1 W.L.R. 9; 104 Sol. Jo. 16; 39
Digest (Repl.) 529, 665 .. .. 69, 98, 99, 104

ldring's Case. *See* Eastern Distributors, Ltd. *v.* Goldring.

ss *v.* Nugent (1833), 5 B. & Ad. 58; 2 Nev. & N.K.B. 28; 2 L.J.K.B. 127; 17 Digest
(Repl.) 313 145

ulston Discount, Ltd. *v.* Clark, [1967] 2 Q.B. 493; [1967] 1 All E.R. 61; [1966] 3
W.L.R. 1280; 110 Sol. Jo. 829, C.A.; Digest Supp... 346

acie (Owners) *v.* Argentino (Owners), The Argentino. *See* Argentino, The

aham (Thomas), Ltd. *v.* Glenrothes Development Corporation 1968 S.L.T.2 211, 226

ant *v.* Australian Knitting Mills, Ltd., [1936] A.C. 85, [1935] All E.R. Rep. 209;
105 L.J.P.C. 6; 154 L.T. 18; 52 T.L.P. 38; 79 Sol. Jo. 815, P.C.; 39 Digest
(Repl.) 541 .. .. .. 68, 88, 92, 98, 99, 125, 126, 127

eat Eastern Rail. Co. *v.* Lord's Trustee, [1909] A.C. 109; 78 L.J.K.B. 160; 100 L.T.
130; 25 T.L.R. 176; 16 Mans. 1, H.L.; 7 Digest (Repl.) 21 320

eat Northern Rail. Co. *v.* Witham (1873), L.R. 9 C.P. 16; 43 L.J.C.P. 1; 29 L.T. 471;
22 W.R. 48; 12 Digest (Repl.) 231 87

eaves *v.* Ashlin (1813), 3 Camp. 426; 39 Digest (Repl.) 677 376

ebert-Borgnis *v.* Nugent (1885), 15 Q.B.D. 85; 54 L.J.Q.B. 511; 1 T.L.R. 434, C.A.;
39 Digest (Repl.) 811 413

een *v.* All Motors, Ltd., [1917] 1 K.B. 625; [1916–17] All E.R. Rep. 1039; 86
L.J.K.B. 590; 116 L.T. 189, C.A.; 26 Digest (Repl.) 669 13

enfell *v.* E. B. Meyrowitz, Ltd., [1936] 2 All E.R. 1313; 39 Digest (Repl.) 535 .. 71

iffiths *v.* Peter Conway, Ltd., [1939] 1 All E.R. 685, C.A.; 39 Digest (Repl.) 552
85, 88, 119, 428

imoldby *v.* Wells (1875), L.R. 10 C.P. 391; 44 L.J.C.P. 203; 32 L.T. 490; 39 J.P.
535; 23 W.R. 524; 39 Digest (Repl.) 561 268

ist *v.* Bailey, [1967] Ch. 532; [1966] 2 All E.R. 875; [1966] 3 W.L.R. 618; 110 Sol.
Jo. 791; Digest Cont. Vol. B. 545 123

H

dley *v.* Baxendale (1854), 9 Ex 341; [1843–60] All E.R. Rep. 461; 23 L.J. Ex. 179;
23 L.T.O.S. 69; 18 Jur. 358; 2 W.R. 302; 2 C.L.R. 517; 8 Digest (Repl.) 152
388, 409, 416

dley *v.* Droitwich Construction, Ltd., [1967] 3 All E.R. 911; [1968] 1 W.L.R. 37;
111 Sol. Jo. 849, C.A.; Digest Supp... .. .. 86, 428

ll *v.* Smith (1887), 3 T.L.R. 805, C.A.; 7 Digest (Repl.) 4 307

ll (J. and E.), Ltd. *v.* Barclay, [1937] 3 All E.R. 620, C.A.; 46 Digest (Repl.) 512 .. 380

Hall (R. and H.), Ltd. and W. H. Pim & Co. Arbitration, *Re* (1928), 139 L.T. 50; [1928] All E.R. Rep. 763; 33 Com. Cas. 324; 30 Ll.L.R. 159, H.L.; 39 Digest (Repl.) 818 .. ..

Hammonds *v.* Barclay (1802), 2 East 227; 1 Digest (Repl.) 644

Hanson *v.* Meyer (1805), 6 East 614; 2 Smith, K.B. 670; 39 Digest (Repl.) 620 .. 164,

Harbutt's Plasticine, Ltd. *v.* Wayne Tank and Pump Co., Ltd., [1970] 1 Q.B. 447; [1970] 1 All E.R. 225; [1970] 2 W.L.R. 198; 114 Sol. Jo. 29; [1970] 1 Lloyd's Rep. 15, C.A.
51, 144, 360,

Hardwick Game Farm *v.* Suffolk Agricultural and Poultry Producers Association, Ltd., [1964] 2 Lloyd's Rep. 227; on appeal, [1966] 1 All E.R. 309; [1966] 1 W.L.R. 287; 110 Sol. Jo. 11; [1966] 1 Lloyd's Rep. 197, C.A.; affd. *sub nom.* Kendall (Henry) & Sons, Ltd. (a firm) *v.* William Lillico & Sons, Ltd., [1969] 2 A.C. 31; [1968] 2 All E.R. 444; [1968] 3 W.L.R. 110; 112 Sol. Jo. 562; [1968] 1 Lloyd's Rep. 547, H.L.; Digest Supp. 80, 84, 85, 86, 88, 92, 98, 99, 100, 132, 137, 139,

Hardy (E.) & Co. (London) *v.* Hillerns and Fowler, [1923] 2 K.B. 490; [1923] All E.R. Rep. 275; 92 L.J.K.B. 930; 129 L.T. 674; 39 T.L.R. 547; 67 Sol. Jo. 618; 29 Com. Cas. 30, C.A.; 39 Digest (Repl.) 726 .. .. .. 269, 399,

Harlow and Jones, Ltd. *v.* Panex, Ltd., [1967] 2 Lloyd's Rep. 509 .. ..

Harrison *v.* Knowles and Foster [1917] 2 K.B. 606; 86 L.J.K.B. 1490; 117 L.T. 363; 33 T.L.R. 467; 61 Sol. Jo. 695; 22 Com. Cas. 293; on appeal, [1918] 1 K.B. 608; [1918–1919] All E.R. Rep. 306; 87 L.J.K.B. 680; 118 L.T. 566; 34 T.L.R. 235; 14 Asp. M.L.C. 249; 23 Com. Cas. 282, C.A.; 39 Digest (Repl.) 514 .. .. 74, 75,

Harrison and Jones, Ltd. *v.* Bunten and Lancaster, Ltd., [1953] 1 Q.B. 646; [1953] 1 All E.R. 903; 97 Sol. Jo. 281; 35 Digest (Repl.) 113 .. .. ..

Hartley *v.* Hymans, [1920] 3 K.B. 475; [1920] All E.R. Rep. 328; 90 L.J.K.B. 14; 124 L.T. 31; 36 T.L.R. 805; 25 Com. Cas. 365; 39 Digest (Repl.) 523 145, 147,

Hayman *v.* Flewker (1863), 13 C.B.N.S. 519; 1 New Rep. 479; 32 L.J.C.P. 132; 9 Jur. N.S. 895; 1 Digest (Repl.) 384 .. ..

Head (Phillip) & Sons, Ltd. *v.* Showfronts, Ltd. (1969), 113 Sol. Jo. 978; [1970] 1 Lloyds Rep. 140

Healing (Sales), Pty., Ltd. *v.* Inglis Electrix, Pty., Ltd., [1969] A.L.R. 533; 42 A.L.J.R. 280 .. .. 65, 276, 415,

Healy *v.* Howlett & Sons, [1917] 1 K.B. 337; 86 L.J.K.B. 252; 116 L.T. 591; 39 Digest (Repl.) 601 .. .. 168, 172, 244,

Heap *v.* Motorists' Advisory Agency, Ltd., [1923] 1 K.B. 577; [1922] All E.R. Rep. 251; 92 L.J.K.B. 553; 129 L.T. 146; 39 T.L.R. 150; 67 Sol. Jo. 300; 39 Digest (Repl.) 650 .. .. 207, 213,

Hedley Byrne & Co., Ltd. *v.* Heller and Partners, Ltd., [1964] A.C. 465; [1963] 2 All E.R. 575; [1963] 3 W.L.R. 101; 107 Sol. Jo. 464; [1963] 1 Lloyd's Rep. 485, H.L.; Digest Cont. Vol. A 53 .. .. .. 50, 120, 129, 130,

Heil *v.* Hedges, [1951] 1 T.L.R. 512; 95 Sol. Jo. 140; 39 Digest (Repl.) 542 ..

Heilbut *v.* Hickson (1872), L.R. 7 C.P. 438; 41 L.J.C.P. 228; 27 L.T. 336; 20 W.R 1005; 39 Digest (Repl.) 561 .. .. 110, 180, 270,

Heilbutt, Symons & Co. Buckleton, [1913] A.C. 30; [1911–13] All E.R. Rep. 83; 82 L.J.K.B. 245; 107 L.T. 769; 20 Mans. 54, H.L.; 9 Digest (Repl.) 259 .. ..

Helby *v.* Matthews, [1895] A.C. 471; [1895–9] All E.R. Rep. 821; 64 L.J.Q.B. 465; 72 L.T. 841; 60 J.P. 20; 43 W.R. 561; 11 T.L.R. 446; 11 R. 232, H.L.; 26 Digest (Repl.) 660 .. .. 12, 222, 223, 228,

Hemmings *v.* Stoke Poges Golf Club, [1920] 1 K.B. 720; [1918–19] All E.R. Rep. 798; 89 L.J.K.B. 744; 122 L.T. 479; 36 T.L.R. 77; 64 Sol. Jo. 131, C.A.; 15 Digest (Repl.) 800

Henderson & Co. *v.* Williams, [1895] 1 Q.B. 521; 64 L.J.Q.B. 308; 72 L.T. 98; 43 W.R. 274; 11 T.L.R. 148; 14 R. 375, C.A.; 1 Digest (Repl.) 431 190, 192, 193,

Henderson (John M.) & Co., Ltd. *v.* Montague L. Meyer (1941), 85 Sol. Jo. 166; 46 Com. Cas. 209; 12 Digest (Repl.) 68

Henry Kendall & Sons, Ltd. (a firm) *v.* William Lillico & Sons, Ltd. *See* Hardwick Game Farm *v.* Suffolk Agricultural and Poultry Producers Association, Ltd.

Heron II, The, Koufos *v.* Czarnikow, [1969] 1 A.C. 350; [1967] 3 All E.R. 686; [1967] 3 W.L.R. 1491; 111 Sol. Jo. 848; [1967] 2 Lloyd's Rep. 457; Digest Supp. .. ..

Herschtal *v.* Stewart and Arden, Ltd., [1940] 1 K.B. 155; [1939] 4 All E.R. 123; 109

PAGE

L.J.K.B. 328; 161 L.T. 331; 56 T.L.R. 48; 84 Sol. Jo. 79; 45 Com. Cas. 63; 36
Digest (Repl.) 83 .. .. 125, 126, 284

skell v. Continental Express, Ltd., [1950] 1 All E.R. 1033; 94 Sol. Jo. 339; 17 Digest
(Repl.) 131 .. .. 332, 411

wison v. Ricketts (1894), 63 L.J.Q.B. 711; 71 L.T. 191; 10 R. 558; 26 Digest (Repl.)
201 .. .. 347, 362, 372

yman v. Darwins, Ltd., [1942] A.C. 356; [1942] 1 All E.R. 337; 111 L.J.K.B. 241;
166 L.T. 306; 58 T.L.R. 169, H.L.; 2 Digest (Repl.) 492 .. .. 360, 361

kman v. Haynes (1875), L.R. 10 C.P. 598; 44 L.J.C.P. 358; 32 L.T. 873; 23 W.R.
872; 39 Digest (Repl.) 799 148

l & Sons v. Edwin Showell & Sons, Ltd. (1918), 87 L.J.K.B. 1106; 119 L.T. 651; 62
Sol. Jo. 715, H.L.; 39 Digest (Repl.) 813 384

l (Christopher), Ltd. v. Ashington Piggeries, Ltd., [1969] 3 All E.R. 1496; [1969] 2
Lloyd's Rep. 425, C.A.; Digest Supp. .. 71, 72, 76, 84, 85, 87, 92, 101, 102, 114

las & Co., Ltd. v. Arcos, Ltd., [1932] All E.R. Rep. 494; 147 L.T. 503; 38 Com.
Cas. 23, H.L.; 39 Digest (Repl.) 448 21

tchcock v. Humfrey (1843), 5 Man. & G. 559; 6 Scott, N.R. 540; 12 L.J.C.P. 235;
1 L.T.O.S. 109; 7 Jur. 423; 26 Digest (Repl.) 70 346

are v. Rennie (1859), 5 H. & N. 19; 29 L.J. Ex. 73; 1 L.T. 104; 8 W.R. 80; 39 Digest
(Repl.) 700 279

lden (Richard), Ltd. v. Bostock & Co., Ltd. (1902), 50 W.R. 323; 18 T.L.R. 317; 46
Sol. Jo. 265, C.A.; 39 Digest (Repl.) 589 425

llins v. Fowler (1875), L.R. 7 H.L. 757; [1874–80] All E.R. Rep. 118; 44 L.J.Q.B.
169; 33 L.T. 73; 40 J.P. 53, H.L.; 1 Digest (Repl.) 787 377

lmes v. Ashford, [1950] 2 All E.R. 76; 94 Sol. Jo. 337, C.A.; 36 Digest (Repl.) 87 125,
126

nck v. Muller (1881), 7 Q.B.D. 92; 50 L.J.Q.B. 529; 45 L.T. 202; 29 W.R. 830, C.A.;
39 Digest (Repl.) 701 279

ng Kong Fir Shipping Co. v. Kawasaki Kisen Kaisha, [1962] 2 Q.B. 26; [1962] 1 All
E.R. 474; [1962] 2 W.L.R. 474; 106 Sol. Jo. 35; [1961] 2 Lloyd's Rep. 478, C.A.;
41 Digest (Repl.) 363 51

okway (F. E.) & Co. Isaacs & Sons, [1954] 1 Lloyd's Rep. 491 108

rn v. Minister of Food, [1948] 2 All E.R. 1036; 65 T.L.R. 106; 39 Digest (Repl.) 554 254

rst (Clemens E.) Co. v. Biddell Brothers, [1912] A.C. 18; [1911–13] All E.R. Rep.
93; 81 L.J.K.B. 42; 105 L.T. 563; 28 T.L.R. 42; 56 Sol. Jo. 50; 12 Asp. M.L.C.
17; 17 Com. Cas. 55, H.L.; 39 Digest (Repl.) 704 273

undsditch Warehouse Co., Ltd. v. Waltex, Ltd., [1944] 1 K.B. 579; [1944] 2 All E.R.
518; 113 L.J.K.B. 547; 171 L.T. 275; 60 T.L.R. 517; 39 Digest (Repl.) 562 .. 104

usehold Machines, Ltd. v. Cosmos Exporters, Ltd., [1947] K.B. 217; [1946] 2 All
E.R. 622; [1947] L.J.R. 578; 176 L.T. 49; 62 T.L.R. 757; 39 Digest (Repl.) 811 412, 413

ward v. Furness Houlder Argentine Lines, Ltd. and Brown, Ltd., [1936] 2 All E.R.
781; 80 Sol. Jo. 554; 41 Com. Cas. 290; 36 Digest (Repl.) 82 125

well v. Coupland (1876), 1 Q.B.D. 258; 46 L.J.Q.B. 147; 33 L.T. 832; 40 J.P. 276;
24 W.R. 470, C.A.; 39 Digest (Repl.) 490 255

well v. Evans (1926), 134 L.T. 570; 42 T.L.R. 310; 39 Digest (Repl.) 739 277

ll Ropes Co., Ltd. v. Adams (1895), 65 L.J.Q.B. 114; 73 L.T. 446; 44 W.R. 108; 40
Sol. Jo. 69; 26 Digest (Repl.) 659 222

mphries v. Carvalho (1812), 6 East 45; 17 Digest (Repl.) 57 179

rst v. Picture Theatres, Ltd., [1915] 1 K.B. 1; [1914–15] All E.R. Rep. 836; 83 L.J.K.B.
1836; 111 L.T. 972; 30 T.L.R. 642, C.A.; 17 Digest (Repl.) 207 330

draulic Engineering Co. v. McHaffie (1878), 4 Q.B.D. 670; 27 W.R. 221, C.A.; 17
Digest (Repl.) 133 .. .. 412, 421

man v. Nye (1881), 6 Q.B.D. 685; [1881–5] All E.R. Rep. 183; 44 L.T. 919; 45 J.P.
554; 3 Digest (Repl.) 96 86

I

lependent Automatic Sales, Ltd. v. Knowles and Foster, [1962] 3 All E.R. 27; [1962]
1 W.L.R. 974; 106 Sol. Jo. 720, Digest Cont. Vol. A 182.. 309

glefield (George), Ltd., Re [1933] Ch. 1; [1932] All E.R. Rep. 244; 101 L.J. Ch. 360;
147 L.T. 411; 48 T.L.R. 536; [1931] B. & C.R. 220, C.A.; 35 Digest (Repl.) 280 310

P.

Inglis *v.* Robertson and Baxter, [1898] A.C. 616; 67 L.J.P.C. 108; 79 L.T. 224; 14
  T.L.R. 517; H.L.; 44 Digest (Repl.) 194   ..   ..   223, 224, 225,
Inglis *v.* Stock (1885), 10 App. Cas. 263; 54 L.J.Q.B. 582; 52 L.T. 821; 23 W.R. 877;
  5 Asp. M.L.C. 422, H.L.; 39 Digest (Repl.) 649   ..   ..
Ingram *v.* Little, [1961] 1 Q.B. 31; [1960] 3 All E.R. 332; [1960] 3 W.L.R. 504; 104 Sol.
  Jo. 704, C.A.; 35 Digest (Repl.) 104   188,
Interoffice Telephones, Ltd. Freeman Co., Ltd., [1958] 1 Q.B. 190; [1957] 3 All E.R.
  479; [1957] 3 W.L.R. 971; 101 Sol. Jo. 958, C.A.; 3 Digest (Repl.) 116. .   379,
Isaacson, *Re, ex parte* Mason, [1895] 1 Q.B. 333; 64 L.J.Q.B. 191; 71 L.T. 812; 43 W.R.
  278; 11 T.L.R. 101; 39 Sol. Jo. 169; 2 Mans. 11; 14 R. 41, C.A.; 7 Digest (Repl.)
  36   ..   ..

J

Jackson *v.* Rotax Motor and Cycle Co., [1910] 2 K.B. 937; 80 L.J.K.B. 38; 103 L.T.
  411, C.A.; 39 Digest (Repl.) 556   ..   ..   ..   81, 277,
Jackson *v.* Union Marine Insurance Co., Ltd. (1874), L.R. 10 C.P. 125; 44 L.J.C.P. 27;
  31 L.T. 789; 23 W.R. 169; 2 Asp. M.L.C. 435; 29 Digest (Repl.) 301 ..
Jackson *v.* Watson & Sons, [1919] 2 K.B. 193; 78 L.J.K.B. 587; 100 L.T. 799; 25 T.L.R.
  454; 53 Sol. Jo. 447, C.A.; 39 Digest (Repl.) 589
James Finlay & Co., Ltd. *v.* N. V. Kwik Hoo Tong. *See* Finlay (James) & Co., Ltd. *v.*
  N. V. Kwik Hoo Tong.
Janesich *v.* Attenborough & Son (1910), 102 L.T. 605; 26 T.L.R. 278; 37 Digest (Repl.)
  20   ..   ..
Jay's Furnishing Co. *v.* Brand & Co., [1915] 1 K.B. 458; [1914–15] All E.R. Rep. 811;
  84 L.J.K.B. 867; 112 L.T. 719; 31 T.L.R. 124; 59 Sol. Jo. 160, C.A.; 18 Digest
  (Repl.) 295
Jerome *v.* Bentley & Co., [1952] 2 All E.R. 114; [1952] 2 T.L.R. 58; 96 Sol. Jo. 463; 1
  Digest (Repl.) 655
Jewelowski *v.* Propp, [1944] 1 K.B. 510; [1944] 1 All E.R. 483; 113 L.J.K.B. 335; 171
  L.T. 234; 60 T.L.R. 559; 17 Digest (Repl.) 112
Joblin *v.* Watkins and Roseveare (Motors), Ltd., [1949] 1 All E.R. 47; 64 T.L.R. 464; 1
  Digest (Repl.) 390
Jobson *v.* Eppenheim (1905), 21 T.L.R. 468; 39 Digest (Repl.) 755   ..   ..
Johnson *v.* Credit Lyonnais Co. (1877), 3 C.P.D. 32; 47 L.J.Q.B. 241; 37 L.T. 657; 42
  J.P. 548; 26 W.R. 195, C.A.; 17 Digest (Repl.) 67 ..
Johnson *v.* Rees, (1915), 84 L.J.K.B. 1276; 113 L.T. 275; 7 Digest (Repl.) 19   ..
Jones *v.* Just (1868), L.R. 3 Q.B. 197; 9 B. & S. 141; 37 L.J.Q.B. 89; 18 L.T. 208; 16
  W.R. 643; 39 Digest (Repl.) 531
Jorden *v.* Money (1854), 5 H.L. Cas. 185; 23 L.J. Ch. 865; 24 L.T.O.S. 160, H.L.; 7
  Digest (Repl.) 237   ..   ..   148, 185,

K

Karflex, Ltd. *v.* Poole, [1933] 2 K.B. 251; [1933] All E.R. Rep. 46; 102 L.J.K.B. 475;
  149 L.T. 140; 49 T.L.R. 418; 26 Digest (Repl.) 665   16, 55, 58, 60, 61, 62,
Karsales, Ltd. *v.* Wallis, [1956] 2 All E.R. 866; [1956] 1 W.L.R. 936; 100 Sol. Jo. 548,
  C.A.; 26 Digest (Repl.) 666   70, 86, 116, 141, 291,
Kasler and Cohen *v.* Slavouski, [1928] 1 K.B. 78, 96 L.J.K.B. 850; 137 L.T. 641   413,
Keith Prowse & Co. *v.* National Telephone Co., [1894] 2 Ch. 147; 63 L.J. Ch. 373; 70
  L.T. 276; 58 J.P. 573; 42 W.R. 380; 10 T.L.R. 263; 8 R. 776; 28 Digest (Repl.)
  821
Kelly *v.* Lombard Banking, Ltd., [1958] 3 All E.R. 713; [1959] 1 W.L.R. 41; 103 Sol.
  Jo. 34, C.A.; 26 Digest (Repl.) 667   375,
Kemp *v.* Falk (1882), 7 App. Cas. 573; 52 L.J. Ch. 167; 47 L.T. 454; 5 Asp. M.L.C.
  1; 31 W.R. 125, H.L.; 39 Digest (Repl.) 771   ..   ..
Kemp *v.* Ismay Imrie & Co. (1909), 100 L.T. 996; 14 Com. Cas. 202; 39 Digest (Repl.)
  754   ..   ..
Kempler *v.* Bravington, Ltd. (1925), 133 L.T. 680; 41 T.L.R. 519; 69 Sol. Jo. 639, C.A.;
  39 Digest (Repl.) 625   ..
Kendrick *v.* Southeby & Co., [1967] C.L.Y. 42; 111 Sol. Jo. 470; Digest Supp.   ..

Table of Cases

xxxix

PAGE

nnedy v. Panama etc. Mail Co. (1867), L.R. 2 Q.B. 580; 8 B. & S. 571; 36 L.J.Q.B. 260; 17 L.T. 62; 15 W.R. 1039; 35 Digest (Repl.) 126 358

nahan, Ltd. v. Parry, [1910] 2 K.B. 389; 79 L.J.K.B. 1083; 102 L.T. 826; Revsd. [1911] 1 K.B. 459; 80 L.J.K.B. 276; 103 L.T. 867, C.A.; 1 Digest (Repl.) 405.. 185

ng's Norton Metal Co., Ltd. v. Edridge, Merrett & Co., Ltd. (1897), 14 T.L.R. 98, C.A.; 39 Digest (Repl.) 654 199

ngsley v. Stirling Industrial Securities, Ltd., [1967] 2 Q.B. 747; [1966] 2 All E.R. 637; [1966] 2 W.L.R. at p. 1277; 110 Sol. Jo. 267, C.A.; Digest Cont. Vol. B 334

riri Cotton Co., Ltd. v. Dewani, [1960] A.C. 192; [1960] 1 All E.R. 177; [1960] 2 W.L.R. 127; 104 Sol. Jo. 49, P.C.; Digest Cont. Vol. A 1094 .. 39, 280, 296

rkham v. Attenborough, [1897] 1 Q.B. 201; [1895–99] All E.R. Rep. 450; 66 L.J.Q.B. 149; 75 L.T. 543; 45 W.R. 213; 13 T.L.R. 131; 41 Sol. Jo. 141, C.A.; 39 Digest (Repl.) 624 39

tto v. Bilbie, Hobson & Co. (1895), 72 L.T. 266; 11 T.L.R. 214; 2 Mans. 122; 15 R. 188; 5 Digest (Repl.) 1171 .. .. 178, 206

h Hor Khoon (Official Assignee of Property), Bankrupts v. Ek. Liong Hin, Ltd., [1960] A.C. 178; [1960] 1 All E.R. 440; [1960] 2 W.L.R. 250; 104 Sol. Jo. 84, P.C.; 35 Digest (Repl.) 232 218

ufos v. Czarnikow. See Heron II, The, Koufos v. Czarnikow 303

ell v. Henry, [1903] 2 K.B. 740; 72 L.J.K.B. 794; 89 L.T. 328; 52 W.R. 246; 19 T.L.R. 711, C.A.; 12 Digest (Repl.) 435 254

bach v. Hollands, [1937] 3 All E.R. 907; 53 T.L.R. 1024; 81 Sol. Jo. 766; 36 Digest (Repl.) 87 126

rsell v. Timber Operators and Contractors, Ltd., [1927] 1 K.B. 298; 95 L.J.K.B. 569; 135 L.T. 223; 42 T.L.R. 435; C.A.; 12 Digest (Repl.) 452 159, 165, 172, 254

wei Tek Chao (Trading as Zung Fu Co.) v. British Traders and Shippers, Ltd., [1954] 2 Q.B. 459; [1954] 3 All E.R. 165; [1954] 2 W.L.R. 365; 98 Sol. Jo. 163; sub nom. Chao (Trading as Zung Fu Co.) v. British Traders and Shippers, Ltd., [1954] 1 All E.R. 779; [1954] 1 Lloyd's Rep. 16; 39 Digest (Repl.) 721 58, 60, 397, 400, 401, 402, 405, 412, 417, 418, 423

L

cis v. Cashmarts, [1969] 2 Q.B. 400; [1969] 2 W.L.R. 329; 112 Sol. Jo. 1005; Digest Supp. 163

ng (Sir James) & Sons, Ltd. v. Barclay, Curle & Co. Ltd., [1908] A.C. 35; 77 L.J.P.C. 33; 97 L.T. 816; Asp. M.L.C. 583, H.L.; 39 Digest (Repl.) 612.. 171

ncashire Waggon Co. v. Fitzhugh (1861), 6 H. & N. 502; 30 L.J. Ex. 231; 3 L.T. 703; 21 Digest (Repl.) 593 369

ngdom Trust, Ltd. v. Hurrell, [1955] 1 All E.R. 839; [1955] 1 W.L.R. 391; 99 Sol. Jo. 239; Digest Cont. Vol. A 470 394

ngton v. Higgins (1859), 4 H. & N. 402; 28 L.J. Ex. 252; 33 L.T.O.S. 166; 7 W.R. 489; 39 Digest (Repl.) 610 .. .. 170, 171, 172

rner v. Fawcett, [1950] 2 All E.R. 727, C.A.; 32 Digest (Repl.) 264.. .. 240

urie and Morewood v. Dudin & Sons, [1926] 1 K.B. 223; [1925] All E.R. Rep. 414; 95 L.J.K.B. 191; 134 L.T. 309; 42 T.L.R. 149; 31 Com. Cas. 96, C.A.; 39 Digest (Repl.) 639 .. .. 157, 158, 192

af v. International Galleries, [1950] 2 K.B. 86; [1950] 1 All E.R. 693; 66 (pt. 1) T.L.R. 1031, C.A.; 39 Digest (Repl.) 831 192

e v. Bayes and Robinson (1856), 18 C.B. 599; 26 L.T.O.S. 221; 20 J.P. 694; 2 Jur. N.S. 1093; 1 Digest (Repl.) 79 .. .. 358, 401, 403

e v. Butler, [1893] 2 Q.B. 318; [1891–4] All E.R. Rep. 1200; 62 L.J.Q.B. 591; 69 L.T. 370; 42 W.R. 88; 9 T.L.R. 631; 4 R. 563, C.A.; 26 Digest (Repl.) 659 12, 14, 221, 222, 227, 229

gh v. Paterson (1818), 8 Taunt. 540; 2 Moore C.P. 588; 39 Digest (Repl.) 818 236

ster Leather and Skin Co., Ltd. v. Home and Overseas Brokers, Ltd., (1948), 64 T.L.R. 569; 92 Sol. Jo. 646, C.A.; 39 Digest (Repl.) 819 411

vy v. Green (1859), 1 E. & E. 969; 28 L.J.Q.B. 319; 33 L.T.O.S. 241; 5 Jur. N.S. 1245; M.W.R. 486; 39 Digest (Repl.) 693 391

vy & Co. v. Goldberg, [1922] 1 K.B. 688; 91 L.J.K.B. 551; 127 L.T. 298; 38 T.L.R. 446; 28 Com. Cas. 244; 12 Digest (Repl.) 402 .. .. .. 148, 266

PA

Libau Wood Co. v. H. Smith & Sons, Ltd. (1930), 37 Ll. L. Rep. 296 4

Lickbarrow v. Mason (1787), 2 Term Rep. 63; reversed *sub nom.* Mason v. Lickbarrow (1790), 1 Hy. Bl. 357; (1793), 4 Bro. Parl. Cas. 57; 6 East 22, n., H.L.; subsequent proceedings (1794), 5 Term Rep. 683; 39 Digest (Repl.) 750 .. .. 188, 194,

Liesbosch, Dredger v. Edison Steamship (Owners), [1933] A.C. 449; 102 L.J.P. 73; 77 Sol. Jo. 176; 38 Com. Cas. 267; 18 Asp. M.L.C. 380; 45 Ll.L. Rep. 123; *sub nom.* The Edison, [1933] All E.R. Rep. 144; 149 L.T. 49; 49 T.L.R. 289, H.L.; 42 Digest (Repl.) 946 .. .. 378, 380, 381, 387,

Lincoln Waggon and Engine Co. v. Mumford (1879), 41 L.T. 655; 7 Digest (Repl.) 121 ..

Linz v. Electric Wire Co., Ltd., [1948] A.C. 371; [1948] 1 All E.R. 604; [1948] L.J.R. 1836; 92 Sol. Jo. 308, P.C.; 9 Digest (Repl.) 295 ..

Litchfield v. Dreyfus, [1906] 1 K.B. 584; 75 L.J.K.B. 447; 22 T.L.R. 385; 50 Sol. Jo. 391; 35 Digest (Repl.) 232 .. ..

Liverpool and County Discount Co., Ltd. v. A.B. Motor Co. (Kilburn), Ltd., [1963] 1 All E.R. 396; [1963] 1 W.L.R. 611; 107 Sol. Jo. 270, C.A.; Digest Cont. Vol. A 652 .. .. 49, 290,

L'Estrange v. Graucob, Ltd., [1934] 2 K.B. 394; [1934] All E.R. Rep. 16; 103 L.J.K.B. 730; 152 L.T. 164; 12 Digest (Repl.) 70 ..

Lloyds and Scottish Finance, Ltd. v. Modern Cars and Caravans (Kingston), Ltd., [1966] 1 Q.B. 764; [1964] 2 All E.R. 732; [1964] 3 W.L.R. 859; 108 Sol. Jo. 859; Digest Cont. Vol. B 630 .. .. 57, 65, 66, 240, 391,

Lloyds and Scottish Finance, Ltd. v. Williamson, [1965] 1 All E.R. 641; [1965] 1 W.L.R. 404; 109 Sol. Jo. 10, C.A.; Digest Cont. Vol. B 10 .. 185, 205, 213,

Lloyds Bank, Ltd. v. Bank of America National Trust and Savings Association, [1938] 2 K.B. 147; [1938] 2 All E.R. 63; 107 L.J.K.B. 538; 158 L.T. 301; 54 T.L.R. 599; 82 Sol. Jo. 312; 43 Com. Cas. 209, C.A.; 1 Digest (Repl.) 387 154, 184,

Loder v. Kekule (1857), 3 C.B.N.S. 128; 27 L.J.C.P. 27; 30 L.T.O.S. 64; 4 Jur. N.S. 93; 5 W.R. 884; 39 Digest (Repl.) 591 ..

Lombard, Ltd. v. Excell, [1964] 1 Q.B. 415; [1963] 3 All E.R. 486; [1963] 3 W.L.R. 700, C.A.; Digest Cont. Vol. A 470 .. ..

London Jewellers, Ltd. v. Attenborough, [1934] 2 K.B. 206; [1934] All E.R. Rep. 270; 103 L.J.K.B. 429; 151 L.T. 124; 50 T.L.R. 436; 78 Sol. Jo. 413; 39 Com. Cas. 290, C.A.; 39 Digest (Repl.) 624 .. .. 178, 179,

London Plywood and Timber Co., Ltd. v. Nasic Oak Extract and Steam Sawmills Co., Ltd., [1939] 2 K.B. 343; 108 L.J.K.B. 587; 55 T.L.R. 826; 83 Sol. Jo. 607; 39 Digest (Repl.) 694 ..

Long v. Lloyd, [1958] 2 All E.R. 402; [1958] 1 W.L.R. 753; 102 Sol. Jo. 488, C.A.; 39 Digest (Repl.) 830 .. .. .. 270, 358, 400, 402,

Longbottom & Co., Ltd. v. Bass, Walker & Co., [1922] W.N. 245 277,

Lorymer v. Smith (1822), 1 B. & C. 1; 1 L.J.O.S.K.B. 7; *sub nom.* Lorimer v. Smith, 2 Dow & Ry. K.B. 23; 39 Digest (Repl.) 559 109,

Lovegrove, *Re ex parte* Lovegrove & Co. Sales, Ltd., [1935] 1 Ch. 464; [1935] All E.R. Rep. 749; 104 L.J. Ch. 282; [1934–5] B. & C.R. 262; 152 L.T. 480; 79 Sol. Jo. 145; 51 T.L.R. 248; C.A.; 5 Digest (Repl.) 751 299,

Lowe v. Lombank, Ltd., [1960] 1 All E.R. 611; [1960] 1 W.L.R. 196; 104 Sol. Jo. 210, C.A.; Digest Cont. Vol. A 645 .. .. 88, 93, 94, 139, 142, 193, 194, 310,

Lowther v. Harris, [1927] 1 K.B. 393; 96 L.J.K.B. 170; 136 L.T. 377; 43 T.L.R. 24; 1 Digest (Repl.) 386 .. .. 204, 205, 206,

Lubert's Case. *See* Bentworth Finance, Ltd. v. Lubert

Lucy v. Manflet (1860), 5 H. & N. 229; 29 L.J. Ex. 110; 39 Digest (Repl.) 562 ..

Lynch v. Thorne, [1956] 1 All E.R. 744; 100 Sol. Jo. 225, C.A.; 7 Digest (Repl.) 347

Lyons v. Hoffnung (1890), 15 App. Cas. 391; [1886–90] All E.R. Rep. 1012; 59 L.J.P.C. 79; 63 L.T. 293; 39 W.R. 390; 6 Asp. M.L.C. 551, P.C.; 39 Digest (Repl.) 758

Lyons (J. L.) & Co., Ltd. v. May and Baker, Ltd., [1923] 1 K.B. 685; 92 L.J.K.B. 675; 129 L.T. 413; 39 Digest (Repl.) 743 .. ..

M

Maas v. Pepper, [1905] A.C. 102; 74 L.J.K.B. 452; 92 L.T. 371; 53 W.R. 513; 21 T.L.R. 304; 12 Mans. 107; H.L.; affirming *sub nom.* Mellor's Trustee v. Maas,

PAGE

[1902] 1 K.B. 137; 71 L.J.K.B. 26; 85 L.T. 490; 50 W.R. 111; 8 Mans. 341; on appeal, [1903] 1 K.B. 226; 72 L.J.K.B. 82; 88 L.T. 50; 18 T.L.R. 139; 10 Mans. 26, C.A.; 7 Digest (Repl.) 19 .. .. 33, 294, 295

Donald (Gerald) & Co. v. Nash & Co., [1924] A.C. 625; [1924] All E.R. Rep. 601; 93 L.J.K.B. 610; 131 L.T. 428; 40 T.L.R. 530; 68 Sol. Jo. 594; 29 Com. Cas. 313, H.L.; 6 Digest (Repl.) 296

Entire v. Crossley Brothers, [1895] A.C. 457; [1895-9] All E.R. Rep. 829; 64 L.J.P.C 345 129; 72 L.T. 731; 2 Mans. 334; 11 R. 207, H.L.; 26 Digest (Repl.) 661.. .. 10

cleod v. Kerr 1965 S.L.T. 358 10

cpherson Train & Co., Ltd. v. Ross & Co., Ltd., [1955] 2 All E.R. 445; [1955] 1 W.L.R. 200 640; 99 Sol. Jo. 385; [1955] 1 Lloyd's Rep. 518; 39 Digest (Repl.) 522.. .. 73

Rae v. The Commonwealth Disposals Commission (1951), 84 C.L.R. 377 251, 252, 254

gee v. Pennine Insurance Co., Ltd., [1969] 2 Q.B. 507; [1969] 2 All E.R. 891; [1969] 2 W.L.R. 1278; 113 Sol. Jo. 303, C.A.; Digest Supp.

nbre Saccharine Co., Ltd. v. Corn Products, Ltd., [1919] 1 K.B. 198, [1918-19] 123 All E.R. Rep. 980; 88 L.J.K.B. 402; 120 L.T. 113; 35 T.L.R. 94; 24 Com. Cas. 89; 39 Digest (Repl.) 705 .. .. 73, 247

nchester Diocesan Council for Education v. Commercial and General Investments, Ltd., [1969] 3 All E.R. 1593; [1970] 1 W.L.R. 241; 114 Sol. Jo. 70; 21 P. & C.R. 38; 212 Estates Gazette 34

nchester Liners, Ltd. v. Rea, Ltd., [1922] 2 A.C. 74; [1922] All E.R. Rep. 605; 91 147 L.J.K.B. 504; 127 L.T. 405; 38 T.L.R. 526; 66 Sol. Jo. 421; 27 Com. Cas. 274, H.L.; 39 Digest (Repl.) 547 .. .. 80, 92

nchester Sheffield and Lincolnshire Rail. Co. v. North Central Wagon Co. (1888), 13 App. Cas. 554; 58 L.J. Ch. 219; 59 L.T. 730; 37 W.R. 305; 4 T.L.R. 728, H.L.; 8 Digest (Repl.) 161 .. .. 293, 294, 297, 311

nders v. Williams (1849), 4 Exch. 339; 18 L.J. Ex. 437; 13 L.T.O.S. 325; 39 Digest (Repl.) 625 177

ple Flock Co., Ltd. v. Universal Furniture Products (Wembley) Ltd., [1934] 1 K.B. 148; [1933] All E.R. Rep. 15; 103 L.J.K. 513; 150 L.T. 69; 50 T.L.R. 58; 39 Com. Cas. 89, C.A.; 39 Digest (Repl.) 699 278

redelanto Compania Naviera S.A. v. Bergbau-Handel G.m.b.H., The Mihalis Angelos, [1970] 1 All E.R. 673; [1970] 2 W.L.R. 907; 114 Sol. Jo. 30; [1970] 1 Lloyd's Rep. 118; reversed, [1970] 3 All E.R. 125; [1970] 3 W.L.R. 601; 114 Sol. Jo. 548, C.A. 52, 115, 266, 361, 379, 381

rgarine Union G.m.b.H. v Cambay Prince Steamship Co., Ltd., [1969] 1 Q.B. 219; [1967] 3 All E.R. 775; [1967] 3 W.L.R. 1569; 111 Sol. Jo. 943; [1967] 2 Lloyd's Rep. 315; Digest Supp.

rgaronis Navigation Agency, Ltd. v. Peabody & Co. of London, Ltd., [1965] 2 Q.B. 249 430; [1964] 3 All E.R. 333; [1964] 3 W.L.R. 873; 108 Sol. Jo. 562; [1964] 2 Lloyd's Rep. 153, C.A.; 41 Digest (Repl.) 202

ritime Electric Co., Ltd. v. General Dairies, Ltd., [1937] A.C. 610; [1937] 1 All E.R. 74, 77 748; 106 L.J.P.C. 81; 156 L.T. 444; 53 T.L.R. 391; 81 Sol. Jo. 156, P.C.; 20 Digest (Repl.) 228

ritime National Fish, Ltd. v. Ocean Trawlers, Ltd., [1935] A.C. 524; [1935] All E.R. 191 Rep. 86; 104 L.J.P.C. 88; 153 L.T. 425; 79 Sol. Jo. 320; 18 Asp. M.L.C. 551; P.C. 12 Digest (Repl.) 388

rket Overt Case (1596), 5 Co. Rep. 83b; sub nom. Bishop of Worcester's Case, Moore 254 K.B. 360; sub nom. Palmer v. Woolley, Cro. Eliz. 454; sub nom. Anon, Poph 34; 1 and 344; 33 Digest (Repl.) 491

rshall (W. E.) v. Lewis and Peat, Ltd., [1963] 1 Lloyd's Rep. 562.. 237

rten v. Whale, [1917] 2 K.B. 480; 86 L.J.K.B. 1305; 117 L.T. 137; 33 T.L.R. 330, 397 C.A.; 17 Digest (Repl.) 56

sh and Murrell, Ltd. v. Joseph I. Emmanuel, Ltd., [1961] 1 All E.R. 485; [1961] 1 7, 114 W.L.R. 862; 105 Sol. Jo. 468; [1961] 1 Lloyd's Rep. 46; Reversed, [1962] 1 All E.R. 77, n; [1962] 1 W.L.R. 16, n.; 105 Sol. Jo. 1007; [1961] 2 Lloyd's Rep. 326, C.A.; 39 Digest (Repl.) 545 82

son v. Burningham, [1949] 2 K.B. 545; [1949] 2 All E.R. 134, [1949] L.J.R. 1430; 65 T.L.R. 466; 93 Sol. Jo. 496, C.A.; 13 Digest (Repl.) 475 .. 65, 66, 378, 416

son v. Lickbarrow. See Lickbarrow v. Mason

PA

Mason v. Williams and Williams and Thomas Turton & Sons, Ltd., [1955] 1 All E.R.
   808; [1955] 1 W.L.R. 549; 99 Sol. Jo. 338; Digest Cont. Vol. A 1162 .. 127, 1
May and Butcher v. R., [1934] 2 K.B. 17, n; 103 L.J.K.B. 556, n.; 151 L.T. 246, n; H.L.
   39 Digest (Repl.) 448 .. ..
Medd v. Cox (1940), 67 Ll. L. Rep. 5 .. ..
Medway Oil, Ltd. v. Silica Gel Corporation (1928), 33 Com. Cas. 195, H.L.; 39 Digest
   (Repl.) 548 .. ..
Melachrino v. Nickoll and Knight, [1920] 1 K.B. 693; [1918–19] All E.R. Rep. 857; 89
   L.J.K.B. 906; 122 L.T. 545; 36 T.L.R. 143; 25 Com. Cas. 103; 39 Digest (Repl.)
   818 .. .. 410, 4
Mellor's Trustee v. Maas. See Maas v. Pepper
Mendelssohn v. Normand, Ltd., [1970] 1 Q.B. 177; [1969] 2 All E.R. 1215; [1969] 3
   W.L.R. 139; 113 Sol. Jo. 263, C.A.
Mercantile Bank of India, Ltd. v. Central Bank of India, Ltd., [1938] A.C. 287; [1938]
   All E.R. 52; 107 L.J.P.C. 25; 158 L.T. 269; 54 T.L.R. 208; 81 Sol. Jo. 1020,
   P.C.; 3 Digest (Repl.) 311 .. .. 184, 188, 191, 2
Mercantile Credit Co., Ltd. v. Hamblin, [1965] 2 Q.B. 242; [1964] 3 All E.R. 592;
   [1964] 3 W.L.R. 798; 108 Sol. Jo. 674, C.A.; Digest Cont. Vol. B 49 37, 197, 1
   285,
Mercantile Credit, Ltd. v. Cross, [1965] 2 Q.B. 205; [1965] 1 All E.R. 577; [1965] 2
   W.L.R. 687; 109 Sol. Jo. 47, C.A.; Digest Cont. Vol. B 334 .. ..
Mercantile Union Guarantee Corporation, Ltd. v. Wheatley, [1938] 1 K.B. 490;
   [1937] 4 All E.R. 713; 107 L.J.K.B. 158; 158 L.T. 414; 54 T.L.R. 151; 81 Sol. Jo.
   1002; 26 Digest (Repl.) 666 .. ..
Merchant Banking Co. of London v. Phoenix Bessemer Steel Co. (1877), 5 Ch. D. 205;
   46 L.J. Ch. 418; 36 L.T. 395; 25 W.R. 457; 39 Digest (Repl.) 711 .. ..
Mersey Steel and Iron Co. v. Naylor Benzon & Co. (1884), 9 App. Cas. 434; 53 L.J.Q.B.
   497; 51 L.T. 637; 32 W.R. 989, H.L.; 39 Digest (Repl.) 518 .. ..
Metal and Ropes, Ltd. v. Tattersall, [1966] 3 All E.R. 401; [1966] 1 W.L.R. 1500; 110
   Sol. Jo. 510; [1966] 2 Lloyd's Rep. 166, C.A.; Digest Cont. Vol. B 730 ..
Midland Counties Motor Finance, Ltd. v. Slade, [1951] 1 K.B. 346; [1950] 2 All E.R.
   821; 94 Sol. Jo. 704, C.A.; 26 Digest (Repl.) 664 346,
Midland Motor Showrooms, Ltd. v. Newman, [1929] 2 K.B. 256; [1929] All E.R. Rep.
   521; 98 L.J.K.B. 490; 141 L.T. 230; 45 T.L.R. 499, C.A.; 26 Digest (Repl.) 663
Mihalis Angelos, The. See Maredelanto Compania Naviera S.A. v. Bergbau-Handel
   G.m.b.h., The Mihalis Angelos
Milgate v. Kebble (1841), 3 Man. & G. 100; Drinkwater 225; 3 Scott N. R. 358; 10
   L.J.C.P. 277; 39 Digest (Repl.) 777 .. ..
Millett v. Van Heek & Co., [1921] 2 K.B. 369; [1921] All E.R. Rep. 519; 90 L.J.K.B.
   671; 125 L.T. 51; 37 T.L.R. 411; 65 Sol. Jo. 356, C.A.; 39 Digest (Repl.) 674..
Milroy v. Lord (1862), 4 De G. F. & J. 264; [1861–73] All E.R. Rep. 783; 31 L.J. Ch.
   798; 7 L.T. 178; 8 Jur. N.S. 806; 8 Digest (Repl.) 631 .. .. ..
Ministry of Housing and Local Government v. Sharp, [1970] 2 Q.B. 252; [1970] 1 All
   E.R. 1009; [1970] 2 W.L.R. 802; 134 J.P. 358; 114 Sol. Jo. 109; 68 L.G.R. 187;
   21 P. & C.R. 166; 213 Estates Gazette 1145, C.A.
Mischeff v. Springett, [1942] 2 K.B. 331; [1942] 2 All E.R. 349; 111 L.J.K.B. 690; 167
   L.T. 402; 106 J.P. 279; 58 T.L.R. 385; 40 L.G.R. 264; 17 Digest (Repl.) 472 155,
Mitchell v. Jones (1905), 24 N.Z.L.R. 932; 39 Digest (Repl.) 657 216,
Mitchell-Henry v. Norwich Union Life Insurance Society, [1918] 2 K.B. 67; 87
   L.J.K.B. 695; 119 L.T. 111; 34 T.L.R. 359; 62 Sol. Jo. 487, C.A.; 12 Digest
   (Repl.) 534 .. ..
Modern Light Cars, Ltd. v. Seals, [1934] 1 K.B. 32; [1933] All E.R. Rep. 539; 102
   L.J.K.B. 680; 149 L.T. 285; 49 T.L.R. 503; 77 Sol. Jo. 420; 26 Digest (Repl.) 658 2
Molling & Co. v. Dean & Sons, Ltd. (1901), 18 T.L.R. 217; 39 Digest (Repl.) 716.. 2
   425,
Montforts v. Marsden (1895), 12 R.P.C. 226 .. ..
Moorcock, The (1889), 14 P.D. 64; [1886–90] All E.R. Rep. 530; 58 L.J.P. 73; 60 L.T.
   654; 37 W.R. 439; 5 T.L.R. 316; 6 Asp. M.L.C. 373, C.A.; 47 Digest (Repl.) 774
Moore & Co. and Landauer & Co., Re, [1921] 2 K.B. 519; [1921] All E.R. Rep. 466; 90

PAGE

L.J.K.B. 731; 125 L.T. 372; 37 T.L.R. 452; 26 Com. Cas. 267, C.A.; 39 Digest
(Repl.) 528 .. .. 74, 78, 79

oorgate Mercantile, Ltd. *v.* Finch and Read, [1962] 1 Q.B. 701; [1962] 2 All E.R. 467;
[1962] 3 W.L.R. 110; 106 Sol. Jo. 284, C.A.; Digest Cont. Vol. A 651 .. 356, 377

oralice (London), Ltd. *v.* E. D. and F. Man, [1954] 2 Lloyd's Rep. 526 74

ordaunt *v.* British Oil and Cake Mills, Ltd., [1910] 2 K.B. 502; 79 L.J.K.B. 967; 103
L.T. 217; 54 Sol. Jo. 654; 15 Com. Cas. 285; 39 Digest (Repl.) 769 .. 186, 187

orelli *v.* Fitch and Gibbons, [1928] 2 K.B. 636; [1928] All E.R. Rep. 610; 97 L.J.K.B.
812; 140 L.T. 21; 44 T.L.R. 737; 72 Sol. Jo. 503; 39 Digest (Repl.) 528.. .. 98

organ *v.* Russell & Sons, [1909] 1 K.B. 357; 78 L.J.K.B. 187; 100 L.T. 118; 25 T.L.R.
120; 53 Sol. Jo. 136; 39 Digest (Repl.) 444 19

orison *v.* Lockhart 1912 S.C. 1017; 39 Digest (Repl.) 617 160

orris *v.* Baron & Co., [1918] A.C. 1; 87 L.J.K.B. 145; 118 L.T. 34, H.L.; 12 Digest
(Repl.) 398 145

oss *v.* Hancock, [1899] 2 Q.B. 111; 68 L.J.Q.B. 657; 80 L.T. 693; 63 J.P. 517; 47 W.R.
698; 15 T.L.R. 353; 43 Sol. Jo. 479; 19 Cox C. C. 324; 39 Digest (Repl.) 449 18

oss *v.* Sweet (1851), 16 Q.B. 493; 20 L.J.Q.B. 167; 16 L.T.O.S. 341; 15 Jur. 536; 39
Digest (Repl.) 627 179

otor Trade Finance, Ltd. *v.* H. E. Motors, Ltd. (1926), unreported, cited in, [1933]
Ch. at p. 20 .. .. 298, 299, 300

ount (D. F.), Ltd. *v.* Jay and Jay (Provision) Co., Ltd., [1960] 1 Q.B. 159; [1959] 3 All
E.R. 307; [1959] 3 W.L.R. 537; 103 Sol. Jo. 636; 39 Digest (Repl.) 607.. 186, 225

owbray *v.* Merryweather, [1895] 2 Q.B. 640; 65 L.J.Q.B. 50; 73 L.J. 459; 59 J.P. 804;
44 W.R. 49; 12 T.L.R. 14; 40 Sol. Jo. 9; 14 R. 767, C.A.; 36 Digest (Repl.) 62.. 86

ucklow *v.* Mangles (1808), 1 Taunt. 318; 39 Digest (Repl.) 612 171

unro *v.* Willmott, [1949] 1 K.B. 295; [1948] 2 All E.R. 983; [1949] L.J.R. 471; 64
T.L.R. 627; 92 Sol. Jo. 662; 1 Digest (Repl) 328 380

unro (Robert) & Co ., Ltd. *v.* Meyer [1930] 2 K.B. 312; [1930] All E.R. Rep. 241; 99
L.J.K.B. 703; 143 L.T. 565; 35 Com. Cas. 232; 39 Digest (Repl.) 533 76, 277, 278

uskham Finance, Ltd. *v.* Howard, [1963] 1 Q.B. 904; [1963] 1 All E.R. 81; [1963] 2
W.L.R. 87; 106 Sol. Jo. 1029, C.A.; Digest Cont. Vol. A 473 37

utual Finance, Ltd. *v.* Davidson, [1963] 1 All E.R. 133; [1963] 1 W.L.R. 134; 106
Sol. Jo. 1009, C.A.; Digest Cont. Vol. A 644 22

utual Life and Citizens' Assurance Co. *v.* Evatt, [1970] 11 C.L. 3376, P.C... .. 130

N

gle *v.* Fielden, [1966] 2 Q.B. 633; [1966] 1 All E.R. 689; [1966] 2 W.L.R. 1027; 110
Sol. Jo. 286, C.A.; Digest Cont. Vol. B 323 35

nka-Bruce *v.* Commonwealth Trust, [1926] A.C. 77; 94 L.J.P.C. 169; 134 L.T. 35;
39 Digest (Repl.) 654 167

poli, The, (1898), 15 T.L.R. 56; 39 Digest (Repl.) 621 167

tional Cash Register Co. *v.* Stanley, [1921] 3 K.B. 292; 90 L.J.K.B. 1220; 125 L.T.
765; 37 T.L.R. 776; 65 Sol. Jo. 643; 26 Digest (Repl.) 669 116

wbigging *v.* Adam (1886), 34 Ch. D. 582; [1886–90] All E.R. Rep. 975; 56 L.J. Ch.
275; 55 L.T. 794; 35 W.R. 597; 3 T.L.R. 249, C.A.; on appeal *sub nom.* Adam *v.*
Newbigging (1888), 13 App. Cas. 308; [1886–90] All E.R. Rep. 975; 57 L.J. Ch.
1066; 59 L.T. 267; 37 W.R. 97, H.L.; 31 Digest (Repl.) 193 358

wton of Wembley, Ltd. *v.* Williams, [1964] 2 All E.R. 135; [1964] 1 W.L.R. 1028;
108 Sol. Jo. 621; affd., [1965] 1 Q.B. 560; [1964] 3 All E.R. 532; [1964] 3 W.L.R.
888; 108 Sol. Jo. 619, C.A.; Digest Cont. Vol. B 635 201, 202, 224, 227, 228, 230

olett *v.* Confectioners' Materials Co., [1921] 3 K.B. 387; [1921] All E.R. Rep. 459;
90 L.J.K.B. 984; 125 L.T. 552; 37 T.L.R. 653, C.A.; 39 Digest (Repl.) 527 56, 57,
58, 63, 65, 66, 95, 96

chol *v.* Godts (1854), 10 Exch. 191; 2 C.L.R. 1468; 23 L.J. Ex. 314; 23 L.T.O.S.
162; 39 Digest (Repl.) 560 108

cholson *v.* Harper, [1895] 2 Ch. 415; [1895–99] All E.R. Rep. 882; 64 L.J. Ch. 672;
73 L.T. 19; 59 J.P. 727; 43 W.R. 550; 11 T.L.R. 435; 39 Sol. Jo. 524; 13 R. 567;
37 Digest (Repl.) 18 218

cholson and Venn *v.* Smith-Marriott (1947), 177 L.T. 189; 39 Digest (Repl.) 529 76, 123

Nippon Yusen Kaisha v. Ramjiban Serowgee, [1938] A.C. 429; [1938] 2 All E.R. 285;
   107 L.J.P.C. 89; 159 L.T. 266; 54 T.L.R. 546; 82 Sol. Jo. 292; 19 Asp. M.L.C.
   154; 43 Com. Cas. 223, P.C.; 41 Digest (Repl.) 244.. 3
Nocton v. Lord Ashburton, [1914] A.C. 932; [1914–15] All E.R. Rep. 45; 83 L.J. Ch.
   784; 111 L.T. 641, H.L.; 35 Digest (Repl.) 57 1
Norman v. Ricketts (1886), 3 T.L.R. 182, C.A.; 12 Digest (Repl.) 533.. .. 2
North Central Wagon Co., Ltd. v. Brailsford, [1962] 1 All E.R. 502; [1962] 1 W.L.R
   1288; 106 Sol. Jo. 878; Digest Cont. Vol. A 71   295, 301, 302, 3
North General Wagon and Finance Co., Ltd. v. Graham, [1950] 2 K.B. 7; [1950] 1 All
   E.R. 780; 66 (Pt. 1) T.L.R. 707, C.A.; 26 Digest (Repl.) 670 .. .. 16, 3

O

Official Assignee of the Property of Khoon v. Ek Liong Hin, Ltd. See Koh Hor Khoon
   (Official Assignee of Property) Bankrupts v. Ek Liong Hin, Ltd.
Ogg v. Shuter (1875), L.R. 10 C.P. 159, C.A. 1
Ogle v. Earl of Vane (1868), L.R. 3 Q.B. 272; 9 B. & S. 182; 37 L.J.Q.B. 77; 16 W.R.
   463; 39 Digest (Repl.) 819 4
Olds Discount, Ltd. v. Cohen (1937), [1938] 3 All E.R. 281, n.; 159 L.T. 335; 35 Digest
   (Repl.) 232 .. .. 301, 3
Olds Discount, Ltd. v. John Player, [1938] 3 All E.R. 275; 159 L.T. 332; 82 Sol. Jo.
   648; 35 Digest (Repl.) 233 3
Olds Discount, Ltd. v. Krett and Krett, [1940] 2 K.B. 117; [1940] 3 All E.R. 36; 109
   L.J.K.B. 641; 163 L.T. 151; 56 T.L.R. 708; 84 Sol. Jo. 441; 39 Digest (Repl.) 655 2
                                                                                 2
Ollett v. Jordan, [1918] 2 K.B. 41; [1918–19] All E.R. Rep. 1069; 87 L.J.K.B. 934; 119
   L.T. 50; 82 J.P. 221; 62 Sol. Jo. 636; 16 L.G.R. 487; 26 Cox C. C. 275; 25 Digest
   (Repl.) 119 1
Oppenheimer v. Attenborough & Son, [1907] 1 K.B. 510; 176 L.J.K.B. 177; 96 L.T.
   501; 23 T.L.R. 182; 12 Com. Cas. 88; affd., [1908] 1 K.B. 221; [1904–7] All E.R.
   Rep. 1016; 77 L.J.K.B. 209; 98 L.T. 94; 24 T.L.R. 115; 52 Sol. Jo. 76; 13 Com.
   Cas. 125, C.A.; 1 Digest (Repl.) 392 .. 204, 212, 213, 214, 1
Ornstein v. Alexandra Furnishing Co. (1895), 12 T.L.R. 128; 39 Digest (Repl.) 628 1
Oscar Chess, Ltd. v. Williams. See Chess (Oscar), Ltd. v. Williams
Overseas Tankship (U.K.), Ltd. v. Morts Dock and Engineering Co., Ltd., [1961] A.C.
   388; [1961] 1 All E.R. 404; [1961] 2 W.L.R. 126; 105 Sol. Jo. 85; [1961] 1 Lloyd's
   Rep. 1; [1961] A.L.R. 569, P.C.; Digest Cont. Vol. A 1149 3
Overstone, Ltd. v. Shipway, [1962] 1 All E.R. 52; [1962] 1 W.L.R. 117; 106 Sol. Jo.
   14, C.A.; Digest Cont. Vol. A 1149 .. .. 330, 360, 374, 379, 3

P

Pacific Motor Auctions Pty., Ltd. v. Motor Credits (Hire Finance), Ltd., [1965] A.C.
   867; [1965] 2 All E.R. 105; [1965] 2 W.L.R. 881; 109 Sol. Jo. 210; [1965] A.L.R.
   1084, P.C.; Digest Cont. Vol. B 634 .. .. 191, 212, 214, 217, 219, 2
Page v. Cowasjee Eduljee (1886), L.R. 1 P.C. 127; 3 Moo. P.C.C. N.S. 499; 14 L.T. 176;
   12 Jur. N.S. 361; 39 Digest (Repl.) 780 .. .. 367, 3
Pagnan and Fratelli v. Corbisa Industrial Agropacuaria Limitada, [1970] 1 W.L.R. 1306;
   114 Sol. Jo. 568, C.A. 379, 390, 4
Palmer v. Woolley. See Market-Overt Case
Panchard Frères S.A. Co. v. Establissements General Grain Co., [1970] 1 Lloyd's Rep.
   53 4
Panoutsos v. Raymond Hadley Corporation of New York, [1917] 2 K.B. 473; [1916–17]
   All E.R. Rep. 448; 86 L.J.K.B. 1325; 117 L.T. 330; 33 T.L.T. 436; 61 Sol. Jo. 590;
   22 Com. Cas. 308, C.A.; 39 Digest (Repl.) 576 1
Pantanassa, The, Norsk Bjergnings Kompagni A/S v. Owners of Steamship Pantanassa,
   [1970] 1 All E.R. 848; [1970] 2 W.L.R. 981; 114 Sol. Jo. 372; [1970] 1 Lloyd's Rep.
   153 .. .. 119, 125, 1
Parker v. Oloxo, Ltd., and Senior, [1937] 3 All E.R. 524; 36 Digest (Repl.) 87
Parker v. South Eastern Rail. Co. (1877), 2 C.P.D. 416; 46 L.J.Q.B. 768; 36 L.T. 540;
   41 J.P. 644; 25 W.R. 564, C.A.; 3 Digest (Repl.) 93 .. .. ..

PAGE

asley *v.* Freeman (1789), 3 Term Rep. 51; 39 Digest (Repl.) 512 129

atrick *v.* Russo-British Grain Export Co., [1927] 2 K.B. 535; [1927] All E.R. Rep.
692; 97 L.J.K.B. 60; 137 L.T. 815; 43 T.L.R. 724; 33 Com. Cas. 60; 39 Digest
(Repl.) 812 412

aul and Frank, Ltd. *v.* Discount Bank (Overseas), Ltd., [1967] Ch. 348; [1966] 2 All
E.R. 922; [1966] 3 W.L.R. 490; 110 Sol. Jo. 423; Digest Cont. Vol. B 108 .. 309

ayzu, Ltd. *v.* Saunders, [1919] 2 K.B. 581; [1918–19] All E.R. Rep. 219; 89 L.J.K.B.
17; 121 L.T. 563; 35 T.L.R. 657, C.A.; 17 Digest (Repl.) 110 275, 390, 391

earl Mill Co. *v.* Ivy Tannery Co., [1919] 1 K.B. 78; [1918–19] All E.R. Rep. 702; 88
L.J.K.B. 134; 120 L.T. 28; 24 Com. Cas. 169; 39 Digest (Repl.) 806 274, 275, 362

earson *v.* Rose and Young, Ltd., [1951] 1 K.B. 275; [1950] 2 All E.R. 1057; 66 (Pt. 2)
T.L.R. 886; 94 Sol. Jo. 778, C.A.; 1 Digest (Repl.) 388 205, 206, 208, 210, 213, 214, 215

eirce *v.* London Horse and Carriage Repository, Ltd., [1922] W.N. 170, C.A.; 39
Digest (Repl.) 654 .. .. 202, 234

enarth Dock Engineering Co., Ltd. *v.* Pounds, [1963] 1 Lloyd's Rep. 359 .. 274, 381

ennington *v.* Crossley & Son (1897), 77 L.T. 43; 13 T.L.R. 513; 41 Sol. Jo. 661, C.A.;
12 Digest (Repl.) 533 272

ennington *v.* Reliance Motor Works, Ltd., [1923] 1 K.B. 127; [1922] All E.R. Rep.
466; 92 L.J.K.B. 202; 128 L.T. 384; 38 T.L.R. 670; 66 Sol. Jo. 667; 32 Digest
(Repl.) 288 324

erkins *v.* Bell, [1893] 1 Q.B. 193; [1891–94] All E.R. Rep. 884; 62 L.J.Q.B. 91; 67
L.T. 792; 41 W.R. 195; 9 T.L.R. 147; 37 Sol. Jo. 130; 4 R. 212, C.A.; 39 Digest
(Repl.) 562 270

erry *v.* Davis (1858), 3 C.B.N.B. 769; 31 Digest (Repl.) 177 147

eruvian Guano, Ltd. *v.* Dreyfus Brother & Co., Ltd., [1892] A.C. 166; 61 L.J. Ch. 749;
66 L.T. 536; 8 T.L.R. 327; 7 Asp. M.L.C. 225, H.L.; 17 Digest (Repl.) 125 .. 333

eter Darlington, Ltd. *v.* Gosho, Ltd. *See* Darlington (Peter), Ltd. *v.* Gosho, Ltd.

eter Dumenil & Co., Ltd. *v.* Ruddin. *See* Dumenil (Peter) & Co., Ltd. *v.* Ruddin

hillip Head & Sons, Ltd. *v.* Showfronts, Ltd. *See* Head (Phillip) & Sons, Ltd. *v.* Showfronts, Ltd.

hillips *v.* Brooks, [1919] 2 K.B. 243; [1918–19] All E.R. Rep. 246; 88 L.J.K.B. 953;
121 L.T. 249; 35 T.L.R. 470; 24 Com. Cas. 263; 39 Digest (Repl.) 653.. 162, 199

hoenix Distributors, Ltd. *v.* L.B. Clarke (London), Ltd., [1967] 1 Lloyd's Rep. 518,
C.A. .. ..

ickard *v.* Sears (1837), 6 Ad. & El. 469; 2 Nev. & P.K.B. 488; Will. Woll. & Dav. 678;
21 Digest (Repl.) 369 92

ignatoro *v.* Gilroy, [1919] 1 K.B. 459; 88 L.J.K.B. 726; 120 L.T. 480; 35 T.L.R. 191;
63 Sol. Jo. 265; 24 Com. Cas. 174; 39 Digest (Repl.) 607 194

ilkington *v.* Wood, [1953] Ch. 770; [1953] 2 All E.R. 810; [1953] 3 W.L.R. 522; 97
Sol. Jo. 572; 43 Digest (Repl.) 120 172, 175, 176, 241

lasticmoda Societe Per Azione *v.* Davidsons, Ltd., [1952] 1 Lloyd's Rep. 527 .. 390

olar Refrigeration Service, Ltd. *v.* Moldenhauer (1967), 60 W.W.R. 284; 61 D.L.R.
(2 d) 462; Digest Supp. 148

olemis and Furness, Withy & Co., Ltd., *Re*, [1921] 3 K.B. 560; [1921] All E.R. Rep. 40;
90 L.J.K.B. 1353; 126 L.T. 154; 37 T.L.R. 940; 15 Asp. M.L.C. 398; 27 Com.
Cas. 25, C.A.; 36 Digest (Repl.) 38 168

olenghi Brothers *v.* Dried Milk Co., Ltd. (1904), 92 L.T. 64; 53 W.R. 318; 21 T.L.R.
118; 49 Sol. Jo. 120; 10 Com. Cas. 42; 39 Digest (Repl.) 562 387

ollock *v.* Macrae 1922 S.C. 192; S.L.T. 510; 60 Sc. L.R. 11; 39 Digest (Repl.) 578.. 108, 110, 269

olsky *v.* S. and A. Services, Ltd., [1951] 1 All E.R. 185; affd., [1951] 1 All E.R. 1062,
n.; 95 Sol. Jo. 414, C.A.; 7 Digest (Repl.) 18 142

oole *v.* Smith's Car Sales, Ltd., [1962] 2 All E.R. 482; [1962] 1 W.L.R. 744; 106 Sol.
Jo. 284, C.A.; 39 Digest (Repl.) 624 282, 295, 297, 300, 302

otts (W.) & Co., Ltd. *v.* Brown, Macfarlane & Co., Ltd. (1924), 30 Com. Cas. 64,
H.L.; 39 Digest (Repl.) 679 .. .. 177, 180

rager *v.* Blatspiel, Stamp and Heacock, Ltd., [1924] 1 K.B. 566; [1924] All E.R. Rep.
524; 93 L.J.K.B. 410; 130 L.T. 672; 40 T.L.R. 287; 68 Sol. Jo. 460; 39 Digest
(Repl.) 777 270

reist *v.* Last, [1903] 2 K.B. 148; 72 L.J.K.B. 657; 89 L.T. 33; 51 W.R. 678; 19 T.L.R.
527; 47 Sol. Jo. 566, C.A.; 39 Digest (Repl.) 545 .. .. 84, 88, 89, 92

Premor, Ltd. *v.* Shaw Brothers, [1964] 2 All E.R. 583; [1964] 1 W.L.R. 978; 108 Sol.
  Jo. 375, C.A.; Digest Cont. Vol. B 547 .. .. 302, 30
Printing and Numerical Registering Co. *v.* Sampson (1875), L.R. 19, Eq. 462; 44 L.J.
  Ch. 705; 32 L.T. 354; 23 W.R. 463; 45 Digest (Repl.) 499
Produce Brokers Co., Ltd. *v.* Olympia Oil and Cake Co., Ltd., [1916] 1 A.C. 314; 85
  L.J.K.B. 160; 114 L.T. 94; 32 T.L.R. 115; 60 Sol. Jo. 74; 21 Com. Cas. 320, H.L.;
  2 Digest (Repl.) 602 1
Produce Brokers Co., Ltd. *v.* Olympia Oil and Cake Co., Ltd., [1917] 1 K.B. 320;
  [1916–17] All E.R. Rep. 753; *sub nom.* Olympia Oil and Cake Co. *v.* Produce Brokers
  Co., 86 L.J.K.B. 421; 116 L.T. 1; 33 T.L.R. 95, C.A.; 39 Digest (Repl.) 604 .. 1
Pye *v.* British Automobile Commercial Syndicate, Ltd., [1906] 1 K.B. 425; 75 L.J.K.B.
  270; 22 T.L.R. 287; 17 Digest (Repl.) 151 3

Q

Qualcast (Wolverhampton), Ltd. *v.* Haynes, [1959] A.C. 743; [1959] 2 All E.R. 38;
  [1959] 2 W.L.R. 510; 103 Sol. Jo. 310, H.L.; 39 Digest (Repl.) 259 1

R

R. *v.* R. W. Proffitt, Ltd., [1954] 2 Q.B. 35; [1954] 2 All E.R. 798; [1954] 2 W.L.R.
  1001; 98 Sol. Jo. 352; 38 Cr. App. Rep. 102; 26 Digest (Repl.) 659 .. ..
R. *v.* Sutton, [1966] 1 All E.R. 571; [1966] 1 W.L.R. 236; 130 J.P. 183; 110 Sol. Jo. 51;
  50 Cr. App. Rep. 114, C.C.A.; Digest Cont. Vol. B 201 1
Read *v.* J. Lyons & Co., Ltd., [1945] 1 K.B. 216; [1945] 1 All E.R. 106; 114 L.J.K.B.
  232; 172 L.T. 104; 61 T.L.R. 148, C.A.; affd., [1947] A.C. 156; [1946] 2 All E.R.
  471; [1947] L.J.R. 39; 175 L.T. 413; 62 T.L.R. 646; 91 Sol. Jo. 54, H.L.; 24 Digest
  (Repl.) 1021 1
Reddall *v.* Union Castle Mail Steamship Co. Ltd. (1914) 84 L.J.K.B. 360; 112 L.T. 910;
  13 Asp. M.L.C. 51; 20 Com. Cas. 86; 39 Digest (Repl.) 757 3
Reliance Car Facilities, Ltd. *v.* Roding Motors, [1952] 2 Q.B. 844; [1952] 1 All E.R.
  1355; [1952] 1 T.L.R. 1370; 96 Sol. Jo. 360, C.A.; 26 Digest (Repl.) 668 290, 3
Rendell *v.* Turnbull (1908), 27 N.Z.L.R. 1067; 39 Digest (Repl.) 495 2
Reynolds *v.* General and Finance Facilities, Ltd. (1963), 107 Sol. Jo. 889, C.A. 334, 3
Richard Holden, Ltd. *v.* Bostock & Co., Ltd. *See* Holden (Richard), Ltd. *v.* Bostock &
  Co., Ltd.
Rickards (Charles), Ltd. *v.* Oppenheim, [1950] 1 K.B. 616; [1950] 1 All E.R. 420; 66
  (Pt. 1) T.L.R. 435; 94 Sol. Jo. 161, C.A.; Digest Cont. Vol. A 288   23, 146, 148, 26
    274, 3

Robbins Case. *See* Stadium Finance, Ltd. *v.* Robbins
Robert Stewart & Sons, Ltd. *v.* Carapanayoti, Ltd. *See* Stewart (Robert) & Sons, Ltd.
  v. Carapanayoti, Ltd.
Robinson *v.* Graves, [1935] 1 K.B. 579; [1935] All E.R. Rep. 935; 104 L.J.K.B. 441;
  153 L.T. 26; 51 T.L.R. 334; 79 Sol. Jo. 180; 40 Com. Cas. 217, C.A.; 39 Digest
  (Repl.) 445 .. ..
Robophone Facilities, Ltd. *v.* Blank, [1966] 3 All E.R. 128; [1966] 1 W.L.R. 1428; 110
  Sol. Jo. 544, C.A.; Digest Cont. Vol. B 43 3
Rogers, Sons & Co. *v.* Lambert & Co., [1891] 1 Q.B. 318; 10 L.J.Q.B. 187; 64 L.T. 406;
  55 J.P. 452; 39 W.R. 114; 7 T.L.R. 69, C.A.; 3 Digest (Repl.) 106 .. ..
Roper *v.* Johnson (1873), L.R. & C.P. 167; 42 L.J.C.P. 65; 28 L.T. 296; 21 W.R. 384;
  39 Digest (Repl.) 818 .. .. 361, 390, 4
Roscorla *v.* Thomas (1842), 3 Q.B. 234; 2 Gal. & Dav. 508; 11 L.J.Q.B. 214; 6 Jur. 929;
  39 Digest (Repl.) 515 1
Rose (Frederick E.) (London), Ltd. *v.* William H. Pim, Junior & Co., Ltd., [1953] 2
  Q.B. 450; [1953] 2 All E.R. 739; [1953] 3 W.L.R. 497; 97 Sol. Jo. 556; 70 R.P.C.
  238, C.A.; 35 Digest (Repl.) 147 4
Rose and Frank Co. *v.* J. R. Crompton and Brothers, Ltd., [1925] C.A.. 445; [1924] All
  E.R. Rep. 245; 94 L.J.K.B. 120; 132 L.T. 641; 30 Com. Cas. 163, H.L.; 39 Digest
  (Repl.) 781 1
Rosenthal *v.* Alderton & Son, Ltd., [1946] 1 K.B. 374; [1946] 1 All E.R. 583; 115
  L.J.K.B. 215; 174 L.T. 214; 62 T.L.R. 236; 90 Sol. Jo. 163, C.A.; 46 Digest (Repl.)
  515 3

osenthal (J.) & Sons *v.* Esmail (Trading) as H. M. H. Esmail & Sons). *See* Esmail (Trading as H. M. H. Esmail & Sons) *v.* J. Rosenthal & Sons, Ltd.

oss T. Smyth & Co., Ltd. *v.* Bailey Son & Co. *See* Smyth (Ross T.) & Co., Ltd. *v.* Bailey Son & Co.

oth (L.) & Co., Ltd. *v.* Taysen, Townsend & Co. (1896), 12 T.L.R. 211; 1 Com. Cas. 306, C.A.; 12 Digest (Repl.) 87 411

owland *v.* Divall, [1923] 2 K.B. 500; [1923] All E.R. Rep. 270; 92 L.J.K.B. 1041; 129 L.T. 757; 67 Sol. Jo. 703, C.A.; 35 Digest (Repl.) 128 56, 58, 59, 60, 61, 62, 63, 64, 401, 405, 408

uben (F. & S.), Ltd. *v.* Faire Brothers & Co., Ltd., [1949] 1 K.B. 254; [1949] 1 All E.R. 215; [1949] L.J.R. 800; 93 Sol. Jo. 103; 39 Digest (Repl.) 726 .. .. 108, 401

ugg *v.* Minett (1809), 11 East 210; 39 Digest (Repl.) 496 .. .. 164, 167, 407

ylands *v.* Fletcher (1868), L.R. 3 H.L. 330; [1861–73] All E.R. Rep. 1; 37 L.J. Ex. 161; 19 L.T. 220; 33 J.P. 70; 20 Digest (Repl.) 232 124

S

achs *v.* Miklos, [1948] 2 K.B. 23; [1948] 1 All E.R. 67; [1948] L.J.R. 1012; 64 T.L.R. 181, C.A.; 1 Digest (Repl.) 328 185

t. Margaret's Trust, Ltd. *v.* Castle, [1964] C.L.Y. 1685 300

amuels *v.* Davis, [1943] 1 K.B. 526; [1943] 2 All E.R. 3; 112 L.J.K.B. 561; 168 L.T. 296, C.A.; 39 Digest (Repl.) 541 23

an Pedro Compania Aramadora S.A. *v.* Henry Navigation Co., Ltd. and Pablo Compania Maritima ole Desarrollo S.A., The Ranger, [1970] 1 Lloyd's Rep. 32 374

anders *v.* Jameson (1848), 2 Car. & Kir. 557; 39 Digest (Repl.) 559 .. 401

anders *v.* MacLean (1883), 11 Q.B.D. 327, 52 L.J.Q.B. 481; 49 L.T. 462; 31 W.R. 698; 5 Asp. M.L.C. 160, C.A.; 39 Digest (Repl.) 518 .. 182, 264, 322

aunders *v.* Anglia Building Society, [1970] 3 All E.R. 961; [1970] 3 W.L.R. 1078, H.L.; affirming *sub nom.* Gallie *v.* Lee, [1969] 2 Ch. 17; [1969] 1 All E.R. 1062; [1969] 2 W.L.R. 901; 113 Sol. Jo. 187; 20 P. & C.R. 310; 209 Estates Gazette 1435, C.A.; Digest Supp. 196

aunt *v.* Belcher and Gibbons, Ltd., (1920) 90 L.J.K.B. 541; [1920] All E.R. Rep. 142; 125 L.T. 283; 26 Com. Cas. 115; 39 Digest (Repl.) 716 .. .. 37, 196

caliaris *v.* E. Ofverberg & Co. (1921), 37 T.L.R. 307, C.A.; 39 Digest (Repl.) 536.. 270

cammell (G.) and Nephew, Ltd. *v.* Austen, [1941] A.C. 251; [1941] 1 All E.R. 114; 110 L.J.K.B. 197; 164 L.T. 379; 57 T.L.R. 280; 85 Sol. Jo. 224; 46 Com. Cas. 190, H.L.; 39 Digest (Repl.) 448 .. .. 22, 36, 295

carf *v.* Jardine (1882), 7 App. Cas. 345; [1881–5] All E.R. Rep. 651; 51 L.J.Q.B. 612; 47 L.T. 258; 30 W.R. 893, H.L.; 21 Digest (Repl.) 299 200

chotsmans Lancashire and Yorkshire Rail. Co. (1867), 2 Ch. App. 332; 36 L.J. Ch. 361; 16 L.T. 189; 15 W.R. 537; 2 Mar. L.C. 485; 39 Digest (Repl.) 773 326

cotson *v.* Pegg (1861), 6 H. & N. 295; 30 L.J. Ex. 225; 3 L.T. 753; 9 W.R. 280; 12 Digest (Repl.) 238 52

cott *v.* Shepherd (1773), 2 Wm. Bl. 892; 3 Wils. 403; 46 Digest (Repl.) 419 .. 387

cruttons, Ltd. *v.* Midland Silicones, Ltd., [1962] A.C. 446; [1962] 1 All E.R. 1; 106 Sol. Jo. 34; [1961] 2 Lloyd's Rep. 365, H.L.; Digest Cont. Vol. A 271 .. 136, 249

eath & Co. *v.* Moore (1886), 11 App. Cas. 350; 55 L.J.P.C. 54; 54 L.T. 690; 5 Asp. M.L.C. 586, H.L.; 39 Digest (Repl.) 613 158

eddon *v.* North East Salt Co., Ltd., [1905] 1 Ch. 326; [1904–07] All E.R. Rep. 817; 74 L.J. Ch. 199; 91 L.T. 793; 53 W.R. 232; 21 T.L.R. 118; 49 Sol. Jo. 119; 39 Digest (Repl.) 829 359

haffer (James), Ltd. *v.* Findlay Durham and Brodie, [1953] 1 W.L.R. 106; 97 Sol. Jo. 26, C.A.; Digest Cont. Vol. A 289 278

hanklin Pier, Ltd. *v.* Detel Products, Ltd., [1951] 2 K.B. 854; [1951] 2 All E.R. 471; 95 Sol. Jo. 563; [1951] 2 Lloyd's Rep. 187; 39 Digest (Repl.) 579.. .. 120

harp *v.* Christmas (1892), 8 T.L.R. 687, C.A.; 39 Digest (Repl.) 525.. .. 274

harpe & Co., Ltd. *v.* Nosawa & Co., [1917] 2 K.B. 814; 87 L.J.K.B. 33; 118 L.T. 91; 22 Com. Cas. 286; 39 Digest (Repl.) 704 411

hell Mex, Ltd. *v.* Elton Cap Dying Co., Ltd. (1928), 34 Com. Cas. 39; 39 Digest (Repl.) 605 .. .. 371, 429

PA

Shepherd v. Harrison (1871), L.R. 5 H.L. 116; 40 L.J.Q.B. 148; 24 L.T. 857; 20 W.R.
    1; Asp. M.L.C. 66, H.L.; 39 Digest (Repl.) 637   1
Shepherd v. Ready Mix Concrete (London) (1968), 112 Sol. Jo. 518; Digest Supp.   2
Shipton Anderson & Co. v. Weil Brothers & Co., [1912] 1 K.B. 574; 81 L.J.K.B. 910;
    106 L.T. 372; 28 L.T.R. 269; 17 Com. Cas. 153; 39 Digest (Repl.) 690. .
Shipton Anderson & Co. and Harrison Brothers & Co., Re, [1915] 3 K.B. 676; 84
    L.J.K.B. 2137; 113 L.T. 1009; 31 T.L.R. 598; 21 Com. Cas. 138; 12 Digest (Repl.)
    450   ..   ..   181, 2
Sibree v. Tripp (1846), 15 L.J. Ex. 318; 15 M. & W. 23; 6 Digest (Repl.) 37   ..
Simon v. Pawson and Leafs, Ltd. (1933), 148 L.T. 154; [1932] All E.R. Rep. 72; 38
    Com. Cas. 151, C.A.; 17 Digest (Repl.) 129   4
Simpson v. Crippin (1872), L.R. 8 Q.B. 14; 42 L.J.Q.B. 28; 27 L.T. 546; 21 W.R. 141;
    39 Digest (Repl.) 700   ..
Slater v. Hoyle and Smith, [1920] 2 K.B. 11; [1918–19] All E.R. Rep. 654; 89 L.J.K.B.
    401; 122 L.T. 611; 36 T.L.R. 132; 25 Com. Cas. 140, C.A.; 39 Digest (Repl.) 592   3
                                         418, 4
Smart Brothers, Ltd. v. Holt, [1929] 2 K.B. 303; [1929] All E.R. Rep. 322; 98 L.J.K.B.
    532; 141 L.T. 268; 45 T.L.R. 504; 35 Com. Cas. 53; 18 Digest (Repl.) 295   11,
Smart Brothers, Ltd. v. Pratt, [1940] 2 K.B. 498; [1940] 3 All E.R. 432; 109 L.J.K.B.
    952; 163 L.T. 259; 56 T.L.R. 975; 84 Sol. Jo. 465, C.A.; 26 Digest (Repl.) 675   3
Smeaton Hanscomb & Co., Ltd. v. Sassoon I Setty, Son & Co., [1953] 2 All E.R. 1471;
    [1953] 1 W.L.R. 1468; 97 Sol. Jo. 862; [1953] 2 Lloyd's Rep. 580; 39 Digest (Repl.)
    582   1
Smith v. Parkinson. See Bigge v. Parkinson
Smyth (Ross T.) & Co., Ltd. v. Bailey, Son & Co., [1940] 3 All E.R. 60, 164 L.T. 102;
    56 T.L.R. 825; 84 Sol. Jo. 572; 67 Ll. L. Rep. 147; 45 Com. Cas. 292; 39 Digest
    (Repl.) 611   ..   ..   175, 247, 277, 278, 3
Snell v. Unity Finance, Ltd., [1964] 2 Q.B. 203; [1963] 1 All E.R. 417; [1963] 3 W.L.R.
    559; 107 Sol. Jo. 533, C.A.; Digest Cont. Vol. A 326
Snook v. London and West Riding Investments, Ltd., [1967] 2 Q.B. 786; [1967] 1 All
    E.R. 518; [1967] 2 W.L.R. 1020; 111 Sol. Jo. 71, C.A.; Digest Supp. 29, 280, 296, 2
Solle v. Butcher, [1950] 1 K.B. 671; [1949] 2 All E.R. 1107; 66 (Pt. 1) T.L.R. 448, C.A.;
    31 Digest (Repl.) 675   ..   1
Somes v. British Empire Shipping Co. (1860), 8 H.L. Cas. 338; 30 L.J.Q.B. 229; 2 L.T.
    547; 6 Jur. N.S. 761; 8 W.R. 707, H.L.; 12 Digest (Repl.) 627   ..   3
South Bedfordshire Electrical Finance, Ltd. v. Bryant, [1938] 3 All E.R. 580; 82 Sol. Jo.
    681, C.A.; 26 Digest (Repl.) 673   3
Southern Industrial Trust (Trading as Starnes Motors) v. Brooke House Motors, Ltd.
    (1968), 112 Sol. Jo. 798, C.A.   ..
Southern Livestock Producers, Ltd., Re, [1963] 3 All E.R. 801; [1964] 1 W.L.R. 24;
    108 Sol. Jo. 15; Digest Cont. Vol. A 1116   3
Spencer v. North Country Finance, Ltd., [1963] C.L.Y. 212; Guardian, February 20th   2
Spencer Trading, Ltd. v. Devon, [1947] 1 All E.R. 284; 39 Digest (Repl.) 550   ..
Springer v. Great Western Rail. Co., [1921] 1 K.B. 257; [1920] All E.R. Rep. 361; 89
    L.J.K.B. 1010; 124 L.T. 79; 15 Asp. M.L.C. 86, C.A.; 41 Digest (Repl.) 411   1
Square v. Model Farm Dairies, (Bournemouth), Ltd., [1939] 2 K.B. 365; 108 L.J.K.B.
    198; 160 L.T. 165; 55 T.L.R. 384; 83 Sol. Jo. 152, C.A.; 25 Digest (Repl.) 141
Stadium Finance, Ltd. v. Helm (1965), 109 Sol. Jo. 471, C.A...   3
Stadium Finance, Ltd. v. Robbins, [1962] 2 Q.B. 664; [1962] 2 All E.R. 633; [1962] 2
    W.L.R. 453; 106 Sol. Jo. 369, C.A.; Digest Cont. Vol. A 7   205, 206, 208, 209, 21
                                           213, 2
Staffs Motor Guarantee, Ltd. v. British Wagon, Ltd., [1934] 2 K.B. 305; [1934] All
    E.R. Rep. 322; 103 L.J.K.B. 613; 151 L.T. 396; 1 Digest (Repl.) 387   206, 217, 21
                                           2
Standard Manufacturing Co., Re, [1891] 1 Ch. 627; [1891–4] All E.R. Rep. 1242; 60
    L.J. Ch. 292; 64 L.T. 487; 39 W.R. 369; 7 T.L.R. 282; 2 Meg. 418, C.A.; 7
    Digest (Repl.) 32   2
Steels and Busks, Ltd. v. Bleeker Bik & Co., Ltd., [1956] 1 Lloyd's Rep. 228   72 92, 99, 1
Stein, Forbes v. County Tailoring Co. (1916), 86 L.J.K.B. 448; 115 L.T. 215; 13 Asp.
    M.L.C. 422; 39 Digest (Repl.) 794   ..   ..   168, 3

PAGE

teinberger v. Atkinson & Co., Ltd. (1914), 31 T.L.R. 110; 39 Digest (Repl.) 744 .. 318

tennett v. Hancock and Peters, [1939] 2 All E.R. 578; 83 Sol. Jo. 379; 36 Digest (Repl.) 82 125

tephens v. Wilkinson (1831), 2 B. & Ad. 320; 9 L.J.O.S.B. 231; 39 Digest (Repl.) 780 367, 369

terling Industrial Facilities, Ltd. v. Lydiate Textiles, Ltd. (1962), 106 Sol. Jo. 669.. 290, 346

terns, Ltd. v. Vickers, Ltd., [1923] 1 K.B. 78; [1922] All E.R. Rep. 126; 92 L.J.K.B. 331; 128 L.T. 402, C.A.; 39 Digest (Repl.) 647 .. .. 243, 244, 245, 253

tewart v. Reavell's Garage, [1952] 2 Q.B. 545; [1952] 1 All E.R. 1191; [1952] 1 T.L.R. 1266; 96 Sol. Jo. 314; Digest Cont. Vol. B 33 .. .. .. 23, 121

tewart (Robert) & Sons, Ltd. v. Carapanayoti, Ltd., [1962] 1 All E.R. 418; [1962] 1 W.L.R. 34; 106 Sol. Jo. 16; [1961] 2 Lloyd's Rep. 387; Digest Cont. Vol. A 470 412

tockloser v. Johnson, [1954] 1 Q.B. 467; [1954] 1 All E.R. 630; [1954] 2 W.L.R. 439; 98 Sol. Jo. 178, C.A.; 20 Digest (Repl.) 549 .. .. .. 330, 373

toneleigh Finance, Ltd. v. Phillips, [1965] 2 Q.B. 537; [1965] 1 All E.R. 513; [1965] 2 W.L.R. 508; 109 Sol. Jo. 68, C.A.; Digest Cont. Vol. B 107 .. .. 189, 296

trand Electric, Ltd. v. Brisford Entertainment, Ltd., [1952] 2 Q.B. 246; [1952] 1 All E.R. 796; [1952] 1 T.L.R. 939; 96 Sol. Jo. 260, C.A.; 46 Digest (Repl.) 486 .. 381

treet v. Blay (1831), 2 B. & Ad. 456; 39 Digest (Repl.) 581 161

trongman (1945), Ltd. v. Sincock, [1955] 2 Q.B. 525; [1955] 3 All E.R. 90; [1955] 3 W.L.R. 360; 99 Sol. Jo. 540, C.A.; Digest Cont. Vol. A 482 38

uisse Atlantique Societe D'Armement Maritime S.A. v. N.V. Rotterdamsche Kolen Centrace, [1967] 1 A.C. 361; [1966] 2 All E.R. 61; [1966] 2 W.L.R. 944; 110 Sol. Jo. 367; [1966] 1 Lloyd's Rep. 529, H.L.; Digest Cont. Vol. B 652 136, 143, 145, 379

ummer Permain & Co. v. Webb & Co., [1922] 1 K.B. 55; [1921] All E.R. Rep. 680; 91 L.J.K.B. 228; 126 L.T. 294; 38 T.L.R. 45; 66 Sol. Jo. 17; 27 Com. Cas. 105, C.A.; 39 Digest (Repl.) 556 .. .. 85, 91, 96, 98, 101

wan v. North British Australasian Co., Ltd. (1862), 7 H. & N. 603; (1863), 2 H. & C. 175; 9 Digest (Repl.) 220 197

T

.C. Trustees, Ltd. v. J. S. Darwen, Ltd., [1969] 2 Q.B. 295; [1969] 1 All E.R. 271; [1969] 1 W.L.R. 81; 112 Sol. Jo. 864, C.A. 330

ailby v. Official Receiver (1888), 13 App. Cas. 523; [1886–90] All E.R. Rep. 486; 58 L.J.Q.B. 75; 60 L.T. 162; 37 W.R. 513; 4 T.L.R. 726, H.L.; 47 Digest (Repl.) 135 307

arling v. Baxter (1827), 6 B. & C. 360; 9 Dow & Ry. K.B. 272; 5 L.J.O.S.K.B. 164; 39 Digest (Repl.) 617 162

aylor v. Caldwell (1863), 3 B. & S. 826; [1861–73] All E.R. Rep. 24; 2 New Rep. 198; 32 L.J.Q.B. 164; 8 L.T. 356; 27 J.P. 710; 11 W.R. 726; 12 Digest (Repl.) 418 254

aylor v. Combined Buyers, Ltd., [1924] N.Z.L.R. 627.. .. .. 75, 90, 98

aylor v. Great Eastern Rail. Co., [1901] 1 K.B. 774; 70 L.J.K.B. 499; 84 L.T. 770; 49 W.R. 431; 17 T.L.R. 394; 45 Sol. Jo. 381; 6 Com. Cas. 121; 39 Digest (Repl.) 488 .. .. 327, 328

aylor v. Oakes, Roncoroni & Co., (1922), 127 L.T. 267; 38 T.L.R. 517; 66 Sol. Jo. 556; 27 Com. Cas. 261, C.A.; 39 Digest (Repl.) 727 .. .. 149, 266

aylor & Sons, Ltd. v. Bank of Athens (1922), 91 L.J.K.B. 776; 128 L.T. 795; 27 Com. Cas. 142; 39 Digest (Repl.) 590 422

eheran-Europe, Ltd. v. S. T. Belton (Tractors), Ltd., [1968] 2 Q.B. 545; [1968] 2 All E.R. 886; [1968] 3 W.L.R. 205; 112 Sol. Jo. 501; [1968] 2 Lloyd's Rep. 37, C.A.; Digest Supp. 92

hames Ironworks Co. v. Patents Derrick Do. (1860), 1 John & H. 93; 29 L.J. Ch. 714; 2 L.T. 208; 6 Jur. N.S. 1013; 8 W.R. 408; 39 Digest (Repl.) 743.. .. 315

hames Sack and Bag Co., Ltd. v. Knowles & Co., Ltd. (1919), 88 L.J.K.B. 585; 119 L.T. 287; 39 Digest (Repl.) 519 274

homas Graham, Ltd. v. Glenrothes Development Corporation. See Graham (Thomas), Ltd. v. Glenrothes Development Corporation.

homas Young, Ltd. v. Hobson. See Young (Thomas), Ltd. v. Hobson

PAG

Thompson (W. L.), Ltd. *v.* Robinson (Gunmakers), Ltd., [1955] Ch. 177; [1955] 1 All
    E.R. 154; [1955] 2 W.L.R. 185; 99 Sol. Jo. 76; 39 Digest (Repl.) 795 38
Thornett and Fehr *v.* Beers & Sons, [1919] 1 K.B. 486; 88 L.J.K.B. 684; 120 L.T. 570;
    24 Com. Cas. 133; 39 Digest (Repl.) 555 .. 68, 10
Thornett and Fehr and Yuills, Ltd., *Re*, [1921] 1 K.B. 219; 90 L.J.K.B. 361; 124 L.T.
    218; 37 T.L.R. 31; 26 Com. Cas. 59; 39 Digest (Repl.) 806 37
Three Rivers Trading Co. *v.* Gwinear and District Farmers (1967), 111 Sol. Jo. 831,
    C.A.; Digest Supp. 14
Tiffin *v.* Pitcher, [1969] C.L.Y. 3234 .. .. 401, 40
Times Furnishing Co. *v.* Hutchings, [1938] 1 K.B. 775; [1935] 1 All E.R. 422; 107
    L.J.K.B. 432; 158 L.T. 335; 54 T.L.R. 390; 82 Sol. Jo. 315; 18 Digest (Repl.) 296 9
Tolly's Case. *See* Charterhouse Credit, Ltd. *v.* Tolly
Tommey *v.* Finextra, Ltd. (1962), 106 Sol. Jo. 1012 .. .. 146, 375, 4?
Tool Metal Manufacturing Co., Ltd. *v.* Tungsten Electric Co., Ltd., [1955] 2 All E.R.
    657, [1955] 1 W.L.R. 761; 99 Sol. Jo. 470; 72 R.P.C. 209; H.L.; Digest Cont. Vol. A
    1250 14
Torkington *v.* Magee, [1902] 2 K.B. 427; [1900–3] All E.R. Rep. 991; 71 L.J.K.B. 712;
    87 L.T. 304; 18 T.L.R. 703; Affd, [1903] 1 K.B. 644; 72 L.J.K.B. 336; 88 L.T.
    443; 19 T.L.R. 331; 8 Digest (Repl.) 556 3
Towers *v.* Barrett (1786), 1 Term Rep. 133; 12 Digest (Repl.) 262 40
Townley *v.* Crump (1836), 4 Ad. & El. 58; 39 Digest (Repl.) 761 32
Trans Trust S.P.R.L. *v.* Danubian Trading, Ltd., [1952] 2 Q.B. 297; [1952] 1 All E.R.
    970; [1952] 1 T.L.R. 1066; 96 Sol. Jo. 312; [1952] 1 Lloyd's Rep. 348, C.A.; 39
    Digest (Repl.) 781 .. .. 275, 351, 383, 38
Transport and General Credit Corporation, Ltd. *v.* Morgan, [1939] Ch. 531; [1939] 2
    All E.R. 17; 108 L.J. Ch. 179; 160 L.T. 380; 55 T.L.R. 483; 83 Sol. Jo. 338; 35
    Digest (Repl.) 233 .. .. 311, 31
Travers (Joseph) & Sons. Ltd. *v.* Longel, Ltd. (1947), 64 T.L.R. 150; 39 Digest (Repl.)
    560 10
Tredegar Iron and Coal Co., Ltd. *v.* Hawthorn Brothers & Co. (1902), 18 T.L.R. 716,
    C.A.; 39 Digest (Repl.) 799 30
Tsakiroglou & Co., Ltd. *v.* Noblee and Thorl G.m.b.H., [1962] A.C. 93; [1961] 2 All
    E.R. 179; [1961] 2 W.L.R. 633; 105 Sol. Jo. 346; [1961] 1 Lloyd's Rep. 329, H.L.;
    39 Digest (Repl.) 569 24
Tucker *v.* Farm and General Investments Trust, Ltd. [1966] 2 Q.B. 421; [1966] 2 All
    E.R. 508; [1961] 2 W.L.R. 1241; 110 Sol. Jo. 267, C.A.; Digest Cont. Vol. B 22 .. 2·
Tucker *v.* Linger (1883), 8 App. Cas. 508; 52 L.J. Ch. 941; 49 L.T. 373; 48 J.P. 4; 32
    W.R. 40, H.L.; 2 Digest (Repl.) 51 1
Turner *v.* Sampson (1911), 27 T.L.R. 200; 1 Digest (Repl.) 432 20

U

U.S.A. *v.* Motor Trucks, Ltd., [1924] A.C. 196; 93 L.J.P.C. 46; 130 L.T. 129; 39
    T.L.R. 723, P.C.; 44 Digest (Repl.) 151 4
Underwood, Ltd. *v.* Burgh Castle Brick and Cement Syndicate, [1922] 1 K.B. 123;
    on appeal [1921] 1 K.B. 343; [1921] All E.R. Rep. 515; 91 L.J.K.B. 355; 126 L.T.
    401; 38 T.L.R. 44, C.A., 39 Digest (Repl.) 619 .. .. .. 165, 10
Union Transport Finance, Ltd. *v.* Ballardie, [1937] 1 K.B. 510; [1937] 1 All E.R. 420;
    106 L.J.K.B. 268; 156 L.T. 142; 53 T.L.R. 240; 81 Sol. Jo. 159; 1 Digest (Repl.)
    389 2
United Dominion Trust (Commercial), Ltd. *v.* Eagle Aircraft, Ltd., [1968] 1 All E.R.
    104; [1968] 1 W.L.R. 74; 111 Sol. Jo. 849, C.A.; Digest Supp. .. 137, 29
United Dominions Trust (Commercial), Ltd. *v.* Ennis, [1968] 1 Q.B. 54; [1967] 2 All
    E.R. 345, [1967] 3 W.L.R. 1; 111 Sol. Jo. 191, C.A.; Digest Supp. .. 385, 3?
United Dominions Trust (Commercial), Ltd. *v.* Kesler (1963), 107 Sol. Jo. 15, C.A. : 3.
United Dominions Trust, Ltd. *c.* Kirkwood, [1966] 2 Q.B. 431; [1966] 1 All E.R. 968;
    [1966] 2 W.L.R. 1083; 110 Sol. Jo. 169; [1966] 1 Lloyd's Rep. 418, C.A.; Digest
    Cont. Vol. B 45 .. .. 301, 302, 303, 30
United Dominions Trust (Commercial), Ltd. *v.* Parkway Motors, Ltd., [1955] 2 All
    E.R. 557; [1955] 1 W.L.R. 719; 99 Sol. Jo. 436; 26 Digest (Repl.) 670 .. ..

PAGE

ited Motor Finance Corporation, Ltd. *v.* Turner, [1956] 2 Q.B. 32; [1956] 1 All E.R.
623; [1956] 2 W.L.R. 730; 100 Sol. Jo. 209, C.A.; 26 Digest (Repl.) 675 .. 339
ited States of America and Republic of France *v.* Dollfus Mieg Et. Compagnie S.A.
and Bank of England, [1952] A.C. 582; [1952] 1 All E.R. 572; [1952] 1 T.L.R. 541;
96 Sol. Jo. 180, H.L.; 3 Digest (Repl.) 287 363
ited States Steel Products Co. *v.* Great Western Rail. Co., [1916] 1 A.C. 189;
1914–1915] All E.R. Rep. 1049; 85 L.J.K.B. 1; 113 L.T. 886; 31 T.L.R. 561; 59
Sol. Jo. 648; 21 Com. Cas. 105, H.L.; 39 Digest (Repl.) 749 329
ity Finance, Ltd. *v.* Hammond (1965), 109 Sol. Jo. 70, C.A. 36
ity Finance, Ltd. *v.* Woodstock, [1963] 2 All E.R. 270; [1963] 1 W.L.R. 455; 107
Sol. Jo. 214, C.A.; Digest Cont. Vol. A 628 346
iversal Cargo Corporation *v.* Citati, [1957] 2 Q.B. 401; [1957] 2 All E.R. 70; [1957]
2 W.L.R. 713; 101 Sol. Jo. 320; [1957] 1 Lloyd's 174; *Affd.,* [1957] 3 All E.R. 234;
[1957] 1 W.L.R. 979; 101 Sol. Jo. 762; [1957] 2 Lloyd's Rep. 191, C.A.; Digest
Cont. Vol. A 291 267

V

cwell Engineering Co., Ltd. *v.* B.D.H. Chemicals, Ltd., [1969] 3 All E.R. 1681;
[1969] 3 W.L.R. 927; 113 Sol. Jo. 639; on appeal, [1970] 3 All E.R. 553; [1970]
3 W.L.R. 67, 114 Sol. Jo. 472, C.A. 85, 92, 112, 126, 130, 389
rley *v.* Whipp, [1900] 1 Q.B. 513; 69 L.J.Q.B. 333; 48 W.R. 363; 44 Sol. Jo. 263; 39
Digest (Repl.) 528 .. .. 68, 74, 75, 159, 162
: Mill, Ltd., *Re,* [1913] 1 Ch. 465; 82 L.J. Ch. 251; 108 L.T. 444; 57 Sol. Jo. 404,
C.A.; 39 Digest (Repl.) 797 384
ctoria Laundry (Windsor), Ltd. *v.* Newman Industries, Coulson & Co., Ltd., [1949]
2 K.B. 528; [1949] 1 All E.R. 997; 65 T.L.R. 274; 93 Sol. Jo. 371, C.A.; 39 Digest
(Repl.) 816 .. .. 378, 388, 413, 420
gers Brothers *v.* Sanderson Brothers, [1901] 1 K.B. 608; 70 L.J.K.B. 383; 84 L.T.
464; 49 W.R. 411; 17 T.L.R. 316; 45 Sol. Jo. 328; 6 Com. Cas. 99; 39 Digest (Repl.)
575 168
gan & Co. *v.* Oulton (1899), 81 L.T. 435; 16 T.L.R. 37, C.A.; 3 Digest (Repl.) 97 428

W

ddington & Son *v.* Neale & Sons (1907), 97 L.T. 786; 23 T.L.R. 464; 1 Digest (Repl.)
393 212
gon Mound, The. *See* Overseas Tankship (U.K.), Ltd. *v.* Morts Dock and Engineering Co., Ltd.
it, *Re,* [1927] 1 Ch. 606; [1926] All E.R. Rep. 433; 96 L.J. Ch. 179; 136 L.T. 552;
43 T.L.R. 150; 71 Sol. Jo. 56; [1927] B. & C.R. 140, C.A.; 39 Digest (Repl.)
821 .. .. 158, 173, 246, 294, 429
it *v.* Baker (1848), 2 Exch. 1; 17 L.J. Ex. 307; 39 Digest (Repl.) 602 .. 170
it and James *v.* Midland Bank (1926), 31 Com. Cas. 172; 39 Digest (Repl.) 658 158
llace *v.* Woodgate (1824), 1 C. & P. 575; Ry. & M. 193; 32 Digest (Repl.) 271 .. 322
llis *v.* Russell, [1902] 2 I.R. 585; 39 Digest (Repl.) 546 .. .. 87, 88, 91
llis, Son and Wells *v.* Pratt and Haynes, [1910] 2 K.B. 1003, 79 L.J.K.B. 1013;
103 L.T. 118; 26 T.L.R. 572, C.A.; on appeal, [1911] A.C. 394; 80 L.J.K.B. 1058;
105 L.T. 146; 27 T.L.R. 431; 55 Sol. Jo. 496, H.L.; 39 Digest (Repl.) 588 .. 5,
51, 139, 415
rd (R. V.), Ltd. *v.* Bignall, [1967], Q.B. 534; [1967] 2 All E.R. 449; [1967] 2 W.L.R.
1050; 111 Sol. Jo. 190, C.A.; Digest Supp. .. 163, 317, 361, 366, 367, 368, 383
rder's Import and Export Co., Ltd. *v.* W. Norwood & Sons Ltd., [1968] 2 Q.B. 663;
[1968] 2 All E.R. 602; [1968] 2 W.L.R. 1440; 112 Sol. Jo. 310; [1968] 2 Lloyd's
Rep. 1, C.A.; Digest Supp. 241, 265
rman *v.* Southern Counties Finance Corporation, Ltd., [1949] 2 K.B. 576; [1949]
1 All E.R. 711; [1949] L.J.R. 1182; 93 Sol. Jo. 319; 26 Digest (Repl.) 666 .. 55,
60, 61, 62, 416
tson, *Re ex parte* Official Receiver in Bankruptcy (1890), 25 Q.B.D. 27; 59 L.J.Q.B.
394; 63 L.T. 209; 38 W.R. 567; 6 T.L.R. 332; 7 Morr. 155, C.A.; 7 Digest (Repl.)
6 292

P.

Watson *v.* Buckley, Osborne Garrett & Co., Ltd. and Wyrovoys Products, Ltd., [1940]
   1 All E.R. 174; 36 Digest (Repl.) 87 ..   ..   6, 119,
Watteau *v.* Fenwick, [1893] 1 Q.B. 346; 67 L.T. 831; 56 J.P. 839; 41 W.R. 222; 9
   T.L.R. 133; 37 Sol. Jo. 117; 1 Digest (Repl.) 358 ..   ..
Watts *v.* Seymour, [1967] 2 Q.B. 647; [1967] 1 All E.R. 1044; [1967] 2 W.L.R. 1072;
   131 J.P. 309; 111 Sol. Jo. 294; Digest Supp.
Webb's Case. *See* Summer Permain & Co. *v.* Webb & Co.
Webster *v.* Higgin, [1948] 2 All E.R. 127; 92 Sol. Jo. 454, C.A.; 26 Digest (Repl.) 665
Weiner *v.* Gill, [1906] 2 K.B. 574; [1904–07] All E.R. Rep. 773; 75 L.J.K.B. 916;
   95 L.T. 438; 22 T.L.R. 699; 50 Sol. Jo. 632; 11 Com. Cas. 240, C.A.; 39 Digest
   (Repl.) 627   177,
Weiner *v.* Harris, [1910] 1 K.B. 285, [1908–10] All E.R. Rep. 405; 79 L.J.K.B. 342;
   101 L.T. 647; 26 T.L.R. 96, 54 Sol. Jo. 81; 15 Com. Cas. 39, C.A.; 1 Digest (Repl.)
   387   ..   ..   180, 205,
Weld-Blundell *v.* Stevens, [1920] A.C. 956, [1920] All E.R. Rep. 32; 89 L.J.K.B. 705;
   123 L.T. 593; 36 T.L.R. 640; 64 Sol. Jo. 529, H.L.; 45 Digest (Repl.) 296   ..
Wells (Merstham), Ltd. *v.* Buckland Sand and Silica Co., Ltd., [1965] 2 Q.B. 170;
   [1964] 1 All E.R. 41; [1964] 2 W.L.R. 453; 108 Sol. Jo. 177; Digest Cont. Vol. B
   632   ..   ..   52.
Wertheim *v.* Chicoutimi Pulp Co., [1911] A.C. 301; [1908–10] All E.R. Rep. 707; 80
   L.J.P.C. 91; 104 L.T. 226; 16 Com. Cas. 297, P.C.; 39 Digest (Rep.) 815   ..
Western Credit, Ltd. *v.* Alberry, [1964] 2 All E.R. 938; [1964] 1 W.L.R. 945; 108 Sol.
   Jo. 423, C.A.; Digest Cont. Vol. B 326   346,
White *v.* John Warwick & Co., [1953] 2 All E.R. 1021; [1953] 1 W.L.R. 1285; 97 Sol.
   Jo. 740, C.A.; 3 Digest (Repl.) 96   ..   ..   ..   126, 140,
White and Carter (Councils), Ltd. *v.* McGregor, [1962] A.C. 413; [1961] 3 All E.R.
   1178; [1962] 2 W.L.R. 17, 105 Sol. Jo. 1104, H.L.; Digest Cont. Vol. A 291   371,
White Sea Trust Timber, Ltd. *v.* North, Ltd. (1933), 148 L.T. 263, [1932] All E.R. Rep.
   136; 49 T.L.R. 142; 77 Sol. Jo. 30; 18 Asp. M.L.C. 367; 39 Digest (Repl.) 719 ..
Whitehorn Brothers *v.* Davison, [1911] 1 K.B. 463; [1908–10] All E.R. Rep. 885; 80
   L.J.K.B. 425; 104 L.T. 234, C.A.; 39 Digest (Repl.) 654 ..   ..   ..
Whiteley, Ltd. *v.* Hilt, [1918] 2 K.B. 808; [1918–19] All E.R. Rep. 1005; 78 L.J.K.B.
   1058; 119 L.T. 632; 34 T.L.R. 592; 62 Sol. Jo. 717, C.A.; 3 Digest (Repl.) 470   ..
   59, 63,
Whitfield *v.* Le Despenser (1778), 2 Comp. 754; 1 Digest (Repl.) 784   ..   ..
Wickham Holdings, Ltd. *v.* Brooke House Motors, Ltd., [1967] 1 All E.R. 117; [1967]
   1 W.L.R. 295, C.A.; Digest Supp.   13,
Wiehe *v.* Dennis Brothers (1913), 29 T.L.R. 250; 3 Digest (Repl.) 66   ..   ..
Wilensko Slasko Towarzy Stwo Drewno *v.* Fenwick & Co. (West Hartlepool), Ltd.,
   [1938] 3 All E.R. 429; 54 T.L.R. 1019; 44 Com. Cas. 1; 61 Ll.L. Rep. 249; 39
   Digest (Repl.) 724   ..   ..
Wilkinson *v.* Downton, [1897] 2 Q.B. 57; 66 L.J.Q.B. 493; 76 L.T. 493; 45 W.R. 525;
   13 T.L.R. 388; 41 Sol. Jo. 493; 1 Digest (Repl.) 29   ..   ..   124, I
William Barker (Junior) & Co., Ltd. *v.* Ed. Agius, Ltd. *See* Barker (William) (Junior)
   & Co., Ltd. *v.* Ed. Agius, Ltd.
William Cory & Son *v.* I.R. Comrs. *See* Cory (William) & Son *v.* I.R. Comrs.
Williams *v.* Reynolds (1865), 6 B. & S. 495; 6 New Rep. 293; 34 L.J.Q.B. 221; 12 L.T.
   729; 11 Jur. N.S. 973; 13 W.R. 940; 39 Digest (Repl.) 817   4
Williams Brothers *v.* E. T. Agius, Ltd., [1914] A.C. 510; [1914–15] All E.R. Rep. 97;
   83 L.J.K.B. 715; 110 L.T. 865; 30 T.L.R. 351; 58 Sol. Jo. 377; 19 Com. Cas.
   200, H.L.; 39 Digest (Repl.) 812   ..   ..   410, 4
Williams Case. *See* Newtons of Wembley Ltd. *v.* Williams
Wilson *v* Lombank, Ltd., [1963] 1 All E.R. 740; [1963] 1 W.L.R. 1294; 46 Digest
   (Repl.) 415   ..   ..
Wilson *v.* Rickett, Cockrell & Co., Ltd., [1954] 1 Q.B. 598; [1954] 1 All E.R. 868;
   [1954] 2 W.L.R. 629; 98 Sol. Jo. 233, C.A.; 39 Digest (Repl.) 556   ..   8
   88, 90, 98, 99, 4
Wimble, Sons & Co. *v.* Rosenberg & Sons, [1913] 3 K.B. 743; 82 L.J.K.B. 1251; 109
   L.T. 294; 29 T.L.R. 752; 57 Sol. Jo. 784; 12 Asp. M.L.C. 373; 18 Com. Cas. 65,
   302, C.A.; 39 Digest (Repl.) 703   2

PAGE

Winkfield, The, [1902] P. 42; [1900-3] All E.R. Rep. 346; 71 L.J.P. 21; 85 L.T. 668; 50 W.R. 246; 18 T.L.R. 178; 46 Sol. Jo. 163; 9 Asp. M.L.C. 259; 3 Digest (Repl.) 111 380

Winterbottom v. Wright (1848), 10 M. & W. 109; 11 L.J. Ex. 415; 36 Digest (Repl.) 107 126

Wood v. Leadbitter (1835), 13 M. & W. 838; 14 L.J. Ex. 161; 4 L.T.O.S. 433; 9 J.P. 312; 9 Jur. 187; 19 Digest (Repl.) 26 330

Woodhouse A.C. Israel Cocoa, Ltd. v. Nigerian Produce Marketing Co., Ltd., [1970] 2 All E.R. 124; [1970] 1 Lloyd's Rep. 295; reversed, [1970] 11 C.L. 327b; *Times,* November 25th, C.A. 192, 378

Woodley v. Coventry (1863), 2 H. & C. 164; 2 New Rep. 35; 32 L.J. Ex. 185; 8 L.T. 249; 9 Jur. N.S. 548; 11 W.R. 599; 21 Digest (Repl.) 405 192

Woolfe v. Horn (1877), 2 Q.B.D. 355; 46 L.J.Q.B. 534; 36 L.T. 705; 41 J.P. 501; 25 W.R. 728; 39 Digest (Repl.) 524 274

Worcester's (Bishop) Case. *See* Market-Overt Case

Workman Clark & Co. Ltd. v. Lloyd Brazileno, [1908] 1 K.B. 968; 77 L.J.K.B. 953; 99 L.T. 477; 24 T.L.R. 458; 11 Asp M.L.C. 126, C.A.; 39 Digest (Repl.) 782 .. 371

Wren v. Holt, [1903] 1 K.B. 610; 72 L.J.K.B. 340; 88 L.T. 282; 67 J.P. 191; 51 W.R. 435; 19 T.L.R. 292, C.A.; 39 Digest (Repl.) 555 .. .. 68, 90, 99, 426

Wright (Frank H.) (Constructions), Ltd. v. Frodoor, Ltd., [1967] 1 All E.R. 433; [1967] 1 W.L.R. 506; 111 Sol. Jo. 210; Digest Supp. 303

Y

Yeoman Credit, Ltd. v. Apps, [1962] 2 Q.B. 508; [1961] 2 All E.R. 281; [1961] 3 W.L.R. 94; 105 Sol. Jo. 567, C.A.; Digest Cont. Vol. A 649 .. .. 83, 86, 93, 361, 374, 403, 407, 414, 424

Yeoman Credit, Ltd. v. Latter, (1961) 2 All E.R. 294; [1961] 1 W.L.R. 828; 105 Sol. Jo. 300, C.A.; Digest Cont. Vol. A 628 346

Yeoman Credit, Ltd. v. Odgers (Vosper Motor House (Plymouth) Ltd. Third Party), [1962] 1 All E.R. 789; [1962] 1 W.L.R. 215, 106 Sol. Jo. 75, C.A.; Digest Cont. Vol. A 325 .. .. 283, 423, 427

Yeoman Credit, Ltd. v. Waragowski, [1961] 3 All E.R. 145; [1961] 1 W.L.R. 1124; 105 Sol. Jo. 588, C.A.; Digest Cont. Vol. A 650 .. .. .. 385, 393

Yorkshire Railway Wagon Co. v. Maclure (1882), 21 Ch. D. 309; 51 L.J. Ch. 857; 47 L.T. 290; 30 W.R. 761, C.A.; 10 Digest (Repl.) 756 292

Young v. Matthews (1866), L.R. 2 C.P. 127 166

Young (Thomas), Ltd. v. Hobson (1949), 65 T.L.R. 365 246

Young and Marten, Ltd. v. McManus, Childs, Ltd., [1969] 1 A.C. 454; [1968] 2 All E.R. 1169; [1968] 3 W.L.R. 630; 112 Sol. Jo. 744; 67 L.G.R. 1, H.L.; Digest Supp. 23, 141

Bibliography

ALLEN, *Law in the Making* (7th edn., 1966).

AMERICAN RESTATEMENT, Restatement of the Law of Torts (1965)

ATIYAH, *Sale of Goods* (3rd edn., 1966).

BENJAMIN, *The Law of Sale* (8th edn., by Finnemore & James, 1950).

BLACKBURN, *On Sale* (3rd edn., by Raeburn & Thomas, 1910).

BOWER, SPENCER, *Estoppel by Representation* (2nd edn. by Turner, 1966).

BUCKLEY, *On the Companies Acts* (13th edn. by Lindon, Williams & Parker, 1957).

CHALMERS, *Sale of Goods Act* 1893 (15th edn., by Mark, 1968).

CHESHIRE & FIFOOT, *Law of Contract* (7th edn., 1969).

CLERK & LINDSELL, *Law of Tort* (13th edn., by Armitage, 1969).

COOTE, *Exception Clauses* (1964).

CROSS, *On Evidence* (3rd edn., 1967).

CROWTHER, Report on Consumer Credit.

DIAMOND (ed.), *Instalment Credit* (1970).

DICEY & MORRIS, *Conflict of Laws* (8th edn., 1967).

DUNSTAN, *Law Relating to Hire Purchase* (4th edn., 1939).

EARENGAY, *Law Relating to Hire Purchase* (2nd edn., 1938).

FLEMING, *Law of Torts* (3rd edn., 1965).

FRIDMAN, *Law of Agency* (2nd edn., 1966).
         Sale of Goods (1966).

GOFF & JONES, *Law of Restitution* (1966).

GOODE, *Hire Purchase Law and Practice* (2nd edn., 1970).

GOODE & ZIEGEL, *Hire Purchase and Conditional Sale* (1965).

GUEST, *Law of Hire Purchase* (1966).

GUEST (ed.), Oxford Essays in Jurisprudence (1961).

HALSBURY, *Laws of England* (3rd edn., 1952–1964).

HOGAN, *Hire Purchase Act* 1965 (annotations in Current Law).

LAW COMMISSION, First Report on Exemption Clauses in Contracts (No. 24) (1969).

LAW REFORM COMMITTEE, Twelfth Report (Transfer of Title to Chattels) (Cmnd. 2958) (1966).

MALONEY, Report on Consumer Protection (Cmnd. 1781) (1961).

MAYNE & McGREGOR, *On Damages* (12th edn., by McGregor, 1961).

PATON, *Bailment in the Common Law* (1952).

PAYNE, Report on the Enforcement of Judgment Debts (Cmnd. 3909) (1969).

POWELL, *Law of Agency* (2nd edn., 1961).

SALMOND & WILLIAMS, *The Law of Contracts* (2nd edn., 1945).

SCHMITTHOFF, *Sale of Goods* (2nd edn., 1966).

              The Export Trade (5th edn., 1969).

SMITH & THOMAS, *Casebook on Contract* (4th edn., 1969).

STOLJAR, *Law of Agency* (1961).

          Mistake and Misrepresentation (1968).

STREET, *Law of Torts* (4th edn., 1968).

      Law of Damages (1962).

STROUD, *Judicial Dictionary* (3rd edn., by Burke & Allsop, 1952).

TREITEL, *Law of Contract* (3rd edn., 1970).

VAINES, CROSSLEY, *Personal Property* (4th edn., 1967).

WILD, *The Law of Hire Purchase* (2nd edn., 1965).

WILLIAMS, GLANVILLE, *Joint Torts and Contributory Negligence* (1951).

              The Law Reform (Frustrated Contracts) Act 1943 (1944).

WILLIAMS, *Law and Practice in Bankruptcy* (18th edn., by Hunter & Graham, 1968).

WINFIELD, *On Tort* (8th edn., ed. Jolowicz & Ellis Lewis, 1967).

WOLL, *Administrative Law* (1963).

The Nature of the Contract

CHAPTER 1

Introduction

1 THE SCOPE OF THE ENQUIRY

1 The categories of the law

This book is concerned with what the layman might term "sales of goods". Whilst the basic situation to be examined is the contract for the sale of goods, we shall not confine ourselves to contracts of sale *simpliciter*. For example, the contract of sale may provide for immediate delivery and subsequent payment of the price by instalments, in which case the transaction may be termed a "credit sale" or "conditional sale". Alternatively, the parties may not even use the legal form of a contract of sale to achieve their object of immediate delivery and subsequent payment of the price by instalments: their contract may take the form of a "hire-purchase" agreement (hereafter referred to as a h.p. agreement) or even a contract of simple hire (hereafter referred to as a rental agreement). Often, the different types of transaction just mentioned are dealt with in entirely separate works, because they are analytically distinguishable in legal terms. However, the layman is not concerned with legal analysis, but with the achievement of an economic object. It may therefore be useful to compare the different legal forms to see how effective they are in achieving this economic object.

The basic form, the contract for the sale of goods, is dealt with by the Sale of Goods Act 1893 (hereafter called the S.G.A.). This Act expressly leaves the general principles of the law of contract untouched save in so far as they are inconsistent with the terms of the Act (s. 61 (2)); and it purports to do no more than "codify the law relating to the sale of goods". Thus, it does not apply to contracts for the sale of other types of property, such as realty, negotiable instruments or choses in action; nor does it refer to all dispositions of goods. The Act expressly excludes from its ambit

> "any transaction in the form of a contract of sale, which is intended to operate by way of mortgage, pledge, charge or other security". (s. 61 (4)).

Whilst falling outside the S.G.A., these other types of disposition may be governed by other statutes, e.g., the Bills of Sale Acts or Pawnbrokers Acts.

However, in the context of the sale of goods, the draftsman of the S.G.A., Sir Mackenzie Chalmers, endeavoured to capture the spirit of

3

the common law rules. The underlying philosophy behind the nine-teenth century rules was that their function was to hold the ring be-tween two equal parties whilst they achieved a true bargain[1], the rules themselves being displaceable by contrary agreement. Whilst Chalmers for the most part succeeded in embodying this philosophy in his draft, the conception may itself be criticised. The assumption of equality of bargaining power must clearly be fictitious in some cases, and it would seem an almost impossible task to formulate a set of even *prima facie* rules which would do justice to all parties in all circumstances. For rather different reasons Parliament had already found it necessary to restrict the use of trade marks on goods offered for sale by means of the Merchandise Marks Act 1862.

In one sense, both these Acts were typical of the nineteenth century: the 1893 Act reflected the principle of freedom of contract; and the 1862 Act was designed to protect the proprietary interest in trade marks. However, in the twentieth century both pieces of legislation have to some extent been adapted to serve a new interest, that of the con-sumer. Yet the scope for judicial interpretation is necessarily limited; and, what is more, one increasingly important vehicle for consumer transactions, that where payment is made by instalments subsequent to delivery, falls partly outside the S.G.A. Thus, the explosive growth of h.p. and the inevitable abuses which followed it led to the pressure for the statutory protection of the consumer, which bore fruit in the Hire Purchase Act 1938. After 1945, the increasingly vocal movement for consumer protection led to the passing of such measures as the Con-sumer Protection Act 1961, and the appointment of the Molony Committee on Consumer Protection, whose Final Report sparked off a chain of legislative activity perhaps not yet exhausted. In particular, the law relating to h.p. transactions was consolidated in the Hire Purchase Act 1965 (hereafter called the H.P.A.); and the Merchandise Marks Acts were recast with the primary object of protecting the con-sumer in the Trade Descriptions Act 1968. These Acts are typical of the changed philosophy and technique underlying legislation in this field. Thus, the Trade Descriptions Act seeks to protect the consumer largely by the imposition of criminal sanctions, whilst the H.P.A. largely prevents the parties from contracting out of even its civil provisions.

2 The Interpretation of the Acts

The history of the S.G.A. is to be found in the preface to the com-mentary on the Act written by Chalmers, where the author says that the pre-Act cases are only law in so far as they illustrate the words of the

---

1. See *per* JESSEL M.R. in *Printing and Numerical Registering Co.* v. *Sampson* (1875), L.R. 19, Eq. 462, at p. 465.

statute. The problem of whether to interpret these decisions in the light of the Act, or *vice versa*, is at once a difficult and a vital one. Discussing another codifying Act, Lord Herschell took the view that previous decisions should only be considered where the Act was ambiguous, but that the Act should be interpreted in the light of subsequent decisions[2]; and speaking of the S.G.A. Lord Alverstone said[3]:

> "I think it is very important to bear in mind that the rights of people in regard to these matters depend now upon the statute. To a large extent the old law, I will not say has been swept away, but it has become unnecessary to refer to it."

In the nineteenth century, the typical judicial attitude to codifying Acts, such as the S.G.A., was that they should be interpreted according to the literal rule of statutory construction[4]; but it may be wondered whether a similar attitude will obtain in relation to the twentieth century legislation referred to above. Whilst the S.G.A. is avowedly neutral as between seller and buyer, the later legislation certainly is not; and, in the latter case it is at least arguable that the evident bias of the legislation should lead to the adoption of the mischief rule of interpretation[4]. The argument, however, is weaker in the case of the Trade Descriptions Act, because criminal sanctions are normally interpreted restrictively.

This work is chiefly concerned with the statutory rules of the S.G.A. and H.P.A., both of which are mainly concerned with the civil law. Surely, it would not be surprising if the differences in object were to lead to a different approach to interpretation? Yet the position is not quite so simple as this, because there has been a tendency on the part of the courts in this century to interpret the provisions of the S.G.A. in favour of the buyer, as shown by their restriction of the principle *caveat emptor*.

2 DEFINITION OF A CONTRACT OF SALE

The contract of sale is defined by section 1 of the S.G.A., and Chalmers suggests that this definition is merely declaratory of the common law. In fact, the S.G.A. expressly saves the rules of common law except in so far as they are inconsistent with the express provisions of the Act (s. 61 (2)). The contract of sale must, however, be distinguished from several other transactions which it resembles. Even since the repeal of the requirement (derived from the Statute of Frauds) that certain contracts for the sale of goods must usually be evidenced in

---

2. *Bank of England* v. *Vagliano Brothers*, [1891] A.C. 107, H.L., at 144–145.
3. *Wallis, Son and Wells* v. *Pratt and Haynes*, [1911] A.C. 394, H.L., at 398.
4. See generally, Allen, *Law in the Making* (7th Edn.), 482–503; Willis (1938) 16 Can.B.R. 1.

writing (S.G.A., s. 4)[5], the distinction may still be important, e.g. in relation to the implied terms as to quality and fitness.   Yet it must be borne in mind that the relevance of the distinction may be lessened by the tendency of the courts to model the common law rules relating to analogous transactions on those in the S.G.A.   In some cases, moreover, the courts have even treated a contract as being partly of sale and partly of something else[6].

A contract of sale is defined by section 1 (1) of the S.G.A. as follows:

> "A contract of sale of goods is a contract whereby the seller transfers or agrees to transfer the property in the goods to the buyer for a money consideration, called the price.   There may be a contract of sale between one part owner and another."

This definition requires that the following components should be present.

1. A contract.   The Act makes no attempt to interfere with the ordinary rules concerning the formation of contracts: it just requires that there should be a contract[7].

2. A contract of sale.   The object of the contract must be "to transfer the property in the goods" from the seller to the buyer, though the Act does not insist on an immediate transfer of property[8].   The Act provides that "property" means.

> "the general property in the goods, and not merely a special property" (s. 62 (1)).

However, the general property in the goods is not always the most important consideration. Thus, the Act distinguishes between property and title, and sometimes allows a person to pass a good title even though he does not possess the property in the goods[9].   Moreover, the Act contemplates that the parties may contract out of the implied obligation on the part of the seller that he will transfer a good title[10]. It will be argued later that the Act does not insist that the seller must always transfer the general property in the goods to the buyer; but what it does insist is that he either does agree to transfer the general property to the buyer, or that he agrees to do so in so far as he has the property in the goods[11].   Even this obligation is qualified by section 1 (2), which provides that

> "A contract of sale may be absolute or conditional."

---

5. See below, p. 32.
6. E.g. *Watson* v. *Buckley*, [1940] 1 All E.R. 174, at 179–180.
7. See below, Chapter 3,
8. See the definition of "contract of sale" in s. 62 (1); and also below, pp. 8–9.
9. See below, Chapter 14.
10. See below, Chapter 5.
11. See below, p. 56.

Condition in this subsection does not refer to conditions in the sense of essential stipulations, but to conditions precedent or subsequent to the sale itself. In *Marten* v. *Whale*[12].

> M. agreed to buy a plot of land from T. subject to M.'s solicitor's approval of title; and in consideration of this agreement T. agreed to buy M.'s car. T. took possession of the car and sold it to a b[ona] f[ide] p[urchaser]. Subsequently, M.'s solicitor disapproved T.'s title to the land.

The Court of Appeal held that, as the two sales were interdependent, there was a conditional contract for the sale of the car within s. 1 (2); and that, even though the condition never materialised, T. was able to pass a good title under the S.G.A. s. 25 (2)[13]. This insistence of the Act on at least an agreement to transfer the general property in the goods, combined with its evident indifference as to whether there is any transfer of possession[14], serves to distinguish a contract for the sale of goods from the following transactions:

(i) A bailment. The essential element of a bailment is a transfer of possession. A bailment merely gives the bailee a right to retain possession under the terms of the bailment; and the law assumes that the bailor will eventually get back the actual object bailed. The rights and duties of the parties are governed by the ordinary law of bailment[15].

(ii) A pledge. A pledge is a particular type of bailment, under which the pledgee will obtain a special property in the goods pledged; he will receive possession, plus the right to retain possession until the pledge is redeemed, with a right of sale in default[16]. Thus, the objects of sale and pledge are quite different, and the S.G.A. is expressed not to be applicable to pledges (s. 61 (4)).

(iii) A mortgage. A mortgage is a transfer of the property in goods by way of security for the discharge of an obligation; and, if it is evidenced in writing it will usually fall within the ambit of the Bills of Sale Act 1882. Theoretically, a mortgage may be distinguished from a sale by the equity of redemption, though in practice it may be difficult to differentiate between the two transactions[17]. The S.G.A. does not apply to bills of sale granted by way of mortgage (s. 61 (4)), but it does apply to absolute bills of sale (s. 61 (3))[18].

(iv) A h.p. agreement. As we shall see in the next section, the essence

12. [1917] 2 K.B. 480, C.A. See further below, p. 114.
13. See below, p. 220.
14. Thus, s. 62 (1) provides that "sale" "includes a bargain and sale as well as a sale and delivery". And see *Watts* v. *Seymour*, [1967] 2 Q.B.647; [1967] 1 All E.R. 1044, D.C.
15. See Crossley Vaines, *Personal Property* (4th Edn.) Chapter 6.
16. See s. 1 (5), F.A. 1889 (below, p. 211); and Crossley Vaines, *op. cit.*, Chapter 22.
17. See below, pp. 291–300.
18. Crossley Vaines, *op. cit.*, Chapters 20, 21.

of a h.p. agreement is that it is a contract of hire with an option to purchase; and it can be distinguished from a sale in that the hirer has not agreed to buy.

3. *A contract for the sale of goods.* The meaning of the term "goods" will be dealt with later[19]. There must be a contract *for* the sale of goods: it is not sufficient that there is a contract for services between the parties under which the general property in goods is transferred from one to the other[20].

4. *A transfer of property from seller to buyer.* The essence of a sale is the transfer of the property in goods from one person to another. Indeed, the common law rule was that a man could not purchase his own goods; but this would seem to be amended to the extent that the Act allows one part-owner to sell to another. It has been argued that the old common law rule was resuscitated by a case on the Liquor Licencing Acts in 1902[1]. However, this was a criminal case, the S.G.A. was not mentioned, and, in view of the special interpretation put on statutes imposing strict criminal liability, it seems doubtful whether the case has qualified the clear words of the S.G.A. Moreover, it is clear that the S.G.A. will cover the situation where an owner of goods buys them back from one who has a legal right to dispose of them, such as a sheriff[2]. The requirement seems to be that the buyer must stand to gain some part of the general property in the goods from the seller; and for this reason it is essential to distinguish carefully a contract of sale from a contract of agency, one who purchases from one who acts as agent in effecting a purchase. Whilst theoretically quite clear, the distinction may be difficult to apply in practice, particularly where the alleged agent is a commission agent or a *del credere* agent (one who guarantees performance by his principal).

5. *A price.* Section 1 (1) requires that the transfer of property be for "a money consideration, called the price". This topic is considered below[3].

Finally, it should be noticed that the S.G.A. clearly recognises that the two elements of contract and conveyance are both present in the one transaction of a contract of sale. Indeed, the Act uses different terminology according to whether or not the property has passed under the contract. Section 1 says:

"(3) Where under a contract of sale the property in the goods is transferred from the seller to the buyer the contract is called a sale;

---

19. See below, p. 18.
20. E.g. *Appleby* v. *Sleep*, [1968] 2 All E.R. 265, D.C.
1. Atiyah, *Sale of Goods* (3rd Edn.) 9, citing *Davies* v. *Burnett*, [1902] 1 K.B. 666, D.C. But compare *Doak* v. *Bedford*, [1964] 2 Q.B. 587; [1964] 1 All E.R. 311, D.C.; *French* v. *Hoggett*, [1967] 3 All E.R. 1042, D.C.
2. See below, p. 239.
3. P. 21.

but where the transfer of the property in the goods is to take place at a future time or subject to some condition thereafter to be fulfilled the contract is called an agreement to sell.

(4) An agreement to sell becomes a sale when the time elapses or the conditions are fulfilled subject to which the property in the goods is to be transferred."

Thus, a sharp distinction is drawn between a sale and an agreement to sell: the one is an executed contract, the other executory. The distinction is important, because the executory contract creates only personal rights between the parties whereas an executed contract gives the buyer an interest in the goods themselves.

3 DEFINITION OF A CONTRACT OF HIRE PURCHASE

H.p. is in economic fact, but not in legal theory, a fiction: historically, its evolution consists of increasingly sophisticated attempts by legal draftsmen to devise on behalf of one who "sells on credit" a contract which would preserve for the latter such rights in the goods "sold" as would provide adequate security for the subsequent payment of the "price".

1 Development of the common law form

There are three major dangers which one who "sells on credit" must face. First, he must secure his rights to the goods against the "buyer" and the latter's creditors. Second, he must try to prevent the "buyer" passing any proprietary rights in the goods to a *bona fide* purchaser (hereafter referred to as a b.f.p.) such as will override his interest in them. Third, when the "seller" has secured his legal interest in the goods, he must take steps to ensure that these rights continue to be of adequate value.

Throughout the nineteenth century, the legal form of the contract was evolving to meet these requirements; and it was not until 1895 that the major characteristics of the form were settled. By reason of its complicated nature, the transaction was almost always in writing.

A. Preserving the security against the "buyer" and his creditors. Any appropriate form of words will create a debt in the "buyer", so that in the event of default the "seller" may levy execution on any of the "buyer's" goods[4]. However, as the "seller" also wished to obtain a preferential claim to the goods in the event of the "buyer's" insolvency, one of the following forms was normally used:

(a) A conditional sale; that is, an agreement to sell with a reservation of property until the price was paid.

(b) A h.p. agreement; that is, a letting of the goods with an option to purchase.

---

4. But see the S.G.A., s. 26, considered below, p. 239.

Either form would usually keep the goods out of any execution levied on goods in the possession of the buyer or hirer[4]; but it might still be vulnerable because of the legislation discussed below[5].

(i) The Bills of Sale Act 1882[6]. This Act rendered void almost every chattel mortgage evidenced in writing which was not in the statutory form; and, as the statutory terms did not provide adequate security, creditors would normally seek to avoid the Act altogether. The 1882 Act was expressed to apply to any transaction evidenced by a bill of sale granted by way of security for a loan (s. 3); and the term "bill of sale" is defined by s. 4 of the Bills of Sale Act 1878 to include

> "licences to take possession of personal chattels as security for any debt".

Both a conditional sale and a h.p. agreement will normally contain a licence to seize, and for some time it was thought that they might therefore fall within the 1882 Act. However, in *McEntire* v. *Crossley Brothers*[7] the House of Lords held that such a conditional sale did not fall within the 1882 Act because the grantor of the licence was not, and never had been, the owner of the goods. Lord Herschell explained[8]

> "If the property never passed to the bankrupt [conditional buyer], he can never have . . . given the right to seize . . . within the meaning of the Bills of Sale Act. The . . . Act relates to . . . rights to seize given or conferred by the person who owns the property."

Thus, the House of Lords confirmed that an ordinary b[ona] f[ide] two-party conditional sale or h.p. agreement would avoid the Bills of Sale Acts, simply because the agreement did not pass any sufficient proprietary interest during the period when the licence to seize was operative. The position would, of course, be otherwise if the property passed before the licence to seize expired, or if the agreement were not made in good faith.

(ii) The Bankruptcy Act 1914. Normally a trustee in bankruptcy can acquire no greater rights to the bankrupt's goods than the latter himself had, so that the reservation of ownership is a sufficient protection against the trustee. However, one exception to this rule is set out in s. 38 (2) (c), which provides that the trustee may claim, inter alia,

> "all goods being, at the commencement of the bankruptcy, in the possession, order or disposition of the bankrupt, in his trade or business, by the consent and permission[9] of the true owner, under such circumstances that he is the reputed owner thereof; provided

---

5. Useful summaries of the legislation to be discussed will be found in Crossley Vaines, *Personal Property* (4th Edn.); and Goode, *H.P. Law & Practice* (2nd Edn.) 63–81. See also below, pp. 32–33.
6. The full title is the Bills of Sale Act (1878) Amendment Act 1882.
7. [1895] A.C. 457, H.L.   8. At p. 462.   9. See below, note 12.

that things in action other than debts due or growing due to the bankrupt in the course of his trade or business shall not be deemed goods within the meaning of this section".

This provision is probably inapplicable on the insolvency of a limited company[10]; and, anyway, the exception only applies to traders, and is frequently rebutted by proof of notoriety of a custom that goods of that particular description are in that trade normally hired on h.p. terms rather than purchased. Furthermore, the H.P.A. provides that the doctrine of reputed ownership shall not apply whilst goods are subject to a notice of default, or a postponed order for delivery (s. 53 H.P.A). Despite the infrequency with which the doctrine is likely to affect the owner of goods let on h.p., it is normal for the agreement to contain a clause providing for the automatic termination of the agreement on the bankruptcy of the hirer.

(iii) The Law of Distress Amendment Act 1908. This Act was designed to deal with the situation where goods taken by a landlord in distress did not belong to the tenant; and it provided that, in general, the owner of the goods might safeguard his rights by serving a statutory declaration on the distrainor. However, section 4 (1) of this Act provides that this rule

"shall not apply . . . to goods comprised in any bill of sale, hire purchase agreement, or settlement made by such tenant, nor to goods in the possession, order, or disposition of such tenant by the consent and permission of the true owner under such circumstances that the tenant is the reputed owner thereof . . ."

To escape section 4 and bring themselves within the protection of the 1908 Act, owners of goods let on h.p. eventually produced the clause tested in *Smart Brothers Ltd.* v. *Holt*[11], which provided that where the hirer was in breach of the agreement the owners might alternatively

(a) without prejudice to their already-accrued rights "forthwith without notice terminate the hiring and repossess themselves of and remove the goods"; or

(b) "by written notice . . . forthwith and for all purposes absolutely determine and end this agreement and the hiring thereby constituted and thereupon the hirer shall no longer be in the possession of the goods with the owner's consent, nor shall either party thereafter have any rights hereunder, but such determination shall not discharge any pre-existing liability of the hirer to the owners".

Acting under clause (b) the owners in that case purported to terminate the agreement; and, when the hirer's landlord subsequently levied distress on the goods, successfully sued for illegal distress on the

---

10. See *Buckley on Companies Acts* (13th Edn.) 633–634.
11. [1929] 2 K.B. 303, D.C.

grounds that at the time the distress was levied the goods were no longer "comprised in" the h.p. agreement within the meaning of section 4. Most modern h.p. agreements contain a *Smart Brothers* v. *Holt* clause. Such a clause will normally provide adequate protection for the owner[12]; but the complicated manner in which this protection is achieved is a reproach to the law.

B. *Defeating the bona fide transferee for value.* The persons supplying goods on condition that the "price" was subsequently paid by instalments also wished to protect their interest in the goods from the claims of the following persons to whom the "buyer" purported to transfer proprietary or possessory rights in the goods:

(i) The b.f. purchaser or pledgee. In the mid-nineteenth century, the conditional sale with a reservation of property was sufficient to defeat the claims of such persons because of the rule *nemo dat quod non habet*[13]. However, an important exception to that rule was enacted in section 9 of the Factors Act 1889, which provided that, generally speaking, one who had "agreed to buy" goods should be able to pass a good title to a b.f. purchaser or pledgee[14]. In *Lee* v. *Butler*[15], the Court held that a conditional buyer had "agreed to buy" within the meaning of section 9. Whilst in the light of more recent cases it would appear that this decision does not seriously jeopardise the interest of the owner of the goods[16], the form of the contract was immediately altered to a hiring with an option to purchase. This new form was litigated in *Helby* v. *Matthews*[17], where the House of Lords unanimously decided that section 9 could have no application to such a contract.

(ii) The b.f. assignee. If a hirer under a h.p. agreement cannot pass a better title than his own, can he pass such interest as he has? This immediately raises the question of the nature of the hirer's interest, which has two aspects:

(a) a contract of hiring; and
(b) an option to purchase.

The ordinary rule is that, whilst the hirer cannot, generally speaking, assign the burden of the contract[18], he can assign these two rights, either separately or together, unless the parties clearly intend that the rights are not to be assignable. Despite the fact that the owner will normally make careful enquiries into the character of the would-be

---

12. But see *Times Furnishing Co.* v. *Hutchings*, [1938] 1 K.B. 775; [1938] 1 All E.R. 422 criticised by Wild, *Hire Purchase* (2nd Edn.) 153–155. For another way in which s. 4 may apparently be avoided, see *Abingdon R.D.C.* v. *O'Gorman*, [1968] 2 Q.B. 811; [1968] 3 All E.R. 79.
13. See below, p. 183.   14. See below, p. 220
15. [1893] 2 Q.B. 318, C.A.   16. See below, p. 228.
17. [1895] A.C. 471, H.L.   18. See below, p. 306.

hirer before entering the agreement[19], the courts have taken the attitude that this does not evince an intention to restrict the *p[rima] f[acie]* right of assignment[20]. For this reason, most modern h.p. agreements expressly forbid assignment by the hirer of his rights under the agreement. In these cases, a purported assignment by the hirer logically cannot confer any rights on the assignee as against the owner[1], though the assignee will have his remedy as against the hirer[2]. In practice, the owner will frequently relinquish his interest in the goods to the assignee on payment of the outstanding balance of the h.p. price; but he is not generally bound to do so[3], and is in law entitled to the goods or their full value[4].

(iii) A lien-holder. Essentially, a lien is a right to retain possession of goods as security for the performance of some obligation[5]; and in respect of goods let on h.p. the most commonly claimed lien is that of a repairer. Whilst no man can create a lien on goods of another without the other's consent, it has been held that a letting on h.p. normally gives the hirer an implied authority to create a lien for repairs[6], but only whilst the agreement remains in force[7]. To counteract this, the agreement will normally expressly prohibit the hirer from creating any lien over the goods, though the hirer may still be left with an ostensible authority to do so provided that the repairer knows that the goods are on h.p.[8].

C. Maintenance of the security. Where the owner acquires a right to the immediate possession of the goods hired, he may sue in conversion or detinue for their recovery. Moreover, to remove any doubt as to when the owner acquires a right to immediate possession, the agreement will usually spell out in detail the duties of the hirer, and provide that breach of any of them shall entitle the owner to determine the agreement. Having taken elaborate steps to preserve his interest in the goods, the owner will normally seek to protect the value of this interest

---

19. See below, p. 34.
20. E.g. *Whiteley, Ltd.* v. *Hilt*, [1918] 2 K.B. 808, C.A.
  1. *United Dominions Trust (Commercial), Ltd.* v. *Parkway Motors, Ltd.*, [1955] 2 All E.R. 557; doubted by two members of the C.A. in *Wickham Holdings, Ltd.* v. *Brooke House Motors, Ltd.*, [1967] 1 All E.R. 117, at pp. 120, 121.
  2. E.g. *Butterworth* v. *Kingsway Motors, Ltd.*, [1954] 2 All E.R. 694; see below, p. 59.
  3. But see *Wickham Holdings, Ltd.* v. *Brooke House Motors, Ltd.* (above).
  4. See *United Dominions Trust (Commercial), Ltd.* v. *Parkway Motors, Ltd.* (above).
  5. E.g., see the unpaid seller's lien for the price, below, p. 318.
  6. *Green* v. *All Motors, Ltd.*, [1917] 1 K.B. 625.
  7. *Bowmaker, Ltd.* v. *Wycombe Motors, Ltd.*, [1946] K.B. 505; [1946] 2 All E.R. 113, D.C.
  8. *Albermarle Supply Co., Ltd.* v. *Hind*, [1928] 1 K.B. 307, C.A. What if the repairer does not know for certain that the goods are on h.p., but merely that they are likely to be so?

by putting the risk on the hirer[9], and requiring the latter to take out a comprehensive insurance of the goods[10]. In addition, the agreement will usually be designed to ensure that the hirer effectively promises to make good any loss sustained by the owner, by requiring the hirer on termination of the agreement to make certain payments under a "minimum payments clause". This clause will usually stipulate for the following elements of "compensation": (a) the expenses of repossession; (b) sums paid by the owner on the hirer's behalf, e.g. insurance premiums; (c) arrears of rentals to the date of termination; (d) damages for breaches of contract; and (e) "compensation" for depreciation or loss of profit.

2 The statutory definition of h.p.

Upon this common law form of h.p., a number of statutory definitions have been imposed. The leading definition is that to be found in s. 1 of the H.P.A. 1965, which provides that a h.p. agreement means[11]

> "an agreement for the bailment of goods under which the bailee may buy the goods, or under which the property in the goods will or may pass to the bailee".

Thus far, the definition merely repeats that in the H.P.A. 1938, under which it was settled that the time to determine whether a transaction fell within the definition was the time when the agreement was made[12]. The definition in the 1938 Act gave rise to the following difficulties:

1. The meaning of the phrase "under which the property in the goods will or may pass to the bailee". It was at least arguable that the phrase was apt to cover conditional sales of the type litigated in *Lee* v. *Butler*: if this were so, such transactions would appear to be subject to two contradictory sets of legislation, the S.G.A. and the H.P.A.[13]. However, the Legislature intervened in this dispute by the attachment of entirely new incidents to the conditional sale, and carefully distinguished this form from a "credit sale". This latter expression is also given a special meaning by the H.P.A., s. 1. Section 1 provides that[11]

> " 'credit-sale agreement' means an agreement for the sale of goods under which the purchase price is payable by five or more instalments, not being a conditional sale agreement;

---

9. For a discussion of risk, see below, p. 241.
10. Compare c.i.f. contracts of sale, below, p. 247.
11. The agreement may be constituted by two or more documents—ss. 1 (2), 58 (6).
12. *R.* v. *Proffitt, Ltd.,* [1954] 2 Q.B. 35, [1954] 2 All E.R. 798.
13. [1893] 2 Q.B. 318, C.A.; see above, p. 12. This suggestion was strongly denied by Goode, *H.P. Law & Practice* (2nd Edn.) 55–57.

'conditional sale agreement' means an agreement for the sale of goods under which the purchase price or part of it is payable by instalments, and the property in the goods is to remain in the seller (notwithstanding that the buyer is to be in possession of the goods) until such conditions as to the payment of instalments or otherwise as may be specified in the agreement are fulfilled".

Having distinguished between conditional and credit sales largely on the basis of whether the property passes before any of the instalments are paid, the H.P.A. then provides that such conditional sale agreements within the ambit of the Act shall be treated for most (but not all) purposes like h.p. agreements also within the ambit of the Act. The result is that generally speaking the crucial distinction is no longer whether the customer has agreed to buy, but whether the property passes when the contract is made. Unfortunately, the position is not quite so simple as this. First, statutory conditional sales are not assimilated to statutory h.p. agreements for all purposes, so that a new hybrid has been created[14]. Second, the H.P.A. does not cover all transactions. Accordingly, the distinctions in existence before the H.P.A. 1938 are still important: h.p. agreements must be carefully distinguished from sales (whether they be sales *simpliciter*, or on credit, or under which there is a reservation of property). The result is that one fiction has spawned at least six categories without (it is submitted) any apparent advantage. Here indeed is a trap for the unwary draftsman: if the property does not pass immediately under what he thought was a credit sale, it will probably be a conditional sale and invalid for non-compliance with the H.P.A.[15].

2. *Does the statutory definition of h.p. cover perpetual hiring agreements?* These agreements for the perpetual hiring of goods are devices whereby the owner seeks to obtain most of the advantages of a h.p. agreement without attracting the restrictions of the H.P.A.[16]. If the agreement is truly a simple hiring agreement, then it clearly does escape the statutory restrictions[16]; but it is probably a matter of substance, not words, so that, if the agreement provides that all the incidents of property will pass to the bailee, a retention of the outward shell of property by the bailor probably will not prevent the application of the H.P.A.[17].

3. *Does the statutory definition of h.p. cover any bailment out of which the property is capable of passing to the bailee?* If the words were applied

---

14. See Ziegel (1964), 108 Sol. Jo. 788, at 790.
15. What is the effect of the passing of property part-way through the payment of the instalments?
16. *Galbraith* v. *Mitchenall Estates, Ltd.,* [1965] 2 Q.B. 473; [1964] 2 All E.R. 653; cf. *Baker* v. *Monk* (1864), 4 De G.J. & Sm. 388.
17. See *Domestic Electric Rentals, Ltd.* v. *Dawson,* [1943] L.J.N.C.C.R. 31.

literally, then it would appear that the definition would cover both the following types of transaction:

(i) A pledge or deposit, with a power to sell in default; and

(ii) A delivery of goods on sale or return or approval.

Perhaps such an undesirable result could be avoided by interpreting the word "bailment" in the definition to mean "hiring"[18].

3 Difficulties arising from the legal form

It is now possible to consider a number of difficulties arising from the dual nature of h.p. In practice the two elements of bailment and sale may be embodied in either of the following forms:

(i) The hirer agrees to take the goods on hire, with an option to purchase once he has paid a stipulated amount of hire rent, that option being exercisable on payment of a further sum (usually nominal), which in practice is added to the last instalment.

(ii) The price of the option is paid at the outset, or included in the hire-rent, so that the property in the goods necessarily passes automatically unless the hirer is given a power to terminate.

Because of the dual nature of the h.p. agreement, the courts have frequently been faced with the problem of whether to apply to it the rules of sale or bailment. It purports to be a species of bailment; and the courts have so treated it when deciding such issues as who may maintain an action in conversion[19], or the measure of damages to which an owner is entitled in respect of breach by the hirer[20]. Yet, the economic object of the transaction is obviously to effect a sale; and the courts have looked exclusively at this element when determining such issues as the damages to which the hirer is entitled in respect of breach by the owner[1], or when the hirer may plead a total failure of consideration[2]. Similar inconsistencies of approach may be found in the decisions in relation to h.p. agreements in respect of such matters as risk[3] and illegality[4]. As it is apparently impossible to decide whether h.p. has more in common with sale or bailment[5], it has sometimes simply been labelled as a form of contract *sui generis*[6]. The whole problem is neatly illustrated by the difficulty of deciding the extent of the hirer's

---

18. See Goode, *H.P. Law & Practice* (2nd Edn.) 59–61.
19. E.g. *North Central Wagon and Finance Co., Ltd.* v. *Graham*, [1950] 2 K.B. 7; [1950] 1 All E.R. 780, C.A. But not the rules of *ius tertii*: see below, p. 377.
20. See below, p. 384.
1. See below, p. 423.   2. See below, p. 404.
3. See below, p. 241.   4. See below, p. 37.
5. See the *obiter* of the C.A. in *Felston Tile Co., Ltd.* v. *Winget, Ltd.*, [1936] 3 All E.R. 473, C.A.; criticised *obiter* in *William Cory & Son* v. *I.R. Comrs.*, [1964] 3 All E.R. 66, at pp. 71, 75.
6. E.g. *per* GODDARD J. in *Karflex, Ltd.* v. *Poole*, [1933] 2 K.B. 251, at pp. 264, 265.

proprietary interest in the goods. During the continuance of the hiring, the value of that interest may be measured by the proportion of the h.p. price which has been paid: every instalment paid *pro tanto* reduces the value of the owner's interest in the goods and increases that of the hirer. Yet the hirer's proprietary interest is of a peculiarly uncertain nature, inasmuch as the owner, by lawfully terminating the agreement in accordance with its terms, will "automatically" bring the hirer's interest to an end[7].

---

7. See below, p. 33.

CHAPTER 2

Subject-Matter of the Contract

1 THE MEANING OF "GOODS"

As a species of bailment, the contract of h.p. is only applicable to goods. Moreover, the term "goods" is in fact used in the definition section of the H.P.A. (s. 1), and subsequently that Act provides that the term shall have the same meaning as that assigned to it in the S.G.A. (s. 58 (1) H.P.A.). Similarly, the term "goods" is used in the definition section of the S.G.A. (s. 1), and is subsequently defined in s. 62 (1) of that Act. Section 62 (1) provides that, "unless the context or subject matter otherwise requires", "goods"

> "include all chattels personal other than things in action and money . . . The term includes emblements, industrial growing crops, and things attached to or forming part of the land which are agreed to be severed before sale or under the contract of sale".

This definition may be analysed as follows:

1. Chattels personal other than things in action and money. The term "chattels personal" covers all tangible moveable personal property, and even gas and water, and probably electricity as well. However, the following two types of personal chattels are excluded:

(a) Things in action[1]. Thus, an assignment of a chose in action, e.g., a negotiable instrument or debt, can never amount to a sale of goods.

(b) Money. This excludes money *qua* money[2], but not money bought as a curio[3], or trading stamps[4].

2. Emblements and industrial growing crops. These are incorporated in the old term *fructus industriales*, and include growing crops of the soil which are produced by the labours of the cultivator, e.g. wheat, barley, potatoes.

3. Things attached to or forming part of the land. This phrase covers fixtures and what was known as *fructus naturales*, the latter expression comprehending natural products of the soil, such as grass

---

1. See the definition by CHANNELL J. in *Torkington* v. *Magee*, [1902] 2 K.B. 427, at pp. 429–430.
2. Including foreign currency? What of gold sovereigns bought as an investment?
3. *Moss* v. *Hancock*, [1899] 2 Q.B. 111, D.C.
4. See the Trading Stamps Act 1964; *Building etc., Ltd.* v. *Post Office*, [1966] 1 Q.B. 247; [1965] 1 All E.R. 163.

and timber. At common law, the sale of fixtures and of *fructus naturales* (but not *fructus industriales*) was normally regarded as a sale of an interest in land, unless the thing was to be detached from the soil before the property was to pass. However, since products of the soil must always be sold with a view to their ultimate severance, it has been suggested that the S.G.A. has done away with the distinction between *fructus naturales* and *industriales*, and abolished the relevance of the time when property is to pass. Thus, there is always a sale of goods so long as severance of the subject-matter is envisaged under the contract; and therefore such contracts are always outside s. 40 (1) of the Law of Property Act 1925[5]. Another view is that the word "goods" may have a different meaning under the S.G.A. from that under the L.P.A., so that one transaction may be both a sale of goods within the S.G.A. and a sale of an interest in land within the L.P.A.[6]. Whatever the position of *fructus naturales*, it is still necessary to distinguish "goods" within the S.G.A. from the actual land itself; and this may involve difficult questions of construction[7].

2 DIFFERENT TYPES OF GOODS

Section 5 of the S.G.A. appears to envisage the following three different types of goods:

1. **"Existing goods".** This term is explained by s. 5 (1) as follows:

> "The goods which form the subject matter of a contract of sale may be . . . existing goods, owned or possessed by the seller . . ."

Thus, the seller does not have to be the owner of the goods so long as they are in his possession[8]; and *vice versa*.

2. **"Future goods".** This term is defined by ss. 5 (1) and 62 (1) in exactly the same terms, namely

> "goods to be manufactured or acquired by the seller after the making of the contract of sale".

It is clear from this definition that goods may be "future goods" notwithstanding that they are in existence somewhere at the time when the contract is made, and even though the parties have their eyes on certain identified goods. It is, of course, impossible in this situation to effect an actual sale: whereas the property may pass immediately in the case of "existing goods", the Act specifically recognises that a contract for the

---

5. *Benjamin on Sale* (8th Edn.) 189; Fridman, *Sale of Goods* 12.
6. See Atiyah, *Sale of Goods* (3rd Edn.) 20; Cheshire & Fifoot, *Law of Contract* (7th Edn.) 177; Hudson, [1958] Conv. 137.
7. E.g. *Morgan* v. *Russell & Sons*, [1909] 1 K.B. 357, D.C.
8. The question of whether there can be a sale of goods in which the seller does not promise to transfer the title is considered below, p. 55.

sale of "future goods" must initially be only an agreement to sell (s. 5 (3)). The property in the goods cannot pass unless and until the seller does some act irrevocably appropriating them to the contract. The difficult question whether, prior to this stage, the seller has any equitable interest in the goods will be examined later[9].

3. "A Chance". The sale of "a chance" is envisaged by section 5 (2), which provides

> "There may be a contract for the sale of goods, the acquisition of which by the seller depends upon a contingency which may or may not happen."

The distinction between the sale of "a chance" and of "future goods" is not at first sight very clear, for both may depend on a chance. However, it is submitted that the distinction probably lies in whether or not the seller promises that he will manufacture or obtain the goods: if he does so promise, then there is a sale of future goods; but, if he does not, there is only a sale of a chance[10]. At one time, it was thought that there could never be a sale of future goods or of a chance, because of the element of wagering involved; but it is now clear that such circumstances do not even raise a presumption that the transaction amounts to a wager within the Gaming Act 1845[11].

Whilst s. 5 is obviously intended to deal with the different types of goods, there is a further classification which cuts right across the distinctions drawn in that section and is in practice far more important. This is the dichotomy between "specific" and "unascertained" goods.

a. "Specific goods". These are defined by s. 62 (1), which lays down that, subject to a contrary intention,

> " 'Specific goods' means goods identified and agreed upon at the time a contract of sale is made".

b. "Unascertained goods". These are nowhere defined by the Act; but the Act does use the expression by way of contrast to "specific" goods, so that "unascertained" goods must, *prima facie*, be goods which are not identified and agreed upon at the time when the contract is made, but will become ascertained at some later stage. "Unascertained" goods may be of any of the following three types:

(a) To be manufactured or grown by the seller;
(b) Generic goods, i.e. of a designated type;
(c) An unascertained part of a specific whole.

---

9. P. 173.
10. Compare Atiyah, *Sale of Goods* (3rd Edn.) 21.
11. See *Ellesmere* v. *Wallace*, [1929] 2 Ch. 1, C.A. See further *Benjamin on Sale* (8th Edn.) 533–541.

Thus, the distinction between "specific" and "unascertained" goods will frequently only be one of degree: contracts for the sale of *any* hundred tons of wheat, for the sale of 99 tons out of a particular stock of 100 tons, or for the sale of *that* 100 tons may look similar, but the first two are for the sale of "unascertained" goods and the last for the sale of "specific" goods. The distinction is important in the contexts of the passing of property and impossibility of performance, though for the purposes of specific performance the essential distinction is between specific and ascertained goods on the one hand and unascertained goods on the other[12].

3 THE PRICE

In order that the S.G.A. can apply to a transaction, the Act requires that the property be transferred for "a money consideration, called the price" (s. 1 (1)); and s. 8 provides for the manner in which that price is to be determined, laying down the following rules:

"(1) The price in a contract of sale may be fixed by the contract, or may be left to be fixed in a manner thereby agreed, or may be determined by the course of dealings between the parties.

(2) Where the price is not determined in accordance with the foregoing provisions the buyer must pay a reasonable price. What is a reasonable price is a question of fact dependent on the circumstances of each particular case."

Thus, s. 8 assumes that a contract has been made; but it must be borne in mind that the determination of the price is often an important factor in deciding *whether* a contract has been concluded[13]. Agreements to sell at a valuation are dealt with by s. 9 in the following terms:

"(1) Where there is an agreement to sell goods on the terms that the price is to be fixed by the valuation of a third party, and such third party cannot and does not make such valuation, the agreement is avoided; provided that if the goods or any part thereof have been delivered to and appropriated by the buyer he must pay a reasonable price therefor.

(2) Where such third party is prevented from making the valuation by the fault of the seller or buyer, the party not in fault may maintain an action for damages against the party in fault."

"Fault" is rather unhelpfully defined by the Act as "wrongful act or default" (s. 62 (1)), but presumably comprehends breach of contract or

---

12. See below, pp. 157, 249, 428.
13. Compare *May and Butcher* v. *R.*, [1934] 2 K.B. 17n, H.L.; *Hillas & Co., Ltd.* v. *Arcos, Ltd.*, [1932] All E.R. Rep. 494, H.L.; *Foley* v. *Classique Coaches, Ltd.*, [1934] 2 K.B. 1, C.A.

tort. Section 9 (1) assumes that the contract is void in the circumstances there set out, though it is conceivable that the seller or buyer may *promise* that the third party will make the valuation[14]. Do the same rules apply to h.p. agreements[15]?

The H.P.A., which applies to many credit sales, conditional sales and h.p. agreements, is much more explicit on the question of price: it has to be, because the operation of the Act depends on the price falling within certain ranges[16]. Section 58 (1) of the H.P.A. provides that, unless the context otherwise requires,

> "hire-purchase price . . . means the total sum payable by the hirer under a hire-purchase agreement in order to complete the purchase of goods to which the agreement relates . . ."

> "total purchase price . . . means the total sum payable by the buyer under a credit-sale agreement or a conditional sale agreement . . ."

Both definitions are expressed to be

> "exclusive of any sum payable as a penalty or as compensation or damages for breach of the agreement";

and to be subject to s. 58 (2), which expands the concept of price to include

> "any sum payable . . . under a[n] . . . agreement . . . by way of a deposit or other initial payment, or credited or to be credited to him under the agreement on account of any such deposit or payment, whether that sum is to be or has been paid to the owner or seller or to any other person or is to be or has been discharged by a payment of money or by the transfer or delivery of goods or by any other means . . ."

Section 58 (2) is obviously intended to cover not just cash deposits, but also part-exchanges[17], and to apply whether the transaction involves two or three parties. Whether it also includes sums payable by way of installation, maintenance or service charges depends on whether the parties intend those sums to be part of the price[18].

It is now possible to compare sales and h.p. agreements with the following transactions:

1. Gifts. A gift involves a transfer of goods without any consideration. Unlike sales, and h.p. agreements, a gift of goods is incomplete

---

14. Compare the discussion on s. 6 of the S.G.A., below, **p.** 250.
15. What, if any, is the relevance here of *Scammell* v. *Ouston,* [1941] A.C. 251, H.L.?
16. See below, p. 30.
17. See further below, p. 271.
18. See *Mutual Finance, Ltd.* v. *Davidson,* [1963] 1 All E.R. 133, C.A. Compare s. 55 (1) H.P.A.

and ineffectual until delivery, unless effected by deed or declaration of trust[19].

2. Sale of skill and labour. For many purposes, it makes no difference whether a transaction is a sale or letting of goods, or of skill and labour. Thus, in many cases the courts have applied to sales of skill and labour similar rules to those applicable to sales and lettings on h.p. of goods, e.g. in relation to delivery[20] and the implied term as to fitness[1]. Yet, even since the abolition of the statutory requirement of writing for certain sales of goods[2], the distinction may still be important, in particular, because the Law Reform (Frustrated Contracts) Act 1943 does not apply to certain contracts for the sale of goods[3]. It is well settled that employees in a furniture factory are not selling the furniture they make, but hiring out their skill and labour. Equally clearly, a carpenter may produce an article of furniture which subsequently becomes the subject-matter of a contract for the sale of goods between himself and another. Yet there are a number of difficult borderline cases, and the criteria for distinguishing between the two categories were considered in *Robinson* v. *Graves*[4]. In this case, the Court of Appeal unanimously held that the commissioning of a portrait from an artist was a sale of skill and labour, notwithstanding that the canvas and frame would pass under the contract: the court said that everything depended on the substance of the contract.

3. Barter or exchange. Section 1 (1) of the S.G.A. seems to envisage that the consideration for the promise to transfer goods shall be money, for it calls that consideration "the price"; and, in defining "goods", s. 62 (1) explicitly excludes money. It therefore seems that where each party merely promises to transfer goods to the other, then the contract is merely one of barter, and outside the S.G.A. The more difficult situation is where the consideration for the transfer of goods is expressed to be partly goods and partly money. In *Dawson, (G. J.) (Clapham) Ltd.* v. *Dutfield*[5]

the defendants agreed to buy two lorries for £475, of which £250 was to be paid in cash and the rest made up by two lorries taken in part-exchange, provided they were delivered within one month.

---

19. See *Milroy* v. *Lord* (1862), 4 De G.F. & J. 264.
20. *Charles Rickards, Ltd.* v. *Oppenheim*, [1950] 1 K.B. 616; [1950] 1 All E.R. 420, C.A.: set out below, p. 148.
1. E.g. *Samuels* v. *Davis*, [1943] 1 K.B. 526; [1943] 2 All E.R. 3, C.A.; *Stewart* v. *Reavell's Garage*, [1952] 2 Q.B. 545; [1952] 1 All E.R. 1191; *Young and Marten, Ltd.* v. *McManus, Childs, Ltd.*, [1968] 2 All E.R. 1169.
2. See above, p. 6.
3. S. 2 (5) (c) of the 1943 Act. See below, p. 257.
4. [1935] 1 K.B. 579, C.A., discussed by Samek (1962), 36 A.L.J. 66.
5. [1936] 2 All E.R. 232. See also *Aldridge* v. *Johnson* (1857), 26 L.J.Q.B. 296, where the contract was treated as being one of sale, the price of £215 to be paid in cattle to the value of £192 and £23 cash.

The money was paid, but the defendants failed to deliver the two lorries within the stipulated time.

If this had been a contract of barter, the plaintiff would have been able to frame his action in detinue for the two lorries promised; but HILBERY J. held that this was an entire contract of sale, on which the plaintiff was entitled to sue for the balance of the price. It is submitted that the case does not turn upon whether the greater proportion of the price was payable in cash or kind; but upon whether the parties intend the transaction to be a sale or a barter. The primary stipulation in this case was for a cash price, which showed that the parties intended a sale. Is the position any different in a h.p. transaction which falls within the H.P.A. by reason of the definitions of hire purchase and total purchase price?

Finally, mention must be made of two other matters pertaining to price. First, the attempts by suppliers to fix the retail price of goods is now largely dealt with by legislation[6]. Second, the statutory regulations to be discussed later contain restrictions as to the deposit, instalments and repayment period of many instalment credit transactions[7].

4 FINANCING SALES

The S.G.A. certainly envisages that the price may be payable subsequent to delivery, perhaps by instalments; and, in a h.p. transaction, the price will always be payable by instalments subsequent to delivery. Now, a considerable amount of capital will be required to conduct business on instalment credit terms, and if the supplier of goods cannot finance his own sales he will need to look elsewhere. Thus, it is becoming increasingly common for such capital to be supplied by specialist finance companies.

The economic function of a finance company is to provide the credit, so that the dealer may have his price whilst the dealer's customer obtains immediate possession of the goods. In return for this service, the finance company will levy a finance charge on the customer, which is added to the cash price of the goods: it is these two items which basically form the hire purchase or total purchase price that the customer will subsequently pay the finance company by instalments. In those trades in which the dealer is in a particularly strong position, e.g., the motor trade, the dealer will be able to stipulate for a percentage of the finance charge as commission for the introduction of the business[8].

It is now necessary to turn to the methods by which the finance company provides the credit, a matter which is of considerable legal

---

6. Restrictive Trade Practices Acts 1956 & 1968; Resale Prices Act 1964.
7. See below, p. 45.
8. See *Re Finance Houses Association, Ltd.'s Agreement*, [1965] 3 All E.R. 509, R.P.C.

significance. Basically, the choice of the "credit-provider" is between directly and indirectly financing the transaction.

1. Direct Financing[9]. Where the goods involved have a sufficiently large unit value to bear the administrative costs of individual treatment, the more expensive directly financed transaction is usually undertaken. Under this system, the customer selects his goods, typically a motor vehicle, from the dealer's stock, and then completes a proposal form in respect of the goods. This proposal form will normally have the terms of the proposed instalment credit agreement printed on the back, and in law the signed form usually amounts to an offer by the customer to take the goods on those terms. In addition to completing the proposal form, the customer may have to find a surety, and will normally have to pay a substantial deposit to the dealer. The dealer will retain this deposit, unless the proposal is not accepted by the finance company—in which case the deposit should be returned to the customer. The next step is for the dealer to forward the proposal form (plus any guarantee required) to the finance company, together with an invoice, which will contain details of the goods and their cash price, and will constitute an offer to sell the goods to the finance company: the invoice may contain the conditions of the proposed sale, or be subject to a "master agreement"[10]. If the finance company decides to accept the business, the proposal form will usually be signed by one of its officers and a copy dispatched to the customer; and, at the same time, the finance company will notify the dealer that the proposal has been accepted, and that it is in order for him to deliver the goods. The dealer will obtain the signature of the customer on a delivery receipt; and the finance company will pay the dealer the cash price less the deposit against this receipt. The result of this complicated transaction will thus be (1) a contract of sale from dealer to finance company and (2) an instalment credit contract from company to customer. No primary contractual relationship will arise between the dealer and the customer[11], although there may be a collateral contract between the two of them[11a]. Finally, the dealer may guarantee to the finance company that the customer will perform his obligations under the instalment credit contract, this guarantee being termed a "recourse provision".

2. Indirect Financing[11b]. Where the unit value of the goods involved is insufficient to justify individual treatment, e.g. most domestic appliances, the cheaper indirect financing will probably be used. The normal course of business here is that the dealer enters into an instalment

---

9. See Goode, *H.P. Law & Practice* (2nd Edn.) 129–132b.
10. See below, p. 26.
11. *Drury* v. *Victor Buckland, Ltd.*, [1941] 1 All E.R. 269, C.A.
11a. E.g. *Brown* v. *Sheen and Richmond Car Sales, Ltd.*, [1950] 1 All E.R. 1102.
11b. See Goode, *op. cit.*, 657–661.

credit contract with the customer, so that initially the dealer is extending the credit to the customer. Subsequently, the dealer may assign part or all of his interest in the agreement to the finance company in return for the whole or part of the outstanding "price". In practice, the dealer will not enter into a separate transaction with the finance company in respect of every agreement, but transfers them in blocks to the company at agreed intervals: hence, this method of business is frequently known as "block-discounting". Whilst master agreements are uncommon in direct financing, the transfer of interest from dealer to finance company in indirect financing will normally be closely regulated by an elaborate master agreement. This agreement will usually specify whether the dealer is to transfer to the company either or both his contractual and proprietary rights, and whether that transfer is to be absolute, or by way of mortgage or declaration of trust. An absolute transfer of proprietary rights is, of course, a sale of goods within the S.G.A. A non-absolute transfer of proprietary rights, however, does not fall within the S.G.A.; nor does any sort of transfer of contractual rights, as these are merely choses in action.

The implications for the parties of the transaction being financed either directly or indirectly will be considered further in Chapter 17; but these modes of business have repercussions that will be observed throughout this work.

5 CONSUMER PROTECTION

1 Contracts of purchase

The attitude of the common law in the nineteenth century towards the consumer may be summed up in the maxim *caveat emptor*: let the buyer beware. It has already been mentioned that the S.G.A. embodied the twin themes of freedom and sanctity of contract[12]. Nominally a policy of equality, this attitude was plainly based on a fiction in the field of consumer standard-form contracts; and, in the twentieth century, the courts have increasingly sought to protect the weaker consumer by progressively interpreting the S.G.A. in his favour and restricting the use of exclusion clauses. However, the ambit of such contractual liability is clearly limited by the doctrine of privity of contract; and the courts sought to avoid this problem by developing the doctrine of the collateral contract. Simultaneously, the courts have gradually extended the protection offered to the consumer by the law of tort[13].

However, the rules of contract and tort are not the only techniques available to the law for the protection of the weaker party. In some

---

12. See above, p. 4.
13. See further Chapter 10, below.

ways the imposition of criminal sanctions is more effective; and the nineteenth century saw an enormous increase in the legislation imposing criminal sanctions in this area, much of it directed to foodstuffs. In this century, the scope of this legislation has become significantly wider, and may presently be considered under the following heads:

1. Weights and Measures. The major enactment of 1878 has recently been replaced by the Weights and Measures Act 1963, which provides for the inspection of weighing devices and the compulsory labelling of correct quantities on packages.

2. Standards. There are a number of Acts regulating the composition or construction of particular types of goods. For instance, the Road Traffic Act 1960, and regulations made under it, specify the standards of crash-helmets and also vehicles sold for use on the roads; and the Food and Drugs Act 1955 closely regulates the composition and purity of food sold. Many of the statutes in this field empower the Government to issue statutory regulations; and the Consumer Protection Act 1961 gives a rather more general power than most to make regulations to protect the public from risk of death or personal injury.

3. Advertisements. Some protection against misleading advertisements inducing the purchase of goods by consumers is contained in the Food and Drugs Act, and the Merchandise Marks Acts mentioned below; and rather more specific protection in this regard is now to be found in the Advertisements (Hire Purchase) Act 1967.

4. Trade Description Legislation. The Merchandise Marks Acts 1887 to 1953 were primarily intended to protect the trader from unfair competition, but were subsequently utilised to confer a measure of protection on consumers. However, those Acts have now been replaced by the Trade Descriptions Act 1968, whose primary object is the protection of consumers. This Act carefully defines a trade description, and makes it an offence to apply a false trade description to goods, whether orally or in writing; and it also prohibits certain misleading statements as to price. Particularly in its institution of an elaborate system of enforcement, the 1968 Act may herald the first tentative step towards a system like the United States Federal Trade Commission[14].

All the enactments mentioned above impose criminal sanctions in default, which raises two problems for the civil law. First, will the attractions of criminal sanctions taint the contract with illegality[15]? Second, will default also give rise to civil liability for breach of statutory duty? A few statutes, such as the Consumer Protection Act 1961, specifically give such a right; and, where the Act is silent, there are

---

14. See further, Woll, *Administrative Law*, 116–124.
15. See further, below, p. 37.

sometimes decisions on the point[16]; but in the remaining cases it is difficult to forecast whether the courts will grant a right of action[17].

2 Instalment credit contracts[18]

The explosive growth in the use by consumers of instalment credit in the twentieth century was mainly conducted through the medium of the h.p. transaction. Not only did this form in itself allow the development of a number of abuses, but the very inequality of the parties led to oppression of the consumer. First, many people were induced to enter into elaborate written agreements which they did not understand, and of which they could obtain no subsequent record. Second, by the inclusion in the h.p. agreement of stringent repossession clauses[19], and by encouraging customers to incur debts beyond their means, dealers could be reasonably certain of default by the customer; and, if he delayed repossession or "snatch-back" until late in the day, the dealer could usually obtain most of the price by way of rent and still recover the goods. This result was made possible by the decision that h.p. was not a form of mortgage, and that the hirer had no equity of redemption in the goods[20]. Not only was the letter of the law often enforced by intimidation and violence, but the misery of the hirer was frequently compounded by the device of "linked-on" agreements, whereunder the hirer was induced to cancel an almost completed agreement and undertake a fresh agreement in respect of those goods and further goods, thereby giving the dealer additional security at no cost to himself. Third, the goods let by dealers practising this type of business were frequently extremely shoddy, yet the dealer was normally protected by widely drawn exclusion clauses. Fourth, if the hirer sought to exercise his option to determine the agreement, he was often faced with an exorbitant minimum payments clause[1]. Fifth, it was often impossible for the hirer to ascertain the cash price of the goods, and hence work out the finance charge. Sixth, it was not unknown for dealers to persuade hirers to sign blank h.p. forms, and thereafter to insert more onerous terms than those orally agreed.

The first statutory attempt to curb these abuses was made in the H.P.A. 1938, which was expressed to apply to all h.p. and credit sale agreements under which the h.p. or total purchase price did not exceed certain stated amounts. The Act required that the customer should be informed of the cash price of the goods before entering the

---

16. E.g. *Square* v. *Model Farm Dairies, (Bournemouth), Ltd.,* [1939] 2 K.B. 365, C.A.; *Badham* v. *Lambs, Ltd.,* [1946] K.B. 45; [1945] 2 All E.R. 295.
17. See Fleming, *Torts* (3rd Edn.) 126–136.
18. See generally Diamond in *Instalment Credit* (Ed. Diamond) 1–24.
19. See further, below, p. 355.
20. See below, p. 330.
1. These clauses are explained above, p. 14.

transaction, and be given a memorandum of the agreement he signed (s. 2); and that at any subsequent stage during the continuance of the agreement the customer should be entitled to a further copy and a notice of the state of accounts between the parties (s. 7). The Act further provided that, where a hirer had paid more than one-third of the h.p. price, the owner could not repossess the goods against the wishes of the hirer otherwise than by court order (s. 11); and it gave the court such wide powers to impose a just solution where such applications were made (ss. 12–18), that the "snatch-back" and "linked-on" agreement virtually disappeared as a method of trade. Section 4 of the Act gave the hirer an inalienable right to return the goods on payment of the instalments in arrears and a certain sum for depreciation; and thereafter the hirer might well return the goods if his "equity" in them fell below the outstanding debt. Furthermore, the Act made it more likely that the finance company might be responsible for the representations of the dealer (s. 5), and made it more difficult to contract out of the implied conditions as to quality and fitness (s. 8).

Since the war, the success of h.p. has been linked with the development of the affluent society and the mushroom growth of finance companies; and these companies may be said to have achieved a measure of financial respectability in 1954 with the direct participation in their affairs of the Clearing Banks[2]. Meanwhile, the soaring inflation of the post-war period rendered the 1938 Act applicable to a decreasing amount of h.p. business; and the H.P.A. 1954 was intended to restore the ambit of the legislation to its 1938 scope by raising the monetary limits simply to take into account the decline in value of money. The terrific increase in the use of advertising in this period led to the passage of the Advertisements (Hire Purchase) Act 1957, which was designed to curb misleading advertisements.

From the early 1950's onwards, there was an increasing body of opinion in favour of widening the application of the H.P. Acts, in particular to cover new, and the more expensive used, motor vehicles; and this, combined with the more general consumer protection movement, led to the appointment of the Molony Committee on Consumer Protection in October 1959. The Final Report of this Committee appeared in July 1962 (Cmnd 1781); and many of its recommendations have since found their way into the statute book, e.g. the H.P.A. 1964 and the Trade Description Act 1968. The H.P.A. 1964 was noteworthy in that, not only was it the first piece of Government-sponsored legislation in this field, but it also made some really important

---

2. Thus, in *Snook* v. *London and West Riding Investments, Ltd.*, [1967] 2 Q.B. 786; [1967] 1 All E.R. 518, at p. 527, Diplock L.J. said: "it is not a presumption of law that a h.p. finance company cannot be innocent. It is not even a p.f. presumption of fact."

innovations. However, the 1964 Act was an extreme example of legislation by reference, being almost incomprehensible in parts (see s. 34
(3)); and it was replaced by a consolidating Act in 1965. Unless otherwise specified, all subsequent references in this book will be to the
H.P.A. 1965[3].

The financial limits of the H.P.A. are to be found in Part I, which
provides that the Act can only be applicable to the following transactions[4]:

(a) Conditional sale and h.p. agreements where the "price" does not
exceed £2,000 (s. 2 (2));

(b) Credit-sale agreements where the "price" exceeds £30 but does
not exceed £2,000 (s. 2 (3)), though the minimum figure does not apply
in some cases (s. 2 (4)). To meet the problem of devaluation of the
currency, s. 3 allows these financial limits to be raised by Order in
Council. It was not intended, however, that the H.P.A. should apply
to other than consumer transactions; and Parliament sought to achieve
this object by laying down in s. 4 that the transactions covered by the
Act

> "do not include any agreement which is made by or on behalf of a
> body corporate (whether incorporated in the United Kingdom or
> elsewhere) as the hirer or buyer of the goods to which the agreement
> relates".

Three points should be noticed. First, the section only purports to
exclude agreements made by incorporated bodies, so that the Act still
applies where the hirer or buyer is a partnership. Second, s. 4 only
excludes those transactions made by an incorporated body as hirer or
buyer: it is irrelevant whether or not the owner or seller is an incorporated body. Third, the section refers to agreements "made by or on
behalf of a body corporate"; an agreement made by an individual but
subsequently assigned to a corporate body would not appear to fall
within this expression.

It is convenient to summarise here some of the innovations made by
the 1964 Act which are now to be found in the 1965 Act. First, to
meet the objection that the customer often does not realise until too late
the nature of the document he has signed, the Act provides that the
document shall contain a clearly-labelled "signature-box" with appropriate cautionary wording (s. 7 (2)), that the customer shall in all cases
obtain a copy of the document he signs (ss. 8, 9), and that the agreement

---

3. For general criticism of the H.P.A. 1965, see Hughes (1967), J.B.L. 307.
4. The hirer or buyer cannot estop himself out of the protection offered by the
   Act by representing that the price falls outside these limits—*Campbell
   Discount Co., Ltd.* v. *Gall*, [1961] 1 Q.B. 431; [1961] 2 All E.R. 104, C.A.
   See below, p. 287.

must be signed by the customer personally, and by or on behalf of all other parties (s. 5 (1)). Second, the Act sought to deal with the abuses prevalent in door-to-door selling by giving the customer a limited right of cancellation, and a "cooling-off" time in which to exercise it (ss. 9, 11–14). Third, the Act expressly makes the dealer the agent of the finance company for some purposes (ss. 12 (3), 16). Fourth, within the four corners of the agreement the Act considerably strengthens the implied terms as to quality and fitness, imports new implied terms as to sample and description, and makes it more difficult to contract out of all of them (ss. 17–19, 29). Fifth, the right of the owner or seller to repossess goods is further restricted by the requirement of a notice of default and the introduction of a sort of statutory equity of redemption (ss. 25, 26); and any provision terminating the agreement on the death of the customer is struck out (s. 30). Sixth, the Act extends its protection to persons guaranteeing performance by the customer (ss. 5, 22, 23), and makes it clear that its provisions extend to conditional sales[5].

Yet the H.P.A. 1965 does not embody all the statutory provisions relating to conditional sales and h.p. agreements. Part III of the 1964 Act, which extends a measure of protection to one who purchases a motor vehicle in good faith from a hirer or conditional buyer, still stands; and it should be noted that the ambit of these provisions is not restricted by Part I of the 1965 Act (nor by the equivalent provisions of the 1964 Act). Furthermore, the provisions of the h.p. legislation which related to advertisements were not incorporated in the 1965 Act, but have now been consolidated in the Advertisements (Hire Purchase) Act 1967.

---

5. See above, pp. 14–15.

CHAPTER 3

Formalities and Formation

The requirements of the S.G.A. and H.P.A. in relation to the formalities and formation of agreements falling within their ambit differ markedly; and those differences mirror the differing functions of the two Acts. The S.G.A. is designed as a general code to deal with every type of sale transaction, from the sale of a box of matches, to the sale of a car, to the sale of a cargo of a ship. It is therefore essential that it be general and permissive rather than detailed and obligatory. On the other hand, the H.P.A. is designed to deal with one particular type of transaction, namely, consumer instalment credit, and is particularly interested in protecting one party to that transaction. It is therefore not surprising that the H.P.A. is often both detailed and obligatory.

I FORMALITIES OF THE AGREEMENT

1 Sales

The common law required no special formalities in the conclusion of a contract of sale; but certain statutory requirements were to be found in ss. 3 and 4 of the S.G.A. Section 4 was repealed in 1954[1], and s. 3 lays down no requirements as to form whatsoever. Certain formalities are, however, required by the following Statutes:

(1) The H.P.A., which is discussed below.

(2) The Merchant Shipping Act 1894 imposes certain formalities in the sale of a ship or a share therein (s. 24).

(3) The Law of Property Act 1925 requires a note or memorandum of a sale of an interest in land signed by the party sought to be charged therewith[2].

(4) The Bills of Sale Acts, which apply to most documents transferring proprietary interests in chattels without any transfer of possession[3]. The S.G.A. expressly saves these provisions (s. 61 (3)), and the Acts themselves draw a distinction between the two following types of transfer effected by bill of sale:

(a) Absolute transfers. Where the grantor transfers his entire interest, the transfer must be attested and registered in conformity

---

1. Law Reform (Enforcement of Contracts) Act 1954, s. 1.
2. S. 40. See also, above, p. 19.
3. See above, p. 10. But note documents of title, below, p. 207.

with the Bills of Sale Act 1878, but otherwise are governed by the S.G.A.[4].

(b) Non-absolute transfers. When the grantor transfers less than his entire interest, the S.G.A. is inapplicable to the transaction (s. 61 (4)), which is wholly governed by the Bills of Sale Act 1882. The 1882 Act requires the bill to be in the form set out in the schedule to that Act[5].

2 Consumer sales

The elaborate safeguards developed by owners ensured that h.p. agreements would usually be in writing[6], and the H.P.A. 1938 required a note or memorandum of the agreement. Nowadays, the statutory orders invariably require the actual agreement to be in writing, and further substantial provisions as to the formalities of agreement are to be found in the H.P.A. 1965 (ss. 5–7). These provisions of the 1965 Act are expressed to be applicable to h.p. agreements, conditional and credit sales; and the Act provides that, subject to the discretion of the court under s. 10, enforcement shall be conditional on compliance with the requirements there laid down (s. 5 (1))[7]. The effects of such unenforceability are spelt out by s. 5 (2) as follows:

(a) The owner or seller cannot enforce any related contract of guarantee (s. 5 (2) (a));

(b) No security given by the customer or guarantor is enforceable (s. 5 (2) (b));

(c) The owner cannot enforce any right to recover the goods from the hirer or buyer (s. 5 (2) (c)); but it would seem that he probably can recover the goods from any third party to whom the hirer or buyer transfers them[8].

Section 6 requires that the cash price of the goods be clearly stated to the customer before he enters the transaction[9], and the Act then lays down certain other formalities. These formalities are obligatory, though all except the first are subject to the dispensing power granted to the court by s. 10.

a. Signature. Section 5 (1) (a) insists that

> "the agreement is signed by the hirer or buyer, and by or on behalf of all the other parties to the agreement".

---

4. See, for instance, indirect financing, below, p. 307.
5. E.g. *Maas* v. *Pepper*, [1905] A.C. 102, H.L.; set out below, p. 294.
6. See above, p. 9.
7. Can the hirer or buyer sue on the agreement whilst refusing to perform his side of the bargain?
8. *Eastern Distributors, Ltd.* v. *Goldring*, [1957] 2 Q.B. 600; [1957] 2 All E.R. 525, C.A.; see below, p. 189. Does it follow that the hirer or buyer may retain and use the goods indefinitely without payment of any rent?
9. What if the dealer refuses to sell for cash?

Not only must the customer sign personally, but the exact location of his signature is important, and he must sign the *agreement*[10].

b. Signature-boxes. The Molony Report recommended that the agreement should contain a signature-box with suitable cautionary wording in which the customer be required to sign; and the Board of Trade have utilised the powers granted to them by the Act to issue regulations designed to achieve this object (ss. 7 (1) (c), (2)).

c. Statements of price. It is required that the h.p. or total purchase price and certain other information is inserted in the agreement (s. 7 (1) (a)).

d. Identification of the goods. A list of the goods sufficient to identify them is required (s. 7 (1) (b)).

e. Legibility. Section 7 (1) (d) requires the agreement to comply with the rules relating to legibility laid down by the Board of Trade under the powers granted them by s. 32.

f. Statutory notices. Section 7 (1) (e) requires that the agreement contain a notice "which is at least as prominent as the rest of the contents of the agreement", in the form laid down in Schedules 1 and 2, which notice informs the hirer or buyer of his statutory right to terminate the agreement and of the statutory restrictions on the owner's powers of repossession.

Finally, the H.P.A. prevents any evasion of these elaborate requirements (insofar as there might be any doubt on the matter) by laying down in s. 29 (4) that

> "Any contract, whether oral or in writing, which apart from this subsection would have effect as a contract to enter into a hire-purchase agreement, a credit-sale agreement or a conditional sale agreement (as distinct from a contract constituting such an agreement) shall be void".

2 FORMATION OF THE AGREEMENT

1 The pre-contract stage

Where business is to be done on credit terms, the credit-provider's first line of defence is usually to have recourse before the credit is granted to a credit bureau. Perhaps the most well-known of these is the specialised H.P. Information Ltd., which keeps a record of all motor vehicles which are subject to h.p. transactions. What if that company wrongly said that a vehicle was not on h.p., or *vice versa*? The enquirer who paid his fee to the Company and suffered damage by reason of the inaccuracy of information given to him no doubt has his

---

10. Does this imply that *all* the terms must be in the written agreement, so that there is no room for importing extra terms in the light of representations made by the dealer?

remedies in contract, deceit or even possibly negligent misstatement. But what of the innocent owner of a vehicle who suffers loss because his vehicle is wrongly listed as being subject to an agreement? These sorts of problem arise in a yet wider field in relation to credit bureaux generally; and such problems seem likely to increase in significance as the scope of these bureaux becomes nation-wide, and the individual's credit-rating all-important[11]. Is there any remedy for refusal to grant a credit-rating[12]? Is the communication of a credit-rating protected by qualified privilege against the law of defamation[13]? Does the bureau owe a duty of care to the person being rated[14]?

This is not to say that the consumer is entirely without protection in this pre-contract stage. Some statutes which provide protection against a number of malpractices that are likely to occur during this period by imposing criminal sanctions on those who practise them have already been discussed[15].

2 The general principles of formation

1. Offer and Acceptance. The S.G.A. assumes that a contract for the sale of goods will be made according to the ordinary principles of the law of contract[16]; and only in the case of infancy and auction sales does it lay down any rules[17]. Nor does the H.P.A. really interfere with the general rules, except by its insistence on the form in which the parties should signify their intention to be bound[18], and the introduction of the cancellation provisions[19]. Similarly, the ordinary rules of construction will apply to the standard-form contracts by which many of these transactions are effected.[20]. However, the matter which causes problems particular to this area is the method of financing instalment credit contracts[1], though it is only direct financing that causes any real difficulty. In *Financings, Ltd.* v. *Stimson*[2] the parties intended to set up a directly financed transaction, and the facts were as follows:

> On March 16th the defendant signed a h.p. proposal form produced by a dealer; and two days later the dealer allowed him to take away the car to which that document related. On March 20th, the defendant returned the car to the dealer, saying that he did not want

---

11. For a general discussion of the problems, see *Law and Contemporary Problems*, Spring 1966, p. 342.
12. Cf. *Nagle* v. *Fielden*, [1966] 2 Q.B. 633; [1966] 1 All E.R. 689, C.A.
13. See *Clerk & Lindsell on Tort* (13th Edn.), para. 1755.
14. Cf. *Ministry of Housing and Local Government* v. *Sharp*, [1970] 1 All E.R. 1009, C.A.
15. See above, pp. 27–28; and also Strachan (1970), 114 Sol. Jo. 660.
16. See above, pp. 6, 9.   17. Ss. 2, 58.
18. See above, p. 33.   19. See below, p. 42.
20. For an interesting article on "sold notes", see Hoggett (1970), 33 M.L.R. 518.
1. See above, p. 24.   2. [1962] 3 All E.R. 386, C.A.

it and (believing himself to be bound by a contract) offered to forfeit his deposit. During the night of March 24/25 the car was stolen from the dealer's premises and recovered badly damaged. On March 25th, the finance company (not having been informed that the defendant had returned the car to the dealer) signed the agreement.

The finance company's action against the "hirer" for breach of the h.p. agreement failed before the Court of Appeal. Their Lordships unanimously took the view that the defendant's completed proposal form constituted an offer[3], but that that offer had come to an end before the finance company purported to accept it on March 25th for the following reasons:

(i) (PEARSON L.J. dissenting) the return of the car by the defendant to the dealer on March 20th amounted to a revocation of his offer, as the dealer had an ostensible authority to accept the revocation of the offer on behalf of the finance company[4];

(ii) (unanimously) the offer was conditional on the car being in substantially the same condition at the time of acceptance as at the time of offer, and therefore the offer terminated on the night of March 24/25[5].

Presumably, if the matter had been decided on ordinary common law principles, the court would have found that the defendant's offer had been accepted on March 18th when the dealer communicated to the defendant the finance company's oral acceptance[6]. But the proposal form contained the following clause:

"This agreement shall become binding on the [finance company] only upon acceptance by signature on behalf of the [company] and the hiring shall be deemed to commence on such date of acceptance".

Their Lordships therefore took the view that the offer contained in the proposal form had not been accepted before March 25th[7]; and they also rejected the argument that there was a preliminary oral contract containing most of the terms embodied in the proposal form[8]. Finally, it should be pointed out that in the normal case communication of acceptance will be achieved by the finance company sending the customer a copy of the signed agreement in pursuance of some such

---

3. *Contra* if the customer completes the form in blank and the dealer subsequently inserts different terms from those agreed between himself and the customer—*Unity Finance, Ltd.* v. *Hammond* (1965), 109 Sol. Jo. 70, C.A.
4. See below, p. 285.
5. See below, p. 116.
6. But see *Scammell, Ltd.* v. *Ouston*, [1941] A.C. 251; [1941] 1 All E.R. 14, H.L.
7. Can the offeree stipulate that he need not communicate his acceptance?
8. Presumably because of the clause cited above. See now s. 29 (4) of the H.P.A. 1965, set out above, p. 34.

clause as that set out in the text[9]; and that, where the H.P.A. applies, this procedure will satisfy the rules as to copies[10].

2. Mistake. The circumstances where the parties reach agreement, but the subject-matter does not, or ceases to, exist will be considered in Chapter 15. Apart from this question of impossibility of performance, the S.G.A. expressly saves the common law rules of mistake (s. 61 (2)); and the H.P.A. is altogether silent on the matter. Whilst exposition of the common law rules of mistake may be left to the standard works on contract, two particular types of fraud by a dealer in a directly financed transaction are likely to cause difficulty in this connexion. First, the dealer may trick the customer into signing a proposal form, and then submit that form to the finance company. In such circumstances, the customer can only escape from his signature on a plea of *non est factum* if he can show that he took all reasonable care in signing the document[11], and that that document was fundamentally different in character from that which he thought it was[12]. Second, the dealer may persuade the customer to sign the proposal form in blank, and subsequently insert different terms from those orally agreed between himself and the customer, and submit the proposal to the finance company. In such event, it seems clear that the customer is not stopped from pleading the protection of the H.P.A.; that the dealer is the agent of neither party; and that there is no *consensus ad idem* between the customer and the finance company[13].

3. Invalidity. Whilst the S.G.A. has nothing to say in general terms on the question of invalidity (s. 61 (2)), it does provide that auction sales without reserve "may be treated as fraudulent" if the seller bids either himself or through an agent (s. 58 (3))[14]. On the other hand, the H.P.A. includes a number of provisions rendering a contract unenforceable for non-compliance with certain of its requirements, e.g. the rules as to copies. In addition, there are a number of offences, mostly statutory, which may be committed in the course of completing a contract of sale or h.p. The difficulty is to know what is to be the effect of transgression on the agreement. Now, the H.P.A. spells out

---

9. If there were no such clause, would acceptance date from when (1) the letter was posted; or (2) it was received; or (3) opened?
10. See below, p. 40.
11. This is not an instance of negligence operating by way of estoppel, as to which see below, pp. 196–198.
12. *Saunders* v. *Anglia Building Society*, [1970] 3 All E.R. 961, H.L., affirming C.A. *sub. nom Gallie* v. *Lee*, [1969] 2 Ch. 17. Compare *Muskham Finance, Ltd.* v. *Howard*, [1963] 1 Q.B. 904; [1963] 1 All E.R. 81, C.A. and *Mercantile Credit Co., Ltd.* v. *Hamblin*, [1965] 2 Q.B. 242; [1964] 3 All E.R. 592, C.A. (set out below, p. 197).
13. See below, p. 286.
14. Does this mean: "treated as illegal"? See also the Auctions (Bidding Agreements) Acts, 1927 and 1969: and the Mock Auctions Act 1961.

some of these effects[15]; and, at the other extreme, the Trade Descriptions Act 1968 expressly provides that transgression is to have no effect on the contract (s. 35). But in most cases, we must fall back on general principles. Now, these criminal offences[16] may be committed at the following different stages in the life of the transaction of sale or h.p.:

(i) The offence may occur prior to the formation of contract, as for instance under the Advertisements (Hire Purchase) Act 1967.

(ii) The formation of the contract may constitute the criminal offence, as under the Consumer Protection Act 1961, or the statutory orders controlling deposit and repayment period.

(iii) The contract may be legal in its formation, but the illegality occur subsequently in performance, as where a vehicle is supplied in a state which is unroadworthy within the meaning of the Road Traffic Act 1960, s. 68[17].

Leaving aside the questions of severance of an illegal contract and illegality of performance (case (iii)) which are adequately dealt with in the ordinary contract books, we must consider the effect of the illegality in cases (i) and (ii). Whilst it is clear that the illegality taints the contract in case (ii), this is by no means so clear in case (i): the illegality may be totally unconnected with the contract, in which event the contract presumably may not be tainted, e.g., an obscene advertisement for a sale of a first edition of *Lady Chatterley's Lover*; but where the statute is intended to protect one party in his entering into such transactions, e.g. the Advertisements (Hire Purchase) Act 1967, it is arguable that the illegality should taint the transaction[18]. Assuming that a contract is tainted with illegality, the effect may be as follows:

(a) To prevent either party relying on the illegal contract in any litigation[19], though it may be that a party who entered into the transaction under an innocent mistake as to the facts which constitute the offence can sue on the contract[20], or in tort[1] or under a collateral contract[2].

---

15. See also the Auctions (Bidding Agreements) Act 1927, s. 2.
16. Does this include all conduct which contravenes s. 58 (3) of the S.G.A.?
17. Does a reception which amounts to a contravention of s. 40 of the Administration of Justice Act 1970 (discussed below, p. 330) fall within this category?
18. But see Goode, *H.P. Law & Practice* (2nd Edn.) 151, note 9.
19. *Snell* v. *Unity Finance, Ltd.*, [1964] 2 Q.B. 203; [1963] 3 All E.R. 50, C.A.
20. *Archbolds, Ltd.* v. *Spanglett, Ltd.*, [1961] 1 Q.B. 374; [1961] 1 All E.R. 417, C.A. But not where he made an innocent mistake of law—*Allan (J.M.), (Merchandising), Ltd.* v. *Cloke*, [1963] 2 Q.B. 340; [1963] 2 All E.R. 258, C.A.
   1. *Belvoir Finance Co., Ltd.* v. *Stapleton*, [1970] 3 All E.R. 664, C.A.; [1970] 3 W.L.R. 530.
   2. *Strongman (1945), Ltd.* v. *Sincock*, [1955] 2 Q.B. 525; [1955] 3 All E.R. 90, C.A.; *Southern Industrial Trust* v. *Brooke House Motors* (1968), 112 Sol. Jo. 798, C.A.

(b) Recovery of money or property. The general rule is that title passes under an illegal contract notwithstanding the illegality, so that goods[3] or money[4] transferred cannot be recovered: but exceptionally property may be recovered, either by one who belongs to a class that the statute infringed was intended to protect[5], or the action can be pursued without reference to the illegal conduct[6].

3 Statutory provisions

1 Agency for the purposes of receiving notices

It is sometimes a difficult question at common law whether a dealer in a directly financed transaction is the agent of either or both the other parties; and between the wars it was common for the proposal-form to provide expressly that the dealer was to be regarded as the agent of the hirer. This was thought to be unfair, and such clauses were avoided by the H.P.A. 1938, whose provisions were re-enacted in s. 29 (2) of the H.P.A. 1965. Section 29 (2) avoids any provision in any agreement (whether h.p. or conditional or credit sale or not):

> "(d) whereby any person acting on behalf of an owner or seller in connection with the formation or conclusion of a hire-purchase agreement, credit-sale agreement, or conditional sale agreement is treated as, or deemed to be, the agent of the hirer or buyer, or
>
> (e) whereby an owner or seller is relieved from liability for the acts or defaults of any person acting on his behalf in connection with the formation or conclusion of a hire-purchase agreement, credit-sale agreement or conditional sale agreement".

These provisions neither make the dealer the agent of the finance company, nor prevent his being the agent of the company: they merely allow the court to look at the true facts. However, the H.P.A. 1964 actually increased the liability of the finance company by laying down that for the following two purposes the dealer was to be deemed to be the agent of the finance company:

(i) making representations to the customer with respect to the goods[7]; and

---

3. *Kingsley* v. *Stirling Industrial Securities, Ltd.*, [1967] 2 Q.B. 747; [1966] 2 All E.R. 414, C.A.
4. *Berg* v. *Sadler and Moore*, [1937] 2 K.B. 158; [1937] 1 All E.R. 637, C.A.
5. *Kiriri Cotton Co., Ltd.* v. *Dewani*, [1960] A.C. 192; [1960] 1 All E.R. 177, P.C.
6. *Bowmakers, Ltd.* v. *Barnet Instruments, Ltd.*, [1945] K.B. 65; [1944] 2 All E.R. 579, C.A.: foll. *Belvoir Finance Co., Ltd.* v. *Harold Cole & Co., Ltd.*, [1969] 2 All E.R. 904; *Belvoir Finance Co., Ltd.* v. *Stapleton*, [1970] 3 All E.R. 664, C.A. The 1945 case has been severely criticised by academic writers: see Treitel, *Law of Contract* (3rd Edn.) 422–424; Cheshire & Fifoot, *Law of Contract* (7th Edn.) 305–306; Goode, *H.P. Law & Practice* (2nd Edn.) 153–155.
7. Now s. 16, H.P.A. 1965, which is considered below, p. 288.

(ii) receiving notices on behalf of the finance company.

The second of these innovations is now to be found in ss. 12 (3) and 31 of the H.P.A. 1965. Section 12 (3) specifically makes the dealer the agent of the finance company for the purposes of receiving a notice of cancellation[8]; and, additionally, s. 31 widens the common law right[9] of the hirer under a h.p. agreement or a buyer under a conditional or credit sale agreement to withdraw his offer or rescind the agreement. Section 31 provides that

> "any person who conducted any antecedent negotiations shall be deemed to be the agent of [the finance company] for the purpose of receiving . . ."

notice from the customer that his offer is withdrawn (s. 31 (1)) or the agreement rescinded (s. 31 (2))[10]. Thus, the section confirms in rather wider terms the common law rule that the dealer is the agent of the finance company for the purpose of receiving notice from the customer that his offer is withdrawn[11]; and it also extends that rule to include receipt of notice by the customer of his intention to exercise any common law right of rescission[9]. For good measure, s. 29 (3) (b) expressly avoids any provision

> "excluding or restricting the operation of any enactment contained in section 16 or section 31 of this Act".

2 Copies of the agreement

The H.P.A. 1938 required that a copy of the note or memorandum of the agreement was sent to the hirer within seven days of the agreement being made; and this provision was amended by the H.P.A. 1964, which required that the customer be provided with a copy of the actual agreement. However, the rule laid down by the 1938 Act was also thought to be defective in that the customer was not immediately entitled to a copy of the document he signed, and the 1964 Act therefore stipulated that he should always be supplied with a copy of the document at the time when he signed it. These provisions are now to be found in the H.P.A. 1965, which divides the problem according to whether or not the customer signed the proposal form at "appropriate trade premises". This expression is defined by s. 58 (1), which provides that, unless the context otherwise requires,

> " 'appropriate trade premises', in relation to a document, means

---

8. See below, p. 43, note 2.
9. S. 31 does not apply to the statutory rights of cancellation and termination—s. 31 (3), (4).
10. S. 31 does not actually describe the principal as the "finance co.", but as the "owner or seller" (s. 31 (2)), or the person who would become such (s. 31 (1) & (3)). The person who conducted the "antecedent negotiations" includes the dealer, and his servants and agents—s. 58 (3), (4), (5).
11. See above, p. 36.

premises at which either the owner or seller (as defined by section 11 (5) of this Act) normally carries on a business, or goods of the description to which the document relates, or goods of a similar description, are normally offered or exposed for sale in the course of a business carried on at those premises".

Thus, "appropriate trade premises" may be of either of the following types:

(i) Normal business premises of the owner or seller. The business of the owner or seller need not be connected with retail selling at all; and, to make it clear that the expression is apt to include finance companies, s. 11 (5) seeks to cope with the problem that the finance company may not become the actual owner or seller of the goods until quite late in the transaction.

(ii) Normal business premises of the dealer. Only in a tripartite transaction will this be the premises of a different person from that covered in (i) above.

In the definition provided by s. 58, both the words "normal" and "premises" are likely to give rise to some difficulty[12]. Irrespective of where the prior negotiations are conducted, the H.P.A. distinguishes according to where the customer *actually signed the proposal* that may become a h.p. agreement or a conditional or credit sale agreement.

A. On-trade-premises agreements. Whilst the cancellation provisions do not apply, s. 8 deals with two situations:

(i) Where both parties to the agreement are present on the trade premises, s. 8 (2) provides that, whether the customer signs immediately before or after the dealer, one copy of the executed agreement must be delivered immediately to the customer. This will cover two-party transactions, indirectly financed transactions, and also those directly financed transactions where the dealer completes the agreement as agent for the finance company.

(ii) In all other cases, the customer's signature on the document will only constitute an offer, and the Act therefore speaks of the "relevant document"[13]. The Act requires that a copy of the relevant document be delivered to the customer "immediately after he signed it" *and* that a copy of the executed agreement be sent to him within seven days of execution (s. 8 (3)).

B. Off-trade-premises agreements. Here, the rules as to copies are

---

12. Does "normal" exclude stalls at trade fairs and exhibitions? What are "premises"?
13. This expression is defined by s. 8 (4) as
   "the document which, on being signed by the hirer or buyer and by or on behalf of all other parties to the agreement, became the hire-purchase agreement, credit-sale agreement or conditional sale agreement, as the case may be".

reinforced by the cancellation provisions (see below); and provide that the customer must receive the following documents[14]:

(i) The first statutory copy. This must be either presented to the customer when he signs the "relevant document", or sent to him with that document (s. 9 (2)).

(ii) The second statutory copy. Within seven days of execution, a copy of the executed agreement must be sent by post to the customer (s. 9 (3)); and the court is only allowed to dispense with this requirement in cases where the second statutory copy is sent, but not within seven days (s. 10 (2))[15].

Both statutory copies must contain certain specified information; namely,

(a) a statement of the customer's right of cancellation (s. 9 (4)), there being no dispensing power in default (s. 10 (3)); and

(b) the name and address of the person to whom notice of cancellation may be sent (s. 9 (5)), the court having a dispensing power in respect of this requirement (s. 10 (1)).

Thus, where the agreement is signed off trade premises, the customer should *always* obtain two copies, one of the document he signed, and the other of the executed agreement[16].

3 Cancellation of the agreement

The Molony Report recommended that, in order to protect the customer from unfair selling practices exercised in his home, a person signing instalment credit documents other than at a retail establishment should be allowed a "cooling-off" period of 72 hrs within which he could withdraw from the transaction. The H.P.A. 1964 sought to give effect to the recommendation by the introduction of a "right of cancellation" in respect of all off-trade-premises agreements[17]. It was found impossible to draft the provision so that it covered only unfair selling practices exercised in the home. Accordingly, the provision strikes at all off-trade-premises agreements, even though there be no unfair selling practices; but it does not apply to agreements signed on trade premises, notwithstanding that prior negotiations were conducted at the customer's home and included unfair selling practices. Thus, the unscrupulous salesman need only ensure that the proposal form is signed by the customer at appropriate trade premises to avoid the cancellation provisions. The cancellation provisions are now to be found in ss. 11 to 15 of the 1965 Act, and are expressed to apply wherever a customer at a

---

14. At the prescribed standard of legibility—s. 9 (6).
15. What if it never arrives?
16. S. 29 (4) prevents off-trade-premises forms from being used for on-trade-premises transactions.
17. To obtain the customer's signature off trade premises is still significant because, if the customer thereafter does nothing he will be bound.

place other than trade premises signs a document (in the Act referred to as the "relevant document") which constitutes, or would if executed by the other party constitute, a h.p. agreement or a conditional or credit sale agreement (s. 11 (1)). Section 11 (2) provides that:

> "At any time after he has signed the relevant document and before the end of the period of four days beginning with the day on which he receives the second statutory copy, the prospective hirer or buyer may serve a notice under this section (in this Act referred to as a 'notice of cancellation')—
> (a) on the owner or seller, or
> (b) on any person who (whether by virtue of section 12 (3) of this Act or otherwise) is the agent of the owner or seller for the purpose of receiving such a notice".

There are a number of points arising from this provision.

(i) The right of cancellation is only available to the prospective hirer or buyer; and, even if he exercises that right, the finance company does not, *ipso facto*, acquire the right to escape from any contract it may have made to purchase the goods from the dealer[18].

(ii) The rules as to copies go some way towards ensuring that the customer will be aware of his right of cancellation.

(iii) The right of cancellation may only be exercised within four days of receipt of the second statutory copy[19]. On whom does the onus of proof of receipt of the second statutory copy lie? How late may service of that copy be? Can a notice of cancellation be effective when served after judgment; or is the matter *res judicata*[20].

(iv) Section 11 (2) provides that the notice of cancellation may be served on either of the following:

(a) "the owner or seller". This term is widely defined by s. 11 (5)[1].

(b) "the agent of the owner or seller". This expression covers not only those who are agents at common law but also those who are deemed to be agents under the Act[2].

---

18. However, it is arguable that that contract is (1) subject to an implied condition precedent that the hirer or buyer will not cancel, or (2) is frustrated by that cancellation.
19. Where there is no valid exercise of any right of cancellation, the notice might operate as a repudiation or termination of the agreement—see below, Chapter 19.
20. Compare Goode, *H.P. Law & Practice* (2nd Edn.) 179.
 1. See above, p. 41.
 2. S. 12 (3) provides:
   "Any person who conducted any antecedent negotiations, but is not the owner or seller, shall be deemed to be the agent of the owner or seller for the purposes of receiving any notice of cancellation served by the prospective hirer or buyer".
   See also above, p. 40, note 10.

(v) Section 29 (3) (a) avoids any provision in any agreement (whether the h.p. or conditional or credit sale agreement or not)—

"excluding or restricting the operation of any enactment contained in sections 11 to 15 of this Act or the exercise of any right conferred by such an enactment or imposing any liability in consequence of the exercise of such a right, other than or in addition to any liability imposed by such an enactment".

(vi) Section 12 deals with the mechanics of service of a notice of cancellation in terms that makes it clear that it is preserving the common law right to revoke an offer[3]. The terminology seems to envisage that the notice of cancellation will be in writing; but s. 11 (3) provides that a notice of cancellation

"shall have effect if, however expressed, it indicates the intention of the prospective hirer or buyer to withdraw from the transaction to which the relevant document relates".

Does the notice, therefore, have to be in writing? The effect of the service of a valid notice of cancellation is to rescind *ab initio* any agreement or to revoke any offer (s. 11 (4)); and this power must be carefully distinguished from the common law and statutory powers of termination, which extinguish a contract subject to any already-accrued rights[4]. On serving a valid notice of cancellation, a customer is given certain rights. First, he may recover any sums paid as simple contract debts (s. 14 (2) and (4)). Any obligation to pay such sum is extinguished (s. 14 (3)), and any contract of guarantee deemed never to have had effect (s. 14 (1)). Further, the dealer may not recover any expenses by levying a cancellation fee[5]. Second, where the customer has already delivered goods to the dealer in part-exchange (s. 15 (1), (6) (a)), s. 15 (2) provides that

"Unless, before the end of the period of ten days beginning with the date of service of the notice of cancellation, the goods in question are delivered to the prospective hirer or buyer, and are then in a condition which is substantially as good as when they were delivered to the dealer, the prospective hirer or buyer shall be entitled to recover from the dealer a sum equal to the part-exchange allowance".

Thus, the dealer has an option to return the part-exchange goods[6]; but that option is subject to two conditions, and failure to comply with both will render the dealer liable for the part-exchange allowance or a reasonable sum[7], on payment of which the customer's title to the part-

---

3. See above, p. 40.   4. See Chapter 19, below.
5. Ss. 14 (2), (3) and 29 (3).
6. Unless the effect of cancellation is merely to revoke an offer, the customer can never insist on the return of the part-exchange goods, but he can waive the conditions.   7. S. 15 (2), (4), (6) (b).

exchange goods will, if it has not already done so, vest in the dealer (s. 15 (5)). Third, the Act confers on the customer a lien as against the dealer over the intended subject-matter of the transaction for the following purposes: (a) repayment of any sum recoverable under s. 14 (2); and (b) return of the part-exchange goods in the statutory condition or payment of the allowance (s. 15 (3)). Finally, the Act takes elaborate steps to deal with the situation where the intended subject-matter of the transaction has already been delivered to the customer at the time of his cancellation (s. 13 (1)). Section 13 deals in great detail with the customer's duty to redeliver, providing that he shall be under no duty to redeliver "except at his own premises" (s. 13 (2)), but giving him the power to take the goods back to the dealer should he so desire (s. 13 (3), (9)). Until redelivery, or the expiry of a period of 21 days from the date of service of a notice of cancellation, the section provides that the customer "shall be under an obligation[8] to take reasonable care of the goods" (s. 13 (4)): this obligation will cease on redelivery (s. 13 (5)), or expiry of the 21 days (s. 13 (8)), and may be extended indefinitely by his wrongful refusal to redeliver (s. 13 (6)); but, apart from this statutory duty, the customer who has served a notice of cancellation

> "shall not be under any obligation (whether arising by contract or otherwise) to take care of the goods by reason of their having come into his possession . . ."

in pursuance of the transaction (s. 13 (8))[9].

4 The terms controls[10]

The Government was first given power to regulate the deposit and repayment period in a regulation made under the Emergency Powers (Defence) Act 1939: and the device was thought to be such an effective way of controlling the volume of sales on the home market that, whilst the other emergency powers were progressively dismantled after the War, the power to impose terms controls was expressly preserved by the Emergency Laws (Re-enactments and Repeals) Act 1964, s. 1. Over the years, the regulations have steadily become more comprehensive, and today cover dispositions by way of h.p., conditional and credit sale and simple hire. Unlike the H.P.A., their scope is not defined by reference to the price of the goods, but according to their type. Where they apply, the regulations require that a certain minimum deposit

---

8. To the person for the time being entitled to possession of the goods (s. 13 (7)).
9. This does not oust any common law duty of care in the period before service of a notice of cancellation. But, when s. 13 (8) does operate, it would seem to put the customer into the position of an involuntary bailee, who must merely refrain from wilful damage.
10. See generally Oliver & Runcie in *Instalment Credit* (ed. Diamond), 141–174.

should be taken when the agreement is entered into, that the subsequent payments should be made in roughly equal instalments, and
that unless the disposition is of simple hire the subsequent payments
should be spread over a specified maximum period. Any infringement
of the orders is made a statutory offence by s. 13. The effect of contravention would appear to be to render the contract illegal, and prevent
either party relying on it, though it would seem that the owner or seller
may be able to recover goods let or sold under an illegal agreement
provided that he can do so without relying on that agreement.[11]

---

11. See above, p. 39. Suppose the agreement contravenes s. 5 of the H.P.A.
and the terms controls. Can the owner or seller recover the goods, despite
the fact that s. 5 clearly intended the sanction to be that he shall not be able
to recover the goods ? See Goode, *H.P. Law & Practice* (2nd Edn.) 155.

PART 2

The Contents of the Contract

CHAPTER 4

Contractual Terms

I REPRESENTATIONS AND TERMS

In the course of the negotiations which precede a contract, it is common for the parties to make certain representations either by words or conduct. The common law refused to grant damages for innocent misrepresentation, but would do so in the tort of deceit if the representation were fraudulent[1], or in contract if the representation became a term of a contract between the parties. Whilst deceit required the plaintiff to discharge the heavy burden of proving that the defendant did not honestly believe his statement to be true (always a difficult matter), liability in contract was strict, and fraud need not be proved[2]. This relative attractiveness of the contractual action led litigants to frame actions based on misrepresentation in contract rather than tort, so that the vital question was frequently whether the representation had attained contractual status. The courts decided that this issue turned on the intention of the parties.

Where the contract stated in terms that the defendant warranted the truth of the statement, then it was easy to infer such an intention[3]; but in many other cases the enquiry led the courts into considerable difficulty, because the parties may not have adverted their minds to the question. Alternatively they may not have exhibited any clear intention, or may have exhibited contrary intentions[4]. In view of such possibilities, the criterion of the intention of the parties may be criticised as elusive, artificial and almost useless. However, the persistence of litigants has forced the courts to return to the question time and again, though the amount of light generated has been slight[5]. All that can be said is that, in the field of consumer transactions, the courts appear to be making a determined effort to impose on a dealer contractual liability for the representations he makes[6]. Fortunately, it may be that recent developments in the law will shift attention away from the dichotomy of contractual term and mere representation. First, the

1. *Derry* v. *Peek* (1889), 14 App. Cas 337, H.L.   See also below, p. 128.
2. See also below, p. 129.
3. E.g. *Liverpool and County Discount Co., Ltd.* v. *A.B. Motor Co. (Kilburn), Ltd.*, [1963] 2 All E.R. 396, C.A.
4. See Gilmore & Axelrod (1948), 57 YALE L.J. 517, 518, note 3.
5. See *Heilbut, Symonds & Co.* v. *Buckleton*, [1913] A.C. 30, H.L.
6. E.g. *Dick Bentley, Ltd.* v. *Harold Smith (Motors), Ltd.*, [1965] 2 All E.R. 65, C.A.

House of Lords decided in 1963 that there might be liability in tort for negligent misstatement[7]. Second, the Misrepresentation Act 1967 will now in some cases give a statutory right of action in respect of innocent misrepresentations[8].

2 THE NATURE OF TERMS

The nature of contractual terms is subject to considerable confusion, largely because of the nomenclature involved: the appellations "condition" and "warranty" have been used by the courts without any precise definition and the same expressions have been used to explain different phenomena[9]. Perhaps the key to understanding the present "system" lies in the origin and development of the warranty. Whilst starting as an action in tort for deceit, towards the end of the eighteenth century the action began to be declared in assumpsit, and soon came to be thought of in a contractual rather than a tortious context[10]. This process had particular repercussions in the law relating to the sale of goods, then fast-developing; and the legacy is to be seen in Chalmers' definition of a "warranty" in s. 62 (1) of the S.G.A. as

> "an agreement with reference to goods which are the subject of a contract of sale, but collateral to the main purpose of such contract, the breach of which gives rise to a claim for damages, but not to a right to reject the goods and treat the contract as repudiated".

After a breach of warranty by the seller, a buyer might, in theory, wish to reject the goods tendered and affirm the contract; but it would seem that the meaning of the Act is that he may neither reject nor rescind for breach of warranty[11].

Leaving aside for the moment the meaning of "collateral", it will be observed that Chalmers in part defined a warranty according to the effect of its breach. The term "condition", however, is nowhere expressly defined in the Act, but is inferentially defined in s. 11 of the S.G.A. as a term, breach of which will give rise to a right to reject and rescind. Here again, Chalmers was reflecting a common law development, though it has been convincingly demonstrated that that development was itself based on a misconception[12]. In fact, the Act employs the word "condition" in at least two important senses[13]:

---

7. *Hedley Byrne & Co., Ltd.* v. *Heller & Partners, Ltd.*, [1964] A.C. 465; [1963] 2 All E.R. 575, H.L.; see further below, p. 129.
8. See below, p. 121.
9. See Stoljar (1952), 15 M.L.R. 425; (1953), 16 M.L.R. 174.
10. See also below, p. 129.
11. See *Benjamin on Sale* (8th Edn.) 983.
12. See Stoljar, *ibid.*
13. See Stoljar (1953), 69 L.Q.R. 485. See further Montrose (1937), 15 Can. B.R. 308, 323.

in s. 1 it is utilised in the sense of a condition precedent[14], whereas in ss. 11–15 it means an essential term of that contract, breach of which will give rise to a right to rescind.

Under the scheme adopted by the S.G.A. a condition in the sense of an essential stipulation is clearly superior to a warranty, the relationship between them being partly explained by s. 11 (1) (a)[15].

In view of the rigid distinction drawn between the two types of term, it may therefore be important to determine whether a particular term is a condition or a warranty. Section 11 (1) (b) of the S.G.A. says that in each case it depends on the construction of the contract, and adds unhelpfully that[16]

> "A stipulation may be a condition, though called a warranty in the contract".

In many cases, the S.G.A. and H.P.A. avoid this problem by expressly assigning a status to a particular term; but, in the absence of such statutory specification the question can only be determined on common law principles. Perhaps the most widely accepted test is that laid down by FLETCHER MOULTON L.J. in *Wallis, Son and Wells* v. *Pratt and Haynes*[17], where his Lordship said that the issue turned on whether the term went to the substance of the contract, or was

> "so essential to its very nature that [its] non-performance may fairly be considered by the other party as a substantial failure to perform the contract at all".

A new approach to the question of the remedies available for breach of contract was made by DIPLOCK L.J. in the *Hong Kong Fir Shipping Co.* v. *Kawasaki Kisen Kaisha*[18]: whilst agreeing that some terms could be categorised as conditions or warranties, his Lordship argued that there were other more complex contractual undertakings,

> "and the legal consequences of a breach of such an undertaking . . . depend on the nature of the event to which the breach gives rise and do not follow from a prior classification of the undertaking as a 'condition' or a 'warranty' ".

Obviously, this new approach allows for a greater flexibility; but it does

---

14. See above, p. 6. Conditions precedent are further discussed below, pp. 115–116.
15. Set out below, p. 147.
16. Perhaps in recognition of the lack of consistency in nomenclature used by the courts. Was it also designed to enable the courts to restrict exemption clauses?
17. [1910] 2 K.B. 1003, C.A., at p. 1012. The dissenting judgment of FLETCHER MOULTON L.J. was adopted by the H.L. in [1911] A.C. 394.
18. [1962] 2 Q.B. 26, C.A., at p. 70. App. *Harbutt's Plasticine, Ltd.* v. *Wayne Tank and Pump Co., Ltd.*, [1970] 1 Q.B. 447; [1970] 1 All E.R. 225, C.A.

so at the expense of the element of predictability[19].   The question is:
to what extent has the traditional approach pre-empted the ground?
Plainly, the traditional approach is inescapable where Statute has
specified the status of particular terms or there is a binding authority on
the point.   But which approach should be adopted, for instance, where
an implied term is being imported into a h.p. agreement at common
law, but on the analogy of one of the statutory implied terms to be found
in the S.G.A. or H.P.A.?

Returning to the warranty, it will be recalled that the S.G.A. defines
the warranty as being "collateral to the main purpose of" a contract of
sale.   No doubt, this formula faithfully reflects case-law developments
in the nineteenth century; but it has been pointed out that the ordinary
warranty in the contract of sale certainly is not a separate agreement as
distinct from the rest of the contract, since no further consideration is
required[20].   Indeed, we must carefully distinguish the collateral term
from the collateral contract, the latter being supported by its own
consideration.   The collateral contract may be of one of the following
types:

(1) A makes a representation to B, as a result of which B enters into
a contract with C[1];

(2) A makes a representation to B, as a result of which B enters into
a contract with A.

In *Wells (Merstham), Ltd.* v. *Buckland Sand and Silica Co., Ltd.*[2],
the facts fell within case (1), and EDMUND DAVIES J. said:

> "As between A . . . and B . . . two ingredients, and two only, are . . .
> required in order to bring about a collateral contract containing a
> warranty: (1) a promise or assertion by A as to the nature, quality
> or quantity of the goods which B may reasonably regard as being
> made animo contrahendi and (2) acquisition by B of the goods in
> reliance on that promise or assertion".

It is submitted that this *dictum* should also be applied to case (2), and
the two cases treated in the same manner, though case (2) does involve
an additional factor in that it may circumvent the parol evidence rule.

3 EXPRESS AND IMPLIED TERMS

The express terms of a contract may range from agreement on the
barest essentials to an elaborate written agreement.   In the former case,

---

19. Per MEGAW L.J. in *The Mihalis Angelos*, [1970] 3 All E.R. 125, C.A., at
p. 138.
20. Stoljar (1952), 15 M.L.R. 425, 430-432.
 1. E.g. *Andrews* v. *Hopkinson*, [1957] 1 Q.B. 229; [1956] 3 All E.R. 422; cf.
Scotson v. *Pegg* (1861) 6 H. & N. 295.
 2. [1965] 2 Q.B. 170, at p. 180.

the law undertakes to fill in the details of the agreement by implying further terms. In the latter case, there may be little room for the implication of terms.

A good example of the elaborate written agreement is the standard-form contract, which has considerable advantages to a party engaged in numerous transactions. First, it saves time, and hence money. Not only does this save the cost of individual drafting[3], but it may be extremely convenient to businessmen to be able to make a contract, perhaps orally, merely by reference to one of the standard-forms well known in their particular trade. Thus, the standard-form contract is a useful device for allocating the many risks of a transaction between the parties, who can bear this allocation in mind in fixing the price. Second, the standard-form contract has been used to exploit economic advantage. This is particularly the case in respect of those enterprises doing business with the consumer: the terms and price are rigidly laid down, and the only choice available to the individual consumer is whether or not to contract at all[4].

Whilst the scope for the application of implied terms at common law may well depend on the degree of elaboration in the express terms of the agreement, statute law is not necessarily so inhibited. Indeed, the technique of the "implied term" has frequently been used by the Legislature to limit the express terms. Sometimes, the social need has been felt to be so great that Parliament has dictated in full the only terms on which the parties may contract, as happened in relation to chattel mortgaging[5]. At other times, Parliament may suggest or prescribe some of the contents of a contract, or prevent a party enforcing certain of his rights. Thus, the S.G.A. implies certain terms as to quality and fitness into contracts for the sale of goods (s. 14): it is true that the seller may always prevent the implication of these terms, but their significance lies in the fact that, if the seller does nothing, the terms will automatically be imported into the contract. On the other hand, whilst the H.P.A. uses the terminology of implied terms, their implication is often imperative: in many cases, the terms set out in the Act must be read into the contract, and cannot be avoided (s. 29). Plainly, such implication does not rest on the intention of the parties; and it may therefore be unfortunate that we use in this situation the common law terminology, because, at least in theory, the implication of terms at common law depends on the intention of the parties[6].

---

3. For instance, a master agreement for indirect financing drafted by counsel may well cost a business several thousand pounds in legal fees.
4. He may not even have that choice with the monopoly supplier of essential goods and services.
5. The Bills of Sale Act 1882, Schedule.
6. See Glanville Williams (1945), 61 L.Q.R. 384, 401–406.

The major obligations imposed on the parties to a sale or h.p. transaction by common law or statute are as follows:

1. Identification of the goods. The law imports a condition that the goods delivered will correspond with their contract description. This undertaking will be examined in Chapter 6.

2. Title to goods. Recognising that the object of the buyer or hirer is normally to acquire title to the goods, the law imports certain undertakings by the seller or owner as to title. These will be examined in Chapter 5.

3. Quality and fitness. As the "use-value" of goods is perhaps the most important aspect of the transaction to the buyer or hirer, the law imports certain obligations designed to ensure the usability of the goods. These will be examined in Chapter 7.

4. Delivery and payment. As the primary object of both sale and h.p. is the transfer of goods for a sum of money, the obligation to deliver will be considered together with payment of the price in Chapter 16.

5. Risk. Because of the association of risk with the property in goods it is convenient to deal with it in that context. The passing of risk will be discussed in Chapter 15.

The above obligations started life in the contract of sale, and were later imported into h.p. because the latter transaction was obviously analogous to sale. Yet the h.p. agreement is also analogous to simple bailment, and the law has also imported into h.p. agreements some of the obligations developed in the ordinary law of bailment. These obligations are discussed in Chapter 9.

CHAPTER 5

Undertakings as to Title

1 INTRODUCTION

Section 12 of the S.G.A. provides for an implied condition as to the seller's title to the goods sold, and implied warranties by him of quiet possession and freedom from encumbrances. It seems probable that these implied undertakings were largely declaratory of the common law[1]; and, subsequently, the courts implied similar undertakings in h.p. agreements. To do so, the courts rejected the ordinary rule of bailment that a bailee is estopped from denying his bailor's title[2], and introduced a presumption to the opposite effect[3]. Where a transaction falls within the H.P.A., that Act imports undertakings as to title similar to those found in section 12 of the S.G.A. (s. 17 (1)). Furthermore, it is the provisions of the H.P.A., not the S.G.A., which apply to conditional sales within the ambit of the H.P.A. (s. 20 (3) H.P.A.).

Can the implied undertakings as to title be excluded? Obviously, such a result can only be achieved by an unmistakable contractual intention to this effect[4]; and even clear words to this effect may be struck out on grounds of repugnancy if a seller or owner also gives an express guarantee as to title. Thus, in *Karflex, Ltd.* v. *Poole*[5] the courts were able to ignore such an exclusion clause on the grounds that the references in the h.p. agreement to "the owner" amounted to an express term that the person named as "the owner" was the true owner. For this reason, it is unlikely that a purported exclusion of all the undertakings as to title in a h.p. agreement will be effective at common law; and where the H.P.A. applies, that Act provides that the implied undertakings as to title there laid down

"shall be implied notwithstanding any agreement to the contrary" (s. 18 (3)).

However, the opening words of s. 12 of the S.G.A. only say that the undertakings in that section are to be implied

"unless the circumstances are such as to show a different intention",

---

1. S. 12 largely follows s. 7 of the Conveyancing Act 1881.
2. E.g. *Rogers* v. *Lambert*, [1891] 1 Q.B. 318, C.A.
3. *Karflex, Ltd.* v. *Poole*, [1933] 2 K.B. 251, D.C.
4. See below, Chapter 11.
5. [1933] 2 K.B. 251, D.C. Foll. in *Warman* v. *Southern Counties Finance, Ltd.*, [1949] 2 K.B. 576; [1949] 1 All E.R. 711: set out below, p. 60.

and s. 55 of the Act also states that any of the implied terms may be negatived. One view is that, despite these provisions, a contract of sale without any express or implied undertakings as to title would amount to a sale of a chance, and not to a sale of goods within the S.G.A., on the grounds that such a sale cannot be brought within the definition of a sale of goods contained in section 1 (1)[6]. On the other hand, it has been argued that section 1 does not require an absolute promise to transfer the general property in the goods, and that a conditional promise to do so will be sufficient[7]. Certainly, the language of the Act would appear to favour the latter view[8], and it seems likely that the position is as follows: there will be a sale within the meaning of the S.G.A. where the seller agrees to transfer such title as he has; but not where he does not promise to transfer even such title as he has[9]. The Law Commission have accepted this, but have recommended that the implied condition as to title should only be excludable where it is clear that this is what was intended, and that the implied warranties as to title should never be totally excludable[10].

2 THE IMPLIED CONDITION AS TO TITLE

Where there is a sale of goods, s. 12 (1) of the S.G.A. provides that, unless a contrary intention appears, "there is"

> "An implied condition on the part of the seller that in the case of a sale he has a right to sell the goods, and that in the case of an agreement to sell he will have a right to sell the goods at the time when the property is to pass".

In the case of a h.p. or conditional sale agreement within the H.P.A., s. 17 (1) (a) of that Act lays down that "there shall be implied"

> "A condition on the part of the owner or seller that he will have a right to sell the goods at the time when the property is to pass".

Two matters must be considered: first, what amounts to a "right to sell"; and second, the effect of a breach of this obligation.

---

6. E.g. Atiyah, *Sale of Goods* (3rd Edn.) 40; Cheshire & Fifoot, *Contract* (7th Edn.) 149–150; Guest (1961), 77 L.Q.R. 98. Whilst these authors place reliance on *Rowland* v. *Divall*, [1923] 2 K.B. 500, C.A., the plea was not raised therein, and it does not appear that the decision *necessarily* supports their conclusion.
7. E.g. Hudson (1957), 20 M.L.R. 236 and (1961), 24 M.L.R. 690; Samek (1959), 33 A.L.J. 392 and (1961), 35 A.L.J. 437; Reynolds (1963), 79 L.Q.R. 534; Coote, *Exception Clauses*, 61–69.
8. See ss. 1 (2), 5 (2), and the opening words of s. 12. See also *per* ATKIN L.J. in *Niblett* v *Confectioners' Materials Co.*, [1921] 3 K.B. 387, C.A., at p. 401.
9. See Thornley (1958), C.L.J. 123, at p. 125; Reynolds (1963), 79 L.Q.R. 534, 542.
10. *The First Report on Exemption Clauses in Contracts* (Law Com. No. 24), paras. 16–18.

1 The "right to sell"

The H.P.A. plainly envisages that a h.p. agreement may result in a sale (s. 1 (1) H.P.A.); and the definition of a sale recites that the object of the transaction is to transfer the property in the goods from the seller to the buyer (s. 1 (1) S.G.A.). In 1895, LORD RUSSELL C.J. drew the (apparently logical) deduction that the duty was merely to pass the general property in the goods[11]; but a different view of the transferor's obligation has since been taken by the Court of Appeal. In *Niblett* v. *Confectioners' Materials Co.*[12] the facts were as follows:

> The seller agreed to sell 3,000 tins of condensed milk, to be shipped from America to England. The price was paid on tender of the shipping documents; but, what those documents did not reveal, was that the tins were labelled "Nissly" brand, which was a colourable imitation of Nestlé's trade-mark, and gave the latter company the right to restrain their sale in England by injunction. The buyer therefore had to strip off the labels, and sell the tins of milk un-branded for the best price obtainable. He then sued the seller to recover the difference between the price obtained, and that which the milk would have fetched as a branded article, alleging breach of the implied undertakings of (1) the right to sell, (2) quiet enjoyment and (3) merchantable quality.

At this point, we are only interested in the right to sell[13]. Upon this matter the trial judge followed Lord Russell's view. However, he was unanimously reversed by the Court of Appeal, and ATKIN L.J. commented[14]:

> "The Lord Chief Justice is using the right to sell in two different senses. The right to pass the property is one thing, and no doubt the [sellers] could have passed the property in the milk but for the intervention of the Nestlé Company; but the existence of a title superior to that of the vendor, so that the possession of the vendee may be disturbed is another thing ... The owners of the patent had no right or ability to pass the property, but they had a right to disturb the possession of the [vendee] in that case".

It would appear from this case that "right to sell" must be read as meaning "power" or "ability" to sell: if the vendors could have been prevented by injunction from selling, they had no power or ability to sell. Plainly, if the vendor does not possess the property in the goods, and cannot pass it, there is a breach of the undertaking[15]; but what if

---

11. *Montforts* v. *Marsden* (1895), 12 R.P.C. 266, at p. 269.
12. [1921] 3 K.B. 387, C.A. Compare *Lloyds and Scottish Finance, Ltd.* v. *Modern Cars and Caravans, Ltd.*, [1966] 1 Q.B. 764: set out below, p. 65.
13. The other pleas are considered below, pp. 65, 95.
14. At p. 402.
15. What if he can pass the general property, but subject to the special property of, e.g., a pledgee?

the seller can pass a good title under one of the exceptions to the
nemo dat rule? It is submitted that it is a question, not of what the
seller gives, but of what the buyer obtains, so that there is then no
breach of this undertaking[16].

When must the seller or owner have the right to sell? In the case of
a sale of goods, section 12 provides that the crucial time is when the
property in the goods is to pass. However, when a similar obligation
was imported into h.p. agreements, the courts rejected the existing rule
as to time, and decided that the transferor must have a right to sell at
the time of delivery[17]. The H.P.A. restored the test of the time when
the property is to pass (s. 17 (1) (a)); but it also preserved the common
law rule (s. 17 (5)). Thus, unless the h.p. agreement effectively ousts
the common law term, the result will be that where a h.p. agreement falls
within the H.P.A. the owner or seller must have a right to sell *both* at the
time of delivery *and* when the property is to pass.

2 Breach of the undertaking

Where the seller or owner is in breach of the undertaking that he has
the right to sell the goods, the buyer or hirer, *prima facie*, has two
courses open to him: he may elect either to rescind or to affirm the
agreement[18].

1. Rescission. If the buyer or hirer takes this course, it has been said
that the proper method of recovering the price paid is by an action in
quasi-contract on the grounds of total failure of consideration[19].
Ordinarily, a party who brings such a claim will not have obtained any
benefit at all; but in the present context it would seem that the buyer or
hirer may have his cake and eat it as well. The leading case is *Rowland
v. Divall*[20].

> The plaintiff dealer bought a car from the defendant, and two
> months later sold it to X. After a further two months, it was dis-
> covered that the car had been stolen by the person who sold it to the
> defendant. The plaintiff refunded his price to X., and then sought
> to rescind his contract with the defendant, and to recover his price
> on the grounds of total failure of consideration.

BRAY J. found that there had not been a total failure of consideration
because the plaintiff had had the use of the car for a considerable time,

---

16. See *per* ATKIN L.J. in *Niblett's Case* (above), at p. 401. Compare Atiyah,
    Sale of Goods (3rd Edn.) 36.
17. *Mercantile Union Guarantee Corporation, Ltd.* v. *Wheatley*, [1938] 1 K.B.
    490; [1937] 4 All E.R. 713.
18. These remedies are considered further in Chapter 19, below.
19. *Per* DEVLIN J. in *Kwei Tek Chao* v. *British Traders, Ltd.*, [1954] 2 Q.B.
    459, at p. 457. See further below, p. 404.
20. [1923] 2 K.B. 500, C.A. See also *Karflex, Ltd.* v. *Poole*, [1933] 2 K.B.
    251, D.C.

and that the breach of condition could only be treated as a breach of warranty. This decision was unanimously reversed by the Court of Appeal, who held that, as the buyer had not received any part of that for which he bargained, his use of the car was immaterial[1], and there had been a total failure of consideration. The majority avoided the problem of whether the condition was converted into a warranty by the resale and delivery[2]. The implications of this decision were spelt out in *Butterworth* v. *Kingsway Motors, Ltd.*[3]:

> X. let a car to Miss R. under a h.p. agreement. Mistakenly thinking that she had a right to sell the car subject to her continuing to pay the instalments, Miss R. sold the car to K. before she had completed payments. K. resold to H.; H. resold to the Kingsway Motors; and the latter resold the car to Butterworth for £1,275. After making full use of the car for eleven months, Butterworth was notified by X. of his title, and immediately wrote to the Kingsway Motors claiming the return of his price. About a week later, Miss R. paid the remaining instalment due to X. and exercised her option to purchase, upon which X. notified Butterworth that he, X., had no further interest in the car. Nevertheless, Butterworth continued his action against the Kingsway Motors; and H., K. and Miss R. were joined in the action. Owing to the fall in market values, the car which Butterworth had bought for £1,275 was only worth about £800 when he repudiated, and £400 by the date of the hearing.

PEARSON J. held that the sale by Miss R. to K. was a clear breach of s. 12 (1), as was each succeeding sale in the chain, but observed that a great deal of trouble would have been saved if Butterworth had merely bought off X., and recovered that sum from Miss R.[4]. His Lordship agreed that the Kingsway Motors, H. and K. were reduced to claiming damages for breach of warranty, but held, on the authority of *Rowland* v. *Divall*, that Butterworth was entitled to rescind, notwithstanding his use of the car for eleven months, because the issue of total failure of consideration was to be tested at the date Butterworth purported to rescind. PEARSON J. further held that, in assessing the value of what Kingsway Motors received for the purposes of mitigating their loss as against H., the material date was when Miss R. exercised her option and her newly-acquired title "fed down the line" to the Kingsway Motors. Accordingly, Butterworth recovered his £1,275 from the Kingsway Motors; and the latter recovered £475 (£1,275 − £800) from H. Thus, Kingsway Motors lost £400, and the other £475 was the amount of damages arising from the breach of warranty of title, and

---

1. This might have been material if he had held onto the car with knowledge of the facts, and thereby affirmed: see below, p. 405.
2. See further below, p. 60.
3. [1954] 2 All E.R. 694.
4. As in *Whiteley, Ltd.* v. *Hilt*, [1918] 2 K.B. 808, C.A.

this was passed down the line to Miss R., together with the cumulative costs[5]. Quite apart from the obvious injustice of the decision, the immediate problem is to know why the buyer is not in these circumstances reduced to claiming damages by his acceptance of the goods. As will be seen later[6], acceptance will usually have such a result by reason of s. 11 (1) (c) of the S.G.A.[7]. In *Rowland* v. *Divall* BRAY J. would seem to have based his decision at least in part on the application of s. 11 (1) (c); but in the Court of Appeal only ATKIN L.J. referred to this provision, and he merely said that it had no application to breaches of the implied condition as to title, without offering any convincing reasons[8]. On the other hand, it has since been accepted that, if the buyer were to take delivery with knowledge of the seller's lack of title, he would be reduced to claiming damages[9]; and in *Butterworth* v. *Kingsway Motors, Ltd.* none of the intermediate parties was allowed to rescind[10]. It is submitted that there is logically no reason why s. 11 (1) (c) should never apply to breaches of the implied condition as to title[11], and that it would be desirable if the view of ATKIN L.J. were not followed.

2. Affirmation. The buyer or hirer may elect, with knowledge of the breach, to affirm the agreement, as occurred in *Warman* v. *Southern Counties Finance Corporation, Ltd.*[12]:

> In pursuance of a directly financed transaction, the plaintiff entered into a h.p. agreement with the defendants. Before payments were completed, the plaintiff received notice from the true owner, X., of his claim to the hired car. Nevertheless, the plaintiff continued to pay the instalments due and eventually exercised the option to purchase on the very day that X. served a writ on him claiming the return of the car. The plaintiff returned the car to X., and sued the defendants for damages for breach of the implied term as to title, claiming all the sums paid under the h.p. agreement, together with the cost of insurance, repairs and legal expenses[13].

Following *Karflex, Ltd.* v. *Poole*[14], FINNEMORE J. held that there was an express condition that the defendants were the owners of the car. He added that that condition was to be tested on delivery, and that any

---

5. See below, p. 427.   6. See below, p. 397.
7. This provision would have been inapplicable if Butterworth had been a conditional buyer within the H.P.A. (s. 20 (1)).
8. At pp. 506–507.
9. See *per* DEVLIN J. in the *Kwei Tek Chao Case*, as reported in [1954] 1 All E.R. 779, at p. 788. See also *Warman's Case* below.
10. But the plaintiff in *Rowland* v. *Divall* was an intermediate party.
11. See Atiyah, *Sale of Goods* (3rd Edn.) 40; Samek (1960) 33 A.L.J. 392.
12. [1949] 2 K.B. 576; [1949] 1 All E.R. 711. See also *Bowmaker (Commercial), Ltd.* v. *Day*, [1965] 2 All E.R. 856.
13. The action for damages is further considered below, p. 416.
14. [1933] 2 K.B. 251, D.C.; see above, p. 55.

knowledge gained by the hirer thereafter was therefore irrelevant[15]. The defendants, however, counter-claimed for a reasonable sum for hire of the vehicle for the seven months during which the plaintiff hirer had had the use of it, and raised a point which GODDARD J. had expressly left open in *Karflex, Ltd.* v. *Poole.* The counter-claim was rejected by FINNEMORE J. who said[16]:

> "If [the plaintiff] wanted to make an agreement merely to hire a car he would make it, but he enters into a hire purchase agreement because he wants to have the right to purchase the car; that is the whole basis of the agreement . . . I should have thought that, even on broad principle, that if the defendants break their contract or are unable to carry it out they are not entitled to claim on a sort of *quantum meruit* . . ."

Actually, the loss in this case did not fall on the defendant finance company, because the company brought in the dealer as third party, alleging breach of warranty of title, and FINNEMORE J. held that the dealer must indemnify the company for all loss arising from the breach.

In the normal case, there will be at least three innocent parties involved in breach of the undertaking as to title; namely, the original owner, the intermediate buyer, and the ultimate buyer or hirer. Let us take a typical example, where the goods are stolen from the original owner (O.) by a thief (X.), who sells them to A., who resells to B., who resells to C., who resells or lets on h.p. to D.:

O.

X. → A. → B. → C. → D.

Besides the complications necessarily arising from the number of parties involved, certain other factors must be borne in mind. First, the value of the goods may rise, fall or fluctuate as they pass down the chain. Second, O. may, though he will not necessarily, sue any or all of the parties in the chain in conversion or detinue, because any of the acts of selling, buying, letting or hiring is sufficient ground for such actions. Third, depending on the circumstances and the actions taken by the parties, the property in the goods may at the end of the day be found in any one of the parties. It is now possible to consider the rights of the various innocent parties.

1. The original owner (O.). Assuming that at the beginning O. has the property in the goods, it may be that he will recover possession and still have the best title to the goods[17]. On the other hand, it may be that

---

15. The answer might have been different if the plaintiff had made the agreement with knowledge of the defect in the defendants' title.
16. At p. 582.
17. E.g. *Rowland* v. *Divall*, [1923] 2 K.B. 500, C.A.; *Warman's Case*, [1949] 2 K.B. 576.

either A. or B. or C. or D. has acquired the best title either by buying off O.[18], or by satisfying a judgment in conversion or detinue obtained by O.[19]; and, on acquisition, such title is immediately fed down the chain to each party in succession, stopping only when and where the chain has been broken by rescission[1]. On principle, it would seem that the risk of any change in the value of the goods should be borne by the transferee in whom the title is vested[2].

2. The innocent intermediate parties (A. B. or C.). Each may complain that his seller is in breach of the undertaking as to title, and recover damages on this ground, such damages being passed back up the chain, so that the loss is suffered by the first innocent party[3]. Such a result follows the normal pattern of the law that the party A., who bought from the thief, X., should be left to seek his remedy from X.; but it is a little harsh when X. is instead an innocent hirer under a h.p. agreement[4]. Two particular problems arise with the intermediate parties:

(i) Can they be made to pay for any use of the goods which they may have had? It has been shown that, whoever is sued by O. in conversion or detinue, the loss is passed back up the line, no allowance being made for any use of the goods by the intermediate parties[5]. Further, a counter-claim for use has been rejected by the courts[3]; and, of course, the common law has no power to apportion, though it may be that the courts now have a statutory power to apportion in these circumstances under s. 6 of the Law Reform (Married Women and Tortfeasors) Act 1935[6].

(ii) Can each intermediate party rescind and claim the price he has paid as on total failure of consideration? Such a possibility would seem to follow from *Rowland* v. *Divall*[7], but gives rise to a number of legal problems. Can a contract be rescinded after resale and delivery[8]? Is the quasi-contractual claim dependent on the ability to rescind[9]? Must a breach of the condition as to title necessarily amount to a total failure of consideration[10]?

3. The ultimate buyer or hirer (D.). The major problem here is whether D can be made to pay for his use of the goods. This involves the issues

---

18. E.g. *Karflex, Ltd.* v. *Poole*, [1933] 2 K.B. 251, D.C.; *Butterworth's Case*, [1954] 2 All E.R. 694.
19. See below, p. 363.   1. E.g. *Butterworth's Case* (above).
2. It is on this ground that the Kingsway Motors had to bear the loss of £400 in *Butterworth's Case*. On risk, see Chapter 15, below.
3. E.g. *Warman's Case*, [1949] 2 K.B. 576.
4. E.g. Miss R. in *Butterworth's Case*, [1954] 2 All E.R. 694.
5. E.g. *Butterworth's Case* (above).
6. See Williams, *Joint Tortfeasors* 19, 98; Treitel, *Law of Contract* (3rd Edn.), pp. 862–863.
7. [1923] 2 K.B. 500 C.A. But see *Butterworth's Case* (above).
8. See below, p. 401.
9. See below, pp. 405–406.   10. See below, pp. 63–64.

of his right to rescind[8], and the relationship of the quasi-contractual claim to rescission[9].

The ordinary rule in quasi-contract is that he who seeks the return of any benefit given, must, *prima facie*, restore any benefit gained[11]. In *Rowland* v. *Divall*[12] the car had been returned to the true owner, and the defendant therefore argued that the plaintiff could not maintain his claim because he could not return the car to the defendant; but this argument was rejected by the Court of Appeal, who pointed out that the very reason for the plaintiff's inability to return the car to the defendant was that of which he was complaining, namely, the defendant's lack of title. The defendant also argued unsuccessfully that the plaintiff's use and enjoyment of the car made restitution impossible; but ATKIN L.J. replied[13]:

> "To my mind [the use] makes no difference at all ... The buyer has not received any part of that which he contracted to receive—namely, the property and right to possession—and, that being so, there has been a total failure of consideration".

The result is that the plaintiff had free use of the goods[14]. Now, it is well settled that the quasi-contractual remedy requires that the failure of consideration be total, not partial; that is, that the claimant did not receive any part of that for which he bargained[15]. Yet, despite the fact that the transferee in these circumstances will be bargaining for title *and* possession, it has been held that if he gets possession but not title there is a total failure of consideration[16]. It is difficult to know how far this principle extends. First, does it apply to any breach of the under-taking as to title[17], or merely to inability to transfer the property in the goods? Second, would the answer be the same if the buyer or hirer acquired a good title, but the goods were never delivered to him[18]? Third, suppose the transferor does not initially pass a good title, but the transferee subsequently acquires one: he may buy off the true owner[19]; or an intermediate party may do so[20]; or D. may utilise the goods for the

---

11. See below, p. 408.
12. [1923] 2 K.B. 500, C.A. See generally Goff & Jones, *Law of Restitution*, pp. 343–346.
13. At p. 507. See also BANKES L.J., at p. 504.
14. In *Butterworth's Case*, [1954] 2 All E.R. 694 the plaintiff had eleven months' free use of the car.
15. See below, pp. 406–407.
16. E.g. *Rowland* v. *Divall* (above); *Butterworth's Case* (above).
17. E.g. such as occurred in *Niblett's Case*, [1921] 3 K.B. 387, C.A.: this case is set out above, p. 57.
18. It has been suggested that it follows from *Rowland* v. *Divall* that there will be no total failure of consideration—Atiyah, *op. cit.*, 39. *Contra* Samek (1959), 33 A.L.J. 392, 397.
19. E.g. *Whiteley, Ltd.* v. *Hilt*, [1918] 2 K.B. 808, C.A.
20. E.g. *Butterworth's Case* (above).

whole of their useful life, or otherwise destroy them[1]. Could D. still claim total failure of consideration? Would it make any difference if D. did not discover the defect in title until after it had been cured by an intermediate party[2]?

In view of these many difficulties, it is sometimes suggested that *Rowland* v. *Divall* is wrong; or, alternatively, that the implied condition as to title should be excised from this branch of the law[3]. Yet, many of the difficulties outlined above flow from the disregard of substantial enjoyment of possession if that enjoyment be tortious. Perhaps those difficulties would be resolved if this rule were reversed for both the contractual and quasi-contractual claim, and if it were made clear that the courts have a power of apportionment: D. would usually be reduced to claiming damages, would only receive compensation for his actual loss, and would have to account for any benefit gained[4].

3 THE IMPLIED WARRANTIES AS TO TITLE

Where there is a sale of goods, s. 12 of the S.G.A. provides that, unless a different intention appears, "there is":

"(2) An implied warranty that the buyer shall have and enjoy quiet possession of the goods:
(3) An implied warranty that the goods shall be free from any charge or encumbrance in favour of any third party, not declared or known to the buyer before or at the time when the contract is made".

It is still uncertain whether similar warranties will be implied by common law in a h.p. agreement; but, where a h.p. or conditional sale agreement falls within the H.P.A., s. 17 of that Act lays down that there "shall be implied":

"(b) a warranty that the hirer or buyer shall have and enjoy quiet possession of the goods:
(c) a warranty that the goods shall be free from any charge or encumbrance in favour of any third party at the time when the property is to pass".

Whilst the warranties implied by the S.G.A. may be excluded, those implied by the H.P.A. may not[5].

Not only will a breach of the implied condition as to title frequently

---

1. See the "whisky problem" in Atiyah, *Sale of Goods* (3rd Edn.) 38–39.
2. In *Butterworth's Case* (above), PEARSON J. felt some difficulty on this point. Compare Samek (1959), 33 A.L.J. 392, 398; Treitel, *Law of Contract* (3rd Edn.) 862; Atiyah, *op. cit.*, 38, note 1.   3. See Atiyah, *op. cit.*, 40.
4. See the *First Report on Exemption Clauses in Contracts*, para 16, Law Com. No. 24.
5. See above, pp. 55–56.

involve a breach of one or both of these warranties[6], but it has sometimes been doubted whether the warranties cover any cases which do not also amount to breaches of the implied condition. However, the usefulness of the implied warranties was demonstrated in *Lloyds and Scottish Finance, Ltd.* v. *Modern Cars, Ltd.*[7].

> In pursuance of a writ of execution, a sheriff took "walking possession" of a caravan occupied by the judgment debtor. But subsequently, the debtor sold the caravan to the defendant dealer, who removed it, and resold it to the plaintiff finance company as part of a directly financed h.p. transaction with W. By the dealer's invoice to the finance company, he expressly warranted that "the goods are . . . our sole property unencumbered and that we have the right to sell such goods free from any lien". Later, the sheriff seized the caravan, and W. repudiated the h.p. agreement. The plaintiffs claimed damages from the defendant for breach of warranty of title.

EDMUND DAVIES J. held that the sheriff had effectively seized the caravan by taking "walking possession" of it[8]; and he concluded that[9]

> "although the defendants transferred a good title in the caravan to the plaintiffs, they did so in breach of the express warranty in their dealer's invoice that it was unencumbered, and also in breach of the warranties as to quiet possession and freedom from encumbrance implied by s. 12 of the [S.G.A.]".

He therefore held that the plaintiffs were entitled to recover the price they paid for the caravan, the h.p. charges that were irrecoverable from the hirer, and also the expenses to which they had been put in asserting title to the caravan[10].

Even where the act of the defendant amounts to a breach of the condition and of either or both of the warranties as to title, it has been suggested that the scope of the warranties may be wider than that of the condition in the following respects:

(1) *Prima facie*, it might appear that additional damages could be recovered. In *Mason* v. *Burningham*[11], however, the buyer of a typewriter recovered the purchase price under s. 12 (1), and then successfully claimed under s. 12 (2) the money she had expended on having the machine overhauled. SINGLETON L.J. pointed out that the buyer could,

---

6. E.g. *Niblett's Case*, [1921] 3 K.B. 387, C.A. The buyer pleaded ss. 12 (1) & (2): only ATKIN L.J. referred to s. 12 (2), and he thought that there had been a breach of that subsection.
7. [1966] 1 Q.B. 764; [1964] 2 All E.R. 732. See also *Healing Sales Pty., Ltd.* v. *English Electrix Pty., Ltd.* (1968), 42 A.L.J.R. 280, H.C. (seller seized goods after delivery).
8. See below, p. 240.   9. At p. 781.
10. The measure and mitigation of damages are discussed below, pp. 416, 391.
11. [1949] 2 K.B. 545; [1949] 2 All E.R. 134, C.A.

at her option, have treated the breach of condition as a breach of warranty, and have recovered both the price and cost of overhaul under s. 12 (1). The conclusion would seem to be that the measure of damages is the same whichever subsection is pleaded[12].

(2) There may be a difference in the limitation period. The statutory condition is expressed to take effect at the time when the property is to pass, whereas the implied warranties are expressed *in futuro*. On the analogy of the covenants in respect of land, it has therefore been suggested that in the case of the condition the limitation period runs from sale, whereas in the case of the two warranties time does not begin to run until breach[13]. However, the analogy with sales of land was expressly rejected by LORD GREENE M.R. in *Mason* v. *Burningham*[14]; and it has been suggested that it would be a little odd if such a difference were brought about in such an obscure manner[15].

It has been argued that the implied warranty of freedom from encumbrances is a mistake, or of little importance[16]. But, suppose in the *Lloyds and Scottish Case*[17] the sheriff had not traced the caravan until some time after W. had paid all the instalments and exercised his option to purchase. Leaving aside any question of limitation of actions, the position would appear to be as follows: W. could claim for breach of the warranties of quiet possession and freedom from encumbrances; but the finance company could only claim for breach of the warranty that the goods be free from encumbrance, because there has been no interference with their quiet enjoyment whilst they had any right to enjoyment.

---

12. See further below, p. 416.
13. *Per* ATKIN L.J. in *Niblett's Case*, [1921] 3 K.B. 387, C.A., at p. 403. Supported by *Benjamin on Sale* (8th Edn.) 681, 683; Atiyah, *Sale of Goods* (3rd Edn.) 41; Cheshire & Fifoot, *Contract* (7th Edn.) 141.
14. [1949] 2 K.B. 545, C.A., at p. 563.
15. Atiyah, *Sale of Goods* (3rd Edn.) 41, note 6.
16. *Benjamin on Sale* (8th Edn.) 683; Crossley Vaines, *Personal Property* (4th Edn.) 334.
17. [1966] 1 Q.B. 764; [1964] 2 All E.R. 732.

CHAPTER 6

Undertakings as to Description and Quantity

1 INTRODUCTION

In a sense, the S.G.A. marks the beginning of the movement away from *caveat emptor*. It is true that the common law had to some extent modified its attitude where this was found to be excessively inconvenient or unfair; but the S.G.A. may have taken the process somewhat further when it laid down a number of implied terms. Sections 13 and 14 of the S.G.A. include three major implied conditions: that the goods correspond with their description (s. 13); that in a "trade sale"[1] they are merchantable under that description (s. 14 (2)); and that in a "trade sale" they are fit for the purpose for which they are supplied (s. 14 (1)). These provisions have since been more or less consistently interpreted by the courts in favour of the buyer. Particularly important has been the gradual extension of the scope of "sales by description": today it covers most if not all contracts for the sale of goods, with the result that all three implied conditions may today apply to almost any "trade sale". This development of the concept of sales by description is dealt with in s. 2 of this chapter.

The undertakings as to correspondence with description in both sale and h.p. transactions will be examined in the remainder of this chapter; but within the discussion the undertakings as to quantity will receive separate treatment because they are separately dealt with by the S.G.A. The undertakings as to fitness and merchantability will be considered in Chapter 7; and the undertakings in sale by sample will receive separate treatment in Chapter 8 because the S.G.A. in part makes separate provision for them (s. 15).

2 SALES BY DESCRIPTION[2]

The common law drew a sharp distinction between sales of specific goods and sales by description, and this dichotomy was adopted by Chalmers when he drafted the S.G.A. At its simplest, the dichotomy depended on the idea that a buyer would know the subject-matter of his

---

1. Where the seller is a dealer in goods of that description: see below, pp. 86, 101.
2. See generally, Montrose (1937), 15 Can.B.R. 760; Stoljar (1952), 15 M.L.R. 425, at pp. 441–445; and (1953), 16 M.L.R. 174.

contract either by acquaintance or by description.   However, perhaps because there are many cases which do not fall neatly into one or other of the two categories, the ambit of each of them was never clearly defined. *Benjamin* divides sales by description into two types[3]:

(1) Sales "of unascertained or future goods, as being of a certain kind or class, or to which otherwise a 'description' is applied".   Here, it is essential that the contract is by description, for in no other way can the parties achieve certainty of subject-matter[4].

(2) Sales "of specific goods, bought by the buyer in reliance, at least in some part, upon the description given, or to be tacitly inferred from the circumstances, and which identifies the goods".

Category (2) does not fit easily into any simple dichotomy of goods known *either* by acquaintance *or* description; and it has been within this category that the crucial developments have taken place.

The first step was to interpret the concept of sales by description to cover all sales of specific goods where the buyer had not seen the goods either before or at the time of contracting, but was relying on the description alone[5].   Then, the concept was extended to cover those situations where the buyer was contracting in the presence of goods which he had no opportunity to inspect before purchase, such as beer bought in a public house[6].   From this point, it was a small step to the decision in *Thornett* v. *Beers*[7]:

> The buyers of specific barrels of glue declined the invitation to inspect the glue as they were pressed for time.   The court accepted that this was a sale of goods by description for the purposes of the S.G.A., s. 14 (2), but the buyers failed on other grounds.

Within a few years, the courts appear to have been willing to find that there was a sale by description without troubling to enquire whether the parties were negotiating over goods in their actual presence.   Thus, in *Grant* v. *Australian Knitting Mills, Ltd.*[8] LORD WRIGHT said:

> "It may also be pointed out that there is a sale by description even though the buyer is buying something displayed before him on the counter: a thing is sold by description, though it is specific, so long as it is sold not merely as the specific thing but as a thing corresponding to a description, e.g. woollen undergarments, a hot-water bottle, a second-hand reaping machine, to select a few obvious illustrations".

In this case, the Privy Council decided that a retail sale of undergarments conducted across a shop-counter was a sale by description;

---

3. *On Sale* (8th Edn.) 615.
4. See *per* CHANNELL J. in *Varley* v. *Whipp*, [1900] 1 Q.B. 513, at p. 516.
5. *Varley* v. *Whipp* (above); set out below, p. 74.
6. *Wren* v. *Holt*, [1903] 1 K.B. 610, C.A.
7. [1919] 1 K.B. 486.   8. [1936] A.C. 85, at p. 100, P.C.

and in *Godley* v. *Perry*[9] EDMUND DAVIES J. accepted that a retail sale of a plastic catapult by a newsagent to a six year old boy was a sale by description. A striking case is *Beale* v. *Taylor*[10]:

> The seller advertised a 1961 Herald car for sale. The buyer inspected the car and agreed to buy it, but subsequently discovered something the seller had never realised all the time he had owned the car: that the rear half of the car was a 1961 Herald, but the front half was part of an earlier model, the two halves having been welded together.

The buyer succeeded before the Court of Appeal in his claim for damages for breach of the implied condition that the goods correspond with their description. In delivering the judgment of the Court, SELLERS L.J. said that, even if there were no other terms as to the state of the goods, fundamentally the seller was selling a 1961 Herald. However his Lordship did adopt one limitation to be found in *Chalmers*[11], namely, that the rule be confined to non-apparent defects, and that,

> "when the parties are really agreed on the thing sold, a misdescription of it in the contract may be immaterial".

Today, the position would appear to be that almost every sale, whether of specific or unascertained goods, is a sale by description, though the degree of detail attached to that description will depend on the circumstances. Even if the seller does not himself describe the goods to the buyer, either orally or in writing, it may be that any label attached to the goods may form part of the description and that the physical shape of the goods may itself amount to a description[12]. At this rate, almost every sale in a super-market could be a sale by description[13].

Whether all, or any, of this description does form part of the contractual description is, or should be, another question[14]. However, in *Beale* v. *Taylor*[15] SELLERS L.J. seemed to suggest that s. 13 of the S.G.A. somehow converted all descriptive statements into contractual terms. It is submitted that it is most unlikely that s. 13 has had such a revolutionary result, and that s. 13 pre-supposes that the description has been imported into the contract on ordinary principles. Indeed, perhaps the tidiest explanation of the cases is that every sale can be a sale by description, but in some circumstances part, or all, of that factual description

---

9. [1960] 1 All E.R. 36.   10. [1967] 3 All E.R. 253, C.A.
11. *Sale of Goods* (15th Edn.) 57.
12. See also Diamond (1960), 23 M.L.R. 200; Feltham (1969), J.B.L. 16, at p. 21.
13. But see the doubts expressed by the Law Commission in their *First Report on Exemption Clauses*, paras. 23–25 (Law Com. No. 24).
14. *Oscar Chess, Ltd.* v. *Williams*, [1957] 1 All E.R. 325, C.A.
15. [1967] 3 All E.R. 253, C.A.

never becomes part of the description in law.   Thus, a patent mis-description by the seller of goods which are in the presence of the parties will not usually become part of the contract because the parties will have evinced an intention to contract for *those* goods, regardless of descrip-tion[16].

3 UNDERTAKINGS AS TO DESCRIPTION

Section 13 of the S.G.A. lays down that:

> "Where there is a contract for the sale of goods by description, there is an implied condition that the goods shall correspond with the description; and, if the sale be by sample, as well as by description, it is not sufficient that the bulk of the goods corresponds with the sample if the goods do not also correspond with the description".

It would appear likely that the common law will apply a similar under-taking in h.p. agreements[17]; and, where the H.P.A. applies, s. 19 (2) of that Act provides:

> "Where goods are let under a hire-purchase agreement, or are agreed to be sold under a conditional sale agreement, and are so let or agreed to be sold by description, there shall be implied in the agree-ment a condition that the goods will correspond with the description; and if the goods are let or agreed to be sold under the agreement by reference to a sample, as well as by description, it shall not be sufficient that the bulk of the goods corresponds with the sample if the goods do not also correspond with the description".

The undertakings in sales by sample will be separately considered in Chapter 8; but, leaving these aside, we must now consider the effect of the undertaking that the goods "shall" or "will" correspond with the description.   Several points may be made at the outset.   First, it is rather misleading of the Acts to speak of implying such conditions when the condition will often be an express term of the contract[18].   Second, it has already been argued that s. 13 assumes that the description has become part of the contract according to ordinary principles[19].   Third, unlike the major conditions implied by the S.G.A., s. 14, the under-taking as to correspondence with description is implied whether or not the seller or owner is a dealer[20].   Fourth, if the description has a special trade usage, then the goods may have to comply with that specialised one rather than the ordinary one if it is possible to spell out an agreement

---

16. Compare Atiyah, *Sale of Goods* (3rd Edn.) 56.
17. See *Karsales, Ltd.* v. *Wallis*, [1956] 2 All E.R. 866, C.A., set out below, p. 141.
18. E.g. *Andrews Brothers, Ltd.* v. *Singer, Ltd.*, [1934] 1 K.B. 17, C.A.   Com-pare the *First Report on Exemption Clauses*, paras. 21–22 (Law Com. No. 24).   19. See above, pp. 69–70.
20. Compare s. 14, discussed below, Chapter 7.

by the parties to the term being used in the sense ascribed to it by the trade usage[1]. However, particularly if the trade usage was not known to one of the parties, it may be that there is no contract because the parties were never *ad idem* as to the description of the goods[2].

The extent of the duty that the goods comply with their description is dependent on the degree of precision of description[3]: if the description is vague, the duty may be minimal; and the better the description the more onerous the duty. But within this limitation, does every part of the description fall within the scope of this implied condition? Before the S.G.A. the common law position was as follows: the seller's descriptive statements as to the quality of the goods was a condition where the sale was by description, and a warranty where the sale was of specific goods; and, where the sale was by description, merchantable quality was regarded as being part of that description, so that the contract was regarded as being for the sale of merchantable goods of the designated kind[4]. It is now necessary to consider to what extent this is still the position since the S.G.A.: presumably, the position is the same under the H.P.A., s. 19 (2) as under the S.G.A., s. 13.

Where the identification of the goods depends on the description, s. 13 would appear to embody the common law. The leading case is *Arcos, Ltd.* v. *Ronaasen & Son, Ltd.*[5].

> There was a contract for the sale of a quantity of staves of $\frac{1}{2}''$ thickness. The buyer purported to reject the staves delivered on the grounds that they did not comply with the contract description. The arbitrator found that only 5% of the staves were of $\frac{1}{2}''$ thickness, but that the rest were nearly all less than $\frac{9}{16}''$ thick. Moreover, the staves were required, to the knowledge of the seller, to make cement barrels; and the arbitrator found that they were fit for this purpose, and that they were commercially within and merchantable under the contract description. He therefore held that the buyer was not entitled to reject.

This decision was reversed by WRIGHT J. who was unanimously upheld by the Court of Appeal and the House of Lords. LORD ATKIN said[6]:

> "It was contended that in all commercial contracts the question was whether there was 'substantial' compliance with the contract: there

---

1. E.g. *Grenfell* v. *E. B. Meyrowitz, Ltd.*, [1936] 2 All E.R. 1313, C.A. Compare *Andrews (Brothers) (Bournemouth), Ltd.* v. *Singer & Co., Ltd.*, [1934] 1 K.B. 17, C.A.
2. See *Peter Darlington, Ltd.* v. *Gosho, Ltd.*, [1964] 1 Lloyds Rep. 149. See further, the discussion on mistake, below, p. 122.
3. E.g. *Christopher Hill, Ltd.* v. *Ashington Piggeries, Ltd.*, [1969] 3 All E.R. 1496, C.A.; set out below, pp. 72–73.
4. *Benjamin on Sale* (8th Edn.) 644.
5. [1933] A.C. 470, H.L.   6. At pp. 479–480.

must always be some margin: and it is for the tribunal of fact to determine whether the margin is exceeded or not. I cannot agree. If the written contract specifies conditions of weight, measurement and the like, those conditions must be complied with. A ton does not mean about a ton, or a yard about a yard. Still less when you descend to minute measurements does ½ inch mean about ½ inch. If the seller wants a margin he must, and in my experience does, stipulate for it . . .

"No doubt there may be microscopic deviations which businessmen and therefore lawyers will ignore . . . But, apart from this consideration, the right view is that the conditions of the contract must be strictly performed".

A judicial attempt to modify the rule in *Arcos, Ltd.* v. *Ronaasen & Son, Ltd.* is to be found in *Steels and Busks, Ltd.* v. *Bleeker Bik & Co., Ltd.*[7]

After a series of dealings in similar materials between the parties, there was a sale of a quantity of pale pink rubber "quality as previously delivered", which turned out to be unfit for the buyer's purpose owing to the presence of some new chemical. The buyer sought damages, alleging breach of ss. 13, 14 (1), 14 (2) and 15 (2); but the arbitrator found in favour of the seller on the grounds that the buyer had not relied on the seller's skill and judgment, that the goods were of merchantable quality, and that the goods did correspond with their description.

The decision of the arbitrator was upheld by SELLERS J. The argument with reference to each of the other provisions will be taken up in due course[8], but in respect of s. 13 his Lordship said[9]:

"I think the present case bears no resemblance to [*Arcos, Ltd.* v. *Ronaasen & Son, Ltd.*]. I do not understand that the finding in the award [of the arbitrator] is that the goods approximated to or were near enough to the description, but that by the standard generally applied and accepted in the trade they complied with the description and were of the quality called for by the contract, quality not being affected by the chemical used . . ."

Whilst the decision of SELLERS J. does look very much like the findings of the arbitrator in *Arcos, Ltd.* v. *Ronaasen & Son, Ltd.*[10], it may be possible to justify the decision on the basis that the terminology used in this case had a special trade meaning. Thus, in *Christopher Hill, Ltd.* v. *Ashington Piggeries, Ltd.*[11],

The plaintiff manufacturers habitually undertook the compounding of animal feedstuffs to customers' formulae. The defendants asked

---

7. [1956] 1 Lloyds Rep. 228.
8. See below, pp. 92, 99, 108.   9. At p. 237.
10. [1933] A.C. 470, H.L. See Atiyah, *Sale of Goods* (3rd Edn.) 59.
11. [1969] 3 All E.R. 1496, C.A.

the plaintiffs to compound a vitamin-fortified mink food, to be called King Size, in accordance with a formula to be supplied by the defendants. The plaintiffs made it clear that they knew nothing about mink, but did suggest that herring meal should be substituted for one of the other ingredients. After making satisfactory deliveries for about 12 months, the plaintiffs began to make up the compound with herring meal purchased from N., under a contract which stipulated that it was "fair average quality of the season", and was to be taken "with all faults and defects . . . at a valuation". Unknown to any of the parties, that meal contained D.M.N.A., a chemical produced in the meal by chemical reaction. D.M.N.A was found to be harmless to other animals but (then unknown to the parties) toxic to mink. The plaintiffs sued for the price, the defendants counterclaimed for breach of the S.G.A., ss. 13, 14 (1) and (2), and the plaintiffs brought in N.

The decision of MILMO J.[12] that each seller was liable to his buyer was reversed by the Court of Appeal, the judgment of the court being delivered by DAVIES L.J. At this stage, we need only consider the argument on s. 13[13]. As between the plaintiffs and the defendants, their Lordships held that the compound did correspond with its description, the contract description being "King Size, meaning thereby a food compounded in accordance with an agreed formula", and DAVIES L.J. made the following points: first, the description did not include the suitability of the compound as a food for mink; and second, that D.M.N.A. was a condition of the herring meal, and not an additional unauthorised ingredient[14]. Nor did their Lordships think that there was a breach of s. 13 as between the plaintiffs and N.: they held that the contract description was "Norwegian Herring Meal, fair average quality of the season"; and that the goods complied therewith because that description related only "to such qualities as are apparent on an ordinary examination or analysis of the goods, such as is usually done in the trade in relation to such goods"[15].

The courts have shown themselves willing to extend the principle of *Arcos, Ltd.* v. *Ronaasen & Son, Ltd.* beyond the physical state of the goods themselves. Thus, the courts have held the following to be part of the description: the size of bags containing goods[16]; the average weight of parcels[17]; the date of the arrival of a ship in which the goods were being transported[18]; and that goods have been shipped

---

12. [1968] 1 Lloyds Rep. 457.
13. The other issues are considered below, pp. 87, 92, 101, 102.
14. At pp. 1510–1513. But see Patient (1970), 33 M.L.R. 565, at p. 566.
15. At pp. 1519–1522.
16. *Manbre Saccharine Co., Ltd.* v. *Corn Products, Ltd.*, [1919] 1 K.B. 198.
17. *Ballantine & Co.* v. *Cramp and Bosman* (1923), 129 L.T. 502.
18. *Macpherson Train & Co., Ltd.* v. *Ross & Co., Ltd.*, [1955] 2 All E.R. 445.

under-deck[19]. A particularly striking case is *Re Moore, Ltd.*[20].

> There was a contract for the sale of a quantity of Australian canned fruit, described as being in cases of 30 tins each. Subsequently, the buyer sought to reject on the grounds that half the cases contained only 24 tins instead of 30. The arbitrator found that the contract quantity was delivered, and that there was no difference in the market value of the goods, whether packed in cases of 24 or 30 tins.

ROWLATT J. held that the buyer was entitled to reject for breach of ss. 13 and 30 (3); and this decision was unanimously affirmed by the Court of Appeal, though on slightly different grounds[1]. Of course, it may be that the buyer had contracted to resell these goods to different persons in multiples of 30 tins; but this does not seem to have been the case. It appears that the buyer was merely looking for an excuse to reject[2]. But this is not to say that any breach, however minute, will entitle the buyer to reject: "microscopic deviations" will be ignored, though the scope of this exception is very limited[3].

Where the goods sold by description are really specific, the question arises whether s. 13 has altered the law by elevating what was previously a warranty as to quality to the status of a condition by making it part of the description. In *Varley* v. *Whipp*[4]

> The defendant agreed to buy a second-hand reaping machine which he had never seen, but which the plaintiff seller stated to have been "new the previous year" and very little used. On discovering that the machine did not comply with this description, the defendant returned the reaper to the plaintiff. The defendant pleaded breach of s. 13 as a defence to the plaintiff's action for the price.

CHANNELL J. held that this was a sale by description[5], and that the buyer was entitled to reject for breach of s. 13[6]. His Lordship seems to have thought that s. 13 had not altered the law[7], and that it was still necessary to distinguish the description of the goods from collateral warranties[8]. A similar view of s. 13 was taken by BAILHACHE J. in *Harrison* v. *Knowles and Foster*[9] though his Lordship contrived to come to the opposite answer.

---

19. *White Sea Trust Timber, Ltd.* v. *North, Ltd.*, [1933] 148 L.T. 263. See *Fisher, Reeves & Co.* v. *Armour & Co.*, [1920] 3 K.B. 614, C.A. (ex-store).
20. [1921] 2 K.B. 519, C.A.   1. See below, pp. 78–79.
2. Compare the restrictions on the buyer's right to reject discussed below, p. 397. Why should the buyer have such a wide right of rejection under s. 13?
3. *Margaronis Navigation Agency, Ltd.* v. *Peabody & Co. of London, Ltd.*, [1965] 2 Q.B. 430, C.A. See also *Moralice, Ltd.* v. *Man*, [1954] 2 Lloyds Rep. 526.   4. [1900] 1 Q.B. 513.   5. See above, p. 68.
6. It was difficult to reconcile this decision with ss. 11 (1) (c), 18. See below, p. 162.
7. *Sed quaere?* Compare above, p. 67.   8. Esp. at p. 515.
9. [1917] 2 K.B. 606. Affd. on other grounds; [1918] 1 K.B. 608, C.A.

In the course of negotiations over the sale of certain ships, the seller furnished the buyer with certain written particulars, which included a statement that the deadweight capacity of each ship was 460 tons. The buyer subsequently agreed to buy the ships, and signed a memorandum of sale which did not refer to the written particulars. After delivery, the buyer discovered that the deadweight capacity of each ship was only 360 tons, and sought damages.

As the contract excluded liability for breach of warranty, but not for breach of condition, the buyer could only succeed if he could show that there had been a breach of condition. BAILHACHE J. sought to distinguish between conditions and warranties as to description in sales of existing specific chattels as follows[10]:

> "a statement as to some quality possessed by or attaching to such chattel is a warranty, and not a condition, unless the absence of such quality or the possession of it to a smaller extent makes the thing sold different in kind from the thing as described in the contract. Applying this principle here, . . . it seems to me that the difference is essentially one of degree and not of kind, and that the statement as to deadweight capacity was a warranty and not a condition".

His Lordship's decision in favour of the seller was affirmed by the Court of Appeal on the preliminary point that the representation as to deadweight never became a term of the contract[11]; but all three members of the Court of Appeal doubted the criterion suggested by BAILHACHE J.[12]. Certainly, it is difficult to distinguish between *Varley* v. *Whipp* and *Harrison* v. *Knowles and Foster* according to the criterion suggested by BAILHACHE J. However, it has been suggested that it may be possible to reconcile the two cases on the following basis: where the buyer relies wholly on the description *Varley* v. *Whipp* applies; but where the buyer sees the goods then *Harrison* v. *Knowles and Foster* obtains[13]. On the other hand, this may be thought to introduce undesirable complications, so that it may be better to choose between the two cases. Whether the cases are reconciled, or one chosen in preference to the other, it seems clear that s. 13 has brought about a change in the law, and the real question is as to the extent of this change[14].

Finally, some consideration must be given to the effect of any exclusion clause. Whilst this subject will be examined in more general

---

10. At p. 610. Accepted by SALMOND J. in *Taylor* v. *Combined Buyers, Ltd.*, [1924] N.Z.L.R. 627, at pp. 641–644. See also Feltham (1969), J.B.L. 12, 22–24.
11. But see now s. 2 (1) of the Misrepresentation Act 1967, below, p. 121.
12. See esp. PICKFORD L.J., at p. 609.
13. Stoljar (1953), 16 M.L.R. 174, at pp. 185–186.
14. Compare Stoljar, *ibid.*, and Atiyah, *Sale of Goods* (3rd Edn.) 57.

terms in Chapter 11, it is convenient to discuss here the effect of exclusion clauses on breaches of undertakings as to description[15]. Of course, the clause will be construed strictly, as against the *proferens*[16]; but a distinction must also be drawn between those clauses which exclude and those which limit liability: the clause may either prevent any obligation from arising or merely limit liability for breach of an obligation once it has arisen[17]. If the contract goods are unascertained, an attempt to *exclude* all undertakings as to description would destroy any certainty of subject-matter[18]; but this argument would not obtain where the contract goods are specific. Thus, if the only objection to clauses excluding undertakings as to description was on grounds of certainty of subject-matter[19], the position would appear to be as follows: the seller could always *limit* his liability: he could *exclude* it where the contract were for the sale of specific goods; and, even where the contract were for the sale of unascertained goods, he could probably *exclude* liability for such trivial breaches as those which occurred in *Arcos, Ltd.* v. *Ronaasen & Son, Ltd.*[20]. Finally, it should be noticed that, where a transaction falls within the H.P.A., that Act avoids any provision purporting to exclude or modify the undertaking as to description implied by s. 19 (s. 29 (3) (c)).

4 UNDERTAKINGS AS TO QUANTITY

Section 30 of the S.G.A. makes it clear that it is the seller's duty to deliver the contract quantity of the specified goods[1]. Of course, s. 30 is dealing with express conditions, whereas s. 13 is devoted to implied ones; but, in a sense, s. 30 is clearly an aspect of the undertaking as to description found in s. 13. No doubt, the fact that the two provisions are to be found in different Parts of the Act follows from the scheme of arrangement adopted. However, there may also be a distinction in substance between the two sections in the following: where the breach is merely as to quality, it will usually be clear that the seller is merely performing defectively, whereas a tender of a different quantity of goods is far more likely to show an intention to make a counter-offer[2].

---

15. See generally, Coote, *Exceptions Clauses*, Chapter 3; and also below, Chapter 11.
16. See *Munro & Co., Ltd.* v. *Meyer*, [1930] 2 K.B. 312; *Harrison* v. *Knowles and Foster*, [1918] 1 K.B. 608, C.A.; *Nicholson and Venn* v. *Smith-Marriott* (1947), 177 L.T. 189; *Christopher Hill, Ltd.* v. *Ashington Piggeries, Ltd.*, [1969] 3 All E.R. 1496, C.A., at pp. 1522–1523 (the exclusion clause in the contract between the plaintiffs and N.). See generally below, pp. 138–145.
17. See below, p. 137.
18. See *Benjamin on Sale* (8th Edn.) 622–623.
19. See *First Report on Exclusion Clauses in Contracts*, para. 21 (Law Com. No. 24): see further below, pp. 141–145.
20. See Atiyah, *Sale of Goods* (3rd Edn.) 61.
 1. See below, Chapter 16.   2. *Sed quaere?*

Whether a tender of delivery amounts to a defective performance or a counter-offer may depend on what constitutes a performance. As in the case of s. 13 exact performance is required, subject to two exceptions. First, s. 30 (4) lays down that:

> "The provisions of this section are subject to any usage of trade, special agreement, or course of dealing between the parties".

Whilst allowing for the importation of a special trade meaning[3] or an agreed tolerance[4], this provision also envisages that the parties may contract beforehand as to what is to happen if the seller is in breach of his duty under s. 30. Second, the strict duty of performance is qualified by the *de minimis* rule in a manner similar to that of s. 13, and the courts have likewise been strict in their interpretation of this exception[5]. Subject to these exceptions, s. 30 lays down the following rules:

(1) Section 30 (1) provides that:

> "where the seller delivers to the buyer a quantity of goods less than he contracted to sell, the buyer may reject them, but if the buyer accepts the goods so delivered he must pay for them at the contract rate".

In *Behrend & Co.* v. *Produce Brokers, Co.*[6].

> There was a contract for the sale of 700 tons of cotton seed *ex* the *Port Inglis*. The ship discharged 37 tons in London, and then left for Hull in order to discharge there other goods which had been loaded on top of the remainder of the seed. Without undue delay, the ship returned to London and discharged the remainder of the cotton seed.

BAILHACHE J. held that the buyer was entitled to keep the part actually delivered and pay for it at the contract rate, and to reject the balance of the goods and reclaim the remainder of the price as on total failure of consideration[7]. In a subsequent case, WRIGHT J. held that the buyer could not be taken to have exercised the option conferred on him by s. 30 (1) unless and until he knew the true facts[8].

---

3. See above, pp. 70–71.
4. E.g. *Shipton Anderson & Co.* v. *Weil Brothers*, [1912] 1 K.B. 574.
5. Compare *Shipton Anderson & Co.* v. *Weil Brothers* (above) with *Wilensko Slasko Towarzy Stwo Drewno* v. *Fenwick & Co., Ltd.*, [1938] 2 All E.R. 429. And see *per* DIPLOCK L.J. in *Margaronis Navigation Agency, Ltd.* v. *Peabody & Co. of London, Ltd.*, [1965] 2 Q.B. 430, C.A., at p. 448.
6. [1920] 3 K.B. 530.
7. See below, p. 408. An alternative explanation is that recovery was made on the basis of money held and received.
8. *Barrow, Lane and Ballard, Ltd.* v. *Phillips & Co., Ltd.*, [1929] 1 K.B. 574: set out below, p. 252. Compare rescission: below, p. 400.

(2) Section 30 (2) provides that:

> "Where the seller delivers to the buyer a quantity of goods larger than he contracted to sell, the buyer may accept the goods included in the contract and reject the rest, or he may reject the whole. If the buyer accepts the whole of the goods so delivered he must pay for them at the contract rate".

Thus, if the seller sends too many goods of the contract type, this rule saves the buyer from the trouble and expense of separating the contract goods from the others.

(3) Section 30 (3) provides that:

> "Where the seller delivers to the buyer the goods he contracted to sell mixed with goods of a different description not included in the contract, the buyer may accept the goods which are in accordance with the contract and reject the rest, or he may reject the whole".

It should be noticed immediately that, unlike subsections (1) and (2), this provision does not say that the buyer has the option to accept the goods delivered. Are we to infer from this that in s. 30 (3) the buyer does not have such an option[9]?

The wording of s. 30 (3) seems to cause some difficulty as to the scope of the provision. The difficulties start with the meaning of the words "mixed with", and the two possible meanings of those words may be illustrated by reference to a contract for the sale of a bag of beans: first, "mixed with" may mean *intermixed*, e.g. where there are some peas included in the bag of beans delivered; second, the phrase may mean *accompanied by*, e.g. where a bag of peas is delivered together with the bag of beans. In *Barker, Ltd.* v. *Agius, Ltd.*[10], SALTER J. indicated that, had the matter been of first impression, he would have taken the view that the subsection covered the situation where the seller delivered *all* the contract goods *intermixed* with other goods. However, his Lordship recognised that s. 30 (3) had been interpreted in *Re Moore, Ltd.*[11] to apply to the situation where the seller tried to deliver just the contract goods, but part of those goods did not comply with the contract description. This gives rise to several difficulties:

(a) Does "mixed with" mean only *accompanied by*, or does it also include *intermixed*? The former view was taken by ROWLATT J. in *Re Moore, Ltd.*[12]; and, on this basis, it has been suggested that where the goods are *intermixed* the buyer's right to reject depends on s. 13,

---

9. See further, below, p. 79.
10. (1927), 33 Com. Cas. 120, at p. 132.
11. [1921] 2 K.B. 519, C.A.: set out above, p. 74. See also *Dawood, Ltd.* v. *Heath*, [1961] 2 Lloyds Rep. 512.
12. At first instance: [1921] 1 K.B. 73, at p. 76.

not on s. 30 (3)[13]. However, whilst SALTER J. reluctantly followed *Re Moore, Ltd.*[14] he does not appear to have considered that the decision necessarily restricted "mixed with" to the one meaning; and it may therefore be that s. 30 (3) is apt to cover both situations.

(b) How much of the contract goods need be delivered before s. 30 (3) is applicable? SALTER J. appears to have taken the view that, *prima facie*, the provision only covered the situation where the seller delivered *all* the contract goods *plus* some other goods; but he felt bound by *Re Moore, Ltd.* to hold that the subsection also covered the situation where the seller delivered part of the contract goods, and also some goods of a "different description"[14].

It has already been observed that in one sense s. 30 merely deals with an aspect of the undertaking to be found in s. 13. Yet there is a good reason for distinguishing between the two situations. The availability of the right to reject may vary according to whether the goods tendered constitute merely a defective performance or a counter-offer: if the latter, the "buyer" must always have a right to reject the offer; but in the former situation the availability of the right to reject may be restricted by the terms of the contract or the general law[15]. By expressly giving the buyer a right to accept the whole of the goods delivered, s. 30 (1) and (2) seem to envisage that the delivery will constitute a counter-offer; and it has been argued that the position should be the same under s. 30 (3)[16]. Assuming that s. 30 gives way to a contrary intention[17], the position would appear to be as follows: a breach of s. 30 will *prima facie* amount to a counter-offer, whereas a breach of s. 13 will *prima facie* merely amount to a defective performance.

Section 30 of the S.G.A. will, of course, apply not merely to sales *simpliciter*, but also to credit and conditional sales. What of h.p. transactions? In so far as s. 30 is merely an enactment of the ordinary common law rules of offer and acceptance, the same position will presumably apply in h.p. The H.P.A. does not mention the matter; but this is not really surprising, since the sort of transaction envisaged by that Act will usually involve just one item of a given description, and the rules as to quality will be far more important than the rules as to quantity.

---

13. Fridman, *Sale of Goods*, 211.
14. See below, p. 398.
15. For the restrictions imposed by law, see below, p. 397.
16. Atiyah, *Sale of Goods* (3rd Edn.) 53. But how is the price to be fixed?
17. Section 30 does not expressly state that it is to give way to a contrary intention; but there is a general provision to this effect in s. 55: set out below, p. 132.

CHAPTER 7

Undertakings as to Fitness and Merchantability

I INTRODUCTION

The S.G.A. probably narrowed the scope of the maxim *caveat emptor* by providing that, subject to a contrary intention, there shall be implied into a contract of sale conditions as to the merchantable quality of goods and their fitness for the purpose for which they are supplied[1]. On the other hand, it does largely reproduce the common law in respect of these two undertakings. The position before the Act was as follows: where there was a sale by description, there was an implied condition that the goods were merchantable under that description[2]; and where there was a sale of specific goods there might be an undertaking as to fitness. However, by the process of judicial interpretation, the ambit of the two undertakings has been increased in much the same way as that of the undertaking that the goods correspond with their description[3]. The result is that today all three undertakings may apply in many cases, and it has been pointed out that the three represent a series of graduated duties[4]. The undertaking as to correspondence with description applies to almost all sales, but may offer the buyer only minimal protection. The undertaking as to merchantability affords a greater degree of protection to the buyer, though it does not cover such a wide area: goods may correspond with their description and still be unmerchantable. The greatest degree of protection is that afforded by the undertaking as to fitness, which applies in still more limited circumstances: this undertaking may be broken even though the goods correspond with their description and are merchantable under it.

In this chapter, the two undertakings of fitness and merchantability will be considered separately. However, before so doing, it is convenient to mention several points which they have in common.

---

1. See *per* Lord BUCKMASTER in *Manchester Liners, Ltd.* v. *Rea, Ltd.*, [1922] 2 A.C. 74, H.L., at p. 79.
2. It has already been pointed out that Chalmers separated the two undertakings that the goods (1) comply with their description, and (2) were merchantable under it—see above, p. 71.
3. "There has been a tendency to construe [the undertaking as to merchantability] too narrowly and to compensate for that by giving a wide construction to [the undertaking as to fitness]". *Per* Lord REID in *Henry Kendall & Sons* v. *William Lillico & Sons, Ltd.*, [1969] 2 A.C. 31, H.L., at p. 79.   4. Atiyah, *Sale of Goods* (3rd Edn.) 55.

(1) The undertakings apply not just to the contract goods, but also to other goods "supplied under the contract of sale". Thus, in *Geddling* v. *Marsh*[5]

> The plaintiff shop-keeper purchased bottles of mineral water from the defendant manufacturer on the basis that one penny was return-able on every bottle the shop-keeper returned to the manufacturer. Whilst the plaintiff was handling a bottle, it burst and injured her.

Despite the fact that the contract in respect of the bottles seems to have been one of hire rather than sale, the plaintiff successfully claimed damages before the Divisional Court: BAILHACHE J. pointed out that the goods could not be supplied except in some sort of container; and BRAY J. found support in the fact that the opening words of the relevant provision of the S.G.A. (s. 14) speaks of "goods supplied under the contract of sale". A spectacular application of those statutory words by the Court of Appeal is to be found in the case of *Wilson* v. *Rickett Cockerell, Ltd.*[6].

> The plaintiff purchased a ton of Coalite from the defendant coal merchant. Subsequently, the plaintiff was injured when there was an explosion in the grate by reason of the inclusion of an explosive substance in the consignment.

The Court of Appeal unanimously rejected the defendant's plea that there was nothing wrong with the Coalite as Coalite, and DENNING L.J. explained[7]:

> "Coal is not bought by the lump. It is bought by the sack, or by the hundred-weight or by the ton. The consignment is delivered as a whole and must be considered as a whole; not in bits. A sack of coal, which contains a hidden detonator, is not fit for burning, and no sophistry should lead us to believe that it is fit . . .
>
> "It is no answer for the seller to say that there was nothing wrong with the coal as coal. There was a great deal wrong with the con-signment as a consignment".

(2) If it is in the contemplation of the parties that something be done to the goods by the buyer before they are used, they must comply with the undertaking after, though not necessarily before, this has been done[8].

(3) The buyer will, *prima facie*, be able to reject the goods where only part of them do not comply with the undertaking, except in the follow-ing circumstances: (a) the contract is severable; or (b) the *de minimis* rule applies. Both exceptions were considered in *Jackson* v. *Rotax Motor and Cycle Co.*[9].

---

5. [1920] 1 K.B. 668, D.C.
6. [1954] 1 Q.B. 598, C.A.   7. At p. 606.
8. *Heil* v. *Hedges*, [1951] 1 T.L.R. 512.   9. [1910] 2 K.B. 937, C.A.

A contract for the sale of about 600 motor horns provided for delivery at the buyer's request; and, at his request, the goods were delivered to a certain carrier in 19 cases at varying dates over a period of two months. Upon delivery of the last case, the buyer inspected the goods, and he thereupon determined to reject the whole of them, except for one case which he had legally accepted by reason of his having resold it. The buyer alleged that 364 horns were defective; but the official referee found that the horns were substantially in accordance with the contract, and that "most if not all . . . could at a very slight cost have been made merchantable".

The Court of Appeal unanimously held that each consignment must be treated as a separate contract[10], so that acceptance of one case did not bar rejection of the others[11], and that the goods were not of merchantable quality so that the buyer might reject them. Their Lordships rejected the attempt to apply the *de minimis* rule, and said that if the buyer had to expend money on the goods to make them saleable, albeit a trifling amount, there was a breach of the undertaking[12].

(4) There is the question of for how long after delivery the goods must continue to comply with the undertaking. The common law took the view that the goods ought to comply with the undertaking for long enough for the buyer to deal with them in the ordinary way of business[13]; but for some time after the passage of the S.G.A. it was thought that this rule might have been abrogated by s. 33 of the Act[14]. In *Mash and Murrell, Ltd.* v. *Joseph I. Emmanuel, Ltd.*[15]

The plaintiff dealer contracted to buy c. & f. from the defendant 2,000 half-bags of Cyprus Spring potatoes then afloat the SS. Ionian bound for Liverpool. The seller knew that the potatoes were required for human consumption. After a normal voyage, the goods were found on arrival to be unfit for human consumption; and the buyer alleged breach of ss. 14 (1) and (2).

Having held as a fact that the potatoes were not fit to travel to Liverpool when they were loaded in Cyprus, DIPLOCK J. held that there had been a breach of both undertakings. His Lordship explained[16]:

"A necessary and inevitable deterioration during transit which will render [the goods] unmerchantable upon arrival is normally one for which the seller is liable".

---

10. See below, p. 277.
12. See COZENS HARDY M.R., at p. 943.
13. *Beer* v. *Walker* (1877), 46 L.J.Q.B. 677.
14. This section is considered below, pp. 244–245.
15. [1961] 1 All E.R. 485; reversed on a question of fact: [1962] 1 All E.R. 77, C.A.
16. At p. 493.

11. See below, p. 398.

This decision was reversed by the Court of Appeal simply on the grounds that there was insufficient evidence on which DIPLOCK J. could have based his finding of fact[17].

(5) Do the undertakings apply where the contract goods are not in the United Kingdom at the time when the property is to pass[18]?

(6) Does the designation of the statutory undertakings as conditions mean that any similar common law undertakings will also be regarded as conditions[19]?

2 UNDERTAKINGS AS TO FITNESS

1 The undertakings

In the absence of an express undertaking as to the fitness of goods, such an undertaking may only be imported by operation of law. In the case of sales, s. 14 (1) of the S.G.A. provides as follows:

> "Where the buyer, expressly or by implication, makes known to the seller the particular purpose for which the goods are required, so as to show that the buyer relies on the seller's skill or judgment, and the goods are of a description which it is in the course of the seller's business to supply (whether he be the manufacturer or not), there is an implied condition that the goods shall be reasonably fit for such purpose, provided that in the case of a contract for the sale of a specified article under its patent or other trade name, there is no implied condition as to its fitness for any particular purpose".

Comparatively recently, it has been settled that the common law will imply a similar obligation into h.p. transactions[20]. Where a h.p. or conditional sale falls within the H.P.A., s. 17 (4) of that Act provides:

> "Where the hirer under a hire-purchase agreement, or the buyer under a conditional sale agreement, whether expressly or by implication—
>
> (a) has made known to the owner or seller, or to a servant or agent of the owner or seller, the particular purpose for which the goods are required, or
>
> (b) in the course of any antecedent negotiations has made that purpose known to any other person by whom those negotiations were conducted, or to a servant or agent of such a person, there shall, subject to the provisions of section 18 of this Act, be implied a condition that the goods will be reasonably fit for that purpose".

---

17. The burden of proof is discussed by Sassoon (1965), 28 M.L.R. 180, 191–192.
18. This is primarily a problem of conflict: see Dicey & Morris, *Conflict of Laws* (8th Edn.) Rules 128–129; Goode & Ziegel, *Hire Purchase and Conditional Sales*, Part V; Uniform Law on International Sales Act 1967.
19. See above, p. 52.
20. *Yeoman Credit, Ltd.* v. *Apps*, [1962] 2 Q.B. 508, C.A., esp. *per* HOLROYD PEARCE L.J., at p. 516.

Section 18 (4) lays down the conditions under which the undertaking may be excluded[1].

In the next three subsections, we shall consider (1) the content of the undertakings as to fitness, (2) the limitations on them, and (3) exclusion of the undertakings.

2 **The content of the undertakings**

The S.G.A. requires that the goods be "reasonably fit" for the purpose for which they are supplied. Whether the goods are "reasonably fit" must be tested in relation to the purpose for which they are supplied, and must depend on the degree of precision with which that purpose is specified. For instance, in *Christopher Hill, Ltd.* v. *Ashington Piggeries, Ltd.*[2] the Court of Appeal held that the plaintiffs' claim against N. under s. 14 (1) failed, *inter alia*, because they could not show[3] "that the herring meal sold was not suitable as food for at least one type of animal to which this herring meal could fairly and reasonably have been expected to be fed (in which case it might not matter that mink was not a type of animal to which herring meal would normally be fed)"[4]. The words "reasonably fit" must now be examined.

The statutory undertaking by the seller that the goods are "reasonably fit" does not imply that his liability is to be founded on carelessness. On the contrary, his liability is strict, as may be seen from *Frost* v. *Aylesbury Dairy Co.*[5]:

> Typhoid germs were found in milk sold for "family use". As these germs could only be discovered by prolonged scientific investigation, the sellers argued that they could not reasonably have discovered the defect by the exercise of reasonable care.

Notwithstanding this, the Court of Appeal unanimously held the sellers liable for breach of s. 14 (1). Nor is it any answer for the seller to plead that he promised two contradictory things, so that in *Baldry* v. *Marshall*[6] the seller was held liable for breach of s. 14 (1) in promising to sell a Bugatti car that was suitable for touring. Thus, the seller is under a strict duty to see that the goods are "reasonably fit". How-

---

1. See below, p. 93.
2. [1969] 3 All E.R. 1496, C.A.: see above, p. 72.
3. The plaintiffs alleged that the meal should be reasonably fit for the particular purpose of "inclusion in animal feeding-stuffs to be compounded by the plaintiffs".
4. At p. 1523. This test is related to the question of remoteness: see below, p. 388.
5. [1905] 1 K.B. 608, C.A.: see also *Preist* v. *Last*, [1903] 2 K.B. 148, C.A.; and *Henry Kendall & Sons, Ltd.* v. *William Lillico & Sons, Ltd.*, [1969] 2 A.C. 31, H.L. (set out below, p. 88).
6. [1925] 1 K.B. 260, C.A.: see also below, p. 90. Cf. *Lynch* v. *Thorne*, [1956] 1 All E.R. 744, C.A.

ever, the seller's duty, though strict, is necessarily limited by the nature of the undertaking. In *Griffiths* v. *Peter Conway, Ltd.*[7].

> The plaintiff contracted dermatitis from a Harris Tweed coat which she had purchased from the defendants. It was found as a fact that the plaintiff had an unusually sensitive skin, and that the coat would not have harmed a normal person.

The Court of Appeal held that there was no breach of s. 14 (1); and Lord GREENE M.R. explained that, if a person suffering from such abnormality desires to obtain the benefit of the implied condition[8]:

> "The essential matter for the seller to know . . . consists in the particular abnormality or idiosyncrasy from which the buyer suffers. It is only when he has that knowledge that he is in a position to exercise his skill or judgment . . . The fact that those essential characteristics are not known . . . to the buyer does not seem to me to affect the question".

His Lordship would seem to be implying that, if the plaintiff had made known her particular abnormality to the seller, then the seller would have been in breach of s. 14 (1)[9]. Certainly, if the buyer does make clear to the seller the particular purpose for which he requires the goods the seller may be strictly liable, notwithstanding that he could not reasonably have prevented the harm[10], nor even that the buyer himself was unaware of the possibility of harm[11]. Alternatively, it may be that the circumstances show that the seller's duty is merely to warn the buyer of possible hazards connected with the purpose for which the goods are required[12].

What is the ambit of this strict liability? According to Lord GREENE in *Griffiths* v. *Peter Conway, Ltd.*[13], it might seem that the seller should be liable for any injury to the buyer which flows from the range of "essential characteristics" made known. Yet it is submitted that there must be some limitation on the rule. The burden of the rule must be limited by the circumstances of the transaction: A., who buys a 1937 car for £50 cannot expect it to be as fit for driving as the

---

7. [1939] 1 All E.R. 685, C.A.   8. At p. 691.
9. But could the buyer realistically expect the seller to know about the effect of the garment on her skin? Compare the cases in note 10 with the discussion of reliance below, pp. 90–93.
10. E.g. *Frost* v. *Aylesbury Dairy Co.*, [1905] 1 K.B. 608, C.A.; *Henry Kendall & Sons, Ltd.* v. *William Lillico & Sons, Ltd.*, [1969] 2 A.C. 31, H.L.
11. *Henry Kendall & Sons, Ltd.* v. *William Lillico & Sons, Ltd.*, [1969] 2 A.C. 31, H.L. See also *Sumner, Permain & Co.* v. *Webb*, [1922] 1 K.B. 55, C.A.: set out below, pp. 95–96, where the C.A. decided against the buyer on other grounds. Contra *Christopher Hill, Ltd.* v. *Ashington Piggeries, Ltd.*, [1969] 3 All E.R. 1496, C.A.: but see *Patient* (1970), 33 M.L.R. 565, 568–569.
12. E.g. *Vacwell Engineering Co., Ltd.* v. *B.D.H. Chemicals, Ltd.*, [1969] 3 All E.R. 1681: set out below, p. 389.
13. [1939] 1 All E.R. 685, C.A.

1959 car purchased by B. for £500; and B. cannot expect his car to be as fit as the new car purchased by C. for £1,000[14]. It may be that this is the proper meaning of the words "reasonably fit": the goods must be as fit for the purpose supplied as goods of that description and in those circumstances usually are[15].

Where the H.P.A. applies, the same words "reasonably fit" are used (s. 17 (4)); and there has been a tendency on the part of the courts to use the same expression to describe the common law undertaking[16]. Does the expression mean the same in these contexts as within the S.G.A.? The problem is whether to apply to h.p. the rules of sale or hire. Whereas in sale the duty is a strict one, in simple hire it has been variously formulated as follows[17]:

    (1) An undertaking to exercise reasonable care[18];

    (2) Strict liability, except for latent defects[19]; or

    (3) Strict liability, even for latent defects[20].

In relation to h.p. (1) is open to the objection that it does not go beyond the ordinary duty of care in the tort of negligence[1]. There is much to be said for adopting (3), which would bring the rule into line with that in sale. However, judicial pronouncements would seem to favour (2)[2]. The matter is as yet unresolved.

3 The qualifications of the undertakings

The statutory provisions embodying the undertakings as to fitness contain a number of qualifications, though unfortunately these qualifications are by no means the same in each case. The qualifications are as follows:

1. Sales by a dealer. Section 14 (1) of the S.G.A. only applies where

> "the goods are of a description which it is in the course of the seller's business to supply (whether he be the manufacturer or not)".

A similar limitation is imposed by the implied undertaking as to merchantable quality in the S.G.A. (s. 14 (2))[3]; but no such restriction

---

14. Would the M.O.T. test have any effect on the position?

15. And see Lord PEARCE in *Henry Kendall & Sons, Ltd.* v. *William Lillico & Sons, Ltd.*, [1969] 2 A.C. 31, H.L., at p. 115.

16. See PARKER L.J. in *Karsales (Harrow), Ltd.* v. *Wallis*, [1956] 2 All E.R. 866, at p. 870, C.A.; and HARMAN L.J. in *Yeoman Credit, Ltd.* v. *Apps*, [1962] 2 Q.B. 508, at p. 522, C.A.

17. See Guest, *Law of H.P.* 277; Paton, *Bailment* 289–299.

18. *Mowbray* v. *Merryweather*, [1895] 2 Q.B. 640, C.A. Cf. *Hadley* v. *Droitwich Construction, Ltd.*, [1967] 3 All E.R. 911.

19. *Hyman* v. *Nye* (1881), 6 Q.B.D. 685; but see Goode, *H.P. Law & Practice* (2nd Edn.) 233–235.

20. *Bentley Brothers* v. *Metcalfe*, [1906] 2 K.B. 548, C.A.

  1. Guest, *Law of H.P.* 278.

  2. See *Yeoman Credit, Ltd.* v. *Apps*, [1962] 2 Q.B. 508; [1961] 2 All E.R. 281, C.A., set out below, pp. 141–142.   3. See below, p. 101.

is to be found in the H.P.A., s. 17 (4). The limitation in s. 14 (1) makes it clear that, under the S.G.A., the seller must be a dealer in the class of goods sold; and it has been held that the words in brackets do not imply that the undertaking is only to be applicable to manufactured goods[4]. In *Spencer Trading Ltd.* v. *Devon*[5] the court accepted that it was sufficient that the goods fall within the general description of goods supplied by the seller, although in a particular instance they take a special form or are designed for a special use. Whilst approving that case, the Court of Appeal in *Christopher Hill, Ltd.* v. *Ashington Piggeries, Ltd.*[6] held that it was not in the course of his business for the plaintiff manufacturer of animal foodstuffs to compound mink food, this being the first arrangement under which he had ever done so, although he had supplied the buyer with quantities of the mink food over a period of about a year[7]. Whether the particular goods contracted for fall within the ambit of the seller's business is a question of degree. In practice, the effect of the limitation would seem to be that only manufacturers, wholesalers, retailers and dealers will be caught[8]; but it is submitted that only sales which such persons make in the course of business as opposed to those made by private treaty are within the provision. The Law Commission have recommended that any article sold in the course of business should be within the provision, regardless of whether the supplier has previously traded in the same line[9]. Whilst no such limitation is to be found in the H.P.A., most h.p. transactions are effected through the trade[10], so that in practice the position will not be very different.

2. *Knowledge of particular purpose.* Section 14 (1) of the S.G.A. is expressed only to apply

> "where the buyer, expressly or by implication, makes known to the seller the particular purpose for which the goods are required".

The courts have consistently interpreted this limitation in favour of the buyer. First, they have refused to read "particular" in the sense of special as opposed to general purpose. For instance, in *Frost* v.

---

4. *Wallis* v. *Russell*, [1902] 2 I.R. 585, C.A., *per* PALLES C.B. at p. 592. See also *Frost* v. *Aylesbury Dairy Co.*, [1905] 1 K.B. 608, C.A.; *Christopher Hill, Ltd.* v. *Ashington Piggeries, Ltd.*, [1969] 3 All E.R. 1496, C.A., at pp. 1518–1519.
5. [1947] 1 All E.R. 284.
6. [1969] 3 All E.R. 1496, C.A.: set out above, pp. 72–73.
7. At pp. 1516–1517, 1519. Their Lordships thought that all the goods were supplied under the original contract, which was conditional on orders being placed from time to time. Cf. *Great Northern Rail Co.* v. *Witham* (1873), L.R. 9 C.P. 16.
8. Atiyah, *Sale of Goods* (3rd Edn.) 69.
9. *First Report on Exemption Clauses in Contracts* (Law Com. No. 24), para. 31.
10. Atiyah, *Sale of Goods* (3rd Edn.) 259.

Aylesbury Dairy Co.[11] the Court of Appeal held that milk required for human consumption is required for a particular purpose. Second, the courts have shown themselves very ready to make the implication that the buyer's purpose has been made known to the seller, particularly where the goods are ordinarily only used for one purpose[12]. Both these points are illustrated by the decision of the House of Lords in *Henry Kendall & Sons, Ltd.* v. *William Lillico & Sons, Ltd.*[13].

> K. and G. Ltd were both wholesale dealers and members of the London Cattle Food Trade Association. K. sold to G. Ltd a quantity of "Brazilian ground nut extraction" under a contract which purported to exclude liability for any defects rendering the goods unmerchantable which would not be apparent on a reasonable examination. K. knew that G. Ltd required the goods for resale for compounding as food for cattle and poultry. However, the goods contained a toxic substance (unsuspected at this time) which resulted in their being fit for use as food for cattle, but not for poultry. G. Ltd orally agreed to sell part of the goods to one of their long-standing customers, SAPPA Ltd, a dealer, and subsequently sent SAPPA Ltd one of their ordinary "sold notes" which stated that the buyer took liability for latent defects. SAPPA Ltd made known to G. Ltd that the goods were required for compounding into food for pigs and poultry. SAPPA Ltd then compounded the goods bought from G. Ltd into food for birds, and sold some to the Hardwick Game Farm. Many of their pheasants having died as a consequence of being fed the compound, the farmers sued SAPPA Ltd, who admitted liability under the S.G.A. ss. 14 (1) and (2) and negotiated a reasonable settlement. SAPPA Ltd brought in G. Ltd, and G. Ltd brought in K., each buyer alleging similar breaches of s. 14 against his seller.

The Court of Appeal[14] held each seller liable to his buyer for breach of s. 14 (1), but decided that there had been no breaches of s. 14 (2)[15]. The Court explained that, whilst the exclusion clause on the "sold note" became part of the contract between G. Ltd. and SAPPA Ltd.[16], it did not protect G. Ltd. from liability for breach of s. 14 (1)[17]. This decision was affirmed by the House of Lords, who agreed with the Court

---

11. [1905] 1 K.B. 608, C.A. See also *Wallis* v. *Russell*, [1902] 2 I.R. 585, C.A. (retail purchase of two crabs "for tea").
12. E.g. *Preist* v. *Last*, [1903] 2 K.B. 148, C.A. (hot-water bottle); *Frost* v. *Aylesbury Dairy Co.* (above); *Grant* v. *Australian Knitting Mills, Ltd.*, [1936] A.C. 85, P.C.; *Griffiths* v. *Peter Conway, Ltd.*, [1939] 1 All E.R. 685, C.A. (clothing); *Wilson* v. *Rickett Cockerell, Ltd.*, [1954] 1 Q.B. 598; [1954] 1 All E.R. 868, C.A. (Coalite); *Lowe* v. *Lombank, Ltd.*, [1960] 1 All E.R. 611, C.A. (car).
13. [1969] 2 A.C. 31, H.L. See generally Davies (1969), 85 L.Q.R. 74.
14. *Hardwick Game Farm* v. *Suffolk Agricultural Poultry Producers Association*, [1966] 1 All E.R. 309, C.A.
15. See below, p. 100.
16. See below, p. 132.   17. See below, p. 139.

of Appeal that the purpose for which each buyer required the goods, even though their normal and obvious purpose, was a sufficient particular purpose made known to his seller. Lord MORRIS said[18]:

> "The degree of precision or definition which makes a purpose a particular purpose depends entirely on the facts and circumstances of a purchase and sale transaction. No need arises to define or limit the word 'particular' . . . There is no magic in the word 'particular'. A communicated purpose, if stated with reasonably sufficient precision, will be a particular purpose . . .
>
> "The next question that arises is whether that particular purpose was made known so as to show that the buyers relied on the skill and judgment of the sellers . . . Again, there is no magic in any particular word in the section".

Thus far, we have been considering goods which ordinarily are only required for one purpose. The difference between goods capable of ordinary use for many purposes and those ordinarily used for only one purpose was explained by COLLINS M.R. in *Preist* v. *Last*[19], where he said that in the former case

> "in order to give rise to the implication of a warranty, it is necessary to show that, though the article sold was capable of general use for many purposes, in the particular case it was sold with reference to a particular purpose. But in a case where the discussion begins with the fact that the description of the goods by which they were sold points to one particular purpose only, it seems to me that the first requirement of the sub-section is satisfied . . . The sale is of goods which, by the very description under which they are sold, appear to be sold for a particular purpose".

The effect of the cases would therefore appear to be as follows: if the goods have only one ordinary use, the seller is impliedly promising that the goods are fit for that use; if they have more than one ordinary use, there is no implication that the goods are fit for any one of those ordinary uses unless the buyer specifies for which use he requires the goods[20]; and if the buyer wishes to put the goods to an extraordinary use, he must specify that use in order to obtain the benefit of the undertaking[1]. Presumably, the common law would apply similar rules with respect to h.p. transactions[2], and the only real difficulty arises in respect of directly financed transactions. At common law, it may be difficult to say that a particular purpose made known to the dealer is necessarily

---

18. At pp. 93-94. See also *per* Lord PEARCE, at pp. 114-115.
19. [1903] 2 K.B. 148, C.A., at p. 153.
20. See also *First Report on Exemption Clauses in Contracts* (Law Com. No. 24), para. 35.
1. *B. S. Brown, Ltd.* v. *Craiks, Ltd.*, [1970] 1 All E.R. 823, H.L. But see the undertaking as to merchantable quality, below, p. 99.
2. See also Guest, *Law of H.P.* 279.

communicated to the finance company[3]; but s. 17 (4) of the H.P.A. successfully avoids any such problem[4].

3. Reliance. Under the S.G.A. the implied undertaking as to fitness will only exist where it can be shown that the buyer was buying in reliance on the seller's skill and judgment. This question arises in two different forms in s. 14 (1):

(1) The proviso to the subsection says that there shall be no implied condition as to fitness

> "in the case of a contract for the sale of a specified article under its patent or other trade name".

The courts have given a very restricted meaning to this proviso. Not only has the phrase "patent or other trade name" been interpreted restrictively[5], but in *Baldry* v. *Marshall*[6] the Court of Appeal held that, even if goods had a "patent or other trade name", they were not necessarily sold thereunder within the meaning of the proviso. The Court in that case held that the buyer's action for breach of s. 14 (1) was not defeated by the proviso, and BANKES L.J. explained[7]

> "The test of an article having been sold under its trade name within the meaning of the proviso is: Did the buyer specify it under its trade name in such a way as to indicate, rightly or wrongly, that it will answer his purpose, and that he is not relying on the skill or judgment of the seller, however great that skill or judgment may be?"

Speaking rather in terms of the seller who manufactured the goods, ATKIN L.J. suggested a slightly different test that would give the proviso a rather wider application[8]. Yet, if a distinction is to be drawn between a possibly culpable manufacturer and a probably innocent retailer, there is much to be said for giving the proviso a rather wider application in the case of the retailer. Certainly, most of the cases where the proviso has been successfully invoked have involved a retail seller[9]: in the only

---

3. See below, p. 285.
4. For the purposes, *inter alia*, of s. 17 (4), the Act gives a wide meaning to the phrase "antecedent negotiations"—see above, p. 40; and s. 58 (5) adds that
   > "anything received by a servant or agent, if received by him in the course of his employment or agency, shall be treated as received by his employer or principal".
5. See *Bristol Tramways Carriage Co.* v. *Fiat Motors, Ltd.*, [1910] 2 K B. 831, C.A.   6. [1925] 1 K.B. 260, C.A.
7. At p. 267. See also SARGANT L.J., at p. 270.
8. His Lordship thought that the proviso was based on *Chanter* v. *Hopkins* (1838), 4 M. & W. 399. It may be that he misunderstood that case, but Chalmers quotes it as authority: *Sale of Goods* (15th Edn.) 62.
9. E.g. *Wren* v. *Holt*, [1903] 1 K.B. 610, C.A.; *Taylor* v. *Combined Buyers, Ltd.*, [1924] N.Z.L.R. 627; *Daniels and Daniels* v. *White & Sons*, [1938] 4 All E.R. 258; *Wilson* v. *Rickett Cockerell, Ltd.*, [1954] 1 Q.B. 598; [1954] 1 All E.R. 868, C.A.

case where the court has considered a plea by a manufacturer that he should escape under the proviso the plea was refused[10]. BANKES L.J. clearly thought that the question raised by the proviso is whether the buyer has relied on the seller's skill and judgment; and it has therefore been suggested that the proviso has been "virtually interpreted out of existence" since it is merely an example of non-reliance[11]. Presumably for this reason, the proviso was not included in s. 17 (4) of the H.P.A.[12]. The Law Commission have recommended its deletion from the S.G.A.[13].

(2) The subsection expressly requires that the buyer must make known to the seller the particular purpose for which he requires the goods

"so as to show that the buyer relies on the seller's skill or judgment".

At common law, it would seem that a mere opportunity on the part of the buyer to inspect the goods would prevent the implication of the undertaking as to fitness; and s. 14 (1) is clearly more favourable to the buyer in that it raises no such implication. Once again, the courts have interpreted the requirement in favour of the buyer. Thus, in delivering the judgment of the House of Lords in a case in 1928, Lord SUMNER said *obiter*[14]

"The buyer's reliance is a question of fact . . . [and] . . . must be such as to constitute a substantial and effective inducement which leads the buyer to agree to purchase the commodity".

Merely because the buyer inspects the goods, this does not necessarily prevent there being any implication of reliance[15]; and it is possible to rely in part on the seller's skill. Thus, in *Cammell Laird, Ltd.* v. *Manganese Bronze and Brass, Ltd.*[16]

The purchaser of ships' propellers stipulated for certain specifications. The propellers supplied were found to be unfit for the purpose supplied because they were not thick enough, a matter not covered by the specifications.

The House of Lords found for the buyer on the grounds that in respect of matters not specified by the buyer he was relying on the seller's skill and judgment. The converse situation is to be found in *Christopher*

---

10. *Bristol Tramways Carriage Co.* v. *Fiat Motors, Ltd.*, [1910] 2 K.B. 831, C.A. In *Sumner, Permain & Co.* v. *Webb*, [1922] 1 K.B. 55, at p. 57 n., the C.A. avoided this issue by deciding as a matter of fact that the buyer had not relied on the seller's skill or judgment.
11. Atiyah, *Sale of Goods* (3rd Edn.) 70.
12. For a common law h.p. decision, see *Farnworth Finance Facilities, Ltd.* v. *Attryde*, [1970] 2 All E.R. 774 (below, p. 143).
13. *First Report on Exemption Clauses in Contracts* (Law Com. No. 24), para. 33. See also Davies (1969), 85 L.Q.R. 74, 87–89.
14. *Medway Oil, Ltd.* v. *Silica Gel Corporation* (1928), 33 Com. Cas. 195, H.L., at p. 196.
15. *Wallis* v. *Russell*, [1902] 2 I.R. 585, C.A.   16. [1934] A.C. 402, H.L.

Hill, Ltd. v. *Ashington Piggeries, Ltd.*[17], where the Court of Appeal pointed out that the defendants had made known to the plaintiffs the purpose for which the compound was required so as to show that they relied on the plaintiffs' skill to select and compound ingredients suitable to feed to animals generally but not necessarily to mink.   As the ingredient D.M.N.A. was harmful only to mink, their Lordships held that there was no breach of the undertaking as to fitness[18].   In this, as in many other cases, the court stressed that the issue was essentially one of fact.   In practice, the courts have shown themselves fairly ready to make an inference of reliance where the seller is the more expert in the goods sold to the knowledge of the buyer; and *vice versa*[19].   However, in the case of retail sales the courts would appear to be fairly ready to make the inference of reliance regardless of relative expertise[20].   Of course, the relative expertise is not the only criterion in making the implication of reliance, and in *Henry Kendall & Sons, Ltd.* v. *William Lillico & Sons Ltd.*[1] such an implication was made in respect of a sale between two wholesale dealers who were members of the same trade association.   Whilst the S.G.A. is neutral on the question of reliance, the case of *Manchester Liners, Ltd.* v. *Rea*[2] has sometimes been taken as authority for the proposition that, where the buyer makes known to the seller the purpose for which he requires the goods, that in itself raises a presumption of reliance.   In *Henry Kendall & Sons, Ltd.* v. *William Lillico & Sons, Ltd.* the judges were divided on this point[3]; but in *Teheran-Europe Ltd.* v. *Belton Ltd.*[4] the Court of Appeal unanimously found that the buyer had failed to prove his reliance on the seller's skill and judgment, and Lord DENNING M.R. said that it was necessary to revert to the words of the Act[5].   The opinion of the Master of the Rolls was accepted by REES J. in *Vacwell Engineering, Ltd.* v. *B.D.H. Chemicals, Ltd.*[6], though in that case it was found that there had been reliance.   In respect of h.p. transactions, the common

---

17. [1969] 3 All E.R. 1496, C.A.: set out above, pp. 72–73.
18. At pp. 1513–1516.   But see Patient (1970), 33 M.L.R. 565, at pp. 567–568.
19. E.g. *Cammell Laird & Co., Ltd.* v. *Manganese Bronze and Brass Co., Ltd.*, [1934] A.C. 402, H.L.; *Christopher Hill, Ltd.* v. *Ashington Piggeries, Ltd.* (above)—but see Patient, *op. cit.*, at p. 568.
20. E.g. *Preist* v. *Last*, [1903] 2 K.B. 148, C.A.; *Grant* v. *Australian Knitting Mills, Ltd.*, [1936] A.C. 85, P.C.; *Ashford Shire Council* v. *Dependable Motors, Ltd.*, [1961] A.C. 336; [1961] 1 All E.R. 96, P.C.
 1. [1969] 2 A.C. 31, H.L.   (HAVERS J., DIPLOCK L.J. and Lord GUEST disagreed on this point.)   Compare *Steels and Busks, Ltd.* v. *Bleeker Bik & Co., Ltd.*, [1956] 1 Lloyds Rep. 228; *Phoenix Distributors, Ltd.* v. *L. B. Clarke (London), Ltd.*, [1967] 1 Lloyds Rep. 518, C.A.   2. [1922] A.C. 74, H.L.
 3. Lord PEARCE (at p. 115), HAVERS J. and all three members of the C.A. thought that there was such a presumption.   Lords REID, GUEST and WILBERFORCE disagreed (at pp. 84, 107, 125).
 4. [1968] 2 All E.R. 886, C.A.
 5. At p. 890.   But see SACHS L.J., at p. 896.
 6. [1969] 3 All E.R. 1681: set out below, p. 389.

law similarly insists that there will only be an implied undertaking as to fitness where it can be shown that the hirer relied on the owner's skill or judgment, and that such reliance is a question of fact[7]. It would appear that neither the hirer's knowledge of minor defects nor the mere opportunity to examine the goods will oust the undertaking[8]: there must be something to show that the hirer took the risk on himself[9]. Once again, directly financed transactions are apt to cause trouble, because it is difficult to say that the hirer has relied on the skill or judgment of the finance company. In *Yeoman Credit, Ltd.* v. *Apps*[10] the Court of Appeal assumed that the hirer had shown reliance on the skill or judgment of the finance company, notwithstanding that their Lordships also found that the dealer was not the agent of the company. There is a certain logical difficulty about accepting this; but s. 17 (4) of the H.P.A. has been drafted with a view to avoiding any such problems. It is suggested that there remains much room for further simplification of the statutorily implied undertakings as to fitness, particularly in the case of the S.G.A., s. 14 (1)[11].

4 Exclusion of the undertakings

The general limitations which the common law imposes on the exclusion of liability will be considered in Chapter 11, and we are concerned here with those rules which are particular to the undertakings as to fitness. Whilst the undertaking in the S.G.A. is comparatively easily excluded[12], the courts have taken a somewhat stricter view in relation to h.p. agreements, particularly in the case of consumer transactions[13]. Where the transaction falls within the H.P.A., s. 18 (4) lays down that[14]

> "The owner or seller shall not be entitled to rely on any provision in a hire-purchase agreement or conditional sale agreement excluding or modifying the condition referred to in section 17 (4) of this Act unless he proves that before the agreement was made that provision was brought to the notice of the hirer or buyer and its effect made clear to him".

To exclude the undertaking as to fitness, the owner or seller must therefore comply with all three of the following requirements: (1) use words

---

7. See *per* HOLROYD PEARCE L.J. in *Yeoman Credit, Ltd.* v. *Apps*, [1962] 2 Q.B. 508, at p. 516, C.A.; and *per* PEARSON L.J. in *Astley Industrial Trust, Ltd.* v. *Grimley*, [1963] 2 All E.R. 33, at pp. 40–41, C.A. These cases are further discussed below, p. 141, *et seq.*
8. *Yeoman Credit, Ltd.* v. *Apps* (above).
9. *Astley Industrial Trust, Ltd.* v. *Grimley* (above).
10. [1962] 2 Q.B. 508; [1961] 2 All E.R. 281, C.A.
11. See *First Report on Exemption Clauses in Contracts* (Law Com. No. 24), paras. 37–38.
12. E.g. *Bartlett* v. *Sidney Marcus, Ltd.*, [1965] 2 All E.R. 753, C.A.
13. *Lowe* v. *Lombank, Ltd.*, [1960] 1 All E.R. 611, C.A.: set out below, pp. 139–140.
14. A similar provision is to be found in the H.P.A. 1938, s. 8 (3).

in the agreement which are apt to exclude the undertaking; (2) draw
the customer's attention to these words; and (3) make their effect clear
to him. When engaged in direct financing, finance companies have
been acutely conscious that they are dependent on the good faith and
competence of the dealer in respect of requirements (2) and (3). Some
companies therefore made attempts to avoid such reliance on the dealer
by the insertion in the proposal form of a clause reciting that the hirer
acknowledged that the dealer had complied with requirements (2) and
(3). The failure of such a device to protect the finance company in
Lowe v. *Lombank, Ltd.*[15] has led to doubts as to whether such a device
can ever be effective[16].

3 UNDERTAKINGS AS TO MERCHANTABILITY

1 The undertakings

In the absence of an express undertaking as to merchantability, such
an undertaking may only be imported by operation of law. In the case
of sales, s. 14 (2) of the S.G.A. provides as follows:

> "Where goods are bought by description from a seller who deals in
> goods of that description (whether he be the manufacturer or not),
> there is an implied condition that the goods shall be of merchantable
> quality; provided that if the buyer has examined the goods, there
> shall be no implied condition as regards defects which such examina-
> tion ought to have revealed".

In addition, the S.G.A. makes special provision with regard to sales by
sample[17], and s. 15 (2) (c) of the Act provides that in such a case:

> "There is an implied condition that the goods shall be free from any
> defect, rendering them unmerchantable, which would not be
> apparent on reasonable examination of the sample".

In the twentieth century, the courts have frequently taken the view that,
as these provisions are so largely declaratory of the common law,
similar undertakings should be implied into analogous types of agreement, such as contracts for the sale of work and labour or contracts of
h.p.[18]. Where a transaction falls within the H.P.A., then s. 17 of that
Act provides as follows:

> "(2) Subject to the next following subsection, and to section 18 of
> this Act, in every hire purchase agreement and in every conditional
> sale agreement there shall be implied a condition that the goods will
> be of merchantable quality.

---

15. [1960] 1 All E.R. 611, C.A.
16. Guest, *Law of H.P.* 291.
17. See generally, below, Chapter 8.
18. See the cases collected in *Chalmers' Sale of Goods* (15th Edn.) 61, note (t).

(3) Where the hirer or buyer has examined the goods or a sample of them, the condition referred to in subsection (2) of this section shall not be implied by virtue of that subsection in respect of defects which the examination ought to have revealed".

Section 18 of the H.P.A. lays down certain conditions under which the undertaking as to merchantability may be excluded[19]. It should be noticed that the H.P.A. makes no separate provision as to merchantability where goods are let or sold by reference to a sample.

In the next three subsections, we shall consider (1) the content of the undertakings as to merchantability, (2) limitations on them, and (3) exclusion of the undertakings.

2 The content of the undertakings

The common law required that goods sold by description be merchantable under that description; and in 1815 Lord ELLENBOROUGH defined "merchantable" as meaning that the goods[20]

"shall be saleable in the market under the denomination mentioned in the contract . . ."

However, when Chalmers codified the law of sale, he wrote into s. 14 (2) the requirement that the goods be of "merchantable quality". The first question is therefore whether the addition of the word "quality" has brought about an alteration in the law.

According to the Oxford Dictionary, "quality" means "nature, kind or character"; and s. 62 (1) of the S.G.A. provides that the

" 'quality of goods' includes their state or condition".

Unfortunately, in the two leading cases on the point, the same Court of Appeal appear to have come to opposite conclusions as to the meaning of the word "quality". In *Niblett's Case*[1], the majority[2] held that there had been a breach of s. 14 (2), as well as of s. 12 (1)[3]; and BANKES L.J. said[4]:

"Quality includes the state or condition of the goods. The state of this condensed milk was that it was packed in tins bearing labels. The labels were as much a part of the state or condition of the goods as the tins were. The state of the packing affected the merchantable quality of the goods".

On the other hand, in *Sumner, Permain & Co.* v. *Webb*[5] the Court of Appeal found that there was no breach of s. 14 (2).

---

19. See below, p. 104.
20. *Gardiner* v. *Gray* (1815), 4 Camp. 144, at p. 145.
1. [1921] 3 K.B. 387, C.A.
2. BANKES and ATKIN L.JJ.
3. See above, p. 57. 4. At p. 395. 5. [1922] 1 K.B. 55, C.A.

The defendant was the manufacturer of a product known as "Webb's Indian Tonic Water". As the defendant knew, the plaintiff purchased some of this tonic water from him for the purpose of shipment to the Argentine. However, the defendant was unaware of two vital facts: (1) his product contained a small quantity of salicylic acid; and (2) the sale of any article of food or drink containing salicylic acid was prohibited in the Argentine. After the Argentine authorities had seized and condemned his tonic water, the plaintiff claimed damages for breach of s. 14 (1) and (2).

The decision of BAILHACHE J. in favour of the buyer on both points was unanimously reversed on appeal[6]. In respect of s. 14 (2), the Court of Appeal were clear that the fact that the goods were unsaleable in the Argentine did not prevent their being of merchantable quality. Very naturally, the buyer in *Webb's Case*[5] relied on *Niblett's Case*[7], which he alleged turned on the fact that the milk could not be sold in this country because of the law of registered trade marks. However, BANKES L.J. replied[8]:

> "Our decision . . . was wholly independent of any question of the state of the law. What we were directing our attention to was the condition of the goods . . . The packing of the milk was an essential part of its condition. There is nothing of that kind here. The 'quality' of the tonic was perfectly good, its 'state' was perfectly good, and so was its 'condition'. The only objection that could be taken to it was that one of its ingredients prevented it from being lawfully sold in the Argentine".

SCRUTTON L.J., who had ventured no opinion on the matter in *Niblett's Case*[7], was clear that merchantable quality did not cover "the legal title to goods or the legal right to sell them"[9]; and ATKIN L.J. sought to explain his decision in the earlier case as follows[10]:

> ". . . nobody would buy those tins, because, if they did, they would probably be buying a law-suit, and the tins in that state and condition were unsaleable, not merely in this country by reason of a law peculiar to this country, but unsaleable anywhere . . ."

Logically, it might be thought that the decisions should be the other way round if a distinction is to be made between the two cases: in *Niblett's Case*[7] there was no complaint as to quality of the actual milk, yet the goods were found not to be of merchantable quality; and in *Webb's Case*[5] the complaint was not about the label, but about the quality of the contents of the bottles, and the court thought the goods

---

6. As to s. 14 (1), see above, p. 91.
7. [1921] 3 K.B. 387, C.A.   8. At p. 61.
9. At p. 63.   10. At pp. 65–66.

were of merchantable quality. Perhaps some satisfaction is to be gained from the distinction suggested by ATKIN L.J.: the condensed milk with those labels was treated as not being saleable anywhere, and not merely by reason of the law peculiar to this country[13]; but the tonic water could be sold almost anywhere as such, except in the Argentine[14].

Yet it would be unfortunate if too much emphasis were attached to the word "quality". Whereas that word appears in s. 14 (2) of the S.G.A. and s. 17 (2) of the H.P.A., it is not to be found in s. 15 of the S.G.A. A sale by sample is, after all, a type of sale by description; and it is submitted that it would be undesirable if the scope of the under-taking as to merchantability varied according to whether or not a sample were used. The H.P.A. draws no such distinction.

We must now consider how the meaning of the term "merchantable" has been developed by the courts since 1893. In most of the cases, the courts were considering s. 14 (2) of the S.G.A.; but it may be assumed that the term means the same in s. 15 of the S.G.A., in s. 17 of the H.P.A., and in the present day common law.

It has already been pointed out that at common law the primary meaning attached to merchantability was "saleability" under the contract description. An example of the application of the test of "saleability" is to be found in *Bristol Tramways Carriage Co.* v. *Fiat Motors, Ltd.*[15].

> There was a written contract for the sale of a Fiat Omnibus and six Fiat Chassis, the goods to be of certain specifications. Upon delivery, they proved to be very unsatisfactory, and had to be entirely reconstructed before use. The buyer sought damages, alleging breach of ss. 14 (1) and (2).

The buyer's action succeeded before the Court of Appeal on both grounds[16]. On the subject of merchantable quality, FARWELL L.J. said[17]:

> "The phrase is . . . used as meaning that an article is of such a quality and in such condition that a reasonable man acting reason-ably would after a full examination accept it under the circumstances of the case in performance of his offer to buy that article whether he buys for his own use or to sell again".

---

13. Is this so? Did ATKIN L.J. have in mind the conflict rule that, if no evi-dence of foreign law is produced, it is assumed to be the same as English Law? Does this rule apply to statute law? See Dicey & Morris, *Conflict of Laws* (8th Edn.) pp. 1118–1119. Would there have been a reasonable distinction if ATKIN L.J. had said "not saleable anywhere *by reason of English Law*"?
14. This would fit in with the general maxim that the undertaking as to mer-chantability is not usually an undertaking that the goods will be fit for any particular purpose—see below, p. 99.
15. [1910] 2 K.B. 831, C.A.
16. The decision on s. 14 (1) is considered above, p. 91.   17. At p. 841.

This definition was obviously inaccurate in so far as it suggested that latent defects would not render the goods unmerchantable, which is not the case[18]. Accordingly, the definition was amplified by DIXON J. in *Australian Knitting Mills Ltd.* v. *Grant*[19], where he explained that the goods

> "should be in such an actual state that a buyer fully acquainted with the facts and, therefore, knowing what hidden defects exist and not being limited to their apparent condition would buy them without abatement of the price obtainable for such goods if in reasonably sound order and condition and without special terms . . ."

Two criticisms may be made of this definition offered by FARWELL L.J., even in its amended form. First, it is circular, as a reasonable buyer would only accept the goods if he were legally bound to do so[20]. Second, the suggested test must in many cases be fictitious for the following reasons: the test does not seem to be intended to depend on whether there is a demand for the goods in question[1]; and it will frequently be clear that the goods are bought for consumption, not resale. This last point is met by the following amended *obiter dictum* by Lord WRIGHT in *Cammell Laird, Ltd.* v. *Manganese Bronze and Brass, Ltd.*[2]:

> "What subsection (2) now means by "merchantable quality" is that the goods in the form in which they were tendered were of no use for any purpose for which *goods which complied with the description under which these goods were sold* would normally be used, and hence were not saleable under that description".

Whilst Lord REID has recently said that it is impossible to give a complete definition of merchantable quality[3], a penetrating analysis of the concept is to be found in the judgment of SALMOND J. in *Taylor* v. *Combined Buyers, Ltd.*[4], where there was a sale of a "new Calthorpe car", which proved defective. During the course of his judgment, the learned Judge made the following points[5]:

(1) Merchantable does not mean merely saleable. Goods may be

---

18. *Per* Lord WRIGHT in *Grant* v. *Australian Knitting Mills, Ltd.*, [1936] A.C. 85, P.C., at p. 100.   See also *Morelli* v. *Fitch and Gibbons*, [1928] 2 K.B. 636; *Daniels and Daniels* v. *White & Sons, Ltd.*, [1938] 4 All E.R. 258 (set out below, p, 125); *Wilson* v. *Rickett Cockerell, Ltd.*, [1954] 1 Q.B. 598; [1954] 1 All E.R. 868, C.A.; *Godley* v. *Perry* [1960] 1 All E.R. 36.
19. (1933), 50 C.L.R. 387, H.C., at p. 418.
20. *Per* SALMOND J. in *Taylor* v. *Combined Buyers, Ltd.*, [1924] N.Z.L.R. 627, at p. 646.
 1. *Per* SCRUTTON L.J. in *Webb's Case*, [1922] 1 K.B. 55, C.A., at p. 63,
 2. [1934] A.C. 402, H.L., at p. 430.   The italicised amendment was introduced by Lord REID in *Henry Kendall & Sons, Ltd.* v. *William Lillico & Sons, Ltd.*, [1969] 2 A.C. 31, H.L., at p. 77, and was approved by the House of Lords in *B. S. Brown & Son, Ltd.* v. *Craiks, Ltd.*, [1970] 1 All E.R. 823.
 3. *B. S. Brown & Son, Ltd.* v. *Craiks, Ltd.* (above), at p. 825.
 4. [1924] N.Z.L.R. 627.   5. At pp. 644-647.

saleable, yet not of merchantable quality: few goods are so defective that they cannot be disposed of at any price or for any purpose[6].

(2) Goods are not necessarily merchantable simply because they comply with the description under which they were sold: they may be truthfully described, and still be unmerchantable.

(3) Merchantable does not mean of good, fair or average quality. Goods may be of inferior or even bad quality, and yet be merchantable: there is no implied condition that the goods are of any particular quality, and the buyer must accept inferior goods as long as they are merchantable under the contract description[7].

(4) Goods are not unmerchantable merely because they are not fit for the particular purpose for which the buyer requires them[8]; and *vice versa*: goods may be fit for their particular purpose, and yet be unmerchantable.

This last point brings us to the relationship of the undertakings of merchantability and fitness. Particularly in view of the extension of the concept of sale by description[9], and of "particular purpose" to include usual purpose[10], there will be many situations where both undertakings are applicable. Where there is such an overlap, it may be that the rather stricter limitations of s. 14 (1) prevent the buyer from relying on that subsection; and, in order to give the buyer a remedy in such circumstances, the courts have sometimes reasoned that, if the goods have only one ordinary use, they are unmerchantable if they are unfit for that use[11]. However, in *Bartlett* v. *Sidney Marcus, Ltd.*[12] Lord DENNING pointed out that

> "There is a considerable territory where on the one hand you cannot say that the article is "of no use" at all, and on the other you cannot say that it is entirely "fit for use". The article may be of some use though not entirely efficient use for the purpose. It may not be in perfect condition but yet it is in usable condition. It is, then, I think merchantable".

---

6. Cf. *Asfar & Co.* v. *Blundell*, [1896] 1 Q.B. 123, C.A. See also *per* WRIGHT J. in *Canada Export Co.* v. *Eilers* (1929), 35 Com. Cas. 90, at p. 102.
7. *Per* Lord REID in *Hardwick Game Farm* v. *S.A.P.P.A.*, [1969] 2 A.C. 31, H.L., at p. 75. Compare *Empire Cream Co.* v. *Quinn* (1928), 154 N.Y. App. Div. 302, where merchantable quality defined as "at least of medium quality or goodness" or "such as would bring the average market price at least".
8. E.g. *Steels and Busks, Ltd.* v. *Bleeker Bik & Co., Ltd.*, [1956] 1 Lloyds Rep. 228; *B. S. Brown & Son, Ltd.* v. *Craiks, Ltd.*, [1970] 1 All E.R. 823, H.L.
9. See above, p. 67, *et seq.*
10. See above, p. 87, *et seq.*
11. E.g. *Wren* v. *Holt*, [1903] 1 K.B. 610, C.A.; *Grant* v. *Australian Knitting Mills, Ltd.*, [1936] A.C. 85, P.C.; *Wilson* v. *Rickett Cockerell, & Co., Ltd.*, [1954] 1 Q.B. 598; [1954] 1 All E.R. 868, C.A.; *Godley* v. *Perry*, [1960] 1 All E.R. 36.
12. [1965] 2 All E.R. 753, C.A., at p. 755.

Thus, in *Henry Kendall & Sons, Ltd.* v. *William Lillico & Sons, Ltd.*[13], the evidence showed that buyers who only compounded poultry food would not be prepared to buy the contaminated goods at any price; but that compounders of cattle food would be prepared (with complaints) to pay the full price, test the goods, and use the less highly contaminated goods in their cattle foodstuffs. At first instance, HAVERS J. applied the test suggested by Lord WRIGHT[14], and concluded that the goods were of merchantable quality as they were of use for one of their ordinary purposes[15]. A unanimous Court of Appeal[16] and two members of the House of Lords[17] agreed that HAVERS J. had applied the correct test, and that the goods were merchantable. However, the majority of their Lordships[18] thought that Lord WRIGHT's test[14] was defective in that it omitted all reference to price, and therefore preferred, with modifications, the test propounded by FARWELL L.J.[19], Lord PEARCE explained[1]:

> "One could not say that a new carpet which happens to have a hole in it or a car with its wings buckled are of no use for their normal purpose and hence would be unsaleable under that description. They would no doubt, if their price was reduced, find a ready market. In return for a substantial abatement of price a purchaser is ready to put up with serious defects, or use part of the price reduction in having the defects remedied. In several classes of goods there is a regular retail market for "seconds", that is, goods which are not good enough in the manufacturer's or retailer's view to fulfil an order and are therefore sold off at a cheaper price. It would be wrong to say that 'seconds' are necessarily merchantable".

Applying this test, Lords PEARCE and WILBERFORCE concluded that the goods were unmerchantable[2]; but Lord GUEST disagreed[3]. The Law Commission have accepted the majority view of the House of Lords, and have suggested the following new definition for the purposes of ss. 14 (2) and 15 of the S.G.A.[4]:

> "Goods of any kind are of merchantable quality within the meaning of this Act if they are as fit for the purpose or purposes for which

---

13. [1969] 2 A.C. 31, H.L.: set out above, p. 88.
14. See above, p. 98.
15. *Hardwick Game Farm* v. *Suffolk Agricultural and Poultry Producers Association, Ltd.*, [1964] 2 Lloyds Rep. 227.
16. *Hardwick Game Farm* v. *Suffolk Agricultural and Poultry Producers Association, Ltd.*, [1966] 1 All E.R. 309, C.A.
17. Lords REID and MORRIS (the former with some qualification), at pp. 76–79, 96–98.
18. Lords GUEST, PEARCE and WILBERFORCE, at pp. 108, 118, 126.
19. See above, p. 97.
 1. At p. 118.   2. At pp. 119, 126.
 3. At p. 108. See also *B. S. Brown & Son, Ltd.* v. *Craiks, Ltd.*, [1970] 1 All E.R. 823, H.L.
 4. *First Report on Exemption Clauses in Contracts* (Law Com. No. 24), paras. 43, 44.

goods of that kind are commonly bought as it is reasonable to expect having regard to their price, any description applied to them and all the other circumstances . . ."

The Law Commission took the view that the overlap between the undertakings as to fitness and merchantable quality was desirable in the interests of consumer protection[5]. With a similar object in view, one commentator has gone even further, and suggested that the two undertakings should be read together, so that, for instance, where the buyer has made his particular purpose known to the seller[6], that particular purpose should be included in the description of the goods and the goods be unmerchantable if they are unfit for it[7].

3 The qualifications of the undertakings

The statutory provisions embodying the undertakings as to merchantability contain a number of qualifications, though unfortunately these qualifications are by no means the same in each case. These are as follows:

1. Sales by description. Section 14 (2) of the S.G.A. is only expressed to apply "where goods are bought by description", and s. 15 (2) (c) "in the case of a contract for sale by sample". It is submitted that sales by sample are just a special example of sales by description[8]; and it has been decided[9] that the term "sale by description" means the same here as it does in s. 13 of the S.G.A. discussed above[10]. The undertaking in s. 17 (2) of the H.P.A. is not expressed to be subject to any such limitation; and the Law Commission have recommended that the provisions of the S.G.A. be freed from the limitation[11].

2. Sales by a dealer. Section 14 (2) of the S.G.A. only applies where goods are bought by description

> "from a seller who deals in goods of that description (whether he be the manufacturer or not)".

Rather oddly, this limitation does not apply where the sale is by sample and the undertaking is imported by the S.G.A., s. 15 (2) (c)[12]. Nor is any such limitation to be found in s. 17 (2) of the H.P.A. An apparently similar limitation is to be found in the implied undertaking

---

5. *Ibid.*, para. 39.
6. So as to show reliance?
7. Davies (1969), 85 L.Q.R. 74, esp. at pp. 77–80. This would probably have enabled the buyer to succeed in *Webb's Case*, [1922] 1 K.B. 55, C.A.: set out above, p. 96. But see *Christopher Hill, Ltd.* v. *Ashington Piggeries, Ltd.*, [1969] 3 All E.R. 1496, C.A.: set out above, pp. 72–73.
8. See further below, p. 106.
9. *Christopher Hill, Ltd.* v. *Ashington Piggeries, Ltd.* (above), at p. 1518.
10. See above, p. 67, *et seq.*
11. *First Report on Exemption Clauses in Contracts* (Law Com. No. 24), para. 45.
12. Sales by sample by sellers who are not dealers are probably exceptional.

as to fitness in s. 14 (1) of the S.G.A.[13]; but in *Christopher Hill, Ltd.* v. *Ashington Piggeries, Ltd.*[14] the Court of Appeal argued that the verbal dissimilarities between the two subsections led to a difference in effect. Their Lordships held that the phrase "that description" in the limitation referred back to the description under which the goods were sold, and that the plaintiff was not liable for breach of s. 14 (2) because he was not a dealer in goods of the contract description: they thought that "that description" in s. 14 (2) was narrower than "a description" in s. 14 (1). Before this case, it was usually thought that the difference in wording between ss. 14 (1) and (2) in this respect was merely to make the section as a whole more readable, and that the two limitations were co-extensive. It is submitted that such uniformity would be desirable.[15] The Law Commission recommended that s. 14 (2) of the S.G.A. be freed from this restriction as to dealers and apply to every article sold in the course of business[16], including articles sold through an auctioneer or other agent in the course of the agent's business[17].

3. Examination by transferee. Each of the statutory undertakings as to merchantability mentions pre-contract examination by the transferee[18]. Section 14 (2) of the S.G.A. lays down that

> "if the buyer has examined the goods, there shall be no implied condition as regards defects which such examination ought to have revealed".

Section 15 (2) (c) of the S.G.A. only imposes a condition as to merchantability in respect of freedom from defects

> "which would not be apparent on reasonable examination of the sample".

Section 17 (3) of the H.P.A. provides:

> "Where the hirer or buyer has examined the goods or a sample of them, the condition . . . [as to merchantability] . . . shall not be implied . . . in respect of defects which the examination ought to have revealed".

It is probable that the common law rule in sale was that the implied undertaking was excluded by the mere opportunity for examination, but s. 14 (2) brought about two changes: (1) the exclusion of the undertaking was made to rest on an examination in fact; and (2) even if there was an examination, the undertaking was only ousted in respect of

---

13. See above, pp. 86–87.
14. [1969] 3 All E.R. 1496, C.A., at p. 1518: set out above, pp. 72–73.
15. And see Patient (1970), 33 M.L.R. 565, at pp. 569–570.
16. *First Report on Exemption Clauses in Contracts* (Law Com. No. 24), para. 46.
17. *Ibid.*, paras. 53–55.
18. This should not be confused with the buyer's right to examine on delivery, considered below, p. 269.

defects which such examination ought to have revealed. A case which is at first sight difficult to reconcile with the plain wording of the section is *Thornett* v. *Beers*[19], where the buyers' claim for breach of s. 14 (2) failed on the grounds that they had brought themselves within the proviso. Before entry into the contract, the buyers told the sellers that they had inspected the barrels of glue, though in fact they had not done so because they were pressed for time. BRAY J. said[20]:

> "I do not think that the Statute requires[1] a full examination, because the words that follow show that the proviso deals with the case where the buyer has not made a full examination. Was there an examination?... Both parties intended a full examination... It may be a question whether, after this statement [that they had examined the glue], the [buyers] could be heard to say that they had not examined the glue, but however that may be, I think they examined the goods within the meaning of the sub-section. There can be no doubt that such an examination if made in the ordinary way would have revealed the defects complained of".

It has been suggested that the examination was, in effect, waived[2]; but it is difficult to reconcile this suggestion with the clear words of s. 14 (2), which seems to mean that the undertaking will only be excluded in respect of *such defects as the examination actually made* ought to have revealed[3]. If this is correct, then it would seem that the decision in *Thornett* v. *Beers*[19] can only be reconciled with s. 14 (2) on the basis that the buyers were estopped from denying that they had inspected the goods; that the case proceeded on the basis that the inspection had been made; and that that inspection ought to have revealed the defects. Thus, the effect of the limitation would appear to be that the seller is saved from liability where the buyer's loss is due to his own negligent inspection[4]. The position under s. 14 (2) may be compared with that under s. 15 (2) (c), which excludes liability for defects which would be apparent on a reasonable examination, whether or not the buyer made any examination; and the reason for the distinction is presumably that the seller can usually assume that the buyer has examined the sample[5]. Section 15 (2) (c) is largely modelled on the

---

19. [1919] 1 K.B. 486: set out above, p. 68.
20. At p. 489.
 1. The statute does not *require* any examination at all, but merely limits the undertaking where there is an examination.
 2. *Chalmers' Sale of Goods* (14th Edn.), 57, note (t). This suggestion is not repeated in the 15th Edn.
 3. See Stoljar (1953), 16 M.L.R. 174, at p. 183; Atiyah, *Sale of Goods* (3rd Edn.) 62, note 5. The word "ought" suggests an objective standard.
 4. Is this a "reasonable man" test, cf. tort of negligence?
 5. Atiyah, *Sale of Goods* (3rd Edn.) 63; *Benjamin on Sale* (8th Edn.) 657. The justification for such an assumption in every case is not entirely clear: suppose the seller *knows* that the buyer did not examine the goods.

House of Lords decision in *Drummond* v. *Van Ingen*[6]. In that case, Lord MACNAGHTEN, discussing how far the implied undertaking should be excluded, said[7]:

> "[A sample] cannot be treated as saying more than such a sample would tell a merchant of the class to which the buyer belongs, using due care and diligence, and appealing to it in the ordinary way and with the knowledge possessed by merchants of that class at the time. No doubt the sample might be made to say a great deal more. Pulled to pieces and examined by unusual tests which curiosity or suspicion might suggest, it would doubtless reveal every secret of its construction. But that is not the way business is done in this country".

A similar attitude is to be found in *Godley* v. *Perry*[8], and is, indeed, to the advantage of both parties. The seller is not protected from liability under s. 15 (2) (c) in respect of latent defects; and furthermore, it is also the case that the buyer cannot insist under s. 15 (2) (a) that the goods correspond with their sample in some manner not discoverable on a reasonable examination[9]. It has been said, moreover, that if the buyer, with knowledge of the defect in the sample rendering the goods unmerchantable, "is content to take a delivery which corresponds with the sample, and gets such a delivery, he has no ground for complaint"[10]. The distinction in the width of the limitations in the S.G.A. according to whether or not the sale is by sample is not to be found in the H.P.A., which substantially follows the language of s. 14 (2) and makes no special provision for those transactions involving a sample. The Law Commission have recommended that the limitation be extended so that there is no undertaking in respect of defects to which the seller specifically draws the buyer's attention[11], but that the full paraphernalia of s. 18 (2) of the H.P.A. should not be introduced to ordinary sales[12].

4 Exclusion of the undertakings

The general limitations which the law imposes on the exclusion of liability will be considered in Chapter 11, and the present discussion will be concerned with those rules which are particular to the undertakings as to merchantability. Whilst the undertakings in the S.G.A. may be excluded comparatively easily[13], the H.P.A. lays down that, except in so far as the Act allows, the undertaking as to merchantability

---

6. (1887), 12 App. Cas. 284, H.L. 7. At p. 297.
8. [1960] 1 All E.R. 36. 9. See below, p. 108.
10. *Per* STABLE J. in *Houndsditch Warehouse Co., Ltd.* v. *Waltex, Ltd.*, [1944] 2 All E.R. 518, at p. 519. *Sed quaere?*
11. *First Report on Exemption Clauses in Contracts* (Law Com. No. 24), para. 49.
12. *Ibid.*, para. 50. Section 18 (2) of the H.P.A. is considered below. Compare the view of Davies (1969), 85 L.Q.R. 74, at pp. 90-91.
13. See e.g. *Bartlett* v. *Sidney Marcus, Ltd.*, [1965] 2 All E.R. 753, C.A.

"shall be implied notwithstanding any agreement to the contrary" (s. 18 (3)). Section 18 of the H.P.A. provides that the undertaking as to merchantability imported into h.p. or conditional sales by s. 17 (2) may only be excluded as follows:

(*A*) *In respect of second-hand goods.* Section 18 (1) provides that where the goods are let or agreed to be sold as "second-hand goods", and—

> "(a) the agreement contains a statement to that effect, and a provision that the condition referred to in section 17 (2) of this Act is excluded in relation to those goods, and
> (b) it is proved that before the agreement was made the provision in the agreement so excluding that condition was brought to the notice of the hirer or buyer and its effect made clear to him,
> that condition shall not be implied in the agreement in relation to those goods".

Thus, the undertaking as to merchantability may be totally excluded in respect of "second-hand goods"[14] when all three of the following conditions are satisfied: (1) the agreement contains a statement that the goods are sold or let as second-hand goods; and (2) the agreement contains a clause excluding the statutory undertaking as to merchantability in respect of those goods; and (3) the exclusion clause is pointed out to the hirer or buyer and its effect made clear to him *before* the agreement is made.

(*B*) *In respect of specified defects.* Section 18 (2) provides that

> "Where . . . goods are let or agreed to be sold as being subject to defects specified in the agreement (whether referred to in the agreement as defects or by any other description to the like effect), and—
> (a) the agreement contains a provision that the condition referred to in section 17 (2) of this Act is excluded in relation to those goods in respect of those defects, and
> (b) it is proved that before the agreement was made those defects, and the provision in the agreement so excluding that condition, were brought to the notice of the hirer or buyer and the effect of that provision was made clear to him,
> that condition shall not be implied in respect of those defects".

Thus, s. 18 (2) only allows a partial exclusion of the undertaking. Whether the goods are sold or let as being new or second-hand, the statutory undertaking as to merchantability may be excluded in relation to "specified defects"[15] when all the following conditions are satisfied: (1) the agreement contains a clause excluding the statutory undertaking as to merchantability in relation to those goods *and* in respect of those defects; and (2) the exclusion clause is pointed out to the hirer or buyer and its effect made clear to him *before* the agreement is made.

---

14. When is a motor vehicle "second-hand"?
15. It remains to be seen what degree of certainty the courts will require in the specification of the defects.

CHAPTER 8

The Significance of Samples

I CONTRACTS BY SAMPLE

The classic exposition of the legal function of a sample is that of Lord MACNAGHTEN in *Drummond* v. *Van Ingen*[1], where he said:

> "The office of a sample is to present to the eye the real meaning and intention of the parties with regard to the subject-matter of the contract which, owing to the imperfections of language, it may be difficult or impossible to express in words. The sample speaks for itself".

A sample may be utilised in the sale of specific goods, in which case the sample will be taken from the contract goods; or there may be a sale of unascertained or future goods as corresponding with a particular sample. In either case, the function of the sample is similar to that of the description of the goods sold, and might almost be regarded as a special type of sale by description. Yet it is important to distinguish between the two, because the S.G.A. makes separate provision for sales by sample, and even contemplates that a sale may be both by description and by sample (s. 13)[2].

When does a sample become part of the contract? Section 15 (1) of the S.G.A. rather unhelpfully provides:

> "A contract of sale is a contract for sale by sample when there is a term in the contract, express or implied, to that effect".

Unfortunately, this would appear to import all the pre-1893 learning on the matter. The position at common law seems to have been that, just because a sample is exhibited at the time of sale, there is not necessarily a sale by sample: the seller may decline to sell by sample, and require the buyer to inspect the bulk; or the parties may in some other way show that in their contract they are not relying on the sample, so that, for example, it has been decided that a sample will not become part of a written contract unless it is embodied in the writing[3].

On the other hand, the terminology of the H.P.A. is different, and s. 19 of that Act speaks of goods being "let or agreed to be sold *by*

---

1. (1887), 12 App. Cas. 284, H.L., at p. 297.
2. There would appear to be no post-1893 example where a contract has been held to be a sale by description and by sample, but the point was argued in *Travers, Ltd.* v. *Longel, Ltd.* (1947), 64 T.L.R. 150.
3. See *Benjamin on Sale* (8th Edn.) 653–654.

reference to a sample". It has been said that goods will be let or sold by reference to a sample[4]

> "where a sample is exhibited or supplied . . . during the negotiations for the contract, and there need be no term in the contract, express or implied to this effect".

For example, if a car dealer takes a customer for a demonstration run in a new car, it would seem that if a similar new car is subsequently let to the customer it may be let by reference to the car demonstrated, even if the transaction is directly financed. Thus, the effect of the difference in terminology in the two Acts would appear to be that a sample is more likely to become part of a transaction which falls within the H.P.A. than part of one which is within the ambit of the S.G.A. The position concerning h.p. and conditional sales which fall outside the scope of the H.P.A. is unclear.

2 UNDERTAKINGS IN CONTRACTS BY SAMPLE

1 **Title**

Section 15 of the S.G.A., which sets out the terms which are to be implied into sales by sample, makes no mention of undertakings as to title, but presumably s. 12 is wide enough to cover such transactions. Where a transaction falls within the H.P.A., s. 17 of that Act would appear to introduce such an undertaking irrespective of any sample. These undertakings have been discussed in Chapter 5.

2 **Correspondence with sample**

In the case of a sale by sample s. 15 (2) (a) of the S.G.A. provides that

> "There is an implied condition that the bulk shall correspond with the sample in quality".

Where a transaction falls within the H.P.A., s. 19 (1) (a) lays down that there shall be implied in the agreement

> "A condition that the bulk will correspond with the sample in quality".

It should be noticed that the wording of the two Acts is almost identical, so that they should, presumably, be given the same meaning. Neither of them refers to the question of quantity; and the rules concerning this have been considered above[5].

The undertaking that the goods will correspond with the contract sample in quality is closely related to the undertaking that goods shall

---

4. Guest, *Law of H.P.* 302.   5. P. 76, *et seq.*

correspond with their description[6]. A similarly strict attitude is normally taken to compliance with the undertaking[7]; but it has been held that, if the normal trade practice is that a sample only be subjected to a visual examination, there is no breach of the undertaking if the bulk does not correspond with the sample in some manner not discoverable by such examination[8]. If the two undertakings as to correspondence with sample and description did have exactly the same effect, there would be little point in making special provision for transactions made by reference to both description and sample. Yet both the S.G.A. and H.P.A. stipulate in almost identical terms that in this situation

> "it is not sufficient that the bulk of the goods correspond with the sample if the goods do not also correspond with the description" (s. 13, S.G.A.; s. 19 (2) H.P.A.).

The H.P.A. provision is clearly modelled on the S.G.A. undertaking, which in turn reflects the common law[9].

The undertakings that the bulk shall correspond with the sample are, like the undertakings that the goods shall correspond with their description, specified in the Acts to be conditions. Where the transaction involves unascertained or future goods, breach of the undertakings will clearly, *prima facie*, give rise to a right to reject[10]; but where specific goods are involved, then it would appear that, just as under s. 13 of the S.G.A.[11], the right to reject will rest on proof of a difference in kind[12].

Finally, the effect of any exclusion clause must be considered. Where a transaction falls within the H.P.A., s. 29 (3) (c) avoids any provision

> "excluding or modifying any condition implied by virtue of section 19 of this Act".

On the other hand, where a h.p. or sale transaction falls outside the ambit of the H.P.A. there is no statutory prohibition on contracting out. However, the courts appear to take a strict view of exclusion clauses similar to that adopted in respect of attempts to oust the undertaking

---

6. Above, p. 70, *et seq.*
7. See *per* HILBERY J. in *F. & S. Ruben, Ltd.* v. *Faire Brothers & Co., Ltd.*, [1949] 1 K.B. 254, at p. 260.
8. *Hookway* v. *Isaacs*, [1954] 1 Lloyds Rep. 491; *Steels & Busks, Ltd.* v. *Bleeker Bik & Co., Ltd.*, [1956] 1 Lloyds Rep. 228.
9. See *Nichol* v. *Godts* (1854), 10 Exch 191.
10. *Polenghi Brothers* v. *Dried Milk Co.* (1904), 92 L.T. 64.
11. See above, pp. 74–75.
12. See *Azémar* v. *Casella* (1867), L.R. 2 C.P. 677 (it is arguable that this is not a case of sale by sample).

of correspondence with description[13]. Thus, in *Champanhac & Co., Ltd.* v. *Waller & Co., Ltd.*[14].

> There was a sale of a quantity of government surplus balloons under a contract in which the seller stipulated that the goods were sold "as sample taken away" and "it is distinctly understood that these are government surplus goods and we sell them to you with all faults and imperfections". On delivery, the goods were found to be perished and unmerchantable.

SLADE J. held that there was a sale by sample; and that the goods did not correspond with their sample, which was neither perished nor unmerchantable. In considering the exclusion clause, his Lordship thought that the cases under s. 13 were *in pari materia*, and held that the seller was not protected in respect of breach of the undertaking that the goods should correspond with their sample. He suggested, *obiter*, that the clause might have protected the seller if there were latent defects in the goods and sample which rendered the goods unmerchantable. In this case, the undertaking was express, so that it may be that any exclusion clause must be otiose; but it has been suggested on the basis of this case that the undertaking as to correspondence with sample can never be excluded[15]. The problem would seem to be the same as that considered in relation to attempts to exclude the undertaking that the goods comply with their description.

3 Opportunity for inspection

Both the S.G.A. and the H.P.A. provide in almost identical terms that the buyer or hirer shall have

> "A reasonable opportunity of comparing the bulk with the sample".

The provision of the H.P.A. (s. 19 (1) (b)) is clearly based on that of the S.G.A. (s. 15 (2) (b)), which is itself founded on *Lorymer* v. *Smith*[16]. In this case,

> There was a contract made on Sept. 11th for the sale by sample of two parcels of wheat. On Sept. 19th the buyer went to the seller's warehouse and asked to inspect the wheat. The seller showed the buyer one parcel, but the other was not at that time in his warehouse. The seller offered to send a sample of the second parcel, but refused to let the buyer go and inspect it, saying that he refused to let the buyer into his connections. The buyer replied that under those circumstances he would not have the wheat. Notwithstanding this, the seller a few days later offered the buyer facilities to inspect the whole of the second parcel at his warehouse.

---

13. See above, p. 76   14. [1948] 2 All E.R. 724.
15. *Chalmers' Sale of Goods* (15th Edn.) 57, note (t).
16. (1822), 1 B. & C. 1.

The court held that the buyer was entitled to rescind. HOLROYD J. reasoned that, as the buyer might have insisted on delivery on 19th Sept. when the seller was not ready to comply, the seller could not afterwards insist on performance by the buyer. As ABBOTT C.J. seemed to justify his decision on the grounds that such a transaction smacked of gambling and this objection has long-since been over-ruled[17], it would appear that the rule must be justified, if at all, on the grounds put forward by HOLROYD J.

The statutory formula "reasonable opportunity" must mean "at a reasonable time and place". *Prima facie*, the time and place of delivery is the time and place for comparing the bulk with the sample; and these matters are discussed in Chapter 16 below. However, the exceptional case was considered in *Heilbutt* v. *Hickson*[18], where BRETT J. said of a sale by sample:

> "such a contract always contains an implied term that the goods may under certain circumstances be returned; that such term necessarily contains certain varying or alternative applications, and, amongst others, the following, that, if the time of inspection, as agreed upon, be subsequent to the time agreed for the delivery of the goods, or if the place of inspection, as agreed upon, be different from the place of delivery, the purchaser may, upon inspection at such time and place, if the goods be not equal to sample, return them *then and there* on the hands of the seller".

The result would appear to be that, where there is a sale by sample, the buyer has two rights to reject[19]: he has the ordinary right to reject under s. 34[20] and the special right now under discussion. These may occur in either order, and impose on the buyer different duties to return the goods[1]. Where a transaction falls within the H.P.A., the right of inspection can never be excluded (s. 29 (3) (c)), so that the hirer or buyer must always have two rights to reject the goods, though they may in certain circumstances be co-extensive. Where a contract of sale or h.p. falls outside the H.P.A. then the undertaking may be ousted. However, the courts lean against such exclusion clauses, so that, for example, even an express agreement to pay the price before inspection may not oust the undertaking[2], and exclusion of the one right to inspect may not oust

---

17. ABBOTT C.J. seems to have thought that this was like a sale of future goods (*sed quaere?*), and that such sales are necessarily wagering contracts. The latter point has since been shown to be incorrect—see above, p. 20.
18. (1872), L.R. 7 C.P. 438, at p. 456,
19. Compare Atiyah, *Sale of Goods* (3rd Edn.) 75, who suggests that the right of inspection in sales by sample is merely "a special instance of the general right of examination conferred by s. 34".
20. Discussed below, p. 269.
 1. See *Lorymer* v. *Smith* (1822), 1 B. & C. 1; *Polenghi Brothers* v. *Dried Milk Co.* (1904), 92 L.T. 64.
 2. *Polenghi Brothers* v. *Dried Milk Co.* (above).

the other. Despite the fact that dual rights of inspection possibly increase the power of the consumer to reject, it is difficult to justify this special right of inspection, and it would appear that its abolition would be no great loss[3].

4 Merchantability and fitness

In *Drummond* v. *Van Ingen*[4], the House of Lords accepted that there was ordinarily a presumption that if the bulk corresponded with the sample it satisfied the contract, but that this presumption was rebutted by proving that the goods contained a latent defect rendering them unmerchantable. This rule was embodied in s. 15 (2) (c) of the S.G.A., which is discussed above[5]. It has been shown that the scope of that subsection differs from that of s. 14 (2); what should happen, therefore, if the sale is both by description and by sample? It is submitted that in these circumstances s. 14 (2) can have no application: this would appear to reach an answer consistent with the common law; and, if s. 14 (2) were applicable in these circumstances, the more severe limitations of s. 15 (2) (c) would be pointless.

With respect to h.p. transactions, there is no common law authority as to the undertaking as to merchantability where the transaction is conducted by reference to a sample. Which analogy should be adopted: s. 14 (2) or s. 15 (2) (c) of the S.G.A.? However, where a transaction falls within the H.P.A. there is only the one undertaking as to merchantability which is to be found in s. 17 of that Act, and is expressed to apply to "every" h.p. and conditional sale agreement (s. 17 (2)).

Neither the S.G.A. nor the H.P.A. makes any special reference to an undertaking that the goods are fit for the purpose for which they are supplied where the transaction is by sample (s. 15 S.G.A.; s. 19 H.P.A.); and in both cases the statutory language of the ordinary undertaking appears to be wide enough to cover this situation (s. 14 (1) S.G.A.; s. 17 (4) H.P.A.)[6]. Support for the application of the ordinary undertakings as to fitness to transactions by sample is to be found in the common law[7].

---

3. Compare the *First Report on Exemption Clauses in Contracts* (Law Com. No. 24), paras. 58, 59.
4. (1887), 12 App. Cas. 284, H.L.
5. P. 94 *et seq.*
6. Above, p. 83.
7. *Drummond* v. *Van Ingen* (1887), 12 App. Cas. 284, H.L. See esp. *per* Lords MACNAGHTEN and HERSCHELL, at pp. 295, 293.

CHAPTER 9

Other Implied Terms and Obligations

This subject may be divided according to whether the terms or obligations are derived from (1) statute or (2) common law.

1 TERMS AND OBLIGATIONS DERIVED FROM STATUTE

1 The S.G.A.

The statutory obligations as to delivery and payment will be dealt with in Chapter 16; and it remains to consider here the residue of undertakings as to the character and quality of goods sold. Section 14 (3) provides that

> "an implied warranty or condition as to quality or fitness for a particular purpose may be annexed by the usage of trade".

This rule is a statutory formulation of what is perhaps the best-known example of implied terms at common law[1]. The alleged usage must fulfil all the normal tests of a custom[2]; but, provided that it does so, it will become part of the contract so long as it is reconcilable with the express or implied terms of the contract[3].

2 The H.P.A.

The common law right of an owner or seller to refuse to accept instalments of rent or price tendered after a breach by the hirer or buyer which amounts to a repudiation of the contract is modified by the notice of default procedure considered below[4]; and, where there is more than one debt due from the hirer or buyer, the right of the owner or seller to appropriate payments to a particular debt is excluded by s. 51[5]. On the other hand, the common law duty of a bailee to take reasonable care of the goods bailed receives statutory reinforcement under the termination provisions[6].

---

1. See *per* Lord BLACKBURN in *Tucker* v. *Linger* (1883), 8 App. Cas. 508, at p. 511. See Allen, *Law in the Making* (7th Edn.), Ch. 1 and 2.
2. E.g. *Peter Darlington, Ltd.* v. *Gosho, Ltd.*, [1964] 1 Lloyds Rep. 149; *Three Rivers Trading Co.* v. *Gwinear and District Farmers* (1967), 111 Sol. Jo. 831, C.A.; *Vacwell Engineering, Ltd.* v. *B.D.H. Chemicals, Ltd.*, [1969] 3 All E.R. 1681 (set out below, p. 389).
3. See *Produce Brokers Co., Ltd.* v. *Olympia Oil and Cake Co., Ltd.*, [1916] 1 A.C. 314, H.L.; and further litigation under the same name, [1917] 1 K.B. 320, C.A. 4. Pp. 334–336.
5. See below, pp. 271, 337. 6. See s. 28 (3) of the H.P.A.

Furthermore, the Act seeks to avoid a fertile source of misunderstanding (and even oppression) by ensuring that both parties can ascertain their rights and duties under the agreement at any time during its currency. Thus s. 21 (1) provides that:

> "At any time before the final payment has been made under a hire-purchase agreement, a credit-sale agreement or a conditional sale agreement, any person entitled to enforce the agreement against the hirer or buyer[7] shall, within four days after he has received a request in writing from the hirer or buyer, and the hirer or buyer has tendered to him the sum of 2s. 6d.[8] for expenses, supply to the hirer or buyer a copy[9] of the agreement[10], together with a statement signed by that person or his agent showing—
> (a) the amount paid by or on behalf of the hirer or buyer[11];
> (b) the amount which has become due under the agreement but remains unpaid . . .; and
> (c) the amount which is to become payable under the agreement . . ."

Subsection 2 renders continuous default for a period of a month a summary offence[12] if such default is without reasonable cause[13], and it provides that, whilst such default continues[14], no person shall be entitled to enforce the agreement against the hirer or buyer, nor any guarantee, nor any right to recover the goods[15], nor any security given by the hirer, buyer or guarantor. Almost at a *quid pro quo* for the owner or seller, s. 24 provides:

> "(1) Where by virtue of a hire-purchase agreement or a conditional sale agreement a hirer or buyer is under a duty to keep the goods comprised in the agreement in his possession or control, the hirer or buyer shall, on receipt of a request in writing from the owner or seller, inform the owner or seller where the goods are at the time when the information is given, or, if sent by post, at the time of posting.
> (2) If the hirer or buyer fails without reasonable cause to give that information within fourteen days of receipt of the notice, he shall be liable on summary conviction to a fine not exceeding £25"[16].

---

7. By s. 58 (1), the expressions "hirer" and "buyer" include anyone to whom their rights have passed by assignment or operation of law.
8. For conversion of this sum, see s. 10 of the Decimal Currency Act 1969.
9. Which complies with the legibility requirements: s. 21 (3).
10. But see s. 21 (4).
11. By s. 56, this includes payment otherwise than in money where this has been agreed between the parties, e.g. a part-exchange allowance: see below, p. 271.
12. Does this render the contract illegal? Or does s. 21 (2) exhibit a sufficient contrary intention. Illegality is discussed above, pp. 37–39.
13. Presumably the onus of proof is on the prosecution, cf. the common defence of reasonable excuse.
14. The impairment need only be temporary. Compare s. 5, above, p. 33.
15. Compare s. 34 (2), discussed below, pp. 338–339.
16. Does this render the contract illegal?

3 Other statutes

Apart from the S.G.A. and H.P.A., there are a number of other
statutes which impose obligations on the contracting parties. Often
these provisions are aimed at a particular type of transaction or a transaction involving a specified type of goods, or both.

In imposing such obligations three techniques are available to the
Legislature. First, a statute may import terms into the contract,
breach of which will give the innocent party civil law rights[17]. Second,
the agreement may be rendered unenforceable[18] or terminated[19] in the
event of non-compliance. Third, a statute may impose criminal
sanctions in respect of the prohibited act[20]. This last course tends to
be more favoured nowadays as it is more likely to be effectively enforced, but it does give rise to certain problems: (1) does it render the
agreement illegal; (2) if so, to what extent does this prevent the parties
from relying on the agreement; and (3) does contravention give rise
to an action for breach of statutory duty[1]?

2 TERMS AND OBLIGATIONS DERIVED FROM COMMON LAW

Whether the transaction envisaged is one of sale or h.p., there is
nothing in the Acts to oust any express or implied condition precedent.
Conditions in the sense of essential stipulations have already been
distinguished from conditions precedent[2]; and in relation to conditions
precedent it is further necessary to distinguish between those precedent
to the existence of a contract[3] and those precedent to performance of
some or all of its obligations[4].

We are now in a position to consider the terms implied by common
law into sale or h.p. transactions, whether they are terms within the
contract, or conditions precedent of one sort or the other.

---

17. E.g. Hops (Prevention of Frauds) Act 1866, s. 18; Anchors & Chain Cables
    Act 1899, s. 2; Fertilisers & Feeding Stuffs Act 1926, s. 2; Plants & Seeds
    Act 1964, s. 17.
18. E.g. H.P.A., ss. 5, 22; L.P.A. 1925, s. 40.
19. H.P.A., s. 34. Does the Infants Relief Act 1874, s. 1 fall within this
    category?
20. E.g. Fabrics (Misdescription) Act 1913, s. 3; Rag Flock Material Act 1951,
    s. 10; Food & Drugs Act 1955; Road Traffic Act 1963, s. 68; Consumer
    Protection Act 1961; Weights & Measures Act 1963, s. 22; Plant Varieties
    and Seeds Act 1964, ss. 13, 28; Trade Description Act 1968.
 1. See above, pp. 27–28.
 2. See above, pp. 50–51.
 3. I.e. the offer or acceptance may be conditional, e.g. *Financings, Ltd.* v.
    Stimson, [1962] 3 All E.R. 386, C.A. (see above, p. 36); *Christopher Hill,
    Ltd.* v. *Ashington Piggeries, Ltd.*, [1969] 3 All E.R. 1496, C.A. (see above,
    p. 87, note 7).
 4. E.g. *Marten* v. *Whale*, [1917] 2 K.B. 480, C.A.: set out above, p. 7.

1 In sale

Where a transaction falls within the S.G.A., then the opening words of s. 14 of that Act provide that:

> "Subject to the provisions of this Act and of any statute in that behalf, there is no implied warranty or condition as to the quality or fitness for any particular purpose of goods supplied under a contract of sale . . ."

These words might appear to confirm the full severity of the common law attitude of *caveat emptor*, and to prevent any implication of terms under the doctrine of *The Moorcock*[5]. However, there are a number of ways in which the full severity of this rule may be mitigated. First, the section says "there is no warranty or condition", which seems to imply that "condition" is here used in the sense of essential stipulation. If so, s. 14 does not prevent the implication of conditions precedent. Second, s. 14 does not prevent the prudent buyer from securing an express contractual promise by the seller as to the quality or fitness of the goods sold. Does such an express promise oust the terms which would ordinarily be implied? At common law this turned on whether the parties intended the term to be in addition to the implied term or merely to replace it[6]; and s. 14 (4) now provides:

> "An express warranty or condition does not negative a warranty or condition implied by this Act unless inconsistent therewith".

This subsection would appear to be merely an example of the ordinary rule as to the exclusion of implied terms set out in s. 55[7]. Third, it may be possible to show that the contract falls wholly or partly outside the S.G.A., as being a contract for skill and labour or as a barter[8]. Whilst this may avoid the direct effect of s. 14, the tendency of the courts to model the common law terms on the basis of those to be found in the S.G.A. might result in the opening words of s. 14 being applied by analogy. Fourth, it may be possible for the buyer to bring an action in tort, though such an action will not usually be as likely to succeed as a claim in contract[9]. Fifth, it has been suggested that a person who buys goods with a latent defect may be able to rescind the contract on the grounds of non-disclosure[10].

2 In hire purchase

In contrast to the situation within the S.G.A. the courts have felt themselves able to import a considerable number of implied terms for

---

5. (1889), 14 P.D. 64, C.A. See also *The Mihalis Angelos*, [1970] 3 All E.R. 125, C.A.
6. See *Bigge* v. *Parkinson* (1862), 7 H. & N. 955.
7. Section 55 is reproduced below, p. 132.   8. See above, pp. 23–24.
9. See below, Chapter 10.   10. Atiyah (1968), 2 Ottawa L.R. 337, 339–344.

the benefit of both owners and hirers. Many of these implied terms obviously owe their inspiration to the law of bailment.

For the benefit of the hirer, it has been decided that the hiring does not commence until delivery[11], and that the goods have not been delivered until they have been accepted by the hirer so as to pass into his possession[12]. Furthermore, the courts have implied conditions that the goods should remain in substantially the same condition from the time when the offer is made up to the time of acceptance[13], and from then until the time of delivery[12]. In *Bentworth Finance, Ltd.* v. *Lubert*[14]

> The plaintiff finance company agreed to let a car to L. under a directly financed transaction under which M. agreed to act as surety for L. The dealer left the car, unlicenced and untaxed, outside L.'s house, and L. neither used the car nor paid any instalments.

The Court of Appeal unanimously dismissed the plaintiff's action against L. for arrears of instalments, and against M. under the contract of surety, on the following grounds:

(1) It was an implied condition of the h.p. agreement that the log-book should be supplied, and until it was supplied "there was no contract of h.p. at all", and no instalments fell due;

(2) M. was not liable because the plaintiff's loss did not arise from the contract of h.p. being unenforceable, but from the "plaintiff's allowing the dealers to hand over the car without the log-book"[15].

Now, in all the cases so far cited in this paragraph the owner was suing the hirer, and the courts did no more than hold that performance of a particular act by the owner was a condition precedent to his enforcement of the agreement[16]. It is, however, usually thought that the owner impliedly promises to deliver the goods, and to deliver them in substantially the same condition as they were when inspected by the hirer.

Similarly, the courts implied in favour of the owner obligations that the hirer will accept delivery of goods tendered in performance of the contract[11]. That he will take reasonable care of them during the currency of the agreement[17], that he will not do any act in relation to

---

11. *National Cash Register Co.* v. *Stanley*, [1921] 3 K.B. 292, D.C.
12. *Karsales, Ltd.* v. *Wallis*, [1956] 2 All E.R. 866, C.A.: set out below, p. 141.
13. *Financings, Ltd.* v. *Stimson*, [1962] 3 All E.R. 386, C.A.
14. [1968] 1 Q.B. 680; [1967] 2 All E.R. 810, C.A,
15. See further below, pp. 346, 379.
16. Were they conditions precedent to contract or performance? See Lord DENNING M.R. in *Lubert's Case* (above), at p. 685,
17. The extent of this common law duty is uncertain; and it is unlikely to be settled as the agreement will almost always impose strict liability on the hirer.

the goods which is totally repugnant to the terms of the bailment[18] and that he will pay the sums stipulated in the agreement subject to the ordinary common law rules of payment[19]. Furthermore, where the agreement is determined, the hirer is under a common law duty to redeliver the goods; but, should redelivery become impossible through no fault of the hirer, the hirer is, *prima facie* discharged from this duty[1]. Failure to comply with his duty to redeliver will render the hirer liable to an action for breach of contract, or in tort for conversion or detinue. In the absence of any contractual provision to the contrary, the common law duty of redelivery is merely to hold the goods ready for the owner to fetch them; and the battle of wits to which this rule may give rise is well illustrated by *Capital Finance, Ltd.* v. *Bray*[2].

---

18. See below, p. 356.
19. See below, p. 271.
 1. See subsequent impossibility, below, Chapter 15.
 2. [1964] 1 All E.R. 603, C.A.: set out below, p. 338.

CHAPTER 10

Product Liability[1]

The pattern of liability to consumers for defects in products imposed by English Law demonstrates considerable inconsistency; and in part this is due to the fact that the problem has been approached through two completely independent sets of legal principles, those of contract and those of tort. Where there is a contractual relationship there may be strict liability, whereas outside the contractual nexus liability is likely only to be founded on negligence. In considering product liability, it is therefore necessary to decide whether there is any contractual nexus between any two of the potentially large number of persons in the chain of distribution from the manufacturer to the consumer.

I WITHIN THE CONTRACTUAL NEXUS

Where there is a contractual nexus between the parties, it is again important to distinguish according to whether or not there is any contractual promises as to the state of the product.

1 A contractual promise

Assuming that there is such a contractual promise, the discussion may be conveniently sub-divided according to whether the promise became (1) a term of a single contract for the disposition of goods, or (2) a term of one of a chain of such contracts, or (3) a term of a collateral contract. *1. A single contract.* In the previous Chapters of Part 2, the various undertakings which may be imported into a contract of sale or h.p. have been considered. The major protection of the buyer or hirer rests on the undertakings as to title, correspondence with description, fitness for the purpose supplied and merchantable quality. Potentially, the last two probably offer the most valuable protection to the transferee; and Chapter 7 dealt with the complicated nature of these undertakings, the limitations on them, and the overlap between them. The present position is chaotic and unfair. It is suggested that the first step towards simplification should be to treat consumer sales and h.p. in an identical manner, and to imply the same obligations in both. And is it not time that the last vestiges of *caveat emptor* were swept away from all consumer sales?

---

1. See generally Fleming, *Torts* (3rd Edn.), Chapters 21, 25; Jolowicz (1969), 32 M.L.R. 1; Waddams (1969), 49 U.T.L.J. 157.

2. *A chain of contracts.* The ordinary situation where there is a chain of contracts from manufacturer to consumer is well illustrated by the case of *Parker* v. *Oloxo Ltd.*[2].

> On one occasion, a hairdresser suggested to the plaintiff, one of her regular customers, that she try a new hair dye, Oloxo, and assured her that it was safe to use. As a result of the application of Oloxo, the plaintiff suffered an acute attack of dermatitis. The hairdresser had been induced to purchase Oloxo by the distributor of that product in the U.K.; and, in obtaining the hairdresser's order, the distributor had warranted to her that the product was safe to use, and said that, if she purchased one guinea's worth, she would be entitled to attend certain lectures and demonstrations free of charge. For trade reasons, the distributor supplied the hairdresser through a wholesaler. Thereafter, the hairdresser attended the lectures, at which the distributor promised to indemnify hairdressers for any claims arising out of the use of Oloxo.

In an action by the plaintiff customer against the hairdresser and distributor, HILBERY J. held:

(1) The customer was entitled to recover damages against both the defendants for the following reasons:

(a) The hairdresser was liable to the customer for breach of the express warranty contained in her assurance[3].

(b) The distributor was liable to the customer in the tort of negligence[4].

(2) The hairdresser was entitled to recover from the distributor the damages[5] she paid to the customer on the following grounds:

(a) There was a contract of sale between the two, under which the distributor expressly warranted Oloxo[6].

(b) The distributor was liable to the hairdresser in the tort of negligence[7].

It was further argued by the hairdresser that the distributor was liable to her under the indemnity given at the lectures; but this plea was rejected on the grounds that it was not "made at the time when it can be deemed to be a part of the contract"[8]. Where there is a chain

---

2. [1937] 3 All E.R. 524.
3. What if there had been no express assurance: could one have been implied? Cf. *Griffiths* v. *Peter Conway, Ltd.*, [1939] 1 All E.R. 685, C.A., and *Watson* v. *Buckley, Osborne, Garrett & Co., Ltd.*, [1940] 1 All E.R. 174.
4. See below, pp. 125, 129.
5. It has been said that the damages should include all that was within the contemplation of the parties, including the retailer's costs in defending the action—*per* BRANSON J.
6. The position where there is no contract of sale between the two, but simply a collateral contract of warranty is discussed below.
7. See below, p. 129.
8. At p. 529. If the objection is one of past consideration, surely the hairdresser's subsequent recommendation of Oloxo to her customer would have sufficed.

of contracts for the disposition of goods by way of sale or h.p., the last transferee will normally have a right to rescind for breach of condition; but previous transferees are less likely to be able to rescind[9]. To the extent that the previous transferee can only claim damages, his position is similar to that of a person suing under a collateral contract of warranty. Yet the two situations must be carefully distinguished because only the contract of disposition will attract the whole paraphernalia of implied terms.

3. A collateral contract. Whether there is a single contract or a chain of contracts for the disposition of goods, there may be one or more collateral contracts[10]. Thus, A. may make a misrepresentation to B. which is calculated to, and does, lead B. to enter into a contract to sell to or buy from C.[11]. In the field of product liability, there are two particular situations where this device has been used to impose liability: first, to impose contractual liability on a dealer in a directly financed transaction; and second, to give the consumer a right of action in contract against a manufacturer, distributor or wholesaler. The former situation will be considered later[12], but the use of the device may be illustrated here by reference to the latter situation. The representation may be made personally to the customer by the representative of the manufacturer, distributor or wholesaler[13]. It is more likely, however, that the representation will be made to the customer in a less personal way by sales literature, or other advertisement whether distributed at the point of retail sale, directly mailed or carried in newspapers or on television[14]. One particular device which requires special mention here is the "manufacturer's guarantee". Such a device will normally contain two elements: it will probably purport to confer limited rights on the customer as against the manufacturer in respect of defects in the goods, in consideration for which the customer agrees to forgo his ordinary legal rights against the manufacturer, and also possibly against the retailer. The exclusionary aspect of the document will be considered in Chapter 11, but the device may also raise questions concerning the doctrine of consideration. There is no difficulty where there are two clauses such as those outlined above, each of which provides the consideration for the other. But where there is only one clause, and it is only brought to the notice of the customer after he has purchased

---

9. See s. 35 of the S.G.A., which is discussed below, pp. 400–402.
10. Collateral contracts are discussed above, p. 52.
11. Cf. *Hedley Byrne & Co., Ltd.* v. *Heller, Ltd.*, [1964] A.C. 465; [1963] 2 All E.R. 575, H.L.: see below, p. 129.
12. See below, pp. 282–284.
13. E.g. *Shanklin Pier, Ltd.* v. *Detel Products, Ltd.*, [1951] 2 K.B. 854.
14. Liability is, perhaps, less likely here, because the advertising industry is usually very careful not to make any material representations of fact.

from the retailer, it may be that any consideration is "past"[15]. Similar difficulties arise in respect of the service contracts frequently offered in respect of the more durable consumer goods[16].

2 Other remedies

Even though no contractual promise is made to the consumer, he may be able to rely on the law relating to misrepresentation, illegality, unenforceability or mistake.

1. Misrepresentation[17]. At common law, the remedies available in the case of mere misrepresentation depend on whether the misrepresentation was fraudulent or innocent. In either case, the misrepresentee might rescind[18]; but only if the misrepresentation were fraudulent could he get damages at common law, in the tort of deceit. Whilst the common law will usually only offer an innocent misrepresentee the possibility of rescission and an indemnity, the Misrepresentation Act 1967 may enable him to recover damages in two situations.

(a) Where there is an innocent but negligent misrepresentation. Section 2 (1) provides:

> "Where a person has entered into a contract after a misrepresentation[19] has been made[20] to him by another party thereto and as a result thereof[1] he has suffered loss, then, if the person making the misrepresentation would be liable to damages in respect thereof had the misrepresentation been made fraudulently[2], that person shall be so liable[3] notwithstanding that the misrepresentation was not made fraudulently, unless he proves[4] that he had reasonable ground to believe and did believe up to the time the contract was made that the facts represented were true".

---

15. E.g. *Roscorla* v. *Thomas* (1842), 3 Q.B. 234.
16. E.g. *Stewart* v. *Reavell's Garage*, [1952] 2 Q.B. 545; [1952] 1 All E.R. 1191.
17. See generally Cheshire & Fifoot, *Contract* (7th Edn.) 233–269; Stoljar, *Mistake and Misrepresentation*; Atiyah & Treitel (1967), 30 M.L.R. 369; Fairest, [1967] Camb. L.J. 239; Smith & Thomas, *Casebook on Contract* (4th Edn.) 247–254.
18. The remedy of rescission for misrepresentation will be considered below, pp. 357–359.
19. There is no statutory definition of "misrepresentation", so the common law definition presumably applies.
20. Does the phrase "misrepresentation made" cover non-disclosure?—see Hudson (1969), 85 L.Q.R. 524.
 1. Presumably the misrepresentor must intend the misrepresentee to rely on the misrepresentation before the provision operates. On whom does the burden of proof lie?
 2. The effect of this would appear to be to incorporate by reference the law of deceit. The difficult question of how much of that law is so incorporated is discussed by Atiyah & Treitel, *op. cit.*, pp. 374–375.
 3. Is the measure of damages that in contract or deceit? See Atiyah & Treitel, *op. cit.*, p. 373.
 4. The effect of this *seems* to be to place the legal (?) burden of proof on the misrepresentor. Compare the much lighter onus in an action of deceit, when the legal and evidential burden is on the misrepresentee.

(b) Where there is an innocent misrepresentation, whether negligent or not. Section 2 (2) provides:

> "Where a person has entered into a contract after a misrepresentation[19] has been made[20] to him otherwise than fraudulently, and he would be entitled, by reason of the misrepresentation, to rescind the contract[5], then, if it is claimed, in any proceedings arising out of the contract, that the contract ought to be or has been rescinded, the court or arbitrator may declare the contract subsisting and award damages[6] in lieu of rescission, if of opinion that it would be equitable to do so, having regard to the nature of the misrepresentation and the loss that would be caused by it if the contract were upheld, as well as to the loss that rescission would cause to the other party".

Thus, the representee is only entitled to damages as of right if either (a) the misrepresentation became a term of the contract[7], or (b) it was fraudulent[8], or (c) he can bring himself within s. 2 (1). Where he is induced to contract by an innocent non-negligent misrepresentation, he can only obtain damages under s. 2 (2), and whether he does so lies wholly at the discretion of the court.

2. Illegality and Unenforceability. There are a number of statutory provisions which may taint a contract with illegality or render it unenforceable; and many of these were specifically designed for the protection of a particular group of persons[9]. The effect of these provisions on the contract has already been considered[10].

3. Mistake[11]. Frequently as a line of last resort, the buyer or hirer may claim to avoid contractual liability on grounds of mistake. Immediately, it is vital to decide whether or not the parties have reached agreement. If they have, but are both labouring under the same fundamental mistake, such as where the contractual goods have already been destroyed, this raises the question of initial impossibility considered below[12]. On the other hand, it may be denied that the parties were ever *ad idem.* so that the alleged contract was "void" *ab initio.*

---

5. Does this mean right to rescind for (a) misrepresentation, or (b) misrepresentation or breach? Does it refer exclusively to the common law right to rescind; or to that right as enlarged by s. 1 of the Misrepresentation Act 1967? See Atiyah & Treitel, *op. cit.*, pp. 376–378.
6. It has been pointed out that rescission can be obtained without proof of damage, so that presumably the court could award damages in lieu cf rescission without proof of damage—Street, *Torts* (4th Edn.) 388. What is the measure of damages? See Atiyah & Treitel, *op. cit.*, p. 377. Section 2 (3) enables the court to award damages under both ss. 2 (1) and (2), provided that there is no element of double recovery.
7. See above, pp. 49–50.
8. It is usually assumed that the 1967 Act has not touched the common law action for deceit.
9. See above, pp. 27.   10. See above, p. 37.
11. See generally Treitel, *Law of Contract* (3rd Edn.), Chapter 8; Stoljar, *Mistake and Misrepresentation.*   12. See pp. 250–254.

The possibility of such a mistake has already been considered[13]; and it has been pointed out that such a plea is particularly likely to be raised by the buyer or hirer who finds that the contract goods are defective[14]. Within the English law of contract, there are only two possible solutions:

(1) The goods are at the risk of the buyer or hirer, i.e. the rule *caveat emptor* applies; or

(2) The goods are at the risk of the seller or owner for one of the following reasons:

(a) there is a breach of an express or implied term which puts responsibility on the seller or owner; or

(b) the contract is void, in which case the transferor as owner bears the risk of any defect in his goods.

On this basis, it is clear that the plea of mistake as to quality by the buyer or hirer is really an alternative method of trying to place the risk on the transferor. Such a plea was raised for this purpose by the buyer in *Harrison and Jones, Ltd.* v. *Bunten and Lancaster, Ltd.*[15]:

> There was a contract for the sale by sample of Calcutta Kapok, "Sree" brand. Neither party was aware that this brand of kapok contained an admixture of cotton, which it turned out rendered it unsuitable for use by the buyer on his machines.

PILCHER J. rejected the buyer's plea of mistake, pointing out that there was no finding of fact that the parties directed their minds towards the question of whether the goods contained an admixture of cotton[16]. Nevertheless, his Lordship did consider what would have been the position had they done so. He denied that the mistake would be such as to make the goods "essentially different", so that the contract would be void at common law under the doctrine of *Bell* v. *Lever Brothers, Ltd.*[17]. Nor did he think that the buyer should be able to rescind in equity under the rule in *Solle* v. *Butcher*[18]. Whilst an insurer has recently been allowed by the Court of Appeal to escape from a contract of compromise on grounds of mistake, the authority of this case is weakened by the fact that one of the majority thought that the contract was void at common law and the other that it was only voidable in equity[19].

---

13. Above, p. 37. 14. Atiyah, *Sale of Goods* (3rd Edn.) 83.
15. [1953] 1 Q.B. 646; [1953] 1 All E.R. 903. 16. At p. 657.
17. [1932] A.C. 161, H.L. The only case where a contract for the sale of goods has been held void on grounds of mistake is *Nicholson and Venn* v. *Smith-Marriott* (1947), 177 L.T. 189: but see the criticisms of that case in Atiyah, *Sale of Goods* (3rd Edn.) 86, note 1; Treitel, *Law of Contract* (3rd Edn.) 216, note 44.
18. [1950] 1 K.B. 671; [1949] 2 All E.R. 1107, C.A. See also *Grist* v. *Bailey*, [1967] Ch. 532; [1966] 2 All E.R. 875.
19. *Magee* v. *Pennine Insurance Co., Ltd.*, [1969] 2 Q.B. 507; [1969] 2 All E.R. 891, C.A. See Harris (1969), 32 M.L.R. 688.

Moreover, there is a strong argument for saying that it is undesirable that the law should too frequently allow a buyer or hirer of goods to escape from his contract of sale or h.p. on a plea of mistake, on the grounds that this would unduly interfere with the interests of certainty.

2 OUTSIDE THE CONTRACTUAL NEXUS

With a few limited exceptions, the common law takes an extremely strict view of contractual promises, the promisor being almost regarded as guaranteeing his promise. Yet this strict contractual liability is limited by the doctrine of privity, and those who are not privy can only be liable in tort, where liability usually depends on fault. It has already been noted how the courts have sought to avoid this limitation of strict liability both by tracing breach back along the chain of distribution, and by the collateral contract of warranty; and it has been pointed out the courts have also sought to mitigate the effects of the doctrine of privity by "astute manipulation of the agency concept and a husband's or parent's claim in the case of injury or death to his wife or child"[20].

However, because there are so many claims that cannot be fitted within the framework of contract, we must consider, albeit briefly, the grounds of liability in tort. In this discussion, it is convenient to distinguish between (1) liability for acts or omissions, and (2) liability for statements.

1 Liability for acts or omissions[1]

The supplier of goods will seldom be under any strict liability in tort in relation to defects in the goods causing physical loss: the doctrine in *Rylands* v. *Fletcher* probably has no application in this context[2], and the possibility of an action in trespass will usually be ruled out because the act or omission of the supplier on which the complaint is based will generally have occurred whilst the goods were in his ownership or control[3]. Thus recovery in tort will usually depend on proof of negligence. The difference between liability in contract, and that in

---

20. Fleming, *Torts* (3rd Edn.) 475. See also the comments of the Law Commission in the *First Report on Exemption Clauses in Contracts* (Law Com. No. 24), paras. 60–63.
1. Fleming, *op. cit.*, Chapter 21; Street, *Torts* (4th Edn.) 167–176; Winfield, *Tort* (8th Edn.), Chapter 11.
2. See the judgment of SCOTT L.J. in *Read* v. *Lyons, Ltd.*, [1945] 1 K.B. 216; [1945] 1 All E.R. 106, C.A.; decision affd., [1947] A.C. 156; [1946] 2 All E.R. 471, H.L.
3. Possibly, an action on the case for physical injury might lie on the analogy of *Wilkinson* v. *Downton*, [1897] 2 Q.B. 57. Cf. *Beaudesert Shire Council* v. *Smith* (1966), 40 A.L.J.R. 211, H.C.: see Dworkin & Harari 40 A.L.J. 296, 347.

the tort of negligence is neatly exemplified by *Daniels and Daniels v. White & Sons, Ltd.*[4].

> The male plaintiff sued the retailer in contract and his wife sued the manufacturer in tort when they both suffered injury by reason of the fact that the sealed bottle of lemonade sold to them included a large element of carbolic acid.

Notwithstanding that it seemed extremely likely that the acid was introduced into the bottle whilst at the manufacturer's plant, LEWIS J. held that the manufacturer was not liable in negligence on the grounds that his process was foolproof[5], but that the innocent retailer was liable for breach of the S.G.A., s. 14 (2)[6].

Indeed, it was only with the decision of the House of Lords in *Donoghue v. Stevenson*[7], that a manufacturer owed a duty to the ultimate consumer, that it became clear that participation in the chain of distribution might involve a general liability in the tort of negligence. The scope of the principle, as developed in subsequent cases, may be analysed as follows:

1. The subject-matter. In *Donoghue v. Stevenson* the court was dealing with a bottle of ginger beer and referred to "a manufacturer of products". Subsequently the principle has been extended to other manufactured products[8], and probably includes not only the goods sold, but also any other goods transferred under the contract.[9]

2. The plaintiff. In *Donoghue v. Stevenson*, the court was prepared to contemplate that a donee of goods (her donor having purchased from the retailer) might recover, and the court spoke in terms of the "ultimate consumer". Subsequently, liability has been extended beyond the literal meaning of that expression[10].

3. The defendant. In *Donoghue v. Stevenson*, the defendant was a manufacturer, but the rule has subsequently been extended to cover manufacturers of components[11], assemblers[12], distributors[13] and retailers[14]. Thus, it would seem that any person who forms a link in the chain of distribution may potentially be liable to any later link,

---

4. [1938] 4 All E.R. 258. 5. But see below, p. 127.
6. See above, p. 98. 7. [1932] A.C. 562, H.L.
8. E.g. *Grant v. Australian Knitting Mills, Ltd.*, [1936] A.C. 85, P.C. (underpants); *Parker v. Oloxo, Ltd. and Senior*, [1937] 3 All E.R. 524 (hair-dye); *Herschtal v. Stewart and Arden, Ltd.*, [1940] 1 K.B. 155; [1939] 4 All E.R. 123 (motor car).
9. Cf. *Geddling v. Marsh*, [1920] 1 K.B. 668: set out above, p. 81.
10. See e.g. *Stennett v. Hancock and Peters*, [1939] 2 All E.R. 578; *Barnett v. Packer, Ltd.*, [1940] 3 All E.R. 575.
11. E.g. *Evans v. Triplex, Ltd.*, [1936] 1 All E.R. 283.
12. E.g. *Howard v. Furness, Ltd.*, [1936] 2 All E.R. 781.
13. E.g. *Parker v. Oloxo, Ltd. and Senior*, [1937] 3 All E.R. 524. But compare *Holmes v. Ashford*, [1950] 2 All E.R. 76, C.A.
14. E.g. *Fisher v. Harrods, Ltd.*, [1966] 1 Lloyds Rep. 500; *Andrews v. Hopkinson*, [1957] 1 Q.B. 229; [1956] 3 All E.R. 422 (see below, pp. 283–284).

though the manifestation of the duty may vary according to the defendant's place in the chain: the manufacturer or assembler may be liable for negligent manufacture[15] or failure to warn[16], whereas the distributors are more likely to be liable only for negligent handling or failure to warn[17]. At one time it was thought that a defendant could not be liable in negligence to one with whom he had contracted if the facts were such as to give rise to liability for breach of contract[18]; but it has now been settled that, where there is liability in contract, then *a fortiori* a duty of care is owed in tort[19]. The extent of the duty of care which any of these defendants owes to a donee is still very much open[20].

4. *Intermediate examination.* In *Donoghue* v. *Stevenson* the court stressed that there was "no reasonable opportunity of intermediate examination". Thus, the liability of the manufacturer may be reduced or cancelled by the failure of some later party in the chain of distribution to inspect the goods. The test would seem to be not whether there is the possibility of examination, but whether that party is foreseeably likely to examine the goods for that particular defect[1]. Where that intermediate party is unlikely to examine, he will not be liable to anybody further along the chain of distribution, unless the defect was either caused by his negligence, or he knew of the defect, or unless he is under a contractual obligation to the person injured to examine the goods. On the other hand, where the intermediate party is forseeably likely to inspect the goods, he is liable to anybody further along the chain of distribution injured by his negligent discharge of this duty[2], though such liability will not necessarily exonerate persons through whose hands the goods have earlier passed[3], and liability may be apportioned[4]. It has been suggested that similar principles should apply where the ultimate

---

15. If the goods are inherently dangerous, the manufacturer may also have a duty to warn: cf. *Burfitt* v. *Kille*, [1939] 2 K.B. 743; [1939] 2 All E.R. 372; and *Holmes* v. *Ashford*, [1950] 2 All E.R. 76, C.A.
16. *Vacwell Engineering, Ltd.* v. *B.D.H. Chemicals, Ltd.*, [1969] 3 All E.R. 1681: see below, p. 389.
17. E.g. *Clarke* v. *Army and Navy Co-operative Society*, [1903] 1 K.B. 155; *Andrews* v. *Hopkinson* (above).
18. This rule was unjustifiably deduced from *Winterbottom* v. *Wright* (1848), 10 M. & W. 109: see Fleming, *Torts* (3rd Edn.) 478.
19. *White* v. *John Warwick & Co.*, [1953] 2 All E.R. 1021, at p. 1026.
20. But see Fleming, *Torts* (3rd Edn.) 486.
 1. E.g. *Grant* v. *Australian Knitting Mills, Ltd.*, [1936] A.C. 85, P.C.; *Watson* v. *Buckley, Osborne, Garrett & Co., Ltd.*, [1940] 1 K.B. 155; [1940] 1 All E.R. 174. Cf. *Clay* v. *Crump, Ltd.*, [1964] 1 Q.B. 533; [1963] 3 All E.R. 687, C.A.
 2. E.g. *Herschtal* v. *Stewart and Arden, Ltd.*, [1940] 1 K.B. 155; [1939] 4 All E.R. 123.
 3. See *Kubach* v. *Hollands*, [1937] 3 All E.R. 907.
 4. Under the Law Reform (Married Women and Tortfeasors) Act 1935.

purchaser might reasonably be expected to inspect the goods and discover the fault[5].

The duty owed by each party in the chain of distribution to every subsequent party in the chain is merely to exercise reasonable care. Moreover, a defendant may be exonerated from liability, or that liability reduced, where the plaintiff himself knows of the danger and disregards it, or uses the goods for a purpose which is materially different from that for which they were designed[6], or where the defect is due to wear and tear, inadequate maintenance or faulty repair.

Frequently, the most vital matter in this type of action is proof of causation, a matter which becomes more difficult to prove as more links exist in the chain of distribution between plaintiff and defendant. If the plaintiff can show that the defect arose whilst the goods were within the control of the defendant, then he may be able to rely on the maxim *res ipsa loquitur*. As this presumption is very difficult to rebut[7], the effect of its operation may be the imposition of something very like strict liability in tort. It has been pointed out that the combination of strict liability in both contract and tort is "to make the manufacturer virtually an insurer"[8]. However, it is in the nature of this type of situation that the defect may be caused by the default of any one of a number of people in the chain of distribution, so that it may be very difficult to prove that one person was at fault. As it will usually be impossible for either party to prove whose fault caused the defect, he who bears the burden of proof will normally lose. For instance, in some cases the courts have refused to apply the maxim *res ipsa loquitur*, and have dismissed the plaintiff's action because he could not prove exactly where the defect had occurred[9]. Sometimes, it is possible for the courts to escape from this dilemma by apportioning loss, or because one party is vicariously liable for the torts of the other, or because the evidence clearly establishes the innocence of all but one of the parties in the chain of distribution[10]. Where either A. *or* B. *or both* have been negligent, then it is arguable that it has been shown on the balance of probabilities that *both* A. and B. have been negligent[11]. But what if the

---

5. Fleming, *Torts* (3rd Edn.) 481–482.
6. What of the child who drinks furniture polish?
7. It was successfully rebutted in *Daniels and Daniels* v. *White, & Sons, Ltd.* [1938] 4 All E.R. 258. But what of vicarious liability?
8. Fleming, *Torts* (3rd Edn.) 482.
9. E.g. *Evans* v. *Triplex, Ltd.*, [1936] 1 All E.R. 283; *Daniels and Daniels* v. *White & Sons, Ltd.*, [1938] 4 All E.R. 258. But see *Mason* v. *Williams and Williams and Thomas Turton & Sons, Ltd.*, [1955] 1 All E.R. 808.
10. This last point may provide the explanation of the finding of negligence against the manufacturer in both *Grant* v. *Australian Knitting Mills, Ltd.*, [1936] A.C. 85, P.C., and *Mason's Case* (above).
11. See *Baker* v. *Market Harborough Industrial Co-operative Society, Ltd.*, [1953] 1 W.L.R. 1472 (this is not a sale case).

evidence merely shows that either A. *or* B., *but not both* have been negligent? The maxim *res ipsa loquitur* can have no application[12], and it would seem that the plaintiff is not entitled to succeed against both A. and B.[13], unless perhaps both have refused to give evidence[14].

2 Liability for statements

There are a variety of ways in which an untrue statement may cause loss, but no one action in tort exists to cover all such circumstances. Instead, there are a number of torts giving a partial, sometimes overlapping, protection against loss arising by reason of the untrue statement of another. First, the law of torts offers some protection in respect of injury to reputation of the person or goods by way of defamation, injurious falsehood and passing-off. Second, statements calculated to cause injury to the person may be actionable: for instance, there may be liability for inducing breach of contract, or if a deliberate falsehood is calculated to cause physical harm within the principle of *Wilkinson* v. *Downton*[15]. Third, where reliance on the statement causes injury, it may be possible to bring an action in deceit or negligence. The common factors in all the torts just listed is that liability may arise under each of them through statements made by the defendant to the plaintiff, irrespective of whether there is any contractual relation between the two. However, each tort is subject to its own rules and limited in its scope; and for the details reference must be made to the standard works on tort, though some comments about the third category may be apposite here.

Where the defendant knowingly[16] or recklessly makes a false statement with the intention that the plaintiff should act on it, then the plaintiff may recover in respect of any loss caused by his reliance on it, irrespective of whether the statement was made directly to him. However, to stop litigants avoiding the Statute of Frauds 1677 by suing in deceit in respect of a false statement as to creditworthiness, the Statute of Frauds Amendment Act 1828, s. 6, enacted as follows:

> "No action shall be brought whereby to charge any person upon or by reason of any representation or assurance made or given concerning or relating to the character, conduct, credit, ability, trade or dealings of any other person, to the intent or purpose that such other

---

12. See *per* Finnemore J. in *Mason's Case* (above), at p. 810. Cf. *Cook* v. *Lewis*, [1952] 1 D.L.R. 1; Hogan (1961), 24 M.L.R. 331.
13. *A fortiori*, if either A. or B. or C. have been negligent.
14. *Per* Denning L.J. in *Baker's Case* (above), at p. 1476. And see *per* Jenkins L.J. in *Bray* v. *Palmer*, [1953] 2 All E.R. 1449, C.A., at p. 1451.
15. [1897] 2 Q.B. 57.
16. What if the representation is made innocently, but its falsity is later discovered? See Fleming, *Torts* (3rd Edn.) 600.

person may obtain credit, money, or goods upon[17], unless such representation or assurance be made in writing, signed by the party to be charged therewith".

The independent tort of deceit is a relatively modern one, but its basis may be traced back to the Writ of Deceit in the thirteenth century. This writ was the origin of two separate lines of development: the modern tort of deceit itself[18]; and, quite separately, the old Writ, which had been used to give a remedy for breach of warranty, was absorbed into the action of assumpsit[19]. With the passage of time, the two developments became quite distinct, so that liability for breach of warranty became strict, whilst liability in deceit required proof of a fraudulent intent. Where there is no contractual liability and fraud cannot be proved, there may be a remedy in the tort of negligence.

For some considerable time, at common Law there might be liability for negligent misstatements which caused harm to the person[20]; and, provided it was not too remote, a claim for financial loss might be tacked on to such a claim[1]. However, in the absence of a fiduciary relationship[2], the courts were unwilling to impose liability where the loss was purely financial; and it has been suggested that this is partly due to[3]

"a fancied anxiety not to trench upon the sphere of contract and its basic philosophy that a claim to economic advantage must trace its source to a promise made for a consideration".

Hedley Byrne & Co., Ltd. v. *Heller, Ltd.*[4] appears to mark a change of heart in this respect, though their Lordships were impressed by the need to confine liability for negligent misstatements within fairly narrow limits. They thought that the establishment of liability for negligent misstatements on the same basis as liability for negligent acts would result in a more extensive liability than was desirable[5], and that normally the only duty should be to give an honest answer[6]. Accordingly, they took the view that something more was required in order to establish liability, and that there must be evidence to show

---

17. For the possible meanings of the word "upon", see Fleming, *Torts* (3rd Edn.) 614, note 14.
18. See *Pasley* v. *Freeman* (1789), 3 Term Rep. 51.
19. See above, p. 50.
20. E.g. *De Freville* v. *Dill* (1927), 96 L.J.K.B. 1056 (not a sale case); *Parker* v. *Oloxo, Ltd. and Senior*, [1937] 3 All E.R. 524 (set out above, p. 119).
1. The so-called "parasite damage". See Fleming, *Torts* (3rd Edn.) 173; Atiyah (1967), 83 L.Q.R. 248.
2. E.g. *Nocton* v. *Lord Ashburton*, [1914] A.C. 932, H.L.
3. Fleming, *op. cit.*, 172.
4. [1964] A.C. 465; [1963] 2 All E.R. 575, H.L.: see generally Winfield, *Tort* (8th Edn.) 216–249.
5. See especially Lord PEARCE, at p. 534.
6. *Per* Lords REID, MORRIS, HODSON, and DEVLIN, at pp. 483, 504, 513, 514.

that the defendant had assumed responsibility for his advice. Two of their Lordships characterised this as a "special relationship" between the parties[7]. Moreover, Lord DEVLIN suggested that this requirement would be satisfied "wherever there is a relationship equivalent to contract", and all that was lacking is consideration; and that *a fortiori* there would be a duty of care where there was a contract between the parties[8]. Whilst the courts have continued to show a reluctance in this field[9] to "concede that an action can lie in tort as well as in contract on the same set of facts"[10], the lead given by the House of Lords was accepted by CAIRNS J. in *Anderson Ltd.* v. *Rhodes Ltd.*[11].

> The plaintiffs and defendant were both dealers on the same vegetable market. The defendants carelessly told the plaintiffs that X. was credit-worthy, knowing that the plaintiffs were likely to act on this information in dealing with X. The plaintiffs lost money through giving X. credit in reliance on this advice.

The court held the defendants liable for negligent misstatement, and rejected the argument that the action was barred by the Statute of Frauds Amendment Act 1828 on the grounds that that Act did not constitute a defence to a claim based on negligence.

In his judgment in *Hedley Byrne Ltd.* v. *Heller Ltd.*, Lord DEVLIN explicitly recognised that the imposition of liability for negligent misstatement was a way of avoiding the doctrine of privity, and of escaping from the search for an artificial consideration[12]. Such an attitude may have important implications in the field of product liability, especially if it were accepted that participation in the chain of distribution, from manufacturer to consumer, gives rise to a "special relationship"; the result would be to enable any member of that possibly extensive chain to recover damages in respect of purely financial forseeable loss occasioned by his handling of the product, where that handling was induced by the negligent misstatement of someone else in the chain of distribution[13].

---

7. *Per* Lords DEVLIN and PEARCE, at pp. 528–529, 539. Cf. Lords REID, MORRIS, and HODSON, at pp. 486, 502–503, 514.
8. At pp. 528–529.
9. Compare the overlap of contract and conversion, where there is a restriction as to the amount of damages recoverable: see below, pp. 413–414. Does that restriction also apply here?
10. Poulton (1966), 82 L.Q.R. 346, 369. But see REES J. in *Vacwell Engineering Co., Ltd.* v. *B.D.H. Chemicals, Ltd.*, [1969] 3 All E. R. 1681, at p. 1698.
11. [1967] 2 All E.R. 850. But see *Mutual Life & Citizens' Assurance Co.* v. *Evatt*, [1970] 11 C.L. 3376, P.C., where the majority took a narrow view of liability. Why did the plaintiff in the former case not plead a collateral contract?
12. E.g. *De la Bere* v. *Pearson, Ltd.*, [1908] 1 K.B. 280, C.A.
13. But see the doubts voiced by Lord REID in *Hedley Byrne & Co., Ltd.* v. *Heller, Ltd.*, [1964] A.C. 465, at p. 483, H.L.

3 THE FUTURE[14]

The sharp distinction between contract and tort is clearly logical once it is settled that a contract requires consideration, and may not have mattered much when the chain of distribution was short. However, with the application of the techniques of mass-production to an increasingly sophisticated range of products, problems were bound to occur, and it may be that experience in the United States is relevant to the way in which English law will develop[15]. If so, progress may be expected on two fronts. First, there will be attempts to extend contractual liability, perhaps by use of the collateral contract of warranty[16]. Second, liability in tort for purely financial loss may become more acceptable, and tortious liability may become stricter[17].

---

14. The Law Commission intend to make a special study of the future of product liability: *First Report on Exemption Clauses in Contracts* (Law Com. No. 24), para. 63.
15. See Mueller (1969), 78 Yale L.J. 576; Pasley (1969), 32 M.L.R. 241.
16. See Atiyah (1968), 2 Ottawa L.R. 337, 357–358; Uniform Commercial Code Art. 2–318.
17. See Fleming, *Torts* (3rd Edn.) 474; Restatement (Second) of Torts, para. 402A.

CHAPTER 11

Avoidance and Waiver of Terms

It is common, particularly in standard form contracts, to find that one party has purported to avoid some of his liability[1] and prevent the waiver of some of his rights. In this Chapter, the effectiveness of these clauses, and the restrictions which the law places upon them will be examined.

I PROVISIONS RENDERED VOID BY STATUTE

The S.G.A. allows almost complete freedom of contract. Not only are many of its provisions expressed to give way to a contrary intention, but s. 55 provides:

> "Where any right, duty, or liability would arise under a contract of sale by implication of law, it may be negatived or varied by express agreement or by the course of dealing between the parties, or by usage, if the usage be such as to bind both parties to the contract".

The section envisages three ways in which "any right, duty, or liability" may be "negatived or varied". First, it may be ousted by express agreement, and the rules for interpreting that express agreement will be considered later[2]. Second, it may be impliedly displaced by the course of dealings between the parties, even though no term to such effect could be implied in any single contract standing alone[3]. Third, even where there is neither an express term nor a course of dealings, it may be negatived by a customary usage to this effect[4].

Because it is thought that the dominant party has frequently taken unfair advantage of this freedom of contract, Parliament has subsequently sought to modify it. The H.P. Acts specify a detailed list of contractual provisions which are avoided by those Acts. Some protection is thereby provided for the consumer in an instalment credit transaction, but the cash buyer is left entirely unprotected. On the

---

1. Clauses which achieve this object have been described by judges and text-writers as "exemption", "exclusion" or "exception" clauses. These terms are used interchangeably; and this usage will be adopted here.
2. See below, p. 138, *et seq.*
3. *Henry Kendall & Sons, Ltd.* v. *William Lillico & Sons, Ltd.*, [1969] 2 A.C. 31, H.L., *per* Lords MORRIS, GUEST, and PEARCE, at pp. 90, 105, 113, affirming the unanimous decision of the C.A. on this point: [1966] 1 All E.R. 309, C.A., *per* SELLERS, DAVIES, and DIPLOCK L.JJ., at pp. 322, 328, 331. For the facts of this case, see above, p. 88.
4. *Cointat* v. *Myham* (1914), 84 L.J.K.B. 2253, C.A.

other hand, the Misrepresentation Act 1967 provides less specific protection in both cash and credit transactions. The Law Commission have recently recommended the extension of these statutory prohibitions on "contracting out".

1 The H.P.A.

The technique of specifically prohibiting certain clauses commonly found in h.p. agreements was first utilised in the H.P.A. 1938 (ss. 5, 8), and the list of clauses so avoided was extended by the H.P.A. 1964 (ss. 16, 23). All these provisions are now to be found in the H.P.A. 1965. A general list of prohibitions is set out in s. 29, which avoids any of the following list of provisions

> ". . . in any agreement (whether a hire-purchase agreement, credit-sale agreement[5] or conditional sale agreement or not)"[6]:

(1) A contractual licence for the owner or seller to enter premises of the hirer or buyer (s. 29 (2) (a))[7];
(2) Any excessive imposition of liability on termination of the agreement, or any restriction on the statutory right to terminate (ss. 29 (2) (b), (c))[8];
(3) Any clause purporting to reverse the effect of the common law or statutory rules of agency (ss. 29 (2) (d), (e), (3) (b))[9];
(4) Any clause purporting to exclude the statutory right of cancellation (s. 29 (3) (a))[10];
(5) Any clause purporting to exclude the statutory implied terms as to sample or description (s. 29 (3) (c))[11].
There are separate provisions dealing with attempts to escape from the other statutory implied terms (s. 18 (3))[12], and from clauses purporting to terminate the agreement on the death of the hirer or buyer (s. 30 (4))[13]. Any attempt to avoid any of these restrictions by embodying the prohibited clause in a collateral agreement would appear to be doomed to failure by reason of s. 29 (4)[14].

---

5. See s. 29 (5).
6. Thus, s. 29 also strikes at any of the listed clauses to be found in any collateral agreement.
7. See below, p. 336.
8. See below, pp. 354, 394, 395.
9. See above, p. 39, and below, p. 289.
10. See above, p. 43.
11. See above, pp. 76, 108.
12. See above, pp. 55, 105.
13. See below, p. 344.
14. See above, p. 34.

2 The Misrepresentation Act 1967[15]

By s. 3 of this Act, Parliament intended to curtail the ability of a representor to exclude or restrict liability for any misrepresentation. Section 3 provides:

> "If any agreement[16] (whether made before or after the commencement of this Act)[17] contains a provision which would exclude or restrict—
>
> (a) any liability to which a party to a contract may be subject by reason of any misrepresentation made by him before the contract was made; or
>
> (b) any remedy available to another party to the contract by reason of such a misrepresentation;
>
> that provision shall be of no effect except to the extent (if any) that, in any proceedings arising out of the contract, the court or arbitrator may allow reliance on it as being fair and reasonable in the circumstances of the case".

Unfortunately, the ambit of the section would appear to be the subject of considerable uncertainty.

1. "Any misrepresentation made." There is no definition of these words[17a] and the problem immediately arises whether they are meant to cover non-disclosure[18] and fraud[19]. Moreover, what if the misrepresentation subsequently attains contractual status? Section 3 would appear to be drafted only to cover mere representations, with the possible result that the representee has more rights outside the contract than within it. Can the representee ignore the fact that the misrepresentation has attained contractual status, and sue for misrepresentation, thereby gaining for himself the possible benefit of s. 3? Does s. 3 apply where a single clause purports to exclude liability for both misrepresentations and breaches of contract so that the court may strike down that clause in relation to both of them[20]?

2. The types of clause covered by paragraphs (a) and (b). The words used are very wide, and seem to import merely the requirements that

---

15. See generally, Atiyah & Treitel (1967), 30 M.L.R. 369; Fairest (1967), Camb. L.J. 239; Smith & Thomas, *Casebook on Contract* (4th Edn.) 247–254.
16. As it is contrasted with the word "contract", this presumably means a non-contractual agreement, such as where there is a condition precedent to contract: see above, p. 114.
17. For the difficulty in reconciling the words in parentheses with s. 5, see Atiyah & Treitel, *op. cit.*, 380.
17a. See also above, p. 121.
18. See Hudson (1969), 85 L.Q.R. 524.
19. Even if s. 3 does cover exclusion of fraudulent misrepresentations, it is inconceivable that the court would exercise its discretion to give effect to such a clause.
20. It is arguable that s. 3 should be read so that "the provision shall be of no effect *only* in so far as it purports to exclude . . . liability . . . in respect of the misrepresentation". *Contra* Atiyah and Treitel, *op. cit.*, 383.

(1) the parties must be parties to a contract, and (2) liability must arise by reason of a misrepresentation. But do they cover liquidated damages clauses, or arbitration clauses, or clauses by which one party declares that the other has not made any representation, or that he has not relied on any representation made? The first two types of clause mentioned may be thought to be for the benefit of both parties, and so outside the scope of s. 3; but the latter two are clearly within the mischief of the Act.

The probable effect of s. 3, like its ambit, is uncertain, because the section confers an exceptionally wide discretion on the court. The section lays down no guidelines whatsoever as to how the court should exercise this discretion, and leaves the court such wide powers that it seems unlikely that there will be much precedent-value in any decisions[1]. It is submitted that the effect of s. 3 is to introduce such a large measure of uncertainty, that it may cause more injustice than it avoids; and it has been said that it throws an unfair burden on the courts and amounts to an abdication of Parliamentary responsibility[2].

3 The proposals of the Law Commission

The present position is generally thought to be unsatisfactory. The detailed restrictions of the H.P.A. do not apply to consumer cash sales; and the provisions of the 1967 Act, whilst applying to cash and credit transactions, are too vague, and do not cover contractual promises as to either (1) future conduct, or (2) matters of fact. Nor does any of the legislation deal adequately with the problems in product liability arising from the chain of distribution[3]. In their *First Report on Exemption Clauses*, the Law Commission showed themselves well aware of these problems[4]. The Commission unanimously recommended that "the statutory conditions and warranties implied by ss. 13–15 of the S.G.A. should apply to a sale to a private consumer notwithstanding any term of the contract express or implied to the contrary"[5], but had difficulty in deciding how far, if at all, this absolute ban on contracting out should be extended beyond sales to private purchasers[6]. Outside the ambit of this absolute prohibition, the Commission was seriously divided as to whether there should be (1) a control on exemption clauses similar to that in s. 3 of the Misrepresentation Act 1967, or (2) no control at all[7]. A similar division of opinion occurred in respect of auction sales[8].

---

1. Cf. *per* Lord SOMERVELL in *Qualcast (Wolverhampton), Ltd.* v. *Haynes,* [1959] A.C. 743, H.L., at pp. 757–758.
2. Atiyah & Treitel, *op. cit.,* 384–385. But see the Solicitor-General (Sir Dingle Foot) 741, H.C. Deb. 1370. 3. See above, Chapter 10.
4. Part V, paras. 64–119. See generally Coote (1970) 34 Conv. 254.
5. Para. 80. 6. Paras. 85–90. 7. Paras. 91–113. 8. Paras. 114–119.

2 PROVISIONS RENDERED VOID AT COMMON LAW[9]

In considering how the common law deals with attempts to avoid liability by way of disclaimer or exclusion clause, two questions arise in any action: first, what in fact happened; and second, is the defendant liable to the plaintiff in view of the facts which are proved to have occurred? The first question has very great practical significance; it may be extremely difficult to prove what happened; but the problem of who bears the burden of proof is beyond the scope of this work[10]. The present discussion will concentrate on the second question, which involves the effectiveness of any disclaimer. The disclaimer may be oral, though a written form is usually favoured by those seeking to rely on it, because it is easier to prove, and may be drafted more comprehensively[11]. The disclaimer may originate from the seller, or from any prior party in the chain of distribution; it is frequently printed on the goods, their packaging, or in a sale agreement; and it may purport to protect either the seller or any other prior party in the chain of distribution—or even both of them.

1 The nature and effect of exclusion clauses

Whether the attempt is to exclude tortious or contractual liability, the clause may or may not be embodied in a contract.

1. Non-contractual exclusion clauses. These clauses are sometimes termed "disclaimers" to distinguish them from contractual exclusion clauses, and this terminology will be used here. A disclaimer cannot affect contractual liability, except by way of the doctrine of waiver[12], but may well defeat an action in tort. Perhaps the most obvious example of the operation of a disclaimer in tort is where it ousts liability in negligence because the other party voluntarily assumes the risk[13]. Here, however, the courts may try to restrict the ambit of the disclaimer so as to be free to apportion loss under the Law Reform (Contributory Negligence) Act 1945.

2. Contractual exclusion clauses. A party may seek by contract to exclude either his contractual or tortious liability—or both. The clause may be effective to exclude tortious liability by its express terms; or it may do so impliedly where it purports to exclude a party from an equivalent duty in contract, or it may act as a sufficient warning to

---

9. See generally, Coote, *Exception Clauses.*
10. See Treitel, *Contract* (3rd Edn.) 197–198; Cheshire & Fifoot, *Contract* (7th Edn.) 126–127.
11. See the strictures of Lord REID in the *Suisse Atlantique Societe D'Armement Maritime S.A.* v *N.V. Rotterdamsche Kolen Centrace,* [1967] 1 A.C. 361, H.L., at p. 406.
12. See below, pp. 146–149.
13. E.g. see *per* Lord DENNING (dissenting) in *Scruttons, Ltd.* v. *Midland Silicones, Ltd.,* [1962] A.C. 446, H.L., at pp. 488–489.

discharge or reduce tort liability in any of the ways suggested above. As regards the exclusion of contractual liability, it has been pointed out that exclusion clauses may be of one of two types[14]:

Type A: clauses "whose effect, if any, is upon the accrual of particular primary rights", such as those excluding the undertakings as to fitness or quality, or any liability for breach.

Type B: "clauses which qualify primary or secondary rights without preventing the accrual of any particular primary rights", such as those limiting recovery for breach of the undertakings as to quality or fitness by limitations as to time, or as to the amount of damages recoverable.

The importance of the distinction is as follows[15]: clauses of *type B* do not prevent the initial obligation arising, but merely limit the remedies available on breach, but clauses of *type A* prevent any such obligation from arising in the first place. If a clause of *type A* were sufficiently widely drawn, its effect would be either[16]

(1) to render the contract void for total failure of consideration, because the party claiming the benefit of the exclusion clause had not made any promise at all[17]; or

(2) to transform what appeared to be a bilateral contract into a unilateral one[18].

2 Incorporation of the exclusion clause in the transaction

Suppose that packaged goods bear a notice purporting to exempt the manufacturer and retailer from any liability (whether in contract or tort), the position is as follows: if the retailer is sued by the person to whom he sold the goods (X.), the issue will probably be the effect of the exclusion clause on the contract; but, if the manufacturer is sued by X., or by any person to whom X. transfers the goods, the problem is unlikely, except through the doctrine of agency, to be a contractual one. The question of whether the exclusion clause is incorporated into the transaction may therefore arise both inside and outside the contractual context.

An exclusion clause may become incorporated in a contract in either of the following ways:

1. Incorporation by notice. The incorporation of a clause excluding liability into a contract between two parties is a matter of intention: in the absence of any particular statutory provisions or fraud, such an

---

14. Coote, *Exception Clauses* 9. 15. *Ibid.*, p. 11.
16. See *per* DIPLOCK L.J. in *Hardwick Game Farm* v. *Suffolk Agricultural and Poultry Producers Association, Ltd.*, [1966] 1 All E.R. 309, at p. 347, C.A.
17. The doctrine of total failure of consideration is considered below, p. 404. The effect may be similar to that of the 1913 agreement in *Rose and Frank* v. *J. R. Crompton and Brothers, Ltd.*, [1925] A.C. 445, H.L.
18. See *per* Lord DENNING M.R. in *United Dominions Trust (Commercial), Ltd.* v. *Eagle Aircraft, Ltd.*, [1968] 1 All E.R. 104, C.A., at p. 107.

exclusion will become part of a contract so as to bind one of the parties (irrespective of whether he listened to, or read it) provided that he realised that the other party intended it to form part of the contract between them. Alternatively, in the absence of actual knowledge, a party may be bound, where he ought to have realised that it was intended to have contractual force because the other party took reasonable steps to bring it to his attention[19]. Where an exclusion of liability does not become incorporated in a contract between the parties, it can usually only operate as a disclaimer of liability in tort. Thus, in the example above, the disclaimer on the package may save the manufacturer from liability in the tort of negligence by "discharging" the duty of care[20], or by giving rise to a voluntary assumption of risk[1] or contributory negligence on the part of the claimant. As in the contractual context, there must be adequate notice of the disclaimer before it becomes operative[2]. In the absence of the restraints imposed by the doctrine of consideration, perhaps the most difficult question is to know how far such disclaimer can be effective.

2. Incorporation by signed document. Where the exclusion clause is embodied in a signed contract, the general rule is that, in the absence of fraud or misrepresentation, the signatory is bound by the contents of the document regardless of whether he has read or understood them[3]. On the other hand, the signed document may neither amount to nor evidence a contract. Possibly a disclaimer in that document will become binding on the signatory merely by signature, rather than only by notice[4]?

3. The attitude of the courts to exclusion clauses

In the first place, there are a number of legal rules which will render an exclusion clause ineffective, even though the clause be incorporated in the transaction[5]:

(1) Where the exclusion of liability is contrary to statute[6];

---

19. *Parker* v. *South Eastern Rail. Co.* (1877), 2 C.P.D. 416, C.A. But see further the discussion by Hoggett in (1970), 33 M.L.R. 518.
20. See *Hedley Byrne & Co., Ltd.* v. *Heller, Ltd.*, [1964] A.C. 465; [1963] 2 All E.R. 575, where the H.L. thought that the effect of the disclaimer was to prevent the duty of care from arising.
1. *Ashdown* v. *Samuel Williams, Ltd.*, [1957] 1 Q.B. 409; [1957] 1 All E.R 35, C.A. There is considerable dispute as to the basis of the decision in this case: see *Winfield, Tort* (8th Edn.) 187–190.
2. Adequate notice here is the same as in contract: see *Ashdown* v. *Samuel Williams, Ltd.* (above).
3. *L'Estrange* v. *Graucob, Ltd.*, [1934] 2 K.B. 394.
4. Cf. *Ashdown* v. *Samuel Williams, Ltd.* (above).
5. These rules are generally framed in the law of contract, but there would appear to be no reason why they should be so confined.
6. See e.g. the H.P.A. and Misrepresentation Act 1967 considered above, p. 132.

(2) Where the object of the clause is contrary to public policy, as where it purports to exclude liability for fraud[7];

(3) Where the party for whose benefit the clause is expressed to operate gives an over-riding oral undertaking[8] or misrepresents the contents of the clause[9];

(4) Where in a contractual action there is no privity of contract between the parties, whether the clause purports to confer a benefit[10] or a burden[11].

Where an exclusion clause cannot be struck down on one of the above grounds, its effect will be a matter of construction. In seeking to ascertain the intention of the parties, however, the courts will, if the clause was inserted merely for the benefit of one party, the *proferens*, construe the words against him. Primarily, this is just an attitude of mind in which the courts approach such clauses, but it has been graced with the name of the *contra proferentem* rule. The rule is a general one[12], but has achieved special prominence in the field of contractual exclusion clauses and disclaimers. When faced with such exclusion clauses and disclaimers, the courts have consistently construed them strictly and literally against the *proferens*[13]. For instance, they have attributed precise legal meanings to technical terms, regardless of whether the parties understood the technicalities: clauses excluding warranties have been held ineffective to exclude conditions[14]; and clauses excluding implied terms have been held not to effect liability for breach of express conditions[15]. A striking illustration of the effectiveness of the *contra proferentem* rule is to be found in *Lowe* v. *Lombank, Ltd.*[16].

> The plaintiff, a widow of 65, agreed to enter a directly financed h.p. transaction, and signed a proposal form at her home without reading it. Clause 8 purported to exclude all warranties; and clause 9 read as follows:
> "The hirer acknowledges that he has examined the goods and that there are no defects in the goods which such examination ought to

---

7. Can a clause be struck down purely on grounds of unreasonableness?
8. *Mendelssohn* v. *Normand, Ltd.*, [1970] 1 Q.B. 177; [1969] 2 All E.R. 1215, C.A.
9. *Curtis* v. *Chemical Cleaning Co.*, [1951] 1 K.B. 805; [1951] 1 All E.R. 631, C.A.
10. *Scruttons, Ltd.* v. *Midland Silicones, Ltd.*, [1962] A.C. 446; [1962] 1 All E.R. 1, H.L.
11. *Dunlop Pneumatic Tyre Co., Ltd.* v. *Selfridge & Co., Ltd.*, [1915] A.C. 847, H.L.
12. See Odgers, *Construction of Deeds and Statutes* (5th Edn.) 95 *et seq.*
13. E.g. *Henry Kendall & Sons, Ltd.* v. *William Lillico & Sons, Ltd.*, [1969] 2 A.C. 31; [1968] 2 All E.R. 444, H.L.: set out above, p. 88.
14. E.g. *Wallis, Sons and Wells* v. *Pratt and Haynes*, [1911] A.C. 394, H.L.; *Baldry* v. *Marshall*, [1925] 1 K.B. 260, C.A.
15. E.g. *Andrews Brothers (Bournemouth), Ltd.* v. *Singer & Co., Ltd.*, [1934] 1 K.B. 17, C.A.   16. [1960] 1 All E.R. 611, C.A.

have revealed and that the goods are of merchantable quality. The hirer further acknowledges and agrees that he has not made known to the owners expressly or by implication the particular purpose for which the goods are required, and that the goods are reasonably fit for the purpose for which they are in fact required".

On delivery, the plaintiff signed a "delivery receipt", in which she acknowledged that the goods were in good order; but the car was, in fact, completely unroadworthy owing to a number of serious, but latent, defects.

The Court of Appeal held that the plaintiff was entitled to damages against the finance company for breach of the implied condition as to fitness in the H.P.A. 1938 for the following reasons:

(1) The hirer impliedly made known that she required the car as a means of transport[17];

(2) Clause 8 did not purport to exclude conditions; and, even had it done so, it had not been brought to her attention and its effect made plain to her as the Act required[18];

(3) Clause 9 was merely a statement of past facts, not a contractual promise, and could, at most, give rise to an estoppel; but that there was no estoppel here because (a) the clause did not unambiguously cover the latent defects, (b) there was no evidence either that the plaintiff intended the statements to be acted upon or that the defendants signed the agreement on the basis of the truth of the statement[19].

But it must not be thought that this hostile attitude will always render an exclusion clause devoid of all meaning. The courts will merely construe the clause as narrowly as possible against the *proferens*[20], and it is difficult to so formulate a clause that judicial ingenuity cannot subsequently find room to manœuvre. In the field of contractual exclusion clauses, this has led to considerable embellishment of the *contra proferentem rule*: exclusion clauses have been interpreted so as not to defeat the main object of the contract[1], or on the assumption that the clause was not intended to protect a party when acting entirely outside the four corners of the agreement[2]. It has also been said that there are some terms which are fundamental to a contract, and that no

---

17. See above, p. 88.
18. See above, p. 94.
19. But see below, p. 143. The statement in the agreement that clause 8 had been brought to the hirer's notice, and its effect made plain to her, was not relied on in this action; but in the light of the decision it seems unlikely that it would have helped the finance company: see Goode, *H.P. Law & Practice* (2nd Edn.) 201–202, 252.
20. See e.g. the cases on the exclusion of liability for negligence—*Alderslade* v. *Hendon Laundry, Ltd.,* [1945] K.B. 189, C.A.; *White* v. *John Warrick, Ltd.,* [1953] 2 All E.R. 1021, C.A.
 1. E.g. *Glynn* v. *Margetson & Co.,* [1893] A.C. 351, H.L.
 2. E.g. *Gibaud* v. *Great Eastern Rail Co.,* [1921] 2 K.B. 426, C.A.

exclusion clause can offer protection against their breach[3]. Perhaps an illustration of this is provided by *Karsales (Harrow) Ltd.* v. *Wallis*[4].

> The defendant entered into a directly financed transaction in respect of a Buick car. Prior to signing the agreement, the defendant had inspected the car, and found it to be in good order. Shortly after the date of the agreement, the "car" was (apparently) towed into position outside the defendant's premises at night; and on inspection the following morning was found to be in a deplorable condition, and incapable of self-propulsion. The defendant refused to accept the goods, and the finance company assigned their rights to the dealer under the repurchase provision[5]. In suing for arrears of instalments, the dealer sought to protect himself against the state of the goods by reliance on the exclusion clause in the h.p. agreement.

The Court of Appeal unanimously found for the defendant on the grounds that the object delivered was not the car contracted for, and that such a breach disentitled the plaintiff from relying on the exclusion clause; and DENNING L.J. added that there was an implied condition that the plaintiff would keep the car in good condition between the dates of inspection and delivery[6]. Alternatively, the majority were prepared to decide the case on the further ground that delivery of the car had not been accepted, so that the plaintiff's only possible remedy would be for damages for non-acceptance (which right had not been assigned to him)[7].

This last case leads to the doctrine of fundamental breach: the idea that a breach of contract may be so serious that no exemption clause, however widely drafted, can protect the guilty party. The high-water mark of this doctrine is, perhaps, to be found in *Yeoman Credit, Ltd.* v. *Apps*[8].

> The defendant entered into a directly financed h.p. transaction upon the dealer agreeing to do some repairs before delivery. After the car had been delivered, the defendant ascertained that the repairs had not been done; and the car was found to have such an accumulation of latent defects as to render it unsafe and unroadworthy. The defendant complained, but kept the car for five months and paid some instalments, hoping he could persuade the dealer to meet half the cost of the repairs. The plaintiff finance company sued for arrears of instalments and the defendant counter-claimed to recover the money he had paid on grounds of total failure of consideration.

---

3. *Per* DEVLIN J. in *Smeaton Hanscomb & Co., Ltd.* v. *Sassoon Setty, Son & Co.*, [1953] 2 All E.R. 1471, at p. 1473.
4. [1956] 2 All E.R. 866, C.A.   5. See below, pp. 290–291.
6. See above, p. 116.   7. See below, p. 376.
8. [1962] 2 Q.B. 508; [1961] 2 All E.R. 281, C.A. The history of the doctrine is traced by Coote (1967), 40 A.L.J. 336. See also Treitel, *Law of Contract* (3rd Edn.) 181–198.

The Court of Appeal held:

(1) Where goods are let on h.p., the common law will imply a condition that the goods are reasonably fit for the purpose for which they are required[9];

(2) That the accumulation of defects when added together amounted to such a fundamental breach of contract as to disentitle the plaintiffs from relying on the exemption clause;

(3) That since the defendant had approbated the contract by paying some instalments, there was no total failure of consideration[10]; and that the plaintiffs were therefore entitled to the hire-rent up to the moment of the defendant's rejection of the goods[11];

(4) but that the defendant's rejection was lawful because there was a continuing breach of contract on the part of the plaintiffs[12], and that he was also entitled to damages[13]. This decision bristles with problems; but at present point (2) alone will be discussed. At first sight, the case might seem to be authority for the proposition that a "congeries of defects[14]" may constitute such a fundamental breach as will disentitle a party from relying on *any* exemption clause. However, if the leading judgment of HOLROYD PEARCE L.J. is examined carefully, it will be seen that his Lordship said only that the exclusion clause did not cover the circumstances which in fact occurred, a perfectly unexceptionable approach.

Subsequently, the Court of Appeal has three times considered similar situations. In two cases in 1963 and one in 1970 there have been directly financed transactions in respect of defective motor vehicles, the hirer has eventually repudiated, and the finance company has repossessed the goods and sued for arrears of rentals, relying on the exclusion clause to protect them from the hirer's counterclaim for breach of the implied term as to fitness. In *Astley Industrial Trust, Ltd.* v. *Grimley*[15] the dealer had promised to remedy certain defects before delivery, and the court held him liable under a collateral contract[16]; but their Lordships thought that the finance company had complied with their obligations as to the fitness of the lorry, and PEARSON L.J. said that the hirer's acknowledgement that he had examined the vehicle and found it in good order must at least exempt the finance company from contractual responsibility for visible external defects[17]. In *Charterhouse*

---

9. See above, p. 83.

10. See below, p. 407.

11. See below, p. 374.

12. See below, p. 403.

13. For the measure of damages, see below, pp. 414, 424.

14. The phrase is that of Lord DUNEDIN in *Pollock & Co.* v. *Macrae* 1922, S.C. H.L. 192, at p. 200. Applied in *Farnworth Finance Facilities, Ltd.* v. *Attryde*, [1970] 2 All E.R. 774, C.A.

15. [1963] 2 All E.R. 33, C.A.

16. See below, p. 284.

17. At pp. 44–45. Cf. *Lowe* v. *Lombank*, Ltd., [1960] 1 All E.R. 611, C.A. (set out above, pp. 139–140) and *Farnworth Finance Facilities, Ltd.* v. *Attryde*, [1970] 2 All E.R. 774, C.A.

Credit, Ltd. v. *Tolly*[18] the court accepted that, as the hirer had approbated the agreement, the finance company was entitled to terminate it
for subsequent breaches, and to hire-rent to the date of termination[19];
but the court held that the hirer was not precluded by the exemption
clause from recovering damages from the finance company[20], because
the exemption clause *could* not avail the company in view of their
fundamental breach of contract. In *Farnworth Finance Facilities, Ltd.*
v. *Attryde*[1] the h.p. agreement provided that the hirer

"expressly acknowledges that . . .
2. He has examined the said vehicle and found it in good order and
condition . . .
4. The said vehicle is supplied to him subject to no conditions
or warranties whatsoever expressed or implied . . ."

Ignoring clause 2, the Court of Appeal unanimously held that there
was a "congeries of defects" in the motor cycle amounting to a fundamental breach[2]; that there was a rule of construction that clause 4
"should not be construed as applying to it"[3]; that, notwithstanding
clause 4, the cases[4] showed that "it is an implied condition that the
machine should correspond with the description and that it should be
reasonably fit for the purpose for which it was hired"[5]; and that there
was a breach of those implied terms which entitled the hirer to reject
the motor cycle[6] and claim damages[7].

Only in *Tolly's Case* did the Court of Appeal clearly say that the
exemption clause *could* not protect the finance company from liability
for fundamental breach, which view would raise the *contra proferentem*
rule of construction into a rule of law; but in *Attryde's Case* the Court
seem to have come fairly close to so doing. On the other hand, it would
prima facie seem rather odd to allow the innocent party to plead the
agreement and yet avoid the exclusion clause which it contains: it seems
to allow the innocent party to rewrite the contract so as to have the best
of both worlds. This point was taken by the House of Lords in the
Suisse Atlantique Case[8], where Lord REID commented[9]:

"Where the contract has been affirmed by the innocent party, at
first sight the position is simple. You must either affirm the whole

---

18. [1963] 2 Q.B. 683; [1963] 2 All E.R. 432, C.A.
19. See below, p. 374.
20. The measure of damages is considered below, p. 424.
1. [1970] 2 All E.R. 774, C.A.
2. See above, p. 142.   3. At p. 777. See below.
4. Lord DENNING M.R. cited the *Apps, Grimley* and *Tolly* cases.
5. At p. 777. Are there therefore two implied conditions e.g. as to fitness; or
   is this to give the exclusion clause a *pro tanto* effect?
6. See below, p. 402.   7. See below, p. 414.
8. [1967] 1 A.C. 361, H.L. (not a sale case). See Coote (1967), 40 A.L.J. 336.
9. At p. 398.

contract or rescind the whole contract; you cannot approbate and reprobate by affirming part of it and disaffirming the rest—that would be making a new contract. So the clause excluding liability must continue to apply".

In this case, the House of Lords took the view, *obiter*, that however fundamental the breach, where the innocent party affirmed the contract, it was a matter of construction whether the exclusion clause covered the breach; that there was a presumption that it did not apply to fundamental breaches; but that this was a rule of construction, not of law[10]. Thus, the exclusion clause might cover a fundamental breach; but, if it did not, and the innocent party elected to affirm, the exclusion clause remained in the affirmed contract, and might offer protection against subsequent breaches, even fundamental ones[11]. Logically, it might be thought that the position should be similar where the innocent party seeks to rescind after a fundamental breach; and such a view would appear to be consistent with the subsequent case of *Farnworth Finance Facilities, Ltd.* v. *Attryde*[12], but not with another Court of Appeal case falling between those two decisions. In *Harbutt's Plasticine Ltd.* v. *Wayne Tank and Pump Co., Ltd.*[13].

> The defendant contracted to design and instal equipment at the plaintiff's factory, and thereafter committed a breach falling within the terms of the exclusion clause in the contract[14]. This breach caused a fire which destroyed the factory, and the plaintiff sued for damages. The Court of Appeal unanimously held that this breach necessarily brought the contract to an end; and that therefore the defendant could no longer rely on the exclusion clause.

This decision may be criticised on two points. First, the generally accepted rule is that a fundamental breach merely renders the contract terminable by the innocent party[15], and does not terminate[16] it *ab initio*[17]. Secondly, it seems undesirable that the question of whether an exclusion clause covers a fundamental breach should be a matter of construction if the innocent party affirms, but a matter of law if he rescinds[18]. Certainly, it is difficult to see why the Court of Appeal

---

10. At pp. 392, 399, 410, 426, 432.
11. And see Treitel, *Law of Contract* (3rd Edn.) 195–196.
12. [1970] 2 All E.R. 774, C.A.
13. [1970] 1 Q.B. 447; [1970] 1 All E.R. 225, C.A.   See Baker (1970), 33 M.L.R. 441; Clarke & Tedd (1970), 114 Sol. Jo. 610, 630; Leigh-Jones and Pickering (1970), 86 L.Q.R. 513; Coote, [1970] C.L.J. 221.
14. All three members of the C.A. accepted that the exclusion clause was apt to cover the breach, though Lord DENNING M.R. had some doubt on the point—at p. 464.   15. See below, p. 361.
16. That would be to allow self-induced frustration: see below, p. 254.   See also Treitel, *Law of Contract* (3rd Edn.) 731.
17. If the contract is terminated *ab initio*, what is the basis of the innocent party's action for damages?   See Coote, [1970] C.L.J. 221, 226.
18. What of the intermediate stage before the innocent party elects?

should have gone to such lengths to avoid an exclusion clause in a contract between two businessmen negotiating at arms length. Even if it were in all cases a matter of construction, the need for statutory reform for the protection of consumers does not appear to be quite as pressing as has been suggested[19]. The *contra proferentem* rule will be sufficient to meet most cases.

3 VARIATION AND WAIVER[20]

The subject-matter of this section is the variation and waiver of obligations, whether or not those obligations arise from a contract. Historically, this area has been bedevilled by the Statute of Frauds 1677, though this body of law is no longer applicable to sales of goods[1], and is only relevant here insofar as it relates to contracts of surety[2]. Ignoring the now-largely irrelevant usage under the Statute of Frauds, the terms "variation" and "waiver" will be used to mean the following: "variation" will be reserved for those situations where contractual rights are subsequently altered by another contract; and any attempt to alter accrued rights otherwise than by contract will be called a "waiver"[3]. Both variations and waivers bear some resemblance to the exclusion clauses and disclaimers considered in the previous section; but they must be distinguished from the subject-matter of the previous section in that they take effect, if at all, only after the accrual of contractual or tortious liability.

1 Variation of liability by contract

On ordinary principles, the parties to a contract may always make alterations to their contract by mutual[4] agreement[5]. Normally, even a written contract may be varied by oral agreement; but a guarantee required to be evidenced in writing may only be varied by written agreement[6], though it may be discharged by oral agreement[7]. Leaving

---

19. *Per* Lord REID in the *Suisse Atlantique Case*, [1967] 1 A.C. 361, at p. 406, H.L. Compare Lord Wilberforce, at p. 434. See the Report of the Law Commission considered above, p. 135.
20. See generally Stoljar (1957), 35 Can. B.R. 485.
 1. S. 4 of the S.G.A. was repealed by the Law Reform (Enforcement of Contracts) Act 1954, s. 1: see above, p. 32.
 2. See below, p. 346.
 3. In practice, it may be difficult to decide whether there has been a variation or a waiver: see Hoggett (1970), 33 M.L.R. 518.
 4. See *D. and C. Builders, Ltd.* v. *Rees*, [1966] 2 Q.B. 617; [1965] 3 All E.R. 837, C.A.
 5. *Hartley* v. *Hymans*, [1920] 3 K.B. 475: set out below, p. 147. Will the *contra proferentem* rule apply?
 6. *Goss* v. *Nugent* (1833), 5 B. & Ad. 58.
 7. *Morris* v. *Baron*, [1918] A.C. 1, H.L.

that complication aside, the only matter likely to cause general difficulty in this context is the requirement of consideration. If neither or both of the parties are in breach of contract, then the variation generates its own consideration[8]; but, if only one party is in breach of the original agreement, consideration is not generated automatically[9]. Quite apart from this, instalment credit transactions may give rise to particular difficulties in this context. Is the variation agreement caught by the H.P.A., s. 29 (4)[10]; or does it constitute part of the original agreement, in which case is it caught by the H.P.A., s. 5[11]? Alternatively, the variation may cause the transaction to breach the Terms Controls[12].

2 The doctrine of waiver

A party may waive either the right to sue in tort or contract.

1. Waiver of tort. Where a party indicates before the commission of a tort that he will waive any right of action in respect thereof, this may amount to a consent to the commission of the tort against him, or to a voluntary assumption of risk. A waiver after commission of a tort may operate to discharge the right of action by way of an election of remedies or by reason of a judgment[13]; but otherwise its effect is presumably similar to that in contract.

2. Waiver of contractual rights. The common law has long accepted that contractual rights may be expressly or impliedly waived before or after breach. The effect of a waiver may be to discharge the whole contract[14]: it may evince a mutual intention to abandon the whole agreement[15]; alternatively, a party who wrongfully repudiates his own obligations or disables himself from performing them may thereby impliedly waive his own rights[16]. However, we are concerned here with those waivers which do not discharge the whole contract, but merely purport to relinquish certain rights under it. Whether a contractual right has been waived is primarily a question of intention[17], with this limitation: if the contractual provision is for the benefit of one party alone, he may waive it unilaterally; but, if it is inserted for the

---

8. It may be important to determine whether, in the case of non-performance of the varied agreement, the consideration is the promise to vary or performance of that promise.
9. For a case where consideration was found, see *Tommey* v. *Finextra, Ltd.* (1962), 106 Sol. Jo. 1012.
10. See above, p. 33.
11. See above, p. 34.
12. See Guest, *Law of H.P.*, paras. 1005–1006.
13. See below, pp. 362–363.
14. Discharge of contract is considered below, Chapter 19.
15. E.g. *Fisher, Ltd.* v. *Eastwoods, Ltd.*, [1936] 1 All E.R. 421.
16. See the cases collected in *Benjamin on Sale* (8th Edn.) 560, note (q).
17. See *per* Lord DENNING L.J. in *Charles Rickards, Ltd.* v. *Oppenhaim*, [1950] 1 K.B. 616, at p. 626, C.A.

benefit of both parties, it can only be waived by mutual agreement[18]. Mere neglect or delay in enforcing an agreement does not *per se* amount to a waiver[19]; but, to avoid any doubt, standard-form agreements commonly provide that no relaxation or indulgence shall be construed as a waiver of rights.

The common law rules as to waiver of contractual rights would appear to have been partially embodied in s. 11 (1) (a) of the S.G.A., which provides—

> "Where a contract of sale is subject to any condition to be fulfilled by the seller, the buyer may waive the condition, or may elect to treat the breach of such condition as a breach of warranty, and not as a ground for treating the contract as repudiated".

It should be noticed that the provision speaks of a "waiver" of rights and an "election" of remedies; and the distinction between the two may become important when deciding whether the buyer may go back on his waiver or election. Where the buyer has several alternative remedies at his disposal, the election may be or become irrevocable[20]; and in some circumstances the law may compel the buyer to accept damages rather than rescind for breach of condition[1]. The effect of a waiver is illustrated by *Hartley* v. *Hymans*[2].

> A written contract for the sale of 11,000 lbs of cotton provided for delivery between September and November 15th 1918. By the latter date, the seller had only delivered 550 lbs; and the buyer subsequently repeatedly complained and requested early delivery. Instalments totalling 3704 lbs were delivered between 15.11.1918 and 27.2.1919. On 13.3.1919 the buyer without any previous notice, purported to cancel the order.

In the seller's action for non-acceptance[3], McCardie J. found that the time for tender of delivery was of the essence of the contract[4]; but he held that the buyer was not entitled to insist on delivery in the period ending 15.11.1918 for the following reasons:

(1) he had waived his rights under s. 11 (1) (a); and

(2) he was estopped from asserting that the contract ceased to be valid on that date; and

(3) the parties had made a new agreement extending the period for delivery beyond 15.11.1918[5].

18. See *per* TUCKER J. in the *Fibrosa Spolka Akcyjna* v. *Fairbairn Lawson Combe Barbour, Ltd.*, [1942] 1 K.B. 12, at pp. 20-21 (reversed by the H.L. on other grounds: [1943] A.C. 32); and *per* BUCKLEY J. in *Manchester Diocesan Council* v. *Commercial and General Investments, Ltd.*, [1969] 3 All E.R. 1593, at p. 1598.
19. *Perry* v. *Davis* (1858), 3 C.B. N.B. 769 (not a sale case).
20. See below, pp. 362–363.
  2. [1920] 3 K.B. 475.
  4. See below, p. 273.
  1. See below, p. 397.
  3. See below, p. 409.
  5. See above, p. 145.

Each of the first two reasons appears to refer to a different line of authority, and "reveals the incredible confusion of thought the law ha[s] now reached"[6]. The binding effect of a waiver at common law had already been recognised in the converse case, where the buyer was in breach, and the seller waived the breach[7]; but in a later case DENNING L.J. explained the rule in terms of estoppel[8]. However, a promise as to future conduct cannot amount to an estoppel at common law[9], and could only take effect under the alleged doctrine of equitable estoppel, a matter beyond the scope of this work[10].

Supposing A. does waive a contractual duty owed to him by B., can either party later set up the subsequent non-performance of that term? It seems that the party for whose benefit the waiver is made (B.) is estopped[11], but that A. may go back on his waiver. In *Charles Rickards, Ltd.* v. *Oppenhaim*[12]

> The defendant ordered a Rolls Royce chassis from the plaintiff, and the latter agreed to build a body on it by March 20th. After the plaintiff had failed to complete the work by that date, the defendant continued to press for delivery, but on June 29th gave notice that if the work was not completed within the next four weeks the contract was off.

The Court of Appeal unanimously held that time was of the essence of this contract[13]; that this stipulation was impliedly waived by the buyer's requests for delivery after March 20th; but that the buyer was entitled to, and had, made time of the essence again by his notice of June 29th.

Finally, there is one particular sort of waiver which has given rise to some difficulty. This is the situation where the seller intends to make a delivery which would be a breach of contract[14]; but, before he can tender the goods, the buyer, in ignorance of the seller's intention, intimates that he will not accept delivery, and purports to repudiate for another reason insufficient in law. Can the buyer subsequently rely on

---

6. Stoljar (1957), 35 Can. B.R. 485, 503.
7. *Panoutsos* v. *Raymond Hadley Corporation*, [1917] 2 K.B. 473, C.A. Applied in *Plasticmoda Societe Per Azione* v. *Davidsons, Ltd.*, [1952] 1 Lloyds Rep. 527.
8. *Charles Rickards, Ltd.* v. *Oppenhaim*, [1950] 1 K.B. 616, at p. 623, C.A.
9. *Jorden* v. *Money* (1854), 5 H.L. Cas. 185. But see below, p. 186, note 2.
10. See Cheshire & Fifoot, *Contract* (7th Edn.) 500–503; Treitel, *Contract* (3rd Edn.) 95–99; Stoljar (1957), 35 Can. B.R. 485, 520–528; Spencer Bower, *Estoppel* (2nd Edn.) Chapter XIV.
11. *Hickman* v. *Haynes* (1875), L.R. 10 C.P. 598; *Levey & Co.* v. *Goldberg*, [1922] 1 K.B. 688.
12. [1950] 1 K.B. 616; [1950] 1 All E.R. 420, C.A. See also *Tool Metal Manufacturing Co., Ltd.* v. *Tungsten Electric Co., Ltd.*, [1955] 2 All E.R. 657, H.L.; *Etablissements Chainbaux S.A.R.L.* v. *Harbormaster, Ltd.*, [1955] 1 Lloyds Rep. 303.
13. See below, p. 274.
14. For the duty of delivery, see below, pp. 255–267.

the seller's breach to justify his refusal to accept delivery? *Benjamin*[15] says that he cannot, that "a condition definitely waived is waived once and for all", and cites *Braithwaite* v. *Foreign Hardwood Co.*[16]. In this case, the buyers refused to accept the bill of lading tendered by the seller, and COLLINS M.R. said that the refusal amounted to a "waiver of perform-ance" by the seller, and that "it is not competent for the (buyers) now to hark back and say that . . . if they had known the facts they might have rejected the instalment when tendered to them"[17]. However, in *Taylor* v. *Oakes*[18], GREER J. noted, *obiter*, the

> "long-established rule of law that a contracting party who, after he has become entitled to refuse performance of his contractual obligations, gives a wrong reason for his refusal, does not thereby deprive himself of a justification which in fact existed, whether he was aware of it or not".

His Lordship sought to reconcile this rule with *Braithwaite's Case* by suggesting that the rule applies where there is a refusal to accept an actual tender of delivery, whereas in *Braithwaite's Case* there was a mere offer to tender delivery[19]. The logic of this distinction is not readily apparent: in *Taylor* v. *Oakes* the majority of the Court of Appeal refused to commit themselves to such an argument[20]; and in *British and Benningtons, Ltd.* v. *Cacher Tea, Ltd.*[1], Lord SUMNER reaffirmed the rule enunciated by GREER J. and said that *Braithwaite's Case* was "not quite easy to understand"[2].

---

15. At p. 560.
16. [1905] 2 K.B. 543, C.A.: set out below, p. 266.
17. At p. 551.
18. (1922), 27 Com. Cas. 261, C.A. GREER J. at first instance, at p. 266.
19. At p. 267.
20. *Per* SCRUTTON & ATKIN L.JJ., at pp. 272, 273. But see BANKES L.J., at p. 271.
1. [1923] A.C. 48, H.L.: set out below, pp. 266–267.
2. At pp. 70–72.

PART 3

The Conveyance

CHAPTER 12

The Effects of the Contract

I CONTRACT AND CONVEYANCE

The different types of contract and their contents have now been considered. However, the object of the parties to these transactions is normally to transfer the proprietary rights in the subject-matter of the contract, and the conveyancing aspect of the transaction must now be examined. The difference between contractual and proprietary rights is this: a contractual right merely gives a party a right against the other contracting party, whereas a proprietary right gives an interest in the goods as against the whole world.

At a fairly early stage, the English law of sale rejected the idea that proprietary rights in goods sold automatically passed at the time of either contract or delivery: instead, it was settled that the matter should be left to the agreement between the parties[1]. The S.G.A. lays down rules as to the passing of proprietary rights where the parties do not evince any specific intent in this respect: these rules will be considered in Chapter 13.

Whilst, therefore, the actual conveyance need not take place at the time when the contract is made, it remains true that the contract suffices to effect the conveyance[2]. Unlike certain other systems of law, and even certain other branches of our own law[3], the English law of sale does not require some legal act distinct from the contract to effect the conveyance. An apparently similar position is to be found in contracts of h.p., though here the option cannot be exercised (and the contract of sale made) until the instalments of hire rent have been paid.

2 PROPERTY AND TITLE

Having separated the contract from the conveyance, it is necessary to examine what is conveyed by the transaction. In common parlance, it is usually said that the parties intend to transfer the "ownership" in the goods; but this is not a term of art, and merely obscures the true

---

1. See now ss. 1 (4) and 17 S.G.A.
2. This is recognised by the statutory definition of sale to be found in the S.G.A., s. 62 (1). See also the distinction between "sale" and "agreement to sell", above, pp. 8–9.
3. A delivery, deed or special statutory form may be required in the case of all gifts, transfers for value of choses in action, mortgages or pledges of chattels.

position. At the outset, three points must be made[4]. First, whatever be the effect of the doctrine of seisin in the law of real property, our common law probably did not recognise any theory of absolute ownership in the case of personal property[5]; and whilst ss. 16–20 of the S.G.A. would appear to recognise such an absolute right, when a remedy is sought the courts are only concerned with the relative question of which of the two parties before the court has the better right to the goods[6]. Second, the doctrine of estates in real property has no application to personal property: generally speaking, *successive* interests, e.g. life interests, in personal property can only exist behind a trust, though there may be *concurrent* legal rights in personal property, as for instance where there is a bailment[7]. Third, the distinction between ownership and possession of goods is not always apparent because the courts will normally accept possession as *prima facie* proof of ownership; and this lends some substance to the maxim that "possession is nine-tenths of the law".

In the development of English law, the courts have tended to concentrate on the availability of remedies rather than any *a priori* theory of rights, so that the concept of "ownership" has tended to follow the remedies rather than lead them. In the field of personal property, two concepts involving "ownership" have developed, those of "title" and "property": the former is built upon the availability of an action in conversion or detinue; but the concept of property in goods is peculiar in that there is no action upon which it is obviously founded[8]. A layman might be forgiven for asking whether it is necessary for our law of personalty to have the two concepts of "property" and "title". Yet the S.G.A. draws a clear distinction between the two concepts. Part 2 of the Act is entitled "Effects of the Contract", and is further sub-divided into sections entitled "Transfer of Property as between Seller and Buyer" and "Transfer of Title". "Title" is nowhere defined in the Act[9]; but "property" is defined by s. 62 (1) as, *prima facie*, meaning—

"the general property in goods, and not merely a special property".

At first sight, it is perhaps difficult to see what the Act intended to be the relationship between "property" and "title", though it is reasonably clear when the provisions of the two sub-sections are to operate: the

---

4. See further, Crossley Vaines, *Personal Property* (4th Edn.), Chapter 4; *Oxford Essays in Jurisprudence v. Ownership* (by Honoré).
5. But see Maitland (1885), 1 L.Q.R. 324.
6. See the actions in conversion and detinue considered below, pp. 377–378.
7. To transfer a good title to personal property, all persons with a concurrent interest in it must act together: see *Lloyds Bank, Ltd.* v. *Bank of America*, [1938] 2 K.B. 147; [1938] 2 All E.R. 63, C.A.
8. See Kiralfy (1949), 12 M.L.R. 424.
9. An analogy has been drawn between the title to goods and the title to land: see Llewellyn (1939), 15 New York L.R. 159.

sections under the heading "Transfer of Property as between Seller and Buyer" are concerned with the very many situations where the dispute is solely between the seller and buyer, whereas the sections under the heading "Transfer of Title" provide for the cases where the title to goods is effectively transferred to a person who has no property in them[10].

The distinction drawn by the Act has been severely criticised on the grounds that the chief feature of all proprietary rights is that they are rights *in rem*, and that they bind third parties[11]; but it may be that Chalmers adopted this terminology from the common law because he felt that it was not the place of a codifying statute to reverse completely the theoretical basis of the existing law[12].

What is the relationship of "property" and "title"? It is clear that "property" is the basic residuary notion[13], and that the basic premise is that he who has the property in the goods can usually pass the best title to them. However, once having adopted the rule that property passes merely by the contract, the demands of mercantile convenience made it essential to introduce exceptions in favour of the *bona fide* purchaser for value (hereafter called the B.F.P.) from the person in possession. In fact, so many such exceptions have been introduced that the basic rule is substantially reversed in practice[14]. Property is an absolute concept[15], whereas title is relative: only one person can (apart from the possibility of concurrent interests) have the general property in goods; but a number of persons may have a title to them, and it will be a question of who has the best title. Because of the basic rule that title passes with property, it is usually unnecessary to make an enquiry into title as between the immediate parties to a contract of sale. But where a third party enters the picture, the existence of the exceptions makes an enquiry into title necessary; and, if one of the exceptions operates, then property might be regarded as being attracted from the original owner to the person to whom the law gives the best title. In this sense, title is either superior to property, or the exceptions should be read as transferring best title *and* the general property.

Perhaps the best way of looking at the concept of "property" is as a bundle of rights[16]. Amongst these rights the more important are as follows:

(1) The basic rule is that only the person with the property in the

---

10. See Thornley (1958), C.L.J. 349.
11. Atiyah, *Sale of Goods* (3rd Edn.) 102.
12. See above, pp. 3–4.
13. *Mischeff* v. *Springett*, [1942] 2 K.B. 331; [1942] 2 All E.R. 349.
14. On the question of terminology, see Lawson (1949), 65 L.Q.R. 352.
15. But see below, pp. 400–401.
16. See Atiyah, *Sale of Goods* (3rd Edn.) 104–105; *Benjamin on Sale* (8th Edn.) 297.

goods can pass the best title, so that, if a case cannot be fitted within one of the exceptions, the basic rule applies[17].

(2) *Prima facie*, the risk in the goods lies on the owner, that is, upon the person with the property in the goods[18].

(3) Generally, the seller can only sue for the price when the property has passed, and is otherwise left to claim damages[19]. On the other hand, the buyer's remedies, such as his right to sue in conversion or for specific performance, are not dependent on the passing of property[20].

(4) On the insolvency of a party, any goods in which he has the property will generally fall into his bankruptcy or liquidation[1]. In the case of persons, but not companies, this rule may be displaced by the "reputed ownership" doctrine[2]. The right of a seller in the event of his buyer's insolvency is strengthened by his rights of lien and stoppage in transit[3].

It is clear, therefore, that there are important results which flow from the passing of property. It has been said that, besides the transfer of risk, the other results of the passing of property are "for the most part, if not entirely, illusory"[4]; but this would seem to be an exaggeration. However, whilst the effects of the passing of property may not be illusory, it has been seriously questioned whether we need both concepts, property and title[5].

The rules of property and title must now be examined in rather more detail. In the next Chapter, the rules relating to the passing of property will be considered; and Chapter 14 contains a discussion of the transfer of title. The question of risk is dealt with in Chapter 15.

---

17. See below, Chapter 14.
18. See below, Chapter 15.
19. See below, Chapter 20.
20. See below, Chapter 21.
 1. The ordinary rules of insolvency are preserved by s. 61 (1).
 2. See above, pp. 10–11.
 3. See below, Chapter 18.
 4. Lawson (1949), 65 L.Q.R. 352, 359.
 5. Atiyah, *Sale of Goods* (3rd Edn.) 105.

CHAPTER 13

The Passing of Property

I INTRODUCTION

The basic thesis of the law in respect of the passing of property is a negative one, namely, that the property in the goods cannot pass unless and until the subject-matter of the contract is ascertained. The ascertainment of the goods is, in short, a condition precedent to the passing of property[1]. This is not to say that the property in the goods will pass when they are ascertained, for this also depends on the intention of the parties.

The reason why the property cannot pass until the goods are ascertained is that until then there is no way of identifying them. There are two ways in which the contract goods may be so marked out: they may be identified at the time the contract is made, when they are termed "specific goods", or they may be identified at some later time[2]. Section 16 of the S.G.A. provides for the case where the contract goods are not identified at the time when the contract is made in the following terms:

> "Where there is a contract for the sale of unascertained goods no property in the goods is transferred to the buyer unless and until the goods are ascertained".

This section is mandatory and negative in form; and its effect may be illustrated by *Laurie and Morewood* v. *Dudin*[3].

> A. contracted to sell to W. 200 quarters of maize out of a larger quantity of 618 quarters then owned by him and lodged at a certain warehouse. A. gave W. a delivery order[4], which the latter passed to the warehouseman, X., at the same time notifying X. that he, W., had sold the maize to the plaintiff, to whose order the 200 quarters was to be held. Shortly afterwards, A., who remained unpaid, notified X. to stop delivery, and the plaintiff sued X. in detinue.

The Court of Appeal unanimously affirmed the decision of SANKEY J. in favour of X., and rejected the following contentions put forward by the plaintiff: first, that the property passed by virtue of the delivery

---

1. S.G.A., ss. 1 (3), (4); *Mischeff* v. *Springett*, [1942] 2 K.B. 331; [1942] 2 All E.R. 349.
2. See above, p. 20.　　　　　3. [1926] 1 K.B. 223, C.A.
4. SANKEY J. held that this was not a document of title: [1925] 2 K.B. 383, at p. 390; and on this basis distinguished *Ant. Jurgens Margarinefabrieken* v. *Dreyfus & Co.*, [1914] 3 K.B. 40: see below, p. 225.

order[5]; and second, that the receipt of the delivery order estopped X. from denying that the plaintiff was the owner of the 200 quarters[6].

Once this negative requirement has been satisfied, the Act confirms that the passing of property is a question of intention. Section 17 (1) provides:

> "Where there is a contract for the sale of specific or ascertained goods the property in them is transferred to the buyer at such time as the parties to the contract intend it to be transferred".

Specific and ascertained goods are here coupled together, which seems to suggest that ascertained goods are those which are agreed upon[7] at some time *after* the contract is made[8]. Thus, in *Laurie and Morewood* v. *Dudin*[9] the maize was unascertained because the buyer could not point to any particular grain and say "The seller agreed to sell that to me".   On the other hand, if A., after selling 200 quarters to W., had sold and delivered the remainder of the grain to a third party, it would have become clear which grains were to be delivered to W.: this situation is termed "appropriation by exhaustion"[10].

Assuming that the goods are specific or ascertained, s. 17 (2) reiterates the common law rule[11] that—

> "For the purpose of ascertaining the intention of the parties regard shall be had to the terms of the contract, the conduct of the parties, and the circumstances of the case".

The intention of the parties is thus a matter of construction.   For instance, in *Re Anchor Line, Ltd.*[12].

> There was a contract for the sale of a crane, the price to be paid by instalments subsequent to delivery. Eve J. held that the property passed when the contract was made under s. 18 r. 1.[13]; but the Court of Appeal pointed out that s. 18 gives way to a contrary intention, and held that on a true construction of the written contract the parties had shown an intention that the property should not pass until the full price had been paid.

Whilst it may be possible in some cases to find a common intention express[14] or implied[15] as to the passing of property, most people do

---

5. As there is no mention of bankruptcy in this case, it is difficult to know why the case was argued on the passing of property rather than on the duty to deliver: see *R.* v. *Sutton*, [1966] 1 All E.R. 571, C.C.A.
6. See below, p. 192.   7. See further below, pp. 175–176.
8. *Per* ATKIN L.J. in *Re Wait*, [1927] 1 Ch. 606, C.A., at p. 630. See also Lord BLACKBURN in *Seath* v. *Moore* (1886), 11 App. Cas., 350, H.L., at p. 370.
9. [1926] 1 K.B. 223, C.A.
10. See *Wait and James* v. *Midland Bank* (1926), 31 Com. Cas. 172.
11. See *Ogg* v. *Shuter* (1875), L.R. 10 C.P. 159, C.A., at p. 162.,
12. [1937] 1 Ch. 1; [1936] 2 All E.R. 941, C.A.   13. See below, p. 163.
14. Many standard-form contracts expressly deal with the point.
15. E.g. trade custom: *Lord Eldon* v. *Hedley Brothers*, [1935] 2 K.B. 1, C.A., esp. *per* GREER L.J. at pp. 16–19.

not act so as deliberately to satisfy such esoteric legal criteria; and, because the common law rejected any other objective test as to the passing of property, the courts therefore had to lay down a series of more or less arbitrary rules for attributing such an intention (usually fictitious) to the parties. These rules have been embodied in s. 18 of the S.G.A.; and, in practice, they are very important simply because the parties so seldom evince any intention on this point. On the other hand, s. 18 does make it clear that the intention of the parties is paramount, for the opening words of the section are as follows:

> "Unless a different intention appears, the following are rules for ascertaining the intention of the parties as to the time at which the property in the goods is to pass to the buyer".

The rules that the section contains will apply not just to sales, but also to h.p. transactions: when the hirer exercises his option, a contract of sale comes into existence and the property passes in accordance with the intention of the parties or under the rules laid down in s. 18.

Besides making special provision for "sale or return" transactions, s. 18 carefully distinguishes between (1) sales of specific goods, and (2) sales of unascertained or future goods[16]. As the section applies different rules to the two situations, it is necessary to distinguish between them. The term "specific goods" occurs in the first three rules, and presumably has the same meaning in each of them. According to the definition section (s. 62 (1)):

> " 'Specific goods' means goods identified and agreed upon at the time a contract of sale is made".

Can "future goods" be specific for the purposes of s. 18? It is sometimes suggested that they cannot[17]; but in *Varley* v. *Whipp*[18] all parties proceeded upon the assumption that there was a contract for the sale of "specific goods" within the meaning of s. 18, notwithstanding that at the time of contract the reaper was owned by a third party. Certainly, some future goods do fall literally within the wording of s. 62; and it may be that in the case of future goods which are identified at the time the contract is made there is a contract for the sale of specific goods subject to an implied condition precedent that the property cannot pass until the seller has acquired the property in the goods[19]. The meaning of the term "specific goods" in relation to the passing of property was considered by the Court of Appeal in *Kursell* v. *Timber Operators, Ltd.*[20].

---

16. The meaning "future goods" is considered above, pp. 19–20.
17. See Atiyah, *Sale of Goods* (3rd Edn.) 108; *Chalmers' Sale of Goods* (15th Edn.) 202.
18. [1900] 1 Q.B. 513: set out above, p. 74.
19. But see below, p. 166.   20. [1927] 1 K.B. 298, C.A.

A contract for the sale of uncut timber then standing in a Latvian forest provided that the buyer might cut and remove all timber of certain minimum specifications within the period of the next 15 years. The buyer paid a first instalment of the price, £30,000; but, before the buyer could cut much timber, the forest was nationalised, and thereafter performance of the contract became illegal. The arbitrator found that the contract had been frustrated, and that no further part of the price was payable, despite a clause in the agreement to the effect that, if the buyer were prevented by the Latvian Government from cutting any timber, the 15 years was to be extended by the length of this interruption.

Upon a case stated, Rowlatt J. decided that the contract had been frustrated. This finding was unanimously affirmed by the Court of Appeal, who held that the property in the timber had not passed to the buyer, and that the risk remained in the seller. Several reasons were given for the decision:

(1) The trees were *fructus naturales*, so that the property did not pass until severance[1].

(2) Section 18 rule 1 did not apply to this case[2]. Lord Hanworth M.R. was content to find a contrary intention[3]; but his brethren examined the matter in rather more detail, and concluded that for two reasons there was not a sale of specific goods. First, they thought that it was really a contract for the sale of a right of severance, that the trees did not become "specific or ascertained" for the purposes of s. 17 until put in a deliverable state, and that they were not in a deliverable state until cut[4]. Second, they thought that the trees were not specific goods until cut, because the contract intended the trees to be measured at the date of cutting rather than at the date of contracting[5]; but, even if the requisite date was that of contracting, Sargant L.J. said[6]:

"... I cannot think that the timber sold was at the date of the contract identified, or more than identifiable; and in order that the goods may be specific they must ... be identified and not merely identifiable ... For the purpose of the passing of the actual property in goods as distinguished from a right to ultimately claim a title to the goods as against the vendor or volunteers under him, a present identification of the goods as specific goods appears to be required by the statute".

---

1. *Per* Lord Hanworth M.R., at pp. 309–310; and Sargant L.J. at p. 314. See further above, pp. 18–19.
2. This provision is considered below, p. 162.   3. At pp. 309, 310.
4. *Per* Scrutton and Sargant L.JJ., at pp. 312, 314, who both expressly adopted the reasoning in the Scots case of *Morison* v. *Lockhart* 1912, S.C. 1017. "Deliverable state" is considered further below, pp. 165–166.
5. *Per* Scrutton and Sargant L.JJ., at pp. 311, 313–314. See also Lord Hanworth M.R. at pp. 307–308.
6. At p. 314.

(3) The parties agreed between themselves, and the court appears to have agreed with them, that the commercial object of the contract had become frustrated[7].

Notwithstanding the *dictum* of SARGANT L.J., it is submitted that the contract goods need only be described by the contract in such a way that they are identified or identifiable[8] at the time the contract is made before they will be regarded as specific: in all other cases, the contract is for the sale of unascertained goods, whether or not the goods are identifiable at the time the contract is made. It is also immaterial how soon after the formation of the contract they are ascertained or identified. When the contract is for the sale of unascertained goods, it will *never become* a contract for the sale of specific goods, though there might be a novation.

Having drawn the distinction between specific and unascertained goods, the rules governing the passing of property in the two cases must now be examined. Sales on approval will be treated separately, as will one example of a contrary intention, the reservation of a right of disposal.

2 THE PASSING OF PROPERTY IN SPECIFIC GOODS

The rules of s. 18 of the S.G.A. with respect to the passing of property in specific goods differentiate between conditional and unconditional contracts, making special provision in rule 1 for "unconditional contracts". The two major uses of the term "condition" in the law of contract are that of conditions precedent and essential stipulations[9]; and, at first sight, it appears too obvious for argument that "unconditional contract" in rule 1 means a contract not subject to any conditions precedent to the passing of property. This was the common law position[10]; and it is, moreover, difficult to envisage the possibility of a contract of sale without any essential stipulations. Further support may be found for this view within the Act. First, throughout the Act, the term "conditional contract" seems to be used in the sense of a contract subject to conditions precedent. Second, rule 1 appears to be contrasted with rules 2 and 3, both of which deal with contracts subject to conditions precedent. Third, if "unconditional contract" in rule 1 means a contract without any essential stipulations, this appears to make nonsense of the references in rule 1 itself to the times of payment and delivery. However, in spite of this apparently overwhelming logic, the courts have in several cases since 1893 suggested that "unconditional

---

7. See the judgments at pp. 306, 312, 314–315. See further below, p. 254.
8. E.g. a contract to sell all the black-faced lambs in the seller's flock.
9. See above, pp. 50–51.
10. See *Street* v. *Blay* (1831), 2 B. & Ad. 456.

contract" means one without any essential stipulations[11]. Their
motive for this apparently illogical attitude seems to have been to
avoid the unfortunate effect of the combination of ss. 11 (1) (c) and 18
rule 1, which might deny a buyer any right of rejection at all. However,
this undesirable result has now been removed by the Misrepresentation
Act 1967[12]; and it is submitted that it is now safe to regard "unconditional" in rule 1 as meaning "without conditions precedent".

1 Unconditional contracts
Section 18 rule 1 provides:

> "Where there is an unconditional contract for the sale of specific
> goods, in a deliverable state, the property in the goods passes to the
> buyer when the contract is made, and it is immaterial whether the
> time of payment or the time of delivery, or both, be postponed".

It is usually said that this rule reiterates the position at common law[13];
and an example of the operation of the rule is to be found in *Dennant* v.
Skinner[14].

> A rogue, X, attended an auction, and successfully bid for a van.
> Afterwards, he told the plaintiff auctioneer that his name was King,
> and that he was the son of the proprietor of a well-known firm,
> King's of Oxford. The plaintiff then knocked down five more
> vehicles to X., including a Standard car. Afterwards, X. went to the
> auctioneer's office, and asked to be allowed to pay by cheque,
> repeating that he was from King's of Oxford. The auctioneer
> allowed him to take the Standard away after he had signed a memo-
> randum in the following terms:
> "I agree that the ownership of the vehicles will not pass to me until
> such time as . . . my cheque . . . [is honoured]".
> X. disappeared, and the Standard found its way into the hands of the
> defendant, a B.F.P.

HALLETT J. held there was a contract of sale between the auctioneer and
X. made "by the fall of the hammer" (s. 58 (2)), the identity of X. being
at that time irrelevant; and that the property passed under s. 18 rule 1
to X. at the time the contract was made, this case being indistinguishable from *Phillips* v. *Brooks*[15]. Nor did his Lordship think the mem-

---

11. Only *Varley* v. *Whipp*, [1900] 1 Q.B. 513, seems to have been decided on
    these grounds.
12. See below, p. 398.
13. *Tarling* v. *Baxter* (1827), 6 B. & C. 360, which is usually cited as the
    authority, is only explicable on the basis that the stacked hay had to be cut
    before removal.
14. [1948] 2 K.B. 164.
15. [1919] 2 K.B. 243 (the rogue North obtained a ring from a jeweller by
    misrepresenting his identity, and HORRIDGE J. held that the rogue obtained
    a voidable title to the ring).

orandum aided the auctioneer: he pointed out that it merely stated a legal error. This case has given rise to controversy on several grounds not directly relevant to rule 1. First, did the auctioneer's mistake as to the identy of X. prevent there ever being a contract between the two of them[16]? Second, assuming that there was a contract, why did the defendant not plead title under the S.G.A., s. 25 (2)[17]? Third, why did the memorandum not impliedly revest the property in the auctioneer[18]?

So far as the actual wording of rule 1 is concerned, the meaning of the terms "unconditional contract" and "specific goods" have already been discussed[19]: and the meaning of "deliverable state" will be dealt with later[20]. It only remains to consider the final words of the rule:

"it is immaterial whether the time of payment or the time of delivery, or both, be postponed".

Though immaterial as such, these events are clearly relevant as possibly giving some indication of a contrary intention which may exclude the operation of s. 18 altogether. Thus, in *Ward, Ltd.* v. *Bignall*[1] DIPLOCK L.J. commented:

"The governing rule . . . is in s. 17, and in modern times very little is needed to give rise to the inference that the property in specific goods is to pass only on delivery or payment".

In *Lacis* v. *Cashmarts*[2], moreover, the Divisional Court held that in a supermarket or "cash and carry" shop

"the intention . . . is that the property shall not pass until the price is paid".

Finally, another factor sometimes looked at by the courts in order to ascertain the intention of the parties is any special agreement with respect to the passing of risk, because of the presumption that risk passes with property. However, an agreement with respect to risk is at best an ambiguous indication of the intention of the parties with regard to the passing of property[3].

---

16. See below, p. 198.
17. See below, p. 220.
18. HALLETT J. merely said that it *had* not revested the property, but it has been suggested (it is submitted wrongly) that even by appropriate wording it *could* not have done so: see Atiyah, *Sale of Goods* (3rd Edn.) 106.
19. See above, pp. 161–162, 159–161.
20. See below, pp. 165–166.
 1. [1967] 1 Q.B. 534, C.A., at p. 545.
 2. [1969] 2 Q.B. 400, at p. 407. Compare *Clarke* v. *Reilly* (1962), 96 I.L.T.R. 96.
 3. See *Re Anchor Line, (Hendeson Brothers), Ltd.*, [1937] 1 Ch. 1, C.A.: set out above, p. 158; and *Carlos Federspiel & Co.* v. *Twigg & Co., Ltd.*, [1957] 1 Lloyds Rep. 240: set out below, p. 169.

2 Conditional contracts

Rules 2 and 3 of s. 18 deal with the passing of property in conditional contracts for the sale of specific goods; and, apart from the question of notice, they appear to embody the common law.

Rule 2 provides as follows:

> "Where there is a contract for the sale of specific goods and the seller is bound to do something to the goods, for the purpose of putting them into a deliverable state, the property does not pass until such thing be done, and the buyer has notice thereof".

This rule seems to be based on *Rugg* v. *Minett*[4].

> There was a sale by auction as separate lots[5] of a number of casks containing different quantities of turpentine. The agreement provided that, before delivery, the seller was to top up the casks from two of their number, and the price was to be computed at so much for each full cask and a *pro rata* payment for the remainder. Halfway through the process of topping up, the seller stopped for the night, during which all the casks were destroyed by a fire which occurred without fault on the part of either seller or buyer. The court held that the property did not pass until the barrels were topped up; and hence the property and risk only passed to the buyer in respect of the barrels which had been topped up.

Rule 3 provides as follows:

> "Where there is a contract for the sale of specific goods in a deliverable state, but the seller is bound to weigh, measure, test, or do some other act or thing with reference to the goods for the purpose of ascertaining the price, the property does not pass until such act or thing be done, and the buyer has notice thereof".

This rule appears to be founded on *Hanson* v. *Meyer*[6].

> There was a contract for the sale of all the starch then lying in a certain warehouse at £6 per hundredweight, though the exact weight was unknown to the parties at the time of contracting. The seller gave a note to the buyer which directed the warehousekeeper to weigh and deliver the starch to the buyer. Part of the starch was weighed and delivered, but the buyer became bankrupt; and the rest remained in the warehouse unweighed, and at the seller's expense. The assignees of the buyer sued in trover for the remainder of the starch.

The Court of Kings Bench found for the seller, and Lord ELLENBOROUGH said[7].

---

4. (1809), 11 East 210.
5. See now s. 58 (1). The fact that there were separate lots is important to the doctrine of total failure of consideration: see below, p. 407.
6. (1805), 6 East 614.   7. At pp. 626–627.

"If anything remains to be done on the part of the seller, as between him and the buyer, before the commodity purchased is to be delivered, a complete present right of property has not attached in the buyer . . ."

It would seem that Lord ELLENBOROUGH carefully worded his judgment so as to decide no more than that the contract made the weighing a condition precedent to delivery; but the case was taken as an indication of the opinion of the Court of Kings Bench as to the vesting of the general property in the goods[8]: it was so adopted in a number of cases, and subsequently embodied in the S.G.A.

It will be observed that under rule 2 the property in goods is not to pass until the goods are put in a "deliverable state" by the seller, whereas rules 1, 3 and 5 deal with situations where the goods are already in a deliverable state. Presumably, the phrase "deliverable state" means the same in each case, and is defined by s. 62 (4) as follows:

"Goods are in a 'deliverable state' within the meaning of this Act when they are in such a state that the buyer would under the contract be bound to take delivery of them".

The meaning of the phrase was considered by the courts in *Underwood, Ltd.* v. *Burgh Castle Brick and Cement Syndicate*[9].

There was a contract for the sale "free on rail" of a condensing engine weighing over 30 tons, then cemented to the floor of the seller's premises. It was envisaged by the parties that the process of detaching and loading the engine onto a railway truck would take about two weeks and cost about £100; and the contract provided that this was to be done by the seller at his own expense. The seller subsequently detached the engine; but it was severely damaged whilst being loaded, without any fault on the part of the seller, and, apparently, before the buyer had notice that it had been detached. The buyer refused to accept the damaged engine, and the seller argued that the property and risk had passed to the buyer at the time of the accident.

ROWLATT J. thought the parties intended the sale of a chattel, the severed engine, not of a fixture[10]; and he said[11]:

"Many chattels have to be taken to pieces before they can be delivered—e.g. a sideboard or a billiard table; nevertheless the property in these passes on the sale and is not postponed until the article is actually taken to pieces and delivered. I do not, therefore,

---

8. See *Blackburn on Sale* (3rd Edn.) 187.
9. [1922] 1 K.B. 123, and 343, C.A.
10. In a subsequent case, a contract was interpreted as a sale of a right of severance by two members of the C.A.: *Kursell* v. *Timber Operators, Ltd.*, [1927] 1 K.B. 298 (see above, p. 160).
11. At p. 125.

lay any stress on the fact of the engine having to be taken to pieces. I think the important point is that the parties were dealing with an article which was a fixture to the premises, and that is different from the case of a loose chattel . . . It seems a safe rule to adopt that if a fixture has to be detached so as to make it a chattel again, the act of detaching it has to be done before the chattel can be deliverable".

His decision in favour of the buyer was unanimously affirmed by the Court of Appeal, who stressed the time and money involved in the operation of loading. BANKES and ATKIN L.JJ. were prepared to find a contractual intention that the property should not pass until the engine was loaded on rail[12]; but all three Judges agreed that the engine was not in a deliverable state at the time of the accident. BANKES L.J. said[13]:

"A 'deliverable state' does not depend upon the mere completeness of the subject-matter in all its parts. It depends on the actual state of the goods at the date of the contract, and the state in which they are to be delivered by the terms of the contract".

It would seem then that "deliverable state" does not refer to whether or not the goods are deliverable in any literal sense, but to whether or not the seller has put the goods in such a state that a delivery of the goods in that state would comply with the provisions of the contract *in respect of the state of the goods*[14]. If the buyer is not bound to take delivery, that does not necessarily show that the goods are not in a deliverable state, because the contract may contain conditions precedent to the passing of property other than the state of the goods, e.g. rule 3[15].

It should be noticed that both rules 2 and 3 are expressed in the negative, and are only applicable where something is to be done by the seller. Thus, it does not follow that once the rule is satisfied the property will pass, as there may be other conditions precedent to the passing of property: for instance, if A. agrees to buy a second-hand car from B. provided that (1) B. executes certain repairs and (2) A.'s wife likes it, when the car is repaired it is put in a deliverable state[16] but the property will not pass until A.'s wife approves. Even the negative effect of the rules has a fairly narrow scope: they do not apply where the act is to be done by the buyer[17]; and it has even been suggested that they are only applicable where the act in relation to the goods is to be done by the seller *before* delivery[18]. Moreover, even where it is applic-

---

12. At pp. 345, 346. See also *Young* v. *Matthews* (1866), L.R. 2 C.P. 127.
13. At p. 345.
14. See *Phillip Head & Sons, Ltd.* v. *Showfronts, Ltd.* (1969), 113 Sol. Jo. 978 (sale and laying of carpet).
15. Smith (1957–8), J.S.P.T.L., at p. 192; Thornely (1958), C.L.J. at p. 126; and now also Atiyah, *Sale of Goods* (3rd Edn.) 108, note 7.
16. *Contra* Atiyah, *op. cit.*, 110.
17. Even if done on behalf of the seller?
18. *Benjamin on Sale* (8th Edn.) 311.

able, the presumption contained in rule 3 would appear to be weaker than that in rule 2[19], and has seldom been applied[20].

Where either rule is applicable, it is subject to the requirement that something is done, *and* that the buyer has notice thereof, this last stipulation being an addition to the common law. The Act does not provide that the seller shall give notice, but merely that the buyer shall have notice[1]; and it may be that such notice is to be contrasted with the assent required under rule 5[2]. This requirement of notice may provide one explanation of *Underwood's Case*[3]: even if the engine was in a deliverable state at the time of the accident, the buyer did not know this.

Finally, there is the question of whether rules 2 and 3 can operate to pass the property in part only of the contract goods. At common law property could be passed in part of the goods[4]: but s. 18 would appear to be ambiguous on the point[5]. In *Underwood's Case*[3] the fact that a small part of the engine had already been sent to the buyer does not seem to have been considered significant. Even assuming that the property can pass in part of the contract goods, it would seem that this will not of itself prevent the buyer from rejecting the goods under s. 30 (1) on the grounds that the contract quantity has not been delivered[6].

3 THE PASSING OF PROPERTY IN UNASCERTAINED GOODS

1 The rule

If the contract is for the sale of unascertained goods, then it must initially be an agreement to sell, because s. 16 prevents the property passing until the goods have been ascertained[7]. Once the goods have become ascertained, s. 17 states that the property will pass when the parties intend it to pass[8]; and, in the absence of a contrary intention,

---

19. Atiyah, *Sale of Goods* (3rd Edn.) 110; *Blackburn on Sale* (3rd Edn.) 194.
20. Cf. *The Napoli* (1898), 15 T.L.R. 56 and *Nanka Bruce* v. *Commonwealth Trust, Ltd.*, [1926] A.C. 77, P.C. The former would appear to be the only post-Act case where rule 3 has been applied; and it is difficult to see why the buyer's action in conversion in that case should have depended on the passing of property.
1. *Benjamin on Sale* (8th Edn.) 307 suggests that "notice" is here equivalent to "knowledge".
2. See below, pp. 175–176.
3. [1922] 1 K.B. 343, C.A.: see above, p. 165.
4. See *Hanson* v. *Meyer* (1805), 6 East 614; *Rugg* v *Minett* (1809), 11 East 210.
5. Before the amendment of s. 11 (1) (c) by the Misrepresentation Act 1967, s. 4 (1) (as to which see below, p. 398), the operation of that subsection and s. 18 rule 2 appeared to conflict with s. 30 (1). Is this a reason for deducing that the Act did not intend to pass the property in part of the goods?
6. See *Barrow, Lane and Ballard, Ltd.* v. *Phillip Phillips & Co., Ltd.*, [1929] 1 K.B. 574, discussed below, p. 253.
7. See above, p. 157.
8. See above, p. 158.

the property will pass according to rule 5 of s. 18, paragraph one of which provides:

> "Where there is a contract for the sale of unascertained or future goods by description, and goods of that description and in a deliverable state are unconditionally appropriated to the contract, either by the seller with the assent of the buyer, or by the buyer with the assent of the seller, the property in the goods thereupon passes to the buyer. Such assent may be express or implied, and may be given either before or after the appropriation is made".

Unlike rules 1, 2, and 3, rule 5 is expressed in positive terms: it says that the property will pass when certain requirements are satisfied. These requirements are as follows:

(1) That the contract is for the sale of "unascertained or future goods by description". It has already been suggested that today most sales will be by description[9]; and the concepts of unascertained and future goods have also been considered[10].

(2) That the goods appropriated to the contract are of the contract description and in a deliverable state. The latter expression presumably has the same meaning here as under the other rules[11]. "Contract description" certainly deals with matters of quality[12]; but it probably does not extend to matters of quantity: no purported appropriation, however, can pass the property in goods which do not comply with the contract description[13]. Nevertheless, it has been held that the property passed where less than the contract quantity of goods of the contract description were appropriated to the contract[14], though in this last case it would seem that it is always open to the buyer to reject for breach of s. 30[15].

(3) That the appropriation is unconditional. As in the case of the other rules, it is submitted that this refers to the absence of any condition precedent[16]: it may be that such a condition precedent evinces an intention to oust s. 18 altogether[17].

(4) That there be an appropriation *with* assent. It is this requirement which gives rise to the greatest difficulty; and the two constituent

---

9. See above, p. 69. 10. See above, pp. 157, 19.
11. See above, p. 165–166.
12. *Healy* v. *Howlett & Sons*, [1917] 1 K.B. 337: set out below, p. 245.
13. *Vigers Brothers* v. *Sanderson Brothers*, [1901] 1 K.B. 608.
14. *Aldridge* v. *Johnson* (1857), 26 L.J.Q.B. 296.
15. This would give the same answer as in the case of specific goods: see above, p. 167. But it may be difficult to reconcile with the old cases such as: *Cunliffe* v. *Harrison* (1851), 6 Exch. 903; *Levy* v. *Green* (1859), 1 E. & E. 969.
16. See above, pp. 161–162. *Contra Polar Refrigeration, Ltd.* v. *Moldenhauer* (1967), 61 D.L.R. (2d) 462; *Ollett* v. *Jordan*, [1918] 2 K.B. 41 (criminal case, said by Benjamin (at p. 649) to be wrong).
17. E.g. *Stein, Forbes & Co.* v. *County Tailoring Co.* (1916), 86 L.J.K.B. 448.

parts, appropriation and assent, will be considered separately. However, it must be remembered that there may be little point in searching for an act of appropriation if there is no evidence of assent; and *vice versa*: the two are required before the property will pass.

2 Appropriation

In a contract for the sale of unascertained goods, an act done by one party in relation to certain goods which evinces an intention that the property in those goods should be passed in pursuance of the contract is termed an "appropriation"[18]. Two cases may be cited to illustrate the difficulty of determining when there has been a sufficient appropriation. In *Aldridge* v. *Johnson*[19]

> There was a contract for the sale "free on rail" of 100 quarters of barley from a larger bulk then situated in the seller's granary, the price of £215 to be paid as to £23 in cash and the rest in cattle[20]. It was agreed that the buyer was to send his own sacks, which the seller was to fill. The cattle were delivered, and the sacks sent to the seller. The seller filled most of the sacks, but emptied the barley back onto the pile of grain just before he became bankrupt. The buyer sued the seller's assignees in bankruptcy in conversion and detinue to recover the sacks and the barley.

The court held that the buyer was entitled to his sacks, and also to so much of the barley as had been put into sacks[1], because the property had passed when it was put into sacks[2]. On the other hand, in *Federspiel* v. *Twigg Ltd.*[3] the court came to the opposite conclusion.

> There was a contract for the sale of cycles by a British manufacturer to a foreign buyer, f.o.b. a British port. The seller packed and marked the goods in preparation for shipment, and the buyer paid the price. Before the goods could be dispatched to the port of shipment, the seller went into liquidation. The buyer sued the liquidator for conversion of the cycles, alleging that they had been appropriated to the contract and that the property had passed to him.

In rejecting this contention, PEARSON J. said[4]:

> ". . . usually, but not necessarily, the appropriating act is the last act to be performed by the seller . . . If there is a further act, an important and decisive act to be done by the seller, then there is

---

18. *Per* PEARSON J. in *Carlos Federspiel & Co.* v. *Charles Twigg & Co., Ltd.*, [1957] 1 Lloyds Rep. 240, at p. 255. See also *Denny* v. *Skelton* (1916), 86 L.J.K.B. 280.   19. (1857), 26 L.J.Q.B. 296.   20. See above, p. 23, note 5.
   1. Does it matter that this barley was not traceable?
   2. It has been suggested that such an action will always result in specific recovery: *Williams on Bankruptcy* (18th Edn.) 273.
   3. [1957] 1 Lloyds Rep. 240.   4. At pp. 255–256.

prima facie evidence that probably the property does not pass until the final act is done".

His Lordship was of the opinion that the emphasis throughout was on shipment as the decisive act to be done by the seller, so that *prima facie* it appeared that the earliest time when the parties intended that the property should pass would be on shipment[5]. Nor could his Lordship find anything to displace this presumption.

Perhaps the most obvious example of an appropriation is delivery[6], a matter which receives special mention in rule 5. Paragraph 2 of that rule provides:

> "Where, in pursuance of the contract, the seller delivers the goods to the buyer or to a carrier or other bailee . . . (whether named by the buyer or not) for the purpose of transmission to the buyer, and does not reserve the right of disposal, he is deemed to have unconditionally appropriated the goods to the contract".

To satisfy this rule, the delivery must be made "in pursuance of the contract", which implies that the goods must be of the contract description and in a deliverable state[7]; and, as we shall see later, "delivery" is defined by the S.G.A. in such a way as to include actual and constructive delivery[8]. Whilst rule 5 (2) seems to be couched as if it were merely an example of rule 5 (1), there has been a tendency on the part of the courts to treat appropriation as being synonymous with an actual or constructive delivery[9]. In *Federspiel* v. *Twigg Ltd.*[10] PEARSON J. commented:

> "I think that is right, subject only to this possible qualification, that there may be after such constructive delivery an actual delivery still to be made by the seller under the contract. Of course, that is quite possible, because delivery is the transfer of possession, whereas appropriation transfers ownership. So there may be first an appropriation, constructive delivery, whereby the seller becomes bailee for the buyer, and then a subsequent actual delivery involving actual possession, and when I say that I have in mind in particular two cases cited, namely, *Aldridge* v. *Johnson*[11] and *Langton* v. *Higgins*[12]."

Chalmers concludes that[13]:

> "If the term 'delivery' had been substituted for 'appropriation', probably less difficulty would have arisen . . ."

---

5. On the question of assent, see below, pp. 175–176.
6. *Per* PARKE B. in *Wait* v. *Baker* (1848), 2 Ex. 1, at pp. 7–8.
7. See above, p. 168.   8. See below, p. 264.
9. See *Chalmers' Sale of Goods* (15th Edn.) 85.
10. [1957] 1 Lloyds Rep. 240, at p. 255.
11. (1857), 26 L.J.Q.B. 296 (above, p. 169).
12. (1859), 4 H. & N. 402 (below, p. 171).
13. *Sale of Goods* (15th Edn.) 85.

But would this be so? It may be that an actual delivery would clearly show when property passed; but it is equally clear that there may be an appropriation notwithstanding that there has not been an actual delivery. Thus, in *Aldridge* v. *Johnson*[11] it was held that the property passed when the grain was put into sacks. To say that the difference between this case and *Federspiel* v. *Twigg, Ltd.*[14], is that in the former case there has been a constructive change of possession does not seem to advance matters much further, because this issue too turns on the intention of the parties.

The cases on appropriation may usefully be considered according to the type of unascertained goods involved, as the effect of the rules may vary according to this factor[15].

1. Goods to be manufactured or grown by the seller. These will be future goods; and s. 5 (3) provides that the contract must initially operate as an agreement to sell, though it says nothing about when the property is to pass. The two types of future goods will be considered separately:

(a) Goods to be manufactured by the seller. According to Benjamin[16],

> "the rule is that, *prima facie*, the property will not pass till the goods are completely made and are appropriated with mutual assent".

Thus, in *Federspiel* v. *Twigg, Ltd.*[14], PEARSON J. thought that there had not been a sufficient appropriation, notwithstanding that the goods were packed and marked ready for shipment. A similar reluctance on the part of the courts to find an appropriation in any act by the manufacturer short of delivery is to be seen in the ship-building cases[17]. The explanation for this attitude may be that the courts wish to leave the manufacturer a reasonable amount of freedom to allocate his products between different buyers.

(b) Goods to be grown by the seller. In *Langton* v. *Higgins*[18],

> The parties made a contract in Jan. 1858 for the sale at a price per pound of the whole of a crop of peppermint to be grown by the seller in that year. In Sept. 1858, the buyer sent bottles to the seller; and the latter, having weighed the oil, poured it into these bottles. The Court of Exchequer followed *Aldridge* v. *Johnson*[19], and held that the property passed when the oil was poured into the bottles, and that the buyer might sue for conversion of the oil.

It has been suggested that the considerations of flexibility obtaining in the case of a manufacturing seller "do not apply in the case of goods to

---

14. [1957] 1 Lloyds Rep. 240; above, p. 169.
15. A similar variation may be noticed in relation to the cases on the passing of risk, though there is no necessary connection between the two.
16. *On Sale* (8th Edn.) 344.
17. See *Mucklow* v. *Mangles* (1808), 1 Taunt. 318; *Laing & Sons, Ltd.* v. *Barclay, Curle & Co., Ltd.*, [1908] A.C. 35, H.L.; *Re Blyth Shipbuilding Co. and Dry Docks Co., Ltd.*, [1926] Ch. 494, C.A.
18. (1859), 4 H. & N. 402.   19. (1857), 26 L.J.Q.B. 296.

be grown by the seller, and here it might well be held that the property in the goods, if sufficiently designated, passes as soon as they come into existence"[20].   However, whilst it is true that there cannot be a sale of goods[1] until they come into existence[2], it does not follow that the property should pass at that moment.   Why should the seller not have a similar flexibility in allocating his crop between buyers? Such an argument was suggested in *Langton* v. *Higgins*[18] by BRAMWELL J. who said, *obiter*, that he thought that the property in the goods did not pass when the oil was made up, notwithstanding that the one buyer had contracted for the entire crop.   But it is just possible that there may be one exceptional case, the common law category of "potential property"[3], where the property passes automatically when the goods come into existence[4]; but presumably this will be subject to the requirement that the goods are then in a deliverable state.

2. *Generic goods, or an unascertained part of a specific whole.*   In *Aldridge* v. *Johnson*[5] we saw that the property was held to have passed when the seller put goods which conformed with the contract in containers supplied by the buyer.   Moreover, just as the goods may become ascertained by process of exhaustion[6], so they may become appropriated to the contract by being physically set aside[7].   Thus in *Pignataro* v. *Gilroy*[8],

> There was a contract for the sale by sample of 140 bags of rice to be delivered within 14 days in two lots—125 bags at a certain wharf, and 15 bags at the seller's premises.   In response to the buyer's request, the seller sent the buyer a delivery order for the 125 bags, and also notified him that the 15 bags had been set aside ready for delivery. When the buyer eventually sent for the 15 bags nearly a month after the contractual delivery date, it was found that they had been stolen. The buyer's action to recover part of the price paid was dismissed on the grounds that the property and risk had passed to him.

A common situation which may cause some difficulty is the mail order business.   Where the seller posts goods of the type ordered, this would

---

20. Atiyah, *Sale of Goods* (3rd Edn.) 166.
1. Where the contract is for the sale of an undivided whole, e.g. a cargo, it has been suggested that "goods" means the whole cargo, and that the property cannot pass until the cargo be made up: *Benjamin on Sale* (8th Edn.) 356.
2. E.g. *Langton* v. *Higgins* (above); *Kursell* v. *Timber Operators and Contractors*, [1927] 1 K.B. 298, C.A.: set out above, p. 160.
3. "Potential goods" have been defined as goods which "would grow naturally out of anything already owned by the seller": *Chalmers' Sale of Goods* (15th Edn.) 34.
4. It is debatable whether "potential property" has survived the Act as a separate category: see *Chalmers' op. cit.*, note 0.
5. (1857), 26 L.J.Q.B. 296.   6. See above, p. 158.
7. Provided they conform with the contract description: *Healy* v. *Howlett*, [1917] 1 K.B. 337: set out below, p. 245.
8. [1919] 1 K.B. 459, D.C.

seem to be an act of appropriation[9]. But can any act prior to posting amount to an appropriation? Clearly, where the customer's order constitutes an offer and the posting an acceptance, posting is the earliest moment at which there may be an appropriation: the property may well pass when the contract is made[10]. But if the contract is made at some prior stage, then it is arguable that the buyer may have conferred on the seller a power of selection; and it would seem that the same considerations obtain with regard to appropriation as in the case of goods to be manufactured by the seller.

At very least, the general effect of the cases seems to be that the goods should be identified before they could be regarded as sufficiently appropriated for the property to pass; and this was the common law, even in the case of potential property. However, equity may have taken a somewhat more elastic view of appropriation: there was some indication that a buyer might have been regarded as acquiring an equitable interest in the goods before there was any sufficient appropriation to pass the legal title to him, in which case the buyer would have an interest which was good against all except a b.f.p. If there was such an equitable interest, and if it survived the S.G.A., then it might be particularly useful to a buyer in the event of the seller's insolvency[11]. The issue arose in *Re Wait*[12].

> W. contracted on Nov. 20th to buy a cargo of 1,000 tons of wheat *ex Challenger*, the cargo to be made up the following month. On Nov. 21st, W. agreed to sell 500 tons of this cargo to X. The cargo was duly shipped, and, whilst the *Challenger* was at sea, X. paid the price to W., who shortly afterwards became insolvent.

The claim of W.'s trustee in bankruptcy to the entire cargo succeeded before the Court of Appeal, which by a majority held that X. was not entitled to specific performance under s. 52[13], and had not acquired any equitable interest in the goods. It was common ground that there had been no appropriation sufficient at law to pass the legal title in 500 tons of the wheat to X.; but their Lordships differed on whether this was sufficient to dispose of the case.

(1) *The position in equity before the S.G.A.* It was accepted that X. could not acquire any interest in the goods on Nov. 21st, because the goods were then future goods[14]. But did the position change when

---

9. See the *Badische Anilin und Soda Fabrik* v. *Basle Chemical Works, Bindschedler*, [1898] A.C. 200, H.L., which demonstrates the difficulty of trying to consider this in terms of constructive possession.
10. Compare s. 18 rule 1, considered above, p. 162.
11. See *Williams on Bankruptcy* (18th Edn.) 274, 295.
12. [1927] 1 Ch. 606, C.A.
13. Lord HANWORTH M.R. and ATKIN L.J. at pp. 621, 630; SARGANT L.J. dissented (at p. 656). On specific performance, see generally below, pp. 428–429.
14. See s. 5 (3), above, p. 20.

the cargo was made up, and the contract became one in respect of an unascertained part of a specific whole? There was authority for the proposition that X. might acquire an equitable interest if he could maintain an action for specific performance; but the majority thought that no such action was available. In the absence of specific performance, ATKIN L.J. thought that the buyer could never by reason of the contract of sale acquire any equitable rights in the goods[15]. However, the majority disagreed: SARGEANT L.J. held that X. could, and would prior to the S.G.A., have acquired an equitable lien which floated over the entire cargo once it was made up[16]; but Lord HANWORTH M.R. took the view that such a right could not attach unless and until the actual contract goods became identifiable, which these never did[17].

(2) The position under the S.G.A. It was suggested by ATKIN L.J. that, even if there were such an equitable right, it could not have survived the S.G.A.; and he argued as follows[18]:

> "It would have been futile in a code intended for commercial men to have created an elaborate structure of rules dealing with rights at law, if at the same time it was intended to leave, subsisting with the legal rights, equitable rights inconsistent with, more extensive, and coming into existence earlier than the rights so carefully set out in the various sections of the Code".

SARGANT L.J. disagreed[19]; Lord HANWORTH M.R. did not comment on this point; and even ATKIN L.J. twice said he did not intend to decide the question[20]. Whilst it may therefore be that theoretically the point is still open[1], it seems unlikely that such an argument will ever succeed[2]. However, we must note a restriction which ATKIN L.J. sought to place on his proposition: he distinguished between those matters dealt with by the Act, where the Act was a "complete and exclusive statement of the legal relations both in law and equity", and what he termed rights coming into existence "dehors" the contract of sale. He then explained[3]:

> "A seller or a purchaser may . . . create any equity he pleases by way of charge, equitable assignment or any other dealing with or disposition of the goods, the subject-matter of the sale; and he may, of course, create such an equity as one of the terms expressed in the contract of sale. But the mere sale or agreement to sell or the acts in pursuance of such a contract mentioned in the Code will only produce the legal effects which the Code states".

Finally, the relationship between an ascertainment and an appropriation of goods must be considered. Neither of these processes is defined

---

15. At p. 637.   16. At pp. 645, 649.   17. At pp. 621–625.
18. At pp. 635–636.   19. At p. 655.   20. At pp. 635, 636.
  1. See Fridman, *Sale of Goods*, 37.
  2. See Atiyah, *Sale of Goods* (3rd Edn.) 117.   3. At p. 636.

by the S.G.A.; but appropriation is an act showing an intention that the property in certain goods should pass under the contract; and it has been suggested that ascertained goods are those identified and agreed upon after the contract is made[4]. This implies that ascertainment is the process of identification of the goods as being the contract goods. Thus, both the acts of ascertainment and appropriation are acts evidencing an intention of a party to the contract of sale. However, an ascertainment shows an intention that certain goods be earmarked as the contract goods; but appropriation evinces an intention that the property should pass in those goods under that contract. Of course, the distinction is rarely considered by the parties, and the one act usually fulfils both purposes, so that the ascertainment and appropriation take place at the same moment[5]. It is for this reason sometimes erroneously assumed that the two words ascertainment and appropriation are interchangeable; and confusion is worse confounded by the fact that the courts sometimes, understandably, use the two terms synonymously.

3. The importance of assent

Section 18 rule 5 (1) infers that an act of appropriation by one party cannot pass the property in the goods without the assent of the other; and adds—

> "Such assent may be express or implied, and may be given either before or after the appropriation is made".

Thus the rule requires a common intention to pass the property[6]; but in one case Lord WRIGHT observed that this is generally to be inferred from the terms of the contract or the practices of the trade[7]. Thus, in *Pignataro* v. *Gilroy*[8] ROWLATT J. thought that by asking for a delivery order the buyer had assented in advance to the seller's appropriation; but he was also prepared to find a subsequent assent in the fact that the buyer did nothing for a whole month in response to an appropriation made in consequence of his own request.

In considering the problem of implied assent, two situations have to be distinguished.

(1) Where the buyer appropriates with the assent of the seller. In these circumstances, the goods will usually be in the actual or construc-

---

4. See above, p. 161.
5. But see, e.g., c.i.f. contracts, below, p. 247.
6. E.g. *Carlos Federspiel & Co.* v. *Charles Twigg & Co., Ltd.*, [1957] 1 Lloyds Rep. 240: set out above, p. 170.
7. *Ross T. Smyth & Co., Ltd.* v. *Bailey, Son & Co.*, [1940] 3 All E.R. 60, H.L., at p. 66.
8. [1919] 1 K.B. 459, D.C.: set out above, p. 172. See also *Aldridge* v. *Johnson* (1857), 26 L.J.Q.B. 296: set out above, p. 169.

tive possession of the seller, in which case it will normally be fairly easy to see whether there has been a sufficient appropriation by the buyer and assent by the seller.

(2) Where the seller appropriates with the assent of the buyer. Because the goods will usually be in the actual or constructive possession of the seller, it may be rather more difficult in these circumstances to find an appropriation by the seller and assent by the buyer, as for instance in the mail order business[9]. It is submitted that the buyer may impliedly assent in advance, by conferring on the seller a power of selection, notwithstanding that the buyer has not seen the stock from which the goods are selected[10].

4 "SALE OR RETURN" TRANSACTIONS

Rule 4 of s. 18 seeks to deal with the passing of property—

> "where goods are delivered to the buyer on approval or 'on sale or return' or other similar terms'.

The rule concentrates on when the property passes. However, the formation of a contract of sale must necessarily precede the passing of property, and there would appear to be two possible interpretations of the time of contracting. First, the goods may be delivered to the potential buyer merely as bailee, in which case the bailor has merely made an offer, and some later act of acceptance is required. Second, the parties may intend to enter into a contract of sale immediately, but to give the buyer a right to rescind if he does not approve of the goods after a trial[11]. It is generally assumed that the Act envisages the first alternative alone; but the Act speaks of the bailee as a "buyer", and the second alternative might explain the decision in *P. Edwards, Ltd. v. Vaughan*[12].

The distinction between the two alternatives is, of course, crucial in the period after delivery and before the transferee approves. If there is a contract of sale, the position is governed by the S.G.A.; but if there is a mere bailment then the common law rules of bailment will apply. The distinction may have important effects in the following respects:

(1) Risk. If there is a mere bailment, the underlying risk is on the bailor[13], and the bailee is only liable for breach of the duty of care he

---

9. See also above, pp. 172–173.
10. E.g. *Pignataro* v. *Gilroy*, [1919] 1 K.B. 459, D.C. *Contra* Atiyah, *Sale of Goods* (3rd Edn.) 119.
11. This must be distinguished from the ordinary right of the buyer to rescind for breach: compare below, p. 353 and pp. 360, 397.
12. (1910), 26 T.L.R. 545, C.A.: see below, p. 180.
13. *Elphick* v. *Barnes* (1880), 5 C.P.D. 321; *Alexander* v. *Glenbroome, Ltd.*, [1957] 1 Lloyd's Rep. 157.

owes under the bailment[14]. The incidence of risk in the case of sales is considered below[15].

(2) Rejection. Whereas a buyer's right to reject if he does not approve may be restricted by the terms of the agreement[16], the bailee has an unrestricted right to reject[17] (in which case he becomes a bailee for custody only[18]).

(3) Resale. As a bailee has no general property in the goods, it follows that before he accepts the bailor may sell to a third party: the bailee may bring an action against his bailor for breach of any collateral contract (e.g. of option), but he cannot thereafter acquire for himself the property in the goods. On the other hand, a buyer in possession has an indefeasible right to the goods. The effect of a resale by buyer or bailee is considered below[19].

1 The passing of property

The first difficulty is to ascertain the scope of rule 4, which is expressed to take effect where a person takes possession of goods "on approval" or "on sale or return", or "other similar terms". What are "other similar terms"? There is some authority that it includes deliveries "on free trial" or "on approbation"[20]. But does it include h.p. agreements[1]?

As in the case of all the other rules of s. 18, rule 4 only applies in the absence of a contrary intention. Thus, in *Weiner* v. *Gill*[2]

> Jewellery was delivered to X., together with a memorandum which stated:
> "On approbation. On sale for cash only or return . . . Goods had on approbation or on sale or return remain the property of [the transferor] until such goods are settled for or charged".
> Without paying for the goods, X. pledged them; but the Court held that X. acquired no property in the goods, and could therefore transfer none to the pledgee.

However, assuming that the transaction falls within rule 4 and that there is no contrary intention, that rule provides that the property passes to the buyer as follows:

> "(a) When he signifies his approval or acceptance to the seller or does any other act adopting the transaction.

---

14. *Per* VAUGHAN WILLIAMS L.J. in *Genn* v. *Winkel* (1912), 107 L.T. 434, C.A., at p. 437; and *per* WILLMER L.J. in *Poole* v. *Smith's Car Sales, Ltd.*, [1962] 2 All E.R. 482, C.A., at p. 489.
15. See below, p. 241, *et seq.*   16. See below, p. 269.
17. *Berry & Son* v. *Star Brush Co.* (1915), 31 T.L.R. 603, C.A.
18. But see *Bradley & Cohn, Ltd.* v. *Ramsey & Co.* (1912), 106 L.T. 771: affd. at p. 773 by C.A. on other grounds.
19. At pp. 220, 230.
20. See the list of authorities collected in *Benjamin on Sale* (8th Edn.) 315, note m.   1. See below, p. 181.
2. [1906] 2 K.B. 574, C.A. See also *Manders* v. *Williams* (1849), 4 Exch. 339.

(b) If he does not signify his approval or acceptance to the seller but retains the goods without giving notice of rejection, then, if a time has been fixed for the return of the goods, on the expiration of such time, and, if no time has been fixed, on the expiration of a reasonable time. What is a reasonable time is a question of fact".

1. Approval or acceptance. Normally this will present few problems; but difficult questions of fact may occur where the trial involves a partial consumption or destruction.

2. Adoption. In *Kirkham* v. *Attenborough*[3]

A manufacturing jeweller entrusted some jewellery to W. on sale or return. W. pledged the goods with the defendant pawnbroker, and the plaintiff jeweller claimed the return of the goods or their value.

The action was dismissed by the Court of Appeal, who held that W. had done an "act adopting the transaction" within rule 4, so that the property passed to him, and he passed a good title to the defendant. Lord ESHER M.R. explained that the phrase "act adopting the transaction"[4]

"cannot mean the delivery of the goods on sale or return, because that had been already done, and it must mean that part of the transaction which makes the buyer the purchaser of the goods . . . There must be some act which shews that he adopts the transaction; but any act which is consistent only with his being the purchaser is sufficient".

He held that pawning was such an act, because it was "inconsistent with his free power to return (the goods)". The phrase was again considered by the Court of Appeal in *Genn* v. *Winkel*[5].

The plaintiff diamond merchant delivered stones to the defendant on sale or return on Tuesday, Jan. 4th; and the same day the defendant entrusted them on sale or return to G. On Jan. 6th G. handed the diamonds, probably on sale or return, to X., who lost them.

SCRUTTON J. and the Court of Appeal were unanimous in allowing the plaintiff to recover the price of the goods from the defendant, but differed as to the reasons why the property had passed. SCRUTTON J. and VAUGHAN WILLIAMS L.J. thought that any voluntary parting with possession was an "act adopting the transaction" within the doctrine laid down in *Kirkham* v. *Attenborough*[3]. In view of the prevalence in the diamond trade of the practice that persons taking stones on sale or return immediately handed them to other people on similar terms, the majority of the Court of Appeal were not prepared to find that such an

---

3. [1897] 1 Q.B. 201, C.A.   See also *London Jewellers, Ltd.* v. *Attenborough*, [1934] 2 K.B. 206, C.A.
4. At p. 203.   5. (1912), 107 L.T. 434, C.A.

act was of itself necessarily an act adopting the transaction; but they held that the act of G. in handing the stones to X. was an "act adopting the transaction". The difference, they thought, lay in this: the defendant was entitled to demand the stones from G. just as soon as the original owner, the plaintiff, was entitled to demand them from him. By handing the stones to G., therefore, the defendant "had not lessened or impeded his power of returning the goods when the owner . . . had a right to demand them back"[6]; whereas, by handing the goods to X. on similar terms two days later G. had "done an act which limits and impedes his power of returning the goods"[6], and that the "act of adoption" on G.'s part must necessarily be an "act of adoption" on the part of the defendant. What are the implications of this case? First, it is submitted that the Court of Appeal did not decide that the accidental[7] loss of the goods by X. was an "act adopting the transaction"[8]. Second, the test for what is meant by an "act of adoption" propounded by the majority of the Court of Appeal seems to have been whether a party has impeded his power, or made it impossible for himself to return the goods within the time-period laid down in the transaction by which he obtained the goods. In one sense, any handing over of the goods to a third party impedes the power to return; but the majority of the Court of Appeal did not think that this was necessarily[9] sufficient. On the other hand, it would presumably have been possible for G. to have demanded the return of the goods from X. two days earlier than agreed; but the majority seemed more interested in whether it was consistent with the terms of the transaction for the goods to be held over beyond the time-limit[10].

3. Retention. Rule 4 (b) provides that the property will pass to the buyer if he "retains the goods without giving notice of rejection". This rule substantially reflects the common law position[11], except that, whereas the common law probably required the transferee to return the goods, the Act only requires him to give notice of rejection[12]. Rule 4 (b) assumes that, even without approval or acceptance on the part of the transferee, the property may pass in either of the following circumstances:

    (a) The transferee retains the goods beyond the stipulated time-limit.

---

6. *Per* FLETCHER MOULTON L.J., at p. 437. What if Jan. 4th had been a Saturday?
7. A fraudulent misappropriation is an act adopting the transaction.
8. Yet FLETCHER MOULTON L.J. did suggest that, after handing the goods on, a bailee "could no longer plead that he merely held them as bailee and had not been guilty of negligence" (at p. 437).
9. Would the answer have been different if it had not been the practice for such bailees to hand the goods on on similar terms?
10. Thus pledging has been held to be an "act adopting the transaction": *London Jewellers, Ltd.* v. *Attenborough*, [1934] 2 K.B. 206, C.A.
11. See *Humphries* v. *Carvalho* (1812), 6 East 45; *Moss* v. *Sweet* (1851), 16 Q.B. 493.
12. Though the agreement may show an intention that the goods actually be returned: *Ornstein* v. *Alexandra Furnishing Co.* (1895), 12 T.L.R. 128.

Even though the transferee retains the goods beyond the stipulated time, he will not be deemed to have accepted the goods where the transferor induced him to prolong the trial[13], or his retention was involuntary[14].

(b) Where there is no time limit laid down, but the transferee retains the goods beyond a reasonable time. What is a reasonable time is a question of fact (ss. 18 r. 4 (b), 56), and may depend on trade usage[15].

2 The property/title borderline

The effect of the operation of rule 4 may well be to pass the property in goods without the seller realising it. This has obvious dangers to the seller, and he may therefore oust the operation of rule 4 altogether by reserving the property in the goods until the price is paid[16]. Such a precaution will usually be effective in the event of the buyer's insolvency; but it is less likely to defeat the b.f.p., who may, in particular, acquire a good title under one of the following exceptions to the *nemo dat* rule:

(*1*) *Estoppel.* Whilst the mere transfer of possession to the buyer will not of itself give rise to estoppel[17], there may be other circumstances which would do so[18].

(*2*) *Agency.* It may be that the transferor goes further than merely reserving the property in the goods, and evinces an intention that the transferee is never to become the owner of them; that is, the transferee is not a buyer, but an agent for sale. Thus, in *Weiner* v. *Harris*[19]

> A manufacturing jeweller sent jewellery to a retailer under a standing agreement whereby the property was to remain in the manufacturer until the goods were sold or paid for. The retailer pledged some of the jewellery.

The Court of Appeal unanimously held that the pledgee obtained a good title because the parties only intended the retailer to be an agent for sale, not a buyer: their Lordships distinguished *Weiner* v. *Gill*[20] on the grounds that in that case the property was only to pass to X. when the goods were paid for, whereas in the present case the retailer was precluded by the terms of the agreement from ever becoming the owner of the goods under the sale or return transaction. Accordingly, the Court held that the retailer was in possession as agent for sale, that he was a

---

13. Per Bovill C.J. in *Heilbutt* v. *Hickson* (1872), L.R. 7 C.P. 438, at p. 452.
14. *Re Ferrier, ex parte Trustee* v. *Donald*, [1944] Ch. 295.
15. E.g. *Poole* v. *Smith's Car Sales, Ltd.*, [1962] 2 All E.R. 482, C.A.
16. E.g. *Weiner* v. *Gill*, [1906] 2 K.B. 547, C.A.: set out above, p. 177.
17. Per Bray J. in *Weiner* v. *Gill* (above), at p. 182. And see *Kempler* v. *Bravingtons, Ltd.* (1925), 133 L.T. 680, C.A.
18. See further below, p. 189.
19. [1910] 1 K.B. 285, C.A.
20. [1906] 2 K.B. 547, C.A.

mercantile agent, and that he passed a good title under the Factors Act[1].

(3) *Buyers in possession.* As we shall see in the next Chapter, a person who has agreed to buy goods and is in possession of them may be able to pass a good title[2]. Whilst a mere bailee is not in such a position, and cannot pass a good title under this provision, one who has agreed to buy subject to a right to rescind after trial clearly could do so[3]. An analogous problem is whether a h.p. agreement falls within the ambit of rule 4. There is a clear difference in function between the two types of transaction, which will be mirrored in the terms of the bailments. Perhaps the biggest difference between the two types of transaction concerns the effect of an act inconsistent with the ownership of the bailor: in a sale or return transaction, such an act will usually cause the property to pass to the erstwhile bailee, whereas in a h.p. agreement it will usually amount to an act of conversion, and prevent the bailee from becoming the owner of the goods. Most commentators accept that h.p. agreements are not sale or return transactions; and *vice versa*[4]. If so, s. 18 r. 4 does not apply to h.p. agreements; and the provisions of the H.P.A. are not applicable to sale or return transactions.

5 THE RESERVATION OF A RIGHT OF DISPOSAL

Section 19 of the S.G.A. seems designed to deal with the situation where the parties are negotiating at a distance, and the unpaid seller wishes to safeguard himself against the insolvency of the buyer. The general rule is laid down in s. 19 (1) in the following terms:

> "Where there is a contract for the sale of specific goods or where goods are subsequently appropriated to the contract, the seller may, by the terms of the contract or appropriation, reserve the right of disposal of the goods until certain conditions are fulfilled. In such case, notwithstanding the delivery of the goods to the buyer, or to a carrier or other bailee . . . for the purposes of transmission to the buyer, the property in the goods does not pass to the buyer until the conditions imposed by the seller are fulfilled".

What is the meaning of the phrase "reservation of a right of disposal"? Section 19 (1) says that it will have the effect of reserving the property in the goods; and whether there has been such a reservation is a question of intention[5]. It might, therefore, be objected that, as s. 18 is always subject to a contrary intention, s. 19 (1) seems superfluous. However,

---

1. See further below, p. 205. 2. See p. 220.
3. This may be the explanation of *P. Edwards, Ltd.* v. *Vaughan* (1910), 26 T.L.R. 545, C.A. See also *London Jewellers, Ltd.* v. *Attenborough*, [1934] 2 K.B. 206, C.A., where the point may have been *obiter*.
4. See Guest, *Law of H.P.*, 51; Goode, *H.P. Law & Practice* (2nd Edn.) 60.
5. *Re Shipton Anderson & Co. and Harrison Brothers & Co.*,[1915] 3 K.B. 676, D.C.

the explanation may be that parties do not usually think in terms of the property in goods, but tend to express themselves with regard to risk— which is inconclusive as to the passing of property[6]—and the retention of control. Nor must this retention of control be confused with the unpaid seller's real rights: the two sets of rights only overlap in the one case where goods are delivered to a carrier for the purposes of trans- mission to the buyer, and then the phrase "reservation of a right of disposal" is used by the Act to describe both situations[7].

Section 19 also deals specifically with two common instances within the general principle laid down by s. 19 (1), providing two ways in which the seller who ships goods to the buyer may utilize the bill of lading. A bill of lading has the following special characteristics, which have earned it the title "semi-negotiable"[8]:

(1) During the period of the transit, it is recognised by the common law as the symbol of the goods, and a transfer of it both operates as a symbolic delivery[9], and may pass the property in the goods[10].

(2) It is a document of title within the meaning of the Factors Act[11]: it may be transferred by indorsement and delivery[12], and the effect of such a transfer will be considered later[13].

(3) The Bills of Lading Act 1855 has secured for these documents a limited exception to the rule of privity in contract[14].

Section 19 envisages that the unpaid seller who ships goods may take one of two courses. First, he may take the bill of lading in his own name, making the goods deliverable to the order of himself or his agent, and send the bill to his agent in the port of arrival with instructions to trans- fer it to the buyer only for cash, in which case s. 19 (2) says that the seller is in such circumstances *prima facie* deemed to have reserved a right of disposal[15]. Second, the seller may draw a bill of exchange for the price of the goods on the buyer and send it, together with the bill of lading, to the buyer, in which case s. 19 (3) provides that[16]

> "the buyer is bound to return the bill of lading if he does not honour the bill of exchange, and if he wrongfully retains the bill of lading the property in the goods does not pass to him".

---

6. *Per* Lords Westbury and Cairns in *Shepherd* v. *Harrison* (1871), L.R. 5 H.L. 116, at pp. 129, 131. See also above, pp. 158–159, 163.
7. Ss. 19 (1), 43 (1) (a). See further below, p. 322.
8. See Crossley Vaines, *Personal Property* (4th Edn.) 201–202.
9. See below, p. 264.
10. *Per* Bowen L.J. in *Sanders* v. *MacLean* (1883), 11 Q.B.D. 327, C.A., at p. 341: e.g. f.o.b. and c.i.f. contracts, but not arrival contract—see below, pp. 246-248.   11. See below, p. 207.
12. S. 11 of the Factors Act; see below, p. 225.
13. See p. 220.   14. See below, p. 249.
15. The converse does not follow: it is merely that there is no presumption either way if the goods are made deliverable to the order of the buyer.
16. E.g. *Cahn* v. *Pockett's Bristol Channel Steam Packet Co., Ltd.*, [1899] 1 Q.B. 643, C.A.: set out below, p. 226.

CHAPTER 14

The Transfer of Title

I NEMO DAT QUOD NON HABET

1 The rule

The relationship between property and title was discussed in Chapter 12; and this Chapter will deal with the situations where goods belonging to A. are transferred by B. to C. Both the original owner (A.) and the transferee (C.) may be entirely blameless; and the problem is to determine which of the two is entitled to the goods, and which is to be left to seek his remedy against the intermediate party (B.) In theory, it should not make any difference which of the two is entitled to the goods, because the other will usually have the right to look to B. for recompense: A. could sue B. in conversion or detinue[1]; or C. could sue B. for breach of the implied undertakings as to title[2]. However, in practice a right of action against B. may be worthless, so that the party left to seek recompense from B. may himself have to bear the loss. Thus, the right to the goods may be of vital importance, and will usually be determined through an action of conversion or detinue brought by A. against C.[3]

The basic rule of personal property is that nobody can transfer a better title than he himself possesses, a rule which is conveniently expressed by the Latin maxim *nemo dat quod non habet*[3]. Its operation may be illustrated by the following example: suppose the title of B. is defective in that he did not obtain the property in the goods from A.: B. can only pass a defective title to C., and A. may successfully sue C. in conversion or detinue because he (A.) has a better title than C.

The *nemo dat* rule is embodied in s. 21 (1) of the S.G.A., which provides as follows:

> "Subject to the provisions of this Act, where goods are sold by a person who is not the owner thereof, and who does not sell them under the authority or with the consent of the owner, the buyer acquires no better title to the goods than the seller had, unless the owner of the goods is by his conduct precluded from denying the seller's authority to sell.

---

1. The action in conversion or detinue is considered below, pp. 332–334, 377–378.
2. The implied undertakings as to title are considered above, Chapter 5.
3. *Per* Lord CAIRNS L.C., in *Cundy v. Lindsay* (1878), 3 App. Cas. 459, H.L., at pp. 463–464.

Whilst s. 21 (1) is only expressed to apply to dispositions by way of sale[4] made by a non-owner, the common law rule would appear to be wider than this both in respect of the defect of title itself and the disposition. Any disposition recognised by law[5] may bring the principle into play, so that it is enough that the goods be pledged or given. As regards the infirmity of title, it is clear that the principle applies where B. has only a possessory title[6]; but it has been taken even beyond this. In the *Mercantile Bank of India, Ltd.* v. *Central Bank of India, Ltd.*[7]

> B. purchased some groundnuts, and, in order to pay for them, pledged the documents of title to the A. Bank. The normal commercial practice, which was adopted in this case, was for the bank making the advance to hand the documents back to the pledgor so that he might obtain delivery of the goods on behalf of the bank. B. fraudulently pledged the documents with the C. Bank, who took in good faith. The A. Bank successfully sued the C. Bank for conversion.

Whilst it is true that the A. Bank would not have succeeded if it had given B. authority to sell on its behalf[8], nor if B. were a mercantile agent and could pass a good title under the Factors Act[9], the decision has been severely criticised[10] on the grounds both that it is most unfair that an owner of goods who is in physical possession of them cannot pass a good title, and that it is most unusual that an encumbrance should run with goods[11]. Of course, the decision depends on the technicality that A. Bank retained legal possession, and B. only obtained custody; but the case would appear to create difficulties for the commercial community.

2 Exceptions to the "nemo dat" rule

In setting out the rule, s. 21 (1) provides that it shall not apply where goods are sold by B. "who does not sell under the authority or with the consent of the owner"; that is, in the following cases:

1. Agency. Section 21 (1) recites that the *nemo dat* rule does not apply to a person who sells "under the authority" of the owner; and the common law rules of agency are expressly preserved by the S.G.A.

---

4. "Sale", not agreement to sell—*Anderson* v. *Ryan*, [1967] I.R. 34.
5. But probably not equitable dispositions: see above, p. 174.
6. *Cundy* v. *Lindsay* (1878), 3 App. Cas. 459, H.L.
7. [1938] A.C. 287; [1938] 1 All E.R. 52, P.C.
8. *Babcock* v. *Lawson* (1880), 5 Q.B.D. 284, C.A.
9. *Lloyds Bank, Ltd.* v. *Bank of America National Trust and Savings Association*, [1938] 2 K.B. 147; [1938] 2 All E.R. 63, C.A.: set out below, p. 210.
10. Atiyah, *Sale of Goods* (3rd Edn.) 138–139.
11. The decision appears to run counter to *Dunlop Pneumatic Tyre Co., Ltd.* v. *Selfridge & Co., Ltd.*, [1915] A.C. 847, H.L. Perhaps the two cases can be distinguished on the grounds that the one is concerned with contractual rights and the other with proprietary rights.

(s. 61 (2)). Discussion of these rules is beyond the scope of this work, but it will be recalled that B. may pass a good title in any of the following circumstances:

(1) Where A. confers actual authority on B. whether expressly or by implication[12].

(2) Notwithstanding that there is no actual authority, where A. clothes B. with an appearance of authority. This rule is closely related to estoppel, and shares with it a number of rules, including the rule that a mere handing over of possession to B. generally will not, without more, confer an apparent authority[13].

(3) Notwithstanding that there is no actual or apparent authority, where it is in the usual course of B's business to make such a disposition[14].

(4) Notwithstanding that there is no actual, apparent or usual authority, there may be an agency of necessity, though the courts are today reluctant to find such an agency[15]. The principle has been applied in the case of the sale of perishable goods by a carrier[16], but not to a sale of furniture by a voluntary bailee[17]; and Parliament has extended the list of bailees who have authority to sell by reason of the owner's failure to collect goods[18].

2. *Consent of the owner.* Section 21 (1) allows that a person may sell "with the consent of the owner"; and this saving is also to be found in s. 47, which provides that—

> "Subject to the provisions of this Act, the unpaid seller's right of lien . . . or stoppage in transitu is not affected by any sale, or other disposition of the goods which the buyer may have made, unless the seller has assented thereto".

Thus, if the buyer (B.) resells[19] the goods before he obtains possession of them and the original seller (A.) consents to the resale, the sub-buyer (C.) obtains a good title free from any rights which A. as unpaid seller might have against the goods[20]. Of course, A. could not be estopped on ordinary common law principles from setting up his real rights where he represents to C. that he will not exercise these[1]; but the courts were

---

12. *Lloyds and Scottish Finance, Ltd.* v. *Williamson*, [1965] 1 All E.R. 641, C.A.
13. Estoppel is considered further below, p. 189.
14. *Watteau* v. *Fenwick*, [1893] 1 Q.B. 346; *Kinahan, Ltd.* v. *Parry*, [1910] 2 K.B. 389, C.A.
15. See *Prager* v. *Blatspiel, Stamp and Heacock, Ltd.*, [1924] 1 K.B. 566.
16. *Springer* v. *Great Western Rail. Co.*, [1921] 1 K.B. 257, C.A.
17. *Sachs* v. *Miklos*, [1948] 2 K.B. 23; [1948] 1 All E.R. 67, C.A. The proper remedy of the bailor is under R.S.C. Ord. 29 r. 4: see below, p. 240.
18. Disposal of Uncollected Goods Act 1952. But see s. 41, Matrimonial Proceedings and Property Act, 1970.
19. What if he lets the goods on h.p.?
20. For the real rights of the unpaid seller, see below, pp. 314–315.
1. *Jorden* v. *Money* (1854), 5 H.L. Cas. 185. See also above, p. 148.

prepared to allow a delivery warrant to have such an effect[2]. However, s. 47 would appear to have gone somewhat further than this, in that it only requires that A. in some manner communicate his assent to B.[3]. Presumably, such assent expressed to B. operates to terminate A.'s real rights by way of waiver[4]. The principle embodied in s. 47 must be distinguished from actual authority in agency because the assent here is to B. acting as owner, not agent, though the principle may have something in common with usual authority. A.'s assent to resale by B. may be express or implied, though the courts have experienced some difficulty in deciding whether to imply an assent, as may be illustrated by two cases with similar facts where the courts reached opposite conclusions. In both cases, A. agreed to sell part of a larger quantity of goods to B., and B. agreed to resell that part to C.; B. received the price from C., but neglected to pay A., who stopped delivery. In *Mordaunt* v. *British Oil and Cake Mills, Ltd.*[5]

> B. sent C. a delivery order[6], which order directed A. to deliver the goods to C., and C. forwarded the delivery order to A., who acknowledged that it was "in order".

PICKFORD J. decided that neither party regarded the acknowledgment as an assent, pointing out that C. paid B. before receiving the acknowledgment, so that there could be no question of estoppel. His Lordship added[7]:

> "The assent contemplated by section 47 . . . means . . . an assent given in such circumstances as to shew that the unpaid seller intends that the sub-contract shall be carried out irrespective of the terms of the original contract".

In *Mount, Ltd.* v. *Jay, Ltd.*[8]

> A. and B. agreed that B. should pay A. out of the proceeds of resale, and A. gave B. a delivery order addressed to the wharfingers who held the goods. B. forwarded the orders to the wharfingers endorsed "please transfer to our sub-buyer".

---

2. E.g. *Merchant Banking Co.* v. *Phoenix Bessemer Steel Co.* (1877), 5 Ch.D. 205. Was this because the warrant was a negotiable instrument; or because of some rule of equitable estoppel?
3. *D. F. Mount, Ltd.* v. *Jay and Jay (Provision) Co., Ltd.*, [1960] 1 Q.B. 159. In the pre-Act cases, knowledge of assent was obtained by B. *and* C., and the courts sometimes talked in terms of estoppel: see even now *Benjamin on Sale* (8th Edn.) 872 proposition 3a.
4. See s. 43 (1) (c), considered below, pp. 323–324.
5. [1910] 2 K.B. 502.
6. The answer would be otherwise if the delivery order were a document of title—Atiyah, *Sale of Goods* (3rd Edn.) 137, note 3.
7. At p. 507.
8. [1960] 1 Q.B. 159.

SALMON J. held that C. had obtained a good title on the grounds that:

(1) A. had assented to the resale; and

(2) C. obtained a good title under s. 25 (2), but not under the proviso to s. 47[9].

As regards (1), his Lordship distinguished *Mordaunt* v. *British Oil and Cake Mills, Ltd.* on the grounds that A. was anxious to get rid of the goods on a falling market and knew that B. could only pay for them out of the resale price; the inference was, therefore that A. intended to renounce his rights against the goods and to take the risk of B.'s dishonesty[10]. Both these cases were concerned with an unascertained part of a specific whole, and in both it was suggested by the court that the inference of assent would be more readily drawn if the goods were specific[11]. Finally, whilst the point does not appear to have been considered by the courts, it is suggested that "assent" here probably means actual assent, notwithstanding that it was obtained by fraud: this rule is to be found in the other exceptions to the *nemo dat* rule[12].

Apart from the above two cases, there are a number of exceptions to the *nemo dat* rule, some of which are expressly dealt with by the S.G.A. The major exceptions which are relevant to the disposition of goods to a *bona fide* transferee are as follows:

(1) Estoppel. A. may be estopped from denying that B. can pass a good title[13].

(2) Voidable title. If B. obtains a voidable title from A., B. may pass a good title to C. at any time before A. avoids his title[14].

(3) Mercantile agency. If B. is a mercantile agent he may be able to pass a good title to C. under the Factors Act 1889[15].

(4) Seller in possession. If B. has sold goods to A. yet remains in possession of them, B. may by statute pass a good title to C.[16].

(5) Buyer in possession. If B. has agreed to buy goods from A. and obtained possession of them, B. may by statute pass a good title to C.[17].

(6) Hirer under a h.p. agreement. Under the H.P.A. 1964, if B. is a hirer in possession of goods under a h.p. agreement, he may pass a good title[18].

(7) Sales in market overt. C. may acquire a good title if he buys in market overt, notwithstanding A.'s title[19].

(8) Miscellaneous statutory and common law powers of sale[20]. Each of these heads will be considered separately in succeeding sections.

---

9. See below, p. 225.   10. At p. 167.

11. PICKFORD J. (at p. 506) even went so far as to say that "no such inference could be drawn if the goods were not in existence".

12. See below, pp. 198, 209, 223.   13. See below, p. 189.

14. See below, p. 198.   15. See below, p. 202.

16. See below, p. 215.   17. See below, p. 220.

18 See below, p. 230.   19. See below, p. 236.   20. See below, p. 238.

Before looking at the details, however, it may be helpful to consider the policy of the law in granting exceptions to the *nemo dat* rule. Generally speaking, the courts have tended to favour ownership and to uphold the *nemo dat* rule; and the history of this area of the law has largely been one where the pressure of the mercantile community has secured the adoption of statutory exceptions to the rule, and the courts have consistently interpreted the exceptions against C. and in favour of A. As long ago as 1787, an attempt was made to ascribe a pattern to the rule and counter-balancing exceptions by ASHHURST J. in *Lickbarrow* v. *Mason*[1], where he said:

> "We may lay it down as a broad general principle, that, wherever one of two innocent persons must suffer by the acts of a third, he who has enabled such a third person to occasion the loss must sustain it".

This dictum was applied by the Privy Council in *Commonwealth Trust, Ltd.* v. *Akotey*[2], where that court appeared to hold that the mere handing over of possession of goods to B. is sufficient to estop A. from setting up his title against C. However, such a view was rejected by the Privy Council in the *Mercantile Bank of India Ltd.,* v. *Central Bank of India, Ltd.*[3] where Lord WRIGHT said of the dictum of ASHHURST J.[4]:

> ". . . it is impossible to accept without qualification as a true statement of law the principles there broadly laid down".

Lord WRIGHT would seem to be correct: the issue between A. and C. does not turn on fault, but on the strict application of the *nemo dat* rule and the exceptions thereto; and the dictum by ASHHURST J. remains no more than an aspiration. Moreover, ASHHURST J. was talking about the common law, where there is, of course, no power to apportion. It has been judicially suggested that the courts should have a statutory power to apportion in these circumstances[5]; but this view was rejected by the Twelfth Report of the Law Reform Committee as "unworkable"[6]. The position therefore remains that, unless C. can bring his case within one of the exceptions, he will lose. Curiously, even if C. canbring his case within one of the exceptions, the title he will obtain may vary because he will only get such title as A. has.

---

1. (1787), 2 Term Rep. 63, H.L. at p. 70.
2. [1926] A.C. 72, P.C.
3. [1938] A.C. 287, P.C.: set out above, p. 184.
4. At p. 298.
5. *Per* DEVLIN L.J. in *Ingram* v. *Little*, [1961] 1 Q.B. 31, C.A., at p. 74.
6. (Cmnd. 2958) paras. 12, 40 (1). For criticisms of this Report, see Atiyah (1966), 29 M.L.R. 541; Diamond 29 M.L.R. 413.

2 ESTOPPEL[7]

1 Introduction

According to the latter part of s. 21 (1) of the S.G.A., the *nemo dat* rule may apply—

> "unless the owner of the goods is by his conduct precluded from denying the seller's authority to sell".

Perhaps the leading case where this provision was applied is *Eastern Distributors, Ltd.* v. *Goldring*[8].

> Murphy was the owner of a Bedford van; and he wished to purchase a car as well, but had no money to pay for it, not even enough for the deposit under a h.p. agreement. A dealer suggested to Murphy that he should raise the deposit in the following manner, and Murphy acquiesced: the dealer would pretend to the plaintiff finance company that he was letting on h.p. to Murphy *both* the van and the car, so that the company would send the dealer the balance of the price due on both vehicles. In pursuance of this scheme, Murphy signed in blank h.p. proposal forms in respect of both vehicles. The dealer then filled in his own name as owner of both vehicles and submitted the proposals to the plaintiffs, who rejected that in respect of the car. Nevertheless, the dealer proceeded with that in respect of the van—which was really owned by Murphy. The plaintiffs sent a memorandum of the agreement to Murphy, who promptly told the dealer that the whole transaction was cancelled, and shortly afterwards sold the van to the defendant, a b.f.p. Upon discovering the true state of affairs, the plaintiffs sued the defendants for conversion of the van, alleging title by estoppel[9], and Murphy was joined as third party.

Both defendants pleaded that Murphy had only given the dealer a limited authority to sell, and that anyway they were not privy to the estoppel and were not bound by it. Alternatively, they pleaded that, even if the plaintiffs acquired title by estoppel, they could not recover the van because (a) Murphy had conferred a good title on the defendants under s. 25 (1) of the S.G.A.[10], and (b) Murphy had not signed the memorandum of the h.p. agreement as the H.P.A. required[11], and that Act did not permit of an action in conversion[12]. The Court of Appeal

---

7. See generally Spencer Bower, *Estoppel* (2nd Edn.); Pickering (1939), 55 L.Q.R. 400.
8. [1957] 2 Q.B. 600; [1957] 2 All E.R. 525, C.A.; and see also *Stoneleigh Finance, Ltd.* v. *Phillips*, [1965] 2 Q.B. 537, C.A.: set out below, p. 296. Cf. *Campbell Discount Co., Ltd.* v. *Gall*, [1961] 1 Q.B. 431; [1961] 2 All E.R. 104, C.A.: see below, pp. 287–288.
9. The Factors Act, s. 2 (1), did not apply because the dealer was not in possession: see below, p. 206.   10. See below, p. 217.
11. See above, p. 33.   12. See below, p. 339.

unanimously found that the plaintiffs had acquired a good title by estoppel, and rejected both defences.

Prima facie, the statutory formula in s. 21 (1) would appear to refer to the common law doctrine of estoppel, though that doctrine is nowhere defined by the S.G.A. However, in *Goldring's Case* this assumption was rejected. The Court of Appeal was clear that Murphy was estopped, but thought that s. 21 (1) differed from common law estoppel in the title it transferred. In delivering the judgment of the Court, DEVLIN J. explained the effect of a common law estoppel as follows[13]:

> "An estoppel affects others besides the representor. The way it has always been put is that the estoppel binds the representor and his privies. But it is not easy to determine exactly who, for this purpose, is a privy. There can be no doubt that, although the representation was actually made by [the dealer], Murphy, on the facts of this case was privy to the making and bound by it. . . . It would also appear that anyone whose title is obtained from the representor as a volunteer is a privy for this purpose. But it is very doubtful whether a purchaser for value without notice is bound by the estoppel".

The defendant in this case was a b.f.p. to whom Murphy had purported to sell the car, so that, if s. 21 (1) merely embodied the common law doctrine of estoppel, it would seem that the plaintiff's title could be defeated by a subsequent sale to a b.f.p.[14]. Whatever the position with regard to common law estoppel, however, the Court of Appeal thought that s. 21 (1) referred rather to the wider common law doctrine of apparent authority resting on mercantile convenience[15]. DEVLIN J. said[16]:

> "The apparent ownership or authority has generally taken the form of arming the agent with some indicia which makes it appear that he was either the owner or had the right to sell. But in our judgement the principle applies to any form of representation or holding out of apparent ownership or the right to sell [17] . . .
>
> "We doubt whether this principle ought really to be regarded as part of the law of estoppel . . . The effect of its application is to transfer a real title and not merely a metaphorical title by estoppel . . . The result is that Murphy is, in the words of [the S.G.A. 1893, s. 21(1)], precluded from denying [the dealer's] authority to sell, and consequently the plaintiffs acquired the title to the goods which Murphy himself had and Murphy has no title left to pass to the defendant".

---

13. At pp. 606–607. Cf. *Henderson & Co.* v. *Williams*, [1895] 1 Q.B. 521, C.A.: see below, p. 192.
14. With or without delivery? Cf. Powell (1957), 20 M.L.R. 650, 652.
15. See criticism by Goodhart (1957), 73 L.Q.R. 455, 457; and the discussion in Powell, *Agency* (2nd Edn.) 68–72.   16. At pp. 610–611.
17. Is this rule confined to dispositions by the agent by way of sale?

Of course, the plaintiffs could get no better title than Murphy: if he had merely stolen the van from X., the plaintiffs' title could still have been defeated by X.

Leaving aside the question of the title transferred, the scope of the statutory formula in s. 21 (1) must now be examined. It would appear that the Court of Appeal in *Goldring's Case* thought that the scope of the statutory formula was the same as that of the doctrine of common law estoppel, apart from the question of the title transferred.

2 The common law doctrine of estoppel

It is worth prefacing any discussion of the scope of the common law doctrine of estoppel with the caution sounded by Lord WRIGHT in the *Mercantile Bank of India Case*[18], where his Lordship pointed out:

> "There are very few cases of actions for conversion in which a plea of estoppel by representation has succeeded".

Moreover, it must be borne in mind that estoppel does not itself give rise to a cause of action[19]: it is perhaps best regarded not as a rule of substantive law, but as a rule of evidence having the effect of a substantive rule[20]. Where the owner of goods is involved in litigation, the doctrine of estoppel may preclude him from setting up his title for the reason explained by PARKE B. in *Freeman* v. *Cooke*[1]:

> "If, whatever a man's real intention may be, he so conducts himself that a reasonable man would take the representation to be true, and believe that it was meant that he should act upon it, and did act upon it as true, the party making the representation would be equally precluded from contesting its truth; and conduct, by negligence or omission, when there is a duty cast upon a person, by usage of trade or otherwise, to disclose the truth, may often have the same effect".

This representation relied upon to estop the owner from setting up his title to goods may be to the effect either that another is the owner of goods[2], or that that other has his authority to dispose of them[3]. In this context, it makes no difference whether the representation gives rise to apparent ownership or agency[4].

---

18. [1938] A.C. 287, P.C., at p. 302.
19. *Per* Lord MAUGHAM in *Maritime Electric, Ltd.* v. *General Dairies, Ltd.*, [1937] A.C. 610, P.C., at p. 620.
20. Cross, *Evidence* (3rd Edn.) 290; Crossley Vaines, *Personal Property* (4th Edn. 158.
1. (1848), 2 Ex 654, at p. 663: see Hoggett (1970), 33 M.L.R. 518, 525–528.
2. E.g. *Eastern Distributors, Ltd.* v. *Goldring*, [1957] 2 Q.B. 600, C.A.
3. See the cases cited in Stoljar, *Agency* 26, note 20. In the *Pacific Motor Auctions Pty., Ltd.* v. *Motor Credits (Hire Finance), Ltd.*, [1965] A.C. 867, which is discussed below, p. 218, the Australian courts held that the finance company was estopped; but the point was expressly reserved by the P.C.
4. Compare liens, above, p. 13.

The nature of the representation will be further considered later, but it will immediately be observed PARKE B.'s formulation of the doctrine is hedged around with the following restrictions.

1. The representation must concern an existing state of facts.   It is fundamental to the common law doctrine of estoppel that the representation must be as to existing facts, and not future intention[5].   A representation of future intention can only[6] take effect under other principles considered elsewhere[7].

2. There must be an unambiguous[8] representation made to the person seeking to set it up[9].   The difficult questions of fact which may be involved are illustrated by two similar cases in which the courts contrived to reach different results[10].   In both cases, the owner of goods lying in a warehouse instructed the warehousekeeper to transfer the goods to the order of the rogue, and the rogue sold the goods to a b.f.p., who paid the price to the rogue in return for a delivery order made out by him.   In *Henderson & Co.* v. *Williams*[11].

> The b.f.p. distrusted the rogue, and before paying him obtained confirmation from the warehousekeeper that the sugar was held to the rogue's order.   On discovering the fraud, the owner instructed the warehousekeeper not to deliver the sugar and gave him an indemnity.   The b.f.p. sued the warehousekeeper in conversion, and the Court of Appeal held that, although the property in the goods remained in the owner, the warehousekeeper was estopped as against the b.f.p. from denying the latter's title[12].   Lord HALSBURY also thought that the owner would be estopped as against the warehousekeeper from denying the rogue's right of disposal.

However, in *Farquharson Brothers & Co.* v. *King & Co.*[13]

> The rogue, a confidential clerk of the owner, perpetrated a series of frauds over a period of about four years in the following manner: he instructed the warehousekeeper to transfer some of his master's timber to the order of Brown; and, under the name of Brown, sold

---

5. *Jorden* v. *Money* (1854), 5 H.L. Cas. 185.
6. Unless it is that the representor has such an intention at the time of making the representation.
7. I.e. equitable estoppel and waiver: see above, p. 146.
8. Or one which is reasonably taken as such ?   See *Woodhouse Cocoa, Ltd.* v. *Nigerian Marketing Co., Ltd.*, [1970] 2 All E.R. 124; rev. by C.A., [1970] 11 C.L. 3276.
9. This distinguishes estoppel from assent: cf. above, p. 185.
10. The following judges sat at different stages in both cases: Lords HALSBURY and LINDLEY reached different conclusions in each case; A.L. SMITH L.J. decided that there was an estoppel in both.
11. [1895] 1 Q.B. 521, C.A.: see also *Woodley* v. *Coventry* (1863), 32 L.J.Ex 185.
12. In this sort of situation, the safest course for the warehousekeeper is to interplead.
13. [1902] A.C. 325, H.L.: see also *Laurie and Morewood* v. *Dudin & Sons*, [1926] 1 K.B. 223, C.A.: set out above, p. 157.

this timber to the b.f.p. and gave him delivery orders. The b.f.p. obtained delivery, and the owner sued him in conversion. The majority of the Court of Appeal held that the owner was estopped from setting up his title because he had enabled his clerk to commit the fraud[14]. STIRLING L.J. dissented on the grounds that there had never been any holding out by the owner or warehousekeeper to the b.f.p. as to the clerk's authority; and the House of Lords adopted this dissenting opinion without any hesitation.

It will be observed that in both cases the warehousekeeper was justified as far as the owner was concerned in delivering the goods to the order of the rogue; and in both the rogue gave the b.f.p. a delivery order which at that moment the warehousekeeper was prepared to honour. However, in *Henderson* v. *Williams* the b.f.p. took the precaution of getting the warehousekeeper to confirm that he would honour the delivery order; but in *Farquharson Brothers & Co.* v. *King & Co.* the b.f.p. did not take such a precaution. Such a distinction is intelligible, but makes no allowance for the negligence of the owner over a four year period in the latter case.

3. The representation must be made with the intention that it be acted upon. The test is objective. Thus, in *Eastern Distributors, Ltd.* v. *Goldring*[15] Murphy was estopped from denying the dealer's title to the van because he had signed documents which made it appear as if the dealer were the owner of the van. On the other hand, in *Lowe* v. *Lombank, Ltd.*[16] one of the reasons given by the Court of Appeal for finding that the hirer was not estopped was that there was no evidence that the hirer intended her representations to be acted on.

4. The party acting on the representation must have a genuine belief in its truthfulness. Another ground on which the Court of Appeal refused to find the hirer estopped in *Lowe* v. *Lombank, Ltd.* was that there was no evidence that the finance company had a genuine belief in the truthfulness of the hirer's representation. On the other hand, in *Eastern Distributors, Ltd.* v. *Goldring* the Court of Appeal held that the finance company did in fact act on the implied representation of ownership contained in the proposal form.[17]

5. The representee must act on the representation to his detriment. In *Carr* v. *London and North Western Rail Co.*[18]

> The railway's agent told Carr that the railway held three consignments of goods to his orders when only two had been received. Carr

---

14. [1901] 2 K.B. 697, C.A.
15. [1957] 2 Q.B. 600; [1957] 2 All E.R. 525, C.A.: set out above, p. 189.
16. [1960] 1 All E.R. 611, C.A.: set out above, pp. 139–140.
17. Perhaps the cases may be distinguished on the basis that the representation is in the very act of signing as opposed to being in the small print.
18. (1875), L.R. 10 C.P. 307.

purported to sell three consignments, and had to pay damages to
the buyer. In an action for (1) non-delivery and (2) trover, BRETT J.
found for the railway on the grounds that they were not estopped
from showing that the goods had never reached their hands.

His Lordship gave the following grounds for refusing to find an
estoppel:

(1) The railway did not intend that the representation should be
relied on in order to resell the goods, but only to collect them;

(2) In this sense no reliance was placed on the representation,
because Carr never did send for the goods;

(3) The representation should not, on the evidence of the case, have
misled Carr; and

(4) The railway did not provide the proximate cause of Carr's loss[19].

Similarly, in *Farquharson Brothers & Co.* v. *King & Co.*,[20] Lord
LINDLEY said that the owner was not estopped because the b.f.p. was
misled, not by anything done by or under the authority of the owner,
but by the clerk's fraud; and in *Lowe* v. *Lombank, Ltd.*[1] the Court
of Appeal thought that the finance company inserted the relevant
clause in the proposal form not so that they might rely on the representation contained therein, but simply to preclude the hirer from
invoking the implied undertakings of the H.P.A.

The conduct relied on as amounting to a representation sufficient to
found such an estoppel may or may not be made inadvertently. The
conduct may itself make the representation[2], or it may allow another to
make a representation[3]; and, whilst there will usually be some active
conduct, there may be a representation by omission[4]. However, once
it is settled that there does not have to be active conduct on the part of
the representor himself, it is difficult to decide what is necessary before
there will be a representation sufficient to found an estoppel. The
dictum of ASHHURST J. in *Lickbarrow* v. *Mason*[5] suggests that wherever
the owner has "enabled" the rogue to occasion the loss he should be
estopped[6]. Yet, as Lord HALSBURY pointed out in *Farquharson
Brothers & Co.* v. *King & Co.*,[7]

"in one sense, every man who sells a pistol or a dagger enables an
intending murderer to commit a crime":

---

19. The issue of proximate causation is further discussed below, pp. 197–198.
20. [1902] A.C. 325, H.L.
 1. [1960] 1 All E.R. 611, C.A.
 2. E.g. *Henderson & Co.* v. *Williams*, [1895] 1 Q.B. 521, C.A.; *Eastern
    Distributors, Ltd.* v. *Goldring*, [1957] 2 Q.B. 600, C.A.
 3. *Coventry* v. *Great Eastern Rail. Co.* (1883), 11 Q.B.D. 776, C.A.: see Cross,
    Evidence (3rd Edn.) 287.
 4. E.g. *Pickard* v. *Sears* (1837), 6 Ad. & El. 469.
 5. (1787), 2 Term Rep. 63, H.L., at p. 70.
 6. See above, p. 188.   7. At p. 332.

but that does not make the seller a party to murder. Similarly, in handing possession of his goods to a rogue, an owner in one sense enables the rogue to dispose of them; but it has been settled since *Johnson v. Credit Lyonnais Co.*[8] that the mere transfer of possession of goods to another will not generally raise an estoppel. No doubt this rule is convenient to owners: they would be in a difficult position if any repairer, cleaner, etc, with whom they deposited goods could pass a good title. Yet the rule obviously runs counter to the interests of the mercantile community, who have therefore secured a number of statutory exceptions, where a person in possession can pass a good title if he is either (1) a seller, or (2) a buyer or (3) a mercantile agent[9].

If the mere possession of goods will not raise an estoppel, what more is required? The issue was canvassed in *Central Newbury Car Auctions, Ltd.* v. *Unity Finance, Ltd.*[10].

> The plaintiff dealer purchased a car, in the log-book of which the previous registered owner, Ashley, had not signed his name. The dealer did not register himself as owner because he intended to resell the car. Subsequently, a rogue tricked the dealer into parting with possession of the car and log-book, and then offered the car to X. giving the name Ashley. By this time, ~~X.~~ *not X, but the rogue* had signed the log-book in the name of Ashley. X. compared the signature in the log-book with that which the rogue provided in his presence, and then completed the purchase. X. sold the car to the defendant finance company. The defendants pleaded that the plaintiff was estopped by his negligence from denying the rogue's authority to sell; and the County Court Judge agreed.

However, this decision was reversed by the Court of Appeal, where the majority thought that the result should turn not upon fault, but upon whether the handing over of the log-book was sufficient to take the case outside the general rule. In reaching their decision, the majority pointed out that the log-book is not a document of title[11]; and that it specifically states on every page that

> "The person in whose name a vehicle is registered may or may not be the legal owner of the vehicle".

However, in a strong dissenting judgment DENNING L.J. adopted ASHHURST J.'s dictum, and pointed out that the log-book was best evidence of title. Whilst the majority thought that the plaintiff's

---

8. (1877), 3 C.P.D. 32, C.A.
9. See below, pp. 215, 220, 202.
10. [1957] 1 Q.B. 371; [1956] 3 All E.R. 905, C.A.
11. There might have been an estoppel if it had been. Documents of title are considered below, p. 207.

negligence was, in the absence of any duty of care, irrelevant, Denning L.J. was prepared to find such a duty, arguing as follows[12]:

> "When the original owner handed over the car and log-book to a complete stranger, intending to part with the property in them, he ought to have foreseen the possibility that the stranger might try and dispose of them for his own benefit . . . The original owner owed a duty to anyone to whom the stranger might try to dispose of them".

In the *Central Newbury Car Case*, the majority of the Court of Appeal decided that an owner will not be estopped from setting up his title to a motor vehicle merely because he transfers possession of the vehicle and its log-book to a rogue. On the other hand, in *Goldring's Case*[13], the Court of Appeal unanimously decided that the owner was estopped where he signed a document stating that the dealer was the owner of the vehicle. No doubt, there is an intelligible distinction between a statement of ownership and a mere transfer of possession, but it makes no allowance for the owner's negligence.

The relevance of negligence in the doctrine of estoppel has been raised in cases where an owner has negligently signed a document which appears to divest him of his property, and this document is utilised by a rogue to transfer the property to a b.f.p. In a contest between the owner and the b.f.p. as to the ownership of the property, two separate lines of argument may be possible. First, the b.f.p. may plead title derived from the document, and the owner deny that that document can have any legal effect by pleading *non est factum*[14], and the b.f.p. reply that the owner is "estopped" by his signature[15]. Second, where the document can be construed as making a representation of fact, such as that the rogue is the owner, the b.f.p. may plead that the owner is estopped or precluded by s. 21 (1) from setting up his title. In relation to the plea of *non est factum*, it would appear to be settled that negligence only defeats the plea if the document signed is a negotiable instrument[16]; and in *Campbell Discount Co., Ltd.* v. *Gall* the Court of Appeal took a similar view with regard to estoppel, holding that a hirer who had signed a h.p. proposal form in blank was not estopped by his negligence from showing that there was no *consensus ad idem* between himself and the finance company[17]. However, it was clear from the

---

12. At p. 385.   13. [1957] 2 Q.B. 600, C.A.: set out above, p. 189.
14. See above, p. 37.
15. "This is not a true estoppel, but an illustration of the principle that no man may take advantage of his own wrong": *per* Lord Hodson in *Saunders* v. *Anglia Building Society*, [1970] 3 All E.R. 961, H.L., at p. 966. And see below, p. 198, note 4.
16. See Treitel, *Law of Contract* (3rd Edn.) 269–270; Cheshire & Fifoot, *Law of Contract* (7th Edn.) 225–232.
17. [1961] 1 Q.B. 431; [1961] 2 All E.R. 104, C.A. This case is discussed below, pp. 287–288.

previous cases that the courts had recognised a doctrine of estoppel by negligence as something separate from that of *non est factum*[18]; and in *Mercantile Credit Co., Ltd.* v. *Hamblin* the Court of Appeal accepted that the doctrine of estoppel by negligence was not confined to negotiable instruments[19]. In *Hamblin's Case*[19]

> The defendant asked a motor dealer if he could obtain for her a loan of £1,000 on the security of her Jaguar car, and the dealer agreed to make enquiries of a finance company. In the meantime, the dealer suggested that it would expedite matters if he should give her a blank cheque and she should sign the necessary documents in blank. Accordingly, the defendant signed three documents, which were in fact those appropriate for a directly financed h.p. transaction, though she did not realise this. The dealer later fraudulently completed the forms and tendered them to the plaintiff finance company, who accepted them and paid the dealer; and the latter pocketed the money. The defendant, who thought the transaction had fallen through, refused to pay the plaintiffs any instalments, and they therefore claimed the car. At first instance, the claim was dismissed on the grounds (1) that the defendant could rely on *non est factum*, and (2) she was not estopped from denying the dealer's authority to sell.

The Court of Appeal affirmed the decision: whilst they held that the defendant could not plead *non est factum*[14], the Court dismissed the plaintiff's appeal on the gounds that the dealer had no authority from the defendant to complete the documents. Whilst the dealer obviously had no actual authority to do so, the plaintiffs contended that he had an ostensible authority on the basis of *Eastern Distributors, Ltd.* v. *Goldring*[20]. However, the Court of Appeal unanimously distinguished the latter case on the grounds that Murphy had expressly agreed that the dealer should make the representation to the finance company[1]; and proceeded to consider whether the defendant could be estopped by her negligence. PEARSON L.J. said[2];

> "In order to establish an estoppel by negligence, the finance company has to show (1) that the defendant owed them a duty to be careful, (2) that in breach of this duty she was negligent, (3) that her negligence was the proximate or real cause of it being induced to part with [the money] to the dealer".

---

18. See Crossley Vaines, *Personal Property* (4th Edn.) 160.
19. [1965] 2 Q.B. 242; [1964] 3 All E.R. 592, C.A.
20. [1957] 2 Q.B. 600, C.A.
 1. But why should the scope of the dealer's actual authority here be relevant to his ostensible authority?
 2. At p. 271. Cf. BLACKBURN J. in *Swan* v. *North British Australasian Co.* (1863), 2 H. & C. 175, at p. 182.

Their Lordships were all agreed that there was a sufficiently proximate relationship between the defendant and any person who might advance money on the security of the car to impose on her a duty of care with regard to the preparation and custody of the documents relating to the "loan".   However, on the peculiar facts of this case, they all thought that she was not in breach of this duty as she had good grounds for relying on the dealer[3].   Furthermore, SELLERS and PEARSON L.JJ. were prepared to hold that, even if there had been a breach of duty in leaving the documents signed in blank with the dealer, this was not the proximate cause of the plaintiffs' loss, since the dealer's fraud was not a foreseeable consequence of what she did[4].

Is there a principle of estoppel by negligence applicable to this context?   All three members of the Court of Appeal in *Mercantile Credit Co., Ltd.* v. *Hamblin*[5] were prepared to accept that the defendant might be estopped by her negligence.   SELLERS and PEARSON L.JJ. seemed to accept a general principle to this effect, whilst SALMON L.J. indicated that estoppel by negligence should generally be confined to cases of negotiable instruments[6].   However, even if this principle were accepted, the decision does seem to indicate that it will be extremely limited[7]: and, assuming that a duty existed in both this case and in *Eastern Distributors Ltd.* v. *Goldring*[8], it is difficult to see why there should be breach and proximity in the earlier case but not in the later one.

3 VOIDABLE TITLE

At the outset, we must distinguish between void and voidable contracts.   Suppose B. purports to accept an offer which, by misrepresentation, he has induced A. to make.   If A.'s offer is incapable of being accepted by B. the contract between them is said to be "void"—though this really is a contradiction in terms[9]; but, if A.'s offer is open to acceptance by B., B.'s acceptance gives rise to a contract between them (albeit one that A. may rescind for misrepresentation), in which case the contract is said to be "voidable".   Suppose that in this example, A. offers to sell, pledge or exchange[10] his car.   If the contract with B. is void, B. will acquire no proprietary interest in the car; but, if the con-

---

3. She was well-acquainted with an apparently respectable dealer with a large business and she had been given a blank cheque.
4. Thus, the defendant was precluded by her conduct from pleading *non est factum*, but not from setting up her title.   This neatly illustrates that "negligence" has a different meaning in the context of the doctrines of *non est factum* and estoppel: see further above, p. 196, note 15.
5. [1965] 2 Q.B. 242; [1964] 3 All E.R. 592, C.A.   6. At p. 278.
7. See Cross, *Evidence* (3rd Edn.) 287; Crossley Vaines, *Personal Property* (4th Edn.) 162; Fridman, *Agency* (2nd Edn.) 192.
8. [1957] 2 Q.B. 600, C.A.
9. *Per* GRESSON P. in *Fawcett* v. *Star Car Sales, Ltd.*, [1960] N.Z.L.R. 406, at p. 412; and *per* DEVLIN L.J. in *Ingram* v. *Little*, [1961] 1 Q.B. 31, C.A., at pp. 63–64.   10. *Anderson* v. *Ryan*, [1967] I.R. 34.

tract is merely voidable, he will acquire a defeasible proprietary interest in it. Suppose, further, that B. purports to dispose of the car to C. If the contract between A. and B. is void, B. acquires no title to the goods, and can therefore pass none[11], though C. might acquire a good title under one of the other exceptions to the *nemo dat* rule. Leaving aside this last possibility, the position is the same if the contract between A., and B. is voidable and has been avoided by A. before B. purports to dispose of the goods[12]. On the other hand, if the voidable contract between A. and B. has not been avoided at the time of the disposition by B. to C., C. will at the very least acquire that voidable title[13]; and, if C. is a *bona fide* transferee for value without notice, he will acquire a good title indefeasible by A.[14].

This last rule is a common law exception to the *nemo dat* rule, and where the disposition by B. is by way of sale the exception has been put in statutory form. Section 23 of the S.G.A. provides:

> "Where the seller of goods has a voidable title thereto, but his title has not been avoided at the time of the sale, the buyer acquires a good title to the goods, provided he buys them in good faith and without notice of the seller's defect of title".

Section 62 (2) adds:

> "A thing is deemed to be done 'in good faith' within the meaning of this Act when it is in fact done honestly, whether it be done negligently or not".

The latter provision is usually thought to embody the common law[15]; and "notice" is not even defined in the Act, so that the matter is left entirely to the common law[16]. Nor do the courts seem to regard s. 23 as having made any changes in the common law. In *Whitehorn Brothers v. Davison*[17] the Court of Appeal were of the opinion that the common law exception still stands in respect of pledges by B. to C.[18]; and that, under both statute and common law, if A. seeks to recover the goods from C., the onus is on A. to show that C. did not purchase in good faith and without notice[19].

---

11. *Cundy* v. *Lindsay* (1878), 3 App. Cas. 459, H.L.
12. *Car and Universal Finance Co., Ltd.* v. *Caldwell*, [1965] 1 Q.B. 525; [1964] 1 All E.R. 290, C.A.
13. E.g. if C. is B.'s trustee in bankruptcy, or a purchaser with notice.
14. *King's Norton Metal Co., Ltd.* v. *Edridge, Merrett & Co., Ltd.* (1897), 14 T.L.R. 98, C.A.
15. See further *Chalmers' Sale of Goods* (15th Edn.) 206–207.
16. See further below, p. 226.   17. [1911] 1 K.B. 463, C.A.
18. See also *Phillips* v. *Brooks*, [1919] 2 K.B. 243. And if the disposition by A. to B. is by way of pledge?
19. Is the position the same if A. seizes possession, so that C. is the plaintiff? The *Twelfth Report of the Law Reform Committee* (Cmnd. 2958), para. 25, recommends that the rule be reversed to achieve uniformity with the other exceptions to the *nemo dat* rule: see below, p. 214.

The question as to when a mistake or misrepresentation will render a contract voidable is beyond the scope of this work; but, assuming that the contract between A. and B. is voidable, it is necessary to consider how A. may rescind or avoid it. In one case, Lord BLACKBURN said that a man does not elect simply because he makes up his own mind to elect; and that he has not elected until he[20]

> "has communicated [his intention] to the other side in such a way as to lead the opposite party to believe that he has made that choice ..."

Plainly, where A. communicates his intention to rescind to B., that will be sufficient; but for a long time it was thought that A. could not effectively rescind by any means short of "going to court"[1], except by actual communication with B.[2] or recaption of the property[3]. Such a rule was perfectly adequate where B. was innocent but not if B. was fraudulent. In the latter case, B. would usually effectively dispose of the goods before A. found him or the goods, with the result that it was assumed that B. would normally be able to pass a good title to a b.f.p. However, this assumption was confounded by the Court of Appeal in *Car and Universal Finance Co., Ltd.* v. *Caldwell*[4].

> On Jan. 12th, Caldwell contracted to sell his car to a rogue, X., for £975 and allowed X. to take the car away in return for payment made as to £965 by cheque. The cheque was dishonoured the next morning; and Caldwell immediately went to the police, and also asked the A.A. to try to find his car. On Jan. 15th, X. sold the car to Y., a *mala fide* purchaser, who immediately resold to Z., a *bona fide* purchaser. On Jan. 29th, Caldwell demanded the return of his car from Y. In August, Z. sold the car to the plaintiff. Subsequently, the car was seized by the sheriff, and the case arose on an interpleader summons. It was conceded that Caldwell had taken adequate steps to avoid the contract by Jan. 29th, so that the plaintiff could have no better title than Z.

At first instance, Lord DENNING M.R. held that the title to the car was vested in Caldwell because—

(1) He had avoided the sale to X, on Jan. 13th by communicating with the police and A.A., so that any later disposition by X. was ineffective; or

(2) Y., a motor dealer, was the general agent of Z., a finance company, so that the latter were affected by Y.'s *mala fides*, and their title

---

20. *Scarf* v. *Jardine* (1882), 7 App. Cas. 345, H.L., at p. 361.
 1. See *per* Lord PEARSON in *Garnac Grain Co., Inc.* v. *H. M. F. Faure and Fairclough, Ltd.*, [1968] A.C. 1130; [1967] 2 All E.R. 353, H.L., at p. 360.
 2. *Per* Lord CLYDE in *Macleod* v. *Kerr* 1965 S.L.T. 358, at p. 363.
 3. Reception is considered below, pp. 330–332.
 4. [1965] 1 Q.B. 525, C.A.: see Cornish (1964), 27 M.L.R. 472.

was avoided by Jan. 29th so that the later disposition to the plaintiff was ineffective.

The Court of Appeal found that Y. was not the agent of Z., so that Z. was not affected by Y.'s *mala fides*[5]; but they unanimously dismissed the appeal on the grounds that Caldwell had effectively avoided the rogue's title on Jan. 13th. SELLERS L.J. explained[6]:

> "Where a contracting party could be communicated with, and modern facilities make communication practically world-wide and almost immediate, it would be unlikely that a party could be held to have disaffirmed a contract unless he went so far as to communicate his decision so to do ... But in circumstances such as the present case, the other contracting party, a fraudulent rogue who would know that the vendor would want his car back as soon as he knew of the fraud, would not expect to be communicated with as a matter of right or requirement, and would deliberately, as here, do all he could to evade any such communication being made to him. In such exceptional contractual circumstances, it does not seem to me appropriate to hold that a party so acting can claim any right to have a decision to rescind communicated to him before the contract is terminated ... That another innocent party or parties may suffer does not in my view of the matter justify imposing on the defrauded seller an impossible task. He has to establish clearly and unequivocally, that he terminates the contract ... If he cannot communicate his decision he may still satisfy a judge or jury that he had made a final and irrevocable decision and ended the contract".

At first sight, *Caldwell's Case* would appear to make substantial inroads into one of the principal exceptions to the *nemo dat* rule[7]: whereas the previous rule left very little chance of avoidance, the new one makes it a real possibility. Yet, it would seem that the Court of Appeal were careful to restrict themselves to cases where a contract is voidable by reason of the buyer's fraud and the buyer deliberately evades the seller[8]. Furthermore, another limitation on the effect of this case became apparent with the decision in *Newtons of Wembley, Ltd.* v. *Williams*[9]. In somewhat similar circumstances to those in *Caldwell's Case* it was accepted that the vendor had avoided the contract by doing all in his power to communicate with the rogue; but the Court of Appeal held that the rogue had nevertheless passed a good title as a

---

5. The possible agency relationship between a finance company and dealer is considered below, p. 285, *et seq.*
6. At pp. 550-551. See also UPJOHN and DAVIES L.JJ., at pp. 555, 558.
7. Atiyah, [1965] J.B.L. 130, 131.
8. Does the rule depend on (a) fraud in the sale, or (b) deliberate evasion, or both?
9. [1965] 1 Q.B. 560; [1964] 3 All E.R. 532, C.A. This case is discussed below, pp. 228-229.

buyer in possession: *Caldwell's Case* was distinguished on the grounds that X. was *mala fide*[10].

The implications of *Caldwell's Case* may be illustrated by way of an example. Suppose X. steals goods from O., and sells them to A.; A. resells to B. under a contract voidable by A.; B. resells to C., who resells to D., who resells to E.:

$$O. \quad X.\text{———}A.\text{———}B.\text{———}C.\text{———}D.\text{———}E.$$
voidable

Several questions arise.

(1) Suppose B. sells to C. before A. avoids the contract. Is the effect of the exception to confer on C. the title of O. or A.? It is submitted that C. will only obtain such title as A. has[11].

(2) Suppose B. sells to C. and C. sells to D. before A. avoids the contract, but C. is *mala fide*. In *Caldwell's Case*, the Court of Appeal seem to have thought that D. would obtain a good title as being a b.f.p.[12] before avoidance[13].

(3) Suppose further that the sale by D. to E. took place after avoidance. It was conceded in *Caldwell's Case* that E. had no better title than D. If this is correct, the effect of the exception is that E. will only succeed where he, or a prior party[14], took *bona fide* and for value before A. rescinds.

Finally, it should be noted that the Law Reform Committee have recommended that the rule as to avoidance laid down in *Caldwell's Case* should be reversed, and actual communication required[15]: if enacted, the recommendation would reverse the result in *Caldwell's Case* but not that in *Williams' Case*.[16]

4 MERCANTILE AGENCY[17]

In the series of Factors Acts which begun in 1823, Parliament attempted to increase the protection of b.f. purchasers and pledgees who obtained goods from factors to whom the goods had been entrusted by their owners[18]; and the history of the Acts is one of legisla-

---

10. This distinction has been called a reproach to our law: Cheshire & Fifoot, *Law of Contract* (7th Edn.) 250, note 6.
11. This is the usual result: see below, pp. 215, 219, 230, 234. Cf. Sales in market overt: below, p. 237.
12. Is it important that he is the first b.f.p.? See further below, p. 230.
13. Cf. *Williams' Case*, [1965] 1 Q.B. 560; [1964] 3 All E.R. 532, C.A.
14. See *Peirce v. London Horse and Carriage Repository, Ltd.*, [1922] W.N. 170, C.A.
15. *Twelfth Report* (Cmnd. 2958), paras. 16, 40 (4).
16. I.e. the b.f.p. in *Williams' Case* would now succeed on the basis of s. 23, and would not need to rely on s. 25 (2).
17. See Powell, *Agency* (2nd Edn.) 216–236.
18. See Stoljar, *Agency* 116–121.

tion in favour of the b.f.p., followed by the courts adopting a restrictive interpretation in favour of the owner, followed by further legislation in favour of the b.f.p. The earlier Acts were consolidated and amended by the Factors Act 1889. Whilst expressly providing that nothing in that Act shall affect the Factors Acts (s. 21 (2) (a)), the S.G.A. rather curiously proceeds to repeat some of the more important provisions of the 1889 Act in *almost* identical terms.

There are two major themes running through the Factors Act 1889 (hereafter called the F.A.).

(1) The attempt to increase the power of "mercantile agents". The object of the Act is not to derogate from the powers of an ordinary agent[19], but to increase them for the benefit of his transferee where the latter has paid the consideration to the agent[20] (s. 13). At the same time, the Act is careful not to increase the powers of the agent vis à vis his principal (s. 12 (1))[1].

(2) Parliament was concerned to modify the common law rule that possession does not usually of itself give rise to an apparent authority to dispose of goods[2]. Thus, the F.A. lays down that a buyer or seller in possession may in certain circumstances pass a good title. These provisions will be considered later[3].

Both these themes have certain similarities to the doctrine of estoppel; and they do in fact cover some of the ground covered by estoppel in those situations where a person in possession has an apparent or usual authority to dispose of goods. But there the similarity ends: estoppel demands a representation made to the b.f.p., but the F.A. requires instead that the b.f.p.'s transferor should be a mercantile agent, or a seller or buyer in possession.

In this section consideration will be given to the special powers of disposition which the F.A. confers on a mercantile agent. The key provision is s. 2 (1) of that Act, which provides:

> "Where a mercantile agent is, with the consent of the owner, in possession of goods or of the documents of title to goods, any sale, pledge, or other disposition of the goods, made by him when acting in the ordinary course of business of a mercantile agent, shall, subject to the provisions of this Act, be as valid as if he were expressly authorised by the owner of the goods to make the same; provided that the person taking under the disposition acts in good faith, and has not at the time of the disposition notice that the person making the disposition has not authority to make the same".

---

19. The powers of an ordinary agent are outlined above, pp. 184–185.
20. If the transferee has not paid the price, the "owner" may be able to recover it from him (s. 12 (3)).
 1. Nor of the agent's trustee in bankruptcy (s. 12 (2)).
 2. See above, p. 195.
 3. See below, pp. 220, 215.

Since 1889, this sub-section has become encrusted with case-law, and each phrase of it must be considered with some care.

1 A mercantile agent

The Act requires that he should be (1) an agent *and* (2) a mercantile agent.

1. An agent. The first requirement is that he must be acting as agent: it is not sufficient if he acts as owner[4], nor as any other type of custodian[5]. Difficult questions may arise where he acts in more than one capacity, as, for instance, where he is both a servant and an agent, e.g. a commercial traveller[6].

2. A "mercantile agent". Before 1889, the Acts merely used the term "agent"; but this had been judicially interpreted to cover only those agents which in normal language are termed factors[7]. The term "mercantile agent" appeared for the first time in the 1889 Act; and, according to CHANNELL J., the legislature intended by using this term[8]

> "to express in a compendious form the result of the decisions as to who were agents within the previous Acts, and that the expression or definition "mercantile agent" in s. 1 substantially represents the result of those judicial decisions".

To the extent that this is so, it is permissible to refer to the cases decided before 1889[9]. According to s. 1 (1), for the purposes of the 1889 Act the expression "mercantile agent" shall mean—

> "a mercantile agent having in the customary course of his business as such agent authority either to sell goods, or to consign goods for the purpose of sale, or to buy goods, or to raise money on the security of goods".

Thus, a "mercantile agent" is one who is entrusted with goods as agent for one of the purposes listed in s. 1 (1). For instance, in *Lowther v. Harris*[10].

> L. installed some antiques he wished to sell in a house. He arranged with an antique dealer, X. that X. should take a flat in the house and sell the items on commission, but should first obtain the sanction of L. X. fraudulently sold and delivered two tapestries to a b.f.p. As to one, there had clearly been no consent by L. to delivery, but in

4. *Belvoir Finance, Co., Ltd.* v. *Cole, Ltd.*, [1969] 2 All E.R. 904.
5. The distinction between agents and certain other categories such as servants, independent contractors, trustees and bailees is best left to the works on agency: see Powell, Ch. 1; Stoljar, Ch. 1; Fridman, Ch. 1.
6. See *Cole* v. *North-Western Bank* (1875), L.R. 10 C.P. 354; *Astley Industrial Trust, Ltd.* v. *Miller*, [1968] 2 All E.R. 36; and below, p. 206.
7. E.g. *Hayman* v. *Flewker* (1863), 13 C.B. N.S. 519.
8. *Oppenheimer* v. *Attenborough*, [1907] 1 K.B. 510, at p. 514; affd., [1908] 1 K.B. 221, C.A.: set out below, p. 212.
9. See Parker (1952), 15 M.L.R. 503, 506.   10. [1927] 1 K.B. 393.

respect of the other X. induced L. to consent to its removal by a misrepresentation. L.'s action in conversion against the b.f.p. succeeded in respect of the first tapestry[11], but failed as to the second on the grounds that X. was a mercantile agent and had passed a good title under the F.A.

As X.'s function was not merely to deliver the goods, but also to collect the price and account for it to L., WRIGHT J. concluded that X. was acting in the usual course of business of a fine art dealer. Nor did he think it material that L. was acting in this instance for one principal only. It would therefore seem that a mercantile agency under the F.A. may exist although the agent is acting for one principal only, and has no general occupation as agent[12]: all that is required is that in the particular transaction he is performing one of the functions listed in s. 1 (1) in the manner of a mercantile agent[13]. It would seem to be uncertain whether the entrusting of goods to another for the purposes of obtaining offers falls within s. 1 (1)[14].

It has been pointed out that the F.A. has so strengthened the powers of disposition of a mercantile agent (hereafter called a m.a.) that for all practical purposes he is almost indistinguishable from a person dealing with goods on his own behalf; that the principal has little more control over a m.a. than he has over an independent trader; and that the result would appear to be that owners today frequently prefer to sell outright rather than employ such an agent, with the result that the position formerly occupied by the factor is being taken over by the independent trader[15]. The effect of this is said to be that[15]

> "the kind of factor who today agitates the law is not the factor of old, but is the more casual agent such as the traveller or salesman . . ."

In this kind of situation, it will, of course, be far more difficult to determine whether or not the rogue is a m.a. Now, in the cases so far cited where it has been held that the F.A. applied, the rogue has been working on a commission basis. This point was seized upon by MACNAGHTEN J. in *Budberg* v. *Jerwood and Ward*[16], where he held that the Act did not apply to defeat the title of an owner who entrusted her jewellery to a friend for the purposes of sale, and relied upon the absence of any

---

11. See explanation below, p. 209.
12. E.g. *Weiner* v. *Harris*, [1910] 1 K.B. 285, C.A., discussed above. p. 180; *Lowther* v. *Harris*, [1927] 1 K.B. 393.
13. Cf. *Brown & Co.* v. *Bedford Pantechnicon, Ltd.* (1889), 5 T.L.R. 449, C.A.; and *Kendrick* v. *Southeby & Co.*, [1967] C.L.Y. 42.
14. Accepted without argument in: *Pearson* v. *Rose and Young, Ltd.*, [1951] 1 K.B. 275; [1950] 2 All E.R. 1057, C.A.; *Stadium Finance, Ltd.* v. *Robbins*, [1962] 2 Q.B. 664; [1962] 2 All E.R. 633, C.A. But see *per* SALMON L.J. in *Lloyds and Scottish Finance, Ltd.* v. *Williamson*, [1965] 1 All E.R. 641, C.A., at p. 644.
15. Stoljar, *Agency*, 124.
16. (1935), 51 T.L.R. 99.

commission to negative any suggestion of a business relationship. *Jerome* v. *Bentley*[17] would, however, appear to deny that the presence or absence of commission is decisive.

> T. fraudulently induced the plaintiff to hand a diamond ring to him to sell or return within 7 days under an agreement which stipulated that T. was to try to sell the ring either in his own name or the plaintiff's, and that if he sold it he was to pay the plaintiff £550 and retain any surplus for himself. After the expiration of the 7 days, T. sold the ring to a b.f.p. and absconded. The plaintiff admitted that T. was his agent, and successfully sued the b.f.p. for conversion. DONOVAN J. held that, at the time of sale, T. had no actual, apparent or usual authority to sell.

It has been suggested that T. was not a m.a.[19]; but it would appear that the F.A. was not pleaded in this case: if it had been, the issue might well have turned on whether T. was acting as an agent or principal,[18] because, if he were an agent, the commission arrangement would seem to indicate that he was a m.a.[20]. It may be that the presence of commission does not conclusively show that an agent is a m.a.; but the cases other than *Jerome* v. *Bentley* certainly seem to show that it is strong evidence to that effect.

2 Possession of goods or documents of title

1. Possession. According to s. 1 (2) of the F.A.[1]:

> "A person shall be deemed to be in possession of goods or of the documents of title to goods, where the goods or documents are in his actual custody or are held by any other person subject to his control or for him or on his behalf".

Not only must the m.a. be in possession[2], but he must also be in possession in his capacity as m.a. Thus, in *Staffs. Motor Guarantee, Ltd. v. British Wagon, Ltd.*[3]

> H., a dealer in motor lorries, agreed to sell a lorry to the defendant finance company, and to rehire it from them under a h.p. agreement with a view to sub-letting it to X. H. then fraudulently sold the lorry, of which he had never relinquished possession, to the plaintiff

---

17. [1952] 2 All E.R. 114.
18. If the case had been argued on the basis that T. was a principal, it would have turned on s. 18 r. 4: see *Kirkham* v. *Attenborough*, [1897] 1 Q.B. 201, C.A. (see above, p. 178).
19. Atiyah, *Sale of Goods* (3rd Edn.) 145 says the case is authority for the proposition that
    "a person who induces another to let him have goods on a representation that he knows a third party who will buy them is not without more a m.a."
20. See Parker (1952), 15 M.L.R. 503; Powell, *Agency* (2nd Edn.) 83, note 6.
1. And see the discussion of delivery below, p. 263, *et seq.*
2. *Lowther* v. *Harris*, [1927] 1 K.B. 393: the first tapestry—see above, p. 205.
3. [1934] 2 K.B. 305.

finance company, a b.f.p. When H. fell into arrears, the defendants repossessed the lorry. In their action to recover the lorry, the plaintiffs pleaded that: (1) the h.p. agreement was void under the Bills of Sale Acts[4]; (2) H. could pass a good title under s. 25 of the S.G.A.[5]; and (3) H. could pass a good title under s. 2 (1) of the F.A. The action failed.

MACKINNON J. rejected the plaintiff's plea under s. 2 (1) of the F.A. on the grounds that, after H. sold the lorry to the defendants, it was entrusted by them to H., not in his capacity as m.a., but as hirer[6]. This view has been expressly accepted by the English courts[7]. However, such a distinction in capacity will obviously, if taken too far, nullify the effect of s. 2 (1); and it has recently been rejected by the Privy Council in the somewhat similar context of the exception relating to sellers in possession[8]. Finally, it must be remembered that s. 2 (1) only applies where a person is a m.a. at the time he is entrusted with the goods[9]: the mere fact that he later becomes a m.a. does not bring s. 2 (1) into operation unless the owner consents to his possession in that capacity[10].

2. *Goods or documents of title.* "Goods" are defined by s. 1 (3) of the F.A. to "include wares and merchandise"[11]; and s. 1 (4) provides that:

> "The expression 'document of title' shall include any bill of lading[12] dock warrant, warehousekeeper's certificate, and warrant or order for the delivery of goods, and any other document used in the ordinary course of business as proof of the possession or control of goods, or authorising or purporting to authorise, either by endorsement or by delivery, the possessor of the document to transfer or receive goods thereby represented"[13].

The problem which has exercised the courts most in recent years is the status of a motor vehicle's log-book. Whilst the courts have had to accept that the log-book is not a document of title[14], there has been an attempt by some judges to establish that in the case of a motor vehicle

---

4. See below, p. 292.
5. See below, p. 217.   6. At p. 313.
7. See *per* DENNING L.J. in *Pearson* v. *Rose and Young, Ltd.*, [1951] 1 K.B. 275, C.A., at p. 288; *per* WILLMER L.J. in *Stadium Finance, Ltd.* v. *Robbins*, [1962] 2 Q.B. 664, C.A., at p. 674.
8. *Pacific Motor Auctions, Ltd.* v. *Motor Credits, Ltd.*, [1965] A.C. 867; [1965] 2 All E.R. 105, P.C.: set out below, pp. 217–218. But see *per* CHAPMAN J. in *Astley Industrial Trust, Ltd.* v. *Miller*, [1968] 2 All E.R. 36, at pp. 41–42.
9. *Per* LUSH J. in *Heap* v. *Motorists' Advisory Agency, Ltd.*, [1923] 1 K.B. 577, at pp. 588–589.
10. But see s. 2 (4), discussed below, p. 210.
11. Compare the definition of goods in the S.G.A.: above, p. 18.
12. Bills of lading are explained above, p. 182.
13. Documents of title are expressly excluded from the definition of bills of sale: s. 4, Bills of Sale Act 1878—see above, p. 32.
14. *Joblin* v. *Watkins & Roseveare (Motors), Ltd.*, [1949] 1 All E.R. 47.

"goods" means "vehicle plus log-book". Starting from the premise that the log-book is best evidence of title[15], Lord DENNING in particular has argued that, because of the importance of the log-book and the fact that a vehicle is not ordinarily sold without one, it should be regarded as part of the goods. Perhaps the high-water mark of this view is to be found in *Pearson* v. *Rose and Young, Ltd.*[16].

> The owner of a Morris car left it with a car dealer (a m.a.) to see if the latter could obtain any offers to buy it. At the same time, the dealer tricked the owner into leaving the log-book with him. The dealer sold the car plus log-book to X., who resold to Y., who resold to Z. The owner sued Z. to recover the car, and DEVLIN J. held that Z. obtained a good title by reason of s. 2 (1). His decision was reversed by the Court of Appeal.

While the case was argued on the issue of whether the dealer obtained possession of the goods with the consent of the owner, it also raised the questions as to whether (1) the sale by the dealer to X. was made in the ordinary course of business[17], and (2) X. was a b.f.p.[18]. On the point argued, the best interpretation of the decision would appear to be that the Court agreed that the owner had consented[19] to the dealer having possession of the car as m.a., but had not consented to his having possession of the log-book[20]. Building on this insecure foundation, DENNING L.J. held that[1]

> "in the case of a car, 'goods' in the Act means the car together with the log-book".

In a later case, his Lordship re-affirmed this rather anomalous distinction[2]; but it was unanimously rejected by the Court of Appeal in *Stadium Finance, Ltd.* v. *Robbins*[3].

> The owner of a Jaguar car left it with a car dealer (a m.a.) to see what offers to buy it the latter could obtain. The owner took away the ignition key, but accidentally left the log-book locked in the glove compartment. The dealer opened the glove compartment

---

15. *Per* Scrutton L.J. in *Folkes* v. *King*, [1923] 1 K.B. 282, C.A., at p. 300; and see *per* DENNING L.J. in the *Bishopsgate Motor Finance Corporation, Ltd.* v. *Transport Brakes, Ltd.*, [1949] 1 K.B. 322, at pp. 337–338, C.A.
16. [1951] 1 K.B. 275; [1950] 2 All E.R. 1057, C.A.
17. See below, pp. 211–214. 18. See below, p. 214.
19. The contrary view of SOMERVELL L.J. (at p. 284) would appear inconsistent with the facts and with his own acceptance of *Folkes* v. *King* (above).
20. Consent is discussed below, pp. 209–211.
 1. At p. 290. SOMERVELL L.J. seemed to accept this, but thought that the appeal would succeed irrespective of this question. VAISEY J. refused to commit himself on this point.
 2. In his dissenting judgment in *Central Newbury Car Auctions, Ltd.* v. *Unity Finance, Ltd.*, [1957] 1 Q.B. 371, C.A., at pp. 384–385.
 3. [1962] 2 Q.B. 664; [1962] 2 All E.R. 633, C.A.

with a duplicate key and found the log-book. He subsequently sold the car to the plaintiff finance company in pursuance of a directly financed transaction. The owner retook possession of the car, and the plaintiff's claim under s. 2 (1) failed on the grounds that the sale to them was not made in the ordinary course of business[4].

The County Court Judge had held that "goods" within s. 2 (1) meant "car plus ignition key", but this view was unanimously rejected by the Court of Appeal, who held that "goods" bore its ordinary meaning, and here meant the car alone[5]. The logic of the *Robbins Case* would appear to be impeccable[6]: it is nonsensical to say that, just because further items are obtained without the consent of the owner, the latter's consent to the possession of the motor vehicle is thereby nullified[7].

3 The consent of the owner[8]

1. Consent. The Act nowhere defines "consent", but perhaps the sense of the term is conveyed by the word used in the previous Factors Acts, namely "entrusts". It is clear that only consent to the fact of possession need be shown, and any secret restrictions on the powers of the agent are irrelevant[9]. While there must be a consent to the agent's possession[10], it is irrelevant that that consent was obtained by trick[11]. Moreover, the Legislature obviously intended to lessen the burden of the person seeking to prove consent by providing in s. 2 of the F.A. as follows:

> "(2) Where a mercantile agent has, with the consent of the owner, been in possession of goods or of documents of title to goods, any sale, pledge, or other disposition, which would have been valid if the consent had continued, shall be valid notwithstanding the determination of the consent: provided that the person taking under the disposition has not at the time thereof notice that the consent has been determined.
>
> (3) Where a mercantile agent has obtained possession of any documents of title to goods by reason of his being, or having been, with the consent of the owner, in possession of the goods represented thereby, or of any other documents of title to the goods, his

---

4. See below, p. 213.
5. *Per* ORMEROD, WILLMER and DANCKWERTS L.JJ. at pp. 670–671, 674, 676. See also CHAPMAN J. in *Astley Industrial Trust, Ltd.* v. *Miller*, [1968] 2 All E.R. 36, at p. 43; and DONALDSON J. in *Belvoir Finance, Ltd.* v. *Cole, Ltd.*, [1969] 2 All E.R. 904, at p. 908.
6. See Schofield, [1963] J.B.L. 344, 350. *Contra* Lannerolle, [1967] J.B.L. 329, 333.
7. Obviously, it is a question of degree which is the tail and which is the dog!
8. This requirement is also to be found in s. 25 (2) S.G.A.: see below, p. 223.
9. *Weiner* v. *Harris*, [1910] 1 K.B. 285, C.A.; *Turner* v. *Sampson* (1911), 27 T.L.R. 200; *Stadium Finance, Ltd.* v. *Robbins*, [1962] 2 Q.B. 664; [1962] 2 All E.R. 633, C.A.
10. *Lowther* v. *Harris*, [1927] 1 K.B. 393: the first tapestry: see above, p. 205.
11. *Folkes* v. *King*, [1923] 1 K.B. 282, C.A.

possession of the first-mentioned documents shall, for the purposes of this Act, be deemed to be with the consent of the owner.

(4) For the purposes of this Act the consent of the owner shall be presumed in the absence of evidence to the contrary".

However, the courts have shown some reluctance to apply those provisions. Thus, it is difficult to see why the transfer of the possession of the log-book to the dealer in *Pearson* v. *Rose and Young, Ltd.*[12] was not connected with the business of obtaining offers for sale[13]; or why this was not presumed under s. 2. (4); and, if it were so connected, why s. 2 (2) did not prevent such consent being withdrawn. Similarly, in the *Robbins Case*[14] the majority were of the opinion that the inference under s. 2 (4) that the owner had consented to possession by the dealer had been rebutted as to the log-book, but not as to the car[15]. WILLMER L.J. went even further, and argued that[16]

"without either key or registration book, [the dealer] was not . . . in possession of the car in his capacity of [m.a.]".

It is submitted that it would be undesirable if the view of WILLMER L.J. were to prevail, as it would unduly restrict the operation of s. 2[17].

2. *Owner.* In *Lloyds Bank, Ltd.* v. *Bank of America*[18]

The plaintiff Bank lent money to S. on the security of documents pledged with them; and then returned the documents to S. to enable him to sell the goods as trustee for the plaintiff—S. giving the Bank a trust receipt. Subsequently, S. fraudulently pledged the documents with the defendant b.f.p., who pleaded title under s. 2 (1).

The plaintiffs argued that the division of ownership between themselves and S. brought about by the pledge prevented S. from being in possession with their consent; but this argument was rejected by the Court of Appeal, who held that S. was a m.a.[19] in possession with the consent of the owner. Lord GREENE M.R. explained[20]:

"Where the right of ownership has become divided among two or more persons in such a way that the acts which the section is contemplating can never be authorised save by both or all of them, these persons together constitute the owner".

---

12. [1951] 1 K.B. 275; [1950] 2 All E.R. 1057, C.A.
13. Powell, *Agency* (2nd Edn.) 228, note 4.
14. [1962] 2 Q.B. 664; [1962] 2 All E.R. 633, C.A.
15. ORMEROD and DANCKWERTS L.JJ., at pp. 670–671, 676–677.
16. At p. 674.
17. See Hornby (1962), 25 M.L.R. 719.
18. [1938] 2 K.B. 147; [1938] 2 All E.R. 63, C.A.
19. A factor which distinguishes this case from the *Mercantile Bank of India Case*, [1938] A.C. 287; [1938] 1 All E.R. 52, P.C.: set out above, p. 184.
20. At p. 162.

It has already been pointed out that the term "owner" is not a term of art[1]; and it will be suggested later that it includes persons having something less than best title[2].

4 Dispositions by a m.a. in the ordinary course of business

1. The disposition. Section 2 (1) refers to a "sale, pledge or other disposition". According to s. 5 of the F.A.:

> "The consideration necessary for the validity of a sale[3], pledge,[4] or other disposition[5], of goods, in pursuance of this Act, may be either a payment in cash . . . or any other valuable consideration; but where goods are pledged . . . the pledgee shall acquire no right or interest in the goods so pledged in excess of the value of the goods, documents, or security when so delivered or transferred in exchange".

One of the major purposes of the F.A. was to deal with unauthorised pledges by a m.a., and it tackles this subject in considerable detail. Whilst s. 5 provides that the pledgee's security only extends to the value of the consideration he gives[6], s. 4 restricts this to consideration given by the pledgee at the time of the pledge. However, leaving aside the question of pledges, the implication of s. 5 seems to be that the disposition referred to in s. 2 (1) must be for valuable consideration[7].

2. By a mercantile agent. The F.A. envisages the possibility that the disposition may be made on behalf of a m.a. by his servant or agent. Section 6 provides that[8]

> "For the purposes of this Act an agreement made with a mercantile agent through a clerk or other person authorised in the ordinary course of business to make contracts of sale or pledge on his behalf shall be deemed to be an agreement with the agent".

3. In the ordinary course of business. Plainly, this requirement cannot be taken literally, because it is never in the ordinary course of business (hereafter termed o.c.b.) for any m.a. to dispose of goods contrary to his authority. This dilemma is present in the wording of the statute: according to s. 1 (1), a m.a. is one who in the ordinary course of *his* business has authority to sell, etc[9]; but s. 2 (1) provides that a m.a. can

---

1. See above, p. 153. 2. See below, p. 215.
3. The definition of "sale" is discussed above, pp. 5–9.
4. See above, p. 7. Section 1 (5) provides that "pledge"—
   "shall include any contract of pledging, or giving a lien or security on, goods, whether in consideration of an original advance or of any further or continuing advance or of any pecuniary liability".
5. Presumably, this includes h.p. and mortgage.
6. The effect of the words "pecuniary liability" in s. 1 (5) would appear to be that this covers antecedent liabilities.
7. See Powell, *Agency* (2nd Edn.) 233–234. Cf. *Thomas Graham, Ltd.* v. *Glenrothes Development Corporation*, [1968] S.L.T. 2.
8. See the criticism of s. 6 in Powell, *op. cit.*, 230.
9. See above, p. 204.

pass a good title when acting in the o.c.b. of *a* m.a.[10]. In *Oppenheimer v. Attenborough*[11]

> The plaintiff was induced to entrust a parcel of diamonds to a diamond broker (a m.a.) upon the representation that the broker could sell the diamonds to X. at an agreed minimum price. The broker pledged the diamonds with the defendant, who took *bona fide* and for value. Evidence was given that a diamond broker employed to sell diamonds had no authority to pledge them, and that it was unheard of in the trade to employ a broker to pledge diamonds. The plaintiff argued that a m.a. could only pass a good title under s. 2 (1) when acting in the ordinary course of *his* business, and that it was not in the ordinary course of a diamond broker's business to pledge diamonds.

Nevertheless, the Court of Appeal found in favour of the pledgee. The Court thought it irrelevant that the pledgee did not know that his pledgor was not acting as a principal[12]; and it was further irrelevant that the broker had brought the transaction within s. 2 (1) by acting in the o.c.b. of *a* m.a. BUCKLEY L.J. explained[13]:

> "Section 1 (1) is speaking of the arrangement made between the owner of the goods and his agent ... It deals with the circumstances under which the agent gets his authority; to satisfy the definition he must get [the goods] in the customary course of his business as a mercantile agent. Section 2 (1) deals with another matter. It has to do with the stage at which the agent is going to deal with the goods in his possession with reference to some other person, and the form of the expression is here altered ... [to mean] 'acting in such a way as a mercantile agent acting in the ordinary course of business of a mercantile agent would act'; that is to say, within business hours[14], at a proper place of business, and in other respects in the ordinary way in which a mercantile agent would act, so that there is nothing to lead the pledgee to suppose that anything wrong is being done, or to give him notice that the disposition is one which the mercantile agent had no authority to make".

This decision clearly accords with the purpose of the Act, namely, to reverse the rule that a factor cannot pledge goods[14a]; but the courts have been careful not to extend s. 2 (1) too far. Thus it has been held

that it is not in ordinary course of business that a mercantile agent asks friend to pledge goods for

---

10. See above, p. 203.
11. [1908] 1 K.B. 221, C.A. Cf. *Waddington & Son* v. *Neale & Sons* (1907), 97 L.T. 786, D.C.
12. *Per* Lord ALVERSTONE C.J. and KENNEDY L.J., at pp. 228, 232. But see below, pp. 228–229.
13. At pp. 230–231. But see criticisms in Powell, *Agency* (2nd Edn.) 219.
14. See *Pacific Motor Auctions, Ltd.* v. *Motor Credits, Ltd.*, [1965] A.C. 867; [1965] 2 All E.R. 105, P.C.: discussed below, p. 217, esp. note 18.
14a. See above, pp. 203, 211.

him[15]; nor to ask his buyer to pay the price in part to a third party in satisfaction of a judgment debt against the m.a.[16]; nor where the operation was characterised as "a very peculiar transaction"[17].

In recent years, the question of whether a disposition for value of a motor vehicle by a m.a. has been in the o.c.b. has caused the courts considerable difficulty. In *Pearson* v. *Rose and Young, Ltd.*[18] the Court of Appeal unanimously held that a disposition of a car with its log-book was not in the o.c.b., because the m.a. was in possession of the log-book without the consent of the owner and the latter must therefore be ignored for the purposes of the disposition. It is difficult to accept this reasoning.

(1) Whilst the Court of Appeal took a similar view in *Stadium Finance, Ltd.* v. *Robbins*[19] with respect to both log-book and ignition key, it ignores the distinction drawn in *Oppenheimer* v. *Attenborough* between the circumstances of (a) acquisition and (b) disposition by the m.a.: whilst the test of the owner's consent on acquisition is subjective, that of the o.c.b. on disposition is objective[1].

(2) Even assuming that the disposition was without the log-book, it is difficult to see why it was necessarily not in the o.c.b. SOMERVELL L.J. suggested that the price would be substantially reduced by the absence of the log-book[2]; but there was no such reduction in this case, and, even if there were, this may only go to *bona fides*[3]. VAISEY J. argued that the reason is that a car without a log-book is like a car with only three wheels[4]; but many defective cars are sold in the o.c.b.,[5] and the easy availability of replacements renders the presence or absence of the parts a little significance[6]. DENNING L.J. pointed out that it is not in the ordinary course of anyone's business to sell a second-hand car without a log-book[7], and this argument was adopted in *Stadium Finance Ltd.* v. *Robbins*, where the plaintiff finance company never asked for the log-book[8]. In *Astley Industrial Trust, Ltd.* v. *Miller*[9] CHAPMAN J. indicated that he thought that the two Court of Appeal decisions were wrong on

---

15. *De Gorter* v. *Attenborough* (1904), 21 T.L.R. 19. But see s. 6 of the F.A.
16. *Biggs* v. *Evans*, [1894] 1 Q.B. 88. But see *Lloyds and Scottish Finance, Ltd.* v. *Williamson*, [1965] 1 All E.R. 641, C.A., at p. 644.
17. *Heap* v. *Motorists' Agency*, [1923] 1 K.B. 577, at p. 589.
18. [1951] 1 K.B. 275; [1950] 2 All E.R. 1027, C.A.: set out above, p. 208.
19. [1962] 2 Q.B. 664; [1962] 2 All E.R. 633, C.A.: set out above, pp. 208–209.
1. See *per* CHAPMAN J. in *Astley Industrial Trust, Ltd.* v. *Miller*, [1968] 2 All E.R. 36, at p. 42. See also Goodhart (1951), 67 L.Q.R. 6; Hornby (1962), 25 M.L.R. 722; Schofield, [1963] J.B.L. 344, 350; Powell, *Agency* (2nd Edn.), 232; Crossley Vaines, *Personal Property* (4th Edn.) 186.
2. At p. 283. Cf. *Janesich* v. *Attenborough* (1910), 102 L.T. 605, at p. 606.
3. See further below, p. 214.   4. At p. 291.
5. See Powell, *op. cit.*, p. 231; Lanerolle, [1967] J.B.L. 329, 331–332.
6. See Schofield, [1963] J.B.L. 344, 349.   7. At p. 290.
8. They do not normally do so, it being understood that the hirer will take care of such matters. Does it follow, that, *prima facie*, the o.c.b. is that the hirer will take possession of the log-book?   9. (Above) at p. 44.

this point; but he was prepared if necessary to distinguish the two cases on the grounds that it is in the o.c.b. to buy a new car without a log-book. It is submitted that, on the principle laid down in *Oppenheimer* v. *Attenborough* what should matter is how the transaction ought to appear to the transferee: if the m.a. can supply either a genuine or a genuine-looking log-book, or a good reason for its absence, or if the log-book is not ordinarily handed over, the transaction should be in the o.c.b.

5 The transferee must take *bona fide* and without notice

Neither good faith nor notice is defined by the F.A.[10]; but in *Heap* v. *Motorists' Advisory Agency, Ltd.*[11], LUSH J. held that the burden of proof in these matters lay on the transferee. Perhaps the most important issue here is the relationship between the o.c.b. and the present requirement. It is clear from the decision in *Oppenheimer* v. *Attenborough* that, if the transferee thinks he is dealing with a principal, the fact that he is actually dealing with a m.a. who is not acting in the o.c.b. is irrelevant[12]. However, if the transferee realises that he is dealing with a particular type of m.a., the fact that it is notorious that that type of m.a. never has authority to engage in the kind of transfer undertaken, e.g. a pledge, will usually destroy the transferee's *bona fides*[13]. Similarly, the fact that the goods were bought at a gross under-valuation should not prevent the transaction being in the o.c.b., but may go to *bona fides*[14]. Again, the absence of the log-book or ignition key or the disposition of a car should not necessarily prevent the transaction from being in the o.c.b., but may indicate that the transferee is not acting *bona fide*[15]. It is submitted that there are sound reasons for the dual requirements that the transfer be in the o.c.b. and that the transferee act *bona fide* and without notice[16].

---

10. See the discussions of good faith above, p. 199, and notice below, p. 226.
11. [1923] 1 K.B. 577, esp. at p. 590.
12. *Lloyds and Scottish Finance, Ltd.* v. *Williamson*, [1965] 1 All E.R. 641, C.A.; *Pacific Motor Auctions, Ptd., Ltd.* v. *Motor Credits, Ltd.*, [1965] A.C. 867; [1965] 2 All E.R. 105, P.C., set out below, p. 217.
13. *Per* KENNEDY L.J. in *Oppenheimer* v. *Attenborough & Son*, [1908] 1 K.B. 221, C.A., at p. 231.
14. This may be the explanation of *Pearson* v. *Rose and Young, Ltd.*, [1951] 1 K.B. 275, C.A.: see Thornely, [1962] C.L.J. 139, 141.
15. The crucial factor may often be failure on the part of the transferee to ask for the log-book: *Per* SCRUTTON L.J. in *Folkes* v. *King*, [1923] 1 K.B. 282, C.A., at p. 300. But see *per* ORMEROD and WILLMER L.JJ. in *Stadium Finance, Ltd.* v. *Robbins*, [1962] 2 Q.B. 664, C.A., at pp. 672, 676.
16. *Contra* Atiyah, *Sale of Goods* (3rd Edn.) 148.

6 The effect of the exception

Where the requirements of s. 2 (1) are satisfied, that subsection provides that the disposition by the m.a.—

> "shall, subject to the provisions of this Act, be as valid as if he were expressly authorised by the owner of the goods to make the same".

Whilst s. 2 (1) uses the term "owner", it is submitted that its effect is to transfer only such title as the m.a.'s principal possesses[17]. Even this rule is subject to certain qualifications in the Act. First, it has already been seen how the F.A. restricts the rights of a pledgee to the extent of the value given by him at the time of the pledge[18]. Second, the F.A. enables the m.a. to create a lien over goods which he consigns to another in respect of "advances made to or for the use of" the m.a. by the consignee (s. 7).

In their *Twelfth Report*, the *Law Reform Committee* did not recommend any changes in this exception to the *nemo dat* rule[19]; but the changes they did recommend would appear to offer protection to transferees in the position of the buyers in both *Pearson* v. *Rose and Young, Ltd.* and *Stadium Finance, Ltd.* v. *Robbins*[20].

5 SELLERS IN POSSESSION[1]

The policy behind the provision about to be discussed is as follows: where the seller has sold the same goods to a number of people in succession, the first buyer to get actual possession of the goods or documents of title is to be preferred to the others, although he, perhaps immediately, parts with possession again. This new exception to the *nemo dat* rule was embodied in s. 8 of the F.A. 1889. Unfortunately, the provision was repeated in s. 25 (1) of the S.G.A. 1893 in almost identical language, no attempt being made to repeal the earlier formulation. This provision, with the extra words of the F.A. in italics[2], is as follows:

> "Where a person, having sold goods, continues, or is, in possession of the goods or of the documents of title[3] to the goods, the delivery or transfer by that person, or by a mercantile agent[4] acting for him, of the goods or documents of title under any sale, pledge, or other

---

17. See further below, pp. 219, 230.   18. See above, p. 211.
19. Cmnd. 2958, paras. 18, 40 (5).   20. See below, p. 229.
 1. Compare the unpaid seller's powers and rights of resale: below, pp. 368–369.
 2. The extra words still stand by reason of the S.G.A., s. 21 (2) (a), and note the difference in punctuation.
 3. See the discussions of "goods" and "documents of title" above, pp. 207–208.
 4. S.G.A., s. 25 (3) provides that the term "m.a." shall have the same meaning as in the F.A.; and that meaning is discussed above, pp. 204–206.

disposition[5] thereof, *or under any agreement for sale, pledge, or other disposition thereof*, to any person receiving the same in good faith and without notice of the previous sale, shall have the same effect as if the person making the delivery or transfer were expressly authorised by the owner of the goods to make the same".

Once again, the wording, and its judicial interpretation, requires careful analysis.

1 Seller in possession

This exception to the *nemo dat* rule only applies where a seller is in possession. Notice, first, the provision says "sold", not "agreed to sell": in the latter case, the seller could still pass a good title by virtue of his property in the goods[6]. Second, "possession" here has its ordinary commercial meaning, so that a seller may be in possession by an agent[7]. Third, the provision does not say that the seller need be in possession with the buyer's consent[8].

Most of the litigation in this provision has centred on the meaning of the phrase "continues, or is, in possession". In *Mitchell* v. *Jones*[9]

> X. sold and delivered a horse to the appellant. Thirteen days later, X. leased the horse from the appellant and then sold and delivered it to the respondent b.f.p. The New Zealand Supreme Court held that the respondent was not protected by their equivalent of s. 25 (1).

STOUT C.J. explained that the meaning of the phrase is[10]

> "first, that if a person sells goods and continues in possession, even though he has made a valid contract of sale, provided that he has not delivered them, he may to a *bona fide* buyer make a good title; and, secondly, the putting-in of the words 'or is in possession of the goods' was meant to apply to a case of this character: If a vendor had not the goods when he sold them, but they came into his possession afterwards, then he would have possession of the goods, and if he sold them to a *bona fide* purchaser he could make a good title to them".

The English Courts have similarly insisted that the provision will only operate where the seller is in possession *qua* seller: but they have extended this rule to cover the situation where there has been no actual delivery by the seller, merely a change in the nature of his possession.

---

5. The phrase "sale, pledge, or other disposition" is considered in relation to s. 2 (1) of the F.A.: see above, p. 211; and see below, pp. 225–226.
6. Compare buyers in possession, below, pp. 221–223.
7. See s. 1 (2) of the F.A., set out above, p. 206; and *per* BRANSON J. in *City Fur Manufacturing Co., Ltd.* v. *Fureenbond (Brokers), London, Ltd.*, [1937] 1 All E.R. 799, at p. 802.
8. Cf. ss. 2 (1) & 9 of the F.A.: see above, pp. 209–210, and below, pp. 223–225.
9. (1905), 24 N.Z.L.R. 932, S.C.   10. At p. 935.

In *Staffs. Motor Guarantee, Ltd.* v. *British Wagon, Co., Ltd.*[11] MACKIN-NON J. held that the dealer, who had remained in possession, could not pass a good title under s. 25 (1) because he was no longer in possession as seller, but in the capacity of hirer. This development received the approval of the Court of Appeal in *Eastern Distributors, Ltd.* v. *Goldring*[12], where the Court accepted without question that Murphy could not pass a good title under s. 25 (1) because the character of his possession had changed from that of seller to bailee.

Whilst paying lip-service to *Mitchell* v. *Jones*[9], these decisions clearly go far beyond that case; and it would appear that they have almost interpreted this exception to the *nemo dat* rule out of existence. Indeed, the only reported English case where a plea under s. 25 (1) was successful would appear to be *Union Transport Finance, Ltd.* v. *Ballardie*[13]: this was a very unusual case, and it would seem that on the facts the court accepted that the seller was still in possession as seller because he was not in possession in any other capacity. However, the Privy Council has now rejected the English case-law on this point, and has held that the disputed words refer, not to the nature of the seller's possession, but to the fact of his possession. In *Pacific Motor Auctions, Ltd.* v. *Motor Credits, Ltd.*[14]

> The respondent finance company entered into a stocking plan[15] with a New South Wales motor dealer, the terms of which were to some extent modified by the practice of the parties. When the dealer wished to raise money, he would arrange to sell to, and rehire from, the finance company specified vehicles, in which case the company would advance 90% of the price, this sum being repayable when the vehicles were sold[16]. In Nov. 1960, the dealer was in financial difficulties, and the company withdrew their consent to his selling any vehicle subject to the stocking plan. Subsequently, the dealer sought to appease another of his creditors, the appellant car auctioneer, by entering into the following arrangement after business hours one day[17]: the dealer agreed to sell to the auctioneer 29 cars, which were to be resold to the dealer if within 7 days he paid off a dishonoured cheque[16]. After the dealer became insolvent, it was

---

11. [1934] 2 K.B. 305: set out above, pp. 206–207. See also *Olds Discount, Ltd.* v. *Krett and Krett*, [1940] 2 K.B. 117.
12. [1957] 2 Q.B. 600; [1957] 2 All E.R. 525, C.A.: set out above, p. 189. See Goodhart (1957), 73 L.Q.R. 455, 459.
13. [1937] 1 K.B. 510; [1937] 1 All E.R. 420.
14. [1965] A.C. 867; [1965] 2 All E.R. 105, P.C.
15. Explained below, p. 282.
16. In English Law, both these sales and re-hirings would probably be void under the Bills of Sale Act, 1882: see below, pp. 297–300.
17. The trial judge found that this disposition was not in the o.c.b.; and the point was conceded before the P.C., who expressly agreed that it was not (p. 890). For the effect of this on mercantile agency, see above, p. 212.

ascertained that 16 of the cars sold and delivered to the auctioneer were subject to the stocking plan: but the auctioneer pleaded that he had obtained a good title under the N.S.W. equivalents of (1) s. 25 (1) of the S.G.A. and (2) estoppel under s. 21 (1) of the S.G.A.

The Privy Council held that the auctioneer had obtained a good title under the first head, and expressly reserved their opinion on the second point[18]. On the former point, Lord PEARCE argued as follows[19]:

> "The fact that a person having sold goods is described as *continuing* in possession would seem to indicate that the section is not contemplating as relevant a change in the legal title under which he possesses. For the legal title by which he is in possession *cannot* continue . . . The possession continues unchanged, but the legal title under which he possesses has changed . . . The object of the section is to protect an innocent purchaser who is deceived by the vendor's physical possession of the goods or documents and who is inevitably unaware of legal rights which fetter the apparent power to dispose".

His Lordship therefore concluded that the *Staffs Motor Case*[1] (and *Goldring's Case*[2] in so far as it followed it) were wrongly decided[3]. This new criterion of continuity of physical possession would seem to be both simpler and more fair, and will restore some worthwhile content to the provision: if it is adopted by the English courts, the risk will usually be on the first buyer who has left his seller in possession.

2 Delivery and disposition to a *bona fide* transferee

As the intention of the legislature was to protect the first transferee to take possession[4], the exception is only expressed to protect a person to whom there is a "delivery or transfer"[5]. If the seller in possession makes successive dispositions to different persons, the first to obtain a "delivery or transfer" obtains title under the exception; but, if none of them takes delivery or transfer, the first transferee obtains title under the *nemo dat* rule[6].

Two questions arise in relation to whether the disposition is within the provision. First, since the formula "under any sale, pledge, or other disposition" is also to be found in ss. 2 (1) and 8 of the F.A., does

---

18. See above, p. 191.
19. At p. 886. Part of this reasoning was cited with approval in the *Twelfth Report of the Law Reform Committee* (Cmnd. 2958), para. 20.
1. [1934] 2 K.B. 305.
2. [1957] 2 Q.B. 600; [1957] 2 All E.R. 525, C.A.
3. At p. 889. See also Atiyah, *Sale of Goods* (3rd Edn.) 156.
4. See above, p. 215.
5. "Delivery" seems to refer to goods, and "transfer" to documents of title. It is doubtful whether a transfer of goods by deed falls within these expressions: *Kitto* v. *Bilbie* (1895), 72 L.T. 266.
6. *Nicholson* v. *Harper*, [1895] 2 Ch. 415.

the formula have the same meaning in all three cases[7]?   Second, what significance should be attached to the fact that s. 8 of the F.A. also refers to "any agreement for sale, pledge, or other disposition", whereas s. 25 (1) seems to require that the disposition purport to transfer the property in the goods[8]?

Lastly, both ss. 8 and 25 (1) are only expressed to operate in favour of

> "any person receiving the [goods] in good faith and without notice of the previous sale".

A similar requirement was discussed in relation to mercantile agency[9], and, by the same reasoning, the onus of proof should similarly be on the purchaser.   In *Pacific Motor Auctions, Ltd.* v. *Motor Credits Ltd.*[10], the Privy Council rejected the argument that, because the dealer was a m.a., the disposition must be in the o.c.b.; and accepted the finding of the trial judge that the auctioneer was a b.f.p.[11].

3 Effect of the exception

Where the requirements of ss. 8 and 25 (1) are satisfied, it is provided that the disposition with delivery to a b.f.p.

> "shall have the same effect as if the person making the delivery or transfer were expressly authorised by the owner of the goods to make the same".

Suppose X. steals goods from O., and then sells them successively to A. and B., delivering them to B.:

Presumably, the term "owner" refers to the person with the property in the goods under the disposition from X. to A., so that B. acquires no better title than X. has, and the best title remains in O.[12].

---

7. See above, p. 211.   Does it make any difference that ss. 2–7 of the F.A. may not be applicable here?—see below, p. 224.
8. Compare ss. 9 and 25 (2), considered below, pp. 225–226.
9. See above, p. 214.
10. [1965] A.C. 867; [1965] 2 All E.R. 105, P.C.
11. But the fact that a m.a. disposes of goods outside his o.c.b. may affect his transferee's *bona fides*: see above, p. 214.
12. Compare above, p. 215, and below, p. 230.

6 BUYERS IN POSSESSION

The converse situation to that of the seller in possession is covered by s. 9 of the F.A. and s. 25 (2) of the S.G.A. The provision, with the extra words of the F.A. in italics[13], is as follows:

> "Where a person, having bought or agreed to buy goods, obtains with the consent of the seller possession[14] of the goods or the documents of title[15] to the goods, the delivery or transfer by that person or by a mercantile agent[16] acting for him, of the goods or documents of title, under any sale, pledge, or other disposition thereof, *or under any agreement for sale, pledge, or other disposition thereof*, to any person receiving the same in good faith and without notice of any lien or other right of the original seller in respect of the goods, shall have the same effect as if the person making the delivery or transfer were a mercantile agent in possession of the goods or documents of title with the consent of the owner".

Amazingly, the b.f.p. receives further statutory protection from both s. 10 of the F.A. and the proviso to s. 47 of the S.G.A., which are both expressed to apply—

> "where a document of title to goods has been lawfully transferred to any[17] person as buyer or owner of the goods, and that person transfers the document to a person who takes the document in good faith and for valuable consideration . . ."

Having made it clear that they apply to the same situation, ss. 10 and 47 then differ markedly in the terms in which they seek to protect the b.f.p. Section 10 of the F.A. continues—

> "the last-mentioned transfer shall have the same effect for defeating any vendor's lien or right of stoppage in transitu as the transfer of a bill of lading has for defeating the right of stoppage in transitu".

On the other hand, s. 47 of the S.G.A. says that—

> "if such last-mentioned transfer was by way of sale, the unpaid seller's right of lien . . . or stoppage in transitu is defeated, and if such last-mentioned transfer was made by way of pledge or other disposition for value, the unpaid seller's right of lien . . . or stoppage in transitu can only be exercised subject to the rights of the transferee".

This extraordinary duplication of stautory provisions must now be considered in detail.

---

13. See above, p. 215, note 2.   14. See above, p. 216.
15. See the discussion of "goods" and "documents of title" above, pp. 207–209.
16. See above, p. 215, note 4.
17. Section 10 says "a" instead of "any".

1 Buyer in possession

Sections 9 and 25 (2) are only expressed to be applicable where a person has "bought or agreed to buy". This phrase has given rise to two problems in trying to determine who is a buyer for the purposes of the provision.

First, there is the question of the effect of the word "bought", which implies that the property has passed. If a person has bought goods, and obtained possession of them with the consent of the seller, then at first sight it seems that he should be able to pass a good title by virtue of his property and possession, no exception to the *nemo dat* rule being required. However, it has been suggested that the effect of the exception is that the buyer in possession of his own goods can only pass a good title in conformity with the terms of the exception[18]. Such a result would be startling; and there are two other possible explanations. First, because a good title is only passed under the exception where its terms are complied with, it does not follow that where its terms are not complied with a good title cannot be passed in any other way. Second, it may be that the words "bought or" are redundant, though it has been shown that there may be circumstances where these words are required to pass a good title under ss. 9 and 25 (2)[19].

The second problem involves the meaning of the words "agreed to buy". It is tempting to assume that where the seller has agreed to sell the buyer has agreed to buy; but this will not necessarily be so, because there can clearly be an agreement to sell without any agreement to buy— as where the buyer purchases an option[20]. An early illustration of an "agreement to buy" is to be found in *Lee* v. *Butler*[1].

> Under an agreement made between X. and a furniture dealer, X. was to take immediate possession of some furniture in return for a promise to pay "as and by way of rent" £1 on May 6th and £96 on the following August 1st. *Inter alia*, the agreement provided that, if X. removed the goods, the dealer might repossess them[2], and all sums previously paid should be appropriated to rent only; but, if X. performed all the terms of the agreement, the rent should cease, and the goods should then, but not before, become the property of X. Before all the instalments were paid, X. sold the furniture to a b.f.p. The Court of Appeal found that X. had "agreed to buy" the furniture, and therefore passed a good title to the b.f.p. under s. 9 of the F.A.

---

18. Atiyah, *Sale of Goods* (3rd Edn.) 158.
19. Smith (1963), 7 J.S.P.T.L. 225, 226.
20. The question whether "sale or return" transactions fall within s. 25 (2) is discussed above, p. 181.
 1. [1893] 2 Q.B. 318, C.A.
 2. This licence to seize probably would not infringe the Bills of Sale Act 1882: see above, p. 10.

This decision immediately threw the instalment credit trade into a turmoil, and the new form of contract drafted with an eye to avoiding the consequences of this decision was litigated in *Helby* v. *Matthews*[3].

> The terms of the agreement between the dealer and customer were somewhat similar to those in the previous case: the customer agreed to pay 10/6 per month as rent for hire of a piano, and the property was not to pass until 36 of these instalments had been paid. However, the agreement further provided that the customer might at any time determine the hiring by delivering the piano to the dealer, upon which he should remain liable for all arrears of rent. During the continuance of the agreement, the customer pledged the piano to the defendant, who took b.f. and for value, and pleaded title under s. 9 of the F.A. The House of Lords unanimously held, reversing the Court of Appeal, that the pawnbroker had not obtained a good title.

Lord MACNAGHTEN explained[4]:

> "The contract . . . on the part of the dealer was a contract of hiring coupled with a conditional contract or undertaking to sell. On the part of the customer it was a contract of hiring only until the time came for making the last payment. It may be that at the inception of the transaction both parties expected that the agreement would run its full course, and that the piano would change hands in the end. But an expectation, however confident and however well-founded, does not amount to an agreement, and even an agreement between two parties operative only during the pleasure of one of them is no agreement on his part at law".

Their Lordships distinguished *Lee* v. *Butler* on the grounds that in that case, as soon as the agreement was made, there was a binding agreement to buy on the part of X. and he had no option to return the goods[5]. The effect of this reasoning is to draw a sharp distinction between two very similar transactions on the basis of whether the consumer has agreed to buy: if he has, there is a conditional sale within s. 1 (2) of the S.G.A., and the customer can therefore pass a good title to a b.f.p. under s. 25 (2); but, if he has not agreed to buy[6], the transaction is not a conditional sale and the customer cannot pass a good title under this exception to the *nemo dat* rule. It has already been pointed out that the H.P.A. has settled doubts as to whether that legislation applied to conditional sales by making express provision for such transactions[7].

---

3. [1895] A.C. 471, H.L. The result is the same even if the customer gives a promissory note as collateral security: *Modern Light Cars, Ltd.* v. *Seals*, [1934] 1 K.B. 32.
4. At p. 482. The reasoning is criticised by Atiyah, *Sale of Goods* (3rd Edn.) 5–6.
5. See also *Hull Ropes, Co., Ltd.* v. *Adams* (1895), 65 L.J.Q.B. 114.
6. Or his agreement to buy is void *ab initio*: see above, p. 198.
7. See above, p. 14.

In the course of a partial assimilation of conditional sales and h.p. transactions, the Act sought to bring some conditional sales within the principle of *Helby* v. *Matthews*. Accordingly, s. 54 of the H.P.A. 1965 provides:

> "For the purposes of section 9 of the Factors Act 1889, and of section 25 (2) of the Sale of Goods Act 1893 . . ., the buyer under a conditional sale agreement shall be deemed not to be a person who has bought or agreed to buy goods".

Whilst it is true that the H.P.A. 1964 does introduce an entirely new exception to the *nemo dat* rule[8], the effect of s. 54 is to reduce the statutory protection of the b.f.p. by denying him the protection of a much wider exception in those cases falling within the ambit of the H.P.A. 1965. Not only does this run counter to the general trend of legislation[9], but it adds further complication to an already unduly difficult branch of the law[10].

2 The seller's consent to the buyer's possession

Unlike the provision in respect of sellers in possession[11], the present exception to the *nemo dat* rule is only expressed to operate where the buyer is in possession with the consent of the seller. It will be recalled that consent to possession is similarly required in the case of the mercantile agency exception[12]; and in *Du Jardin* v. *Beadman Brothers, Ltd.*[13], SELLERS J. said:

> "whatever interpretation is given to the word 'consent' in s. 2 [of the Factors Act] must, I think, also be given to the word in . . . s. 25 of the Sale of Goods Act . . ."

On the other hand, s. 2 of the F.A. does fall under sub-heading "Dispositions by Mercantile Agents", which might imply that the provisions of s. 2 do not apply buyers in possession. This point was taken by the House of Lords in *Inglis* v. *Robertson*[14], an appeal from Scotland. In this case

> A wine merchant contracted to buy from R. whisky then lying in a bonded warehouse[15]. Afterwards, the merchant had the whisky transferred to his own name in the books of the warehousekeeper, and obtained a delivery order from the latter. The merchant then pledged the delivery order to I.; but R. subsequently claimed the

---

8. See below, p. 230.   9. Atiyah, *Sale of Goods* (3rd Edn.) 160.
10. The *Twelfth Report of the Law Reform Committee* (Cmnd. 2958), para. 28, thought it inappropriate for the Report to recommend any changes in this area.
11. See above, p. 216.   12. See above, pp. 209-210.
13. [1952] 2 Q.B. 712, at p. 716.   14. [1898] A.C. 616, H.L.
15. The property in the whisky would appear to have passed to the wine merchant: see *per* Lord WATSON, at p. 626.

goods as unpaid seller. I. admitted that the pledge of the goods was defeated by his failure to notify the warehousekeeper[16], but pleaded title under ss. 3 and 9 of the F.A.

The House of Lords held that Scots law applied. Their Lordships accepted that the F.A. was applicable to Scotland by reason of an Act of 1890[17], but unanimously found for the unpaid seller on the following grounds:

(1) that the pledge of the documents did not amount to a pledge of the goods under s. 3, which provides that

"A pledge of the documents of title to goods shall be deemed to be a pledge of the goods",

because ss. 2–7 of the F.A. were only applicable where the transferor was a m.a. (which the wine merchant was not)[18]; and

(2) that s. 9 was not applicable to the present circumstances[19].

Since this decision, the English Court of Appeal has twice held that the issue of consent in ss. 9 and 25 (2) is subject to ss. 2 (2), (3) and (4) of the F.A.[20]; and it is submitted that these decisions will probably be followed in England[1].

Sections 9 and 25 (2) are expressed to cover only those situations where the buyer

"*obtains* with the consent of the seller possession of the goods or the documents of title to the goods . . ."

The meaning of these words was considered by the House of Lords in *Inglis* v. *Robertson*, where their Lordships concluded that s. 9 did not confer on the pledgee, I., a title free of the rights of the unpaid seller, R., because the wine merchant did not obtain the documents of title either from the seller or with his consent, but "in his own right and in his own name"[2]. However it is difficult to see why the warehousekeeper in this case was not treated as the agent of the seller to issue the documents in which event it could be said that the documents were issued by and with the consent of the seller's agent. Thus it seems unlikely that the English courts will follow *Inglis* v. *Robertson*.

In those circumstances where the b.f.p. is relying on the fact that his transferor obtained possession of the documents of title with the con-

---

16. Section 29 (3) of the S.G.A.: set out below, p. 265.
17. The Factors (Scotland) Act 1890.
18. At pp. 624, 628, 630: see *Benjamin on Sale* (8th Edn.) 40, 923.
19. See below.
20. *Cahn* v. *Pockett's Bristol Channel Steam Packet, Ltd.*, [1899] 1 Q.B. 643, C.A.: set out below, pp. 226–227; *Newtons of Wembley, Ltd.* v. *Williams*, [1965] 1 Q.B. 560; [1964] 5 All E.R. 532, C.A.: set out below, p. 228.
 1. But see the recommendations of the *Law Reform Committee*, below, p. 229.
 2. *Per* Lord WATSON at p. 629. See also *per* Lord HERSCHELL, at p. 630.

sent of the seller, ss. 9 and 25 (2) are partially duplicated by s. 10 of the
F.A. and the proviso to s. 47 of the S.G.A. The latter two provisions
are expressed to apply

> "where a document of title to goods has been *lawfully transferred* to
> any person as buyer or *owner* of the goods . . ."

Whilst the terminology employed suggests that ss. 10 and 47 were
intended to be applicable only where a seller transfers to a buyer a
document of title already in existence, they have been interpreted to
cover the situation where the document is created by the seller and
issued to the buyer[3]. As ss. 9 and 25 (2) apply whether the document
of title is issued[4] or otherwise transferred by the seller[5], there is a considerable overlap between the two sets of provisions. Two questions
remain in relation to ss. 10 and 47. First, does the word "lawfully"
import the absence of criminal conduct, or merely actual consent as
under ss. 9 and 25 (2)[6]? Second, does not the reference to "owner"
suggest that it is sufficient that the buyer acquires the document of title
by reason of his ownership[7]?

3 Delivery and disposition to a *bona fide* transferee

1. Delivery and disposition. All four provisions appear to require a
delivery or transfer by the seller to the buyer of the goods or documents
of title: and, as documents of title are normally transferred by delivery,
or by endorsement and delivery, the sections envisage that there will be
a delivery of the goods, or of the documents of title representing them[8].
However, under ss. 10 and 47 one and the same document of title must
be transferred (or issued) to the "buyer or owner", and that same document must then be transferred to the b.f. transferee. Sections 9 and
25 (2) may, however, apply even where there are two separate documents, the one transferred (or issued) to the "buyer or owner" and the
other transferred (or issued) by that person[9]. Another possible distinction is that ss. 10 and 47 specifically require that the disposition by the

---

3. *Ant. Jurgens Margarinefabrieken* v. *Dreyfus & Co.*, [1914] 3 K.B. 40.
4. *D. F. Mount, Ltd.* v. *Jay and Jay (Provisions), Ltd.*, [1960] 1 Q.B. 159;
   [1959] 3 All E.R. 307: set out above, pp. 186–187.
5. *Cahn* v. *Pockett's Bristol Channel Steam Packet, Ltd.*, [1899] 1 Q.B. 643, C.A.:
   set out below, pp. 226–227.
6. See above and *per* COLLINS L.J. in *Cahn's Case* (above), at p. 665. Compare
   the argument on "lawfully" in s. 43 (1) (b) of the S.G.A.: see below, pp.
   322–323.
7. But see *Inglis* v. *Robertson and Baxter*, [1898] A.C. 616, H.L.
8. But see s. 11 of the F.A., which seems to suggest that there may be a transfer
   by endorsement alone.
9. *D. F. Mount, Ltd.* v. *Jay and Jay (Provisions), Ltd.* (above). But see criticisms by Schmitthoff, *Sale of Goods* (2nd Edn.) 170; Borrie (1960), 23
   M.L.R. 100.

buyer should be for valuable consideration, but it is not clear that ss. 9 and 25 (2) impose a similar requirement[10].

2. *The "bona fide" transferee.* Sections 9 and 25 (2) speak of the goods or documents of title being delivered or transferred to—

"any person receiving the same in good faith[11] and without notice of any lien or other right of the original seller in respect of the goods . . ."

As in the cases of sellers in possession and mercantile agency, it seems that the burden of proof is on the transferee[12]. Neither the F.A. nor the S.G.A. defines "notice", so that this matter is left to the common law[13]. According to *Benjamin*[14]

"either knowledge, or the means of knowledge to which a party wilfully shuts his eyes, is enough, but mere suspicion is not enough".

Sections 9 and 25 (2) require that the transferee should take *bona fide* and without notice of the original seller's rights, but ss. 10 and 47 do not require an absence of such notice[15]; and it has been accepted by the courts that *bona fides* may, but will not necessarily, be defeated by notice[16]. Thus, it would appear that ss. 10 and 47 are wider than ss. 9 and 25 (2) in that a b.f.p. with notice may acquire a good title under the former, but not the latter, provisions[17]. Finally, there is the question of what knowledge on the part of the b.f. transferee is fatal to a claim under ss. 9 and 25 (2). The provisions envisage a sale by A. to B., followed by a disposition by B. to C. It is argued below that "original seller" refers to A.[18]; and it is clear that "lien or other right" includes the similar rights available under s. 39 (2) to an unpaid seller who has retained the property in the goods[19].

4 Effect of the exception

The effect of all four statutory provisions is neatly illustrated by *Cahn* v. *Pockett's Channel, Ltd.*[20].

S. contracted to sell ten tons of copper to B. delivery to be made at Rotterdam, and payment to be by B.'s acceptance of a bill of exchange. After shipping the copper, S. forwarded to B., the bill of

---

10. See *Thomas Graham, Ltd.* v. *Glenrothes Corporation*, [1968] S.L.T. 2; and also above, p. 211.
11. See above, p. 191. 12. See above, pp. 214, 219.
13. See *per* TENTERDEN L.C.J. in *Evans* v. *Truman* (1831), 1 Mood. & R. 10.
14. At p. 38.
15. See the explanation in *Chalmers' Sale of Goods* (15th Edn.) 227.
16. *Pacific Motor Auctions, Ltd.* v. *Motor Credits, Ltd.*, [1965] A.C. 867; [1965] 2 All E.R. 105, P.C.: set out above, pp. 217–218.
17. See Schmitthoff, *Sale of Goods* (2nd Edn.) 168. Doubted by Atiyah, *Sale of Goods* (3rd Edn.) 161.   18. At p. 230.
19. *Cahn* v. *Pockett's Bristol Channel Steam Packet, Ltd.*, [1899] 1 Q.B. 643, C.A.   20. (Above.)

lading and an acceptance. Meanwhile, B. had contracted to sell ten tons of copper to the plaintiff, and had then become insolvent. On the arrival of the documents, B. did not accept the draft, but transferred the bill of lading to the plaintiff, who took b.f. and without notice of S.'s rights. S. stopped the copper in transit, and the plaintiff claimed title under ss. 9 and 10 of the F.A. and ss. 25 (2) and 47 of the S.G.A.

The Court of Appeal agreed with MATHEW J. that the delivery of the bill of lading was conditional on acceptance of the draft, and that therefore s. 19 (3) of the S.G.A. prevented the property from passing to B.[1]. However, MATHEW J. had further held that such a conditional consent to B.'s possession of the bill of lading did not fall within s. 25 (2) of the S.G.A.; and on this point he was unanimously reversed by the Court of Appeal, who held that the plaintiff had obtained a good title under all four of the provisions. Their Lordships argued that it was sufficient if there was an actual consent, which could not be withdrawn[2].

Where the conditions laid down by ss. 9 and 25 (2) are satisfied, it is provided thereby that the disposition by the buyer

> "shall have the same effect as if the person making the delivery or transfer were a mercantile agent in possession of the goods or documents of title with the consent of the owner".

This is an obvious reference back to s. 2 (1) of the F.A.[3], but gives no indication how much of that provision was being incorporated[4]. There were at least two possibilities. First, the effect might be to incorporate merely the result of s. 2 (1), so that the disposition by the buyer

> "shall be as valid as if he were expressly authorised by the owner of the goods to make the same".

If so, the result would be the same as in the case of sales by a seller in possession[5]. Second, it might be read so that a disposition by the buyer

> "*made by him when acting in the ordinary course of business of a mercantile agent* shall . . . be as valid as if he were expressly authorised by the owner of the goods to make the same".

The vital difference between the two is whether the buyer is required to dispose of the goods in the o.c.b. of a m.a.; and the Court of Appeal seems to have changed its mind on this point. In *Lee* v. *Butler*[6] the court appeared to take the first view, there being no hint in that case of such a requirement; but in *Newtons of Wembley, Ltd.* v. *Williams*[7] the court took the second view.

---

1. See above, p. 182. 2. See above, pp. 223–225.
3. See above, p. 203.
4. The point was left open in *Cahn's Case* (above).
5. See above, p. 219.   6. [1893] 2 Q.B. 318, C.A.: set out above, p. 221.
7. [1965] 1 Q.B. 560; [1964] 3 All E.R. 532, C.A.

On June 15th, the plaintiff sold and delivered a Sunbeam car to A. for £935, it being agreed that the property should not pass until A.'s cheque was cleared. On June 18th, the plaintiff found that A.'s cheque would not be met, and immediately took steps to try to recover the car. In July, B. bona fide agreed to buy the car from A. in the Warren St. car market; and thereafter B. sold the car to the defendant. In the plaintiff's action to recover the car, the issue thus turned on whether B. had a good title to transfer to the defendant.

Both at first instance[8] and in the Court of Appeal it was held that A. had only obtained a voidable title which had been avoided within a few days of June 18th[9]; but the Courts nevertheless decided that B. had acquired a good title under the F.A. In the course of examining ss. 2, 8 and 9 of that Act, PEARSON L.J. considered that the difference in wording between ss. 8 and 9 must have been intended to bring about some difference in result because the difference in wording was repeated in s. 25 of the S.G.A. He pointed out that the buyer in possession might or might not be a m.a., and continued[10]:

> "When the provisions of s. 2 are applied to the s. 9 position of a buyer in possession, this is the prima facie result: if the transaction is made by the person concerned when acting in the ordinary course of business of a mercantile agent, the transaction is validated: on the other hand, if the transaction is made by him when not acting in the ordinary course of business of a mercantile agent, the transaction is not validated".

On this basis, the Court of Appeal agreed that the determination of the plaintiff's consent was irrelevant under s. 9 by reason of s. 2 (2) of the F.A.[11]; that the test of whether a disposition was made in the o.c.b. for the purpose of s. 9 was the same as that under s. 2[12]; and that the sale by A. in Warren St., where there was an established second-hand car market, was made in the o.c.b.[13].

It is clear that *Newtons of Wembley Ltd.* v. *Williams* is a very unusual case in that A. happened to sell the car in the Warren St. car market. Can the converse be deduced: that, if A. had not appeared to B. to be a m.a. acting in the o.c.b., then B. would not have obtained a good title? Such a conclusion would severely restrict the operation of ss. 9 and 25 (2), and would appear to have rendered unnecessary the development of h.p. on the basis of the device sanctioned in *Helby* v. *Matthews*[14]. On the other hand, such a view would appear to be incompatible with *Oppenheimer* v. *Attenborough*[15], where the b.f.p. thought that the

---

8. [1964] 2 All E.R. 135, DAVIES L.J.   9. See above, p. 201.
10. At p. 578. See also *per* SELLERS L.J., at pp. 574–575.
11. Set out above, p. 209.   12. See above, pp. 211–214.
13. *Per* SELLERS and PEARSON L.JJ., at pp. 575, 580.
14 [1895] A.C. 471, H.L.: see above, pp. 12, 222.
15. [1908] 1 K.B. 221, C.A.: set out above, p. 212.

broker was acting as principal; so that, even if ss. 9 and 25 (2) do require the disposition to be in the o.c.b. as in s. 2 (1), this will not unduly restrict the scope of the exception. Alternatively, it has been suggested that the requirement that the disposition is in the o.c.b. should be confined to those cases where the buyer is in fact a m.a.[16]. However, the *Twelfth Report of the Law Reform Committee* prefers the approach in *Lee* v. *Butler*[17]: it recommends that, where the buyer's voidable title has been avoided, he should no longer be regarded as being in possession with consent for the purposes of s. 25 (2)[18]; but that the b.f.p. should no longer be required to obtain the goods from one who appeared to be acting in the o.c.b. of a m.a.[19]. The Report pointed out that, under these recommendations, the b.f.p. in the *Williams Case* could not claim the benefit of ss. 9 and 25 (2), but would obtain a good title under two of their other recommendations[20].

The effect of ss. 9 and 25 (2) may be compared with that of ss. 10 and 47. Section 10 of the F.A. provides that the disposition

> "shall have the same effect for defeating any vendor's lien or right of stoppage in transitu as the transfer of a bill of lading has for defeating the right of stoppage in transitu".

Presumably, the legislature intended by this formula that the disposition should override the vendor's right of lien or stoppage[1]; but it made its intention rather clearer in s. 47 of the S.G.A., which provides that

> "if . . . [the] . . . transfer was by way of sale the unpaid seller's right of lien . . . or stoppage in transitu is defeated, and if . . . [the] . . . transfer was made by way of pledge or other disposition for value, the unpaid seller's right of lien . . . or stoppage in transitu can only be exercised subject to the rights of the transferee".

In *Cahn* v. *Pockett's Channel, Ltd.*[2] the Court of Appeal rejected the argument that s. 47 contains the only circumstances in which the seller's rights of lien and stoppage could be defeated; and it would therefore seem that s. 47 merely repeats in part the effect of ss. 9 and 25 (2), making it clear that the rights of the owner are overridden *pro tanto* by the disposition.

Finally, the range of operation of this exception must be considered. Suppose X. steals goods from O. and sells them to A., A. agrees to sell

---

16. Atiyah, *Sale of Goods* (3rd Edn.) 163. Yet s. 25 (2) is probably only needed where the buyer is not a m.a.
17. [1893] 2 Q.B. 318, C.A.
18. See above, p. 224. 19. (Cmnd. 2958), paras. 23, 24.
20. *Ibid.*: (1) voidable title—above, p. 198; (2) market overt—below, p. 236.
1. See also s. 12 (2) of the F.A. Was this expectation defeated by *Lyons* v. *Hoffnung* (1890), 15 App. Cas. 391, P.C.? And see below, pp. 234.
2. [1899] 1 Q.B. 643, C.A., *per* A. L. SMITH and COLLINS L.JJ., at pp. 657, 665.

them to B., and B. acquires possession and sells to C., who resells to D.:

$$O. \qquad X.——A. \frac{agrees}{to\ sell} B.——C.——D.$$

Several questions arise. First, what title does C. get? It has been argued that a b.f.p. from B. would acquire O.'s title[3]. However, it is submitted that when ss. 9 and 25 (2) refer at the end to "the owner", it means the person from whom B. agrees to buy the goods, i.e. A., so that under these provisions C. acquires A.'s title and that best title still remains in O.[4]. Second, what is the effect if C. acts in bad faith? On the analogy of *Caldwell's Case*[5], it is arguable that D. could claim the protection of ss. 9 and 25 (2) as the *first* b.f.p. and thereby obtain A.'s title; but perhaps the better view is that the provisions can only operate where B.'s transferee, i.e. C., is *bona fide*[6]. Third, would it make any difference if both B. and C. had only agreed to buy?

7 SALES OF MOTOR VEHICLES[7]

The decision in *Helby* v. *Matthews*[8] to the effect that a hirer under a h.p. agreement could not pass a good title under ss. 9 and 25 (2) is particularly likely to work hardship on a b.f.p. of a motor vehicle and its log-book from the hirer. Accordingly, Parliament introduced a new exception to the *nemo dat* rule in Part 3 of the H.P.A. 1964; and this provision is still in force today, as amended by Schedule 5 of the H.P.A. 1965. Unfortunately, in order to keep this new exception within the ambit of the mischief at which it was aimed, it proved necessary to draft it in extremely complex language, running to some four pages of the Statute Book[9].

The scope of the exception is set out in s. 27 (1), which says that:

"The provisions of this section shall have effect where a motor vehicle has been let under a hire-purchase agreement, or has been agreed to be sold under a conditional sale agreement, and, at a time

---

3. Cornish (1964), 27 M.L.R. 472, 477.
4. This view has the merit of leaving in force the ordinary rule that nobody can get a better title than O. It also achieves a consistency of result with the exceptions previously considered: see above, pp. 191, 202, 215, 219.
5. [1965] 1 Q.B. 525, C.A.: see above, p. 202.
6. See *per* DAVIES L.J. (at first instance) in the *Williams Case*, [1964] 2 All E.R. 135, at p. 139.
7. See generally Goode, *H.P. Law & Practice* (2nd Edn.) 617–630; Guest, *Law of H.P.*, paras. 757–771.
8. [1895] A.C. 471, H.L.: set out above, p. 222.
9. The *Twelfth Report of the Law Reform Committee* (Cmnd. 2958), para. 27, asks whether it is necessary to distinguish between motor vehicles and other goods. One might go further, and ask whether it is necessary to have an exception of this complexity at all.

before the property in the vehicle has become vested in the hirer or buyer, he disposes of the vehicle to another person".

Whilst the terms "hire-purchase" and "conditional sale" are to have the same meaning as in s. 1 of the H.P.A. 1965[10], the other restrictions of Part 1 of the H.P.A. 1965 are not applicable, so that s. 27 (1) applies whatever the value of the goods and whether or not the hirer or buyer is a body corporate[11]. Section 27 is expressed to take effect notwithstanding anything in s. 21 of the S.G.A., but

> "without prejudice to the provisions of the Factors Acts . . . or any other enactment enabling the apparent owner of goods to dispose of them as if he were the true owner". (s. 27 (5).)

Finally, it should be noticed that s. 27 (1) is only expressed to operate where a motor vehicle[12] is disposed of by a hirer or buyer under a h.p. or conditional sale agreement[13]. This insistence on an agreement means that s. 27 can have no application if the proposal form put forward by the hirer or buyer is not accepted[14], or where that agreement is void[15]; but that it can apply where the agreement is merely voidable[16]. It is unclear for how long a person is to be deemed a "hirer or buyer" for the purposes of s. 27. Section 29 (4) explicitly states that such a person is deemed to be a "hirer or buyer" for the purposes of s. 27 "whether the agreement has before (the time of his disposition) been terminated or not", including the situation where the goods are subject to a postponed order for delivery[17]. Whilst s. 29 (4) seems to suggest that once a person has become a "hirer or buyer" he is always to be deemed to be one for the purposes of s. 27, it has been suggested that this must be read in the light of the mischief at which the provision is aimed, and that s. 27 should no longer be applicable once the owner or seller has resumed possession of the motor vehicle[18].

Once the ambit of the exception had been defined in s. 27 (1), the Act then drew a sharp distinction between "a private purchaser" and "a trade or finance purchaser", with the intention that this new exception to the *nemo dat* rule should protect the consumer, but not persons in the business of disposing of vehicles—the latter could, and usually

---

10. See above, p. 14.   11. Compare above, p. 30.
12. As defined by s. 29 (1).
13. It obviously does not apply to a disposal by a person who has stolen the goods from the hirer or buyer: see Atiyah, *Sale of Goods* (3rd Edn.) 167; Guest, *Law of H.P.* 760.
14. See above, p. 35, *et seq.*
15. See above, pp. 37, 198.
16. What if the agreement is illegal, or "void" under the Infants Relief Act 1874?
17. See below, p. 340.
18. See Goode, *H.P. Law & Practice* (2nd Edn.) 620; Guest, *Law of H.P.*, para. 759.

would, protect himself by checking with H.P. Information Ltd.[19].
Section 29 (2) provides that

> "In this Part of this Act 'trade or finance purchaser' means a pur-
> chaser who, at the time of the disposition made to him, carries on a
> business which consists, wholly or partly,—
>   (a) of purchasing motor vehicles for the purpose of offering or
> exposing them for sale, or
>   (b) of providing finance by purchasing motor vehicles for the
> purpose of letting them under hire-purchase agreements or agreeing
> to sell them under conditional sale agreements,
> and 'private purchaser' means a purchaser who, at the time of the
> disposition made to him, does not carry on any such business".

The obvious examples of the two categories of "trade or finance"
purchasers are motor dealers and finance companies[20].

1 Dispositions to private purchasers

Section 27 (2) provides:

> "Where the disposition referred to in the preceding subsection is to
> a private purchaser, and he is a purchaser of the motor vehicle in
> good faith and without notice of the hire-purchase agreement or
> conditional sale agreement, that disposition shall have effect as if
> the title of the owner or seller to the vehicle had been vested in
> the hirer or buyer immediately before that disposition".

1. The disposition. According to s. 29 (1), the term "disposition"

> "means any sale or contract of sale (including a conditional sale
> agreement), any letting under a hire-purchase agreement and any
> transfer of the property in goods in pursuance of a provision in that
> behalf contained in a hire-purchase agreement, and includes any
> transaction purporting to be a disposition (as so defined) . . ."

This definition gives s. 27 an effect which is both wider than that of
s. 25 (2) of the S.G.A. in that it does not require a delivery, and narrower
in that it does not cover pledges and liens.

2. To a private purchaser. According to s. 29 (3),

> "a person becomes a purchaser of a motor vehicle if, and at the
> time when, a disposition of the vehicle is made to him . . .".

Two problems arise here. First, is it sufficient merely to determine
whether a person is "a trade or finance purchaser" at the time of the
disposition to him; or must he also purchase in his business capacity[1]?

---

19. See above, p. 34.
20. What if a finance company only operated by way of credit sale agreements?
    1. See Goode, *H.P. Law & Practice* (2nd Edn.) 622. Cf. s. 2 (1) of the F.A.:
    see above, pp. 206–207.

Second, "disposition" is defined in s. 29 (1) in such a way that there may be two dispositions in the case of a h.p. agreement: (1) when the contract is made; and (2) when the option is exercised. What is the position if the hirer is a motor dealer at the time he signs the agreement, but not when he exercises his option; or *vice versa*[2]?

3. *In good faith, and without notice.* A private purchaser cannot obtain the benefit of s. 27 unless he takes in good faith and without notice of the prior agreement[3]; nor can he pass a good title under s. 27 even to one who does satisfy these requirements[4]. "Good faith" presumably has the same meaning as under the S.G.A.[5]; and, according to s. 29 (3),

> "a person shall be taken to be a purchaser of a motor vehicle without notice of a hire-purchase agreement or conditional sale agreement if, at the time of the disposition made to him, he has no actual notice that the vehicle is or was the subject of any hire-purchase agreement or conditional sale agreement".

It would therefore appear that constructive notice does not prevent a person claiming the benefit of s. 27[6]; but that knowledge that the vehicle was once on h.p. is fatal, even though the hirer assures him that the agreement has been paid off[7].

We are now in a position to consider the effect of a disposition within s. 27 (2). Section 27 (2) provides that

> "that disposition shall have effect as if the title of the owner or seller to the vehicle had been vested in the hirer or buyer immediately before that disposition".

However, s. 29 (5) explains that the reference to "the title of the owner or seller" means

> "such title (if any) to the vehicle as, immediately before that disposition, was vested in the person who then was the owner in relation to the hire-purchase agreement, or the seller in relation to the conditional sale agreement, as the case may be".

Suppose A. is in possession of a motor vehicle which has been stolen from O.; A. lets it on h.p. to B., B. wrongfully sells it to C. during the currency of the agreement, and C. resells to D.:

$$\text{O.} \qquad \text{A.} \xrightarrow[\text{on h.p.}]{\text{let}} \text{B.} \xrightarrow{\text{sale}} \text{C.} \underline{\qquad} \text{D.}$$

---

2. See Goode, *op. cit.*, 623.
3. But s. 28 makes certain presumptions in favour of the b.f.p.: see below, pp. 235–236.
4. See below, p. 234.
5. See above, p. 199.   6. See also above, p. 226.
7. Presumably, this must be restricted to knowledge that the vehicle was once on h.p. to his transferor.

If C. acts *bona fide*[8], the effect of s. 27 is to confer on him A.'s title. Does this imply that, if A. himself could only claim title under one of the other exceptions to the *nemo dat* rule, C. may stand in A.'s shoes and similarly claim title under that exception[9]? If C. acts *mala fide*, neither C. nor D. can claim the benefit of s. 27, which is only expressed to apply where the first purchaser from the hirer acts *bona fide*; but, provided C. acts *bona fide*, D. will have the benefit of s. 27, even though he acts *mala fide* or is a dealer[10]. Finally, it should be noticed that s. 27 (6) provides that:

> "Nothing in this section shall exonerate the hirer or buyer from any liability (whether criminal or civil) to which he would be subject apart from this section . . ."

2 Dispositions to trade or finance purchasers

Suppose A. is in possession of a motor vehicle which has been stolen from O.; A. lets it to B. on h.p., and during the currency of the agreement B. wrongfully sells it to C., a b.f. "trade or finance purchaser"; and C. later resells to D., a b.f. "private purchaser", who resells to E.:

$$O. \qquad A.\xrightarrow[\text{on h.p.}]{\text{let}} B.\xrightarrow{\text{sells}} \underset{\text{(dealer)}}{C.}\xrightarrow{\text{sells}} \underset{\binom{\text{private}}{\text{purchaser}}}{D.}\text{———}E.$$

Section 27 (3) terms C. "the original purchaser", and provides that, where C. is a "trade or finance purchaser",

> "then if the person who is the first private purchaser of the motor vehicle after the disposition (in this section referred to as "the first private purchaser") is a purchaser of the vehicle in good faith and without notice of the hire-purchase agreement or conditional sale agreement, the disposition of the vehicle to the first private purchaser shall have effect as if the title of the owner or seller to the vehicle had been vested in the hirer or buyer immediately before he disposed of it to the original purchaser".

The effect of s. 27 (3) on the example above is that the title of A. ("the original owner or seller") is deemed to have been vested in B. ("the hirer or buyer") immediately before he disposed of the vehicle to C. ("the original purchaser"), with the result that C. can pass *that*[11] title to D. ("the first private purchaser"). So long as D. acts *bona fide*,. D. obtains, and can pass to E., A.'s title, irrespective of whether E. takes *bona fide*; but best title still remains in O.[11]. But notwithstanding

---

8. For the remainder of this section, the term *bona fide* purchaser is used to mean one who takes in good faith and without notice, and the term *mala fide* purchaser for one who does not.
9. See Goode, *H.P. Law & Practice* (2nd Edn.) 624.
10. Cf. *Peirce* v. *London Horse and Carriage Repository, Ltd.*, [1922] W.N. 170, C.A. This must be so, for otherwise C. would have great difficulty in disposing of the vehicle: see Goode, *op. cit.*, 627, note 16.
11. Section 29 (5): see above, p. 233.

that A.'s title passes through B. and C. to D., s. 27 (6) makes it clear that B. and C. are to remain both civilly and criminally liable.

Thus, the basic scheme is that only D., "the first private purchaser", and persons taking the goods from him can claim the benefit of s. 27 (3); but s. 27 (4) deals with the special case where the disposition to D. is by way of a financed h.p. transaction[12]. Section 27 (4) provides that, where the property in the vehicle is transferred to D. or E. under the terms of that h.p. agreement, D. or E., as the case may be, will obtain A.'s title. Once again, the trade purchasers only act as a conduit pipe. Finally, it must be borne in mind that, in order to obtain the benefit of s. 27 (4), D. must exercise his option to purchase, *and* must be *bona fide* at the time he makes the agreement (though not necessarily at the time he exercises the option)[13].

Particularly where some trade or finance purchasers are involved, it is obvious that the chain of title may be lengthy. In such circumstances, it may be difficult to prove those requirements necessary for the operation of s. 27; and Parliament therefore enacted in s. 28 an elaborate series of presumptions in favour of persons seeking to rely on s. 27. According to s. 28 (1), these presumptions are to be applicable for the purposes of s. 27

> "Where in any proceedings (whether criminal or civil) relating to a motor vehicle it is proved—
> (a) that the vehicle was let under a hire-purchase agreement, or was agreed to be sold under a conditional sale agreement, and
> (b) that a person (whether a party to the proceedings or not) became a private purchaser of the vehicle in good faith and without notice of the hire-purchase agreement or conditional sale agreement . . ."

The presumptions embodied in s. 28 will now be examined in relation to the example set out above. If the person seeking to rely on s. 27 can show that either he, or someone through whom he is claiming, X., is the person mentioned in paragraph (b) of s. 28 (1), s. 28 makes the following rebuttable presumptions[14] in his favour:

First presumption. Section 28 (2) assumes that the claimant or X. is in fact C.

Second presumption. If it is proved that this is not the case, s. 28 (3) makes the following presumptions: (1) that C. is a "private purchaser" who could claim the benefit of s. 27; and (2) that the claimant or X. is claiming title through C., i.e., that the claimant or X. is D. or E.

---

12. Why did the draftsman not provide as well for the case where D. takes under a conditional sale agreement?
13. What if D. sells the motor vehicle to E. during the currency of his agreement?
14. It is difficult to know what to make of s. 28 (5): see Goode, *op. cit.*, 630.

Third presumption. If it is proved that neither the claimant nor X. is C., and that C. is a "trade or finance purchaser", s. 28 (4) makes the following presumptions: (1) that D. is the "first private purchaser", *and* is entitled to the protection of s. 27; and (2) that the claimant or X. is in fact E.

The effect of the presumptions is, therefore, that a claimant will, if he can prove the matters mentioned in s. 28 (1), succeed unless his adversary can show that none of the presumptions is true.

8 SALES IN MARKET OVERT

1 The law[15]

The oldest exception to the *nemo dat* rule is the principle that a buyer in market overt should obtain a good title[16]. As developed by the Elizabethan lawyers, this exception was a sensible attempt to balance the conflicting interests of the owner and the b.f.p. Unfortunately, the development of commerce has left the exception of market overt a curious anomaly.

The present basis of the rule is s. 22 (1) of the S.G.A.[17], which provides:

> "Where goods are sold[18] in market overt, according to the usage of the market, the buyer acquires a good title to the goods, provided he buys them in good faith and without notice of any defect or want of title on the part of the seller"[19].

Neither the requirement that the sale should be "in market overt", nor that it should be "according to the usage of the market" is explained in the Act; and in both cases reference must be made to the common law (s. 61 (2) S.G.A.).

1. Market overt. In 1856, JERVIS C.J. described a market overt as "an open, public and legally constituted market"[20]; and the common law has long maintained a dichotomy between what is a market overt in the City of London, and what is a market overt in the rest of England[1].

(a) Within the City of London. In 1596, COKE C.J. said that every

---

15. See generally *Benjamin on Sale* (8th Edn.) 17–30.
16. See Murray (1960), 9 I.C.L.Q. 24.
17. Section 22 (2) was repealed by Part 3 of Schedule 3 of the Criminal Law Act 1967.
18. This would include both credit and conditional sales.
19. "Good faith" and "notice" are considered above, pp. 199, 226. Presumably the onus of proof is on the original owner, as in s. 23: see above, p. 199.
20. *Lee* v. *Bayes and Robinson* (1856), 18 C.B. 599, at p. 601.
 1. Market overt does not apply to Wales: s. 47, Laws in Wales Act 1542.

shop within the City is a market overt for the things which the shop customarily sells[2]; and this is a question of fact[3].

(b) Outside the City of London. A market overt outside London has been defined as[4]

> "the market place or spot of ground set apart by custom (or other legal authority?), for the sale of particular goods . . ."

It is clear that the sale must be a public one; and the fact that public sales are today conducted at a place which was anciently a market is frequently a matter of chance[5].

2. *According to the usage of the market.* The following rules are well-established:

(a) Market overt does not operate against the Crown.

(b) The goods must be within the class of goods normally sold in that market in the o.c.b.

(c) The sale and delivery must take place wholly within the market; and it must be open and above board, the slightest suspicion of *mala fide* ousting the rule.

(d) Whilst it seems that the sale need not be *by* a regular trader in the market (unless the usage requires it), sales *to* a regular trader are not within the rule.

Where the market overt rule operates, it will protect the b.f.p., and those deriving title from him[6]; but all those who handled the goods before the sale in market overt, including the person who sold the goods in the market, will remain liable, however innocent[7]. On the other hand, the rule is particularly favourable to those within it. Subject to the following two exceptions, the effect of the market overt rule is to confer on the b.f.p. and his successors in title the best title to the goods[8]:

(a) If the original seller in market overt reacquires the goods, then, no matter how many dispositions have intervened, the title of the original owner revives[9].

(b) To encourage the prosecution of thieves, it used to be the rule that the title revested in the person from whom the goods had been

---

2. *The Case of Market Overt* (1596), 5 Co. Rep. 83b.
3. See *Clayton* v. *Le Roy,* [1911] 2 K.B. 1031; rev. by C.A. on other grounds, *op. cit.,* 1046.
4. Stroud, *Judicial Dictionary* (3rd Edn.). See also Murray (1960), 9 I.C.L.Q. 24, 26.
5. See *Bishopsgate Motor Finance Corporation, Ltd.* v. *Transport Brakes, Ltd.,* [1949] 1 K.B. 322; [1949] 1 All E.R. 37, C.A.: see Gower (1949), 12 M.L.R. 371.
6. *Bishopsgate Case* (above).
7. *Delaney* v. *Wallis* (1884), 14 L.R.Ir. 31.
8. Compare above, pp. 191, 202, 215, 219, 230.
9. See *Benjamin on Sale* (8th Edn.) 20, note (x).

stolen where the thief was prosecuted to conviction[10]; but this rule has now been repealed by the Theft Act 1968 (s. 31 (2)), s. 28 of which specifically deals with the question of the restitution of stolen property[11].

2 Proposals for reform

The market overt rule would appear to be hopelessly out of date, and it is to be hoped that it will be abolished[12]. However, the *Twelfth Report of the Law Reform Committee* recommended that the market overt rule be denied decent burial. The majority of the committee recommended[13]

> "that section 22 of the Sale of Goods Act should be replaced by a provision that a person who buys goods by retail at trade premises or by public auction acquires a good title provided he buys in good faith and without notice of any defect or want of title on the part of the apparent owner";

and that the onus of proof should be on the purchaser[14].

9 MISCELLANEOUS POWERS OF SALE

Section 21 (2) of the S.G.A. provides that

> ". . . nothing in this Act shall affect—
> (a) The provisions of the Factors Acts, or any enactment enabling the apparent owner of goods to dispose of them as if he were the true owner thereof;
> (b) The validity of any contract of sale under any special common law or statutory power of sale or under the order of a court of competent jurisdiction".

Apart from the provisions of the F.A., which have already been considered[15], it appears to be difficult to see to what s. 21 (2) (a) is referring[16]. Section 21 (2) (b) refers to three different categories of power.

1 Common law powers

Where these powers have not been absorbed by statute, they are expressly preserved by the Act.

---

10. See s. 24 (1) of the S.G.A. and s. 45 (1) of the Larceny Act 1916.
11. See Macleod, [1968] Cmn. L.R. 577.
12. See also Atiyah, *Sale of Goods* (3rd Edn.) 151. *Contra* Ivamy (1956), 9 Current Legal Problems 113.
13. Cmnd. 2958, para. 33. Lord DONOVAN dissented.
14. As in most of the other exceptions to the *nemo dat* rule.
15. See above, pp. 202, 215, 220.
16. *Benjamin on Sale* (8th Edn.) 9, note (d); *Chalmers' Sale of Goods* (15th Edn.) 92, note (k). Perhaps it includes the reputed ownership doctrine, the Bills of Sale Act 1878, and Part III of the H.P.A. 1964.

2 Statutory powers

From the considerable list of statutory powers of sale[17], three are worthy of mention.

1. The creditors' powers of sale. Unpaid sellers[18], distraining landlords[19], pawnbrokers[20], innkeepers[1] and repairers[2] all have varying statutory powers of sale.

2. Insolvency. The trustee in bankruptcy or liquidator has a statutory power of sale; but neither can pass a better title than the insolvent person has, except that the trustee may do so under the reputed owner-ship doctrine[3].

3. Execution[4]. The process of execution may be divided into three stages.

(a) The delivery of the writ to the sheriff. Section 26 (1) of the S.G.A. provides[5]:

> "A writ of fieri facias or other writ of execution against goods shall bind the property in the goods of the execution debtor as from the time the writ is delivered to the sheriff to be executed . . ."

The title of the execution debtor does not at this stage transfer to the sheriff, and the effect of s. 26 (1) is to create a sort of charge over the goods. Special arrangements are made to deal with the situation where the execution debtor becomes bankrupt at this stage[6], and s. 26 (1) pro-ceeds to deal with sales by the execution debtor as follows:

> "Provided that no such writ shall prejudice the title to such goods acquired by any person in good faith and for valuable consideration, unless such person had at the time when he acquired his title notice that such writ or any other writ by virtue of which the goods of the execution debtor might be seized or attached had been delivered to and remained unexecuted in the hands of the sheriff".

Thus, whilst the execution debtor can transfer such title as he has to a third party, the latter will take subject to the sheriff's rights unless the disposition falls within the proviso to s. 26 (1)[7].

---

17. See further *Halsbury's Laws* (3rd Edn.) XXXIV, 16; *Benjamin on Sale* (8th Edn.) 48–49.
18. See below, p. 365, *et seq.*
19. See above, pp. 11–12.
20. See Crossley Vaines, *Personal Property* (4th Edn.) Ch. 22.
 1. See Crossley Vaines, *op. cit.*, 123–130.
 2. Disposal of Uncollected Goods Act 1952.
 3. See Crossley Vaines, *op. cit.*, Ch. 24; and above, pp. 10–11.
 4. See Crossley Vaines, *op. cit.*, Ch. 25. But see s. 17 (2) of the Administration of Justice Act 1970: and generally below, pp. 364–365.
 5. The time of operation has been amended by s. 22, Administration of Justice Act 1965.
 6. See ss. 40, 41, Bankruptcy Act 1914; *Re Cooper*, [1958] Ch. 922; [1958] 3 All E.R. 97.
 7. See *per* DANCKWERTS J. in *Re Cooper* (above), at pp. 928–929.

(b) *The execution of the writ.* Once the sheriff takes possession of goods under a writ of execution, the writ becomes executed and the proviso to s. 26 (1) can no longer operate; and it has been decided that this will be so where the sheriff merely takes "walking possession"[8]. Under the latter arrangement, the goods remain in the actual possession of the execution debtor who merely acknowledges that the sheriff has taken legal possession[9].

(c) *The sale by the sheriff.* Where goods belonging to a third party, but in the possession of the execution debtor, are seized by the sheriff, the interest of the third party is not thereby overridden. However, the sheriff is protected in his seizure and sale of the goods[10]; and the b.f.p. from the sheriff is protected as against the execution debtor's trustee in bankruptcy[11], and also as against the third party[12].

3 Court orders

There are a number of powers conferred on the courts to make an order for the sale of property. Particularly worthy of note are the power to order a sale or division of goods owned by co-owners who cannot reach agreement *inter se* with respect to the goods[13]; the effect of satisfaction of a judgment in an action of conversion or detinue[14]; and the power to order a sale under the Rules of the Supreme Court where the sheriff interpleads because of a dispute as to the title of goods taken in execution[15], or where the subject-matter of any litigation is perishable, or is likely to deteriorate if kept, or which "for any other reason it is desirable to sell forthwith"[16].

---

8. *Lloyds and Scottish Finance, Ltd.* v. *Modern Cars, Ltd.*, [1966] 1 Q.B. 764; [1964] 2 All E.R. 732, C.A.: set out above, p. 65.
9. See the *Modern Cars Case* (above).
10. In his seizure by the writ; and in his sale by s. 15, Bankruptcy & Deeds of Arrangement Act 1913.
11. Section 40 (3), Bankruptcy Act 1914.
12. Section 15, Bankruptcy & Deeds of Arrangement Act 1913; and see *Curtis* v. *Maloney*, [1951] 1 K.B. 736, C.A., as reported at [1950] 2 All E.R. 201 and [1950] 2 All E.R. 982, C.A.
13. See the explanation in *Chalmers Sale of Goods* (15th Edn.) 97–98.
14. See below, p. 363.
15. R.S.C. Ord. 17, rule 6.
16. R.S.C. Ord. 29, rule 4; *Larner* v. *Fawcett*, [1950] 2 All E.R. 727, C.A. See also below, p. 366.

CHAPTER 15

Risk and Impossibility

1 RISK

In the case of sales, the general assumption of the common law was that any risk of loss or chance of gain accrued to the owner. Logically, the term "risk" ought to cover both losses and gains; but the pessimistic lawyer will usually use "risk" solely in the sense of risk of loss. In this sense, the ordinary rule of risk is summed up by the Latin maxim *res perit domino*. This rule is embodied in s. 20 of the S.G.A. which provides:

> "Unless otherwise agreed, the goods remain at the seller's risk until the property therein is transferred to the buyer, but when the property therein is transferred to the buyer, the goods are at the buyer's risk whether delivery has been made or not . . ."

It has already been seen that delivery is the most obvious act of appropriation of unascertained goods[1], so that in sales of unascertained goods property and risk will usually pass on delivery[2]. However, if property and possession do not go together, s. 20 is a reminder that risk will follow property, not possession[3].

The position in respect of sales may be compared with that in bailment and h.p. transactions. In both the latter cases, the maxim *res perit domino* also applies: risk of loss *prima facie* falls on the bailor. However, it is a well-established rule in bailments that any gains *prima facie* accrue to the bailee, on the grounds that the bailor should not be allowed the double benefit of rent and gains; and, in *Tucker* v. *Farm and General Investments Trust Ltd.*[4], the Court of Appeal decided this rule should apply to h.p. agreements notwithstanding the element of sale they contained.

Of the two aspects of risk, loss and gain, the former may operate where a further doctrine is called into play. Where goods are lost without fault, the contract may be or become impossible of performance; but such loss will not always give rise to impossibility in the

---

1. See above, p. 170.
2. E.g. *Warder's Import and Export Co., Ltd.* v. *Norwood*, [1968] 2 Q.B. 663; [1968] 2 All E.R. 602, C.A.
3. E.g. *Pignatoro* v. *Gilroy*, [1919] 1 K.B. 459, D.C.: set out above, p. 172. The rule is criticised by Atiyah, *Sale of Goods* (3rd Edn.) 124.
4. [1966] 2 Q.B. 421; [1966] 2 All E.R. 508, C.A.

legal sense, and the doctrine of impossibility is therefore considered separately[5].

Returning to the question of risk, it is clear that the presumptions outlined above will give way to a contrary intention. It will be recalled that the same is the case with the rules relating to the passing of property[6]. But there is a practical difference between the two situations: the concept of risk is easier for the layman to understand, so that it is, perhaps, more common for a contract to make special provision as to risk, than to deal specifically with the passing of property. Once again, the obligation to insure is at best an ambiguous indication of the intention of the parties: it may or may not show where risk is to lie[7]. Of course, if the contract is a standard-form one, then it is likely to make express provision for risk, property and insurance; and it will do so in the manner most advantageous to the *proferens*. It is, therefore, unlikely that the ordinary standard-form consumer instalment credit contract will leave the matter of risk to the ordinary law. On the other hand, ordinary sales, including retail sales, may well make no provision as to risk of loss, in which case the basic presumption is that *res perit domino*, though there are certain special cases where this presumption is qualified. These special cases must now be examined.

1 Delay in delivery

A distinction must immediately be drawn according to whether the delay in delivery amounts to a breach of contract.

1. Delay amounting to breach of contract. The contractual duties relating to delivery will be considered later[8]; and the first proviso to s. 20 of the S.G.A. reads:

> ". . . where delivery has been delayed through the fault[9] of either buyer or seller the goods are at the risk of the party in fault as regards any loss which might not have occurred but for such fault".

In *Demby Hamilton, Ltd.* v. *Barden*[10]

> There was a contract for the sale of 30 tons of apple juice by sample, the juice to be delivered in weekly instalments. The seller crushed all 30 tons at once in order to ensure correspondence with the sample. After some instalments had been delivered, the buyer in breach of contract gave no further delivery instructions; and the juice went putrid. SELLERS J. decided that the property remained in the seller, but that the loss fell on the buyer under the first proviso to s. 20.

---

5. See below, p. 249.   6. See above, p. 159.
7. Compare above, p. 163.   8. See below, p. 265, *et seq.*
9. Section 62 (1) provides that "fault" means "wrongful act or default". See also above, pp. 21–22.
10. [1949] 1 All E.R. 435.

His Lordship found some difficulty in construing the proviso, but eventually concluded that it applied because it would have been difficult for the seller (a) to ensure correspondence with sample unless he crushed all 30 tons at once, and (b) to replace the juice with other juice equal to sample if he had sold the juice in his possession. Moreover, the proviso clearly requires a causal connection between the fault and the loss, and the test which the Judge seems to have applied was whether the seller acted reasonably after the default of the buyer. The implication seems to be that if the seller had not acted reasonably the proviso would not have applied[11].

2. *Delay which is not a breach of contract.* Where the buyer is entitled to, and does, delay in taking delivery, it may be inferred that the parties intend the risk to pass notwithstanding that property remains in the seller. In *Sterns, Ltd.* v. *Vickers, Ltd.*[12]

> On Jan. 3rd, the defendants bought from X. 200,000 gallons of white spirit then lying in the tanks of Y. on terms that they should have free storage until Jan. 31st. On Jan. 17th the defendants sold by sample to the plaintiffs 120,000 gallons of that spirit, and it was agreed that the plaintiffs should make their own arrangement for storage after Jan. 31st. On Jan. 23rd the plaintiffs resold by sample the 120,000 gallons to Z. on terms that Z. should pay the storage charges. On Jan. 28th, the defendants obtained a delivery warrant from Y. and handed it to the plaintiffs, who endorsed it to Z. Z. did not take delivery for some months; but when he did do so found that the spirit had deteriorated in quality, mainly due to the fact that Y. had topped up the tank with other, slightly different, consignments of spirits in order to save space[13]. Z. claimed damages from the plaintiffs, who in turn claimed from the defendants. On the only point on which the dispute is reported, the Court of Appeal unanimously found in favour of the defendants as against the plaintiffs.

SCRUTTON L.J. thought that the property in the 120,000 gallons remained in the defendants[14], but that this did not preclude the plaintiffs from having an insurable interest in an undivided share and bearing the risk[15]; and he concluded that the risk passed to the plaintiffs because in handing over the delivery warrant the defendants had performed their duty to deliver[16] and had put it out of their power to control the goods. This decision has subsequently received the approval of the House of

---

11. Compare the mitigation of damage: see below, pp. 390–391.
12. [1923] 1 K.B. 78, C.A.
13. The real complaint is against Y., the bailee.
14. The other two judges expressed no opinion on this point.
15. If the spirit had been stored in two tanks, and Y. had only adulterated one, it follows that the buyer should get the contents of the good tank, and a proportion of the bad: see Atiyah, *Sale of Goods* (3rd Edn.) 121.
16. See below, pp. 266–267.

Lords, though their Lordships stressed the exceptional nature of the case[17]. However, *Sterns, Ltd.* v. *Vickers, Ltd.* gives rise to a number of problems. First, did risk pass on Jan 28th with the constructive delivery; or only subsequently on the delay in taking actual delivery[18]? Second, would the decision have been the same if the spirit had deteriorated before Jan. 28th? It does not appear from the reports when the spirit was adulterated; but, if it was before Jan. 28th, then the case would appear to conflict with *Healey* v. *Howlett*[19]. Assuming that the spirit was adulterated after Jan. 28th, it is arguable that contractual permission to delay in taking delivery shows an intention that the goods should remain at the seller's risk[20]. Third, could the Court of Appeal have reached this decision if the goods had been any other than an unascertained part of a specific whole? Whilst the rule could apply to specific goods[1], it is submitted that it could not operate in respect of generic or future goods[2].

2 Transit

Where under a contract of sale the goods are subject to a transit from seller to buyer, we have already seen that the implied undertakings as to fitness and quality are tested at the end of that transit, so that the seller is impliedly promising that his goods will stand up to an ordinary transit[3]. Subject to this understanding, the S.G.A. makes special provision for risks materialising during the course of transit. Section 33 provides:

> "Where the seller of goods agrees to deliver them at his own risk at a place other than that where they are when sold, the buyer must, nevertheless, unless otherwise agreed, take any risk of deterioration in the goods necessarily incident to the course of transit".

Section 33 is expressed to give way to a contrary intention. Moreover, it can only operate where (a) the contract ousts the ordinary assumption that delivery is to be at the seller's place of business[4], and (b) the seller agrees to deliver at his own risk. The section is not expressed very clearly, but was probably intended to reflect the common law, where a distinction was drawn between an ordinary and an extraordinary

---

17. *Per* Lords PORTER and NORMAND in *Comptoir D'Achat* v. *Luis de Ridder Limitada*, [1949] A.C. 293, H.L., at pp. 312, 319.
18. Is the important thing Z.'s delay in taking actual delivery, or the fact that the plaintiffs made a contract under which Z. might, and did, legitimately delay in taking delivery?
19. [1917] 1 K.B. 337.
20. From the position that, if delay had been a breach of contract on the part of the plaintiff, the risk would have been on him: see above, pp. 242–243
 1. E.g. a conditional sale.
 2. See Atiyah, *Sale of Goods* (3rd Edn.) 122.
 3. See above, p. 82.
 4. Section 29 (1) discussed below, p. 265.

deterioration[5]. In those circumstances where it is operative, s. 33 would appear to assume that the parties have agreed to allocate the risk of deterioration because of the contemplated transit as follows:

1. The buyer is to bear the risk of any deterioration which all goods of the contract description would ordinarily suffer during that transit (s. 33); but the seller is to bear the risk of any deterioration due to some inherent vice peculiar to the contract goods[6].

2. The owner—whether that be the seller or buyer—is to bear the risk of any deterioration due to any abnormality of the transit under the ordinary principle *res perit domino*[7].

Thus, in *Healey* v. *Howlett*[8]

> The plaintiff fish exporter, who carried on business in Ireland, contracted to sell 20 boxes of mackerel to the defendant, a Billings-gate fish salesman, this being the first transaction between the parties. The plaintiff consigned by railway 190 boxes of mackerel. He wired instructions to the railway officials at Holyhead to apportion the boxes between three of his customers, including the defendant, and notified the defendant by invoice that the fish was at his risk from the moment it was put on rail. Owing to delays in Ireland, the fish was no longer in a merchantable state by the time it reached the defendant, and he refused to accept it. The plaintiff's action for the price failed before the Divisional Court, which held that the invoice could not transfer the risk because it was subsequent to the agreement[9], that risk therefore went with property, and that the property had not passed.

The Court decided that the property had not passed because there had not been any effective appropriation: they argued that the earmarking took place after the delay, when the fish had already begun to deteriorate, and that the railway officials were then in the impossible position of having to decide who would get the deteriorated fish. Whilst it may be that there cannot be any appropriation sufficient to pass the property in these circumstances[10], *Sterns, Ltd.* v. *Vickers, Ltd.*[11] demonstrates that this does not of itself prevent the risk passing. However, it may be that the two cases can be distinguished on the following grounds: in *Sterns, Ltd.* v. *Vickers, Ltd.* the seller had probably discharged his duty to deliver before the deterioration of the spirit; but in *Healey* v. *Howlett* the deterioration had set in before delivery. In the latter case, the delay in transit took it outside s. 33.

---

5. See *per* ALDERSON B. in *Bull* v. *Robison* (1854), 10 Exch. 342, at p. 346.
6. See above, note 3.
7. Section 20: see above, p. 241.
8. [1917] 1 K.B. 337, D.C.
9. It would be otherwise if this were not the first transaction between the parties: see above, p. 132.
10. See above, p. 168.
11. [1923] 1 K.B. 78, C.A.: set out above, p. 243.

Section 32 makes special provision for those cases where the contract envisages delivery to a carrier for transmission to the buyer; and s. 32 (1) provides that delivery to the carrier shall *prima facie* be deemed a delivery to the buyer[12]. The importance of the other two provisions is primarily in relation to export sales, which are beyond the scope of this work[13]; but it may be convenient if the major types of such contract are listed.[14]

1. Ex-works or ex-store contracts. The designation primarily refers to the place of delivery; and all the ordinary rules as to the passing of property and risk apply.

2. F(ree) o(n) b(oard) contracts. The expense of delivering the goods on board ship *prima facie* lies on the seller. It is unusual in a f.o.b. contract for the property to pass before shipment[15]; and it may not even pass on shipment, as where an unascertained part of a specific whole is sold[16], or there is a reservation of a right of disposal[17]. Although the property does not pass on shipment, the risk will usually do so[18]; but this rule is modified by s. 32 (2), which provides:

> "Unless otherwise authorised by the buyer, the seller must make such contract with the carrier on behalf of the buyer as may be reasonable having regard to the nature of the goods and the other circumstances of the case[19]. If the seller omit so to do, and the goods are lost or damaged in course of transit, the buyer may decline to treat the delivery to the carrier as a delivery to himself, or may hold the seller responsible in damages".

The effect of non-compliance with s. 32 (2) is that the risk does not pass on shipment[20]; and the buyer may recover in respect of any loss, whether or not this loss is due to the breach of s. 32 (2)[1]. Even where the seller complies with s. 32 (2), a further obligation may be cast on him by s. 32 (3), which provides:

> "Unless otherwise agreed, where goods are sent by the seller to the buyer by a route involving sea transit, under circumstances in which it is usual to insure, the seller must give such notice to the buyer as may enable him to insure them during their sea transit, and, if

---

12. Section 32 (1) is set out below, p. 264.
13. See Schmitthoff, *The Export Trade* (5th Edn.).
14. The question of the type to which a particular contract belongs is a matter of construing the intention of the parties: *Couturier* v. *Hastie* (1856), 5 H.L. Cas. 673: see below, p. 251.
15. See *Carlos Federspiel & Co.* v. *Twigg & Co., Ltd.*, [1957] 1 Lloyds Rep. 240: see above, p. 169.
16. See *Re Wait*, [1927] 1 Ch. 606, C.A.: see above, p. 173.
17. See s. 19, S.G.A.: see above, pp. 181–182.
18. *Inglis* v. *Stock* (1885), 10 App. Cas. 263, H.L.
19. This may include insuring on behalf of the buyer.
20. *Thomas Young, Ltd.* v. *Hobson* (1949), 65 T.L.R. 365.
21. Compare the first proviso to s. 20, S.G.A.: see above, p. 242.

the seller fails to do so, the goods shall be deemed to be at his risk during such sea transit".

It would seem that s. 32 (3) is in the nature of a proviso to s. 32 (1)[2].

3. C(ost), i(nsurance) and f(reight) contracts. Under this type of contract, the seller undertakes the following duties:

(1) To deliver the goods to a port and to ship them under a contract for their carriage to the agreed destination;

(2) To insure the goods for the transit; and

(3) To tender to the buyer an invoice, bill of lading[3] and insurance policy.

In law, these documents together represent the goods, a rule which has several important effects on c.i.f. contracts. First, the seller's duty is to tender the documents to the buyer, so that s. 32 (1) is ousted; and delivery of the documents amounts to delivery of the goods[4]. Second, because the seller is under an express obligation to insure, s. 32 (3) is inapplicable. Third, risk in the goods[5] passes on shipment, unless the seller is in breach of his duty under s. 32 (2)[6]. Fourth, it is the transfer of the bill of lading which usually transfers the property in the goods[7], not delivery of the goods to a carrier, or even to the buyer[8]: this rule will usually apply even though the bill of lading be taken in the name of the buyer, or the seller does an act which ascertains the contract goods[9]. Fifth, the buyer has two rights to reject: he may reject the documents if they do not comply with the contract, and subsequently reject the goods if they do not comply with the contract[10]. Sixth, destruction of the goods after shipment cannot frustrate a c.i.f. contract[11]. Perhaps because of the overwhelming importance of the documents in a c.i.f. contract, it is worth remembering that the transaction is still a sale of goods, not of documents[12].

4. Arrival or ex-ship contracts. The seller's obligation is to deliver goods from a ship on arrival at a named port, and not merely to ship goods for transit to that port as in the case of f.o.b. and c.i.f. contracts. Section 32 can have no application to arrival contracts. The bill of

---

2. *Wimble, Sons & Co.* v. *Rosenberg & Sons,* [1913] 3 K.B. 743, C.A.
3. If the seller is entitled to substitute a delivery order for a bill of lading, it is not a c.i.f. contract, but an arrival contract: Schmitthoff, *Sale of Goods* (2nd Edn.) 139.   4. See below, p. 264.
5. But not necessarily in the freight: *The Pantanassa,* [1970] 1 All E.R. 848.
6. *Tsakiroglou & Co., Ltd.* v. *Noblee Thorl G.M.B.H.,* [1962] A.C. 93; [1961] 2 All E.R. 179, H.L.
7. Subject to defeasance if the goods do not conform with the contract.
8. *Cheetham & Co., Ltd.* v. *Thornham Spinning Co., Ltd.,* [1964] 2 Lloyds Rep. 17.
9. Ascertainment does not then amount to an appropriation: see above, p. 175.
10. See below, p. 402.
11. *Manbre Saccharine Co., Ltd.* v. *Corn Products Co., Ltd.,* [1919] 1 K.B. 198.
12. Per Lord WRIGHT in *Ross T. Smyth & Co., Ltd.* v. *Bailey, Son & Co.,* [1940] 3 All E.R. 60, H.L., at p. 70.

lading only operates as a delivery order, so that its transfer does not pass the property in the goods; and the risk remains in the seller until arrival[13].

3 Bailment

It may be that the subject-matter of the contract of sale is for some time in the possession of someone other than the owner of the goods; and that someone may be either one of the parties to the contract of sale or a third party. In either circumstance, we must consider the liability of that person in possession as bailee. Where the loss is not due to any breach of duty by the bailee,[14] the loss will usually fall on the owner. What if the loss is due to a breach of duty by the bailee[15]?

1. A contracting-party bailee. Either the seller or buyer may be in possession as bailee whilst the property is in the other party; and in either case the second proviso to s. 20 of the S.G.A. enacts that

> ". . . nothing in this section shall affect the duties or liabilities of either seller or buyer as a bailee . . . of the goods of the other party".

There are two possibilities:

(1) Property passes before delivery, in which case the seller is in possession under a contract for value (the sale), and, unless otherwise agreed, his duty is to exercise reasonable care[16]. If the buyer fails to take delivery at the contract time, the seller becomes a gratuitous bailee with a correspondingly lower duty of care[17].

(2) Property passes after delivery, in which case the buyer is a bailee for value and *prima facie*[18] under a duty to exercise reasonable care during the continuance of the bailment[19].

2. A third-party bailee. Where the goods are damaged or lost by the act or omission of an independent third party, either of the parties to the contract for the sale of those goods may wish to maintain an action against the third party in contract or tort.

(1) In tort. An action in conversion or detinue may lie at the suit of the person entitled to immediate possession[20]; but an action in negli-

---

13. *Comptoir D'Achat* v. *Luis de Ridder Limitada*, [1949] A.C. 293; [1949] 1 All E.R. 269, H.L.
14. The duties of a bailee are discussed in Crossley Vaines, *Personal Property* (4th Edn.) 97–110.
15. If both bailee and owner are negligent, does the Law Reform (Contributory Negligence) Act 1945 apply?
16. *Wiehe* v. *Dennis Brothers* (1913), 29 T.L.R. 250.
17. *Benjamin on Sale* (18th Edn.) 400.
18. The typical conditional sale will probably specify the buyer's duties as bailee.
19. Presumably the position is the same in respect of a transferee under a sale or return transaction: see above, pp. 176–177.
20. *Bristol and West of England Bank* v. *Midland Rail Co.*, [1891] 2 Q.B. 653, C.A.

gence will lie only at the suit of the person with the property in the goods or entitled to immediate possession of them[1].

(2) In contract. Whilst an action in contract under the terms of the bill of lading may be available to the seller, the buyer to whom the bill is transferred is prevented by his lack of privity from suing on the bill at common law. To surmount this inconvenience, s. 1 of the Bills of Lading Act 1855 provides:

> "Every consignee of goods named in a bill of lading, and every indorsee of a bill of lading to whom the property in the goods therein mentioned shall pass, upon or by reason of such consignment or indorsement, shall have transferred to or vested in him all rights of suit, and be subject to the same liabilities in respect of such goods as if the contract contained in the bill of lading had been made with himself".

The Act further provides that it is not to affect the right of stoppage in transit or claims for freight (s. 2); and that the bill of lading in the hands of the consignee or indorsee shall be conclusive evidence of shipment as against the signer of the bill notwithstanding that the goods have not been shipped (s. 3). Despite the terminology of s. 1, it is clear that the bill is only evidence of the contract; that the property in the goods passes when the parties intend, which is not necessarily on indorsement; and that s. 1 only operates in favour of a consignee or indorsee who has obtained, and retains, the property in goods whilst they remain subject to the bill of lading[2]. Nor does s. 1 cure the defect of lack of privity in respect of any except such a consignee or indorsee[3].

2 IMPOSSIBILITY

Assuming that the parties to a contract of sale or h.p. have reached an agreement, that agreement may be, or become, impossible of performance in the manner envisaged in the contract. This impossibility may be caused by any number of events, ranging from the death, insolvency or imprisonment of a contracting party to the destruction of the subject-matter or illegality of the contract. The question to be discussed in this section is whether the impossibility of performance will discharge either or both of the parties from their contractual obligations; or whether the non-performance caused by the impossibility will constitute a breach of contract actionable by the other party.

---

1. *Margarine Union G.M.B.H.* v. *Cambay Steamship Co., Ltd.,* [1969] 1 Q.B. 219; [1967] 3 All E.R. 775.
2. E.g. *Margarine Union G.M.B.H.* v. *Cambay Steamship Co., Ltd.* (above).
3. E.g. *Scruttons, Ltd.* v. *Midland Silicones, Ltd.,* [1962] A.C. 446; [1962] 1 All E.R. 1, H.L.

Leaving aside void[4] and illegal[5] contracts, the contract may, *prima facie*, be open to any one of the following interpretations in respect of a particular type of impossibility:

(1) The seller or owner promises that the particular type of impossibility has not occurred or will not occur, but the obligations of the buyer or hirer will lapse by reason of the impossibility; or

(2) The buyer or hirer promises that the particular type of impossibility has not occurred or will not occur, but the obligations of the seller or owner will lapse by reason of the impossibility; or

(3) The obligations of both parties will lapse by reason of the impossibility[6]; or,

(4) The obligations of both parties are to remain binding despite the impossibility of performing the primary obligations, because the contract stipulates in these circumstances for an alternative method of performance.

At this point it is necessary to distinguish between initial and subsequent impossibility: the contract may be impossible of performance at the time when it is made; or it may become impossible of performance at some later stage.

1 Initial impossibility

The contract may be initially impossible of performance owing to the act or omission of a contracting party[7]; or by reason of the conduct of some third party[8]; or because of the happening[9] or non-happening[10] of some event. The effect of such impossibility should, *prima facie*, be a question of interpretation; but in one case the matter is apparently dealt with by statute. Section 6 of the S.G.A. provides:

> "Where there is a contract for the sale of specific goods, and the goods without the knowledge of the seller have perished at the time when the contract is made, the contract is void".

Within its ambit[11], s. 6 would appear to admit of only one interpretation of the contract; namely, that neither party will be under any contractual liability. The section was always thought to embody the House of Lords decision in *Couturier* v. *Hastie*[12].

---

4. See above, pp. 122–124.   5. See above, pp. 37–39.
6. See s. 11 (3) of the S.G.A.
7. E.g. where the contract contemplates that the goods be obtained by the "seller" or "owner" from a third party, and he makes no attempt to obtain them from the third party.
8. E.g. where the contract contemplates that the goods be obtained by the "seller" or "owner" from a third party who refuses to supply them.
9. E.g. the destruction of the goods.
10. E.g. the non-arrival of the goods at a specified time and place.
11. This is discussed below, p. 252.
12. (1856), 5 H.L. Cas. 673.

The seller shipped a cargo of corn at Salonica for delivery in England, and then employed a London corn-factor to sell it on a *del credere* commission. However, owing to inclement weather the cargo became unfit for further transit and was sold by the ship's master in Tunis. Unaware of this sale, the corn-factor shortly afterwards negotiated a sale of the cargo "free on board, and including freight and insurance to a safe port in the United Kingdom". On discovering the previous sale by the ship's master, the buyer repudiated the contract[13]. As a *del credere* agent guarantees performance by the party he introduces, the seller sued the corn-factor for the price.

The liability of the corn-factor depended on that of his buyer; and accordingly the argument turned on whether the repudiation by the buyer had been wrongful. The Court of Exchequer held that the true meaning of the contract was that there was a sale of an adventure[14], so that the buyer, and therefore the corn-factor, remained liable for the price[15]. However, the Court of Exchequer Chamber[16] and the House of Lords took the contrary view; namely, that there was a contract for the sale of goods[17], and that the buyer, and therefore the corn-factor, was not liable for the price. Not only was the decision reached as a matter of construction, but strictly it only decided that the buyer was not liable for the price in the absence of delivery[18]. Thus, it did not decide whether the seller was liable for non-delivery, or whether both parties were discharged: but it seems to have been taken by Chalmers to have decided the latter. The only case where the issue has been canvassed since 1893 is *McRae* v. *The Commonwealth Disposals Commission*[19].

The Commission was charged with the task of disposing of the various wrecks lying abandoned in the Pacific at the end of World War Two. By accident, they offered for sale a non-existent tanker on a non-existent reef. The plaintiff, who had submitted the successful tender, incurred considerable expenditure in undertaking an abortive salvage expedition. The plaintiff's action for breach of contract, deceit and negligence succeeded before the High Court of Australia on the first ground.

The Court decided that the equivalent of s. 6 in the State of Victoria did not apply because the goods had never existed; that the question was primarily one of construction; and that the Commission had impliedly

---

13. Because the insurance policy did not cover the loss: Treitel, *Law of Contract* (3rd Edn.) 221, note 63.
14. Compare c.i.f. contracts (above, p. 247); and the explanation by Treitel, *op. cit.*, 223.
15. (1852), 8 Ex. 40.   16. (1853), 9 Ex. 102.
17. For f.o.b. contracts, see above, pp. 246–247.
18. Slade (1954), 70 L.Q.R. 385, 396–397.
19. (1951), 84 C.L.R. 377.

warranted that the tanker existed. On the basis of these two cases, there are a number of possible interpretations of English law.

(1) *Couturier* v. *Hastie* indicates that the contract is void for mistake; and this rule is embodied in s. 6. This implies that *McRae's Case* does not represent English Law, and that a contract falling within the ambit of s. 6 is always void for mistake[20].

(2) *Couturier* v. *Hastie* may be distinguished from *McRae's Case* on the basis that in the latter case the goods never existed, whereas in the former case they did have an existence once. If this view is adopted, then it may be that s. 6 only applies where the goods once existed[1].

(3) *Couturier* v. *Hastie* does not show that the contract is void for mistake; and s. 6 embodies a mere presumption to this effect. Such an argument may be bolstered by reference to s. 55 of the S.G.A.[2]. On the other hand, s. 6 is one of the few which is not expressed to give way to a contrary intention[3], and the terminology of s. 55 is difficult to reconcile with its application here[4].

(4) The contract of sale will always be rendered void by the non-existence of the subject-matter, but that there may be a collateral contract whereby the seller warrants the existence of the goods[5]. Such a device would be of no avail if the contract of sale remained purely executory on both sides[6]. Alternatively, it may be that there is liability in tort for negligent misstatement[7].

The effect of the operation of s. 6 of the S.G.A. is illustrated by *Barrow, Lane & Ballard, Ltd.* v. *Phillips, Ltd.*[8].

> On Oct. 7th, the plaintiff purchased from X. one lot of 700 bags of ground nuts then in the possession of Y., and inspected but did not count the bags. On Oct. 11th, the plaintiff agreed to sell the 700 bags to the defendant, and the next day handed the defendant a delivery order, which the latter immediately presented to Y. The defendant agreed to resell the goods; but when the defendant attempted to take delivery six weeks later it was discovered that Y. only had 150 bags in his warehouse. It was found that 109 bags had been stolen from, or irregularly delivered by, Y. before Oct. 11th; and that 591 bags had similarly disappeared after that date. Y. being insolvent, the plaintiff sued for the price of 591 bags, arguing

---

20. See Cheshire & Fifoot, *Law of Contract* (7th Edn.) 190, 193; *Benjamin on Sale* (8th Edn.) 143; Glanville Williams (1954), 17 M.L.R. 154, 155.
1. The view taken by the High Court of Australia.
2. Section 55 is set out above, p. 132. See Atiyah, *Sale of Goods* (3rd Edn.) 31; *Chalmers' Sale of Goods* (15th Edn.) 36.
3. Treitel, *Law of Contract* (3rd Edn.) 222–223.
4. Smith (1963), J.S.P.T.L. 227.
5. Cheshire & Fifoot, *Law of Contract* (7th Edn.) 193.
6. Treitel, *Law of Contract* (3rd Edn.) 223.
7. See above, pp. 129–130; and Treitel, *op. cit.*, 223–224.
8. [1929] 1 K.B. 575.

that the property had passed on contract (Oct. 11th) or delivery (Oct. 12th).

WRIGHT J. held that the 700 bags was an indivisible parcel[9]; that the present situation fell within s. 6, and that the contract was therefore void; but that the seller was entitled to the "price" of the 150 bags actually received[10]. His Lordship denied that the acceptance of the delivery order by Y. constituted an appropriation of the 591 bags, on the grounds that the parties only intended to appropriate the 700 bags[11]. The seller further argued that the case was to be treated as a tender of the wrong quantity within s. 30, and that the buyer had accepted the offer of 591 bags; but WRIGHT J. disagreed with this on the grounds that (1) s. 30 gives the buyer an option to reject and rescind when he knows the true facts[12], and (2) the contract was void under s. 6. Nor did his Lordship think that the property passed to the buyers by reason of their sub-sale or delay in taking delivery, and pointed out that there was no contract under which the property could pass[13].

In view of the apparently restricting effect which s. 6 has on the ability of the courts to interpret the intention of the parties, it is important to delimit the operation of the section, which is only expressed to be applicable where "specific goods" have "perished".

1. Specific goods. Both ss. 6 and 7 are limited to sales of "specific goods". This term presumably means the same in each case, and will be considered in connection with s. 7[14].

2. Perish. Both ss. 6 and 7 are only expressed to be applicable where the contract goods have "perished." Presumably this term means the same in each case, though it is nowhere defined in the S.G.A. The term obviously covers physical destruction; and it would also seem to include those situations[15] where the goods are unavailable to the parties for the completion of the contract for some reason which is beyond the control of the parties[16]. Can the goods be said to perish whilst they remain identifiable in the hands of the parties? According to *Benjamin*[17], goods have perished where they have "ceased to exist in a

---

9. The answer might have been different if the contract had been divisible: see below, p. 277.
10. Presumably in quasi-contract. But the buyer had already resold, so how could the quasi-contractual remedy be available? See below, p. 408.
11. See above, p. 167.
12. See above, p. 77.
13. Therefore the risk could not pass under *Sterns, Ltd.* v. *Vickers, Ltd.*: set out above, p. 243.
14. See below, p. 258.
15. E.g. *Couturier* v. *Hastie* (1856), 5 H.L. Cas. 673; *Barrow, Lane and Ballard, Ltd.* v. *Phillip Phillips & Co., Ltd.*, [1929] 1 K.B. 575.
16. What if the seller causes the unavailability, but is protected by an exclusion clause? Compare self-induced frustration: see below, p. 254.
17. *On Sale* (8th Edn.) 143.

commercial sense", as where a cargo of cement is submerged, or dates saturated in sewage[18]. But can this be taken further? Can those situations be included where goods have never existed[19], or where they are requisitioned[20], or where the contract is illegal[1]? What if only part of the goods suffers such a calamity[2]? Is it going too far to suggest that the goods have perished where, subject to the *de minimis* rule, any part of them are commercially unavailable to the parties for the performance of the contract?

2 Subsequent impossibility

The contract may become impossible of performance subsequent to its formation. In this situation the rules of risk have an important part to play[3]; but they will not determine whether the supervening impossibility discharges both parties from their obligations under the contract. They will only be so discharged where the contract is frustrated.

(a) When may a contract be frustrated?

Prima facie, a contract may be frustrated by the destruction of the person or thing essential for its performance[4], by legal impossibility[5] or illegality[6], by serious delay inconsistent with the terms of the contract[7], or by the disappearance of the purpose of the contract[8]; but it is clear that a party cannot rely on a self-induced frustrating event[9]. Suppose the parties make specific provision in their contract for the *prima facie* frustrating event. Can reliance be placed on the possible interpretations of contractual intention analysed above[10]; or does the doctrine of frustration prevent this? In part, the answer may depend on the theoretical basis of the doctrine of frustration[11]; but in one

---

18. Cf. *Asfar & Co.* v. *Blundell*, [1896] 1 Q.B. 123, C.A. But see *obiter* to the contrary in *Horn* v. *Minister of Food*, [1948] 2 All E.R. 1036, which is usually thought to be wrong: Atiyah, *Sale of Goods* (3rd Edn.) 34; *Chalmers' Sale of Goods* (15th Edn.) 36. See also *Rendell* v. *Turnbull* (1908), 27 N.Z.L.R. 1067.
19. E.g. *McRae's Case* (1951), 84 C.L.R. 377: set out above, p. 161.
20. Cf. *Re Shipton Anderson & Co.*, [1915] 3 K.B. 676, D.C.
 1. Cf. *Re Badische Co., Ltd.*, [1921] 2 Ch. 331.
 2. See *Barrow, Lane and Ballard, Ltd.* v. *Phillip Phillips & Co., Ltd.*, [1929] 1 K.B. 575: set out above, pp. 252–253.   3. See below, p. 256.
 4. E.g. *Taylor* v. *Caldwell* (1863), 32 L.J.Q.B. 164. But see c.i.f. contracts: above, p. 247.
 5. E.g. *Re Shipton Anderson & Co.* (see above).
 6. *Re Badische* (see above); *Kursell* v. *Timber Operators and Contractors, Ltd.*, [1927] 1 K.B. 298, C.A. (see above, p. 161).
 7. E.g. *Jackson* v. *Union Marine Insurance Co., Ltd.* (1874), L.R. 10 C.P. 125.
 8. E.g. *Krell* v. *Henry*, [1903] 2 K.B. 740 C.A.
 9. *Maritime National Fish, Ltd.* v. *Ocean Trawlers, Ltd.*, [1935] A.C. 524, P.C.
10. See above, p. 250.
11. See Treitel, *Law of Contract* (3rd Edn.) 779–784; Cheshire & Fifoot, *Law of Contract* (7th Edn.) 507–511. And see *Clarke* v. *Bates*, [1913] L.J.C.C.R. 63, Cty. Ct.; affd. by D.C. at p. 114.

situation there has been statutory intervention. Section 7 of the S.G.A. provides:

> "Where there is an agreement to sell specific goods, and subsequently the goods, without any fault on the part of the seller or buyer, perish before the risk passes to the buyer, the agreement is thereby avoided".

This section can only apply to contracts for the sale of goods; and it is further restricted in that it is only applicable where the contract is for the sale of specific goods, the frustrating event is the perishing of those goods, and neither the property nor risk have passed[12]. In all contracts of h.p., and in all contracts for the sale of goods outside the ambit of s. 7, the common law as amended by the Law Reform (Frustrated Contracts) Act 1943 still applies; and it is arguable that the matter should depend on the contractual intention of the parties. Even where s. 7 is applicable, it is arguable that both ss. 6 and 7 give way to a contrary intention[13].

Assuming that there has been an event *prima facie* capable of frustrating a particular contract of sale or h.p., it does not necessarily follow that it will in all circumstances do so. Two questions arise.

First, how far, if at all, is it necessary for the contract goods to be designated before the contract is capable of being frustrated? Clearly, many frustrating events will operate irrespective of whether the contract goods are ascertained[14]; but other cases are not quite so clear. In *Howell* v. *Coupland*[15]

> In March, the parties made a contract for the sale of 200 tons of potatoes to be grown by the seller on his land in Lincolnshire, and to be delivered the following autumn. The acreage planted by the seller would have been sufficient to have produced 200 tons in a normal year; but in August the crop was spoilt by potato blight, and the seller could only salvage 80 tons. The buyer accepted the 80 tons, and sued for non-delivery of the remainder. The Court of Appeal unanimously agreed that there was an implied term that both parties be excused performance in such an event.

The opposite conclusion was reached in *Blackburn Bobbin, Ltd.* v. *T. W. Allen, Ltd.*[16].

> There was a contract for the sale f.o.r. Hull of seventy standards of Finland birch timber. Unknown to the buyer, the seller was following the usual trade practice, namely, to then load timber in

---

12. The ambit of s. 7 is analysed below, p. 258.
13. See above, p. 252.
14. E.g. death of a person essential for performance.
15. (1876), 1 Q.B.D. 258, C.A.
16. [1918] 1 K.B. 540; affd. [1918] 2 K.B. 467, C.A.

Finland for shipment to England. Before delivery commenced, the outbreak of war made shipment impossible. The buyer's claim for damages succeeded before McCARDIE J., who saw no reason why such "a bare and unqualified contract for the sale of unascertained goods" should be frustrated by the outbreak of war; and the Court of Appeal agreed[17].

The explanation of these decisions is that everything turns on the precise nature of the allegedly frustrating event in relation to the terms of the contract: in the former case it was impossible to perform the contract from the contemplated source; but in the latter case there was no source contemplated in the contract and performance could be from any such timber in the world. Such a distinction has sometimes erroneously led to the conclusion that it is possible to frustrate a contract for the sale of goods by the non-availability of the goods where the contract is for the sale of an unascertained part of a specific whole, but not where the goods are generic, i.e., where the contract may be satisfied by any out of the world supply of those goods.

Second, what is the effect, if any, of the incidence of risk on the doctrine of frustration? Leaving aside those cases where the elements of risk and property are themselves divided between the parties, there are four possible situations, depending on whether property has passed, and whether risk goes with property. Suppose a contract for the sale of goods which are destroyed before either delivery or payment.

	Seller	Buyer
Case 1:	P + R	
Case 2:		P + R
Case 3:	P	R
Case 4:	R	P

Case 1: the property and risk are in the seller. This is, perhaps, the most obvious case where the contract may be frustrated by the destruction of the goods, in which case the seller ceases to be liable for non-delivery, and the buyer ceases to be liable for the price.

Case 2: the property and risk are in the buyer. If we were to say that this contract were frustrated by the destruction of the goods, the effect would be that the buyer was no longer liable for the price, thereby effectively throwing the risk back on the seller. Does this show that such a contract cannot be frustrated by the destruction of the goods?

Case 3: the property is in the seller and the risk in the buyer. A contract cannot be executed before the passing of property. But can it be frustrated by the destruction of the goods if risk has passed?

---

17. It has been suggested that the C.A. decision seems to envisage a slightly wider field of operation for the doctrine of frustration: Atiyah, *Sale of Goods* (3rd Edn.), 127. *Sed quaere?*

<u>Case 4</u>: the risk is in the seller and the property is in the buyer. It has been argued that the contract cannot be frustrated by the destruction of the goods because its object, the transfer of property, has been carried out[18]. Yet, if the buyer is held liable for the price, this is in effect to put the risk on him. Does it therefore follow that the contract can be frustrated?

It is tempting to simplify this rather difficult pattern by saying that whether the contract can be frustrated by the destruction of the goods depends on whether the risk has passed[19]: it would follow that it is possible to frustrate in *Cases 1* and *4*. but not in *Cases 2* and *3*. Yet this view assumes that a provision in the contract passing risk ousts the doctrine of frustration[20] and that frustration affects all the terms of the contract[1]. No doubt it is ordinarily true that only in *Cases 1* and *4* will the contract be frustrated; but this may not simply reflect the incidence of risk so much as the fact that within *Cases 2* and *3* there will rarely be any outstanding contractual obligations which survive the frustrating event. If so, it would seem that at very least the contract could be frustrated whilst it fell within *Case 3*[2]. But is it possible to go further and say that a contract can be frustrated while any duty remains to be performed thereunder, in which case it would follow that even contracts within *Case 2* could be frustrated[3]?

(b) What is the effect of frustration?

Assuming that the contract be frustrated, the effect of frustration is governed by the common law, as amended by the Law Reform (Frustrated Contracts) Act 1943 (hereafter called the F.C.A.). That Act is expressed to be applicable to all contracts which have

> "become impossible of performance or been otherwise frustrated . . . subject to the provisions of section 2 of this Act" (s. 1 (1)).

The only important exception for our purposes is that contained in s. 2 (5) (c), which excludes from the operation of the 1943 Act

> "any contract to which section seven of the Sale of Goods Act 1893 . . . applies, or . . . any other contract for the sale, or for the sale and delivery, of specific goods, where the contract is frustrated by reason of the fact that the goods have perished".

In cases falling within s. 2 (5) (c) only the unamended common law rules apply; and it is therefore necessary to determine the scope of this

---

18. Atiyah, *Sale of Goods* (3rd Edn.) 126.
19. See Goff & Jones, *The Law of Restitution* 338. *Contra* Glanville Williams, *The Frustrated Contracts Act* 82, note 30.
20. This is consistent with the implied term theory, but not the just solution approach.
 1. Atiyah, *op. cit.*, 129. But see Glanville Williams, *ibid.*
 2. See Glanville Williams, *op. cit.*, pp. 84–85, and esp. note 35.
 3. Doubted by Atiyah, *Sale of Goods* (3rd Edn.) 129.

provision. The first part of s. 2 (5) (c) refers to contracts falling within s. 7 of the S.G.A.[4]; and it is often said that the second part to s. 2 (5)(c) does not add anything to the first part[5]. However, on the basis of the analysis set out above[6], it is submitted that the first part refers to contracts falling within *Case 1*, and that the second part refers to contracts falling within *Cases 3* and *4*, and probably even *Case 2*. Both parts will only apply where there is a contract for the sale of "specific goods" frustrated by reason of the fact that the goods have "perished", both of which expressions appear in ss. 6 and 7 of the S.G.A. and 2 (5) (c) of the F.C.A. Presumably, the term "specific goods" means the same in all three cases; but there are two possible meanings of the phrase. First, it may attract the definition in the S.G.A., and thus refer to "goods identified and agreed upon at the time a contract of sale is made" (s. 62 (1))[7]. Second, the expression in this context may be somewhat wider, and merely require that the contract goods are sufficiently specific for the contract to be frustrated by their perishing[8]. The stipulation that the goods must "perish" also presumably means the same in all three cases, and is discussed above[9]. But what of the requirement of s. 7 of the S.G.A. that the goods should perish without fault on the part of either party, and the absence of any such requirement from s. 6 of the S.G.A. and s. 2 (5) (c) of the F.C.A.[10]?

The effect of frustration on contracts falling inside and outside s. 2 (5) (c) of the F.C.A. is adequately discussed elsewhere[11]; but there would only seem to be any practical difference between the two situations in respect of advance payments and part delivery.

1. Advance payment. Two situations must be distinguished:

(1) Where the buyer has paid part or all of the price before the frustrating event. If there has been a total failure of consideration, the buyer may recover that sum at common law or under the F.C.A.; but, where the failure of consideration is only partial[12], the buyer cannot recover at common law though he may do so under the F.C.A. (s. 1 (2)).

(2) Where the contract provides for payment of part or all of the price before the frustrating event, and the seller has incurred expenses before that event. The F.C.A. allows the seller to claim reasonable

---

4. Section 7 is set out above, p. 255.
5. E.g. Atiyah, *Sale of Goods* (3rd Edn.) 129–130; Treitel, *op. cit.,* 777–778; Goff & Jones, *The Law of Restitution*, 338.
6. At pp. 256–257.   7. See above, pp. 20, 159.
8. See above, pp. 255–256.   9. At pp. 253–254.
10. See Glanville Williams, *The Frustrated Contracts Act* 83, note 30.
11. See Atiyah, *Sale of Goods* (3rd Edn.) 129–135; Treitel, *Law of Contract* (3rd Edn.) 768–779; Cheshire & Fifoot, *Law of Contract* (7th Edn.) 520–529. See also *Clarke* v. *Bates*, [1913] L.J.C.C.R. 63 and 114, D.C.; *British Berna Motor Lorries, Ltd.* v. *Inter-Transport Co., Ltd.* (1915), 31 T.L.R. 200; *Shepherd* v. *Ready Mix Concrete (London)* (1968), 112 Sol. Jo. 518.
12. See below, pp. 406–408.

expenses out of the sums paid or payable (s. 1 (2)); but he has no such right at common law.

2. Part delivery. Again, a distinction must be drawn:

(1) Where the buyer has paid the price and received part of the goods. At common law, the buyer could not recover the price because there had been no total failure of consideration[13]; but under the F.C.A. the seller can only claim to retain so much of the price as is attributable to any gain which has accrued to the buyer (s. 1 (3)) or any expenses incurred by the seller (s. 1 (2)).

(2) Where the seller has delivered part of the goods but been paid nothing. Under the F.C.A. the seller may be compensated for any benefit which has accrued to the buyer (s. 1 (3)), or may claim his expenses out of any sum payable by the buyer before the frustrating event (s. 1 (2)). However, at common law, the seller cannot recover anything from the buyer at common law, unless he can show an implied contract from the fact that the buyer has voluntarily retained the goods after the frustrating event[14].

---

13. But he might recover a proportionate amount of the price on the grounds that the goods were still at the seller's risk: Atiyah, *Sale of Goods* (3rd Edn.) 131.
14. The claim is quasi-contractual; and it is difficult to fit in with the requirement that the buyer's retention of the benefit be voluntary, the decision in *Barrow, Lane and Ballard, Ltd.* v. *Phillip Phillips & Co., Ltd.*, [1929] 1 K.B. 575: see above, p. 253.

PART 4

The Price

CHAPTER 16

Delivery and Payment

Under both the contract of sale and the contract of h.p. it is normally envisaged that there be a delivery of goods[1] in exchange for the price[2]; and, leaving aside all questions of what must be delivered and what must be paid, this Chapter is concerned with the acts of delivery and payment. As s. 27 of the S.G.A. states,

> "It is the duty of the seller to deliver the goods, and of the buyer to accept and pay for them, in accordance with the terms of the contract of sale".

Whilst this section is subject to a contrary intention, it plainly expresses the normal expectation of the parties to a contract of sale—and also, for that matter, of the parties to a contract of h.p. The duties of delivery and payment will now be separately analysed; and the time for performance of those duties, and performance by instalments is reserved for sections 3 and 4 respectively.

1 DELIVERY

English law differentiates between the passing of property in, and delivery of, the contract goods; and, because of the different incidents attached to the two, they must be carefully distinguished[3]. Three situations are possible:

(1) Property may pass after delivery, as in a conditional sale or h.p. agreement.

(2) Property may pass at the moment of delivery, as where a delivery of unascertained goods constitutes an appropriation of them[4].

(3) Property passes before delivery, at the earliest when the contract is made[5].

1 The meaning and rules of delivery

A. The meaning of delivery. The H.P.A. defines delivery by reference to the S.G.A. (s. 58 (1) H.P.A.); and the S.G.A. provides that, unless the context otherwise requires,

---

1. See above, pp. 18–19.　　　　2. See above, pp. 21–24.
3. The incidents of property are analysed above, pp. 155–156, and those of delivery below.
4. Section 18, rule 5 (2): see above, p. 170.
5. Section 18, rule 1: see above, p. 162.

" 'Delivery' means voluntary transfer of possession from one person to another" (s. 62 (1)).

The most obvious example of a "delivery" is a physical transfer of actual possession; but "possession" clearly includes constructive possession. Whilst detailed discussion of the common law concept of "possession" is beyond the scope of this work[6], certain common instances of a constructive transfer of possession may be noticed.

(1) "Symbolic delivery"; that is, the handing over of the means of control, e.g., the keys to a room.

(2) "Attornment"; that is, an acknowledgement by a third party who has actual control of the goods that he holds the goods on behalf of the buyer.[7]

(3) Delivery of the documents of title. The S.G.A. defines a document of title by reference to the F.A. 1889 (s. 62 (1) S.G.A.); and the definition in the latter Act is set out above[8]. The transfer of the documents of title may itself amount to a sort of symbolic delivery of the goods[9].

(4) Delivery to the buyer's agent. This may amount at common law to a transfer of possession[10]; but special provision is made for one particular case by s. 32 (1) of the S.G.A. as follows:

"Where, in pursuance of a contract of sale, the seller is authorised or required to send the goods to the buyer, delivery of the goods to a carrier, whether named by the buyer or not, for the purpose of transmission to the buyer is primâ facie deemed to be a delivery of the goods to the buyer".

This presumption gives way to a contrary intention, as where the carrier is the agent of the seller[11].

(5) "Attornment" by the seller or owner; that is, where the seller or owner agrees to retain possession as agent of the buyer or hirer[12].

B. *The rules of delivery*. Certain rules of delivery are set out in s. 29 of the S.G.A.; and, whilst there is no authority on the point, it is usually thought that these rules are also applicable to h.p. transactions[13]. The basic rule is set out in s. 29 (1):

"Whether it is for the buyer to take possession of the goods or for the seller to send them to the buyer is a question depending in each case on the contract, express or implied, between the parties. Apart

---

6. See Crossley Vaines, *Personal Property* (4th Edn.) Ch. 4; and also above, p. 206.   7. And see s. 29 (3) S.G.A.   8. At p. 207
9. *Per* BOWEN L.J. in *Sanders* v. *Maclean* (1883), 11 Q.B.D. 327, C.A., at p. 341. See, e.g. c.i.f. and arrival contracts: above, pp. 247–248.
10. But the goods may still be regarded as in the course of transit—s. 45 (1) S.G.A.: set out below, p. 325.
11. E.g. *Galbraith and Grant, Ltd.* v. *Block*, [1922] 2 K.B. 155.
12. Cf. s. 41 (2) S.G.A.: set out below, p. 321.
13. Guest, *Law of H.P.*, para 321; Goode, *H.P. Law & Practice* (2nd Edn.) 220; Atiyah, *Sale of Goods* (3rd Edn.) 232; Wild, *Law of H.P.* (2nd Edn.) 54.

from any such contract, express or implied, the place of delivery is the seller's place of business, if he have one, and if not, his residence: Provided that, if the contract be for the sale of specific goods, which to the knowledge of the parties when the contract is made are in some other place, then that place is the place of delivery".

This provision refers to two things:

(1) The mode of delivery. The Act leaves it to the parties to decide what shall constitute a delivery; and it may be regretted that there is not a more definite *prima facie* rule[14]. The relationship of this rule to the opportunity to examine the goods is discussed below[15].

(2) The place of delivery. The underlying presumption is not that the seller will send the goods[16], but that the buyer will collect them; but this presumption may be displaced, as in f.o.b., c.i.f. and ex-ship contracts[17].

Section 29 also makes provision for the time of delivery as follows:

"(2) Where under the contract of sale the seller is bound to send the goods to the buyer, but no time for sending them is fixed, the seller is bound to send them within a reasonable time[18].

"(3) Where the goods at the time of sale are in the possession of a third person, there is no delivery by seller to buyer unless and until such third person acknowledges to the buyer that he holds the goods on his behalf; provided that nothing in this section shall affect the operation of the issue or transfer of any documents of title to goods[19].

"(4) Demand or tender of delivery may be treated as ineffectual unless made at a reasonable hour. What is a reasonable hour is a question of fact"[20].

2 The duty of delivery

There are two facets of the duty of delivery: the seller or owner is under a duty to tender delivery; and the buyer or hirer is under a duty to accept delivery.

---

14. *Chalmers' Sale of Goods* (15th Edn.) 104.   15. At p. 269.
16. But s. 29 (5) provides that:
    "Unless otherwise agreed, the expenses of and incidental to putting the goods into a deliverable state must be borne by the seller".
17. See above, pp. 246–248.
18. E.g. *Charles Rickards, Ltd.* v. *Oppenhaim*, [1950] 1 K.B. 616; [1950] 1 All E.R. 420, C.A.: set out above, p. 148; and *Thomas Borthwick (Glasgow), Ltd.* v. *Bunge & Co., Ltd.*, [1969] 1 Lloyds Rep. 17. What is a reasonable time is a question of fact: s. 56 S.G.A.; and the effect of s. 37 S.G.A. may be that time runs from the buyer's request for delivery: see below, p. 268.
19. E.g. *Inglis* v. *Robertson*, [1898] A.C. 616, H.L.: set out above, p. 223; *Wardar's Co., Ltd.* v. *Norwood & Sons, Ltd.*, [1968] 2 Q.B. 663; [1968] 2 All E.R. 602.
20. Presumably, this will be related to the ordinary course of business: see above, pp. 211–214.

(*a*) *Tender of delivery.*   In the case of a sale, the seller's duty is to tender delivery in accordance with the rules set out above.   To what extent must the seller go in performing this duty where the buyer indicates that he will refuse to accept the goods or pay the price if the goods are tendered?   Clearly, the seller is entitled to accept an anti-cipatory breach, and need not actually tender delivery[1]. On the other hand, if the seller wishes to sue the buyer for non-acceptance, he must show that at the time of the buyer's repudiation he was ready and willing to perform his side of the bargain[2]: otherwise, the contract will be dis-charged by agreement.   But need the seller show an ability to perform at the time of the buyer's breach?   In *Braithwaite* v. *Foreign Hardwood Co.*[3]

> There was a contract for the sale of rosewood to be paid for by cash against the bills of lading.   When the seller tendered the bills of lading, the buyer refused to accept them for reasons subsequently found to be unjustifiable.   Subsequently, the buyer discovered that some of the consignments covered by the bills presented did not answer the contract description; and he pleaded this fact by way of a defence to the seller's action for non-acceptance.   This defence was rejected by the Court of Appeal on the grounds that by rejecting the bills of lading the buyer had impliedly waived the seller's breach, and could not thereafter complain of it.

It is a well-established principle that the right to repudiate is not lost because the wrong reason is given for it[4]; and it has already been shown how GREER J. in *Taylor* v. *Oakes*[5] sought to reconcile that rule with the decision in *Braithwaite's Case* by distinguishing between an offer to tender and an actual tender of delivery[6].   However, the majority of the Court of Appeal in *Taylor* v. *Oakes* took the view that *Braithwaite's Case* merely decided that, once the anticipatory repudiation had been accepted, "the vendor was relieved of the necessity of proving his readiness and willingness"[7].   This latter view seems to have been accepted by the House of Lords in *British and Benningtons, Ltd.* v. *North Western Cachar Tea Co., Ltd*[8].

> The buyer agreed to buy the crop of tea to be produced on a certain Indian estate, delivery to be made in bonded warehouse in London,

---

1. *Levey & Co.* v. *Goldberg*, [1922] 1 K.B. 688, at p. 692.
2. *Per* Lord ABINGER C.B. in *De Medina* v. *Norman* (1842), 9 M. & W. 820, at p. 827.   3. [1905] 2 K.B. 543, C.A.
4. See e.g. *per* MOCATTA J. in *The Mihalis Angelos*, [1970] 1 All E.R. 673, at p. 676; rev. on other grounds, [1970] 3 All E.R. 125, C.A.
5. (1922), 27 Com. Cas. 261, C.A.   6. See above, p. 149.
7. *Per* SCRUTTON L.J., at p. 273.   See also ATKIN L.J., *ibid.*
8. [1923] A.C. 48, H.L.   But the analysis of GREER J. was accepted *obiter* by SALMON L.J. in *Esmail & Sons* v. *Rosenthal & Sons, Ltd.*, [1964] 2 Lloyds Rep. 447, at p. 466, C.A.: decision approved by H.L. without reference to this point—[1965] 2 All E.R. 860.

but no date for delivery being specified. Subsequently, the buyer agreed to accept delivery at certain out-ports; but after further delays he repudiated the contract on the grounds that delivery had not been made within a reasonable time. In the seller's action for damages for non-acceptance, it was found that a reasonable time for delivery had not expired when the buyer repudiated.

The House of Lords held that the buyer's waiver of delivery in London did not discharge the seller from his contractual duty in this respect[9]; but they considered that, where there was such an anticipatory breach by the buyer, the seller need not tender delivery before commencing the action, nor need he prove that at the date of repudiation he was ready and willing to deliver in London, Lord SUMNER accepted that a buyer could set up his seller's breach of contract in such circumstances[10], but pointed out that in this case the seller might still have tendered delivery in London within the contract period[11]. It is submitted that a seller suing for non-acceptance ought to have to show that he is ready and willing to tender delivery in conformity with the contract; that the *Cachar Tea Case* merely shows that there is in these circumstances a presumption that the seller intends to perform his contract; and that it is in rebutting this presumption that the distinction drawn by GREER J. may be significant. If the buyer repudiates on an actual tender, that tender can be tested against the contract terms; but, if the buyer repudiates in anticipation of tender, the question is whether the seller has done anything which would preclude his performance when the time for tender arrived.

Because delivery is the essence of bailment, the law puts a far greater emphasis on tender of delivery in h.p. transactions. The hiring does not commence until the owner tenders to the hirer goods which conform with the contract *and* the hirer accepts the same[12]. If the hirer does not accept the goods, he cannot be sued for the instalments of rent, even if expressed to be payable in advance[13].

(*b*) *Acceptance of delivery.* Where the seller tenders goods in conformity with the contract, it is the buyer's duty to accept them (s. 27 S.G.A.); and, if the buyer wrongfully refuses to accept delivery, s. 37 provides as follows:

> "When the seller is ready and willing to deliver the goods, and requests the buyer to take delivery, and the buyer does not within a

---

9. See above, p. 149.
10. At pp. 71–72. Three other Law Lords concurred with this judgment; and the relevant passage in Lord SUMNER's judgment was cited with approval by DEVLIN J. in *Universal Cargo Corporation* v. *Citati*, [1957] 2 Q.B. 401, at p. 445.
11. At p. 71. Does this rebut the argument that, as the seller was still in breach, the buyer was still entitled to rescind? See Stoljar (1957), 35 Can. B.R. 485, 509.
12. See above, p. 116.   13. See below, p. 374.

reasonable time[14] after such request take delivery of the goods, he is liable to the seller for any loss occasioned by his neglect or refusal to take delivery, and also for a reasonable charge for the care and custody of the goods[15]: Provided that nothing in this section shall affect the rights of the seller where the neglect or refusal of the buyer to take delivery amounts to a repudiation of the contract".

Whilst s. 37 is not expressed to give way to a contrary intention, it is submitted that it will do so with the following result: if the contract stipulates a time for acceptance of delivery, the section is ousted and delivery must be made at that time; but, if the contract merely stipulates a time for tender of delivery, it is arguable that acceptance of delivery need only be made within a reasonable time thereafter[16]; and, if there is no stipulation as to the time of delivery, s. 37 requires the buyer to take delivery within a reasonable time of the seller's request that he should do so. The proviso to s. 37 expressly recognises that the conduct of the buyer may evince an intention to repudiate the contract[17].

Conversely, where the goods tendered by the seller are not in conformity with the contract, the buyer is *prima facie* entitled to refuse to accept them[18], in which case s. 36 provides:

> "Unless otherwise agreed, where goods are delivered to the buyer, and he refuses to accept them having the right so to do, he is not bound to return them to the seller, but it is sufficient if he intimates to the seller that he refuses to accept them".

This section seems to assume that there is a contract of sale between the parties; and, if the delivery merely amounts to an offer to sell, the ordinary common law rules apply[19]. Where there is a contract of sale, it is open to the buyer who rejects to return the goods to the seller; but s. 36 reaffirms the common law rule that he need not do so, and that *prima facie* the buyer may reject the goods by "any unequivocal act showing that he rejects them"[20]. Again following the common law, it would seem that the buyer who evinces an intention to reject becomes a mere involuntary bailee of the goods, and is only under a duty to exercise reasonable care of them[1]: the underlying risk is in the erstwhile seller, in whom the property in the goods remains or revests[2]; and the

---

14. What is a reasonable time is a question of fact: s. 56 S.G.A.
15. Damages are considered below, p. 376.
16. See *Benjamin on Sale* (8th Edn.) 689, 751.
17. See below, p. 360.
18. For the restrictions on the buyer's right to reject, see below, p. 397, *et seq*.
19. *Chalmers' Sale of Goods* (15th Edn.) 136.
20. *Per* BRETT J. in *Grimoldby* v. *Wells* (1875), L.R. 10 C.P. 391, at p. 395. For an express agreement to reject in a certain manner, see *Docker* v. *Hyams*, [1969] 3 All E.R. 808, C.A.
1. *Benjamin on Sale* (8th Edn.) 765.
2. Cf. above, p. 248.

seller acquires a right to immediate possession of the goods[3]. Whilst the buyer has no lien on the rejected goods for repayment of the price[4], he may be able to recover the price in quasi-contract where the contract of sale is rescinded[5]; and he may maintain an action against the seller for non-delivery of the contract goods[6].

Obviously, it is very important to the buyer to determine whether or not he must accept the goods tendered by the seller; and the S.G.A. therefore gives him a right to examine the goods before he accepts delivery of them[7]. Section 34 provides[8]:

> "(1) Where goods are delivered to the buyer, which he has not previously examined, he is not deemed to have accepted them unless and until he has had a reasonable opportunity of examining them for the purpose of ascertaining whether they are in conformity with the contract.
>
> (2) Unless otherwise agreed, when the seller tenders delivery of goods to the buyer, he is bound, on request, to afford the buyer a reasonable opportunity of examining the goods for the purpose of ascertaining whether they are in conformity with the contract".

As will be seen later, the buyer loses his right to reject by accepting the goods[9]. However, subject to the terms of the contract[10], s. 34 (2) gives the buyer a right, *on request*, to a reasonable opportunity for examination *before* he accepts delivery; and s. 34 (1) provides that, even if the goods have been delivered to the buyer, he is not to be deemed to have accepted them until he has had a reasonable opportunity to examine them unless he has examined them prior to the delivery[11]. Clearly, the buyer must have accepted the transfer of actual or constructive possession to himself for there to have been a delivery[12], so that the purpose of s. 34 (1) must be to preserve the buyer's right to reject *after* he has taken delivery[13]. The object of s. 34 is to allow the buyer the opportunity to ensure that the goods correspond with their description; and it was presumably drafted with sales of unascertained goods in mind[14]. It allows the buyer a reasonable time for examination, envisaging that this may be before or after delivery, and it has been held

---

3. *Per* BANKES L.J. in *E. Hardy & Co. (London)* v. *Hillerns and Fowler*, [1923] 2 K.B. 490, C.A., at p. 496. See also *Commission Car Sales, Ltd.* v. *Saul*, [1957] N.Z.L.R. 144. 4. See below, pp. 313–314.
5. See below, p. 405. 6. See below, p. 409.
7. This right to examine before acceptance of delivery must not be confused with examination before contract: see above, p. 102.
8. Section 34 embodies the common law: *Benjamin on Sale* (8th Edn.) 741, 753.
9. See below, p. 397, *et seq.*
10. Cf. *Polenghi Brothers* v. *Dried Milk Co., Ltd.* (1904), 92 L.T. 64.
11. And s. 15 (2) (b) gives the buyer a reasonable opportunity of comparing the bulk with any sample: see above, p. 109.
12. See above, p. 264.
13. For the relationship of ss. 28 and 34, see below, p. 273.
14. Does it also cover sales of specific goods by description?

that the conduct of the seller must be taken into account in determining what is a reasonable time[15]. What constitutes a reasonable examination must depend on the nature of the goods[16] and any agreement between the parties[17]. The place of examination is *prima facie* the place of delivery[18]; but, if a reasonable examination is not possible at that place, the courts will try to read the contract so that the place where an effective examination is first possible is the place the parties have agreed upon for the examination[19]. This will commonly be the buyer's place of business[20], or the place of delivery to a sub-buyer[1]; but it has been said that the latter will only be the place of examination where[2]

> "the original vendor must know, either because he is told or by necessary inference, that the goods are going further on, and the place at which he delivers must either be unsuitable in itself or the nature or packing of the goods must make inspection at that place unreasonable".

Such an approach has been adopted where the defect was a latent one not discoverable on delivery[3]; or where the delivery was to be made at a wharf where only a cursory inspection was possible[4]; or where the goods were specially packaged for carriage to a sub-buyer[5].

Whilst there is no authority on the point, it is thought that the position of a bailee under a h.p. agreement is similar to that of a buyer in respect of acceptance of delivery. Thus, it is the duty of the bailee to take delivery[6], and failure to do so will render him liable to damages[7], and may even evince an intention to repudiate. Furthermore, it would seem that, before accepting delivery and rendering himself liable to pay instalments of rent, the hirer has a right of examination similar to that of the buyer[7a].

---

15. *Lucy* v. *Mouflet* (1860), 29 L.J. Ex. 110.
16. See e.g. *Esmail & Sons* v. *Rosenthal & Sons, Ltd.*, [1964] 2 Lloyds Rep. 447, C.A.; rev. on other grounds, [1965] 2 All E.R. 860, H.L.
17. *W. Potts & Co., Ltd.* v. *Brown, Macfarlane & Co., Ltd.* (1924), 30 Com. Cas. 64, H.L.
18. *Perkins* v. *Bell*, [1893] 1 Q.B. 193, C.A. (pre-S.G.A.): and *per* PEARCE L.J. in *Long* v. *Lloyd*, [1958] 2 All E.R. 402, C.A., at p. 407.
19. E.g. f.o.b. contracts: *Scaliaris* v. *E. Ofverberg* (1921), 37 T.L.R. 307, C.A.; *Boks & Co.* v. *J. H. Rayner & Co.* (1921), 37 T.L.R. 800, C.A.; *Bragg* v. *Villanova* (1923), 40 T.L.R. 154, D.C.
20. E.g. *B. and P. Wholesale Distributors* v. *Marko*, [1953] C.L.Y. 3266.
 1. E.g. *Heilbutt* v. *Hickson* (1872), L.R. 7 C.P. 438; *Molling & Co.* v. *Dean & Son, Ltd.* (1901), 18 T.L.R. 217, D.C.
 2. *Per* BAILHACHE J. in *Saunt* v. *Belcher and Gibbons, Ltd.* (1920), 26 Com. Cas. 115, at p. 119.
 3. *Heilbutt* v. *Hickson* (above).
 4. *B. and P. Wholesale Distributors* v. *Marko* (above).
 5. *Molling & Co.* v. *Dean & Son, Ltd.* (above).
 6. Guest, *Law of H.P.*, para. 321.
 7. But not to any instalments of hire-rent: see below, p. 374.
7a. *Farnworth Finance Facilities* v. *Attryde*, [1970] 2 All E.R. 774, C.A. See above, p. 143.

2 PAYMENT

The S.G.A. makes it clear that it is the duty of the buyer to pay the price (s. 27); and a h.p. agreement will usually impose a similar obligation on the hirer with respect to the instalments of hire-rent[8]. At the same time, the seller or owner is under an obligation, implied if not express, not to refuse the whole or part of the price where this is tendered in conformity with the contract. At common law, it is *prima facie* the duty of the debtor to seek out and tender[9] the exact amount of his debt in legal tender to the creditor[10], or to such agent as the creditor authorises to receive payment[11]. If the buyer or hirer owes more than one debt to the seller or owner, he is *prima facie* entitled when making a payment to appropriate that payment to a particular debt; but, if the debtor remains silent, the creditor is entitled at common law to make such appropriation as he thinks fit[12].

What constitutes a valid tender will depend on the terms of the agreement and the ordinary law[13], though it should be remembered that where the transaction falls within the H.P.A. the position may be modified by the notice of default procedure[14]. Besides payment in cash, the two commonest examples in domestic sales are the tender of goods in part-exchange, and a cheque (or other bill of exchange)[15].

1. Part-exchanges. It is quite open to the parties to agree that part of the price shall be paid by way of goods taken in part-exchange, and the parties will usually themselves agree on a price to be put on the part-exchange goods[16]. The H.P.A. expressly deems such part-exchange goods to be part of the h.p. or total purchase price[17].

2. Cheques. *Prima facie*, a cheque is given by way of conditional payment, and suspends the creditor's rights either to sue for the debt[18] or

---

8. See above, p. 117.
9. The buyer's duty to tender the price is considered further below, pp. 321–322.
10. *Bradford Old Bank* v. *Sutcliffe*, [1918] 2 K.B. 833, C.A.
11. Under the ordinary rules of agency, which are expressly saved by s. 61 (2) S.G.A.
12. But see the compulsory scheme in 51 H.P.A. 1965.
13. For discussion of legal tender, see *Chalmers' Sale of Goods* (15th Edn.) 158–159; *Halsbury's Laws* (3rd Edn.) VII, 303–305; and also the Decimal Currency Acts 1967 and 1969.   14. See below, pp. 334–336.
15. In export sales, a common method of payment is by way of bankers' commercial credits: see generally Atiyah, *Sale of Goods* (3rd Edn.) Ch. 21; and Cheshire & Fifoot, *Law of Contract* (7th Edn.) 407–408; Treitel, *Law of Contract* (3rd Edn.) 111.
16. In effect, there is a subsidiary contract for the sale of the part-exchange goods, that contract being conditional on the completion of the major contract.
17. Section 58 (2): see above, p. 22.
18. *Bolt and Nut, Ltd.* v. *Rowlands, Nicholls & Co., Ltd.*, [1964] 2 Q.B. 10; [1964] 1 All E.R. 137, C.A.

exercise a seller's lien[19]; but the creditor's rights revive if the cheque is not met[19]. However, there is nothing to prevent a cheque being given and taken by way of absolute payment, in which case it extinguishes the creditor's other rights[20]; or being given by way of collateral security, in which case none of the creditor's remedies are suspended[1]: the parties merely have to evince an intention to displace the ordinary presumption. It has recently been settled that the mere fact of payment of a lesser sum by cheque is no satisfaction of a greater[2].

Who bears any loss if any payment is sent by post? The ordinary rule is that where the creditor expressly or impliedly authorises his debtor to make payment by post—as by sending a letter demanding payment—the posting of a letter containing the price may operate as payment, even if the letter never arrives[3]. *Prima facie*, the risk of such loss is on the creditor[4]; but, if a cheque is not cashed and does not come into the hands of a holder in due course, the creditor is entitled to a duplicate on giving an indemnity[5]. To some extent, the scope of the foregoing rules have been restricted, as the courts have recognised that in the case of large sums of money the ordinary practice is to remit by crossed cheque, and there is therefore no implied authorisation to send large sums in cash, even by registered letter[6]. Despite this restriction, it is common in standard-form agreements, including h.p. agreements, expressly to put the risk of loss in course of post on the debtor.

Finally, reference must be made to the connection between payment of the price and the buyer's right to sue in conversion or detinue. It will be seen later that a plaintiff can only maintain an action in conversion or detinue where he is entitled to the immediate possession of goods[7]; and this in turn depends on whether the seller or owner is bound to deliver immediately. The time-connection between the obligations of delivery and payment are examined in the next section.

3 THE TIME OF DELIVERY AND PAYMENT

Having analysed the duties of payment and delivery, the importance of the time element in their performance must now be examined.

---

19. See below, p. 314.
20. *Sibree* v. *Tripp* (1846), 15 L.J. Ex. 318.
 1. *Modern Light Cars, Ltd.* v. *Seals*, [1934] 1 K.B. 32.
 2. *D. and C. Builders, Ltd.* v. *Rees*, [1966] 2 Q.B. 617; [1965] 3 All E.R. 837, C.A.
 3. *Norman* v. *Ricketts* (1886), 3 T.L.R. 182, C.A.   Cf. *Pennington* v. *Crossley & Son* (1897), 77 L.T. 43, C.A.   What if payment is sent with the order?
 4. Compare risk of loss of goods: above, p. 241.
 5. Bills of Exchange Act 1882, ss. 69, 70.
 6. *Mitchell-Henry* v. *Norwich Union Life Insurance Society*, [1918] 2 K.B. 67, C.A.
 7. See below, p. 377.

Throughout, it must be remembered that each party has two obligations: it is for the seller or owner to tender delivery of the goods and
accept payment of the price; and for the buyer or hirer to accept
delivery of the goods and tender payment of the price. The basic rule
is laid down in s. 28 of the S.G.A. as follows:

> "Unless otherwise agreed, delivery of the goods and payment of
> the price are concurrent conditions, that is to say, the seller must be
> ready and willing to give possession of the goods to the buyer in
> exchange for the price and the buyer must be ready and willing to
> pay the price in exchange for possession of the goods".

Two situations must be considered: first, where the contract contemplates that the basic presumption applies; and second, where it does not.

1 Where delivery and payment are concurrent terms

Where the presumption in s. 28 operates, delivery must be made in
exchange for the price. Usually, this will mean delivery of the goods,
so that the buyer may exercise his right of inspection under s. 34[8].
However, where the contract contemplates delivery of documents of
title, these documents are equivalent to the goods[9], so that on delivery
of the documents the seller is thereupon entitled to the price[10]; but the
buyer retains the right to inspect and reject the goods[11].

In order to appreciate the effect of a delay in performance by either
party, the status of the obligations of delivery and payment must first
be examined.

1. Delivery. In the case of h.p. agreements, the hiring does not commence until delivery[12]; but, subject to this, it is presumed that, in so far
as the agreement does not cover delay in delivery, those rules of sale
which relate to delivery apply by analogy. In fact, the S.G.A. refrains
from laying down any hard and fast rule as to whether the time of
delivery is of the essence of the contract (s. 10 (1)), but does require that
the "demand or tender of delivery be made at a reasonable hour"
(s. 29 (4)), and makes the duty to tender delivery subject to the unpaid
seller's lien[13]. According to McCardie J.[14]:

> "In ordinary commercial contracts for the sale of goods the rule
> clearly is that time is prima facie of the essence with respect to
> delivery".

This statement must obviously be read subject to the statutory rules just
mentioned, and it hides an ambiguity: the learned Judge may be saying

---

8. See above, p. 269.   9. See above, p. 264.
10. *Clemens Horst* v. *Biddell Brothers*, [1912] A.C. 18, H.L.
11. This dual right of rejection is explained below, p. 402.
12. See above, p. 116.   13. See below, pp. 319–320.
14. *Hartley* v. *Hymans*, [1920] 3 K.B. 475, at p. 484. For the facts of this case,
    see above, p. 147.

that delay is always fatal; or that only such delay as causes serious loss amounts to a breach entitling the other party to rescind[15]. In fact, the courts have decided that, if a commercial contract stipulates a time for delivery[16], any breach by the seller entitles the buyer to rescind, even if he has suffered no damage[17]. However, if the contract is not a commercial one, or does not stipulate a time for delivery, the S.G.A. merely requires that the seller must deliver within a reasonable time (s. 29 (2)), though the seller's delay may be so great as to show an intention to repudiate[18]. It might be thought that the law would impose reciprocal obligations with respect to acceptance of delivery[19]. However, the law will only assume that acceptance of delivery is of the essence where the goods are perishable[20] or there is a "spot" contract[1]. In all other cases, it is assumed that the time of acceptance of delivery is not of the essence[2]; that, if no time of acceptance is specified, the buyer is merely required to accept delivery within a reasonable time; and that further delay merely gives the seller the right to damages[3], unless it is so great as to show an intention to rescind[4]. Why should the time of tender of delivery normally amount to a condition in a commercial contract, whilst the time of acceptance of delivery is only a warranty? It has been suggested that, apart from the cases of perishable goods and "spot" contracts, the seller's prime interest is to obtain the price whereas that of the buyer is to obtain delivery, so that it is understandable that tender of delivery is more important to the buyer than acceptance of delivery is to the seller[5]. Yet, it ought to follow that tender of the price by the buyer is also an essential term; but this is not so.

2. *Payment*. It is the duty of the debtor to tender the price and the creditor to accept the price at the time laid down in the contract, or, if no time is stipulated, within a reasonable time[6]. Section 10 (1) of the S.G.A. provides as follows:

---

15. See Stoljar (1955), 71 L.Q.R. 527, at p. 532.
16. Or if a non-commercial contract stipulates a time for delivery *and* makes that time of the essence: *Charles Rickards, Ltd.* v. *Oppenhaim*, [1950] 1 K.B. 616: [1950] 1 All E.R. 420: set out above, p. 148.
17. *Bowes* v. *Shand* (1877), 2 App. Cas. 455, H.L.
18. Cf. *Pearl Mill Co.* v. *Ivy Tannery Co.*, [1919] 1 K.B. 78.
19. See Atiyah, *Sale of Goods* (3rd Edn.) 49, 100.
20. *Sharp* v. *Christmas* (1892), 8 T.L.R. 687, C.A.; cf. s. 48 (3) S.G.A.: see below, p. 366.
 1. A "spot" contract is one which envisages almost immediate delivery, e.g. *Thames Sack & Bag Co., Ltd.* v. *Knowles & Co., Ltd.* (1919), 88 L.J.K.B. 585.
 2. *Woolfe* v. *Horn* (1877), 2 Q.B.D. 355.
 3. *Penarth Dock Engineering Co., Ltd.* v. *Pounds*, [1963] 1 Lloyds Rep. 359.
 4. *Pearl Mill Co.* v. *Ivy Tannery Co.* (above).
 5. Stoljar (1955), 71 L.Q.R. 527, at p. 538. *Sed quaere?*
 6. See *Brighty* v. *Norman* (1862), 3 B. & S. 305 (stipulation for payment on request).

"Unless a different intention appears from the terms of the contract stipulations as to time of payment are not deemed to be of the essence of a contract of sale. Whether any other stipulation as to time is of the essence of the contract or not depends on the terms of the contract".

However, s. 10 (1) appears to conflict with s. 28 of the S.G.A., which states that payment and delivery shall be "concurrent conditions"[7]. Perhaps the explanation lies in the different usages of the word "condition"[8]: it may be that s. 28 is referring to "condition" exclusively in the sense of condition precedent, and not in the sense of a contractual promise[9], whereas s. 10 (1) is dealing with the importance of the contractual promise. Certainly, the courts have acted on s. 10, and held that its effect is to create a presumption that stipulations as to the time of payment are only warranties[10]. Of course, this presumption may be displaced, as where the buyer contracts to open a banker's confirmed credit[11] or the goods are perishable[12]; and it is fairly common to find time of payment expressly made of the essence in a standard-form contract. Even where time is not of the essence, the delay in payment may be so great as to show an intention to rescind[13]; or the seller may by giving notice obtain a right to rescind under s. 48 (3)[12].

The relative importance of the stipulations as to the time of delivery and payment can now be examined. Leaving aside such delays as manifest an intention to repudiate, s. 28 of the S.G.A. appears to create a statutory stalemate; but what it really means is that each party must be ready and willing[14] to perform his part of the bargain before he can demand that the other party performs his obligations[9]. Moreover, the effect of s. 10 (1) would appear to be to allow the time of delivery to remain an essential undertaking, whilst making the time of payment a warranty: if the seller does not deliver on time the buyer may treat the contract as repudiated; but if the buyer does not pay the price on time the seller is only entitled to damages. This state of affairs has been criticised as extending "compulsory credit to the buyer"[15]. But it must be remembered that the unpaid seller is entitled to retain possession of the goods until payment under two provisions of the S.G.A.: s. 28 makes payment of the price a condition precedent to the duty of the

---

7. Stoljar (1955), 71 L.Q.R. 527, at p. 539.
8. See above, pp. 50–51.
9. See Smith & Thomas, *Casebook on Contract* (4th Edn.) 294–295.
10. *Payzu, Ltd.* v. *Saunders*, [1919] 2 K.B. 581, C.A.
11. *Trans Trust S.P.R.L.* v. *Danubian Trading, Ltd.*, [1952] 2 Q.B. 297; [1952] 1 All E.R. 970, C.A.: set out below, p. 383.
12. See s. 48 (3) S.G.A., discussed below, p. 366.
13. Cf. *Pearl Mill Co.* v. *Ivy Tannery Co.*, [1919] 1 K.B. 78.
14. And able? See above, pp. 266–267.
15. Stoljar (1955), 71 L.Q.R. 527, at p. 540.

seller to deliver the goods; and s. 39 gives the seller a lien on the goods for the price[16].

2 Where delivery and payment are not concurrent terms

The parties to a contract of sale are quite at liberty to oust the presumption in s. 28 of the S.G.A., and make performance by one side conditional on prior performance by the other, whether in whole or in part. Where the contract provides for payment in advance of delivery, the seller is entitled to sue for the price without tendering delivery[17]: he merely has to show an intention to continue with the contract. Similarly, if the contract provides for delivery in advance of payment, the buyer is entitled to sue for non-delivery without tendering the price[18]. Alternatively, the buyer in this last situation may maintain an action of conversion or detinue against the seller as he is *prima facie* entitled to immediate possession[19]; but he will lose this right if insolvent, because the unpaid seller's lien will arise by reason of the insolvency[1]. Finally, it must be borne in mind that delay in performance of the obligation to deliver or pay may show an intention to rescind.

4 PERFORMANCE BY INSTALMENTS

It is quite compatible with s. 28 of the S.G.A. that either or both of the obligations of delivery or payment may be discharged by instalments. Indeed, if the parties agree that delivery and payment shall be by matching instalments, they are plainly adhering to the basic presumption of s. 28. On the other hand, it is quite open to the parties to provide that only one of the obligations shall be performed by instalments.

1 Delivery by instalments

Section 31 (1) of the S.G.A. provides that:

> "Unless otherwise agreed, the buyer of goods is not bound to accept delivery thereof by instalments";

and this links up with the basic obligation on the seller to deliver the right quantity of goods (s. 30)[2]. Thus, to permit delivery by instalments, there must be some agreement between the parties to this effect. No doubt, the typical situation where the parties agree to

---

16. See below, p. 314.
17. Section 49 (2) S.G.A.: set out below, p. 371.
18. Section 51 (1) S.G.A.: set out below, p. 409.
19. *Per* BAYLEY J. in *Bloxam* v. *Sanders* (1825), 4 B. & C. 941, at pp. 948–949. It is sometimes said that this case conflicts with *Chinery* v. *Viall* (1860), 5 H. & N. 288, though in both cases it was irrelevant whether the sale was on credit. See also *Healing (Sales), Ltd.* v. *Inglis, Ltd.* (1968), 42 A.L.J.R. 280.
1. Section 41 (1) S.G.A.: see below, p. 319. 2. See above, p. 76, *et seq.*

instalment deliveries involves a "lengthy course of dealings and great quantities of goods"[3]; but it should be remembered that the rules also cover cases such as a retail sale where the consumer takes some of his goods away with him and has the rest delivered.

Whether a contract provides for delivery by instalments is a question of construction[4]; and, where it does so, the contract may be susceptible of any one of the following interpretations:

(1) That the parties intend that there should be not one contract, but a series of contracts between them[5]; or

(2) That the parties intend that there should be a single contract, but that the contract should be divisible or severable in the sense that each instalment is to be paid for separately[6]; or

(3) That the parties intend that there should be a single contract, and that the price be paid as one sum[7].

Which interpretation is adopted may be important for three reasons: first, in determining whether acceptance of part of the goods prevents the buyer subsequently rejecting the remainder[8]; second, in deciding whether breach by the seller or buyer in respect of one of the instalments amounts to a repudiation of the whole contract; and third, in establishing the unpaid seller's real rights[9].

Where there is a series of contracts, then, however serious the breach of one of them, it cannot, without more, amount to a repudiation of the others. But in practice, the courts seem reluctant to treat an instalment contract as a series of contracts; and a provision that each delivery shall be treated as a separate contract tends to be construed as indicating that there is a single contract under which each instalment is to be paid for separately[10]. Assuming that there is a single contract, the next question is whether performance of that contract is divisible. Where performance is indivisible, a serious breach in respect of one instalment is treated as giving a right to rescind in the same manner as partial breach of a non-instalment contract would do[11]; whereas a partial breach of a divisible contract will not necessarily have such an effect. In the latter case, the "question is whether the acts and conduct of the (guilty) party evince an intention no longer to be bound by the

---

3. Stoljar (1955), 71 L.Q.R. 527, at p. 543.
4. E.g. *Howell* v. *Evans* (1926), 134 L.T. 570.
5. E.g. *Jackson* v. *Rotax Motor and Cycle Co.*, [1910] 2 K.B. 937, C.A.: set out above, p. 82.
6. E.g. *Robert Munro & Co., Ltd.* v. *Meyer*, [1930] 2 K.B. 312; *J. Rosenthal, Ltd.* v. *Esmail*, [1965] 2 All E.R. 860, H.L.
7. E.g. *Longbottom & Co., Ltd.* v. *Bass, Walker & Co.*, [1922] W.N. 245, C.A.
8. This issue is discussed below, pp. 398–400.
9. This issue is discussed below, p. 318.
10. *Per* Lord WRIGHT in *Ross T. Smyth & Co., Ltd.* v. *Bailey, Sons & Co.*, [1940] 3 All E.R. 60, at p. 73, H.L.
11. *Longbottom & Co., Ltd.* v. *Bass, Walker & Co.* (above).

contract"[12]; and in conducting this enquiry, the common law today generally assumes that the parties contemplated payment of damages rather than rescission, so that the guilty party can normally set up his willingness to perform the rest of the contract, subject to his compensating the innocent party for the breach[13]. Single divisible contracts are partly[14] covered by s. 31 (2) of the S.G.A., which provides:

> "Where there is a contract for the sale of goods to be delivered by stated instalments, which are to be separately paid for, and the seller makes defective deliveries in respect of one or more instalments, cr the buyer neglects or refuses to take delivery of or pay for one or more instalments, it is a question in each case depending on the terms of the contract and the circumstances of the case, whether the breach of contract is a repudiation of the whole contract or whether it is a severable breach giving rise to a claim for compensation but not to a right to treat the whole contract as repudiated".

Even where it applies, s. 31 (2) poses rather than answers the question, and it is necessary to fall back on common law principles. In *Robert Munro & Co., Ltd.* v. *Meyer*[15] WRIGHT J. found that the seller had no intention of breaking his contract, but nevertheless held that, as there was a persistent breach continuing for nearly half the contract total of goods, the buyer was entitled to rescind. His Lordship explained that[16],

> ". . . in such circumstances, the intention of the seller must be judged from his acts and from the deliveries which he in fact makes, and that being so, where the breach is substantial and so serious as the breach in this case and has continued so persistently, the buyer is entitled to say that he has the right to treat the whole contract as repudiated".

In *Maple Flock Co., Ltd.* v. *Universal Furniture Products (Wembley) Ltd.*[17], the Court of Appeal said that

> ". . . the main tests to be considered in applying the subsection . . . are, first, the ratio quantitatively which breach bears to the contract as a whole, and secondly the degree of probability or improbability that such a breach will be repeated".

---

12. *Per* Lord COLERIDGE C.J. in *Freeth* v. *Burr* (1874), L.R. 9 C.P. 208, at p. 213. See also *per* Lord BLACKBURN in *Mersey Steel and Iron Co., Ltd.* v. *Naylor Benzon & Co.* (1884), 9 App. Cas. 434, H.L., at p. 443.
13. *Per* Lord WRIGHT in *Ross T. Smyth & Co., Ltd.* v. *Bailey, Sons & Co.*, [1940] 3 All E.R. 60, at p. 71, H.L. See e.g. *James Shaffer, Ltd.* v. *Findlay*, [1953] 1 W.L.R. 106, C.A.; *Peter Dumenil & Co., Ltd.* v. *Ruddin, Ltd.*, [1953] 2 All E.R. 294, C.A.
14. Whilst s. 31 (2) mentions the common cases, a number of others are listed in *Benjamin on Sale* (8th Edn.) 727.
15. [1930] 2 K.B. 312.
16. At p. 331.
17. [1934] 1 K.B. 148, C.A., at p. 157 (judgment of HEWART L.C.J., Lord WRIGHT and SLESSER L.J. delivered by the L.C.J.).

In that case, the Court of Appeal found that the delivery complained of amounted to no more than $1\frac{1}{2}$ tons out of a contract for the sale of 100 tons of rag flock, and that the chance of the breach being repeated was for all practical purposes negligible; and they therefore concluded that there was "no sufficient justification to entitle the (buyer) to refuse further deliveries"[18]. Should it make any difference that the breach is in respect of the first instalment? The cases are conflicting[19], and commentators disagree[20]; but the issue must be set against the modern background of reluctance on the part of the courts to find an intention to repudiate.

2 Payment by instalments

Whereas s. 31 (1) enacts that *prima facie* the buyer is not bound to accept delivery of the goods by instalments[1], the S.G.A. contains no counterpart of s. 31 (1) in relation to the obligation to pay the price. However, it may be that it is to be implied from s. 31 (1) that payment is *prima facie* to be made in a lump sum; and certainly, where the time for payment has arrived, there is no room for payment by instalments. Of course, there is nothing to prevent the parties from providing in the contract for payment by instalments; and in this event the contract will commonly specify the times of payment, make time of the essence[2], and provide that on default all outstanding instalments shall be payable immediately.

Sometimes, all the instalments of the price are payable before delivery of the goods[3]; but the situation is rather more complicated where delivery is made in advance of payment of the whole or part of the price[4]. Naturally, the unpaid seller will lose his rights against the goods[5]; and, where the price is payable by five or more instalments, the transaction might amount to a "credit sale" within the H.P.A.[6], in which case the following statutory rules apply:

(1) The statement of the cash price, and the provisions as to the contents and form of the contract[7];

---

18. At p. 158.
19. Compare *Hoare* v. *Rennie* (1859), 5 H. & N. 19 and *Honck* v. *Muller* (1881), 7 Q.B.D. 92, with *Simpson* v. *Crippin* (1872), L.R. 8 Q.B. 14.
20. Compare *Benjamin on Sale* (8th Edn.) 734 with Stoljar (1955), 71 L.Q.R. 527, at pp. 543–544.
 1. Section 31 (1) is set out above, p. 276.
 2. Thus reversing s. 10 (1): set out above, p. 275.
 3. E.g. under certain types of retail "Xmas Club", the goods being selected and set aside for delivery after completion of payment of the price by instalments.
 4. Pre-contract credit enquiries have already been considered: see above, pp. 34–35.   5. See below, p. 314.
 6. See above, pp. 14, 30. This is why many retailers offer their goods with the price payable by four instalments: none of the restrictions of the H.P.A. apply.   7. See above, pp. 33–34.

(2) The provisions as to agency, copies and cancellation[8];

(3) The protection of guarantors[9].

Moreover, if the seller attempts to protect himself by reserving the property in the goods until paid for, then, regardless of the number of instalments by which the price is payable, the transaction may be a "conditional sale" within the H.P.A.[10]. If it does amount to a "conditional sale", the transaction is subject, *inter alia*, to the following:

(1) All the rules applicable to "credit sales" listed above;

(2) All the implied terms of the H.P.A. instead of those of the S.G.A.[11];

(3) The exception to the *nemo dat* rule in favour of buyers in possession is ousted[12], and that in respect of motor vehicles applies[13];

(4) The restrictions on the right to repossess goods[14] and to terminate the agreement[15] apply.

With all the major restrictions of the H.P.A. applicable to "conditional sales" within its ambit, the real choice of the "seller" is thus between a sale without a reservation of property and a h.p. agreement: the former type of transaction offers no security for the price, but is largely, if not wholly, free of the restrictions of the H.P.A.; whereas a h.p. agreement offers a measure of security which must be weighed against the restrictions of the Act[16].

In considering the position of the instalments to be paid under a sale or h.p. transaction, a distinction must be drawn between the first instalment and the rest of the payments. The owner or seller sometimes requires the first payment to be made before delivery, or even before contract; and, where the Statutory Orders apply, there must be "actual payment" of the minimum deposit before the agreement is "entered into"[17], unless goods are lawfully to be taken in part-exchange[18].

The initial payment. If the contract of sale or h.p. is never concluded, then it is a question of intention whether the initial payment is recoverable[19]: normally, it is intended simply to form part of the consideration of the contemplated contract[20], in which case it is recoverable by the

---

8. See above, pp. 39–46.

10. See above, p. 15.

12. Section 54: see above, p. 223.

14. See below, pp. 334–344.

16. See Chapter 18.

9. See below, pp. 347–348.

11. See above, Chapters 5–9.

13. See above, p. 230, *et seq.*

15. See below, pp. 354–355.

17. See e.g. *Kingsley* v. *Stirling Industrial Securities, Ltd.*, [1967] 2 Q.B. 747; [1966] 2 All E.R. 414, C.A.; *Snook* v. *London and West Riding Investments, Ltd.*, [1967] 2 Q.B. 786; [1967] 1 All E.R. 518, C.A.

18. H.P. & C.S. Order 1964, S.I. 942, Sched. 2, Part I, art. 3. Part-exchanges are considered above, p. 271.

19. The question of from whom it may be recoverable in a tripartite transaction is considered below, pp. 286–288.

20. *Chillingworth* v. *Esche*, [1924] 1 Ch. 97, C.A.—a real property case cited by *Benjamin on Sale* (8th Edn.) 947, note (e).

buyer or hirer on grounds of total failure of consideration[1]; but, if it is intended to be by way of security for completion by the buyer or hirer, then in the event of his default it cannot be recovered at common law, though equity may offer relief against the forfeiture[2], or that agreement may be avoided by the H.P.A.[3]. Where the major contract has been concluded, however, the rules in respect of sale and h.p. will differ[4].

(1) *Sale.* Except by subsequent agreement or lawful discharge, a buyer cannot escape from his contract without breaking it; and, if the buyer does repudiate, the seller may elect to affirm and sue for the price, or rescind and claim damages. If the seller rescinds, the position of the initial payment is as above.

(2) *Hire purchase.* At common law, there can usually be no question of the hirer who elects not to go on with the hiring recovering the initial payment. Nor will he be in any better position if he exercises a statutory right of termination; but he will be able to recover the initial payment on exercise of a statutory right of cancellation, or where the owner wrongfully repossesses protected goods[5].

The subsequent instalments. In the case of a sale, the buyer cannot unilaterally terminate his obligations; but, unless the agreement otherwise provides, he may do so under a h.p. agreement, in which case he is not liable for hire-rent in respect of any future period. Where the contract of sale or h.p. provides for sums to be paid or retained by the seller or owner in the event of breach by the buyer or hirer, the whole subject is bedevilled by the rules relating to penalties[6].

---

1. See below, pp. 287, 404.
2. See below, pp. 372–374.
3. Section 29 (4) H.P.A.: see above, p. 34.
4. The remedies of the seller or owner are considered below, Chapter 20.
5. The statutory rights of cancellation and termination are also available to some buyers.
6. See below, pp. 391–395.

CHAPTER 17

Financing of the Price

I INTRODUCTION

The methods by which a "seller" under an instalment credit transaction may seek to finance the transaction have already been examined[1]; and this chapter deals with the legal effects of such transactions. Three parties are involved: the "seller", the "buyer" and the finance company. Normally, these three will be a dealer, his customer, and a finance company respectively; but, in the case of a stocking agreement[2], the parties will be a supplier or manufacturer, his dealer, and a finance company. In either case, the finance company may require a surety to "guarantee" performance by the other two[3]. Direct financing and indirect financing will each receive separate treatment; but first the relationship between the three parties involved in an ordinary transaction must be considered: (1) dealer and customer; (2) finance company and customer; and (3) finance company and dealer.

1 The relationship between dealer and customer

Where there is an indirectly financed transaction, the primary relationship is between the dealer and his customer, and the fact that a finance company will later be involved does alter this. The position is different in a directly financed transaction: there is ordinarily no primary contractual relationship between the dealer and his customer[4]. Frequently, the customer will allege that he was induced to enter into the directly financed transaction by some misrepresentation on the part of the dealer. The question arises whether the customer has any redress against the dealer.

Whilst there may be the possibility of an action in tort for negligent misstatement or deceit[5], can the dealer be made strictly liable in contract? In *Drury* v. *Victor Buckland, Ltd.*[6]

> The customer in a directly financed transaction sued the dealer for breach of an implied warranty under s. 14 of the S.G.A., alleging that there was a contract of sale between herself and the dealer.

---

1. See above, pp. 24–26.
2. Stocking agreements are explained below, p. 289.
3. Sureties are considered in Chapter 18.
4. But see *Polsky* v. *S. & A. Services, Ltd.*, [1951] 1 All E.R. 185; affd., [1951] 1 All E.R. 1062, C.A.: set out below, p. 295.
5. See above, pp. 128–130. 6. [1941] 1 All E.R. 269, C.A.

282

The Court of Appeal rejected her claim on the grounds that there was no contract of sale between the customer and the dealer. However, another possible avenue by which the customer might attack the dealer in contract was suggested by *Webster* v. *Higgin*[7].

> The dealer's agent told the customer that if he bought the car the dealer would guarantee it. Subsequently, the customer entered into a h.p. agreement to hire the car from the dealer.

The customer's claim against the dealer for breach of a collateral contract of guarantee succeeded in the Court of Appeal, Whilst in this last case there was only a two-party transaction, the pointer thus given was soon followed in directly financed transactions[8]. The leading case is *Andrews* v. *Hopkinson*[9].

> The dealer said to his customer in respect of one of his vehicles: "It is a good little bus; I would stake my life on it". The following day, the customer signed a h.p. proposal form in respect of the vehicle; and he subsequently took delivery of it. About a week later, the steering failed, and the customer was involved in an accident. The customer's action against the dealer succeeded before McNair J.

The grounds of the customer's claim were as follows:

> (1) For breach of an express warranty that the car was in good condition . . . whereby he was induced to enter into a hire purchase agreement in respect thereof.

In finding the dealer liable under this head, McNair J. said[10]:

> "There may be an enforceable warranty between A., the intended purchaser of a car, and B. the motor dealer, supported by the consideration that B. should cause the hire purchase finance company to enter into a hire purchase agreement with A. . . ."

In practice, of course, it is usually the signature of the customer on the proposal form that is induced by the misrepresentation[11]. Furthermore, it has rightly been pointed out that the term "warranty" is a misnomer in this context[12]; that the allegation must be of a collateral

---

7. [1948] 2 All E.R. 127, C.A.
8. *Brown* v. *Sheen and Richmond Car Sales, Ltd.*, [1950] 1 All E.R. 1102. On the development of the collateral contract of warranty, see also above, p. 120; and as to the *prima facie* measure of damages, see below, p. 423.
9. [1957] 1 Q.B. 229, [1956] 3 All E.R. 422.
10. At p. 235. For the measure of damages, see also *Yeoman Credit, Ltd.* v. *Odgers*, [1962] 1 All E.R. 789, C.A.; *Wells Merstham, Ltd.* v. *Buckland Sand and Silica Co., Ltd.*, [1965] 2 Q.B. 170; [1964] 1 All E.R. 41.
11. E.g. *Astley Industrial Trust, Ltd.* v. *Grimley*, [1963] 2 All E.R. 33, C.A.: see Goode, *H.P. Law & Practice* (2nd Edn.) 639, note 3.
12. Wild, *H.P.* (2nd Edn.) 195-199.

contract of warranty[13]; and that the representation made by the dealer is at most evidence of such a collateral contract[14].

(2) For breach of an implied warranty that the car was reasonably fit for driving on the public highway.

Whilst preferring to rest his decision on the first ground, McNair J. said[15]:

"Bearing in mind that the statutory implied warranty now embodied in s. 14 (1) of the [S.G.A.] was merely a modification of the long-existing common law in relation to sales, I feel that there is much to be said for the view that in a transaction such as the present, which, though not in law a transaction of sale between the parties, is closely akin to such a transaction, the court ought to imply such a condition or warranty if any contractual relationship between the parties can in fact be established".

His Lordship suggested that the Court of Appeal reached the decision it did in *Drury* v. *Victor Buckland, Ltd.*[16] solely because such an implied warranty was not pleaded[17]. However, there appears to be no subsequent case where the idea has been taken up; and it has been doubted whether an intention to contract would be inferred where there was no express representation[18].

(3) For negligence in that the defendant knew or ought to have known that the car was dangerous.

In *Herschtal* v. *Stewart and Ardern, Ltd.*[19], the dealer in a directly financed transaction was held liable in tort to his customer for the negligent repair of the vehicle which was the subject-matter of the transaction; and McNair J. relied on that decision in finding the dealer in the present transaction liable for negligence by omission, saying[20]

"I have no hesitation in holding that the defendant in the circumstances was guilty of negligence in failing to make the necessary examination, or at least in failing to warn the plaintiff that no such examination has been carried out".

2 The relationship between finance company and customer

Where the transaction is directly financed, there will be a contract of sale or h.p. entered into between the finance company and the customer; and, where the transaction is indirectly financed, the finance company

---

13. Wild, *ibid.*; Goode, *H.P. Law & Practice* (2nd Edn.) 640.
14. See *per* PEARSON L.J. in *Astley Industrial Trust, Ltd.* v. *Grimley*, [1963] 2 All E.R. 33, C.A., at p. 45. 15. At p. 237.
16. [1941] 1 All E.R. 269, C.A. 17. At p. 237.
18. Cf. Goode, *op. cit.* (1st Edn.) 198 and (2nd Edn.) 640.
19. [1940] 1 K.B. 155; [1939] 4 All E.R. 123. See also above, p. 126.
20. At p. 237.

will acquire rights under that contract subsequent to its formation. Is there any way in which the customer can avoid or offset his obligations to the finance company under that contract of sale or h.p.? In some circumstances, the transaction may infringe the legislation in respect of chattel mortgaging or moneylending, in which case the agreement will be void or illegal. Because of the complexity of this legislation it is considered separately below[1]; and for the moment it is intended to concentrate on such other liability as the finance company may incur by reason of the acts of the dealer.

Where the transaction is directly financed, the major question is whether the finance company can be made "responsible" for the acts of the dealer on the basis that the latter acted as the company's agent. There are two diametrically opposed views on this matter. On the one hand, it is argued that the dealer is the finance company's agent on the basis of ostensible authority. For instance, in *Financings, Ltd.* v. *Stimson*[2] Lord DENNING M.R. argued:

> "The dealer holds the necessary forms; he hands them over to the hirer to sign; he forwards them to the finance company; he receives the deposit as agent for the finance company; he receives from the finance company information that they are willing to accept the transaction; and he is authorised to pass on that communication to the hirer . . . It seems to me that, if we take, as we should, a realistic view of the position, the dealer is in many respects and for many purposes the agent of the finance company".

On the other hand, there is considerable authority for the rejection of any general proposition that the dealer is the agent of the finance company. Thus, in *Mercantile Credit, Ltd.* v. *Hamblin*[3] PEARSON L.J. said:

> "There is no rule of law that in a hire-purchase transaction the dealer never is, or always is, acting as agent for the finance company or as agent for the customer. In a typical hire-purchase transaction the dealer is a party in his own right, selling his car to the finance company, and he is acting primarily on his own behalf and not as general agent for either of the other two parties. There is no need to attribute to him an agency in order to account for his participation in the transaction".

No doubt, the two *dicta* are strictly reconcilable; but they were accepted as involving rival views in *Branwhite* v. *Worcester Finance, Ltd.*[4].

---

1. See below, pp. 289, 300.
2. [1962] 3 All E.R. 386, C.A., at p. 388. He was supported in this case by DONOVAN L.J. (at p. 389); but PEARSON L.J. disagreed (at p. 392).
3. [1965] 2 Q.B. 242, C.A., at p. 269. See also HOLROYD PEARCE L.J. in *Campbell Discount Co., Ltd.* v. *Gall*, [1961] 1 Q.B. 431, C.A., at p. 441.
4. [1969] 1 A.C. 552; [1968] 3 All E.R. 104, H.L.

Three members of the House of Lords there expressly adopted the *dicta* cited from the judgment of PEARSON L.J.[5], whereas the other two expressly rejected it in favour of the argument put forward by Lord DENNING M.R.[6]. In practice, the sale or h.p. agreement was usually carefully drawn with the object of denying the dealer any actual authority to commit the finance company[7], so that the real question was whether the dealer had any ostensible authority such as to override the terms of the agreement. Whilst such clauses were avoided by the H.P.A. 1938[8], the courts showed themselves reluctant to accept that the dealer had acted as agent of the finance company: for instance, it was held that the dealer had authority neither to accept the customer's offer contained in the proposal form[9]; nor to receive instalments of hire rent[10]; nor to fix the finance company with knowledge that the transaction was a disguised bill of sale[11], nor that the dealer's title to the goods was defective[12]. Accordingly, the H.P.A. 1965 expressly deemed the dealer to be the agent of the finance company for the following purposes:

(1) to receive notices from the customer of withdrawal of his offer contained in the proposal form, or where that offer had been accepted the cancellation or rescission of the agreement[13]; and

(2) to receive notice from the customer of the particular purpose for which the goods were required so that the customer might invoke the implied undertaking as to fitness[14]; and

(3) for any representations made by the dealer to the customer in the course of negotiating the transaction[15].

The question of whether the finance company is "responsible" for the acts of the dealer in a directly financed transaction has caused particular difficulty in two contexts.

1. The deposit. On signing the proposal form, the customer will usually hand a deposit to the dealer; and where the Statutory Orders apply he must do so. This deposit may be either cash or goods taken in part-exchange. If the finance company does not accept the proposal, then we have seen that it is a question of intention whether the deposit is

---

5. *Per* Lords MORRIS, UPJOHN and GUEST, at pp. 573, 576.
6. *Per* Lords WILBERFORCE and REID, at p. 585.
7. But see the remarks of Lord DENNING M.R. in *Financings, Ltd.* v. *Stimson*, [1962] 3 All E.R. 386, C.A., at p. 388.
8. Section 5 (d) and (e). These provisions were re-enacted in s. 29 (d) and (e) of the H.P.A. 1965: see above, p. 133.
9. See *Financings, Ltd.* v. *Stimson* (above): set out above, pp. 35–36.
10. *Bentworth Finance, Ltd.* v. *White* (1962), 112 L.J. 140, Cty. Crt.
11. *Spencer* v. *North County Finance, Ltd.*, [1963] C.L.Y. 212, C.A.
12. *Car and Universal Finance, Ltd.* v. *Caldwell*, [1965] 1 Q.B. 525; [1964] 1 All E.R. 290, C.A.: set out above, p. 200.
13. Sections 12 (3), 31: see above, pp. 39–40.
14. Section 17 (4): set out above, p. 83.
15. Section 16: see below, pp. 288–289.

recoverable from the dealer[16]. On the other hand, where the finance company accepts the proposal, the dealer will credit the company with the amount of the deposit or part-exchange allowance, so that that amount may be regarded as being given indirectly to the company; and in some circumstances it may be recovered from the company[17]. What of the intermediate situation where the contract of sale or h.p. is void? This issue has arisen in circumstances where the customer has signed the proposal form in blank; the dealer has subsequently fraudulently inserted larger amounts and submitted the proposal to the finance company; and the latter has accepted the proposal and paid the dealer[18]. In *Campbell Discount Co., Ltd.* v. *Gall*[19] the Court of Appeal unanimously decided that the customer was not estopped from pleading the provisions of the H.P.A. 1938 by reason of the dealer having inserted figures outside the ambit of that Act[20]; that on ordinary common law principles the dealer was the agent of neither party in so doing[1]; and that the customer's signature on the proposal form neither gave the dealer an apparent authority to complete the proposal form on behalf of the customer[2], nor estopped the customer from setting up the true facts[3]. The Court therefore held that:

(1) the finance company's claim against the customer for the instalments of hire-rent failed[4]; and

(2) the customer's counter-claim to recover the deposit from the finance company likewise failed.

A claim against the finance company for the return of the deposit[5] was similarly made in *Branwhite* v. *Worcester Finance Ltd.*[6], the claim being put on the following grounds: first, that the dealer was the agent of the finance company to receive and hold the deposit; and second, that irrespective of any agency, the finance company had received actual payment of the deposit, and had received it for a consideration which had wholly failed. The majority of the House of Lords decided that the dealer was not the agent of the finance company[7]; but their

---

16. See above, p. 280.   17. See below, p. 288.
18. Is the position the same if the agreement is illegal or unenforceable?
19. [1961] 1 Q.B. 431; [1961] 2 All E.R. 104, C.A.
20. The court therefore held that the provision in the agreement deeming the dealer to be the agent of the customer was avoided by s. 5 of the H.P.A. 1938: see above, p. 30, note 4.
 1. Accepted by the parties in *Branwhite's Case*, [1969] 1 A.C. 552, H.L. But is not the customer impliedly giving the dealer permission to complete the form as his agent?
 2. See above, p. 185.
 3. See above, pp. 189, 196.   4. See also below, p. 374.
 5. The customer actually claimed the return of the part-exchange allowance; but their Lordships thought that this was equivalent to the deposit—at pp. 570, 580, 590.
 6. [1969] 1 A.C. 552; [1968] 3 All E.R. 104, H.L.
 7. *Per* Lords MORRIS, GUEST and UPJOHN, at pp. 573, 578. Lords REID and WILBERFORCE dissented, at p. 589.

Lordships unanimously held that, as the dealer had credited the finance company with the deposit as against the price paid by the company to him, this was equivalent to an actual payment of the deposit to the company on behalf of the customer in respect of a transaction which had wholly failed, and so the company must return the deposit to the customer[8]. *Pro tanto, Gall's Case* is overruled.

2. Misrepresentations by the dealer. At common law, it is probably the case that the dealer is not the agent of the finance company for the purpose of affecting the company with liability in respect of misrepresentations made by the dealer in the course of negotiating the transaction with the customer[9]. In their *Tenth Report* (on Innocent Misrepresentation), the Law Reform Committee thought that this was unjust, and recommended that the dealer should be deemed to be the agent of the finance company for such purposes[10]. This proposal was adopted in the H.P.A. 1964, and is now to be found in s. 16 of the 1965 Act, subsection 1 of which provides:

> "Where a person (in this section referred to as 'the owner or seller') lets goods under a hire-purchase agreement, or sells or agrees to sell goods under a credit-sale agreement or a conditional sale agreement, any representations with respect to the goods to which the agreement relates which were made, either orally or in writing, to the hirer or buyer by a person other than the owner or seller in the course of any antecedent negotiations conducted by that other person shall be deemed to have been made by him as agent of the owner or seller".

The section will apply wherever the h.p. or total purchase price is less than £2,000[11]; and the liability it imposes is expressed to be in addition to any other liability, civil or criminal, which would arise apart from s. 16 (s. 16 (2)). By virtue of s. 16 (4), "representation" in this section

> "includes any statement or undertaking, whether constituting a condition or a warranty or not, and any references to making representations shall be construed accordingly".

However, it must be borne in mind that s. 16 (1) is only expressed to apply to "representations with respect to the goods"[12] "made . . . by

---

8. At pp. 572, 582, 590.
9. See Guest, *Law of H.P.*, para. 384; Goode, *H.P. Law & Practice* (2nd Edn.) 289.
10. Cmnd. 1782, paras. 19–20.
11. See s. 16 (3).
12. E.g., as to title, description, fitness or quality of the goods. It has been suggested that it probably does not cover such as "representations as to the interpretation of provisions in the agreement not directly related to the goods"—Hogan, annotation in *Current Law Statutes*.

any person"[13] "in the course of any antecedent negotiations", though the last expression is widely defined as[14]

> "any negotiations or arrangements with the hirer or buyer whereby he was induced to make the agreement or which otherwise promoted the transaction to which the agreement relates . . ." (s. 58 (3)).

Where these requirements are satisfied, s. 16 (1) deems the representor to have acted as the agent of the "owner or seller", notwithstanding any agreement to the contrary (s. 29 (3) (b)), with the following possible results:

(1) The representation may become a term of the contract of sale or h.p. between the finance company and the customer; but

(2) Where it does not become a term of that contract, the customer may still pursue his remedies for misrepresentation against the finance company.

The problems discussed above are peculiar to directly financed transactions. Where the transaction is indirectly financed, the ordinary rules will apply as between dealer and customer, the contract of sale or h.p. being made between these two; and, as assignee of the dealer's rights, the finance company can be in no better position than the dealer. Section 16 of the H.P.A. is unnecessary to give the customer contractual rights against the finance company, but may give him rights against the company in respect of mere representations made by the dealer[15].

3 The relationship between finance company and dealer

It is necessary to say something about two phenomena here: (1) stocking plans, and (2) dealer recourse.

1. Stocking plans.[16] Such transactions are most common in the motor trade; and their economic purpose is to "loan" the dealer the value of the stock he must keep in his show-room. Again there are three parties to the transaction, but this time they are the manufacturer or other supplier, the finance company and the dealer. Most of the problems peculiar to stocking plans have arisen from the attempts of finance companies to retain for themselves some rights in the goods which are the subject-matter of the stocking plan by way of security. Perhaps the simplest scheme would be for the supplier to let the

---

13. This will include the dealer, and his agents or servants—see ss. 58 (3), (5) of the H.P.A.
14. It has been said that s. 16 does not cover representations made privately, and outside the course of the representor's business: Goode, *H.P. Law & Practice* (2nd Edn.) 298. *Sed quaere?*
15. Section 58 (1) provides that the terms "owner", and "seller" include assignees of their rights.
16. See generally Allan (1967), 2 Tas. L.R. 382; Ziegel in *Instalment Credit* (Ed. Diamond) 118–135; Goode, *op. cit.*, 670–674.

dealer have the goods on sale or return; but this offers little security as the dealer can pass a good title to a b.f.p. even where there is a reservation of property[17]. Nor would it seem that the finance company can obtain any effective security where the goods have already been sold to the dealer: if it attempts to "advance" the dealer the price by way of a simple purchase and letting back to the dealer on h.p., the transaction may be avoided by the legislation on chattel mortgages[18]; and, if the company tries to escape this danger by a purchase and simple hiring back, the dealer may still be able to pass a good title to a b.f.p., either because he has actual or ostensible[19] authority to sell, or under the Factors Act 1889[20]. In view of the foregoing disadvantages, finance companies modified the system so that the goods were purchased by them direct from the supplier, and then let on h.p. to the dealer. This last type of transaction appears in essence to be very like an ordinary directly financed one; and the possible application to such transactions of the chattel mortgage legislation will be considered later[1]. In view of the difficulties involved in obtaining any effective security, many finance companies have resigned themselves to making unsecured loans, usually on short-term bills of exchange. There is, however, a very real danger of such a course of business infringing the Moneylenders Acts as will be explained later[2].

2. *Dealer recourse.* The finance company will normally consider themselves as bankers, rather than traders in goods, and will therefore stipulate that, where the customer defaults, the dealer will step in and make good their loss[3]. There is usually no question of these recourse provisions amounting to penalties[4]; and the legal formulae used to achieve this object may vary according to whether the transaction with the customer is financed directly or indirectly.

(1) *Directly financed transactions.* The contract of sale from the dealer to the finance company will, of course, subject the dealer to all the implied undertakings discussed in Part 2; and, in addition, that contract may provide that the dealer warrants the truth of all the information contained in the proposal form[5]. Apart from these types of liability, dealer recourse is usually achieved in one of two ways. First, the dealer may be required, as part of the consideration for the finance

---

17. See above, p. 181.   18. See below, pp. 293–294.
19. I.e. apparent or usual authority: see above, p. 185.
20. Sections 2 and 8: see above, pp. 203, 215.
  1. See below, pp. 297–300.   2. See below, p. 300, *et seq.*
  3. The exact time at which the recourse provision becomes operative depends on the construction of the contract: *Reliance Car Facilities, Ltd.* v. *Roding Motors*, [1952] 2 Q.B. 844; [1952] 1 All E.R. 1355, C.A.: see below, p. 356.
  4. *Stirling Industrial Facilities, Ltd.* v. *Lydiate Textiles, Ltd.* (1962), 106 Sol. Jo. 669, C.A. Penalties are considered below, pp. 391–395.
  5. E.g. *Liverpool and County Discount, Ltd.* v. *A.B. Motors, Ltd.*, [1963] 2 All E.R. 396, C.A.

company agreeing to accept the transaction and purchase the goods, to promise that in the event of default by the customer he will repurchase the goods at a price which covers the finance company's "loss". In the event of repurchase, the finance company will usually have promised to assign all its rights against the customer and the goods to the dealer[6], so that the latter is left to enforce the h.p. or sale agreement against the customer[7]. This form of recourse provision suffers from the disadvantage that it cannot be enforced against the dealer unless all the conditions of the repurchase clause are satisfied to the letter[8] and the company is able to redeliver the goods to the dealer[9]. Second, instead of agreeing to repurchase, the dealer may simply agree to indemnify the finance company against all loss it may incur in the transaction, in return for which the dealer has the option of calling for an assignment of the finance company's rights against the customer and the goods[6]. Whilst such recourse provisions are usually expressed as indemnities, they are often interpreted by the courts as being in reality contracts of guarantee[10], in which case the finance company can have no greater rights against the dealer than it has against the customer, and the dealer will be discharged if the company impairs the security[11].

(2) *Indirectly financed transactions.* In some types of indirect financing, full dealer recourse is achieved by reason of the form taken by the transaction[12]. In other cases, a repurchase or recourse clause will have to be inserted in the master agreement, and the effect will be similar to that in directly financed transactions.

2 DIRECT FINANCING[13]

This section will deal with the effect of the legislation restricting chattel mortgaging and moneylending on directly financed transactions; that is, where A. sells goods to B. and B. lets them on h.p. terms, or sells them on credit to C.

1 Chattel mortgaging

It has already been seen that, where a person mortgages goods by a transaction evidenced in writing, it is usually avoided by the Bills of

---

6. If the finance company is in breach of the reassignment provision, the measure of damages is the value of the goods: *Bowmaker (Commercial), Ltd.* v. *Smith*, [1965] 2 All E.R. 304, C.A.
7. E.g. *Karsales (Harrow), Ltd.* v. *Wallis*, [1956] 2 All E.R. 866, C.A.: set out above, p. 141.
8. See *United Dominions Trust (Commercial), Ltd.* v. *Eagle Aircraft, Ltd.*, [1968] 1 All E.R. 104, C.A.
9. Because non-delivery will lead to a total failure of consideration: see below, p. 405.
10. See below, p. 346.
11. See below, p. 347.　　　　12. See below, p. 310.
13. See generally Kirkpatrick & Greene in *Instalment Credit* (Ed. Diamond) 25–43; Goode, *ibid.*, 44–90.

Sale Act 1882 unless registered and in the form set out in the schedule to that Act[14]. Whilst the 1882 Act does not apply to incorporated companies[15], s. 95 of the Companies Act 1948 provides that, if a company grants, *inter alia,*

> "a charge created or evidenced by an instrument which, if executed by an individual, would require registration as a bill of sale" (s. 95 (2) (c)),

that charge must be registered under the 1948 Act. Where the mortgage or charge is avoided by the Acts of 1882 or 1948 the lender will lose his security, though in each case the loan immediately becomes repayable[16]. However, it is necessary to distinguish between loans to individuals and to companies, because the extent of the avoidance is not the same: a loan within the 1882 Act is absolutely void if not in the prescribed form[17]; whereas an unregistered loan falling within the 1948 Act is only void as "against the liquidator and any creditor of the company" (s. 95 (1)). Whilst the degree of avoidance may thus depend on whether or not the borrower is a company, the test of whether the transaction falls within the ambit of the 1882 or 1948 Act is the same: that is, assuming the borrower is not a company, would the transaction require registration under the 1882 Act?

It has already been shown that the essence of a bill of sale is an assurance of property, and that the ordinary two-party h.p. transaction is therefore outside the ambit of the 1882 Act[18]. *A fortiori*, it might therefore seem that *prima facie* a directly financed transaction would fall outside the Act. However, this will not always be so. After the passage of the 1882 Act, numerous attempts were made to avoid its application by disguising what were really chattel mortgages as sales and rehirings on h.p. To prevent such evasions of the 1882 Act, the courts laid down the rule that a sale and rehiring transaction would escape the Act if genuine[19], but not if it were a mere cloak for a loan[20]. It was one thing to lay down such a rule, but quite another to apply it; and the courts have found particular difficulties where there were more than

---

14. See above, p. 10.
15. Section 17 of the 1882 Act: and see *Re Standard Manufacturing Co.*, [1891] 1 Ch. 627, C.A.
16. See *Bradford Advance Co., Ltd.* v. *Ayres*, [1924] W.N. 152 and s. 95 (1) of the 1948 Act respectively.
17. Section 9 of the 1882 Act. There are differing degrees of avoidance for other breaches of the 1882 Act.
18. See above, p. 10.
19. E.g. *Yorkshire Railway Wagon Co.* v. *Maclure* (1882), 21 Ch.D. 309, C.A.; *Staffs Motor Guarantee, Ltd.* v. *British Wagon, Ltd.*, [1934] 2 K.B. 305: set out above, pp. 206–207.
20. E.g. *Re Watson, ex parte the Official Receiver* (1890), 25 Q.B.D. 27, C.A.

two parties involved[1]. Whilst a directly financed transaction in ordinary form will not involve a sale and rehiring between any two of the parties, it may still be used as an indirect way of achieving a chattel mortgage. At first, the courts were adamant that such a transaction could not infringe the Act. In *Manchester, Sheffield and Lincolnshire Rail. Co.* v. *North Central Wagon Co.*[2]

> B. Co. defaulted in payments due under a h.p. agreement with S. Co. in respect of 100 wagons, upon which event S. Co. were entitled to terminate the agreement. B. Co. wanted £1,000 to pay off S. Co. and put themselves in funds, and therefore made the following arrangement: a finance company would purchase the wagons from S. Co. and let them to B. Co. on h.p terms, the finance company paying S. Co. £257 to settle their interest in the wagons and the residue of £743 to B. Co. The House of Lords held that there was a genuine sale of the wagons to the finance company, and that the transaction did not fall within the Bills of Sale Acts.

Their Lordships placed some emphasis upon the fact that the sale to the alleged lender (the finance company) was not by the alleged borrower (B. Co.), and Lord MACNAGHTEN said[3]:

> "At the time when the [finance company] came forward to assist the [B. Co.], the property in the wagons belonged to the [S. Co.]. They alone were the owners. The [B. Co.] had no equity of redemption. They had no equitable rights whatever. At the utmost, assuming the lease not to have been forfeited, they had a contingent interest liable to be defeated by non-compliance with the terms and conditions of the lease. Whatever else may be doubtful, it was clearly the intention of the parties that that interest should be determined. The property in the wagons passed directly from the [S. Co.] to the [finance company] . . ."

However, in subsequent cases the courts began to have second thoughts; and in some instances they accepted that a tripartite transaction did in fact infringe the Acts. The situation under consideration is that where A. sells goods to B., and B. lets them on h.p. terms to C. It is convenient to consider the cases according to whether there is any prior relationship between A. and C. with respect to the goods.

(a) Circular Transactions

The situation where there is a prior relationship between A. and C. with respect to the goods first presented itself to the courts in a line of cases where an impecunious tenant sought to raise money to pay his

---

1. See generally Goode, *H.P. Law & Practice* (2nd Edn.) 81–93; Guest, *Law of H.P.* 111–130; Diamond (1960), 23 M.L.R. 399 and 516; Fitzpatrick [1969] J.B.L. 211.
2. (1888), 13 App. Cas. 554, H.L.
3. At p. 566. See also Lord FITZGERALD at p. 564.

rent by the following arrangement: the landlord levied distress on the
tenant's furniture, which was then sold to a third party, who let it to the
tenant under a h.p. agreement. In the last decade of the nineteenth
century, it became quite clear that such a transaction might well
infringe the 1882 Act[4]. Whilst this step was comparatively easy in that
the device was clearly within the mischief aimed at by the Act, the
decisions did demonstrate that tripartite transactions might be within
the Act. A rather more unusual and difficult situation arose in *Maas* v.
Pepper[5].

> Mellor agreed to buy a hotel and its furniture from Sykes for
> £30,000, of which £3,000 was appropriated to the value of the
> chattels. A deposit was paid, and most of the price raised by means
> of three mortgages; but, being still in need of £2,000, Mellor
> approached Maas for a loan on the security of a fourth mortgage.
> Maas declined a fourth mortgage, and Mellor refused to give a bill
> of sale, at which Sykes said that the only way was for someone to
> purchase the chattels from Sykes and sell them to Mellor on h.p.
> Without seeing the sale agreement between Sykes and Mellor, Maas
> thereupon agreed to buy the chattels from Sykes for £2,000, and
> gave a receipt for the price. Thereafter, Mellor entered into a h.p.
> agreement with Maas in respect of the furniture, and the purchase
> of the hotel was completed.

In a judgment which was unanimously accepted by the Court of Appeal
and the House of Lords, WRIGHT J. held that the true inference from
these facts was that the £2,000 was a loan from Maas to Mellor, and
that the h.p. agreement was a security for that loan and therefore
infringed the 1882 Act. His Lordship pointed out that, at the time
Maas purchased the furniture, Sykes still had the legal title to it
because the original sale was conditional on payment; and continued[6]:

> "The question is, Was there a real sale to [Maas] in [his] own right?
> The object of all the parties was a loan on security . . . No one
> can suppose that [Maas was] to become absolute beneficial [owner],
> free to remove the goods and deal with them as [he] pleased . . .
> It would have defeated the common purpose of selling the business
> as a going concern . . . It seems to me clear that Sykes and Mellor
> could have prevented [Maas] from removing the goods, or from
> selling to anyone but Mellor. Under these circumstances, I think
> that [Maas] must be regarded as [trustee] for Mellor, and Mellor
> as being the real owner, unless the property is taken out of Mellor

---

4. E.g. *Beckett* v. *Tower Assets, Co.*, [1891] 1 Q.B. 638, C.A.
5. [1905] A.C. 102, H.L.; affirming *sub nom. Mellor's Trustee* v. *Maas*, [1902]
   1 K.B. 137; [1903] 1 K.B. 226, C.A.
6. At pp. 140-141. Cf. *Re Wait*, [1927] 1 Ch. 606, C.A.: set out above, p.
   173; and the *Manchester Rail. Co. Case* (1888), 13 App. Cas. 554, H.L.:
   set out above, p. 293.

or charged by the hiring agreement. But, if Mellor is to be regarded as the real owner, then the hiring agreement was an assurance to [Maas] or was an essential part of [his] title, and it operated as a licence by Mellor to [Maas] to take possession of the goods as against Mellor's equitable interest, and it was a security for a loan''.

The facts of *Maas* v. *Pepper* were perhaps slightly unusual; but the issue involved in that case has arisen in a much simpler form in ordinary directly financed h.p. transactions. If the customer (C.) enters into a binding contract to purchase the goods from the dealer (A.) before the parties apply to the finance company (B.), then, in the absence of a contrary intention, the property in the goods will pass from A. to C. under s. 18, rule 1 of the S.G.A.[7]; and the effect will be that the property in the goods will pass from A. to C. to B., and there will in effect be a sale and rehiring between B. and C. in order to reimburse B. for the price which he has advanced on behalf of C. to A. This situation arose in *Polsky* v. *S. & A. Services*[8].

C. purchased a car from A. for £895, and paid for it by cheque. As this cheque would have overdrawn C.'s account, B. was approached to cover the deficiency. The three parties executed forms which would have been appropriate if there had been an ordinary directly financed transaction; that is, they envisaged a sale from A. to B., followed by a letting by B. to C. After taking delivery of the car, C. successfully sued for a declaration that the h.p. agreement was avoided by the 1882 Act.

In granting the declaration, Lord GODDARD C.J. attached some importance both to the inaccuracy of the documents and to the prior sale by A. to C.; and his judgment was unanimously accepted by the Court of Appeal. In the light of this case, it is usual for the finance company to include in their proposal form a clause to the effect that the customer expressly states that all prior negotiations (if any) entered into by him with respect to the purchase of the goods are now at an end, and that he has no interest or property in them. However, the interests of the dealer are in one sense opposed to those of the finance company, in that the dealer will wish to manoeuvre the customer into a binding agreement even if the h.p. proposal is never accepted. What if the dealer, with such an object in view, gives the customer a "sold note"[9]? Whilst the customer has asserted to the finance company in the proposal form that he has not purchased the goods from the dealer, and the dealer has

---

7. Set out above, p. 162.
8. [1951] 1 All E.R. 185; affd. at p. 1062, C.A. Applied in *North Central Wagon Co., Ltd.* v. *Brailsford*, [1962] 1 All E.R. 502; set out below, p 304.
9. If the "sold note" was intended to evidence a contract of sale by A. to B., with an option for C. to take the goods on h.p. terms from B., then it might be contrary to *Scammell, Ltd.* v. *Ouston*, [1941] A.C. 251; [1941] 1 All E.R. 14, H.L., and infringe s. 29 (4) of the H.P.A.: set out above, p. 34.

similarly warranted his title to the company, it seems that estoppel is not available to defeat the Bills of Sale Acts[10]. Thus, the only question is whether the dealer and customer ever made such a contract, the "sold note" being merely evidence of their intention.

In view of the apparent importance of the element of circularity in the cases discussed above, logically the number of parties in the circle should be immaterial. It would follow that the so-called "re-financing" transactions[11] should fall within the ambit of the Act[12]. In this form of business, the customer (C.) sells his goods to the dealer (A.), who resells to the finance company (B.), who lets the goods on h.p. to C. Yet it would seem that these transactions are, in fact, outside the Act. In *Stoneleigh Finance, Ltd.* v. *Phillips*[13]

> A. Ltd., who dealt mainly in "private" transactions, frequently did business with a finance company, B. Ltd. B. Ltd. had made it quite clear to A. Ltd. that they would accept "private", but not "re-financing", transactions. However, on one occasion, A. Ltd. agreed to obtain finance on the security of their vehicles for C. Ltd. by way of "re-financing"; and, unaware of this, B. Ltd. accepted the proposals. Subsequently, C. Ltd. became insolvent, and the liquidator sold the goods. B. Ltd. sued the liquidator in detinue and conversion. McNair J. held that no genuine sale was intended, and dismissed the actions on the following grounds: (1) the parties did not intend title to pass under this transaction, or were estopped from denying this; and (2) the documents involved were bills of sale and void for want of registration under s. 95 of the 1948 Act.

By a majority[14], the Court of Appeal reversed this decision on both points. Their Lordships held that B. Ltd, had obtained a good title to the vehicles for the following reasons:

(1) C. Ltd. and A. Ltd. intended a genuine sale, so that the title to the goods passed from C. Ltd. to A. Ltd. and thence to B. Ltd.[15]; but, even if this was not so, C. Ltd. was privy to the warranty of title given

---

10. See e.g. *Campbell Discount Co., Ltd.* v. *Gall*, [1961] 1 Q.B. 431; [1961] 2 All E.R. 104, C.A.: see above, p. 287.

11. These must be distinguished from "private" transactions, a term applied to the following circumstances: suppose two private persons, X. and C., wish to arrange a sale from one to the other, X. wanting a cash sale and C. desiring credit; then A. would purchase the goods from X. and sell them to B., who would let them to C.

12. E.g. *per* SALMON L.J. in *Mercantile Credit Co., Ltd.* v. *Hamblin*, [1965] 2 Q.B. 242, C.A., at p. 280.

13. [1965] 2 Q.B. 537; [1965] 1 All E.R. 513, C.A.

14. DAVIES and RUSSELL L.JJ. SELLERS L.J. dissented.

15. At pp. 569–571, 575–577; *contra* SELLERS L.J., at p. 562. Cf. *Bennett* v. *Griffin Finance*, [1967] 2 Q.B. 46; [1967] 1 All E.R. 515, C.A.; *Kingsley* v. *Stirling Industrial Securities, Ltd.*, [1967] 2 Q.B. 747; [1966] 2 All E.R. 414, C.A.; *Snook* v. *London and West Riding Investments, Ltd.*, [1967] 2 Q.B. 786; [1967] 1 All E.R. 518, C.A. (Lord DENNING M.R. dissenting).

by A. Ltd. to B. Ltd. and therefore precluded from denying A. Ltd.'s authority to sell[16].

(2) The transaction did not operate as a charge within the ambit of s. 95 because:

(a) For an instrument to be registrable under s. 95 (2) (c)[17], it is not sufficient that it is a bill of sale, it must also create or evidence a charge on the company's property, i.e., it must be a mortgage and not an absolute bill[18]; and

(b) the instruments in the present case did not create or evidence a charge on the company's property, as there was no obligation on C. Ltd. to pay or repay any money to A. Ltd.[19], and B. Ltd. had no intention of lending money on security of the documents[20].

The difference between the attitude of the courts in the sale and re-hiring cases as opposed to the re-financing cases is striking: in the former, the inaccuracy of the documents and the circularity of the transaction seem to have been regarded as significant factors[1]; but the same can hardly be said in the re-financing cases. Frequently, both types of transaction seem to be clearly within the mischief of the chattel mortgage legislation, and it is difficult to find any distinction of principle between the two situations. Perhaps the explanation lies in the increasing judicial reluctance to utilise the Acts to strike down h.p. transactions: the distinction between the cases may be historical rather than logical[2].

(b) Open-ended transactions

Finally, there is the question whether the chattel mortgage legislation can attack open-ended transactions; that is, where there is no prior relationship between A. and C. with respect to the goods. The *Manchester Rail. Co. Case* suggested that this was unlikely[3]; and such a view was expressed by LUSH J. in *Johnson v. Rees*[4], though ATKIN J. disagreed. Unfortunately, the leading case where the view of ATKIN J.

---

16. At pp. 571, 577–578; and see also SELLERS L.J., at p. 566. And see *Snook* v. *London and West Riding Investments, Ltd.* (above). Estoppel is considered above, p. 189.
17. Set out above, p. 292.
18. At pp. 568, 574–575. SELLERS L.J. did not comment on this point.
19. DAVIES L.J., at p. 568. This echoes the reasoning of the H.L. in the *Manchester Rail. Co. Case* (1888), 13 App. Cas. 554, H.L.: set out above, p. 293.
20. *Per* DAVIES and RUSSELL L.JJ., at pp. 572–573, 579–580; *contra* SELLERS L.J., at pp. 564–566. See also *per* DIPLOCK L.J. in *Snook* v. *London and West Riding Investments Ltd.* (above), at p. 802.
 1. E.g. *Polsky* v. *S. and A. Services*, [1951] 1 All E.R. 185 and 1062, C.A.: set out above, p. 295.
 2. See also below, p. 300.
 3. See above, p. 293.
 4. (1915), 84 L.J.K.B. 1276, D.C.

was adopted is the unreported decision of the House of Lords in *Motor Trade Finance Ltd. v. H. E. Motors, Ltd.*[5].

> A manufacturer, A. Ltd., set up a separate sales company, C. Ltd., and to finance C. Ltd. made the following arrangement: A. Ltd. would sell its vehicles to a finance company, B. Ltd., who would then let them to C. Ltd. under h.p. agreements. The h.p. agreements contained the usual provision that the hirer would not sell the goods during the currency of the agreement; and there also existed a Supplemental Agreement, whereby A. Ltd. agreed to indemnify B. Ltd. from any loss incurred in this business; and which provided that, if C. Ltd. defaulted in any of the h.p. agreements, B. Ltd. might repossess all the vehicles then let to C. Ltd. on h.p. by B. Ltd. FRASER J. held that the parties did not intend the transaction to operate according to its tenor as comprised in the documents, but as a loan on the security of the stock for the time being of C. Ltd.[6]. This decision was affirmed by the Court of Appeal and the House of Lords[7]; and all the courts seem to have been impressed by the facts that C. Ltd. was deliberately, to the knowledge of B. Ltd., set up as a sales company, but that the h.p. agreements specifically forbade sales of the stock; and that the Supplemental Agreement gave B. Ltd. rights over the whole of the stock for the time being on h.p.

Of the judges who thought the transaction colourable, Lord SUMNER and ATKIN L.J. thought that B. Ltd. purchased the cars as agent or trustee of C. Ltd., though Lords ATKINSON and SHAW do not seem to have considered whether there was any such special relationship; and Lord CARSON and SARGANT L.J. held that the transaction was not colourable because there was no such special relationship.

It is submitted that the same answer could have been reached in this case by reducing the number of parties to two, A. Ltd. and B. Ltd. This could have been achieved by lifting the corporate veil of C. Ltd.[8], or treating C. Ltd. as the agent of A. Ltd.; and that the fact that the majority of the judges in this case did not take such an easy way out may be indicative of their confidence that the chattel mortgage legislation can, in appropriate circumstances, strike at open-ended directly financed h.p. transactions. However, almost immediately ACTON J. held that an ordinary directly financed h.p. transaction with dealer

---

5. (1926), House of Lords Journal (26.3.26). See also reports in (1960), 23 M.L.R. at p. 526; Dunstan, *Law Relating to H.P.* (4th Edn.) 217; Earengey, *Law Relating to H.P.* (2nd Edn.) 19.
6. The liquidator pleaded s. 93 of the Companies Consolidation Act 1908, the forerunner of s. 95 of the 1948 Act.
7. C.A.: POLLOCK M.R. and ATKIN L.J., with SARGANT L.J. dissenting. H.L.: Lords ATKINSON, SHAW, SUMNER and DARLING, with Lord CARSON dissenting.
8. There was some evidence to justify this, there being a very close connection between A. Ltd., and its subsidiary C. Ltd.

recourse did not fall within the Acts[9]; and a few years later a stocking agreement was found not to be colourable. In *Re Lovegrove*[10]

> A manufacturer, A., entered into the following arrangement with a finance company, B. Ltd., so that B. Ltd. might provide credit facilities for the sale of A.'s goods: a sales company, C. Ltd., was set up, control of C. Ltd. being vested in B. Ltd.; and it was arranged that, when A. obtained orders, he would sell the goods at a 10% discount to C. Ltd. and, as agent of C. Ltd., resell the goods on credit to the customers. It was further agreed that A. should guarantee performance by the customers; but that, should C. Ltd. make a net profit of more than £2,500 in any one year, any excess should be paid to A. FARWELL J. held that the transaction was intended to be one of loan; and, on appeal, the trustee argued that (1) the sales by A. to C. Ltd. were unregistered bills of sale, and (2) the agreement was avoided by s. 43 of the Bankruptcy Act 1914.

The Court of Appeal unanimously found against the trustee on both points[11]. Their Lordships agreed that such a transaction was capable of falling within the Bills of Sale Acts as being merely a cloak for a loan; but MAUGHAM L.J. explained[12]:

> "I do not hesitate to say that this transaction was unusual, and that it was in effect a transaction by which [A.] was financed by [B. Ltd.] . . . so that he was able to carry on the business. But when it is considered that the mischief aimed at by the Bills of Sale Act or of the Bankruptcy Act was not being brought into play by anything that was done, I for my part do not see why we should be astute to come to the conclusion that this was anything other than an unusual form of sale and purchase between [A.] and [C. Ltd.], the intention being that [C. Ltd.] should never hold the furniture in its own possession, but should immediately cause a resale to be made to the old customers of [A.], so that he would be repaid out of the purchase price".

Although the scheme adopted in *Re Lovegrove* contained nothing resembling the Supplemental Agreement in *Motor Trade Finance Ltd.* v. *H.E. Motors Ltd.*, the basic situation in the two cases is a very similar one; but for some reason the earlier case was not cited in *Re Lovegrove*. Whilst it may therefore be tempting to conclude that *Re Lovegrove* is of doubtful authority as being decided *per incuriam*, it is clear that the later case has set the trend for subsequent decisions[13]. The conclusion

9. *Automobile and General Finance Corporation, Ltd.* v. *Morris* (1929), 73 Sol. Jo. 451.
10. [1935] 1 Ch. 464, C.A.
11. Section 43 of the 1914 Act is considered below, p. 307.
12. At p. 495.
13. E.g. *Olds Discount, Ltd.* v. *Krett and Krett*, [1940] 2 K.B. 117; [1940] 3 All E.R. 36.

would appear to be that tripartite transactions[14], even stocking agreements, are probably safe from the chattel mortgage legislation[15]. Moreover, it seems likely that nowadays re-financing transactions will also escape the Acts[16].

Behind this web of case-law, a changing judicial attitude may be discernible. In the nineteenth century, outright suspicion of h.p. induced the courts to search diligently for some ground on which to hold the transaction colourable; but in the present century the courts have become increasingly aware of h.p., and it is probably on grounds of economic convenience and social acceptability that they gradually came to accept the device of h.p. and the whole ramifications of the trade. Looked at in this light, *Motor Trade Finance Ltd.* v. *H.E. Motors Ltd.* and *Polsky* v. *S. & A. Services*[17] appear to stand out as high-water marks, and it may, perhaps, be misleading to take them at their face-value. Indeed, the common law seems to be fast approaching the position where few h.p. transactions will ever infringe the chattel mortgage legislation; and it would be much simpler if such transactions were expressly excluded from the ambit of the Acts. Perhaps the real answer is that the present legislation has outlived its usefulness, and it is to be hoped that it will soon be replaced by a rather more modern legislative scheme[18].

2 Moneylending[19]

It has already been observed that the *economic object* of a finance company is to lend money, usually on the security of chattels; and in the previous sub-section it was demonstrated that some such transactions may amount to a lending. If the finance company makes a business of lending money, it is in danger of bringing itself within the ambit of the Moneylenders Acts 1900 and 1927. If so, then the company must be registered under the Acts and comply with the extremely onerous rules of those Acts, which are designed to curb the activities of the proverbial Shylock. Moreover, whereas infringement of the chattel mortage legislation merely leads to the avoidance of the transaction so that the sum lent is recoverable[20], failure to comply with the Moneylenders Acts, where applicable, is a criminal offence and will render the money-

---

14. Including "private transactions", which are explained above, p. 296, note 11.
15. See above, pp. 296–297.
16. But see *St. Margaret's Trust, Ltd.* v. *Castle,* [1964] C.L.Y. 1685, C.A.; and Ziegel in *Instalment Credit* (Ed. Diamond) 125.
17. [1951] 1 All E.R. 185, and 1062, C.A.: see above, pp. 295, 297.
18. The Crowther Committee on Consumer Credit is presently considering this question.
19. See generally Goode, *H.P. Law & Practice* (2nd Edn.), Chapter 5; Guest, *Law of H.P.*, paras. 131–140.
20. See above, p. 293.

lending contract illegal, so that not only is the contract void, but the sum lent is also irrecoverable[1].

The Moneylenders Acts thus represent a serious threat to finance companies: as it is for all practical purposes impossible for them to conduct their business as registered moneylenders, they do not register under the Acts; and the vital question is therefore whether their activities fall within the ambit of the Acts. According to s. 6 of the Moneylenders Act 1900,

> "The expression 'moneylender' in this Act shall include every person whose business is that of moneylending, or who advertises or announces himself or holds himself out in any way as carrying on that business; but shall not include[2]—
> (d) any person bonâ fide carrying on the business of banking . . . or bonâ fide carrying on any business not having for its primary object the lending of money, in the course of which and for the purposes whereof he lends money; or
> (e) any body corporate for the time being exempted from . . . this Act by order of the Board of Trade made and published pursuant to regulations of the Board of Trade".

Thus, to establish that a finance company is a "moneylender" within the meaning of the Act, three things must be proved. First, it must be shown that the company has been lending money, a question which is substantially the same as that under the chattel mortgage legislation[3]. Second, the section requires that the company must be conducting a business of moneylending, which implies some degree of system[4]. In view of the repetitive nature of the business, it is likely that this requirement will be fairly readily established where it can be shown that certain types of transaction in reality amount to loans. Third, the finance company will only be a "moneylender" where it cannot bring itself within one of the exceptions listed in the section[5].

Three of these listed exceptions are relevant to the situation under discussion.

1. A bona fide banking business. In one sense, the very existence of this

---

1. See *Chapman* v. *Michaelson*, [1909] 1 Ch. 238, C.A.
2. Exceptions (a), (b) and (c) are irrelevant to the present discussion, and are therefore omitted.
3. Except that the Moneylenders Acts also apply to oral loans and to unsecured loans, the courts assumed that the issue is the same as that under the Bills of Sale Acts: *Automobile and General Finance Corporation, Ltd.* v. *Morris* (1929), 73 Sol. Jo. 451; *Olds Discount, Ltd.* v. *Cohen* (1937), [1938] 3 All E.R. 281 n; *North Central Wagon Co., Ltd.* v. *Brailsford*, [1962] 1 All E.R. 502.
4. See *Litchfield* v. *Dreyfus*, [1906] 1 K.B. 584.
5. Where it is shown that the finance company is *prima facie* a moneylender, the (factual?) burden of proof shifts, so that the company must show that it is within one of the exceptions: see the C.A. in *United Dominions Trust, Ltd.* v. *Kirkwood*, [1966] 2 Q.B. 431, at pp. 441–442, 457, 463.

exception makes nonsense of the definition of a "moneylender", because one of the primary objects of a bank is to make a profit by lending money, and the real distinction between a bank and a moneylender is an emotive one: a bank is socially and economically respectable, whereas a moneylender is not.   The finance companies would like to regard themselves simply as bankers, and it would therefore be natural for them to seek to escape from the Moneylenders Acts by way of this exception.   The issue was tested in *United Dominions Trust, Ltd.* v. *Kirkwood*[6].

> U.D.T. Ltd. extended stocking finance to a dealer, the loans being unsecured, except for a guarantee by the dealer in the form of an endorsement on bills of exchange. When the bills were dishonoured, U.D.T. Ltd. sued the dealer on his endorsements; and the dealer pleaded the Moneylenders Acts. U.D.T. Ltd. admitted that they were unlicenced, but pleaded that they carried on a banking business, and that the loans were made in the course of that business. MOCATTA J. concluded that U.D.T. Ltd. did carry on a banking business, and his decision in favour of that company was affirmed by the majority of the Court of Appeal.

In this case, the Courts made extensive enquiries into the nature and scope of the business conducted by U.D.T. Ltd., and, notwithstanding that the financial establishment was mobilised to support the company, it is fairly clear that U.D.T. Ltd. only just obtained the decision.   As U.D.T. Ltd. is by far the largest and most well-connected of the finance companies, the victory was, indeed, a pyrrhic one for the finance companies as a whole; and it does not even seem to guarantee that U.D.T. Ltd. would be safe from future pleas of this sort.   Clearly, the finance companies must look elsewhere for their protection from the Moneylenders Acts.

2. *The residuary exemption of paragraph (d)*. Whilst it is clear the ordinary directly financed transactions do not amount to loans[7], there is plainly a risk that some of the normal business activities of finance companies will amount to lending money.   This is particularly the case with sale and rehiring transactions[8] and stocking plans[9]; and, as the finance company undertaking such transactions is unlikely to be able to shelter behind the banking exemption, an obvious alternative is to plead the residuary exemption in paragraph (d).   This requires that the finance company satisfy all three of the following requirements:

6. [1966] 2 Q.B. 431; [1966] 1 All E.R. 968, C.A.
7. *Automobile and General Finance Corporation, Ltd.* v. *Morris* (1929), 73 Sol. Jo. 451; *Olds Discount, Ltd.* v. *Cohen* (1937), [1938] 3 All E.R. 281 n.
8. E.g. *Polsky* v. *S. and A. Services,* [1951] 1 All E.R. 185, and 1062, C.A.; set out above, p. 295; *North Central Wagon Co., Ltd.* v. *Brailsford,* [1962] 1 All E.R. 502: set out below, p. 304.
9. E.g. *Premor, Ltd.* v. *Shaw,* [1964] 2 All E.R. 583, C.A.

(1) That it *bona fide* carries on a business "not having for its primary object the lending of money". This is usually easily satisfied by finance companies, whose legal primary object is to enter into h.p. transactions[10]; and the Court of Appeal have even accepted that the requirement is fulfilled where the h.p. and lending transactions are conducted by two separate companies in a group[11].

(2) That the lending of money is "in the course of" that business. It has been decided that it is "in the course of" business for a depository to lend money to depositors of goods[12], or an issuing house to a private company which may subsequently become ripe for flotation[13]; but not for a finance company to extend to a dealer general stocking loans unconnected with any specific h.p. transactions[14].

(3) That that lending is "for the purposes of" the business. The Privy Council have taken the benevolent view that "it is sufficient if it is lent in the course of and for the purposes of the business as a whole, and not merely of its primary objects"[15]. However, in *Premor Ltd.* v. *Shaw*[16] the Court of Appeal insisted that the purpose of the loan must be "directly to help the primary business—as distinct from getting a high rate of interest on the loan"[17]; and they unanimously held that the exception did not cover a stocking loan made by a finance company to a dealer at an effective rate of interest of more than 60% *per annum*, notwithstanding the argument that it was made to "keep the dealer sweet". On the basis of the English cases, it would seem that, before a loan can be brought within the exception, it must be extended as a supporting service for the primary business and not with the major object of making a profit by way of interest on the loan[18].

3. Exemption certificates. Because the economic function of finance companies is so clearly moneylending, the most obvious course is to apply to the Board of Trade for exemption under paragraph (e). In their published Regulations made pursuant to the powers granted to them by paragraph (e)[19], the Board of Trade have reserved a wide

---

10. *Per* DENNING M.R. in *Premor, Ltd.* v. *Shaw* (above), at p. 586. *Contra* their economic object: see above, p. 300.
11. See DENNING M.R. in *United Dominions Trust, Ltd.* v. *Kirkwood*, [1966] 2 Q.B. 431, C.A., at p. 450.
12. *Official Assignee of the Property of Khoon* v. *Ek Liong Hin, Ltd.*, [1960] A.C. 178; [1960] 1 All E.R. 440, P.C.
13. *Frank H. Wright (Constructions), Ltd.* v. *Frodoor, Ltd.*, [1967] 1 All E.R 433.
14. *Per* Lord DENNING M.R. in *Premor, Ltd.* v. *Shaw* (above), at p. 587. Presumably his Lordship envisages that the hirer is to be the dealer's customer.
15. *Khoon's Case*, [1960] A.C. 178, at p. 191, P.C.
16. [1964] 2 All E.R. 583, C.A.
17. *Per* Lord DENNING, M.R., at p. 587.
18. See *Frank H. Wright (Constructions), Ltd.* v. *Frodoor, Ltd.* (above).
19. The Moneylenders (Body Corporate) Regulations, 1927 (S.R. & O. 1927, No. 1151).

discretion as to whether to grant an exemption certificate; and in practice the Board will only grant a certificate for a three year period and then only after a careful investigation of the applicant, one of their criteria being that the true rate of interest for the company's loans does not exceed 10% *per annum*. It is, of course, out of the question for a finance company to lend money at such a low rate of interest; and the effect of an exempted company lending at more than the approved rate was considered in *North Central Wagon Co., Ltd.* v. *Brailsford*[20].

> A haulage contractor who owned an Albion lorry wished to raise £1,000 on that lorry for the purpose of making the initial payment under a h.p. agreement in respect of another lorry. The plaintiff finance company agreed to supply the money if the transaction was carried out in the form of a sale and rehiring, and the price paid to a dealer who was to ensure that it was used to make the initial deposit.

CAIRNS J. had little difficulty in holding that the real transaction was a loan on the security of the Albion lorry; and he therefore decided that it was avoided by the Bills of Sale Acts[1]. However, he held that the plaintiffs were entitled to rely on their exemption certificate to save them from the operation of the Moneylenders Acts for the following reasons[2]:

> "First, that the exemption is not conditional on observance of the undertaking . . . [as to the rate of interest to be charged], and in my opinion remains effective unless and until revoked by the Board of Trade; secondly, that it is only on the basis that the [h.p.] agreement was void that the transaction can be regarded as a moneylending transaction . . . and that involves that the interest provisions in the agreement are void . . ."

As it seems probable that the Board of Trade would withdraw, or refuse to renew, a certificate once it was aware of the true rate being charged, this case marks yet another pyrrhic victory for the finance companies.

The foregoing discussion indicates a very real danger that the activities of *bona fide* h.p. finance companies will fall within the ambit of the out-dated and draconian Moneylenders Acts; and it is therefore not surprising that Lord DENNING M.R. in 1965 called for the Board of Trade to be given powers to exempt such companies from the Acts[3]. His suggestion was taken up in the Companies Act 1967, s. 123 (1) of which provides:

---

20. [1962] 1 All E.R. 502.
  1. See above, p. 295.   2. At p. 508.
  3. *United Dominions Trust, Ltd.* v. *Kirkwood*, [1966] 2 Q.B. 431, C.A., at p. 456.

"A certificate given by the Board of Trade that they are satisfied that a person can properly be treated for the purposes of the Money-lenders Acts 1900 to 1927 as being a person bona fide carrying on the business of banking shall, for those purposes, be conclusive evidence that he is so carrying on that business"[4].

The Board of Trade have already made substantial use of these new powers[5]; and it is to be hoped that the subtle learning of the previous paragraph will soon be redundant so far as finance companies are concerned[6].

3 INDIRECT FINANCING[7]

This section is concerned with the legislative pitfalls of indirect financing; that is, where A. lets goods on h.p. terms, or sells them on credit, to C., and subsequently A. transfers part or all of his interest in the transaction to B. in return for the payment of all or part of the outstanding "debt owed" to A. by C. The essence of indirect financing is thus a transfer of A.'s interest, and it is therefore necessary at the outset to analyse that interest. Having entered into an instalment credit transaction, the dealer (A.) has available for transfer the following interests:

(*1*) *Residuary Proprietary Rights.* Where the contract between A. and C. is a conditional sale or h.p. agreement, A. has a residuary proprietary interest in the goods sold or let. This interest may be likened to the interest of a mortgagee in realty, in that, though the nature of the interest is fixed at the outset of the agreement between A. and C., the value of that interest appears to diminish *pro tanto* with every payment made by C. However, whilst the value of the interest of a mortgagee of realty does diminish in the eyes of the law by reason of the mortgagor's equity of redemption; this cannot be said in the case of a conditional sale or h.p. agreement. A. retains the whole of the proprietary rights in the goods until the time comes for the passing of property; and each payment by C. gives him only a contingent right in the goods—contingent on his completion of the agreement. However, as most customers do complete their agreements, A.'s residuary proprietary rights are usually regarded as being of little commercial value in themselves.

---

4. The Board may under certain circumstances make the certificate retrospective—s. 123 (2); and may revoke the certificate—s. 123 (3).
5. See the Board of Trade Annual Reports on Companies. Presumably, many of the successful applicants have been in breach of the Moneylenders Acts for years!
6. The Crowther Committee on Consumer Credit is presumably considering this whole question.
7. See generally Ziegel in *Instalment Credit* (Ed. Diamond) 135–138.

(2) *Contractual Rights.* Unlike A.'s proprietary rights, his contractual rights against C. are valuable. A transferee of A.'s contractual rights will obtain the "right" to the instalments payable by C.; and this may justify him in paying A. a price for those rights which is not too far below the face value of those instalments (notwithstanding that in the case of h.p. there is no legal obligation on C. to pay them). Whilst the agreement between A. and C. will probably expressly permit A. to assign all his contractual rights against C. to another[8], certain rights are regarded by the law as being incapable of assignment. Contractual promises of a personal nature can never be assigned[9]; nor is the burden of any contract freely assignable[10]; and the position of the licence to seize is doubtful[11], though it is clear that the right to immediate possession may pass with a transfer of proprietary rights[12].

It is now possible to consider (1) the effects of the different types of transfer, and (2) the form of indirect financing.

1 The different types of transfer

In the course of indirectly financing his instalment credit business, a dealer may transfer to the finance company either or both of his proprietary and contractual rights under the instalment credit contracts; and those transfers may be either absolute, or by way of mortgage, charge or declaration of trust.

(a) *Absolute transfers*[12a]

It is convenient to discuss absolute transfers according to the type of right being transferred.

1. Transfers of proprietary rights. An absolute transfer of the dealer's proprietary rights will, if made for consideration, amount to a sale of goods within the 1893 Act[13]. The major problem which arises here is whether the finance company assignee (B.) can recover possession of the goods where the customer (C.) is in breach of his instalment credit agreement.

(1) Where C. is in breach after assignment, the rights of B. would appear to be as follows: if the breach *ipso facto* determines the agreement, B. may sue in conversion or detinue; but, if C.'s breach merely renders the agreement terminable by A., B. has no sufficient right to possession to maintain such an action[14].

---

8. This will avoid the argument that an express or implied prohibition prevents assignment: see above, p. 13.
9. See Treitel, *Law of Contract* (3rd Edn.) 602–604.
10. See Treitel, *op. cit.*, 669–672; Diamond (1956), 19 M.L.R. 498, 500.
11. See below, p. 308.　　　　12. See above, p. 13, and below, pp. 308, 347.
12a. See generally Goode, *H.P. Law & Practice* (2nd Edn.) 512–524, 661–670.
13. See above, pp. 5–9.
14. Unless he can persuade A. to terminate; or A. has contracted to terminate in such circumstances; or B. has also taken an assignment of A.'s contractual rights.

(2) Where C. is in breach before assignment, there is a danger that the assignment may be upset in the event of A.'s insolvency as being a fraudulent preference[15], or within the reputed ownership doctrine[16], or a bill of sale within the 1878 Act[17]. Whilst the first restriction also applies where A. is a limited company[18], the latter two do not[19]. Indeed, the 1878 Act only applies where A. is in the "possession or apparent possession" of the goods at the time of the assignment[20]. Ordinarily, this situation will not arise, because the goods will be in the legal possession of C.; but the transfer will fall within the 1878 Act where A. has repossessed the goods, or, it would seem, where he has an immediate right to do so[1].

2. Transfers of contractual rights. Where there is an absolute assignment of rights under a conditional or credit sale, it may operate as a statutory assignment within s. 136 of the Law of Property Act 1925[2]; but an agreement to assign, or an assignment of the right to future hire-rent under a h.p. agreement, can only operate as an equitable assignment[3]. It is, of course, necessary for B. to give notice of the assignment to C. to complete a statutory assignment; and it is wise to give notice of an equitable assignment to C. both to bind C. to pay the instalments falling due to B.[4], and to secure priority over other assignees[5]. Moreover, there are two particular problems which may arise from an assignment of contractual rights.

(1) Where the dealer becomes insolvent, the transfer will escape the chattel mortgage legislation because it is not applicable to transfers of choses in action[6]; but, if the dealer is not a limited company, the transfer may fall into his bankruptcy. Whilst the transfers will usually be of specific "book-debts", and therefore escape s. 43 of the Bankruptcy Act 1914[7], those same "book-debts" might fall within the reputed ownership doctrine[16], as being "debts due[8] or growing due[9] to the bankrupt in the course of his trade or business".

---

15. Within s. 44 of the Bankruptcy Act 1914.
16. Section 38 (2) (c) of the Bankruptcy Act 1914: set out above, pp. 10–11.
17. See above, pp. 32–33.   18. See s. 320 (1) of the Companies Act 1948.
19. See respectively above, pp. 11, 297.
20. Section 8 of the 1878 Act. (This section is not repealed for absolute bills by s. 15 of the 1882 Act.)
 1. *Ancona* v. *Rogers* (1876), 1 Ex.D. 285, C.A.; *Lincoln Wagon Co., Ltd.* v. *Mumford* (1880), 41 L.T. 655; *Hall* v. *Smith* (1887), 3 T.L.R. 805, C.A.
 2. See Treitel, *Law of Contract* (3rd Edn.) 579–583; Cheshire & Fifoot, *Law of Contract* (7th Edn.) 460, *et seq.*
 3. See *Tailby* v. *Official Receiver* (1888), 13 App. Cas. 523, H.L.
 4. Until notice is given, B. will have to give credit for any instalments which C. pays to A.
 5. Where A. makes successive assignments of the same rights, the first assignee to give notice to C. will usually be in the strongest position.
 6. They are expressly excluded from the definition in s. 4 of the 1878 Act.
 7. E.g. *Re Lovegrove*, [1935] Ch. 464, C.A.: set out above, p. 299.
 8. *Re Fastnedge, ex parte Kemp* (1874), 9 Ch. App. 383 (a decision under the 1869 Act).   9. *Blakey* v. *Trustees of Pendlebury*, [1931] 2 Ch. 255, C.A.

(2) A h.p. or conditional sale agreement will normally contain a licence for the owner or seller (A.) to repossess the goods in the event of a default by the hirer or buyer (C.). It is clear that such licences to seize usually do not fall within definition of a bill of sale[10], nor does an assignment of them[11]. However, it has been suggested in several cases that such a licence to seize is personal and therefore incapable of assignment[12], though it may be that there is merely a presumption to this effect[13].

3. Transfers of proprietary and contractual rights. Assuming that B. can thereby acquire a contractual licence to seize, we have seen that that licence and the assignment of it will both escape the Bills of Sale Act 1878; and it seems clear that B. is unlikely to be in a worse position by taking an assignment of both types of right rather than one of them, because the agreement can usually be severed[14]. The dangers that the licence to seize will be held to be unassignable or that both sets of rights will fall into A.'s bankruptcy by way of the reputed ownership doctrine remain the same.

(b) Non-absolute transfers[15]

The dealer (A.) may effect a transfer to the finance company (B.) of something less than the whole of either or both of his proprietary and contractual rights in respect of the instalment credit transaction with C.; and such a non-absolute transfer may amount to (1) a legal mortgage, or (2) an equitable mortgage or charge, or (3) a declaration of trust. The position of such non-absolute transfers with respect to the Money-lenders Acts is the same as in the case of direct financing[16]; and the present discussion deals with the effect of certain other restrictive enactments on such transfers.

1. Legal mortgage. Where A. purports to transfer his proprietary rights to B. by way of legal mortgage, the transfer may be completely avoided by the Bills of Sale Act 1882[17] or by the reputed ownership doctrine[18]; and, if A. is a limited company, the transfer, whilst escaping the reputed ownership doctrine, may be partially avoided by s. 95 of the Companies Act[1]. A legal mortgage of contractual rights under a conditional or credit sale may operate as a statutory assignment; but an agreement

---

10. See above, p. 10.
11. See above, note 6, and also *Re Isaacson, ex parte Mason,* [1895] 1 Q.B. 333, C.A.
12. *Re Davis & Co., ex parte Rawlings* (1888), 22 Q.B.D. 193, C.A.; *Chatterton v. Maclean,* [1951] 1 All E.R. 761.
13. See Goode, *H.P. Law & Practice* (2nd Edn.) 512–513.
14. See *Re Isaacson, ex parte Mason* (above).
15. See Goode, *op. cit.,* 541–554.
16. See above, p. 300; and see also the cases referred to at p. 311, note 2.
17. See above, p. 10.
18. See above, pp. 10–11.
 1. Section 95 (2) (c): set out above, p. 292.

to assign, or an assignment of the right to future hire-rent under a h.p. agreement, can only operate as an equitable assignment[2]. This latter type of transfer is considered below. Where A. is not a limited company, a legal mortgage of his contractual rights will escape the 1882 Act[3], but not the reputed ownership doctrine; and, if A. is a limited company, this will avoid the latter pitfall, but will amount to "a charge on the book-debts of the company" within s. 95[4]. Again, it is unlikely to do any greater harm to take a legal mortgage of A.'s proprietary and contractual rights[5].

2. Equitable mortgage or charge. An equitable mortgage may be created where there is an intention to create a legal mortgage, and, either the mortgage is not perfected, or the subject-matter is only an equitable interest[6]; or where the intention is merely to create an equitable mortgage or charge, a common example being a deposit of h.p. agreements with an intention of creating a charge over them[7]. The position with regard to such transfers of either or both of A.'s proprietary or contractual rights is the same as in the case of a legal mortgagee. However, it must be remembered that the interest of an equitable mortgagee or chargee is always liable to be defeated by a subsequent transfer by A. of the legal interest to a b.f.p. without notice, so that it is a wise precaution to take possession of the instalment credit agreements mortgaged or charged. Furthermore, the rights of the equitable mortgagee or chargee against the goods, or against C., are somewhat weaker than those of a legal mortgagee.

3. Declaration of trust. The ordinary rules for the creation of a trust apply here, so that A. must use imperative words, and must make it clear which of his interests are held in trust and for whose benefit the trust is created. Once again, B.'s interest is likely to be defeated where A. makes a subsequent transfer of the legal interest to a b.f.p. without notice. Nor would a declaration of trust of A.'s proprietary rights in favour of B. put B. in any better position than if he had been a legal mortgagee as regards the subsequent insolvency of A. Further, a declaration of trust of A.'s contractual rights will, as against C., have "much the same effect as an equitable assignment made without notice"[8]; but it will impress all sums received by A. from C. with a trust, so that if A. subsequently becomes insolvent those sums will

---

2. See above, p. 307. 3. See above, p. 307, note 6.
4. Section 95 (2) (e). See *Independent Automatic Sales, Ltd.* v. *Knowles and Foster*, [1962] 3 All E.R. 27; *Paul and Frank, Ltd.* v. *Discount Bank, Ltd.*, [1967] Ch. 348; [1966] 2 All E.R. 922.
5. See above, p. 308.
6. A second or subsequent mortgage must be in writing: s. 53 (1) (c), Law of Property Act 1925.
7. E.g. *Independent Automatic Sales Case* (above). But see s. 95 (6) of 1948 Act.
8. See Goode, *H.P. Law & Practice* (2nd Edn.) 554.

escape the 1882 Act and, probably s. 95 of the 1948 Act[9]; but, if A. is not a limited company, the declaration of trust may be caught by the reputed ownership doctrine[10].

2 The form of indirect financing

The course of business between a dealer (A.) and a finance company (B.) engaged in indirect financing will normally be governed by a Master Agreement; and some consideration must now be given to the form of that agreement.

The first objective of B. will be to ensure that the transaction in which he is involved will be subject to as few risks as possible. First, B. will wish to ensure that the instalment credit agreements made between A. and his customer (C.) are drawn in the manner most advantageous to B.[11]: the Master Agreement will therefore normally stipulate that A. should conduct his business on agreement-forms provided by, or approved by, B. Second, even well drawn agreements may be unenforceable if they do not comply with the statutory regulations[12]; and B. will therefore require an assurance both that A. is able and willing to complete those agreements in the manner required by law, and that A. will guarantee in the Master Agreement that he has done so. Third, in order to avoid buying a law-suit, B. will wish to ensure that C. has taken delivery of the goods and is satisfied with them[13]; and so the Master Agreement will usually stipulate that A. shall produce a "satisfaction note" signed by C. Fourth, B. will usually require that A. should make certain promises designed to protect B. against any loss arising from the transaction such as the following: an express warranty of A.'s title to the goods[14]; a promise that he will disclose any fact which might materially influence B.'s judgment in deciding whether to finance a particular agreement; the provision of collateral security, usually in the form of bills of exchange[15]; and the undertaking of full recourse[16].

The second objective of B. will be to secure an assignment of A.'s rights which will be as effective as possible. In view of the dangers of statutory intervention in non-absolute assignments, B. will usually take care that the Master Agreement expresses the assignment to be absolute. The leading case on the construction of such provisions is *Re George Inglefield, Ltd.*[17].

---

9. The term "charge" in s. 95 (2) (e) hardly seems apt to describe such a transaction: see *Re David Allester, Ltd.*, [1922] 2 Ch. 211.
10. *Blakey* v. *Pendlebury Property Trustees*, [1931] 2 Ch. 255, C.A. It seems odd that neither in argument nor in any of the judgment is there an express reference to s. 38 (1) of the 1914 Act.
11. See Chapters 1 and 2.   12. See Chapter 3.
13. But see *Lowe* v. *Lombank, Ltd.*, [1960] 1 All E.R. 611, C.A.: set out above, pp. 139–140.
14. See Chapter 5.   15. See above, p. 272.
16. See above, pp. 290–291.   17. [1933] Ch. 1, C.A.

A furniture dealer, A., indirectly financed his business by entering into a Master Agreement which provided, *inter alia*, that the finance company, B., would purchase the goods and the benefit of the h.p. agreements for their "collection value"[18], of which 75% was to be payable immediately and the rest paid by instalments which matched the payments due under the h.p. agreements. The assignment to B. was expressed to be absolute, but clause 18 provided that once B. had received, either from A. or C., the full amount due to it in respect of a particular h.p. agreement, B. "shall allow [A.] to retain all subsequent instalments of rent . . . and shall account to [A.] for all such sums in excess [thereof] as may be received by [B.]". Notwithstanding the terms of the Master Agreement, the usual course of business was for A. to collect the instalments from customers, deduct a sum equal to the instalment payable from B. to himself, and forward the balance to B. Eve J. agreed with A.'s liquidator that the effect of the transaction, and particularly of clause 18, was that B. was making a secured loan to A.; but this decision was unanimously reversed by the Court of Appeal.

The Court of Appeal accepted that the matter was one of substance not of form[19]; but held that clause 18 did not amount to an equity of redemption[1]. Particularly in view of clause 18, and of the fact that the parties did not even carry out the full terms of the Master Agreement, this case is a fairly strong one, and does indicate that the courts will not be over-anxious to find that the assignment in an indirectly financed transaction is non-absolute and hence infringes the legislation in restraint of chattel mortgages[2]. Furthermore, it provides yet another illustration of the *dictum* by Lord MacNaghten that[3]

"there is all the difference in the world between a mortgage and a sale with a right of repurchase. But if the transaction is completed by redemption or repurchase as the case may be there is no difference in the actual result".

Nor, it is submitted, should it make any difference whether the repurchase provision works for the benefit of the dealer or finance company.

Whether or not the assignment is absolute, B.'s third objective will be to secure for itself the benefit of the assignment; and the obvious precautions available to B. are to take possession of the instalment credit

---

18. That is, the face value of the instalments yet to be paid less a finance charge.
19. *Per* Lord Hanworth M.R., and Lawrence and Romer L.JJ., at pp. 17, 24, 27.
1. See esp. *per* Lord Hanworth M.R. and Lawrence L.J., at pp. 20, 26.
2. See also the cases under the Moneylenders Acts: *Olds Discount, Ltd.* v. *Playfair*, [1938] 3 All E.R. 275; *Transport and General Credit Corporation, Ltd.* v. *Morgan*, [1939] Ch. 531; [1939] 2 All E.R. 17.
3. In *Manchester, Sheffield and Lincolnshire Rail. Co.* v. *North Central Wagon Co.* (1888), 13 App. Cas. 554, H.L., at pp. 567-568. For the facts of this case, see above, p. 293.

agreements and to give notice of the assignment to C.[4]. Whilst the former step will usually be taken, one of the objects of the dealer in financing his business indirectly is to preserve undisturbed his business relationship with his customers.   To this end, it is normal for the transfer effected by the Master Agreement to remain executory, and for that Agreement to provide that, until default by the dealer, all instalments are to be collected by A. on behalf of B.   Such a concession by B. has obvious dangers in the event of the fraud or insolvency of A.; and it is therefore common to find that B. has taken certain precautions against these eventualities in the Master Agreement.   First, the Agreement may provide that, on default by A., B. may immediately give notice to C. to pay all further instalments direct to B.; and that A. is also required to execute an irrevocable power of attorney authorising B. to execute any necessary assignment on A.'s behalf.   Second, as B. may be unable to act in time, the Master Agreement may impress any money collected by A. on behalf of B. with a trust.

---

4. For the dangers thereby avoided, see respectively above, pp. 309, 307.

CHAPTER 18

Security for the Price

This chapter will deal with the ways in which a seller or owner of goods sold or let on h.p. can obtain security in respect of the "price". Immediately, a distinction must be drawn between the rights of the seller or owner against the goods sold or let, and his rights against the buyer, hirer or some third party. The personal rights of the seller or owner against the buyer or hirer which arise by reason of the contract of h.p. have already been considered[1]; and in this chapter two matters will be discussed: (1) the rights of a seller and an owner against the goods; and (2) the various ways in which the seller or owner may obtain further personal rights against a third party by way of surety for the performance of the buyer or hirer.

I SECURITY THROUGH POSSESSION

There is much truth in the old adage that possession is nine-tenths of the law: to retain possession of the goods sold may well be the safest way in which a seller can ensure payment, or, at least, minimise his loss. In part, this is because Part IV of the S.G.A. gives the unpaid seller in possession certain rights against the goods sold.

1 The unpaid seller

Part IV of the S.G.A. is expressed to operate only in favour of an "unpaid seller". This expression is given a special meaning.

1. A seller. Section 62 (1) defines a seller as

"a person who sells or agrees to sell goods";

but s. 38 (2) further provides that

"In this Part of this Act the term "seller" includes any person who is in the position of a seller, as, for instance, an agent of the seller to whom the bill of lading has been indorsed, or a consignor or agent who has himself paid, or is directly responsible for, the price".

Thus, any agent who has made himself personally liable on the contract *as if he were the seller* may exercise these remedies; but this does not include a buyer who justifiably rejects the goods after paying the

---

1. See above, Chapter 16.

price[2]. The latter should only reject if satisfied of the seller's solvency, as rejection will revest the property in the seller so that he will be reduced to a personal claim for the return of the price[3].

2. *An unpaid seller.* According to s. 38 (1),

> "The seller of goods is deemed to be an "unpaid seller" within the meaning of this Act—
>
>   (a) When the whole of the price has not been paid or tendered;
>
>   (b) When a bill of exchange or other negotiable instrument has been received as conditional payment, and the condition on which it was received has not been fulfilled by reason of the dishonour of the instrument or otherwise".

Notwithstanding that stipulations as to the time of payment are only warranties[4], Part IV of the S.G.A. allows an unpaid seller who has not granted credit to retain the goods until payment. This fits in neatly with his duty under s. 28 to deliver when the buyer is ready and willing to pay the price[5]. Alternatively, where the seller has taken a cheque for the price[6] his rights under Part IV are suspended; but they revive if the cheque "bounces", for s. 38 (1) (b) then deems him to be an "unpaid seller" again.

2 The unpaid seller's rights against the goods

The rights of the unpaid seller against the goods are set out in s. 39 as follows:

> "(1) Subject to the provisions of this Act, and of any statute in that behalf, notwithstanding that the property in the goods may have passed to the buyer, the unpaid seller of goods, as such, has by implication of law—
>
>   (a) A lien on the goods or right to retain them for the price while he is in possession of them;
>
>   (b) In the case of the insolvency of the buyer, a right of stopping the goods in transitu after he has parted with the possession of them;
>
>   (c) A right of re-sale as limited by this Act.
>
>   (2) Where the property in goods has not passed to the buyer, the unpaid seller has, in addition to his other remedies, a right of withholding delivery similar to and co-extensive with his rights of lien and stoppage in transitu where the property has passed to the buyer".

The rights of the unpaid seller enumerated in s. 39 (1) are as follows:

1. A right of lien. At common law, a lien merely conferred a right to

---

2. *J. L. Lyons & Co., Ltd.* v. *May and Baker, Ltd.,* [1923] 1 K.B. 685.
3. Atiyah, *Sale of Goods* (3rd Edn.) 185–186.
4. See s. 10 (1), discussed above, p. 275.
5. See above, pp. 275–276.
6. Distinguish the situation where the cheque is merely taken by way of collateral security: see above, p. 272.

retain possession of goods until certain demands were met[7]: it only gave a right to retain possession, not to sell goods[8]; the party entitled lost his lien by parting with possession; and anyway the lien only existed in certain clearly defined circumstances[9]. The repairer's lien has already been discussed[10]; and the common law lien of the unpaid seller of goods has now been embodied in the S.G.A.[11], which has been said to replace entirely the common law on the subject[12].

2. A right of stoppage. Whilst the common law lien was only available to an unpaid seller whilst he retained possession, and was lost where the goods passed into the possession of the buyer, the common law recognised an intermediate stage where the goods were in transit from seller to buyer. In this last situation, the unpaid seller was given a limited right to stop the goods and recover possession from the carrier, whereupon the seller's lien arose once more[13]. This right of stoppage in transit has now been enacted in the S.G.A.[14], but is still limited in that it is only available where the buyer is insolvent.

3. A right of resale. In some cases, the unpaid seller's rights of lien and stoppage will meet his primary object: they will ensure that he is paid the contract price of the goods sold. However, where the buyer is unable or unwilling to pay the price, the exercise of the rights of lien and stoppage is a mere preliminary to resale. The common law granted a limited right of resale to an unpaid seller in possession; and this right is now embodied in the S.G.A. However, as it is in the nature of a remedy rather than a mere security, detailed discussion of it will be postponed to Chapter 20.

Before embarking on a detailed discussion of the rights of lien and stoppage as regulated by ss. 41–46[15], some further thought must be given to s. 39. Section 39 (1) says that the three rights there enumerated are to arise "by implication of law", thereby implying that they may be excluded or varied by the terms of the agreement[16]. Furthermore, care must be taken not to confuse two things: (1) the *powers* of the unpaid seller to pass a good title to a second buyer either by virtue of his property in the goods or one of the exceptions to the *nemo dat*[17] rule; and (2) the *rights* of the unpaid seller as against the first buyer, which are listed in s. 39. In order to distinguish between the rights and

---

7. *Per* GROSE J. in *Hammonds* v. *Barclay* (1802), 2 East 227, at p. 235.
8. *Thames Ironworks Co.* v. *Patents Derrick Co.* (1860), 1 John & H. 93.
9. See generally Crossley Vaines, *Personal Property* (4th Edn.) Ch. 7.
10. See above, p. 13.   11. See below, pp. 318–319.
12. *Transport and General Credit Corporation, Ltd.* v. *Morgan*, [1939] 1 Ch. 531, at p. 546.
13. *Per* BULLER J. in *Lickbarrow* v. *Mason* (1793), 6 East 21, at p. 27 n.
14. See below, p. 325.
15. See below, pp. 318, 325.
16. See s. 55 of the S.G.A., set out above, p. 132.
17. See above, Chapter 14.

powers of the unpaid seller, it is convenient to set out the four basic permutations of possession and property.

Case 1. The property has passed to the buyer, who has taken possession of the goods. In this situation, the unpaid seller can have no rights against the goods, nor any power to sell them; and he is reduced to a personal action against the buyer for the price.

Case 2. The property has passed to the buyer, but the seller retains possession. Here, the seller has power to pass title to a b.f.p. under one of the exceptions to the *nemo dat* rule[17]; but whether he has a right, as against the first buyer, to resell is another question.

Case 3. The seller retains the property in the goods, but transfers possession to the buyer. In this case, the seller has the power to pass a good title to a third party by reason of his property in the goods; but it may be a breach of his contract of sale to do so.

Case 4. The seller retains the property in and possession of the goods. He can, of course pass a good title to a third party by reason of his property in the goods; and the resale could only be a breach of the first contract where it could be shown that goods annexed to that contract had been resold[18].

It will be noticed that the first two of the three rights enumerated in s. 39 (1) are appropriate to a seller who has retained possession of the goods; and the provision itself is expressed to operate "notwithstanding that the property in the goods may have passed to the buyer". Thus, where the property and possession have passed (*Case 1*), the unpaid seller can have no right of lien or stoppage under s. 39 (1); and the apparent object of that subsection is to confer on a seller who has parted with property but retained possession (*Case 2*) "not merely the power to deal with the goods, but also the right to do so as against the buyer"[19]. Strictly speaking, an unpaid seller can only have a lien where he has parted with the property in goods because a man cannot have a lien over his own goods[20]. However, in the pre-Act case of *Re Edwards, ex parte Chalmers*[1] the Court of Appeal in Chancery held that an unpaid seller who had retained both property and possession (*Case 4*) should not have any less right to retain possession than one who had merely retained possession (*Case 2*). The question arises whether s. 39 (2) has the effect of restricting the unpaid seller who has retained property and possession to what *Benjamin* terms this "quasi-lien"[2]. It has been argued that it is "inconceivable" that s. 39 (2) should fetter the seller's discretion to deal with goods which he intended to use in per-

---

18. See Atiyah, *Sale of Goods* (3rd Edn.) 185.
19. Atiyah, *op. cit.*, 184.
20. *Per* Lord WRIGHT in *Nippon Yusen Kaisha* v. *Ramjiban Serowgee*, [1938] A.C. 429, P.C., at p. 444.
1. (1873), L.R. 8 Ch. App. 289.
2. *On Sale* (8th Edn.) 347.

formance of the contract, but which have not yet become earmarked as contract goods[3]. Perhaps the better view is that s. 39 (2) was intended to reflect the philosophy existing before the Act; that the words "in addition to his other remedies" in s. 39 (2) will allow s. 61 (2) to save any other rights which the seller may have in respect of his goods; and that s. 39 (2) merely ensures that a seller who has retained the property in the goods will be no worse off than one who has not done so as regards the rights of lien and stoppage.

The third right enumerated in s. 39 (1) is a right of resale. Clearly, the unpaid seller has a power of resale where he has retained either or both of possession and property[4]; and the question is whether s. 39 gives him a right to do so as against the original buyer. The obvious case where s. 39 (1) confers on the unpaid seller a right of resale is where he has retained possession but parted with the property in goods (*Case 2*)[5]. However, it is sometimes deduced from the existence of s. 39 (2) that s. 39 (1) is only applicable where the property has passed; and then inferred from the absence of any mention of a right of resale in s. 39 (2) that an unpaid seller who has retained both possession and property (*Case 4*) has no right of resale[6]. It would be possible to avoid this undesirable result by denying that the absence of a right of resale from s. 39 (2) has such a significance; but in *Ward Ltd.* v. *Bignall*[7] the Court of Appeal escaped the dilemma by another route, deciding that the unpaid seller who retained property and possession had a right of resale under s. 39 (1). Does the unpaid seller have any right of resale in *Cases 1* and *3*; that is, where possession of the goods has passed to the buyer? Section 39 (1) (c) gives a "right of resale as limited by this Act"; and these limitations are to be found in ss. 48 (3) and (4)[8]. In one case, TURNER J. said that the New Zealand equivalent of s. 48 conferred a power only on "those vendors who have never lost possession"[9], though the wording of s. 48 does not appear to support this view. Where both property and possession have passed to the buyer (*Case 1*), clearly the unpaid seller has neither the power nor the right of resale. However, where the unpaid seller takes the precaution of reserving the property in the goods whilst parting with possession (*Case 3*), it is arguable that he has a statutory right of resale under s. 39: he certainly has the power to do so by virtue of his retention of property.

---

3. Atiyah, *op. cit.*, 187.
4. See further below, pp. 368–369.
5. E.g. *Gallagher* v. *Shilcock*, [1949] 2 K.B. 765; [1949] 1 All E.R. 921: set out below, p. 369.
6. See Atiyah, *op. cit.*, where the author suggests that the courts are likely to avoid such an incredible result. And see Fridman, *Sale of Goods*, 254.
7. [1967] 1 Q.B. 534, C.A.: set out below, pp. 367–368.
8. Sections 48 (3) and (4) are discussed below, pp. 365–366.
9. *Commission Car Sales, Ltd.* v. *Saul*, [1957] N.Z.L.R. 144, at p. 146.

3 The unpaid seller's lien

(a) The nature of the lien

The ordinary rule is that the seller's lien is for the whole of the price; but the question arises as to the effect of a part-delivery. Leaving aside the situation where the non-payment manifests an intention to repudiate, the seller's rights will, in the first place, depend on whether there is a single contract or a series of contracts[10]. Where there is a series of contracts, the unpaid seller's rights against the goods only attach to each instalment in respect of the price attributable to it[11]; but it may be otherwise where there is a single contract. Assuming that part-delivery under a single contract does not constitute delivery of the whole[12], and that the other requirements for the exercise of a lien are satisfied[13], s. 42 provides[14]:

> "Where an unpaid seller has made part delivery of the goods, he may exercise his right of lien . . . on the remainder, unless such part delivery has been made under such circumstances as to show an agreement to waive the lien . . ."

Suppose there is a contract for the sale of goods at a price of £100; the contract envisages payment on delivery; but the seller delivers half the goods, valued at £50, before receiving any payment. *Prima facie*, this part-delivery indicates a waiver by the seller of his lien[15]. However, there are three possible interpretations of the seller's conduct: (1) the seller has waived his lien for the £100, and converted the transaction into a sale on credit; or (2) the seller has waived his lien over the goods delivered, but still retains a lien for £50 over the goods in his possession; or (3) the seller has waived his lien over the goods delivered, but retains a lien for £100 over the goods in his possession. Where the seller's conduct is not such as to indicate the first interpretation, the common law appears to have assumed that the lien over the remainder of the goods was for the £100, even where the contract was divisible[16]; and this presumed "indivisibleness of the lien seems to be recognised by the Act"[17].

Whilst the S.G.A. twice says that the lien granted thereby is for the price[18], it is submitted that this should not prevent the seller from

---

10. See above, p. 277.
11. *Steinberger* v. *Atkinson* (1914), 31 T.L.R. 110.
12. As to which, see the cases cited in *Benjamin on Sale* (8th Edn.) 853–856.
13. See below, pp. 319–321.
14. For the right of stoppage in transit, see s. 45 (7), set out below, p. 328.
15. See s. 43 (1) (c), discussed below, pp. 323–324.
16. *Re Edwards, ex parte Chalmers* (1873), 8 Ch. App. 289. For the distinction between divisible and indivisible contracts, see above, p. 277.
17. *Benjamin on Sale* (8th Edn.) 841. See also *Longbottom* v. *Bass, Walker & Co.*, [1922] W.N. 245, C.A. *Sed quaere?*
18. Sections 39 (1) (a) and 41 (1).

exercising any particular lien to which he may otherwise be entitled at common law[19]. Thus, a seller who agrees to repair goods for his buyer will have a lien in respect of the cost of those repairs: where the sale and repair were two independent transactions, he will have two separate liens, one for the price and the other for the cost of repairs; but, where there is a contract for the sale of repaired goods, it may be that the cost of repairs is subsumed under his seller's lien. However, there is no common law lien for storage charges[20], and the unpaid seller may therefore wish to subsume these under his seller's lien. In the pre-Act decision of *Somes* v. *British Empire Shipping Co.*[1], the House of Lords unanimously agreed with the lower courts that an unpaid shipwright exercising his repairer's lien could not add to that lien charges for keeping the goods during the period he exercised his lien. This case is sometimes said to rule out the possibility of including storage charges in the lien[2], though it does not appear to do so[3]. It is submitted that storage charges may fall within the seller's lien if bargained for in the price; and it has even been argued that, where the buyer defaults in taking delivery[4], "it is hard to see why he should not have a lien for such charges"[5].

(*b*) *The conditions under which the lien is exercisable*

Section 41 (1) provides as follows:

"Subject to the provisions of this Act, the unpaid seller of goods who is in possession of them is entitled to retain possession of them until payment or tender of the price in the following cases, namely:—

(a) Where the goods have been sold without any stipulation as to credit;

(b) Where the goods have been sold on credit, but the term of credit has expired;

(c) Where the buyer becomes insolvent".

Not only does the lien granted by the S.G.A. only exist for the price of goods sold, but s. 41 (1) insists that three conditions be fulfilled before it is exercisable.

(1) The person seeking to exercise the lien must be an "unpaid seller" within the meaning of s. 38[6].

(2) The price must be due, or the buyer insolvent. Leaving aside the case where the buyer becomes insolvent, the position where the

---

19. See s. 61 (2).
20. See *Re Southern Livestock Producers, Ltd.*, [1963] 3 All E.R. 801.
1. (1860), 8 H.L. Cas. 338.
2. See Schmitthoff, *Sale of Goods* (2nd Edn.) 156; *Chalmers' Sale of Goods* (15th Edn.) 142.
3. See Atiyah, *Sale of Goods* (3rd Edn.) 189.
4. The seller has an action for damages under s. 37: set out above, pp. 267–268.
5. Atiyah, *op. cit.*, 189. *Contra* Fridman, *Sale of Goods*, 257, note 28.
6. See above, pp. 313–314.

unpaid seller refuses to deliver the goods would appear to be as follows: in the absence of credit terms, the seller's lien and s. 28[7] will prevent the buyer from having a right to immediate possession sufficient to succeed in an action of conversion or detinue against the seller; but, where the granting of credit terms shows an intention that delivery shall be made before payment (thereby ousting s. 28)[8], the buyer may bring such an action[9]. However, even where the seller has agreed to deliver in advance of payment, the unpaid seller's lien arises once more when[10] and if the term of credit expires[11] or the buyer becomes insolvent[12]. According to s. 62 (3),

> "A person is deemed to be insolvent within the meaning of this Act who either has ceased to pay his debts in the ordinary course of business, or cannot pay his debts as they become due, whether he has committed an act of bankruptcy or not . . ."

Insolvency or bankruptcy does not necessarily amount of itself to a repudiation of the contract, so that it is still open to the buyer, his representative, or a sub-buyer to tender the price and claim delivery; but the effect of s. 41 (1) (c) is that the seller cannot, against his will, be reduced to claiming a dividend.

(3) The person claiming the lien must be in possession of the goods. Thus, the seller's lien depends on one of the most difficult concepts in English Law, namely, "possession". Not only does this term have different meanings in different branches of the law[13], but the extent of the control necessary to exercise an innkeeper's lien differs from that required for a repairer's lien[14], and neither may be applicable to the unpaid seller[15]. Whilst the S.G.A. nowhere defines possession, that concept is important in three contexts within the Act: (1) the exceptions to the *nemo dat* rule[16]; (2) the seller's duty of delivery[17]; and (3) the unpaid seller's rights of lien and stoppage[18]. In the present context,

---

7. Section 28 is set out above, p. 273.
8. If the granting of credit shows no more than that delivery *and* payment are to be postponed, and are to remain concurrent terms, the buyer has no right to immediate possession before tendering the price.
9. See *per* BAYLEY J. in *Bloxam* v. *Sanders* (1825), 4 B. & C. 941, at pp. 948–949.
10. Presumably, the seller is liable in conversion or detinue for the period before payment fell due.
11. But does not the granting of credit show an intention to contract out of the statutory lien?
12. And if the buyer is insolvent at the time of contracting?
13. See generally, Crossley Vaines, *Personal Property* (4th Edn.) Part 2; *Oxford Essays in Jurisprudence*, IV *Possession* (by Harris).
14. See Atiyah, *Sale of Goods* (3rd Edn.) 188.
15. *Per* Lord MACNAGHTEN in *Great Eastern Rail. Co.* v. *Lord's Trustee*, [1909] A.C. 109, H.L.; at p. 115.
16. See above, p. 184, *et seq.*   17. See above. pp. 266–267.
18. See below, p. 324.

difficult problems can arise where actual control and the legal right to possession are separated. Leaving aside the situation where actual control is being exercised by a third party[19], possession may be divided between seller and buyer as follows:

(a) The seller is in actual control as agent for the buyer. Section 41 (2) provides:

> "The seller may exercise his right of lien notwithstanding that he is in possession of the goods as agent or bailee . . . for the buyer".

On the other hand, these facts may be evidence that the seller has waived his lien[20].

(b) The buyer is in actual control as agent of the seller. Whilst the common law rule may have been that the seller with "legal possession" retained his lien, the S.G.A. seems to suggest that, at least where actual control passes to the buyer, the lien is lost[1]. In other words more regard is now paid to actual control than to the legal right to control[2].

(c) *Termination of the lien*

The seller may lose his right to exercise a lien for the price in any of the ways set out below.

(*1*) *Where he ceases to be an "unpaid seller"*. According to s. 41 (1), the seller's lien only lasts "until payment or tender of the price"[3]; but s. 43 (2) provides that the unpaid seller

> "does not lose his lien . . . by reason only that he has obtained judgment . . . for the price of the goods"[4].

One difficulty here is that s. 41 (1) appears to suggest that the seller's lien, and hence his right to retain possession, does not cease until the buyer at very least tenders the price, whereas s. 28 expressly says that payment and delivery are concurrent conditions[5]. Whilst the two provisions are usually reconciled by inferring that actual tender of the price is not necessary provided that the buyer is ready and willing to pay the price[6], it has been argued that it is difficult to avoid giving effect to the literal words of s. 41 (1)[7]. It is submitted that a solution may be found as follows: that the buyer's duty to tender the price is similar to

---

19. See below, p. 322.
20. Waiver of lien is considered below, pp. 323–324.
 1. See s. 43 (1) (b), considered below, pp. 322–323.
 2. See Schmitthoff, *Sale of Goods* (2nd Edn.) 156.
 3. And see s. 38 (1) (a), considered above, p. 314.
 4. *Quaere* whether in these circumstances the lien extends only to the price, or also to the costs on the judgment?
 5. See above, p. 273.
 6. See *Chalmers' Sale of Goods* (15th Edn.) 112–113; Schmitthoff, *op. cit.*, 121–122.
 7. Atiyah, *Sale of Goods* (3rd Edn.) 190.

the seller's duty to tender delivery[8]; and that actual tender is not usually required because it is presumed the buyer will perform his contract.

(2) *Delivery to a carrier.* Section 43 (1) (a) provides that the seller will lose his lien

> "When he delivers the goods to a carrier or other bailee . . . for the purpose of transmission to the buyer without reserving the right of disposal of the goods".

The scheme of the Act is that the unpaid seller will have a right of lien whilst he retains possession of the goods, and a right of stoppage whilst they are in transit to the buyer. Not surprisingly, the Act uses the same test both for the termination of the lien and the commencement of the transit, namely, "delivery to a carrier or other bailee for the purposes of transmission to the buyer"; and this expression will be examined in the latter context[9]. However, s. 43 (1) (a) allows one exception to the rule which it lays down: when the seller reserves "a right of disposal". In the context of the sections dealing with the passing of property this expression clearly denotes a reservation of property[10]; but it has been argued that, to avoid any inconsistency with s. 39 (2), it must in s. 39 (2) refer only to a reservation of possession[11]. Perhaps the better view is that in s. 43 the phrase denotes a reservation of property and possession[12]; and that in s. 43 (1) (a) it is referring to the "quasi-lien" under s. 39 (2)[13].

(3) *The buyer obtains possession.* Section 43 (1) (b) lays down that the lien is lost

> "When the buyer or his agent lawfully obtains possession of the goods".

It is submitted that "possession" must here mean actual control; for it is difficult to speak of the buyer's agent as having a legal right to control[14]. The other difficulty in this subsection concerns the meaning of the word "lawfully", as to which there are several theories. First, it may refer to the absence of criminal conduct on the part of the buyer[15]. However, there has been some reluctance to import the law of theft into this branch of the civil law. Thus, *Atiyah* has suggested a second possible meaning; namely, that "lawfully" in this context means "with the consent of the seller" so as to bring it into line with the provisions in respect of dispositions by buyers in possession to be

---

8. See above, pp. 266–267.
9. See below, p. 326. 10. See above, p. 181.
11. Schmitthoff, *Sale of Goods* (2nd Edn.) 157.
12. See *Benjamin on Sale* (8th Edn.) 848, citing *Sanders* v. *Maclean* (1883), 11 Q.B.D. 327, C.A., at p. 341.
13. See above, pp. 316–317. 14. See also above p. 321.
15. E.g. *Wallace* v. *Woodgate* (1824), 1 C. & P. 575.

found in ss. 25 (2) and 9 of the S.G.A. and F.A. respectively[16]. Perhaps the strongest argument in favour of this view is that the term "lawfully" is used in ss. 47 and 10 of the respective Acts. However, it has been pointed out that (1) this view rather strains the language of s. 43 (1) (b), and (2) there is no reason why s. 43 (1) (b) need be brought into line with this exception to the *nemo dat* rule[17]. Furthermore, it is quite conceivable that "lawfully" has a different meaning in ss. 47 and 10 from that which it bears in s. 43 (1) (b)[18]; and it is submitted that it is logically possible that the seller's lien binds all except a b.f. transferee under one of the exceptions to the *nemo dat* rule[19]. Third, *Benjamin* has suggested that "lawfully" in s. 43 (1) (b) means that "the possession must not be obtained tortiously as against the seller"[20]. Whilst this test may be circular if one thinks in terms of the torts of conversion and detinue, it does seem satisfactory in relation to the tort of trespass[1]. In the last analysis, then, it may be that "lawfully" in s. 43 (1) (b) denotes the absence of a trespassory taking by the buyer, irrespective of whether that taking amounts to theft.

(4) Waiver. Section 39 (1) gives the unpaid seller a lien by implication of law[2]; s. 55 allows such rights to be waived expressly or by implication[3]; and s. 43 (1) (c) expressly states that the lien may be lost by waiver. Thus, the unpaid seller may expressly waive his statutory lien, or a waiver of it may be inferred. Examples of implied waiver are where the contract includes the reservation of an express lien[4]; or where the seller wrongfully deals with the goods in a manner inconsistent with the rights of the buyer, e.g. by consuming or reselling them[5]; or where the seller agrees to retain possession as agent of the buyer[6]. Can the unpaid seller who is still in possession go back on any waiver of his statutory lien? The Act itself envisages that, notwithstanding that the seller accepts payment by bill of exchange or sells on credit, he may exercise his lien where the bill is not met[7] or the term of credit expired[8]; and it is possible to see these two instances in terms of an initial waiver and subsequent exercise of the unpaid seller's lien[9].

---

16. *Sale of Goods* (3rd Edn.) 190–191.
17. Smith (1963), J.S.P.T.L. 225, at 226. 18. See above, p. 225.
19. Atiyah, *Sale of Goods* (3rd Edn.) himself appears to accept this possibility (at pp. 158, 191). 20. *On Sale* (8th Edn.) 849.
 1. These torts are discussed below, pp. 376–378.
 2. See above, p. 314. 3. See above, p. 132.
 4. See *Chalmers' Sale of Goods* (15th Edn.) 145.
 5. Chalmers, *op. cit.*, 146; Atiyah, *op. cit.*, 191.
 6. See Atiyah, *ibid.*; and above, p. 321.
 7. Section 38 (1) (b): set out above, p. 314.
 8. Sections 41 (1) (b) and (c): set out above, p. 319. It seems to be sensible to read s. 43 (1) (c) subject to ss. 41 (b) and (c): see Atiyah, *op. cit.*, 192; *Benjamin on Sale* (8th Edn.) 853.
 9. Alternatively, it may be agreed that the lien arises *de novo* upon the happening of these two events.

Moreover, the common law will normally allow a party to go back upon a waiver of his rights if he gives adequate notice[10]; and it was decided before the Act that the unpaid seller might revive his waived lien where he was still in possession[11]. The better view would therefore appear to be that the statutory lien may be revived after waiver by giving adequate notice[12].

(5) *Dispositions by the buyer.* The basic rule embodied in s. 47[13] is that no disposition of the goods by the buyer can affect the rights of the unpaid seller against the goods, unless the disponee takes under one of the exceptions to the *nemo dat rule*[14]. Of course, the facts which fall within the scope of one of the exceptions to the *nemo dat* rule may also operate to terminate the unpaid seller's lien under one of the rules discussed above. However s. 47 specifically deals with one circumstance where it may not do so, namely, where the buyer transfers a document of title to the goods to a b.f.p. for value[15]; and it provides that in these circumstances the unpaid seller's lien is overridden *pro tanto* by the disposition[16]. Presumably, the position is the same in any other case where facts giving rise to an exception to the *nemo dat* rule do not also terminate the lien under one of the above heads. Assuming that the unpaid seller's rights against the goods are overridden by the b.f. transferee, does the unpaid seller have any right to the proceeds of the disposition? At common law, the better opinion would appear to be that he did not[17]; and such a view would seem to be consistent with the terminology of the S.G.A.[18], so that probably the position has not changed[19].

Generally speaking, once the unpaid seller relinquishes possession, his lien is lost; and it will not revive merely because he regains possession, even though he do so with the consent of the buyer[1]. However, an exception to this rule is where the unpaid seller validly stops the goods in transit and recovers possession. It would seem that the exercise of a right of lien or stoppage by the unpaid seller will not necessarily show an intention on his part to rescind the contract[2], but it will defeat an action against him by the buyer in conversion or detinue[3]. On the other hand, where the unpaid seller wrongfully purports to exercise a lien or to stop the goods, he will be liable in conversion or

---

10. *Charles Rickards, Ltd.* v. *Oppenhaim,* [1950] 1 K.B. 616, C.A.: set out above, p. 148.
11. See *Townley* v. *Crump* (1836), 4 Ad. & El. 58.   12. See Atiyah, *ibid.*
13. Set out above, p. 185.   14. See Chapter 14.
15. See above, p. 220.   16. See above, p. 229.
17. *Per* Lord SELBOURNE in *Kemp* v. *Falk* (1882), 7 App. Cas. 573, H.L., at p. 577.
18. See *Benjamin on Sale* (8th Edn.) 927.
19. *Benjamin, ibid.*; Atiyah, *op. cit.*, 198; Fridman, *Sale of Goods,* 272.
 1. See *Pennington* v. *Reliance Motor Works, Ltd.,* [1923] 1 K.B. 127.
 2. See s. 48 (1), set out below, p. 366.
 3. *Milgate* v. *Kebble* (1841), 3 Man. & G. 100.

detinue, but damages will only be the value of the buyer's actual interest in the goods[4].

4 The unpaid seller's right of stoppage in transit

In the eighteenth and nineteenth centuries, the right of stoppage in transit was an extremely valuable weapon in the armoury of the unpaid seller in domestic and international sales; but in the twentieth century, the importance of this right has been declining, perhaps partly because of better communications, speedier carriage, better credit control, and a higher volume of trade compensating for bad debts. Moreover, in the field of international sales the development of the system of payment by bankers' confirmed credits[4a] and government export guarantees[4b] may have rendered the doctrine more or less obsolete[4c]; and in domestic sales, the right of stoppage has never applied to one of the largest carriers, the Post Office[5], which offers its own alternative—the "cash on delivery" service[6]. In the view of the above considerations, treatment of the right of stoppage in transit has been reduced to a minimum.

The basic principle is set out in s. 44 of the S.G.A., which provides that:

"Subject to the provisions of this Act.[7] when the buyer of goods becomes insolvent[8], the unpaid seller[9] who has parted with possession of the goods has the right of stopping them in transitu, that is to say, he may resume possession of the goods as long as they are in course of transit, and may retain them until payment or tender of the price"[10].

The most difficult questions involved here are probably the meaning of "possession" and the duration of the transit, matters upon which s. 45 lays down a series of rules. According to s. 45 (1),

"Goods are deemed to be in course of transit from the time when they are delivered to a carrier by land or water, or other bailee . . . for the purpose of transmission to the buyer, until the buyer, or his agent in that behalf, takes delivery of them from such carrier or other bailee . . ."

---

4. *Chinery* v. *Viall* (1860), 5 H. & N. 288: set out below, p. 413.
4a. See Schmitthoff, *The Export Trade* (5th Edn.) 199–220.
4b. See Schmitthoff, *op. cit.*, Ch. 22.
4c. But cf. Schmitthoff, *op. cit.*, 89.
5. The P.O. does not enter into any contract of carriage—*Whitfield* v. *Le Despenser* (1778), 2 Comp. 754; it is not generally liable for torts connected with the postal services—see now s. 29, Post Office Act 1969; and would not act on an order to stop—s. 58, Post Office Act 1953.
6. Part 8, Inland Post Regulations 1963.
7. This refers principally to ss. 39, 45, 46, 47.
8. Notice the rather wider grounds which s. 39 (1) allows for the exercise of the unpaid seller's lien: see above, pp. 319–321.
9. See above, pp. 313–314. 10. See above, pp. 321–322.

It is quite clear that, where goods are in the legal possession and actual control of the seller, he has the more efficacious right of lien[11]; and that, where the legal possession and actual control of the goods have passed to the buyer, the seller has lost his rights of lien[12] and stoppage[13]. Thus the right of stoppage can only exist in the intermediate situation, where the goods are in the hands of a third party, whom s. 45 calls "a carrier[14] or other bailee"[15], as agent for either seller or buyer. Difficulties immediately arise, however, if it is admitted that either the seller or the buyer may be in legal possession of goods under the actual control of an agent. Leaving aside the situation where either seller or buyer is in actual control as agent of the other[16], the ordinary rule is that the possession of the agent is regarded as being the possession of his principal in this context as elsewhere: where the seller's agent has actual control the seller has the more efficacious right of lien; but where the buyer's agent obtains control the seller loses his real rights entirely. However, if this rule were applied indiscriminately, there would be no room for a right of stoppage at all; and the law is therefore committed to distinguishing between the constructive possession of (1) "a carrier or other bailee", and (2) any other agent in actual control of the goods. Even more difficult, it must distinguish between two different types of constructive possession of "a carrier or other bailee". For instance, the delivery by the seller of the goods to a carrier for transmission to the buyer operates under s. 32 (1) as a constructive transfer of possession to the buyer so as to discharge the seller's duty to deliver[17]. It does not, however, end the transit[18]: otherwise, there would be no transit at all. It is anticipated that this approach will not preclude either seller or buyer from showing that in the circumstances the "carrier or other bailee" was his agent so that the transit has not commenced, or has finished, as the case may be. Support for this approach may be gained from s. 45 (5), which deals with one particular instance as follows:

> "When goods are delivered to a ship chartered by the buyer it is a question depending on the circumstances of the particular case, whether they are in the possession of the master as a carrier, or as agent to the buyer".

As might be expected, the matter which appears to have caused particular difficulty at common law was not so much when the transit

---

11. See above, pp. 320–321.   12. See above, pp. 322–323.
13. Section 45 (3): set out below, p. 327.
14. Presumably, the word "carrier" is wide enough to cover a common carrier.
15. He has been variously described as a "middleman" (*Schotsmans Lancashire and Yorkshire Rail. Co.* (1867), 2 Ch. App. 332, at p. 338) or an "independent contractor" (Atiyah, *Sale of Goods* (3rd Edn.) 194).
16. See above, p. 321.   17. See above, p. 264.
18. This seems consistent with the views of BRETT L.J. in *Re Cock, ex parte Rosevear China Clay Co.* (1879), 11 Ch.D. 560, C.A., at p. 569.

commenced as when it ceased[19]; and s. 45 concentrates on this latter point. Clearly, the transit can at most only last until the goods reach the place at which the contract contemplates that the transit will end[20]; and will in any case be brought to an end where the "carrier or other bailee" hands the goods to the buyer or his agent (s. 45 (1)). However, s. 45 makes special provision for the following difficult cases.

(*1*) *Where the carrier or other bailee attorns to the buyer.* Section 45 (3) provides:

> "If, after the arrival of the goods at the appointed destination the carrier or other bailee . . . acknowledges to the buyer, or his agent, that he holds the goods on his behalf and continues in possession of them as bailee . . . for the buyer, or his agent, the transit is at an end, and it is immaterial that a further destination for the goods may have been indicated by the buyer".

(*2*) *Rejection by the buyer.* According to s. 45 (4),

> "If the goods are rejected by the buyer, and the carrier or other bailee . . . continues in possession of them, the transit is not deemed to be at an end, even if the seller has refused to receive them back".

Where the carrier attorns to the buyer, but the latter rejects the goods, there is an apparent conflict between ss. 45 (3) and 45 (4); but it has been suggested that there is no conflict, because attornment only operates to transfer possession to the buyer provided the latter assented[1], or has not rejected within a reasonable time[2].

(*3*) *Wrongful refusal to deliver.* Section 45 (6) provides that:

> "Where the carrier or other bailee . . . wrongfully refuses to deliver the goods to the buyer, or his agent in that behalf, the transit is deemed to be at an end."

It is submitted that "wrongfully" here means breach by the carrier of his duties under the contract of carriage and this Act.

(*4*) *Interception of the goods.* The transit is not at an end merely because the goods are to be carried in stages, perhaps by different carriers[3]; or because the goods are motionless awaiting delivery to the buyer; or even if it is the buyer who originates the instructions for the transit. However, s. 45 (2) provides that

> "If the buyer or his agent in that behalf obtains delivery of the goods before their arrival at the appointed destination, the transit is at an end".

---

19. The moment of commencement of the transit would only be material where the buyer was not insolvent.
20. *Jobson* v. *Eppenheim* (1905), 21 T.L.R. 468.
1. Atiyah, *Sale of Goods* (3rd Edn.) 196; *Chalmers' Sale of Goods* (15th Edn.) 150.
2. *Taylor* v. *Great Eastern Rail. Co.* (1901), as reported in 17 T.L.R. 394.
3. E.g. *Kemp* v. *Ismay Imrie & Co.* (1909), 100 L.T. 996.

In the words of BAILHACHE J.[4]:

> "Where the original *transitus* is interrupted by the buyers, I think the test is whether the goods will be set in motion again without further orders from the buyers; if not, the transit is ended and the right to stop lost".

Thus, if the carrier agrees to the interception, the transit may be prematurely ended, and with it the unpaid seller's rights against the goods, though it may be that the carrier is in breach of the contract of carriage by his compliance with the buyer's request.

(5) *Part delivery*. According to s. 45 (7),

> "Where part delivery of the goods has been made to the buyer, or his agent in that behalf, the remainder of the goods may be stopped in transitu, unless such part delivery has been made under such circumstances as to show an agreement to give up possession of the whole of the goods".

The effect of a part delivery has already been examined in the context of the unpaid seller's lien[5].

The method by which a right of stoppage in transit may be exercised is set out in s. 46 in the following terms.

> "(1) The unpaid seller may exercise his right of stoppage in transitu either by taking actual possession of the goods, or by giving notice of his claim to the carrier or other bailee . . . in whose possession the goods are. Such notice may be given either to the person in actual possession of the goods or to his principal. In the latter case the notice, to be effectual, must be given at such time and under such circumstances that the principal, by the exercise of reasonable diligence, may communicate it to his servant or agent in time to prevent a delivery to the buyer.
>
> "(2) When notice of stoppage in transitu is given by the seller to a carrier, or other bailee . . . in possession of the goods, he must re-deliver the goods to, or according to the directions of, the seller. The expenses of such re-delivery must be borne by the seller".

This section says nothing about two important matters. First, it assumes that the seller has the right to stop the goods: if not, the seller issuing the order and the carrier or other bailee who complies are both liable to the buyer in conversion or detinue[6]. On the other hand, if the seller has the right to stop, but the carrier or other bailee refuses to comply with such an order, he is liable to the seller in conversion or detinue, or possibly for breach of statutory duty[7]; so that, if in doubt, his safest

---

4. *Reddall* v. *Union Castle Steamship Co.* (1914), 84 L.J.K.B. 360, at p. 362.
5. See above, p. 318.
6. E.g. *Taylor* v. *Great Eastern Rail. Co.* (1901), as reported in 17 T.L.R. 394.
7. See s. 57.

course is to interplead or make delivery dependent on an indemnity. Second, the Act does not define the relationship between the carrier or other bailee and the seller, merely providing that the expenses of redelivery are to be borne by the seller (s. 46 (2)). However, it has been decided that the stoppage of goods by the seller gives the carrier or other bailee a prior lien over the goods for his charges[8]; and that, after stopping the goods, the seller is under a duty to give orders for their disposal[9].

2 SECURITY WITHOUT POSSESSION

Despite the advantages in security accruing to an unpaid seller who retains possession, commercial considerations frequently dictate that the seller delivers the goods before payment. In these circumstances, perhaps the obvious step for the seller intent on maintaining some rights against the goods would be to reserve the property in the goods until payment. However, the security so obtained is somewhat vulnerable. Not only may the buyer in possession pass a good title to a b.f.p.[10], but the seller may be defeated by certain of the buyer's creditors: for, though the agreement will probably escape the Bills of Sale Acts[11], the goods may fall into the buyer's bankruptcy by way of the doctrine of reputed ownership[12], or be taken by way of distress[13], or seized in execution[14]. Moreover, if the purchase price were less than £2,000, the transaction may fall within the H.P.A., and be subject to the restrictions considered below[15].

It was to escape the dangers just outlined that the form of the contract was gradually altered from one of sale to one of h.p.; and this section is primarily concerned with the security by way of rights against the goods offered by a h.p. agreement. At the outset, it should be pointed out that these rights of the owner of goods let under a h.p. agreement have been significantly weakened by the H.P. Acts. Indeed, the H.P.A. 1965 made such significant inroads into the owner's rights against the goods that any further erosion would probably render the form pointless as a commercial proposition: it is to be hoped that the only workable form of chattel mortgage in English Law does not suffer an accidental demise.

---

8. See *United States Steel Products Co.* v. *Great Western Rail. Co.*, [1916] 1 A.C. 189, H.L.
9. *Booth Steamship Co., Ltd.* v. *Cargo Fleet Iron Co., Ltd.*, [1916] 2 K.B. 570, C.A. But see the comment by Atiyah, *Sale of Goods* (3rd Edn.) 199–200.
10. See above, p. 220.
11. See above, p. 10.
12. See above, pp. 10–11.
13. See above, pp. 11–12.
14. See above, p. 239.   15. See p. 334, *et seq.*

1 Agreements outside the H.P.A.

Assuming that the owner of goods let on h.p. terms has a good title to the goods[16], and that he has obtained an immediate right to their possession[17], it is now necessary to examine his rights to the goods. The agreement will usually impose on the hirer a duty in these circumstances to return the goods to the owner; and, despite recent doubts[18], it is well settled that equity has no jurisdiction to grant relief to the hirer[19]. Assuming that the hirer refuses or neglects to return the goods to the owner, how may the latter enforce his right to repossession?

(a) Repossession through self-help

A rightful recaption of goods by the owner will not deprive him of his other remedies under the h.p. agreement[20]; but a wrongful recaption will constitute both a tort and a repudiation of the agreement[1]. Leaving aside special statutory restrictions[2], recaption gives rise to three problems. First, is the owner entitled to use force to repossess the goods? The position would appear to be that, after a failure by the hirer to return the goods after a request, the owner may use reasonable force to recapt the goods[3], but that unreasonable force will amount to an assault[4]. To avoid the uncertainty of what is reasonable force in a confrontation with a hirer, recaption is sometimes achieved in the early hours. Second, is the owner entitled to enter the hirer's premises to recapt the goods? Because the common law is uncertain, the agreement will usually confer on the owner a licence to enter the hirer's land and seize the goods. Such a contractual licence is probably irrevocable[5], and will give the owner immunity from an action in trespass where only reasonable force is used[6]. However, as the entry to recapt may amount to the offence of forcible entry[7], it is common for the owner to take the precaution of employing repossession agents. Third, recaption might amount to an offence under s. 40 of the Administration of Justice Act 1970. The *Report of the Payne Committee* recommended that the un-

---

16. See Chapter 5.   17. See below, p. 355.
18. See *Stockloser* v. *Johnson*, [1954] 1 Q.B. 467; [1954] 1 All E.R. 630, C.A.: discussed below, pp. 373–374.
19. *Cramer* v. *Giles* (1883), Cab. & El. 151; affd. (1884), *Times*, May 9th. Nor has the court any discretion where the creditor seeks a writ of execution: see *T.C. Trustees, Ltd.* v. *J. S. Darwen, Ltd.*, [1969] 2 Q.B. 295; [1969] 1 All E.R. 271, C.A.
20. *Overstone, Ltd.* v. *Shipway*, [1962] 1 All E.R. 52, C.A.: see below, p. 374.
1. *Abingdon Finance, Ltd.* v. *Champion*, [1961] C.L.Y. 3931.
2. See Guest, *Law of H.P.* 531; and Goode, *H.P. Law & Practice* (2nd Edn.) 19–20.
3. *Blades* v. *Higgs* (1861), 10 C.B.N.S. 713, *obiter* at p. 720.
4. *Dyer* v. *Munday*, [1895] 1 Q.B. 742, C.A.
5. *Hurst* v. *Picture Theatres, Ltd.*, [1915] 1 K.B. 1, C.A.; cf. *Wood* v. *Leadbitter* (1835), 13 M. & W. 838.
6. *Hemmings* v. *Stoke Poges Golf Club*, [1920] 1 K.B. 720, C.A.
7. Statute of Forcible Entry 1381.

lawful harassment of debtors be made a criminal offence[8], and Parliament sought to give effect to this suggestion by s. 40. Section 40 (1) provides that

> "A person commits an offence if, with the object of coercing another person to pay money claimed from the other as a debt due under a contract, he—
>
> (a) harasses the other with demands for payment which, in respect of their frequency or the manner or occasion of making any such demand, or of any threat or publicity by which any demand is accompanied, are calculated to subject him or members of his family or household to alarm, distress or humiliation; . . ."

Section 40 (2) extends this offence to any person who

> "concerts with others in the taking of such action . . ., notwithstanding that his own course of conduct does not by itself amount to harassment".

On the other hand, the scope of the offence is limited by s. 40 (3), which provides—

> "Subsection (1) (a) above does not apply to anything done by a person which is reasonable (and otherwise permissible in law) for the purpose—
>
> (a) of securing the discharge of an obligation due, or believed by him to be due, to himself or to persons for whom he acts, or protecting himself or them from future loss; or
>
> (b) of the enforcement of any liability by legal process".

Some idea of the types of conduct which s. 40 was intended to prohibit may be gathered from the *Report of the Payne Committee*[9]; but it is to be regretted that the section is "sadly lacking in precision"[10]. For instance, the Payne Committee intended that the provision should cover "visiting the home of the debtor . . . under the guise of collecting chattels let under a hire purchase agreement"[11], though s. 40 gives rise to several problems in this context. First, is the act of recaption done "with the object of coercing another person to pay money claimed" contrary to s. 40 (1); and is it a "demand for payment" within s. 40 (1) (a)? Or is it only the threat of recaption which is prohibited? The latter interpretation would produce the undesirable result of encouraging recaption without warning. Second, as s. 40 (1) is only expressed to be applicable where money is claimed "as a debt due under a contract", can s. 40 be avoided entirely by the simple expedient of obtaining a judgment for debt prior to recaption? Third, what is the criterion

---

8. *The Report of the Committee on the Enforcement of Judgment Debts* (1969), Cmnd. 3909, para. 1238. See further below, pp. 364–365.
9. See generally paras. 1230–1244.
10. Borrie & Pyke (1970), N.L.J. 588, at p. 589.   11. Para. 1233 (i).

for the establishment by the recaptor of the defence that his action was "reasonable" within the meaning of s. 40 (3)[12]?

(b) *Repossession through court action*

As an alternative to recaption, the owner may seek to obtain judgment for the return of the goods and have that judgment executed by court officers. Leaving aside the summary process of replevin[13], and a claim for restitution in criminal proceedings[14] or quasi-contract[15], the only action which will normally be available to the owner is detinue, to succeed in which the owner must prove the following matters. First, the owner must show that he was entitled to immediate possession of the goods, and remained so entitled down to the date of judgment[16]. Second, the owner must prove that the hirer has unlawfully[17] detained the goods after proper demand was made for their return. Whilst mere possession by the hirer may amount to a breach of the contract of h.p.[18], it is insufficient to found an action in detinue: the owner must show a refusal or neglect to return the goods which is adverse to his right to immediate possession, and the battle of wits to which this may give rise is well illustrated by *Capital Finance, Ltd.* v. *Bray*[19]. Normally, adverse possession is proved by showing that the owner demanded redelivery, and that the hirer unreasonably refused to comply[20]; but it is sufficient to show that the hirer has improperly parted wth possession of, or has destroyed, the goods, or they have become lost or damaged as a result of the hirer's negligence[1]. Whilst detinue will not lie where the goods are destroyed without fault on the part of the hirer, the contract will usually make him strictly liable[2], and the goods will probably be insured as well[3].

At common law, the judgment in an action of detinue directed the defendant to deliver up the goods to the plaintiff *or* to pay their value, and in either case damages for their detention; but, if the defendant tendered the goods in reasonable condition before judgment, the plaintiff was bound to accept them and could not insist on their value, because the essence of the action was a demand for the return of the goods[4]. The quantification of damages and the assessment of the value

---

12. See Borrie & Pyke (1970), 114 N.L.J. 588, at p. 589.
13. See Guest, *Law of H.P.* 847; *Winfield on Tort* (8th Edn.) 492–493.
14. See Macleod (1968), Crim. L.R. 577.
15. See below, pp. 404-408.
16. See the discussion of conversion, below, p. 377.
17. See *Winfield on Tort* (8th Edn.) 488, note 18.
18. *Heskell* v. *Continental Express, Ltd.*, [1950] 1 All E.R. 1033.
19. [1964] 1 All E.R. 603, C.A.: set out below, p. 338.
20. He must be allowed adequate time to verify the plaintiff's title: *Winfield on Tort* (8th Edn.) 489.
 1. The first two, but not the third, are acts of conversion: see below, p. 377.
 2. See above, p. 116, note 18.   3. See above, p. 14.
 4. *Crossfield* v. *Such* (1852), 8 Exch. 159.

of the goods will be considered later, but it may be pointed out here that the plaintiff will not necessarily recover the whole value of the goods, but possibly only the value of his interest in them[5]. Whilst at common law the defendant had the option whether to return the goods or pay their value, Statute has vested this power in the court, whose judgment may take any of the following forms[6]:

(1) For specific delivery of the goods and damages for their detention. This form gives the defendant no option to pay their value, and the plaintiff is allowed to recover the goods by execution. It has been suggested, however, that the defendant should receive an allowance for any increase in value which he has contributed to the goods before judgment[7].

(2) For delivery of the goods to the plaintiff unless payment of their value is made within a specified time, plus damages for their detention. Before the time-limit expires, the defendant may prevent the initiation of process for recovery of the goods by paying their value; but thereafter he must pay their value[8], though the court has a power to stay execution even out of time.

(3) Payment of the value of the goods to the plaintiff, with damages for their detention[9]. A judgment in this form means that neither party can insist on the return of the goods; but this does not prevent the owner from seizing the goods[10], which continue to belong to him until judgment is satisfied[11]. If the plaintiff does recapt the goods, he is deemed to have waived his right under the judgment to their value; but, if judgment is satisfied, the plaintiff's title to the goods passes to the defendant[12].

Whilst detinue is the appropriate form of action where the plaintiff wishes to recover possession, he will not necessarily recover possession by such action. The form of the order is at the discretion of the court, and specific delivery will seldom be ordered[13]; and it has been said that it ought not to be granted[14]

---

5. See below, p. 380.
6. See *Winfield on Tort* (8th Edn.) 490-492. Compare the orders under s. 35 (4) of the H.P.A.: see below, p. 340.
7. *Per* Lord MacNaghten in *Peruvian Guano, Ltd.* v. *Dreyfus, Brother & Co., Ltd.*, [1892] A.C. 166, H.L., at p. 176.
8. *Metals and Ropes, Ltd.* v. *Tattersall*, [1966] 3 All E.R. 401, C.A.; *Astley Industrial Trust, Ltd.* v. *Miller*, [1968] 2 All E.R. 36.
9. The court must put a separate figure on the value of the goods: *General and Finance Facilities, Ltd.* v. *Cook Cars (Romford), Ltd.*, [1963] 2 All E.R. 314, C.A.
10. Recaption is considered above, pp. 330–332.
11. *Brinsmead* v. *Harrison* (1872), L.R. 7 C.P. 547.
12. See below, p. 363.
13. And see the restriction in *Cohen* v. *Roche*, [1927] 1 K.B. 169: see below, p. 414.
14. *Per* Swinfen Eady M.R. in *Whiteley, Ltd.* v. *Hilt*, [1918] 2 K.B. 808, C.A., at p. 819.

"when the chattel is an ordinary article of commerce and of no special value or interest, and not alleged to be of any special value to the plaintiff, and where damages would fully compensate".

Hence, the judgment is likely to be in form (2) or (3); and even an action in detinue is unlikely to result in recovery of possession by the plaintiff owner under a h.p. agreement.

2 Agreements within the H.P.A.

It is common for h.p. agreements to give the owner the right to re-possess the goods in the event of any default by the hirer; and, in view of the use made by some owners of this device to engineer "snatch-backs"[15], the H.P.A. 1938 forbade the owner from seizing the goods where more than one-third of the h.p. price had been paid, and provided that he might only recover possession by court action. To this principle, the H.P.A. 1964 added two further elements of protection: first, the obligatory notice of default procedure in the case of monetary default; and second, the avoidance of any provision terminating the agreement solely by reason of the death of the hirer. Furthermore, these protections were extended to the buyer under a conditional sale agreement. All these restrictions are now to be found in the H.P.A. 1965.

(a) Notice of default

One of the commonest causes of repossession at common law was default by the hirer in payment of the instalments of hire-rent: as the hirer had no equity of redemption[16], the owner was not required to give the hirer any latitude in this respect, though in practice the courts were very willing to find that the owner had waived the fault by accepting late payment[17]. However, this dependence of the hirer on the whim of the owner was thought to be wrong; and the H.P.A. 1964 therefore introduced what was almost a limited statutory equity of redemption, which is now to be found in s. 25 of the H.P.A. 1965.

Section 25 is expressed to apply wherever goods are let under a h.p. agreement or sold under a conditional sale agreement within the ambit of the Act[18], and that agreement contains a provision that certain "specified consequences" will follow where there is

"a default in the payment of one or more instalments or other sums payable by the hirer or buyer" (s. 25 (1)).

According to s. 25 (2), the "specified consequences" are that the

"agreement, or (in the case of a hire-purchase agreement) the bail-ment of the goods, shall terminate, or shall be terminable, or that

15. See above, p. 28.   16. See above, p. 330.
17. E.g. *Reynolds* v. *General and Finance Facilities, Ltd.* (1963), 107 Sol. Jo. 889, C.A. See generally above, pp. 146–148.
18. See above, p. 30.

the owner or seller shall have a right to recover possession of the goods".

Thus, s. 25 does not apply to a clause providing that other consequences will follow the type of default mentioned in s. 25 (1), nor even that the "specified consequences" will follow from any other type of default[19]: the section is only concerned with the monetary obligations of the hirer or buyer[20], though this may result in some rather artificial distinctions[1]. However, the section does apply irrespective of how much of the h.p. or total purchase price has been paid by the hirer or buyer[2].

Where the requirements of the section are fulfilled, s. 25 (3) provides that the "specified consequences"

"shall not follow by reason of that default unless the owner or seller serves on the hirer or buyer, by post or otherwise, a notice (in this Act referred to as a 'notice of default') stating the amount which has become due[3], but remains unpaid, in respect of sums to which the relevant provision applies, and requiring the amount so stated to be paid within such period (not being less than seven days beginning with the date of service of the notice) as may be specified in the notice".

Section 25 (4) further provides:

"Where a notice of default is served, the specified consequences shall not follow before the end of the period specified in the notice by reason of any default to which the notice relates; and, if before the end of that period the amount specified in the notice is paid or tendered by or on behalf of the hirer or buyer or any guarantor, the specified consequences shall not follow thereafter by reason of any such default".

If the "specified consequences" are merely that the contract is terminable, the notice of default may also include a notice terminating it at the end of the specified period

"subject to a condition that the termination is not to take effect if before the end of that period the amount specified in the notice of default is paid or tendered as mentioned in . . . [s. 25 (4)]"[4].

---

19. E.g. bankruptcy of, or assignment by, the hirer or buyer.
20. It does not say that the money must be payable to the owner or seller: see Guest, *Law of H.P.* 484, note 11.
1. See Goode, *H.P. Law & Practice* (2nd edn.) 343, note 10.
2. Compare the restrictions on the right to repossess: see below, pp. 336–337.
3. Perhaps the notice is invalid if the wrong amount is stated: Goode, *op. cit.* 343, note 12.
4. Section 25 (5). If the notice is not expressed to be subject to this condition, it has been suggested that it may be ineffective to terminate the agreement or bailment: Goode, *op. cit.,* 343.

Section 26 contains certain supplementary provisions as to service of a notice of default[5].

(b) Repossession

The H.P.A. 1938 introduced two restrictions on the owner's right to repossess goods within the ambit of that Act[6].

(1) Any contractual provision authorising the owner to enter the hirer's premises to recapt goods was avoided; and this measure is now incorporated in s. 29 of the 1965 Act, which avoids any provision

> "whereby an owner or seller, or any person acting on his behalf, is authorised to enter upon any premises for the purpose of taking possession of goods which have been let under a hire-purchase agreement or agreed to be sold under a conditional sale agreement, or is relieved from liability for any such entry" (s. 29 (2) (a)).

All this subsection does is to avoid any contractual licence to enter[7], thereby making entry a trespass[8]: it in no way restricts the right of the hirer or buyer to terminate the agreement[9]. He is not prevented from giving the owner or seller express leave to enter the premises[10]; nor is he prevented from agreeing in advance to the owner or seller repossessing the goods[11].

(2) Where the hirer had paid more than one-third of the h.p. price, the 1938 Act prevented the owner from enforcing any right to immediate possession other than by court action, and laid down some substantive and procedural provisions in respect of such actions. The H.P.A. 1964 extended certain of these procedural restrictions to those cases where one-third of the h.p. price had not yet been paid, and rendered both the substantive and procedural restrictions applicable to conditional sales. All these matters are now dealt with in Part III of the H.P.A. 1965.

Part III of the 1965 Act carefully distinguishes according to whether or not the goods are "protected goods"; and s. 33 (1) explains that this expression is applicable where the following conditions are fulfilled:

> " (a) that the goods have been let under a hire-purchase agreement, or agreed to be sold under a conditional sale agreement[12];
> (b) that one third of the hire-purchase price or total purchase

---

5. Compare service of a notice of cancellation under s. 12: see above, p. 44.
6. See now Part I of the H.P.A. 1965: above, p. 30.
7. See above, p. 330.   8. See above, p. 330.
9. The right to terminate is considered below, pp. 353–355.
10. See below, p. 337. What if entry is gained with the customer's permission, but the goods then removed against his will? See Goode, *H.P. Law & Practice* (2nd Edn.) 203.
11. See Guest, *Law of H.P.* 544, note 60.
12. It has been suggested that these restrictions should be extended to simple hiring agreements: *Report on the Enforcement Judgment Debts* (1969), Cmnd. 3909, para. 1339—see further below, pp. 364, 374.

price has been paid (whether in pursuance of a judgment or otherwise) or tendered by or on behalf of the hirer or buyer or a guarantor;
(c) that the hirer or buyer has not terminated the hire-purchase agreement or conditional sale agreement, or (in the case of a hire-purchase agreement) the bailment, by virtue of any right vested in him".

In computing the fraction of the h.p. or total purchase price which has been paid, the Act makes special provision for part-exchange allowances[13], installation charges[14], and for the situation where the hirer or buyer is making payments under two or more agreements[15]; and s. 47 prevents the owner or seller from avoiding the restrictions of Part III by the device of "linked-on" agreements[16].

1. Unprotected goods. Where the goods are not "protected goods", the owner or seller retains his common law right to recapt the goods, though he cannot rely on any contractual right of entry[17]. However, where he seeks to recover possession by court action, the Act offers the hirer or buyer a purely procedural protection in that s. 49 (1) requires that[18]

"the action shall be brought in the county court for the district in which the hirer or buyer resides or carries on business, or resided or carried on business at the date on which he last made a payment under the hire-purchase agreement or conditional sale agreement".

2. Protected goods. Section 34 (1) provides that the owner or seller

"shall not enforce any right to recover possession of protected goods from the hirer or buyer otherwise than by action".

This restriction does not apply where the owner or seller seeks to recover possession from a third party[19]; nor does it protect the hirer or buyer where he has exercised his statutory power to terminate the agreement[1], or has voluntarily returned the goods, even though in ignorance of his rights[2]. The effect of s. 34 (1) is merely in all other cases to prevent the owner or seller from taking any active steps to

---

13. By s. 56, the amount paid includes payment otherwise than in money where this has been agreed between the parties, e.g. a part-exchange allowance: see above, p. 271.
14. See s. 55 (1) (b).
15. See s. 51, which imports a compulsory scheme of appropriation.
16. See above, p. 28.
17. See s. 29 (2) (a): above, p. 336.
18. See further ss. 49 (2), (3), (4), 50.
19. But remember that the expressions "hirer" and "buyer" include any assignee therefrom: s. 58 (1).
1. See s. 28 (4): below, pp. 354–355. See *Bentruck, Ltd.* v. *Cromwell Engineering Co.*, [1971] 1 All E.R. 33, C.A.
2. *Mercantile Credit, Ltd.* v. *Cross*, [1965] 2 Q.B. 205; [1965] 1 All E.R. 577, C.A. But see *F. C. Finance, Ltd.* v. *Francis* (1970), 114 Sol. Jo. 568, C.A.

recover the goods[3]. However, if the owner or seller does recover possession of protected goods in contravention of s. 34 (1), it is provided in s. 34 (2) that "the agreement, if not previously terminated, shall terminate", and the owner or seller should be subject to the following penalties:

(1) "the hirer or buyer shall be released from all liability under the agreement, and shall be entitled to recover from the owner or seller, in an action for money had and received, all sums paid by the hirer or buyer under the agreement or under any security given by him in respect thereof" (s. 34 (2) (a)).

The effect of a similar provision in the 1938 Act was considered by GODDARD L.J. in *Carr* v. *James Broderick, Ltd.*[4].

> The owners of goods let under a h.p. agreement seized them in contravention of the Act after one third of the h.p. price had been paid. Subsequently, the owners admitted their error, and offered to repay the sums already paid by the hirer. The hirer refused to accept the money, and sued to recover the goods.

His Lordship held that the agreement had been determined by the Act; and that the hirer was not entitled to claim the goods either in detinue or in conversion, but merely to the sums paid under the agreement. However, he did suggest that the Act contemplated that a hirer might recover damages in respect of something other than the recaption[5]. Thus, once the owner recaps the goods, the hirer cannot recover possession by court action[6]. Nor will the agreement be revived simply because the goods are returned to the hirer: it is conceivable that the parties might make a new agreement on identical terms; but the courts will require very cogent evidence before reaching such a conclusion. In *Capital Finance, Ltd.* v. *Bray*[7]

> The owners of a car seized it in contravention of the Act. Within a few hours, the owners realized their mistake, took the car back, and left it outside the hirer's house. As the hirer continued to make no repayments, the owners some five months later sued to recover the car.

Despite evidence that the hirer had continued to use the car in the intervening five months, the Court of Appeal refused to imply that the agreement had been revived, and held:

(a) that the hirer was not liable in detinue as there was no adverse

---

3. Even if the goods have been abandoned: *United Dominions Trust (Commercial), Ltd.*, v. *Kesler* (1963), 107 Sol. Jo. 15, C.A.
4. [1942] 2 K.B. 275; [1942] 2 All E.R. 441.
5. Under what is now s. 40 (3).
6. What if the hirer seizes the goods?
7. [1964] 1 All E.R. 603, C.A.

possession on the grounds that the hirer was under no legal obligation to return the car to the owners as distinct trom allowing them to collect it[8]; and

(b) the hirer was entitled under the Act to recover all sums that he had paid under the agreement.

(2) "any guarantor shall be entitled to recover from the owner or seller, in an action for money had and received, all sums paid by him under the contract of guarantee or under any security given by him in respect thereof" (s. 34 (2) (b)).

The protection offered by this provision extends to one who has signed a contract of indemnity[9], and applies whether or not the surety entered into his obligation at the behest of the customer[10].

Assuming that the owner or seller has not recapted any part of "protected goods" in contravention of s. 34, the Act lays down a number of rules to govern the action for repossession (s. 35 (1)). However, it first saves the owner from the dilemma that he cannot show adverse possession by the hirer or buyer by reason of the restrictions imposed by s. 34. Section 48 (1) provides that, if the owner or seller in these circumstances made a request in writing to the hirer or buyer to surrender the goods,

"then, for the purposes of the claim of the owner or seller to recover possession of the goods, the possession of them by the hirer or buyer shall be deemed to be adverse to the owner or seller"[11].

On the other hand, whilst s. 48 is expressed not to affect a claim for damages for conversion (s. 48 (2)), s. 52 provides that the refusal by the hirer or buyer to relinquish possession of protected goods shall not render hirer or buyer liable in conversion[12]. Thus, the owner or seller cannot avoid the restrictions of the Act by suing in conversion. Where a claim for repossession is brought under the Act, not only is the hirer or buyer entitled to the procedural protections of s. 49 (1)[13], but it is laid down that all parties to the agreement, including any surety, shall be made parties to the action (s. 35 (2))[14]; and that the court shall have power, on the application of the owner[15],

---

8. See above, p. 332.
9. Section 58 (1). Contracts of surety are considered further below, pp. 344–348.
10. E.g. a dealer under a recourse agreement: see below, p. 345.
11. See *Smart Brothers, Ltd.* v. *Pratt*, [1940] 2 K.B. 498; [1940] 3 All E.R. 432, C.A.; and Guest, *Law of H.P.* 545.
12. Section 52 does not bar an action in conversion against a third party: *Eastern Distributors, Ltd.* v. *Goldring*, [1957] 2 Q.B. 600; [1957] 2 All E.R. 525, C.A.: set out above, p. 189.
13. See above, p. 337.
14. See *United Motor Finance Corporation, Ltd.* v. *Turner*, [1956] 2 Q.B. 32; [1956] 1 All E.R. 623, C.A.
15. Section 45 renders ss. 35 to 44 applicable to conditional sales.

> "to make such orders as the court thinks just for the purposes pro-
> tecting the goods from damage or depreciation, including orders
> restricting or prohibiting the use of the goods or giving directions as
> to their custody" (s. 35 (3)).

At the hearing of the action s. 35 (4) empowers the court, "without
prejudice to any other power", to make any of the following orders[16]:
1. Specific delivery order. The court may "make an order for the
specific delivery of all the goods to the owner" (s. 35 (4) (a)), or all the
rest of the goods if the owner has already recovered some (s. 40 (1)).
If the court makes such an order, the hirer must return the goods, and
has no option to pay their value (s. 35 (5)); but, if he fails to return
them, the court has power to revoke the order and give a money
judgment (s. 42).
2. Split order. The court may "make an order for the specific delivery
of a part of the goods to the owner and for the transfer to the hirer of
the owner's title to the remainder of the goods" (s. 35 (4) (c)). The
court is, however, precluded from making such an order unless it is

> "satisfied that the amount which the hirer has paid[17] in respect of
> the hire-purchase price exceeds the price of that part of the goods[18]
> by at least one-third of the unpaid balance of the hire-purchase
> price" (s. 37 (1)).

3. Postponed order. This power is the one most commonly exercised;
and the Act lays down that the court may

> "make an order for the specific delivery of all the goods to the owner
> and postpone the operation of the order on condition that the hirer
> or any guarantor pays the unpaid[17] balance of the hire-purchase price
> at such times and in such amounts as the court, having regard to the
> means of the hirer and of any guarantor, thinks just, and subject to
> the fulfilment by the hirer or a guarantor of such other conditions
> as the court thinks just" (s. 35 (4) (b)).

However, the Act expressly provides that a postponed order cannot be
made unless the hirer "satisfies the court that the goods are in his
possession or control at the time when the order is made" (s. 36 (1));
and it implies that the court must hear evidence of the means of the
hirer or guarantor[19]. But these requirements may be dispensed with,
subject to safeguards for the guarantor (s. 36 (3)), where

> "an offer as to the conditions for the postponement of the operation
> of an order is made by the hirer, and accepted by the owner . . ."
> (s. 36 (2)).

---

16. The ordinary orders in an action of detinue are set out above, p. 333.
17. See further, s. 40.   18. See s. 37 (2).
19. See s. 35 (4) (b). What if the hirer merely fails to appear in court?

The effect of a postponed order is set out in s. 38. Section 38 (1) provides that

> "While the operation of an order for the specific delivery of goods to the owner is postponed, the hirer shall, subject to the following provisions of this section, be deemed to be a bailee of the goods under and on the terms of the agreement".

Whilst s. 38 (1) envisages that the agreement will continue, the Act makes the following alterations:

(1) Once the owner has commenced an action under s. 35, the Act forbids any separate money claim in respect of the agreement or any related contract of guarantee[20]; and, where the owner in that action claims a sum under the minimum payments clause[1], s. 43 (3) enacts that, except as provided in s. 44[2],

> "the court shall not entertain the claim in respect of that sum unless and until the postponement is revoked, and shall then deal with the claim as if the agreement had just been terminated".

(2) In making the postponed order, s. 38 (3) states that

> "The court may make such further modification of the terms of the agreement, and of any contract of guarantee relating thereto, as the court considers necessary having regard to the variation of the terms of payment";

and, when the order has been made, s. 38 (2) provides that

> "No further sum shall be or become payable by the hirer or a guarantor on account of the unpaid balance of the hire-purchase price, except in accordance with the terms of the order".

(3) During the operation of a postponed order[3], the court has power under s. 39 (1) to (a) vary the conditions of the postponement and vary the agreement and any contract of guarantee; or (b) revoke the postponement; or (c) replace that order by a split order[4].

(4) The Act provides that the hirer shall be entitled to obtain the owner's title to the goods by paying the unpaid balance of the h.p. price either in accordance with the terms of the order (s. 38 (5)) or otherwise (s. 39 (4)).

(5) Notwithstanding that the hirer is in breach of the postponed order, or with the agreement as amended, that Act provides that, not only will the hirer retain the option to purchase (s. 39 (4)), but that,

---

20. Section 41: set out below, p. 375.
 1. See above, p. 14, and below, p. 395.
 2. See below, p. 376.
 3. Even after breach of its terms: s. 39 (2).
 4. The situation where a warrant for delivery has been issued is dealt with by s. 39 (3).

except where there has been a default in the payment of the instalments of hire-rent[5],

> "the owner shall not take any civil proceedings against the hirer or guarantor otherwise than by making an application to the court by which the order was made" (s. 38 (4)).

In view of the substantial alterations which the Act makes, or allows the court to make, in the terms of the h.p. agreement, it has been suggested that the effect of the Act is really to abrogate the original agreement, and to create a new statutory contract of bailment[6].

If, after the owner had obtained an order for the specific delivery of the goods, the hirer disposed of them to a third party, then under the 1938 Act the owner used to be in a rather difficult position[7]. The redress introduced by the 1964 Act is now to be found in s. 42 of the 1965 Act, which provides that, where the owner has obtained an order for the specific delivery of goods[8], but has not recovered possession, he may apply to the court for the substitution of a money judgment. The court is empowered to make an order for the payment (either in a lump sum or by instalments[9]) of a sum "equal to the balance of the price of the unrecovered goods"[10], less any allowance for accelerated payment[11], against

> "any person who, at the time when the order is made, is (apart from the previous order) liable to pay any sum which has then accrued due under the agreement; and on the making of such an order the owner's title to the unrecovered goods shall vest in the person against whom the order is made" (s. 42 (5))[12].

(c) Death of the hirer or buyer

On the death of the hirer or buyer, the general rule is that most causes of action subsisting against or vested in him survive against the estate or for its benefit[13]. However, the death of the hirer or buyer must usually at best result in a temporary cessation of payments; and over the years owners have therefore taken steps to safeguard their interests. Sometimes, they have taken the benevolent step of providing that the

---

5. It has been suggested that, where the hirer is in breach of the terms of the postponed order, the agreement comes into force so that the arrears of rental are immediately recoverable: Prince (1957), 20 M.L.R. 620, 624; Cunliffe (1968), 118 New L.J. 377. Denied by Guest, *Law of H.P.*, *1st Supplement* to paras. 554, 559, 605.
6. Guest, *Law of H.P.* 554.
7. See Goode (1963), 113 L.J. 808.
8. Whichever of the three forms taken by the original order: s. 42 (1).
9. Section 99 of the County Courts Act 1959.
10. Section 39 (4). See the definitions in s. 39 (8).
11. Section 42 (6).
12. Note that the title vests on the making of the order, not on payment. Cf. ss. 38 (5), 39 (4): see above, p. 341.
13. Law Reform (Miscellaneous Provisions) Act 1934, s. 1 (1).

property shall pass without payment of any further instalments. Rather more commonly, the agreement was expressed to terminate, or be terminable, on the death of the hirer or buyer; and such a step would obviously be likely to compound the distress of a family which had just lost its bread-winner (the agreement usually being in his name).

The only contribution made to this problem by the 1938 Act was to provide that the expression "hirer" should include

". . . a person to whom the hirer's rights or liabilities under the agreement passed by assignment or by operation of law" (s. 21 (1))[14].

This had the effect of extending the statutory restrictions on the recovery of possession in appropriate circumstances to the hirer's personal representatives; but it did not prevent the operation of a clause providing for termination of the agreement, or the recovery of the goods, in that event. As a matter of grace, some owners were prepared to accept tender of the outstanding balance of the h.p. price from a personal representative or other interested party; but it was felt that the hirer's interest should be given some measure of legal protection. However, the 1964 Act eschewed the simple, and benevolent, answer of a compulsory transfer of property and cessation of payments, and instead merely avoided any provision terminating the agreement on the death of the hirer or buyer[15]. This latter course made it necessary to introduce complicated provisions to deal with in these circumstances. All these provisions are now to be found in the H.P.A. 1965.

The major provision concerning death is s. 30. Sub-section one provides that it

"shall have effect where goods are let under a hire-purchase agreement[16], or are agreed to be sold under a conditional sale agreement[16], and that agreement, or any other agreement[17], provides that, on the occurrence of, or at a time to be ascertained by reference to, one or more events referred to in the provision in question,—

(a) the hire-purchase agreement or conditional sale agreement, or (in the case of a hire-purchase agreement) the bailment of the goods, shall terminate, or shall be terminable, or the owner or seller shall have a right to recover possession of the goods to which the hire-purchase agreement or conditional sale agreement relates, or

(b) any sum shall become payable by the hirer or buyer or any guarantor, or any liability of the hirer or buyer or any guarantor shall be increased or accelerated, or

---

14. See now s. 58 (1) of the 1965 Act, which extends to buyers under conditional sales.
15. It would have saved a lot of trouble and subtle learning if the provisions had also applied on the insolvency of the hirer or buyer.
16. Within the ambit of the Act: see above, p. 30.
17. E.g. a contract or guarantee.

(c) any right of the hirer under the hire-purchase agreement or of the buyer under the conditional sale agreement shall cease to be exercisable, or shall be, or shall become liable to be, restricted or postponed".

If the only event specified as having any of the effects mentioned in s. 30 (1) is the death of the hirer or buyer, the provision is void (s. 30 (2), and, if other events are also specified, the provision shall be read

"as if any reference to the death of the hirer or buyer were omitted" (s. 30 (3)).

Nor can the owner or seller achieve any of the prohibited objects indirectly (as by making the agreement personal to the hirer or buyer), because any such provision

"shall be void in so far as it would have that effect" (s. 30 (4)).

In itself, s. 30 does not suspend any of the rights of the owner or seller to the payment of the instalments due under the agreement. Clearly, where the hirer or buyer dies, there is a considerable likelihood that one or more of the instalments will become in arrears before anyone can act. If the goods are in the possession of the personal representatives of the hirer or buyer, there is no real problem, because they are entitled to the statutory protections previously outlined in this section. On the other hand, the goods may be in the possession of some third party, usually the widow of the hirer or buyer; and there will probably be a lapse of time before the deceased's rights vest in his personal representatives. The Act avoids the hiatus, by providing that the notice of default procedure shall operate "as if the deceased person had not died" (s. 26 (2) (b)); and s. 46 deals with the problem that the statutory defence of possession of "protected goods" does not extend to the third party in possession by reference to Schedule 3. The complicated provisions of Schedule 3 are beyond the scope of this work[18]; but the necessity for this scheme, or something like it, itself throws doubt on the wisdom of the statutory solution of the difficulties raised by the death of the hirer or buyer[19].

3 THE PERSONAL SECURITY PROVIDED BY A SURETY

Particularly where there is some doubt as to the legal efficacy of the obligations imposed on the hirer or buyer[20], or of his ability to meet the obligations[1], it is fairly common in instalment credit transactions for

---

18. See Guest, *Law of H.P.* 569–576; and Goode, *H.P. Law & Practice* (2nd Edn.) 561–574.
19. See also Guest, *op. cit.*, 576.
20. E.g. minors.   1. E.g. married women.

the "lender" to insist on the security of some personal right of action against a third party in the event of default by the hirer or buyer. Whilst it is true that Part II of the Administration of Justice Act 1970 sets up an apparently viable system for the attachment of earnings[2], the system is only available in respect of debts where there is a court order following a default in payment[3]. Hence, there seems little possibility of obtaining such an order as a security for payment when the credit transaction is set up; and, as the system only has significance as a remedy, it is more properly considered in Part 5[2]. This matter aside, the obvious form of personal security is the surety.

Sureties will usually fall into one of the following categories: (a) a friend or relative of the hirer or buyer; or (b) a dealer or supplier signing a recourse provision; or (c) a director of the hiring or buying company. In any particular instalment credit transaction, there may be sureties from any or all of these classes; and the owner or seller may use any of the following techniques to achieve his object:

1. Co-principals. Particularly where the surety belongs to category (a), the "lender" may make him a party to the contract of h.p., conditional sale or credit sale. If the intention is that he should act as guarantor, the surety's liability is conditional on default by his co-principal; but, if it is intended that he be a genuine principal, his liability may be joint only, or both joint and several[4].

2. Indorsees. A form more frequently used with sureties from categories (b) and (c) is to require them to "back" (indorse) a bill of exchange. Where a third party signs a bill of exchange intending to guarantee payment, the Bills of Exchange Act 1882 provides that

> "he thereby incurs the liabilities of an indorser to a holder in due course" (s. 56);

and it has been decided that the owner or seller may take advantage of this liability even though he is not a holder in due course but a payee[5].

3. Guarantors. Into whatever category the surety may fall, a common technique is to require the surety to guarantee the principal contract[6]. It is this device which will be discussed in the present section.

Finally, it should be pointed out that a surety may have a right to claim a contribution from any other surety of the instalment credit transaction, whether or not he was aware of the existence of the co-surety at the time he entered the contract.

---

2. See below, p. 365.
3. See ss. 14 (3), 13 (5) (a).
4. See further Goode, *H.P. Law & Practice*, (2nd Edn.) 471.
5. *McDonald v. Nash*, [1924] A.C. 625, H.L.
6. Beware of the past consideration rule: see *Astley Industrial Trust, Ltd.* v. *Grimston, Ltd.* (1965), 109 Sol. Jo. 149.

1 Sureties at common law

Many of the difficulties in this subject may be traced back to s. 4. of the Statute of Frauds 1677; and to the distinction drawn in consequence of that provision between a surety who guarantees performance by the principal debtor, and one who takes on the primary obligation himself and agrees to indemnify the creditor[7]. The distinction between contracts of guarantee and of indemnity is a question which is both important in law and uncertain in practice. For instance, the courts have had some difficulty in deciding to which category belongs a contract of surety made by both a friend of the hirer or buyer[8] and a dealer under a recourse provision[9].

We must now examine the position of the surety.

1. Liability. The surety will not be liable unless the other party's loss is caused by the act in respect of which he has agreed to act as surety[10], and unless any condition precedent to which his promise is subject has been fulfilled[11]. At this point, we must distinguish between a guarantee and an indemnity, because the liability of a guarantor, but not of an indemnifier, is further subject to the following restrictions: it is necessary for the secured party first to call on the hirer or buyer to make good his default[12]; the guarantor only promises that the hirer or buyer will perform such obligations as he has; and his liability is co-extensive with that of the hirer or buyer[13].

2. Rights. The surety has certain rights against the other two parties. As against the owner or seller, he has the right to secure his discharge by paying the amount due, and is then entitled to the right of subrogation discussed below; and a guarantor has the additional right of exercising any set-off or counterclaim against the owner or seller that would have been available to the hirer or buyer[14]. As against the hirer or buyer, the surety has the following rights:

(1) An express or implied[15] right of indemnity[16] in respect of sums

---

7. See generally, Cheshire & Fifoot, *Law of Contract* (7th Edn.) 170–175; Treitel, *Law of Contract* (3rd Edn.) 135–137.
8. Cf. *Yeoman Credit, Ltd.* v. *Latter*, [1961] 2 All E.R. 294, C.A. (indemnity); and *Western Credit, Ltd.* v. *Alberry*, [1964] 2 All E.R. 938, C.A. (guarantee).
9. Cf. *Unity Finance, Ltd.* v. *Woodcock*, [1963] 2 All E.R. 270, C.A. (guarantee); and *Goulston Discount, Ltd.* v. *Clark*, [1967] 2 Q.B. 493; [1967] 1 All E.R. 61, C.A. (indemnity).
10. *Bentworth Finance, Ltd.* v. *Lubert*, [1968] 1 Q.B. 680; [1967] 2 All E.R. 810, C.A.: set out above, p. 116.
11. *Midland Counties Motor Finance, Ltd.* v. *Slade*, [1951] 1 K.B. 346; [1950] 2 All E.R. 821, C.A.
12. See *Hitchcock* v. *Humfrey* (1843), 5 Man. & G. 559.
13. E.g. *Stadium Finance, Ltd.* v. *Helm* (1965), 109 Sol. Jo. 471, C.A.
14. *Sterling Industrial Facilities, Ltd.* v. *Lydiate Textiles, Ltd.* (1962), 106 Sol. Jo. 669, C.A.
15. E.g. where the surety undertook the obligation at the request, express or implied, of the hirer or buyer. But see Guest, *Law of H.P.* 423, note 52.
16. And see his rights in equity: *Ascherson* v. *Tredegar Dry Dock and Wharf Co., Ltd.*, [1909] 2 Ch. 401.

paid out in discharge of his obligations under the contract of surety. This rule appears to cause difficulty where the surety has indemnified the owner or seller; the result of its application to a situation where the hirer or buyer is saved from liability to the owner or seller by the H.P.A. is that the protection of the Act may be indirectly avoided if the owner or seller sues the surety and the hirer or buyer is brought in as a third party. It has been suggested that this dilemma should be avoided by making the surety entitled merely to an indemnity to the legal liability of the hirer or buyer[17].

(2) When the surety pays the owner or seller he is entitled[18] to a right of subrogation; that is, that the owner or seller must assign to him all his rights against the hirer or buyer, including any securities[19], in so far as those rights are not purely personal ones[20].

3. *Discharge.* The surety may be discharged from liability under his contract of guarantee or indemnity in any of the ways in which a contract can normally be discharged[1]. In addition, there are a number of situations where a surety may be discharged in pursuance of the rule that the owner or seller must not do anything to prejudice the rights of the surety without his consent[2]: for example, where the owner or seller releases the hirer or buyer; or there is a novation or material alteration in the terms of sale or h.p. agreement[3]; or possibly a waiver of its terms[4]. Where the sale or h.p. agreement is terminated, a surety who has agreed to indemnify the owner or seller may be liable for the full "price"; but a guarantor is only liable to a maximum[5] of the accrued liabilities of the hirer or buyer[6].

2 Sureties under the H.P.A.

Whilst the 1938 Act offered little protection to sureties of agreements within the ambit of the Act[7], their position was considerably improved by the 1964 Act and was consolidated in the 1965 Act. Section 58 (1) of the 1965 Act provides that the expression "contract of guarantee"

---

17. Goode, *H.P. Law & Practice* (2nd Edn.) 508. But see *Re Chetwynd's Estate*, [1938] Ch. 13; [1937] 3 All E.R. 530, C.A.
18. Except in so far as he has expressly or impliedly waived such right: *Re Lord Churchill* (1888), 39 Ch.D. 174.
19. Section 5, Mercantile Law Amendment Act 1856.
20. *Chatterton* v. *Maclean*, [1951] 1 All E.R. 761.
1. See Chapter 19 below.
2. See *Midland Counties Motor Finance, Ltd.* v. *Slade*, [1951] 1 K.B. 346; [1950] 2 All E.R. 821, C.A.
3. E.g. *Midland Motor Showrooms, Ltd.* v. *Newman*, [1929] 2 K.B. 256, C.A.
4. The effect of a waiver is considered above, p. 146. *et seq.*
5. See *Hewison* v. *Ricketts* (1894), 63 L.J.Q.B. 711, D.C.: set out below, p. 372.
6. E.g. *Western Credit, Ltd.* v. *Alberry*, [1964] 2 All E.R. 938, C.A. (lawful termination by a hirer).
7. See above, p. 30.

"in relation to a hire-purchase agreement, credit-sale agreement or conditional sale agreement, means a contract, made at the request (express or implied) of the hirer or buyer, either to guarantee the performance of the hirer's or buyer's obligations under the hire-purchase agreement, credit-sale agreement or conditional sale agreement, or to indemnify the owner or seller against any loss which he may incur in respect of that agreement, and 'guarantor' shall be construed accordingly".

Thus, for the purposes of the Act, the distinction between contracts of guarantee and indemnity is partially abrogated; but s. 58 (1) only applies to contracts made at the request of the hirer or buyer, so presumably it will not cover dealer recourse[8].

Where a contract of surety falls within s. 58 (1), the Act offers considerable protection to the surety. Section 22 provides that, subject to the dispensing power of the court (s. 22 (3))[9], neither the guarantee nor any security given by the guarantor shall be enforceable, unless, within seven days of making whichever is the later of the contract of sale or h.p., or the contract of guarantee, there is delivered or sent to the guarantor the following documents which comply with the "legibility requirements"[10]: (a) a copy of the sale or h.p. agreement; *and* (b) a note or memorandum of the contract of guarantor signed by the guarantor or someone authorised by him to sign it on his behalf (s. 22 (1)). At any time whilst the contract of surety remains in force, s. 23 provides that the guarantor has the right to obtain from the person entitled to enforce the contract of guarantee against him further copies of those agreements and also the information to which the hirer or buyer is entitled under s. 21 (1)[11]. In addition, the H.P.A. also extends to the surety the protection offered to the hirer or buyer where the owner or seller fails to comply with his duties as to the statement of the cash price[12], the form and contents of the agreement[13], the supply of copies[14], the failure to supply documents or information[15], or the wrongful recovery of protected goods[16]; and the position of the surety is also affected by the provisions relating to cancellation of the sale or h.p. agreement[17], notice of default[18], death of the hirer or buyer[19], and proceedings to recover possession under Part III of the Act[20].

---

8. The dealer may be indirectly protected if the recourse provision only amounts to a guarantee.
9. Cf. s. 10: see above, p. 42.
10. Section 22 (2): see above, p. 34.   11. See above, p. 113.
12. Section 6: see above, p. 33.   13. Section 7: see above, p. 34.
14. Sections 8 and 9: see above, p. 40–42.
15. Section 21 (2) (b): see above, p. 113.
16. Section 34 (2) (b): see above, p. 339.
17. Section 14 (1): see above, p. 44.
18. Section 25 (4): see above, p. 335.
19. Section 30 (1) (b): see above, p. 343.   20. Section 35 (s): see above, p. 339.

PART 5

Discharge and Remedies

CHAPTER 19

Discharge of Contractual Obligations

This Chapter is devoted to an examination of the ways in which contractual obligations may be discharged. Leaving aside such matters as discharge by frustration[1] and rescission for mistake[2], the subject may be divided on the basis of whether or not the discharge takes place in accordance with the terms of the contract.

1. DISCHARGE IN ACCORDANCE WITH THE CONTRACT

In considering the discharge of contractual obligations in accordance with the contract, a distinction may be drawn as to whether that discharge is brought about by (a) performance, or (b) the happening of some other event.

1 Discharge by performance[3]

Performance by A. of a contractual obligation which he owes to B. may be important for two reasons: first, non-performance may prevent A. enforcing B.'s promises to him; and second, performance will discharge his obligations to B.

1. Enforcement of B.'s obligations. When sued by A., B. may set up A.'s failure to perform as a defence; and the general rule is that A. cannot succeed unless he can show that he has performed his side of the bargain to the letter. This may be because performance by A. is a condition precedent either to the existence of the contract or to performance by B.[4]: if precedent to contract, A. is not bound to perform, though neither party is bound unless he does so; but, if precedent merely to performance, there is a binding contract. In the latter case, it may be that A. cannot enforce B.'s performance until he has performed his own side of the bargain[5]; or that the promises on each side are concurrent[6].

2. Discharge of A.'s obligations. Generally speaking, A. will only be discharged by exact performance of his obligations; and the remedies available to B. where A. is in breach have already been discussed[7].

---

1. See above, pp. 254–259.   2. See above, pp. 122–124.
3. See generally, Treitel, *Law of Contract* (3rd Edn.) Ch. 19: Cheshire & Fifoot, *Law of Contract* (7th Edn.) 486–495.
4. See above, p. 114.
5. E.g. *Trans Trust S.P.R.L.* v. *Danubian Trading Co., Ltd.*, [1952] 2 Q.B. 297; [1952] 1 All E.R. 970, C.A.: set out below, p. 383.
6. E.g. s. 28 of the S.G.A.: set out above, p. 273.   7. See above, pp. 50–52.

The general rule of exact performance first raises the question of what amounts to an exact performance. Unless a contract of sale is divisible[8], performance of the various obligations laid upon a party to that contract must be viewed as a whole; but it has been said that in the case of a h.p. contract the obligations of the hiring and the option may sometimes be treated separately[9]. Subject to the foregoing, the common law takes an extremely strict view of contractual promises[10]; and it generally insists that performance must be exact, though allowing alternative stipulations as to performance[11]. However, this principle may work hardship where performance by A. is a condition precedent to performance by B. If A. has conferred a benefit on B. in partial performance of his obligations, its effect may be unjustly to enrich B.: A. cannot claim under the contract because he has not fully performed the condition; nor may he claim in quasi-contract where such a claim is inconsistent with the contract[12]. The injustice of this rule is most easily seen in the case of the so-called "entire contracts", where performance by A. of *all* his obligations is a condition precedent to the performance by B. of *any* of his obligations[13].

For these reasons, the common law has been driven to accept in some circumstances a lower standard than exact performance; and there are a number of circumstances where A. may sue B. for breach of contract notwithstanding his own non-performance.

(1) Where B. has wrongfully[14] prevented A. from completing performance.

(2) Where the contract provides for performance by B. before performance by A. as where there is a sale on credit terms from B. to A.[15]

(3) Where there are in fact a number of separate contracts, or where a single contract is divisible[16]. It has been pointed out that, in the latter context, it is more accurate to speak of divisible obligations rather than a divisible contract, for it is quite possible for one contract to contain both divisible and entire obligations[17]. The effect of deciding that a particular obligation is divisible is that A. may sue B. for breach of contract notwithstanding his own non-performance of the

---

8. See above, p. 277.
9. See Goode, *H.P. Law & Practice* (2nd Edn.) 328.
10. E.g. *Arcos, Ltd.* v. *Ronaasen & Son, Ltd.*, [1933] A.C. 470, H.L.: set out above, p. 71.
11. E.g. alternative places for delivery.
12. *Britain* v. *Rossiter* (1879), 11 Q.B.D. 123, C.A.; *Forman & Co., Pty., Ltd.* v. *S. S. Liddesdale*, [1900] A.C. 190, P.C.
13. E.g. *Cutter* v. *Powell* (1795), 6 Term Rep. 320.
14. *Contra* if B. is entitled to prevent A. performing, as where A. has already repudiated the contract—*British and Bennington, Ltd.* v. *Northwestern Casher Tea Co., Ltd.*, [1923] A.C. 48, H.L.: set out above, pp.266–267.
15. See above, p. 276.
16. See above, p. 277.
17. Treitel, *Law of Contract* (3rd Edn.) 681.

divisible obligation, but is liable to a counter-claim for damages for that non-performance.

(4) Where B. is only entitled to damages in respect of A.'s breach of contract[18]. In these circumstances, A. may sue B. for his non-performance, subject to a counter-claim for damages. The only real question is how to fit the doctrine of substantial performance into this scheme[19].

(5) Where A. has committed such a breach as would entitle B. to rescind, but B. elects merely to claim damages[20]. Alternatively, it may be possible in these circumstances to infer from B.'s acceptance of partial performance a fresh agreement, with payment to be made on a *quantum meruit* basis, from the fact that B. has received a benefit. This can only be done, however, where B. has the option to accept or reject the benefit conferred on him by the partial performance[1], and will not necessarily be inferred even then[2].

2 Discharge by stipulated event

The contract may provide for the discharge of one or both parties on the happening of some event other than performance. For example, a sale or return transaction envisages that the transferee may not complete a contract of purchase, but may discharge his obligations by returning the goods[3]; and s. 48 (4) of the S.G.A. provides that a contract of sale is rescinded where the seller exercises an express power of resale[4]. However, it is in the context of h.p. agreements that it is most common to find stipulated events upon the happening of which one or both of the parties are to be discharged from some or all of their obligations; and this subject may be sub-divided according to whether or not there is a termination of the agreement by the transferee.

(a) Termination by the transferee

At common law, it was quite possible for a hirer under a h.p. agreement or a buyer under a conditional or credit sale agreement to be given the right to terminate or rescind the agreement at any time before all the instalments had been paid even where the owner or seller was not in breach of the agreement. However, it was only in h.p. that the law required that the transferee have a right to terminate without cause[5], so that it was hardly ever available in other cases. Even in the context of

---

18. See above, p. 50.
19. See Treitel, *Law of Contract* (3rd Edn.) 681–683; Cheshire & Fifoot, *Law of Contract* (7th Edn.) 491–492.
20. For voluntary and statutory elections, see below, pp. 362, 397.
 1. See e.g., s. 30 (1) of the S.G.A.: above, p. 77. Cf. *Forman & Co., Pty., Ltd. v. S. S. Liddesdale*, [1900] A.C. 190, P.C.
 2. E.g. where there is an "entire contract": see above, p. 352.
 3. See above, p. 176.
 4. Set out below, p. 365.   5. See above, p. 12.

h.p., the right to terminate was almost always subject to some restrictions: sometimes these were merely designed to ensure that the owner recovered the goods[6]; but at other times the restrictions were designed to ensure that the owner did not make a loss on the transaction[7], or to discourage the hirer from exercising his option to terminate[8], or even primarily to increase the hirer's liability on a "snatch-back"[9]. However, the H.P. Acts have severely curtailed the owner's freedom of contract in this respect.

Where the transaction falls within the ambit of the H.P.A., there are two provisions which may modify the position at common law. In the first place, whether the contract is one of h.p. or conditional sale or credit sale, s. 31 (2) enables the hirer or buyer to exercise any common law right to rescind by serving notice on "any person who conducted the antecedent negotiations"[10]. In the second place, s. 27 (1) grants an indefeasible[11] right to terminate in the following terms:

> "At any time before the final payment under a hire-purchase agreement or conditional sale agreement falls due, the hirer or buyer shall (subject to the next following subsection) be entitled to terminate the agreement by giving notice of termination in writing to any person entitled or authorised to receive the sums payable under the agreement".

The Act makes it clear that this statutory right to terminate is to be without prejudice to any right to terminate "otherwise than by virtue of this section" (s. 27 (4)); but rather curiously s. 27 (1) sets out a different test of the person to whom notice of termination may be given; and the Act further makes it clear that the two provisions do not overlap (s. 31 (3) (b)). The statutory right to terminate only lasts until the final payment "falls due"; and the effect of such a termination is to terminate the contract from when notice is given[12]. Section 28 restricts the financial liability of the hirer or buyer on the exercise of this statutory right[13], but s. 28 (4) provides that, where the hirer or buyer, having exercised his statutory right to terminate,

> "wrongfully retains possession of the goods, then, in any action brought by the owner or seller to recover possession of the goods from the hirer or buyer, the court, unless it is satisfied that having regard to the circumstances it would not be just and equitable to do

---

6. E.g. a requirement that the hirer give notice or return the goods to the owner.
7. See the "minimum payments clauses" discussed below, p. 392.
8. The transaction being viewed essentially as a secured loan of the price rather than a sale.
9. See above, p.28.   10. See above, p. 40.
11. Section 29 (2) (b): see above, p. 133.
12. Compare the effect of the exercise of a right of cancellation; see above, p. 44.   13. See below, pp. 394–395.

so, shall order the goods to be delivered to the owner or seller without giving the hirer or buyer an option to pay the value of the goods".

This provision may be compared with the powers which a court will ordinarily have to order specific delivery in an action of detinue[14] or under s. 35 (4) where there are "protected goods"[15].

So far as h.p. agreements are concerned, the effect of s. 27 is to nullify any attempt to restrict the right of the hirer to terminate the agreement; but, in the case of conditional sales, the section creates a right to terminate without cause which is entirely new, thus partially assimilating h.p. and conditional sale agreements. However, the new right of the buyer under a conditional sale to terminate without cause is a limited one, for s. 27 (2) provides that

"In the case of a conditional sale agreement, where the property in the goods, having become vested in the buyer, is transferred to a person who does not become the buyer under the agreement, the buyer shall not thereafter be entitled to terminate the agreement under this section".

Thus, a person who stands in the shoes of the conditional buyer by reason of assignment or operation of law may enjoy the statutory right to terminate; but no other third party who obtains the property in the goods may do so. Where the statutory right to terminate is exercised by a conditional buyer after the property in the goods has passed to him, s. 27 (3) provides that the property in the goods shall revest in

"the person[16] . . . in whom it was vested immediately before it became vested in the buyer . . ."

(b) *Termination by other stipulated event*

In order to protect the interests of the owner, a h.p. agreement will commonly stipulate a number of events that will either terminate the agreement or render it terminable. Examples are death, insolvency or levying of distress against the hirer, or any attempt on his part to assign his rights[17]. Furthermore, to avoid any dispute as to whether the common law would allow the owner to rescind in the following cases, the agreement will usually expressly so provide in the case of (a) any material inaccuracy in the proposal form[18], (b) arrears in the payment of any instalments, and (c) any other breach of the agreement[19]. The

---

14. See above, pp. 333–334.
15. See above, p. 340.
16. Section 27 (3) terms him the "previous owner"; and provides that this expression shall include his assignees by operation of law.
17. See above, pp. 9–13.
18. But see *Lowe* v. *Lombank, Ltd.*, [1960] 1 All E.R. 611, C.A.: set out above, pp. 139–140.
19. See below, p. 360.

insertion of an enormous variety of such stipulated events is, of course, part of the technique of the "snatch-back"[20].

To some extent, the H.P. Acts have alleviated the position of the hirer: this has been achieved largely by restricting the power of the owner to repossess[1]; but in one case the Acts have completely struck out a common stipulated event, namely, the death of the hirer[2]. Moreover, the common law will, in any case, insist that such stipulations be read *contra proferentem*[3]. Nevertheless there is still a considerable scope for the operation of such clauses, and their effect must now be considered.

First, a distinction must be drawn between provisions effecting automatic termination on the happening of a stipulated event, and those merely giving the owner the right to terminate[4]. Automatic termination happens *ipso facto* on the occurrence of the stipulated event, whereas, if the agreement is merely terminable, it will not terminate unless and until the owner so elects[5]. Moreover, a terminable agreement will commonly impose some condition precedent to termination, for example, that the owner gives notice to the hirer: if it does so, there will be no termination until notice is given[6]; but, if it does not so stipulate, the owner is not obliged to give notice[7]. Second, whilst the phrase "termination of the agreement" has so far been used, it is necessary to distinguish between termination of the hiring and termination of the agreement, as it is possible to terminate the hiring without terminating the agreement for all purposes[8].

1. Termination of the hiring. At common law, the bailment will be determined by any act of the bailee inconsistent with the terms of the agreement, such as a sale or a pledge of the goods; but in practice it is normal for the agreement to make specific provision about this matter. The question of whether the hiring is terminated automatically or merely terminable[9] may be important for the following reasons: first, whether the owner is entitled to immediate possession of the goods[10]; second, whether the goods are "in the possession, order or disposition"

---

20. See above, p. 28.
2. See above, pp. 342–344.
4. It may be difficult to distinguish between the two, e.g. *Jay's Furnishing Co.* v. *Brand & Co.*, [1915] 1 K.B. 458, C.A.: see Goode, *H.P. Law & Practice* (2nd Edn.) 326.
5. See below, pp. 362–363.
6. *Reliance Car Facilities, Ltd.* v. *Roding Motors*, [1952] 2 Q.B. 844; [1952] 1 All E.R. 1355, C.A.
7. *North Central Wagon Co., Ltd.* v. *Graham*, [1950] 2 K.B. 7, C.A.; *Moorgate Mercantile, Ltd.* v. *Finch and Read*, [1962] 1 Q.B. 701; [1962] 2 All E.R. 467, C.A.
8. This distinction may not be all that important in practice: see Goode, *op. cit.*, pp. 339–341.
9. This is a matter of interpretation: see Guest, *Law of H.P.* 477–478.
10. See the cases cited in notes 6 and 7 above.

1. See above, p. 336. *et seq.*
3. See above, p. 138, *et seq.*

of the hirer for the purposes of the reputed ownership doctrine in bankruptcy and distress[11]; and third, whether the hirer can create a lien, such as a repairer's lien, over the goods[12].

2. *Termination of the agreement.* This will necessarily also terminate the hiring; but, unless the agreement manifests a contrary intention, it will not discharge either party from any obligations which have already accrued under the agreement. Once again, it may be important to know whether the specified event automatically terminates the agreement or merely renders it terminable: first, because of its effect on the hiring, and those considerations turning upon that matter; second, whether the hirer has any proprietary interest which he can, if the agreement so permits, assign to a third party[13], or which can be seized in execution[14] or fall into his bankruptcy[15]; and third, whether the goods are still "comprised in any hire-purchase agreement" for the purposes of the law of distress[16].

2 OTHER TYPES OF DISCHARGE

A party may be discharged from his contractual obligations otherwise than in accordance with the terms of the contract by (1) rescission of the contract or (2) a subsequent act or event.

1 Discharge by rescission

A contract may be rescinded[17] on the grounds of (a) a misrepresentation or (b) a breach by the other party.

(a) *Rescission for misrepresentation*

Wherever a party is induced to enter into a contract by a material misrepresentation, whether innocent or fraudulent, *prima facie* he has a right to rescind, though the contract will continue in force until he so elects. This election may be made in court, either by asking the court to declare the contract rescinded[18], or by setting up rescission as a defence to a claim for specific performance[19]; or it may be made at some earlier date, as by avoidance of a voidable contract[20]. Where the misrepresentation was fraudulent, the effect of rescission at common law was to avoid the contract *ab initio*[1]; and, whilst the common law

---

11. See above, pp. 10–12.   12. See above, p. 13.
13. See above, pp. 12–13.   14. See above, p. 9.
15. See above, pp. 10–11.   16. See above, pp. 11–12.
17. Does "rescission" refer to (a) the act of the party recognised by the court; or (b) the act of the court; or (c) either?
18. See below, pp. 362–363.
19. See below, pp. 428–429.   20. See below, p. 200.
 1. *Per* Lord ATKINSON in *Abram Steamship Co. Ltd.,* v. *Westville Steamship Co.,* [1923] A.C. 773, H.L., at p. 781.

would not allow rescission for innocent misrepresentation[2], equity recognised a *prima facie* right to rescind *ab initio*. Under the Misrepresentation Act 1967, the court has power to award damages in lieu of the rescission claimed where the misrepresentation is made "otherwise than fraudulently" (s. 2 (2))[3].

Even assuming there is a *prima facie* right to rescind on grounds of innocent or fraudulent misrepresentation, there are a number of ways in which that right may be lost[4].

1. "Restitutio in integrum" impossible. The common law took the strict view that there could be no rescission for misrepresentation unless there could be a complete handing back and taking back of benefits transferred under the contract; and it is for this reason that rescission was barred at common law where the representor had transferred a benefit gained under the contract to a b.f.p.[5] Whilst equity recognised the overriding claims of the b.f.p., it took a rather more realistic view of the situation: in the case of fraud, the victim did not have to make restitution in so far as this was impossible by reason of the fraud; and, in the case of innocent misrepresentation, equity was prepared, within reason, to accept substantial restitution and a financial allowance for depreciation of the subject-matter[6].

2. Affirmation. If the representee, with knowledge of the misrepresentation[7], elects to affirm the contract, his election is determined forever[8]. For instance, in *Long* v. *Lloyd*[9] the court held that the buyer had elected to affirm in accepting the seller's offer to pay half the cost of making good the defect.

3. Lapse of time. In one case, MELLOR J. said[10]:

> "lapse of time without rescinding will furnish evidence that [the representee] has determined to affirm the contract; and when the lapse of time is great, it probably would in practice be treated as conclusive evidence to shew that he has so determined".

In *Leaf* v. *International Galleries*[11],

---

2. *Kennedy* v. *Panama Royal Mail Co.* (1867), L.R. 2 Q.B. 580.
3. Set out above, p. 122.
4. At one time, it was thought that the right to rescind for misrepresentation had not survived the S.G.A.; but it is now clear that it has done so: see Howard (1963), 27 M.L.R. 272, 282–285.   5. See above, p. 199.
6. *Per* BOWEN L.J. in *Newbigging* v. *Adam* (1886), 34 Ch.D. 582, C.A., at pp. 594–595; and *per* PEARCE L.J. in *Long* v. *Lloyd*, [1958] 2 All E.R. 402, C.A. at p. 407.
7. Or, perhaps, if he ought to have known: see Treitel, *Law of Contract* (3rd Edn.) 326.
8. *Per* MELLOR J. in *Clough* v. *London and North Western Rail. Co.* (1871), L.R. 7 Exch. 26, at p. 34.
9. [1958] 2 All E.R. 402, C.A.: set out below, p. 402.
10. In *Clough's Case* (above), at p. 35.
11. [1950] 2 K.B. 86; [1950] 1 All E.R. 693, C.A. See further below, pp. 401, 403.

There was a misrepresentation that the painting sold was by Constable, and this became a term of the contract. Five years later the buyer discovered the truth, and immediately sought to rescind for misrepresentation. The Court of Appeal held that, even if there were a right to rescind, it was barred by lapse of time.

It would seem from this case that, where there is an innocent misrepresentation, time *prima facie* begins to run from the date the contract is executed[12]; but it has been suggested that in the case of fraud time only runs from the date of discovery[13].

At common law, there were two further possible bars to rescission; but these have now been removed by s. I of the Misrepresentation Act 1967, which provides that

> "Where a person has entered into a contract after a misrepresentation has been made to him, and—
> (a) the misrepresentation has become a term of the contract; or
> (b) the contract has been performed;
> or both, then, if otherwise he would be entitled to rescind the contract without alleging fraud, he shall be so entitled, subject to the provisions of this Act, notwithstanding the matters mentioned in paragraphs (a) and (b) of this section".

Paragraph (a). This resolves a conflict as to the effect of the incorporation in a contract of an innocent misrepresentation made before contract. Two situations are possible:

(1) The misrepresentee acquires the right to rescind for breach of contract. Two questions arise: first, does rescission for breach of contract have the same effect as rescission for misrepresentation[14]; and second, is the right to rescind for misrepresentation lost when the right to rescind for breach of contract is lost[15]?

(2) The misrepresentee only acquires a right to damages for breach of contract. Section I appears to grant him a right to rescind for misrepresentation[16]. But, can the representee also claim damages for breach of contract[17]?

Paragraph (b). This replaces the so-called rule in *Seddon* v. *North East Salt Co., Ltd.*[18]; and instead of that rigid rule the court now has a discretion to award damages in lieu of rescission "if it would be just and equitable to do so"[19].

---

12. But see below, p. 402.
13. Treitel, *Law of Contract* (3rd Edn.) 327.
14. See below, p. 361.
15. See below, pp. 403–404.   16. See below, p. 404.
17. As rescission operates *ab initio*, is there any contract left on which he can sue?
18. [1905] I Ch. 326: see Howard (1963), 23 M.L.R. 272.
19. Section 2 (2) of the Misrepresentation Act 1967: set out above, p. 122.

(b) Rescission for breach of contract

B. may be entitled to rescind a contract on the grounds of breach by A. where A. without lawful excuse[20] either performs his side of the bargain defectively or altogether repudiates his obligations under the contract.

1. Defective performance[1]. Whilst not every defective performance by A. will justify B. in refusing to continue with the contract, it will do so in the following circumstances: where there is a breach of an essential stipulation, or a breach which deprives B. of substantially the whole benefit of the contract[2]; or where the contract expressly entitles B. to refuse to continue if A. commits *any* breach of contract[3]; or where performance by A. is a condition precedent to performance by B.[4].

2. Repudiation. Any unequivocal refusal by A. to perform a contractual obligation[5] may amount to a repudiation[6], though it has been said that repudiation "is a serious matter and not to be lightly inferred"[7]. The repudiation may be express[8]; or it may be implied, as where A. incapacitates himself from performing his contractual obligations[9], or completely fails to perform his side of the bargain. Obviously, A. may repudiate at the time when performance is due; but the common law has accepted that A. may repudiate before that time, in which case there is what is termed an "anticipatory breach"[10].

Whilst it is easy to draw the above distinctions in theory, it may be difficult to apply them in practice. This is particularly the case in h.p. transactions, where an intimation by the hirer that he no longer intends to proceed with the transaction might amount to any of the following: (1) a notice of cancellation[11]; or (2) a notice exercising his option to terminate[12]; or (3) a breach of contract or repudiation.

Assuming that B. is entitled to rescind on the grounds of breach or repudiation by A., this does not automatically bring the contract to an end[13], except possibly where further performance is impossible by reason of the breach[14]: it is thought that the general rule is that B.

---

20. E.g. frustration: see above, p. 250.
1. This should be distinguished from repudiation: *per* Lord DENNING M. R. in *Harbutt's Plasticine, Ltd.* v. *Wayne Tank, Ltd.*, [1970] 1 Q.B. 447, C.A., at p. 464.
2. See above, p. 51.   3. See e.g. above, p. 355.
4. See above, p. 351.   5. Even a breach of warranty?
6. *Per* Lord COLERIDGE C. J. in *Freeth* v. *Burr* (1874), L.R. 9 C.P. 208, at p. 213: for the difficulty this has caused with instalment contracts, see above, pp. 277–279.
7. *Per* Lord WRIGHT in *Ross T. Smyth & Co., Ltd.* v. *Bailey, Son & Co.*, [1940] 3 All E.R. 60 H.L., at p. 71.
8. E.g. *Overstone, Ltd.* v. *Shipway*, [1962] 1 All E.R. 52, C.A.
9. As by reselling; but see the difficulties with h.p. above, pp. 12–13.
10. The terminology has been criticised by Lord WRENBURY in *Bradley* v. *Newsom, Sons & Co.*, [1919] A.C. 16 H.L., at pp. 53–54.
11. See above, p. 44.   12. See above, pp. 353–355.
13. *Heyman* v. *Darwins, Ltd.*, [1942] A.C. 356, [1942] 1 All E.R. 337, H.L.
14. *Harbutt's Plasticine, Ltd.* v. *Wayne Tank, Ltd.*, [1970] 1 Q.B. 447; [1970] 1 All E.R. 225, C.A.: set out above, p. 144.

merely has an option to treat the contract as discharged, the contract remaining binding on both parties unless and until B. elects to rescind[15]. Nor is this option foreclosed by the duty to mitigate[16]. Thus, it would appear that it is open to B, to elect as to the following mutually exclusive[17] alternatives[18].

1. To treat the contract as discharged. If B. does elect to "avoid" or "rescind"[19] the contract[20], is the effect merely to discharge it *de futuro* from the moment of election; or does it have some retrospective effect? The common law would appear to take the former view[1]; but this view would appear to cause certain difficulties. First, it has been said to follow from this view that the common law does not require *restitutio in integrum* to be possible before B. can take this course[2]; and certainly it is by no means clear that any part-payment must be returned[3]. Second, whilst it is clear that B. is entitled to damages in respect of breaches occurring before discharge, there has been some disagreement as to whether an owner is entitled to damages in respect of subsequent rentals[4]. Third, if rescission for breach only operates *de futuro*, then B.'s right to rescind for mere misrepresentation is greater than his right to rescind for breach of contractual promise; and, furthermore, s. 1 (a) of the Misrepresentation Act 1967 would materially extend B.'s remedies[5].

2. Not to treat the contract as discharged. If B. elects to keep the contract alive, then it continues binding on both parties, unless, perhaps, there is a "continuing breach"[6]: each must perform his side of the contract, but B. may claim damages for breach. In the case of an anticipatory breach, that election may operate to the advantage of either side in respect of subsequent impossibility[7] or the measure of damages[8].

---

15. *Per* Diplock L. J. in *Ward, Ltd.* v. *Bignall*, [1967] 1 Q.B. 534; C.A. at p. 548.
16. *Tredegar Iron Co., Ltd.* v. *Hawthorn Brothers & Co.* (1902), 18 T.L.R. 716, C.A. See further below, p. 391.
17. *Per* Diplock L.J. in *Ward, Ltd.* v. *Bignall*, (above), at p. 550.
18. The question of how A. elects is considered above, pp. 200–201.
19. Perhaps it might have been better had the expression "rescission" been reserved to describe the remedy for misrepresentation.
20. It is irrelevant that B. gives the wrong reason if he has in fact a right to rescind: *The Mihalis Angelos*, [1970] 3 All E.R. 125, C.A.
 1. *Heyman* v. *Darwins, Ltd.*, [1942] A.C. 356; [1942] 1 All E.R. 337, H.L.; *Yeoman Credit, Ltd.* v. *Apps*, [1962] 2 Q.B. 508; [1961] 2 All E.R. 281, C.A.: set out above, pp. 141–142. And see Coote [1970] C.L.J 221.
 2. Cheshire & Fifoot, *Law of Contract* (7th Edn.) 540.
 3. See below, p. 373.
 4. See below, pp. 384–386.
 5. See above, p. 358.
 6. *Yeoman Credit, Ltd.* v. *Apps*, (above).
 7. E.g. *Avery* v. *Bowden* (1855), 5 E. & B. 714. See generally above, p. 254, *et seq.*
 8. E.g. *Roper* v. *Johnson* (1873), L.R. & C.P. 167. See generally below. p. 411.

2 Discharge by subsequent act or event

Leaving aside discharge by breach, there are certain other acts or events occurring subsequent to the formation of the contract and irrespective of the terms of that contract which may bring about its discharge.

1. Subsequent agreement. On ordinary principles, any duty created by one contract may be discharged by another contract; and there may therefore be a total or partial discharge of liability.

(1) Total discharge. Where the parties expressly agree that each shall be totally discharged from his contractual liability, this may be seen almost as a mutual repudiation; but a total repudiation may also be brought about impliedly, as where the parties abandon the contract[9]. If the first contract is executory on both sides at the time of the subsequent agreement, it generates its own consideration[10]; but, if the contract is executory on one side only, it will usually[11] be necessary for the party on that side to give some fresh consideration for his release, in which event it is usually termed an "accord and satisfaction"[12]. One form of total discharge which requires special mention is that where the original contract is replaced by an entirely new one, as where the subject-matter of the original contract is "traded-in" in part-exchange[13], or taken with subsequent goods under a fresh "linked-on" agreement[14].

(2) Partial discharge. The terms of the original contract may be varied by contract or by mere waiver[15]. Whether there has been a contractual variation or total discharge and subsequent agreement is a question of intention[16].

2. Election of remedies. Where a man is entitled to one of two inconsistent rights, any unequivocal act of election to pursue one of them made by him with knowledge of his rights will amount to a binding waiver[17], as where an owner under a h.p. agreement accepts hire-rent after breach[18], or a seller exercises a licence to seize under a conditional sale[19]. Normally, however, it is not a question of choosing between two inconsistent rights, but merely of electing between two alternative remedies, in which case the election is not *per se* irrevocable; but a

---

9. E.g. *Pearl Mill, Ltd.* v. *Ivy Tanneries, Ltd.*, [1919] 1 K.B. 78, D.C.
10. E.g. *Pearl Mill, Ltd.* v. *Ivy Tanneries, Ltd.* (above).
11. But see s. 62 of the Bills of Exchange Act 1882, and the suggestion in Treitel, *Law of Contract* (3rd Edn.) 88.
12. See generally, Treitel, *op. cit.*, 86–88 Cheshire & Fifoot, *Law of Contract* (7th Edn.) 497, 503–506; Guest, *Law of H.P.* 462; Goode, *H.P. Law & Practice* (2nd Edn.) 329–330.
13. See above, p. 271.   14. See above, p. 28.
15. See above, p. 145. *et seq.*
16. See Guest, *Law of H.P.* 462.
17. For a discussion of the use of the term "waiver" in this context, see Spencer Bower, *Estoppel* (2nd Edn.) 295.
18. See below, p. 375.
19. *Hewison* v. *Ricketts* (1894), 63 L.J.Q.B. 711, D.C.: set out below, p. 372.

party will be so bound by a final judgment of a court of competent jurisdiction, whether or not that judgment is satisfied[20].

3. Judgment. Final judgment in any suit has the effect of merging the original cause of action in the judgment, and the plaintiff must rely on the rights created by the judgment[1]. Judgment alone will normally extinguish any alternative claim against that defendant[2], but it will not affect claims against him which are cumulative, such as the right of an owner under a h.p. agreement to arrears of rentals and damages for breach[3]. Nor will judgment alone discharge the claim upon which that judgment is obtained, though satisfaction of the judgment will do so: for instance, a judgment in detinue for the value of the goods, or in conversion for damages amounting to their value, will vest the plaintiff's title in the defendant if satisfied[4], but not if it remains unsatisfied[5].

4. Repossession. The recaption of "protected goods" contrary to Part III of the H.P.A. 1965 terminates the agreement, and releases the hirer or buyer from all liability thereunder[6].

---

20. See Winfield *Tort* (8th Edn.) 778–779; Street *Torts* (4th Edn.) 460–461.
1. See the authorities cited in note 20 above.
2. What of claims against third parties? Compare the two authorities cited in note 20 above.
3. See below, p. 374.
4. *U.S.A.* v. *Dollfus Mieg*, [1952] A.C. 582; [1952] 1 All E.R. 572, H.L.
5. *Ellis* v. *John Stenning & Son*, [1932] 2 Ch. 81.
6. See above, pp. 338–339.

CHAPTER 20

Remedies of the Owner or Seller

Before considering the substantive rules relating to the remedies available to the owner or seller, a brief mention should be made of the procedures of enforcement, because the latter frequently have a considerable bearing on the efficacy of the former. Such matters have recently been considered in the Report of the Payne Committee on the *Enforcement of Judgment Debts*[1]. This reports recommends, *inter alia*[2], that debtors should be protected from unfair practices[3] and harsh contractual provisions[4], but that assignment of debts cannot be satisfactorily controlled by law for this purpose; that in appropriate cases debtors should be restrained by court order from incurring further credit, and creditors deterred from granting it by the postponement of their debt to other creditors[5]; that the court should have power to determine a debtor's instalment credit agreements[6]; that recovery of debts from a multiple debtor should be undertaken jointly by an Enforcement Office administering all methods of enforcement; that attachment of earnings should be introduced, imprisonment for debt abolished, and execution and recaption restricted; that a court should have power to suspend an order for the delivery of goods supplied under a h.p. conditional sale or simple hiring agreement[7], and to grant relief against forfeiture[8]; that all money recovered from a debtor should be channelled through, and distributed rateably by, the Enforcement Office amongst all creditors according to the same priority as on bankruptcy[9]; and that the Office should have an advisory service to help debtors meet their obligations.

Some of these recommendations have been enacted in the Administration of Justice Act 1970[10], though only the provisions in relation to the unlawful harassment of debtors are presently in force (s. 40)[11]. The major recommendations enacted are to be found in Part II of the

1. (1969), Cmnd. 3909.
2. See paras. 38–44, 78.
3. See e.g. "the unreasonable harassment of debtors": paras. 1230–1244.
4. Compare above, pp. 28, 132.
5. For present pre-contract enquiries, see above, pp. 34–35.
6. Compare s. 27 of the H.P.A.: above, p. 354.
7. Compare above, p. 340. 8. See below, p. 374.
9. To displace the present harsh "first-come-first-served" principle: see paras. 304, 1137.
10. See generally Borrie and Pyke (1970), 120 N.L.J. 540, 564, 588.
11. See above, p. 331.

1970 Act: it severely restricts the power to imprison for debt; it introduces an elaborate system of attachment of earnings in respect of judgment debts[12]; and it suspends all other methods of judicial execution upon the making of an attachment order[13]. Unfortunately, in introducing this new system for the enforcement of judgment debts the 1970 Act ignores the one recommendation which the *Payne Report* regarded as central to its implementation, namely, the setting up of a system of Enforcement Offices[14].

I REMEDIES OF THE OWNER OR SELLER AGAINST THE GOODS

This section will deal with the remedies against the goods which are available to the owner or seller in the event of default by his hirer or buyer.

1 Remedies of a seller

It has already been pointed out that the S.G.A. fails to draw a clear distinction between the power of sale and the right to resell[15]; that is, between the effect of resale on (a) the original contract of sale and (b) the title to the goods resold.

(a) The original contract of sale

A "resale" by the seller will not be a breach of the original contract of sale in any of the following circumstances[16].

1. The goods are not ascertained. The very expression "resale" presupposes that the goods "resold" have become the subject-matter of the prior contract of sale so that the buyer has a contractual right to those goods, or to an as yet unascertained part of them.

2. Discharge of the seller. Even if the goods "resold" were specific or ascertained in relation to the original contract of sale, the seller is entitled to resell if the original contract or the obligation to deliver those particular goods is discharged[17]. One instance of this receives special mention in s. 48 (4), which provides that

> "Where the seller expressly reserves the right of resale in case the buyer should make default, and on the buyer making default, re-sells the goods, the original contract of sale is thereby rescinded, but without prejudice to any claim the seller may have for damages."

---

12. It only applies where there is a judgment debt. See further above, p. 345.
13. But not recaption. See further above, p. 330.
14. See paras. 329 and 442. And also Borrie and Pyke, *op. cit.*, at p. 566.
15. See above, pp. 315–317.
16. No comment on the passing of property is intended by the use of the term "resale" in this context.
17. See Chapter 19.

A typical example here is a provision for resale on default in payment; but other types of default may also be stipulated[18].

3. The statutory right of resale.   As the time for payment of the price is *prima facie* not of the essence[19], the unpaid seller may be in a quandary as to what to do with the goods; and s. 48 (3) therefore makes time of the essence in the circumstances there stated.   Section 48 (3) lays down that

> "Where the goods are of a perishable nature, or where the unpaid seller gives notice to the buyer of his intention to re-sell, and the buyer does not within a reasonable time pay or tender the price, the unpaid seller may re-sell the goods and recover from the original buyer damages for any loss occasioned by his breach of contract".

Two situations are mentioned.

(1) The goods are of "a perishable nature"[20].   Where the price for goods of this type is not forthcoming within a reasonable time[1], s. 48 (3) allows the seller to resell; but it should be remembered that he may also have a right to resell under the doctrine of agency of necessity[2], or that it may be possible to persuade the court to exercise its discretion to order a sale[3].

(2) The seller gives notice.   Whatever the types of goods, s. 48 (3) allows the seller to resell if the price is not paid or tendered within a reasonable time of receipt of that notice[4].   As will be seen later[5], the wording of s. 48 (3) is unfortunate; but presumably, at very least, its effect must be to prevent the resale from being a breach of the original contract of sale, as it envisages that he may still sue the buyer for non-acceptance.

It is necessary to consider the effect on the original contract of sale of the exercise by the unpaid seller of his real rights.

1. Lien or stoppage.   Section 48 (1) provides that

> "Subject to the provisions of this section, a contract of sale is not rescinded by the mere exercise by an unpaid seller of his rights of lien . . . or stoppage in transitu".

It has been suggested that the object of this subsection was to protect the unpaid seller where time of delivery was of the essence[6]; but it actually only states the obvious fact that such action by a seller does not,

---

18. *Per* Diplock L.J. in *Ward, Ltd.* v. *Bignall*, [1967] 1 Q.B. 534, C.A., at p. 550.
19. Section 10 (1): set out above, p. 275.
20. The expression "perish" in the S.G.A. was considered above, pp. 253–254.
 1. This is a question of fact: s. 56.   See *per* Finnemore J. in *Gallagher* v. *Shilcock*, [1949] 2 K.B. 765, at p. 770.
 2. See above, p. 185.   3. See above, p. 240.
 4. See *Benjamin on Sale* (8th Edn.) 947.
 5. See below, p. 368.
 6. *Per* Diplock L.J. in *Ward, Ltd.* v. *Bignall* (above).

without more, demonstrate an unequivocal intention to repudiate the contract[7].

2. *Resale.* *Prima facie*, a seller with a right to rescind for breach by his buyer has the following alternatives. First, he may elect to rescind the contract, in which case the property in the goods will, if it has already passed, revest in him; and he may then resell the goods as his own, and sue the buyer for damages for non-acceptance[8]. Secondly, he may affirm the contract, in which case the property will pass under the terms of the contract to the buyer, whom he may sue for damages for non-acceptance[8], and for the balance of the purchase-price[9], meanwhile exercising his unpaid seller's lien until judgment is satisfied[10]. Does a resale by the seller show an intention to rescind or affirm? The question is important because, if the resale were an affirmation of the first sale, any resale would have to be made on behalf of the first buyer.

It is clear that, once the goods have been delivered to the first buyer and the property has passed to him, the seizure and resale can have no effect on the first sale because it is executed, the resale being merely tortious[11]; and in 1949 the court took the same view with regard to a resale by an unpaid seller who had remained in possession after property had passed. In *Gallagher* v. *Shilcock*[12]

> The plaintiff agreed to buy a motor boat from the defendant for £665 and paid a £200 deposit. Although the property in the goods subsequently passed to him, the buyer failed to pay the balance of the price. Having given the buyer due notice, the seller resold the boat for £700; and the plaintiff claimed the return of the deposit. FINNEMORE J. held that the resale did not rescind the contract; and that the defendent was therefore bound to account for any profit and, *a fortiori*, to return the deposit.

However, the Court of Appeal unanimously took the opposite view of a resale in *Ward, Ltd.* v. *Bignall*[13].

> The defendant contracted to buy two motor vehicles for a total purchase price of £850, and paid a £25 deposit; but he later wrongfully refused to take delivery. After giving due notice, the plaintiff seller attempted to resell the vehicles: he only succeeded in reselling one, for which he obtained £350; and sued the defendant for £497-10s[14], being the balance of the purchase price (i.e. £825) less

---

7. See above, p. 360.
8. Damages for non-acceptance are considered below, p. 376, *et seq.*
9. A claim for the price is considered below, pp. 370–374.
10. *Per* DIPLOCK L.J., in *Ward, Ltd.* v. *Bignall* (above), at p. 547.
11. See *Stephens* v. *Wilkinson* (1831), 2 B. & Ad. 320; *Page* v. *Cowasjee Eduljee* (1866), L.R. 1 P.C. 127.
12. [1949] 2 K.B. 765; [1949] 1 All E.R. 921.
13. [1967] 1 Q.B. 534; [1967] 2 All. E.R. 449, C.A.
14. This was assumed by the C.A. to be for damages for non-acceptance.

the £350, plus the expenses of attempting resale, £22-10s. At first instance, the plaintiff was awarded the sum claimed; but the Court of Appeal deducted from the award the market value of the unsold car which the plaintiff still retained (£450), and reduced the award to £47-10s.

The difference between the attitude of the two courts lay in the inference to be drawn from the fact that s. 48 (4) expressly states that the contract is rescinded by resale, whereas s. 48 (3) is silent on this point: in the earlier case, FINNEMORE J. deduced that resale under s. 48 (3) was therefore not intended to rescind the original contract of sale; but in the later case the Court of Appeal took the view that rescission was expressly referred to in s. 48 (4) to remove any doubt, and to bring it into line with s. 48 (3), where on ordinary principles resale would rescind the first contract. At the same time, DIPLOCK L.J. in *Ward, Ltd.* v. *Bignall* pointed out that, if the seller had affirmed and sued for the balance of the purchase price, the first instance award in the case before him would have been correct[15]. The moral for an unpaid seller considering resale would appear to be as follows[16]: leaving aside the question of any deposit[17], he should rescind and resell if he can thereby obtain a better price[18]; but he should affirm the contract if he cannot do better elsewhere[19].

Finally, it should be pointed out that there appears to be no legal obligation on the seller as to the manner in which he exercises any right to resell, nor as to the price which he accepts. The only restraining factor would appear to be that, if he also seeks damages, he is under a duty to mitigate his loss[20].

(b) *The title to the goods*

In discussing the effect of a resale by the seller on the title to the goods, it is convenient to distinguish according to whether or not the seller has ever delivered the goods to the first buyer.

1. Before delivery. Where the resale by the seller before delivery does not amount to a breach of the first contract of sale, the seller can pass the property in the goods to the second buyer, either because the property never passed to the first buyer or because it revested in him on resale. However, where the resale is a breach of the first contract of sale, it does not revest the property in the seller; and therefore he can only pass a good title to the second buyer, either because he has retained

---

15. At p. 547.
16. And see *per* TURNER J. in *Commission Car Sales, Ltd.* v. *Saul*, [1957] N.Z.L.R. 144, at p. 146 (resale by seller after delivery and subsequent repudiation by buyer).
17. See below, pp. 372–374.
18. E.g. *Gallagher* v. *Shilcock*, [1949] 2 K.B. 765; [1949] 1 All E.R. 921.
19. E.g. *Ward, Ltd.* v. *Bignall*, [1967] 1 Q.B. 534; [1967] 2 All E.R. 449, C.A.
20. See below, pp. 390–391.

the property in the goods, or under one of the following exceptions to the *nemo dat* rule:

(1) Sales by a seller in possession[1].

(2) Section 48 (2), which provides that

> "Where an unpaid seller who has exercised his right of lien . . . or stoppage in transitu resells the goods, the buyer acquires a good title thereto as against the original buyer".

Section 48 (2) differs from the other provisions in certain important respects in that the latter: (1) require a delivery or transfer to the second buyer; (2) do not require that the original buyer be in default; and (3) insist that the second buyer act *bona fide* and without notice of the first sale. The right of the first buyer to sue the second buyer in conversion or detinue will, of course, depend on whether the latter has acquired a good title; and he can sue the seller for non-delivery if the resale were a breach of contract[2], or in conversion or detinue where he had a right to immediate possession[3].

2. After delivery. Once the goods have been delivered to the first buyer, the seller can only pass a good title to the second buyer where he has either retained the property in the goods[4], or it has revested in him[5]: a mere bargain and sale neither changes property nor possession[6], nor does it rescind the first contract of sale[7]. Nor should the seller have any greater power to pass title where he merely seizes the goods after delivery to the first buyer[7], except where the resale be in market overt[8]. Thus, if the resale is a breach of the first contract of sale, the position is as follows: the seller does not commit conversion by reselling without delivery[9], though his seizure of the goods would be a trespass[10] and the resale an injurious falsehood; but if the seller resells and delivers to the second buyer the seller commits conversion[11], and the second buyer will do so unless he obtains a good title under one of the exceptions to the *nemo dat* rule[12].

---

1. See above, p. 215. *et seq.*   2. See below, p. 409. *et seq.*
3. See below, p. 377.   4. See s. 19: above, pp.181–182.
5. E.g. on repudiation by the buyer: *Commission Car Sales, Ltd.* v. *Saul*, [1957] N.Z.L.R. 144.
6. *Lancashire Waggon Co.* v. *Fitzhugh* (1861), 6 H. & N. 502.
7. *Stephens* v. *Wilkinson* (1831), 2 B. & Ad. 320.
8. See *Page* v. *Cowasjee Eduljee* (1866), L.R. 1 P.C. 127; and above, p. 236.
9. *Lancashire Waggon Co.* v. *Fitzhugh* (above).
10. If it is a conditional sale within the H.P.A., it may also be a breach of s. 34: see above, p. 337.
11. *Consolidated Co.* v. *Curtis & Son*, [1892] 1 Q.B. 495.
12. See Chapter 14 above.

2 The real remedies of an owner letting goods on h.p.

The ultimate security of any owner who lets goods on h.p. is to exercise his right of repossession[13], and then to sell the goods[14]. However, if the owner repossesses in breach of the h.p. agreement, this will amount to a repudiation at common law[15]; and the hirer can elect either to rescind and claim damages for breach of contract, or to affirm and seek damages for breach of contract or for conversion. Where the owner repossesses "protected goods" within the meaning of the H.P.A., the agreement is automatically terminated (s. 34 (2))[16].

2 PERSONAL REMEDIES OF THE OWNER OR SELLER

Besides any action for damages, the seller or owner may also be able to maintain an action against the buyer or hirer for the price or hire-rent.

1 Action for the price or rent

(a) *Action for the price of goods sold*

Prima facie, a breach by the buyer of his duty to pay the price[17] does not give rise to a right to rescind (s. 10 (1))[18]; and, in considering the right of an unpaid seller to recover the price, two points must be borne in mind: first, the additional leverage provided by the rights of stoppage and lien are lost on delivery[19]; and secondly, for historical reasons a sharp distinction is drawn according to whether the property in the goods has passed to the buyer. Perhaps unfortunately, the S.G.A. has preserved the common law position that, generally speaking, an action for the price is only maintainable where the property has passed; and that, if it has not passed, the seller is confined to an action for damages.

The situation where the property has passed is dealt with by s. 49 (1), which provides that:

> "Where, under a contract of sale, the property in the goods has passed to the buyer, and the buyer wrongfully neglects or refuses to pay for the goods according to the terms of the contract, the seller may maintain an action against him for the price of the goods".

Under s. 49 (1) an action for the price is only maintainable on certain conditions.

1. The property has passed to the buyer. Unless the case falls within s. 49 (2), no action for the price is possible before the passing of property, even where it is the buyer's fault that the property has not passed[20]. It

---

13. See above, p. 329.
14. The duty to mitigate may require that he sells at the best price obtainable: see below, pp. 390–391.　　　　15. See above, p. 330.
16. See above, p. 339. This provision may also apply where a seller repossesses goods sold under a conditional sale.　　　　17. See above, p. 271.
18. Set out above, p. 275.　　　　19. See above, pp. 322–323.
20. *Colley* v. *Overseas Exporters*, [1921] 3 K.B. 302.

has therefore been said that the principle in *White & Carter (Councils) Ltd.* v. *McGregor*[1] does not affect the law of sale, "since the seller cannot transfer the property to the buyer without the latter's consent"[2].

2. The buyer wrongfully neglects or refuses to pay the price. The duty to pay the price has already been examined[3]; and the most common cases where neglect or failure to pay the price is not wrongful are as follows: first, where payment and delivery are concurrent terms and the seller has not yet tendered delivery[4]; and secondly, where the goods have been delivered, but the sale is on credit terms[5].

The exceptional case where an action is maintainable for the price before the passing of property is embodied in s. 49 (2), which provides that:

> "Where, under a contract of sale, the price is payable on a day certain irrespective of delivery, and the buyer wrongfully neglects or refuses to pay such price, the seller may maintain an action for the price, although the property in the goods has not passed, and the goods have not been appropriated to the contract".

Once again the right of action is hedged about by restrictions: first, that the buyer wrongfully neglects or refuses to pay the price (see above); second, that the price is payable irrespective of delivery[6]; and, third that the price is payable on a day certain. With respect to this last requirement the question arises as to whether it should be interpreted literally, or whether that literal meaning can be extended by invoking the maxim *certum est quod certum reddi potest.* In *Workman Clark, Ltd* v. *Lloyd Brazileno*[7] the Court of Appeal were unanimously of the opinion that the wider meaning should be taken; but this view would appear to have been *obiter*, and it has been pointed out that, if it prevailed, the price would almost always be payable on "a day certain"[8]. However, a strict construction was put upon this requirement in *Shell Mex, Ltd.* v. *Elton Cop Dying Co., Ltd.*[9].

> There was a contract for the sale of 1,000 tons of oil to be delivered "as reasonably required" by the buyers in about equal monthly

---

1. [1962] A.C. 413, H.L. See below, p. 391, note 9.
2. Atiyah, *Sale of Goods* (3rd Edn.) 206, note 1. But suppose a contract for the sale of goods where the property passes immediately but delivery is postponed. Is it sufficient to bring the *McGregor* rule into operation that the seller can tender delivery? However, it may be that the doctrine of mitigation is not applicable to actions for an agreed sum: see below, p. 390, note 15a.
3. See above, pp. 271–272.
4. See s. 28: above, p. 273.   5. See above, p. 276.
6. *Stein, Forbes & Co.* v. *County Tailoring Co.* (1916), 86 L.J.K.B. 448, D.C.; *Colley* v. *Overseas Exporters*, [1921] 3 K.B. 302.
7. [1908] 1 K.B. 968, C.A. See esp. at pp. 977, 978, 981.
8. Atiyah, *Sale of Goods* (3rd Edn.) 206.
9. (1928), 34 Com. Cas. 39.

quantities from 23.6.1926 to 22.6.1927, payment to be made within 14 days of the delivery of each consignment. Clause 15 provided: "Sellers have the right at any time to invoice to buyers the due quantities of oil not taken up, and to demand payment of the invoice amounts . . ." The buyers failed to take delivery of the last 466 tons; and, after 22.6.1927, the buyers sued for the price thereof relying on clause 15. The claim failed, WRIGHT J. holding that the price was not due because the property had not passed and the contract did not make provision for payment "on a day certain".

Whilst his Lordship was prepared to read into s. 49 (2) that "the price is payable *by instalments* on days certain"[10], he was not willing to interpret it so that "the price is payable *by* a day certain".

Where the *prima facie* rule is displaced, and non-payment of the price does show an intention on the part of the buyer to repudiate the contract, the seller must elect between two mutually exclusive alternatives[11]: he can affirm the contract and sue for the price under s. 49; or he can rescind, in which case he is entitled to the goods, but not the price. Thus, ordinarily the seller cannot have his cake and eat it too: he cannot have the goods and their price. For instance, in *Hewison* v. *Ricketts*[12]

> The buyer under a conditional sale defaulted, whereupon the seller seized the goods, but returned them when the defendant guaranteed payment of the outstanding instalments. On the buyer's further default, the seller again seized the goods, and then sued the defendant under his guarantee. The Court held that the seller could alternatively seize the goods or sue for the instalments; that in electing to seize the seller had therefore lost his right to the instalments; and that, as the principal debt was extinguished, so was the liability of the guarantor[13].

However, there is one instance where the seller may seek both to have his goods and the price; and that is where he recovers the goods and retains instalments of the price already paid[14]. There can be no question in this situation of applying the rules against penalties[15], because it is not the seller who is seeking to enforce payment of a prescribed sum, but the buyer who is endeavouring to recover a payment already made[16]. In 1842 the common law rejected an attempt by a defaulting buyer to recover a sum already paid on account of the price[17]; but there have

---

10. Approved by *Benjamin on Sale* (8th Edn.) 827.   11. See above, p. 361.
12. (1894), 63 L.J.Q.B. 711, D. C.   13. See above, p. 346.
14. See generally Goff & Jones, *Law of Restitution* 346–350; Treitel, *Law of Contract* (3rd Edn.) 825–828; Cheshire & Fifoot, *Law of Contract* (7th Edn.) 542–544; Mayne & McGregor, *Law of Damages* (12th Edn.) 254–259.
15. See below, pp. 391–395.
16. See *Pye* v. *British Automobile Commercial Syndicate, Ltd.*, [1906] 1 K.B. 425.
17. *Fitt* v. *Cassanet* (1842), 4 Man. & G. 898; and see *Cramer* v. *Giles* (1883), 1 Cab. & El. 151; affd. (1884), *Times*, May 9th. See also below, p. 407.

since been various attempts to avoid this unjust result. Thus, in *Dies* v. *British and International Mining and Finance Corporation, Ltd.*[18] STABLE J. drew a distinction between a deposit, which could be forfeited, and a part payment, which could not. This decision is not easy to reconcile with the 1842 case; and, more recently, attempts have been made to show that even a deposit may be recoverable in equity by the party in breach, on the grounds that, as the common law relieves against penalties *payable after breach*, equity should relieve against forfeiture of sums *already paid*. In *Stockloser* v. *Johnson*[19]

> The plaintiff agreed to buy plant and machinery under a contract which provided that the price was payable by instalments, and that if there was default for more than 28 days in payment of any instalment the seller could rescind, forfeit the instalments already paid, and re-possess the goods[20]. After the buyer's default, the seller exercised these rights; and the buyer sued for the return of the instalments paid. The Court of Appeal refused the buyer relief, whilst of the opinion that in appropriate circumstances relief might be given.

ROMER L.J. took a rather restricted view of where relief would be appropriate: he was prepared to give the defaulting buyer an opportunity (which the buyer did not want) to pay off the arrears; but added that[1]

> "no relief of any other nature can properly be given, in the absence of some special circumstances such as fraud, sharp practice or other unconscionable conduct of the vendor to a purchaser after the vendor has rescinded the contract".

However, the majority took a rather wider view; and DENNING L.J. said that two things were necessary before equitable relief would be granted[2]:

> "First, the forfeiture clause must be of a penal nature, in this sense, that the sum forfeited must be out of all proportion to the damage[3], and, secondly, it must be unconscionable for the seller to retain the money . . ."

Whilst the majority view may be desirable[4], it would appear that the weight of authority was on the side of ROMER L.J.[5]. Certainly, the

---

18. [1939] 1 K.B. 724. C. Salmond & Williams, *Contract* (2nd Edn.) 569, note (b) and Guest, *Law of H.P.* 596.
19. [1954] 1 Q.B. 476; [1954] 1 All E.R. 630, C.A. See Polack, [1965] C.L.J. 17; Crawford (1966), 44 Can.B.R. 142.
20. This was not a licence to seize within the Bills of Sale Acts because it was only to operate after rescission.
1. At p. 501.
2. At p. 490. See also SOMERVELL L.J. at pp. 485, 486–488
3. This first test is the same as that for penalties: see below, p. 394.
4. See Goff & Jones, *Law of Restitution* 349.
5. Goff & Jones, *op. cit.*, 348, note 36; Cheshire & Fifoot, *Law of Contract* (7th Edn.) 543.

narrower view has subsequently prevailed in *Galbraith* v. *Mitchenall Estates, Ltd.*[6]

> The plaintiff entered into a five year simple hiring agreement in respect of a caravan, mistakenly thinking that it was a h.p. agreement, and paid a deposit of £550. The plaintiff failed to pay any instalments, whereupon the owner repossessed the caravan, and resold it for £775. The plaintiff's claim for the return of the deposit was dismissed.

Notwithstanding that he thought the agreement "hideously harsh", SACHS J. preferred the view of ROMER L.J.; but he suggested that there should be statutory protection against repossession in such situations along the lines of that offered by the H.P.A.[7].

(b) Action for arrears of rentals.

If the hirer refuses to accept delivery, the hiring does not commence; so that the owner is not entitled to any hire-rent[8], but must sue for damages for non-acceptance[9]. On the other hand, once the hirer has taken possession under the h.p. agreement[10], the owner is entitled to any hire-rent which accrues due by reason of the period during which the hirer is in possession under the terms of the agreement[11]; but not for any rentals thereafter[12]. The action for arrears of rentals is an entirely separate one from the claim for damages for breach of contract[13].

Generally speaking, where the hirer is in arrears with his instalments of hire-rent the h.p. agreement will, at very least, be expressed to be terminable by the owner[14]. We have already seen that a seller with a right to rescind must elect either to rescind and take the goods or affirm and recover the price[15]; but h.p. is a species of bailment, so that the owner is entitled to the rentals and the goods at the end of the term: it does not matter whether he repossesses and then claims the arrears of rentals[16]; or *vice versa*[17]. In view of the price element in the

---

6. [1965] 2 Q.B. 473; [1964] 2 All E.R. 653. But see *per* PENNYCUICK J. in *Barton Thompson & Co., Ltd.* v. *Stapling Machines Co.*, [1966] Ch. 499, at p. 509; and also *San Pedro Compania Armadora S.A.* v. *Henry Navigation Co., Ltd.* [1970]1 Lloyd's Rep. 32.
7. At p. 659. See the Report on *Enforcement of Judgment Debts* (1969), Cmnd. 3909: see above, p. 364.
8. See above, p. 116.   9. See below, p. 376.
10. If no agreement is ever concluded, there is no liability to pay hire-rent: *Campbell Discount Co., Ltd.* v. *Gall*, [1961] 1 Q.B. 431; [1961] 2 All E.R. 104, C.A.: see above, p. 287. See also above, p. 37.
11. E.g. *Yeoman Credit, Ltd.* v. *Apps*, [1962] 2 Q.B. 508; [1961] 2 All E.R. 281, C.A.: see above, p. 142; *Charterhouse Credit, Ltd.* v. *Tolly*, [1963] 2 Q.B. 683; [1963] 2 All E.R. 432, C.A.: see above, p. 143.
12. *Belsize Motor Supply Co.* v. *Cox*, [1914] 1 K.B. 244.
13. *Overstone, Ltd.* v. *Shipway*, [1962] 1 All E.R. 52, C.A.
14. See above, p. 355.   15. See above, p. 372.
16. *Brooks* v. *Beirnstein*, [1909] 1 K.B. 98 D.C.; *Overstone, Ltd.* v. *Shipway* (above).
17. *South Bedfordshire Electrical Finance, Ltd.* v. *Bryant*, [1938] 3 All E.R. 580, C.A.

rentals, this therefore implies that the owner under a h.p. agreement can to some extent have his cake and eat it too. This element of "double recovery" may be avoided: first, the owner may affirm the contract with knowledge of the breach, in which case he loses the right to repossess[18]; and secondly, the owner may rescind and recover a judgment in conversion which is merely for the value of his interest in the goods[19], but if it is satisfied he will thereupon lose his title to the goods[20]. However, where the owner rescinds and, either recapts the goods[1], or obtains a judgment for their full value in conversion[19], there exists the potential element of "double recovery" which gave rise to the "snatch-back"[2]: the hirer is prevented by the legal fiction of h.p. from pleading either that the owner has made a double recovery in the legal sense[3], or that the sums are a part-payment of the price[4]; and the recent cases discourage any hope of equitable relief[5].

There is no general provision in the H.P.A. empowering the court to grant relief against forfeiture as such; but certain of the provisions of the Act will, where applicable, prevent the owner from having his cake and eating it too.

1. The right of cancellation. Where a hirer under a h.p. agreement or a buyer under a conditional or credit sale agreement exercises his statutory right of cancellation, the owner or seller may recover the goods, but the hirer or buyer is under no further liability and may recover any payments made (s. 14)[6].

2. The repossession of "protected goods". Where the owner or seller wrongfully repossesses "protected goods", the hirer or conditional buyer is released from all further liability and may recover all sums already paid (s. 34 (2))[7]; and, if he follows the procedure laid down by the Act, s. 41 provides that

> "After the owner has begun an action to which section 35 of this Act applies, he shall not take any step to enforce payment of any sum due under the agreement, or under any contract of guarantee relating to the agreement, except by claiming the sum in that action".

---

18. E.g. *Keith Prowse & Co.* v. *National Telephone Co., Ltd.,* [1894], 2 Ch. 147; *Reynolds* v. *General and Finance Facilities, Ltd.* (1963), 107 Sol. Jo. 889, C.A.
19. See below, p. 380.   20. See above, p. 363.
 1. See above, p. 330.
 2. See above, p. 28.
 3. See below, p. 386.
 4. *Ellis* v. *Rowbotham,* [1900] 1 Q.B. 740, C.A.; *Kelly* v. *Lombard Banking, Ltd.,* [1958] 3 All E.R. 713, C.A.
 5. *Galbraith* v. *Mitchenall Estates, Ltd.,* [1965] 2 Q.B. 473; [1964] 2 All E.R. 653; *Tommey* v. *Finextra, Ltd.* (1962), 106 Sol. Jo. 1012. See Diamond (1956), 19 M.L.R. 498, 506; Prince (1957), 20 M.L.R. 620; Diamond (1958), 21 M.L.R. 199.
 6. See above, p. 44.   7. See above, p. 338.

The position with regard to the different orders which may be made under s. 35 (4) is as follows[8]:

(1) Where an order is made for specific delivery of the goods to the owner or seller, his monetary claims are governed by s. 44[9].

(2) Where a split order is made, the Act makes no mention of the position with regard to rentals or instalments[10].

(3) Whilst a postponed order is in force, the position is governed by s. 38 (2)[11]; but, where the owner or seller has recapted the goods or the postponement been revoked, any monetary claims are governed by s. 44[9].

2 Action for damages

The common types of action for damages available to an owner or seller against the hirer or buyer are for breach of contract, tort, or misrepresentation.

1. For breach of contract. The S.G.A. partially covers the possibilities: besides expressly recognising the right of action for damages where the price is not forthcoming[12], the Act in two places deals with the common situation where the buyer fails to take delivery. Section 37 expressly recognises the seller's right to damages for loss occasioned by the failure to take delivery and for storage charges[13]; and s. 50 (1) provides that

> "Where the buyer wrongfully neglects or refuses to accept and pay for the goods, the seller may maintain an action against him for damages for non-acceptance".

It is curious to find two apparently overlapping provisions in different parts of the Act[14]. At all events, it is clear that the Act merely outlines the more common types of claim; and, on the assumption that the Act merely restates the common law, it is usually assumed that these provisions apply by analogy where a hirer under a h.p. agreement fails to take delivery[15].

2. In tort. The buyer or hirer might wrongfully deprive the seller or owner of the goods in several ways.

(1) A wrongful taking of the goods out of the actual or constructive

---

8. See above, p. 340.
9. Section 44 is discussed in Guest, *Law of H.P.* 603 and Goode, *H.P. Law & Practice* (2nd Edn.) 443–445.
10. But see Guest, *Law of H.P.* 604.   11. Set out above, p. 341.
12. Sections 48 (3) and (4): set out above, pp. 365, 366.
13. Set out above, pp. 267–268.
14. See the suggested distinctions in Fridman, *Sale of Goods* 281, 282; *Benjamin on Sale* (8th Edn.) 751, note (*k*). Both entail saying that s. 37 has altered the common law as established in *Greaves* v. *Ashlin* (1813), 3 Camp 426.
15. See *Karsales, Ltd.* v. *Wallis*, [1956] 2 All E.R. 866, C.A.: set out above, p. 141. See also Guest, *Law of H.P.* 321; Goode, *op. cit.*, 354–355.

possession of the plaintiff may amount to a trespass; and the measure of damages is the actual loss suffered, so that a plaintiff who has been permanently deprived of goods is entitled to recover their full value to him, as assessed in an action of conversion[16].

(2) A wrongful detention of goods, evidenced by a refusal to deliver them up on demand, will give rise to an action in detinue by a plaintiff entitled to immediate possession[17]; and the ordinary judgment will be for damages and for the value of the goods as assessed[18] at the date of judgment[19].

(3) A wrongful disposal of goods in such a manner that they are lost to a plaintiff entitled to immediate possession will amount to a conversion. The judgment will be for damages only, one item of which will be the value of the goods as assessed[18] at the date of conversion[20].

Obviously, there is a considerable overlap between the three actions, and, largely for historical reasons[1], conversion has almost entirely overshadowed the other two. Whilst detailed discussion of conversion is beyond the scope of this work[2], several of its rules must be borne in mind. First, the action only lies at the suit of one who at the time of the defendant's act is in possession or has an immediate right to possession[3], and that the defendant can probably[4] only plead *ius tertii* in the latter case[5]. Secondly, the defendant must have interfered with the plaintiff's right to immediate possession by some active assumption of control over the goods[6]: it is immaterial that the defendant acted by mistake, or in good faith[7]; but the act must involve a dealing with the goods which either is done with the intention of denying the plaintiff's rights[8] or involves the assertion of some inconsistent right[9]. Thirdly, in conversion, unlike detinue[10], the defendant always has the option of keeping the goods and paying the value of the plaintiff's interest in them[11]; but, as in detinue[12], the defendant will usually

---

16. *Wilson* v. *Lombank, Ltd.,* [1963] 1 All E.R. 740.
17. See above, p. 332.   18. See below, p. 380.
19. *Rosenthal* v. *Alderton, Ltd.,* [1946] 1 K.B. 374, C.A.; *Astley Industrial Trust, Ltd.* v. *Miller,* [1968] 2 All E.R. 36.
20. See the authorities cited in Winfield, *Tort* (8th Edn.) 517, note 87.
1. See Winfield, *op. cit.,* 485–488; Fleming, *Torts* (3rd Edn.) 53–54.
2. See Winfield, *op. cit.,* 493–520; Street, *Torts* (4th Edn.) 35–58; Fleming, *op. cit.,* 52–76; *Clerk & Lindsell on Torts* (13th Edn.) Ch. 15.
3. For a right to immediate possession in sale and h.p., see above, pp. 272, 356.
4. But see Street, *Torts* (4th Edn.) 41–42.
5. But see *Karflex, Ltd.* v. *Poole,* [1933] 2 K.B. 251, D.C.
6. It does not lie for negligence: *Ashby* v. *Tolhurst,* [1937] 2 K.B. 242; [1937] 2 All E.R. 837, C.A. *Contra* detinue: see above, p. 332.
7. *Hollins* v. *Fowler* (1875), L.R. 7 H.L. 757; *Moorgate Mercantile Co., Ltd.* v. *Finch,* [1962] 1 Q.B. 701; [1962] 2 All E.R. 467, C.A.
8. E.g. an act of detinue: see above, p. 332. But see s. 52 of the H.P.A. above, p. 339.
9. E.g. unjustifiable seizure; destruction or alteration; disposition *and* delivery.
10. See above, p. 333.
11. See Street, *Torts* (4th Edn.) 59.   12. See above, p. 332.

be able to insist that the plaintiff takes the goods back if they are in reasonable condition[13].

3. For misrepresentation. The common law offers a remedy for misrepresentation where it amounts to the tort of deceit[14] or of negligent misstatement[15]; and damages may now be awarded under s. 2 of the Misrepresentation Act 1967[16].

As the owner or seller will thus frequently have the option of suing for damages either in contract or tort, it must be borne in mind that the object of damages is different in the two cases.   In tort, the position is that, with the exception of exemplary damages, the object is *restitutio in integrum*; that is, so far as money can do it, to put the plaintiff in the same position as if the wrong had not been sustained[17].   However, in contract, where exemplary damages may not be recovered[18], the object of damages is not the restoration of the *status quo ante*, but is to put the plaintiff in the same position as if the contract had been performed[19]: certainly, the plaintiff is entitled to expenses incurred in reliance on the promised performance—his "reliance interest"[20]; but he is alternatively entitled to "the value of performance"[1]—his "expectancy interest"[2].   In pursuing the issue of damages[3], we must look first at the principle of quantification, and then at the restrictions on the amount recoverable[4].

(a) Quantification of damages

Before proceeding to some of the special rules by which the courts quantify damages, certain points of general application must be mentioned.   First, the impact of taxation[5] or a foreign currency element[6] are beyond the scope of this work.   Second, there is the question of putting a monetary value on the time element: there is statutory

---

13. See *Clerk & Lindsell, op. cit.*, 999.
14. See above, p. 128.
15. See above, pp. 129–130.
16. See above, pp. 121–122.
17. *Per* Lord WRIGHT in *Liesbosch Dredger* v. *Edison Steamship (Owners)* [1933] A.C. 449, H.L., at p. 459.
18. *Addis* v. *Gramophone, Ltd.*, [1909] A.C. 488, H.L.
19. See *Mayne & McGregor on Damages* (12th Edn.) 358; Treitel, *Law of Contract* (3rd Edn.) 798; and also Treitel (1969), 32 M.L.R. 556.
20. E.g. *Mason* v. *Burningham*, [1949] 2 K.B. 545; [1949] 2 All E.R. 134, C.A.: see above, p. 65.
 1. Waters (1958), 36 Can.B.R. 360, 361.
 2. E.g. *Victoria Laundry, Ltd.* v. *Newman Industries, Ltd.*, [1949] 2 K.B. 528; [1949] 1 All E.R. 997, C.A.: set out below, p. 420
 3. Is the plaintiff entitled to elect whichever cause of action will give him the greater damages?   See Street, *Law of Damages* 252–253.
 4. In practice, they may be considered in the reverse order; *per* Lord ESHER in *The Argentino* (1888), L.R. 13 P.D. 191, at pp. 195–198.
 5. See Street, *Law of Damages* 88–104; Cheshire & Fifoot, *Law of Contract* (7th Edn.) 555–558; Treitel, *Law of Contract* (3rd Edn.) 787, 798–801.
 6. See Atiyah, *Sale of Goods* (3rd Edn.) 207.   And also *Woodhouse A.C. Israel Cocoa, Ltd.* v. *Nigerian Produce Marketing Co., Ltd.*, [1970] 2 All E.R. 124. rev. by C.A. [1970] 11 C.L. 327b.

provision for the award of interest on a debt or damages[7]; and the common law insists on a rebate for accelerated payment[8]. Third, difficulty may sometimes be caused by questions of causation: the defendant is only liable for more than nominal damages where he causes a loss[9]; and conversely, damages should only be diminished where he causes a benefit to accrue to the plaintiff[10]. Further, where the defendant has the option of performing in alternative ways, it is assumed that he would have performed in the manner most advantageous to himself[11]: but, where the defendant's act is merely one of two or more causes of the plaintiff's harm, the other cause is generally ignored[12], unless it is subsequent to the defendant's act and involves questions of remoteness[13]. Fifth, as the quantification of damages can be a very difficult matter, the parties sometimes agree beforehand (usually in the contract) what sum shall be payable in the event of certain breaches[14]. If such a clause is a genuine pre-estimate of damages and works to the advantage of both parties, then it will be accepted by the courts and is termed "a liquidated damages clause"; but, if it works to the advantage of the innocent party, it may be struck down as being a penalty[15]; and if it acts to protect the guilty party it may amount to an exclusion clause[16].

Three of the more important heads of damage require special mention.
1. The value of the goods. Whilst a seller may have the option in some circumstances of suing in contract for the price[17] or in tort for the value of the goods, the former alternative is never available to an owner under a h.p. agreement. It has already been pointed out that a satisfied

---

7. Law Reform (Miscellaneous Provisions) Act 1934, s. 3 (1). See generally, *Benjamin on Sale* (8th Edn.) 831–832; *Chalmers' Sale of Goods* (15th Edn.) 248–249.
8. *Interoffice Telephones, Ltd.* v. *Freeman*, [1958] 1 Q.B. 190; [1957] 3 All E.R. 479, C.A.; *Overstone, Ltd.* v. *Shipway*, [1962] 1 All E.R. 52, C.A.
9. For loss of profit, see below, p. 381.
10. E.g. sub-sales: *Slater* v. *Hoyle*, [1920] 2 K.B. 11, C.A. But see the difficult case of *British Westinghouse Electric and Manufacturing Co. Ltd.*, v. *Underground Electric Rail. Co., Ltd.*, [1912] A.C. 673, H.L.; app. *Pagnay and Fratelli* v. *Corbisa Industrial Agropacuaria Limitada*, [1970] 1 W.L.R. 1306, C.A.; and the discussion in Treitel, *Law of Contract* (3rd Edn.) 817–818; Street, *Law of Damages* 108, 182; *Mayne & McGregor On Damages* (12th Edn.) 170.
11. E.g. *Re Thornett and Fehr and Yuills, Ltd.*, [1921] 1 K.B. 219; cf. *The Mihalis Angelos*, [1970] 3 All E.R 125, C.A.
12 See *Mayne & McGregor on Damages* (12th Edn) 746.
13. See below, p. 390.
14. E.g. minimum payments clauses in h.p.: see above, p. 14.
15. See below, p. 391.
16. See above, Chapter 11. It has been suggested that, where the innocent party rescinds after a repudiation, any exclusion clause should be ignored in the assessment of damages: *per* Lord UPJOHN in *The Suisse Atlantique Case*, [1967] 1 A.C. 361, H.L., at p. 419, See also *per* Lord REID, at p. 398. *Sed quaere?*
17. See above, pp. 370–372.

judgment in an action of conversion or detinue is effectively that of a compulsory sale[18]; and, if the defendant destroys the goods, an action in negligence will have a rather similar effect[19]. However, it is a "sale" with a difference: the defendant in the tort action is not required to pay the contract price[20] but damages calculated by reference to the value of the goods. This is assessed as follows[1]: if the goods have a market value, that value at the place of loss should be taken[2]; but, where the goods have no market value, the courts start with the assumption that the plaintiff should recover the replacement cost[3]. If the goods have fluctuated in value, the plaintiff is entitled to their value at the date of the tort in conversion and the date of judgment in detinue[4]; but further consideration of the effect of this rule is beyond the scope of this work[5]. Finally, it must be borne in mind that the plaintiff may be entitled only to something less than the value of the goods where the price is unpaid[6], or the defendant either has a legal interest in the goods[7] or increases their value[8]; but that otherwise he is entitled, unless the defendant insists on returning them[9], to the full value of the goods notwithstanding his own limited interest in them[10].

2. *"Restitutio in integrum"*. Whether the action is in contract or tort, the plaintiff seller or owner is entitled to be put in the same position as if the wrong had not been committed[11]. Of the potentially enormous number of heads of claim, it is only possible to refer to some of the more common ones. First, the plaintiff is entitled to recover any expenses to which he may have been put by reason of the breach[12]. Second, he must be recompensed for any injury to the goods caused by the defendant's wrongful act[13], or for any depreciation in the goods between

---

18. See above, p. 363.
19. E.g. *Liesbosch Dredger* v. *Edison Steamship (Owners)*, [1933] A.C. 449, H.L.
20. See above, p. 21.
1. See Street, *Law of Damages*, Ch. 8.
2. *Liesbosch Dredger* v. *Edison Steamship (Owners)* (above).
3. E.g. *J. and E. Hall, Ltd.* v. *Barclay*, [1937] 3 All E.R. 620, C.A.; *Harbutt's Plasticine, Ltd.* v. *Wayne Tank, Ltd.*, [1970] 1 Q.B. 447; [1970] 1 All E.R. 225, C.A.
4. See above, p. 377.   5. See Street, *Law of Damages* 212–216.
6. *Chinery* v. *Viall* (1860), 5 H. & N. 288; set out below, p. 413.
7. E.g. *Belsize Motor Supply Co.* v. *Cox*, [1914] 1 K.B. 244. Or the plaintiff is estopped from denying that fact: *Wickham Holdings, Ltd.* v. *Brooke House Motors, Ltd.*, [1967] 1 All E.R. 117, C.A.
8. E.g. *Munro* v. *Willmott*, [1949] 1 K.B. 295; [1948] 2 All E.R. 983. See further, Street, *op. cit.*, 214.
9. See above, pp. 377–378.
10. *The Winkfield*, [1902] P. 42, C.A. But see the *Wickham Holdings Case* (above) discussed by Peden in (1970), 44 A.L.J. 65; and *Belvoir Finance Co., Ltd* v *Stapleton*, [1970] 3 All E.R. 664, C.A.
11. See above, p. 378.
12. E.g. the expenses of care and custody or resale.
13. E.g. *Brady* v. *St. Margaret's Trust, Ltd.*, [1963] 2 Q.B. 494; [1963] 2 All E.R. 275, C.A.

the detainer and judgment in detinue[14]. Third, the plaintiff may seek damages for loss of use of the goods caused by the defendant's wrongful act[15]: if the chattel is one with a profit-earning capability, he may claim for loss of profit; but, whether or not it has such a capability, he is entitled to such as the cost of hiring a replacement[16], though he must prove that he would actually have been using the goods[17].

3. *Loss of profit.* Whilst loss of profit is commonly thought of as an expectancy interest recoverable in an action for breach of contract, such a claim may arise out of an action in tort where a profit-earning chattel is destroyed; and this is an alternative to claiming the cost of hiring a replacement[18]. The principles at issue here were discussed in *Strand Electric, Ltd.* v. *Brisford Entertainments, Ltd.*[19].

> The defendant wrongfully detained some portable switchgear let to him by the plaintiff. In an action of detinue, the plaintiff claimed for loss of profit. In allowing the plaintiff to recover damages calculated at a rate for hiring from the detention to the date of judgment[1], the Court of Appeal rejected as immaterial the defendant's plea that he had not used the switchgear.

The Court of Appeal were careful to confine their remarks to (1) a profit-earning chattel, which (2) the plaintiff normally hired out[2], and which (3) the defendant detained for his own ends[3]. A claim in contract for loss of profit differs in two respects from that just considered: first, the plaintiff is not suing for a prospective profit that he might have made out of some third party, but the profit he would have made out of his contract with the defendant; and secondly, the plaintiff must show that he has actually lost a profit if he is to recover more than nominal damages[4]. The latter point may be illustrated by reference to two cases, in both of which the defendant, a retail buyer of a motor vehicle at a price fixed by the manufacturer, failed to take delivery of it; and the

---

14. E.g. *General and Finance Facilities, Ltd.* v. *Cooks Cars, Ltd.*, [1963] 2 A., E.R. 314, C.A.; *Astley Industrial Trust, Ltd.* v. *Miller*, [1968] 2 All E.R. 36
15. See Street, *op. cit.*, 203–206; *Winfield, Tort* (8th Edn.) 699–701.
16. *Davis* v. *Oswell* (1837), 7 C. & P. 804. But see *Liesbosch Dredger* v. *Edison Steamship (Owners)*, [1933] A.C. 449, H.L.: see below, p. 387.
17. *Berrill* v. *Road Haulage Executive*, [1952] 2 Lloyd's Rep. 490.
18. See Street, *Law of Damages* 206–210.
19. [1952] 2 Q.B. 246; [1952] 1 All E.R. 796, C.A. And see *Penarth Dock, Ltd.* v. *Pounds*, [1963] 1 Lloyd's Rep. 359; *Astley Industrial Trust, Ltd.* v. *Miller*, [1968] 2 All E.R. 36.
 1. DENNING L.J. said, *obiter*, that if the hirer had wrongfully disposed of the goods, the owner would have been entitled to loss of profit until the date of disposal, and the value in conversion at the moment (at p. 255).
 2. Need this be to the knowledge of the defendant?
 3. Compare *General and Finance Facilities, Ltd.* v. *Cook Cars, Ltd.*, (above).
 4. The same rule is applicable where there is an anticipatory breach. *The Mihalis Angelos*, [1970] 3 All E.R. 125, C.A.

plaintiff, a retail seller, then disposed of the vehicle and subsequently claimed for the loss of profit on the sale to the defendant. In *W. L. Thompson, Ltd* v. *Robinson (Gunmakers), Ltd.*[5] it was found as a fact that the supply of that type of car exceeded the demand in the area, and UPJOHN J. held that the plaintiffs were entitled to recover the full sum because they had lost a profit they would otherwise have made. On the other hand, in *Charter* v. *Sullivan*[6], it was shown that there was a shortage of cars of that type, and that the plaintiff could dispose of all he could obtain; and the Court of Appeal therefore awarded the plaintiff only nominal damages for loss of profit because he had not lost a profit. Assuming that the plaintiff can show that he has lost a profit how is that profit to be measured?

In the nineteenth century, the common law took the view that the value of performance in a contract for the sale of goods was[7]

> "in general . . . the difference between the contract price and the market price of such goods at the time when the contract is broken, because the purchaser, having the money in his hands, may go into the market and buy. So, if a contract to accept and pay for goods is broken, the same rule may properly be applied; for the seller may take his goods into the market and obtain the current price for them".

Thus, the approach was to be the same whether the seller or buyer was in breach; and this attitude has been adopted by the S.G.A. It has been said that the Act has the same purpose in dealing with both sellers (s. 50 (3)) and buyers (s. 51 (3))[8]:

> "50 (3) to ensure that the disappointed vendor shall yet have for his item a price at least equivalent to that of the breached sale, and 51 (3) that the disappointed purchaser shall have an equivalent item at a price not higher than that of the breached sale".

However, whilst in the case of breach by the seller it may be that s. 51 (3) will normally provide an adequate level of compensation, this is by no means true in the case of breach by the buyer; and in practice s. 50 (3) is fairly frequently ousted[9]. Section 50 (3) lays down a *prima facie* rule to apply where there is an "available market"[10], and there has

---

5. [1955] Ch. 177; [1955] 1 All E.R. 154.
6. [1957] 2 Q.B. 117; [1957] 1 All E.R. 809, C.A.
7. *Per* TINDAL C.J. in *Barrow* v. *Arnaud* (1846), 8 Q.B. 604, at pp. 609–610.
8. Waters (1958), 36 Can.B.R. 360, 370.
9. It has been suggested that this is because of the built-in element of mitigation in s. 50 (3): *Mayne & McGregor on Damages* (12th Edn.) 153.
10. See generally Waters (1958), 36 Can.B.R. 360; Lawson (1969), 43 A.L.J. 52, 106; *Mayne & McGregor* 425.

been some judicial disagreement as to whether this refers to a market-place[11] or a level of supply and demand[12].

1. Where there is an available market. Section 50 (3) provides:

> "Where there is an available market for the goods in question the measure of damages is primâ facie to be ascertained by the difference between the contract price and the market or current price at the time or times when the goods ought to have been accepted or, if no time was fixed for acceptance, then at the time of the refusal to accept".

The onus of proving the selling[13] price is on the seller[14]; and the time element in fixing that price is examined in relation to s. 51 (3)[15]. The assessment of damages may now be explained by reference to the simplest case, where the buyer is in breach at the time fixed for delivery and the seller resells immediately[16]. In this case, the amount recoverable from the buyer is as follows:

(1) If the market price is below the contract price, the seller is *prima facie* entitled under s. 50 (3) to the difference between the two: if he resells below the market price, he is not entitled to that extra loss because he has not mitigated his loss[17]; and, if he resells above the market price, he will only recover his actual loss[18].

(2) If the market price is equal to or above the contract price, presumably the intention of s. 50 (3) is that he shall only be entitled to nominal damages. However, the courts have shown themselves fairly willing to oust s. 50 (3). For instance, in *Trans Trust S.P.R.L.* v. *Danubian Trading Ltd*[19]

> There was a chain of contracts for the sale of steel from the manufacturer to A., to the plaintiff, to the defendant, to B. It was known to the defendant that the manufacturer would only release the steel against payment; but the defendant, in breach of his contract with the plaintiff, failed to procure the opening of a letter of credit.

The Court of Appeal unanimously (1) allowed the plaintiff substantial damages for loss of profit notwithstanding that the market price was

---

11. See *per* JAMES L.J. in *Dunkirk Colliery Co.* v. *Lever* (1878), 9 Ch.D. 20, C.A. at p. 25.
12. See *per* JENKINS L.J. in *Charter* v. *Sullivan* (above), at p. 128.
13. Where this differs from the buying price.
14. *Per* DIPLOCK L.J. in *R. V. Ward, Ltd.* v. *Bignall*, [1967] 1 Q.B. 534, C.A. at p. 547. The resale price, if any, may be evidence of this.
15. See below, pp. 410–411.
16. If he delays beyond this time, the seller carries the risk of any fluctuation in the market price: *Campbell Mostyn (Provisions), Ltd.* v. *Barnett, Trading Co.*, [1954] 1 Lloyd's Rep. 65, C.A.
17. See below, pp. 390–391.
18. But compare the position of the innocent buyer: see below, p. 410.
19. [1952] 2 Q.B. 297; [1952] 1 All E.R. 970, C.A.

higher than the contract price, because the plaintiff could not have taken advantage of that higher price; but (2) they refused the plaintiff any damages to compensate him for any claim which might have been made against him by A. on the grounds that it was too remote[20]. Similarly, the courts have shown very little enthusiasm for s. 50 (3) when dealing with fixed price goods[1].

2. *Where there is no available market.* There may be no available market for the seller where, for example, goods are specifically manufactured to order[2], or supply exceeds demand[3]; and in such cases s. 50 (3) is obviously inapplicable. *Prima facie*, the seller in such circumstances will be entitled to the profit he would have made on the contract, even where the seller does manage to resell the goods[4]. On the other hand, it is clear that the defaulting buyer is entitled to adduce evidence to show that the seller could not have made the second profit as well[5]; and, if he does so, the seller will only receive nominal damages for loss of profit[6].

Finally, the assessment of damages for breach by the hirer of a contract of h.p. must be considered. We have already seen that, by reason of the element of bailment, the owner is not entitled to any hire-rent where the hirer refuses to accept delivery[7]. However, where there has been a delivery, the rule in bailment is that, if there is a simple hiring for a term certain, the bailor may be able to recover something like the full hire-rent for the entire period[8]. Should the same apply in h.p.? The difficulty is twofold: first, there is an element of price in the hire-rent; and secondly, the agreement[9], or s. 27 of the H.P.A.[10], may give the hirer a right to terminate before the expiry of the full term. In both the leading cases, there were directly financed h.p. transactions in respect of motor vehicles; the hirer neglected to pay any instalments; the finance company, after waiting some while, terminated the hiring and repossessed the vehicle under the terms of the agreement; and the company then sued to recover (1) the arrears of rentals[11], and (2) damages computed on the basis of the future rentals, less the price

---

20. See further below, p. 388.
  1. See *W. L. Thompson, Ltd.* v. *Robinson, Ltd.*, [1955] Ch. 177; [1955] 1 All E.R. 154; *Charter* v. *Sullivan*, [1957] 2 Q.B. 117; [1957] 1 All E.R. 809, C.A.
  2. E.g. *Re Vic Mill, Ltd.*, [1913] 1 Ch. 465, C.A.
  3. *Per* UPJOHN J. in *Thompson, Ltd.* v. *Robinson, Ltd* (above), at p. 187.
  4. E.g. *Re Vic Mill, Ltd.* (above).
  5. *Hill & Sons* v. *Showell* (1918), 87 L.J.K.B. 1106, H.L.
  6. *Charter* v. *Sullivan* (above).
  7. See above, p. 116.
  8. *Interoffice Telephones, Ltd.* v. *Freeman*, [1958] 1 Q.B. 190; [1957] 3 All E.R. 479, C.A.; *Robophone Facilities, Ltd.* v. *Blank*, [1966] 3 All E.R. 128, C.A.
  9. See above, p. 353.
 10. See above, p. 354.
 11. See above, pp. 374-375.

obtained on resale and the option fee. In *Yeoman Credit, Ltd.* v. *Waragowski*[12]

> The h.p. price was payable by 36 monthly instalments, and the company repossessed the vehicle when the hirer failed to pay any of the first six instalments. The Court of Appeal unanimously agreed that the company was entitled to both the items claimed.

This case recognised the commercial reality: it allowed the company to recover both the price it had "lent" to the hirer, and the expected profit thereon. But subsequently, the court sought to avoid this result by heeding the legal fiction rather than the reality[13]. In *Financings, Ltd.* v. *Baldock*[14]

> The finance company repossessed the vehicle after the hirer had failed to pay the first two out of 24 instalments. The Court of Appeal unanimously allowed the company (1), but not (2).

All the members of the Court of Appeal agreed that the *Waragowski Case* might be distinguished on the grounds that in that case the breach by the hirer was such as to repudiate the contract, and the company merely "reasonably"[15] accepted that repudiation, whereas in the present case the breach by the hirer did not amount to a repudiation and the company was only entitled to terminate by reason of the express power in the contract, so that the loss of future rentals flowed from the company's act and not from the hirer's breach[16]. However, whilst such a distinction may be acceptable in principle[17], it does involve the difficult question of when a breach will amount to a repudiation[18]. Moreover, Lord DENNING M.R. pointed out the illogicality of the distinction: the hirer would have been worse off if he had taken the more courteous course of writing to inform the company that he could not pay the instalments, for that would have been a repudiation. He added[19]:

> "No regard seems to have been paid to the fact that the hirer had the right to terminate the hiring at any time and thus bring to an end his obligation to pay any more instalments. I should have thought,

---

12. [1961] 3 All E.R. 145, C.A. Foll: *Overstone, Ltd.* v. *Shipway*, [1962] 1 All E.R. 52, C.A.
13. Compare the approach when the hirer is claiming damages: see below, pp. 414, 423.
14. [1963] 2 Q.B. 104; [1963] 1 All E.R. 443, C.A. Foll: *Brady* v. *St. Margaret's Trust, Ltd.*, [1963] 2 Q.B. 494; [1963] 2 All E.R. 275, C.A.; *Charterhouse Credit, Ltd.* v. *Tolly*, [1963] 2 Q.B. 683; [1963] 2 All E.R. 432, C.A.; *Anglo-Auto Finance, Ltd.* v. *James*, [1963] 3 All E.R. 566, C.A.; *United Dominions Trust (Commercial), Ltd.* v. *Ennis*, [1968] 1 Q.B. 54; [1967] 2 All E.R. 345.
15. The C.A. did not think that this added anything to the *Waragowski Case*: at pp. 113, 115, 122, 123.
16. See *per* Lord DENNING M.R. and UPJOHN L.J. at pp. 113, 116.
17. See above, p. 379. But see Hughes, [1967] J.B.L. 307, 312.
18. See above, p. 360.   19. At p. 113.

on this account, he would not be liable for any more damages than if he had himself given a notice to terminate . . ., and that if he had given notice himself, the damages would be limited to the breaches up to the date of termination and no more . . . As a matter of principle, I should have thought that the damages should be the same in either case, whoever terminated the hiring".

There, for the moment, the matter rests[20]: if the owner terminates, he cannot recover more than the arrears of rentals[1]; if the hirer repudiates, having no power of termination, the owner is entitled to future rentals; but, if the hirer has a power of termination, then whether he repudiates or terminates it may be that owner is only entitled to arrears of rentals for the reason given by Lord Denning above[2].

(b) Common law and statutory restrictions

It is now possible to consider some of the major restrictions which common law or statute imposes on the recovery of damages.

1. The rule against double recovery. As the primary function of the law of damages is to make good loss[3], it follows that the plaintiff can only recover once in respect of any particular loss, even though that loss may be recoverable by more than one cause of action. For instance, a seller may be entitled to recover the value of the goods in conversion from more than one person, but he can only recover it once; similarly, a seller may be able at his option to sue the buyer for the price of the goods in contract or their value in tort, but not both; and likewise in an action for damages for non-acceptance the seller will have to give allowance for the price paid.

2. Contributory negligence[4]. Whilst contributory negligence was a complete defence at common law, the Law Reform (Contributory Negligence) Act 1945 provides that it shall merely reduce the damages. According to s. 1 (1),

"Where any person suffers damage[5] as the result partly of his own fault[6] and partly of the fault of any other person or persons, a claim in respect of that damage shall not be defeated by reason of the fault

---

20. See Guest, *Law of H.P.* 322, 620–622; and Goode, *H.P. Law & Practice* (2nd Edn.) 399–403.
1. A stipulation that any further sum be payable would offend the rule against penalties: see below, p. 391.
2. For the use of the rule against penalties to achieve these ends, see below, p. 393.   3. See above, p. 378.
4. See generally, Glanville Williams, *Joint Torts and Contributory Negligence* Part 2; Street *Torts* (4th Edn.) 151–160; Winfield *Torts* (8th Edn.) 102–117.
5. Section 4 provides that "damage" "includes loss of life and personal injury".
6. Section 4 says that "fault" means

"negligence, breach of statutory duty or other act or omission which gives rise to a liability in tort or would, apart from this Act, give rise to the defence of contributory negligence".

of the person suffering the damage, but the damages recoverable in respect thereof shall be reduced to such extent as the court thinks just and equitable having regard to the claimant's share in the responsibility for the damage: Provided that—

(a) this subsection shall not operate to defeat any defence arising under a contract[7];

(b) where any contract or enactment providing for the limitation of liability is applicable to the claim, the amount of damages recoverable by the claimant by virtue of this sub-section shall not exceed the maximum limit so applicable"[8].

3. Remoteness of damage. Whilst the criteria for quantifying damages have thus far been reasonably logical and scientific, the courts have always sought to retain an element of negative discretion, refusing compensation where the damage was "too remote". In a sense, the courts have been very successful in retaining an unfettered discretion: there remains considerable doubts as to the tests of remoteness in tort and contract, and the extent to which they correspond.

(1) *Remoteness in tort.* Intended consequences cannot be too remote[9]; and for this purpose recklessness is put on a par with intention[10]. However, where the defendant does not intend the consequences of his act, there has been a fundamental difference of opinion on the test to be adopted[11]: one view was that it was unreasonable to make the defendant liable for more than he ought to have expected, and he was therefore to be made liable only for the foreseeable consequences of his act[12]; but on the other hand it was sometimes felt that this test would unjustly deprive the innocent victim of recovery for damage caused by the admitted wrongdoer, and that the latter should be liable for all the consequences which directly flowed from his wrongful act[13]. Besides this disagreement, there is the problem of the difficult decision of the House of Lords in the *Liesbosch Dredger* v. *Edison Steamship (Owners)*[14]. Whilst in the case of personal injuries the foreseeable consequences rule is probably extended by the rule that "you take your plaintiff as you find him", their Lordships apparently decided that the latter rule was to be partly disregarded in the case of damage to property: they allowed recovery of the expenses attributable to the

---

7. E.g. a contractual exclusion clause: see above, p. 136. What about a non-contractual disclaimer?
8. E.g. s. 28 of the H.P.A.: see below, pp. 394–395.
9. *Scott* v. *Shepherd* (1773), 2 W.M.Bl., 892.
10. And see *per* DENNING M.R. in *Doyle* v. *Olby, Ltd.*, [1969] 2 All E.R. 119, C.A. at p. 122.
11. See *Mayne & McGregor on Damages* (12th Edn.) 73a, note 10m; Street, *Torts* (4th Edn.) 146–149; Winfield, *Tort* (8th Edn.) 90, note 64.
12. This view is generally associated with *The Wagon Mound*, [1961] A.C. 388; [1961] 1 All E.R. 404, P.C.
13. E.g. *Re Polemis and Furness Withy & Co., Ltd.*, [1921] 3 K.B. 560, C.A.
14. [1933] A.C. 449, H.L. See Goodhart (1937), 2 U.Tor.L.J. 1.

contract in hand, but not such expenses as were also due to the injured party's impecuniosity, albeit that that impecuniosity itself arose from the contract. The distinction would appear to be a completely arbitrary and illogical one drawn for policy reasons[15]; and it should probably be viewed in the context of remoteness rather than turning on a causation test (as their Lordships suggested)[16].

(2) *Remoteness in contract.* The basic test of remoteness in contract laid down by ALDERSON B. in *Hadley* v. *Baxendale*[17] turned on what the guilty party could have foreseen; and, as this depended on the state of his knowledge, it led to the formulation of two so-called rules.

First rule. The guilty party is assumed to have the knowledge that every person possesses, and to foresee all the damage which would arise according to the ordinary course of things. In the case of sales, this rule has received statutory formulation in s. 50 (2) of the S.G.A., which provides:

> "The measure of damages is the estimated loss directly and naturally resulting, in the ordinary course of events, from the buyer's breach of contract".

Is the statutory rule in sale[18] synonymous with the common law rule applicable in h.p.[19]?

Second rule. If the guilty party has knowledge of some special circumstance which would increase the loss naturally arising from his breach, he may[20] also be liable for that further loss—what the S.G.A. calls "special damage" (s. 54). Claims for such special damage by sellers have normally been unsuccessful[1]. The test to be adopted was reformulated by ASQUITH L.J. in *Victoria Laundry, Ltd.* v. *Newman Industries, Ltd.* where he said[2];

> "to make the contract-breaker liable . . . it is not necessary that he should have actually asked himself what loss is liable to result from a breach . . . It suffices that, if he had considered the question, he would as a reasonable man have concluded that the loss in question was liable to result . . . Nor . . . need it be proved that upon a given state of knowledge the defendant could, as a reasonable man, foresee that a breach must necessarily result in that loss. It is enough if he

---

15. See *Mayne & McGregor* 107; Street, *Torts* 143.
16. See Winfield, *Tort* 88; Street, *Torts* 143.
17. (1854), 9 Ex 341, at p. 354.
18. E.g. *Charter* v. *Sullivan*, [1957] 2 Q.B. 117; [1957] 1 All E.R. 809, C.A.
19. E.g. *Liverpool and County Discount, Ltd.* v. *A.B. Motors, Ltd.*, [1963] 2 All E.R. 396, C.A.
20. Liability depends on "some knowledge and acceptance by one party of the purpose and intention of the other in entering the contract": *per* Lord SUMNER in *Weld-Blundell* v. *Stephens*, [1920] A.C. 956, H.L., at p. 980.
1. E.g. *Trans Trust S.P.R.L.* v. *Danubian Trading, Ltd.*, [1952] 2 Q.B. 297, C.A.: set out above, p. 383.
2. [1949] 2 K.B. 528, C.A., at p. 540.

could forsee it was likely to result . . . [or] . . . a 'serious possibility' or a 'real danger' or 'liable' to result. Possibly the colloquialism 'on the cards' indicates the shade of meaning with some approach to accuracy".

In the ensuing twenty years, this formulation was constantly referred to as the classic exposition of the matter; but in *Koufos* v. *Czarnikow, The Heron II*[3] the House of Lords heavily criticised the use of the expression "on the cards" in the above passage whilst searching for a formula which would indicate a rather higher degree of probability of occurrence[4].

(3) Comparison of remoteness in contract and tort. In *Vacwell Engineering, Ltd.* v. *B.D.H. Chemicals, Ltd.*[5]

> The plaintiff manufacturers of plant were accustomed to obtain supplies of chemicals from the defendant manufacturers of chemicals, which products normally contained an appropriate warning of industrial hazards. The plaintiffs devised a new method of manufacturing plant utilising the chemical, X., and requested that the defendants supply X. to them, making known the purpose for which it was required. X. was supplied in glass ampoules bearing the legend "Harmful Vapour". Unknown to either party, X. was uniquely dangerous in that it exploded violently on contact with water. There having been such an explosion whilst the plaintiff's servant was washing some of the ampoules, the plaintiff claimed for damage to his premises and for loss of profit. REES J. held the defendants liable because their failure to warn constituted (1) a breach of the undertakings implied (a) by s. 14 (1) of the S.G.A.[6], and (b) from the course of dealings between the parties[7], and (2) the tort of negligence[8].

His Lordship held that the damage was not too remote under either (1) or (2): as to the contractual claim, he held that it was sufficient that some damage by explosion was reasonably foreseeable within the rule in *The Heron*[9]; and that the position was similar with regard to the claim in tort[10]. Yet, even if the foreseeability test is adopted in tort, it is by no means clear that the rules of remoteness will produce the same result in those situations where actions in contract and tort are available concurrently[11]. First, the object of damages is different in the two cases[12]. Second, there is a difference in the time at which the

---

3. [1969] 1 A.C. 350; [1967] 3 All E.R. 686, H.L.
4. See Pickering (1968), 31 M.L.R. 203; Hamson (1968), 26 C.L.J. 14.
5. [1969] 3 All E.R. 1681. This case was settled during appeal, [1970] 3 All E.R. 553. See Weaver (1970), 33 M.L.R. 446.
6. See above, p. 85.
7. See above, p. 112.   8. See above, p. 126.
9. At pp. 1696–1697.   10. At p. 1698.
11. See *per* Lord REID in *The Heron*, [1969] 1 A.C. 350, H.L., at pp. 385–386.
12. See above, p. 378.

foreseeability test is directed: in contract, the material date is the time of contract, and in tort, the time of the tort[13]. Third, there may be differences in attitude to concurrent causes[14]. Fourth, there may be differences in the degree of probability of consequences required[15].

4. *Mitigation of damage.*[15a]   As was explained by Lord HALDANE L.C.[16], the law

> "imposes on a plaintiff the duty of taking all reasonable steps to mitigate the loss consequent on the breach, and debars him from claiming any part of the damage which is due to his neglect to take such steps . . ."

This duty to mitigate must be distinguished from those cases where an act of the plaintiff increases the harm, which raises questions of causation and remoteness; and, at very least, it requires the plaintiff to consider whether he could take any reasonable steps to mitigate his loss. At most, his obligation is to take all reasonable steps; but in *Payzu, Ltd. v. Saunders*[17] SCRUTTON L.J. said that

> "in commercial contracts it is generally reasonable to accept an offer from the party in default".

On the other hand, in a more recent case ROSKILL J. said that the plaintiff[18]

> "is not bound to nurse the interests of the contract breaker, and so long as he acts reasonably at the time, it ill lies in the mouth of the contract breaker to turn round afterwards and complain . . . that the plaintiff failed to do that which perhaps with hindsight he might have been wiser to do".

Thus, the standard required of the plaintiff is a fairly low one[19]. It has been held unreasonable for the plaintiff to decline an offer by the defendant to buy back[20], or to enter into a fresh contract on cash instead of credit terms[1]. On the other hand, the plaintiff need not act so as to injure innocent persons and prejudice his commercial re-

---

13. See *Street on Damages* 249.
14. See *Mayne & McGregor* 76–97, 119–121.
15. See *Mayne & McGregor* 360–362; Pickering (1968), 31 M.L.R. 203, 208.
15a. Is the duty to mitigate only relevant to a claim for damages; or does it also apply to a claim for an agreed sum?   See Treitel, *Law of Contract* (3rd Edn.) 833–834.
16. In *British Westinghouse and Electric Manufacturing Co.* v. *Underground Rail. Co., Ltd.*, [1912] A.C. 673, H.L., at p. 689.
17. [1919] 2 K.B. 581, C.A., at p. 589.   See *Paguan & Fratelli* v. *Corbisa Industrial Limitada*, [1970] 1 W.L.R. 1306, C.A.
18. In *Harlow and Jones, Ltd.* v. *Panex, Ltd.*, [1967] 2 Lloyd's Rep. 509, at p. 530.
19. On whom lies the burden of proof?   See *Roper* v. *Johnson* (1873), L.R. 8 C.P. 167.
20. *Medd* v. *Cox* (1940), 67 Ll.L.R. 5, C.A.
 1. *Payzu, Ltd.* v. *Saunders*, [1919] 2 K.B. 581, C.A.

putation[2], nor embark on uncertain litigation[3], nor risk his money too far to mitigate his loss[4]. What if the plaintiff is financially unable to take steps in mitigation[5]? Where the situation does require the plaintiff to take some steps to mitigate his loss the position is as follows: the plaintiff cannot recover in respect of avoidable loss[6]; but if he incurs reasonable expense in attempting unsuccessfully to mitigate he can probably also recover this[7]. Two matters have caused particular difficulty: first, whether to take account of any reduction in the plaintiff's loss brought about by his efforts beyond the duty to mitigate[8]; and second, whether the duty to mitigate requires an innocent party to forgo his right of electing whether to sue immediately after an anticipatory breach[9]. But, whatever the answer to these questions, it is clear that the duty to mitigate does not interfere with any right of the innocent party after breach to elect whether to rescind or affirm[10], as opposed to any question of when he should make that election, and an act of mitigation must be carefully distinguished from an accord and satisfaction[11].

5. *The rule against penalties.* Where a clause in a contract amounts to the imposition of a penalty it will be struck out, and the innocent party will only be able to recover damages representing his actual loss, whether that be less[12] or more[13] than the sum stipulated in the penalty clause. The guiding principle for determining whether a clause falls within this rule has been summed up by Lord DUNEDIN as follows[14]:

> "It will be held to be a penalty if the sum stipulated for is extravagant and unconscionable in amount compared with the greatest loss which could conceivably be proved to have followed from the breach".

---

2. *James Finlay & Co., Ltd.* v. *N.V. Kwik Hoo Tong*, [1929] 1 K.B. 400, C.A.
3. *Pilkington* v. *Wood*, [1953] Ch. 770; [1953] 2 All E.R. 810.
4. *Lesters Leather and Skin Co.* v. *Home Brokers, Ltd.* (1948), 64 T.L.R. 569, C.A. And see *Jewelowski* v. *Propp*, [1944] 1 K.B. 510; [1944] 1 All E.R. 483.
5. Cf. *Clippens Oil Co., Ltd.* v. *Edinburgh and District Water Trustees*, [1907] A.C. 291, H.L. and *Liesbosch Dredger* v. *Edison Steamship (Owners)*, [1933] A.C. 449, H.L.; discussed in *Street on Damages*, 41 and *Mayne & McGregor* 159 (8).
6. *Payzu, Ltd.* v. *Saunders*, [1919] 2 K.B. 581, C.A.
7. *Lloyd's and Scottish Finance, Ltd.* v. *Modern Cars, Ltd.*, [1966] 1 Q.B. 764: set out above, p. 65.
8. See the *British Westinghouse Case*, [1912] A.C. 673, H.L.: see above, p. 379, note 10.
9. See *White and Carter (Councils), Ltd.* v. *McGregor*, [1962] A.C. 413; [1961] 3 All E.R. 1178, H.L.; discussed by Treitel, *Law of Contract* (3rd Edn.) 733–735, ; Cheshire & Fifoot, *Law of Contract* (7th Edn.) 561.
10. See above, p. 361.
11. See above, p. 362.
12. E.g. *Clydebank Engineering and Shipbuilding Co. Case*, [1905] A.C. 6, H.L.
13. See *Mayne & McGregor* 225. *Sed quaere?*
14. In *Dunlop Pneumatic Tyre Co.. Ltd.* v. *New Garage and Motor Co., Ltd.*, [1915] A.C. 79, H.L., at p. 87.

A clause cannot be a penalty for some purposes and not for others, so that, if the clause is expressed to operate in the event of more than one breach, it is to be tested against the smallest breach[15], unless the clause provides for payment of a variable sum whose variations adequately reflect the loss flowing from the different breaches[16]. The foregoing is, of course, subject to the rule that if the breach or breaches is or are of such a nature that the magnitude of the damage flowing therefrom must remain uncertain, the clause may be saved as being a genuine pre-estimate of damage[17]. One area where these principles have been particularly litigated is that of minimum payments clauses in h.p. agreements[18]. Frequently, the largest element in this is the sum expressed to be "compensation" for depreciation of the goods; and the real purpose of such a clause may be to allow the owner to recoup his "loss of profit". The leading case is *Bridge* v. *Campbell Discount Co., Ltd.*[19].

> There was a tripartite h.p. transaction in respect of a Bedford Dormobile van at a h.p. price of £482 10s. The h.p. agreement, dated 20.7.59, required the hirer to pay a deposit and 36 monthly instalments, commencing 20.8.59; and it contained the following clause:
>
> "9. If this agreement or the hiring be terminated for any reason before the vehicle becomes . . . the property of the hirer, then the hirer shall . . . (b) pay to the owners all arrears of hire rent . . . and by way of agreed compensation for depreciation of the vehicle such further sum as may be necessary to make the rentals paid and payable hereunder equal to two-thirds of the h.p. price . . ." Having taken possession of the van and paid by way of deposit and first instalment £115 10s., the hirer on 3.9.59 wrote to the owner:
>
> "Owing to unforeseen personal circumstances I am very sorry but I will not be able to pay any more payments . . . Will you please let me know where and when I will have to return the car. I am very sorry regarding this but I have no alternative".
>
> The owner did not reply; on 14.9.59 the hirer returned the vehicle to the dealer; and subsequently the owner commenced proceedings against the hirer under clause 9 for the balance of two-thirds of the h.p. price (£206 3s. 4d.). The County Court Judge dismissed claim as being for a penalty; but he was reversed by the Court of Appeal on the grounds that the rule against penalties could not apply

---

15. *Ford Motor Co. (England), Ltd.* v. *Armstrong* (1915), 31 T.L.R. 267, C.A.
16. E.g. the *Clydebank Engineering and Shipbuilding Co. Case*, [1905] A.C. 6, H.L.   17. See above, p. 379.
18. Explained above, p. 14: see the discussions in Goode, *H.P. Law & Practice* (2nd Edn.) 383–399; Guest, *Law of H.P.* 625–650; Ziegel, [1964] C.L.J. 108; Hughes, [1962] J.B.L. 252.
   [1962] A.C. 600; [1962] 1 All E.R. 385, H.L.: see the authorities cited in footnote 18; and also *Mayne & McGregor* 243, *Supplement*; Fridman (1963), 26 M.L.R. 198.

where, as here, the hirer had lawfully terminated his agreement[20]. Reversing the Court of Appeal, the House of Lords held that the hirer had broken the agreement; that the owner was asserting rights under clause 9 consequent on that breach; that clause 9 was void as stipulating for a penal sum; and that the owner was therefore only entitled to damages for the loss suffered.

Two issues were involved, to both of which the House of Lords gave affirmative answers: first, whether the rule against penalties was applicable at all; and second, if so, whether clause 9 stipulated for a penal sum.

(1) *The scope of the rule.* On the traditional view that the stipulated sum could only be a penalty if payable on breach[1], it was at first held that a minimum payments clause could not be a penalty because the stipulated sum was payable not just on breach but also on certain other events, such as lawful termination by the hirer[2]. However, this rule offered such an obvious means by which the draftsman of a minimum payments clause could escape the rule against penalties that it was reversed: in *Cooden Engineering, Ltd. v. Stanford*[3] the Court of Appeal held that, where the event which in fact brought the minimum payments clause into operation was a termination by the owner on grounds of breach by the hirer, the rule against penalties was applicable. Since then, the courts have sought to extend the scope of the rule against penalties in two ways. First, they have taken the view of the facts most advantageous to the hirer in deciding how the agreement has been terminated. Notwithstanding the ordinary rule of interpretation that a party should *prima facie* be assumed to have intended to do that which is lawful, in *Bridge's Case* the House of Lords held that the hirer had broken rather than lawfully terminated his agreement. Similarly, in *United Dominions Trust (Commercial), Ltd. v. Ennis*[4] the Court of Appeal took the view that the hirer's letter was probably only an invitation to the owner to terminate so that the hirer was only liable for arrears of rentals under the doctrine in *Financings Ltd. v. Baldock*[5]; but that, if the letter were a repudiation, the owner had affirmed by suing on the minimum payments clause, and therefore could not sue for loss of profit under *Yeoman Credit, Ltd. v. Waragowski*[6]. Secondly, even though the common law rule against penalties is not applicable where the minimum payments clause is activated by an event other than a breach by the hirer, it was suggested by Lord DENNING in *Bridge's Case*

20. [1961] 1 Q.B. 445, C.A.
  1. *Associated Distributors, Ltd. v. Hall*, [1938] 2 K.B. 83, C.A.
  2. *Elsey, Ltd. v. Hyde* (1926), Unreported: see Guest, *Law of H.P.* 628.
  3. [1953] 1 Q.B. 86; [1952] 2 All E.R. 915, C.A.
  4. [1968] 1 Q.B. 54; [1967] 2 All E.R. 345, C.A.
  5. [1963] 2 Q.B. 104; [1963] 1 All E.R. 443, C.A.: see above, p. 385.
  6. [1961] 3 All E.R. 145, C.A.: see above, p. 385.

that a similar equitable principle might be invoked in these circumstances[7].

(2) A penal sum. On Lord DUNEDIN's "weakest link" principle[8], the clause will be judged on the most extreme circumstances which it purports to cover; that is, on the basis of the highest amount payable for the most insignificant breach. On this basis, any attempt to exact a substantial fixed percentage of the h.p. price would appear to be penal[9]. Nor will a sliding scale necessarily suffice: this may prove objectionable if the result is that the owner is always entitled to recover both the full h.p. price and the goods[10], or if the scale slides the wrong way or does not take into account either the acceleration in payment or the resale[11]. In the light of these considerations, and of the difficulties thrown up by such cases as *Lombank, Ltd.* v. *Excell*[12], it may be that the owner has nothing to gain by making the minimum payments clause applicable to breaches of contract by the hirer. Furthermore, the clause may in fact prove positively dangerous[13], and it may well be that such matters are better left to the common law[14].

Whilst the courts have made substantial inroads into the efficacy of minimum payments clauses by rather dubious arguments, statutory intervention has not been much more satisfactory. Only in the case of termination by reference to the death of a hirer or buyer is the minimum payments clause *pro tanto* avoided by the H.P.A. (s. 30 (1) (b))[15]. Where the hirer or buyer exercises his statutory right to terminate under s. 27 of the H.P.A.[16], his maximum liability is compulsorily[17] set out in s. 28: the effect of this section is that he cannot be required to pay more than the amount due in respect of any liability which has accrued before termination[18], plus the difference between the sums paid or payable and half the h.p. or total purchase price (ss. 28 (1) (5))[19];

---

7. At p. 631; and see Lord DEVLIN at p. 634. *Contra* Lords SIMONDS and MORTON at pp. 613, 614.
8. See *Dunlop Pneumatic Tyre Co., Ltd.* v. *New Garage and Motor Co., Ltd.*, [1915] A.C. 79, H.L. at p. 89.
9. E.g. *Landom Trust, Ltd.* v. *Hurrell*, [1955] 1 All E.R. 839: see *Mayne & McGregor* 243.
10. E.g. *Cooden Engineering, Ltd.* v. *Stanford*, [1953] 1 Q.B. 86; [1952] 2 All E.R. 915, C.A.; *Anglo-Auto Finance, Ltd.* v. *James*, [1963] 3 All E.R. 566, C.A.
11. E.g. *Bridge's Case*, [1962] A.C. 600; [1962] 1 All E.R. 385, H.L.
12. [1964] 1 Q.B. 415; [1963] 3 All E.R. 486, C.A.: see Thornley, [1964] C.L.J. 108; Downey (1964), 27 M.L.R. 100; Guest, *Law of H.P.* 638.
13. E.g. *Ennis' Case* [1968] 1 Q.B 54; [1967] 2 All E.R. 345, C.A.: see above p. 393.
14. See above, pp. 384–386.   15. Set out above, p. 343.
16. See above, p. 354.   17. Section 29 (2) (b): see above, p. 133.
18. Including any sum due for failing to take reasonable care of the goods: s. 28 (3).
19. The concept of h.p. or total purchase price is considered above, p. 22. By s. 56, the amount paid includes payment otherwise than in money where this has been agreed between the parties, e.g. a part-exchange allowance: see above, p. 271.

but that a lesser sum shall be payable where either the agreement specifies that lesser amount (s. 28 (1)), or the court is satisfied that an amount
less than either of those two sums ("would be equal to the loss sustained
by the owner or seller in consequence of the termination of the agreement
by the hirer or buyer" (s. 28 (2))[20]. Where a h.p. or conditional sale
agreement is terminated otherwise than by the hirer or buyer acting
under s. 27, the Act lays down no "statutory yardstick"; but s. 29 (2)
(c)[1] invalidates any provision designed to secure for the owner or seller
a sum in excess of the smallest amount that would be recoverable under
s. 28 if it were applicable; and, if the owner or seller commences an
action under s. 35 for the recovery of protected goods[2], any sum
claimed under the agreement can only be claimed in that action (s. 41)[3],
and there are restrictions on claims under the minimum payments
clause (s. 43)[4]. Moreover, where the amount recoverable is not
governed by s. 28, the stipulation must still be tested against the common
law rule in respect of penalties. It is, to say the least, unfortunate, that
the opportunity was not taken in the H.P.A. 1965 to impose in all cases
an obligatory statutory formula as to the amount recoverable: the present
system would appear to be both unfair to the owner or seller, and also
unnecessarily complicated.

---

20. "Loss" in s. 28 (2) may give rise to some difficulties of interpretation: see
    Guest, *Law of H.P.* 609; Goode, *H.P. Law & Practice*, (2nd. Edn.) 406–407.
1. See above, p. 133.
2. See above, p. 340.
3. Set out above, p. 375.
4. The most common situation is dealt with by s. 43 (3), which is set out above,
   p. 341.

CHAPTER 21

Remedies of the Hirer or Buyer

It must be borne in mind that there are a number of difficulties which a hirer or buyer may face when seeking to pursue his remedies. First, the sharp distinction drawn in English Law between remedies in contract and tort is often important in determining such issues as product liability[1], particularly if the transaction is financed[2]. Second, there is the difficulty in enforcing judgment debts mentioned in Chapter 20[3], though even more important to the hirer or buyer is likely to be the cost of litigation and the restricted availability of legal aid.

The substantive remedies which may be available to the hirer or buyer are as follows: (1) rescission for breach of contract or misrepresentation; (2) restitution in quasi-contract; (3) damages for breach of contract, tort or misrepresentation; (4) specific performance. Each of these remedies may be available alone; or more than one of them may be available either alternatively or cumulatively[4], depending on the duty broken and the nature of the breach. For instance, the following remedies may be available to the hirer or buyer: for breach of the undertaking as to title—rescission, damages and the recovery of any money paid in quasi-contract; for non-delivery—either rescission and damages, or affirmation and damages and possibly specific performance; and for personal injury to him caused by act of a third party—damages alone.

I RESCISSION

1 Rescission for breach of contract

It has already been pointed out that the innocent party to the contract will be entitled to rescind it where the other party repudiates it, or sometimes where he defectively performs it[5]; but that the innocent party will lose that right where he elects to affirm the contract[6]. Of particular significance in the present context is the right of the hirer or buyer to reject the goods tendered and rescind on grounds of defective performance, and the fact that he may lose this right by accepting the goods with knowledge of the breach. Such an acceptance of the goods may be treated as an election to affirm in which event the hirer or buyer can only sue for damages; or it may even be treated as an acceptance of

---

1. See above, Chapter 10.
2. See above, pp. 24–26.   3. See above, pp. 364–365.
4. Subject to the rule against double recovery: see above, p. 386.
5. See above, p. 360.   6. See above, p. 361.

an offer to enter into a contract to vary the previous contract, in which case all remedies for breach of the previous contract might be extinguished[7]. The present section is concerned with the former possibility, in which respect it is convenient to consider separately contracts of sale and h.p.

(a) Rescission by the buyer

It will be recalled that it is the duty of the seller to tender goods in conformity with the contract (s. 27)[8], and that the buyer has a right to inspect any goods tendered to ascertain whether they do so conform (s. 34)[9]. The inference is that the buyer may reject goods tendered in breach of contract[10]. But does this breach also give the buyer the right to rescind the contract?

Under the scheme adopted by the S.G.A., many of the seller's duties are conditions, and even relatively minor breaches of those conditions would give the buyer the right to rescind[11]. Accordingly, the Act seeks to restrict the buyer's rights by providing that he may neither reject the goods nor rescind the contract unless he acts quickly. Section 11 (1) (c) provides as follows:

> "Where a contract of sale is not severable, and the buyer has accepted the goods, or part thereof, *or where the contract is for specific goods, the property in which has passed to the buyer*, the breach of any condition to be fulfilled by the seller can only be treated as a breach of warranty, and not as a ground for rejecting the goods and treating the contract as repudiated, unless there be a term of the contract, express or implied, to that effect".

Notice that the sub-section does not say that if the buyer can and does reject the goods he must rescind the contract[12], but merely imposes a *prima facie* restriction on the right to reject and rescind[13]. This restriction cannot apply to conditional sales within the H.P.A.[14]; and in respect of all other sales may be expressly[15] or impliedly[16] excluded. Nevertheless, the *prima facie* rule contained in s. 11 (1) (c) is important,

---

7. See above, pp. 145–146.   8. Set out above, p. 263.
9. Set out above, p. 269.
10. For the effect on this of the buyer's duty to mitigate, see above, p. 391.
11. But the buyer may neither reject nor rescind for breach of warranty: ss. 11 (1) (b), 62 (1): see above, p. 50.
12. This would deprive him of any right to specific performance. But see *per* DEVLIN J. in *Kwei Tek Chao* v. *British Traders and Shippers, Ltd.*, [1954] 2 Q.B. 459, at p. 480.
13. See *per* SALTER J. in *William Barker & Co., Ltd.* v. *Agius, Ltd.* (1927), 33 Com. Cas. 120, at p. 130.
14. Section 20 (1). Thus, the conditional buyer is in this respect in the same position as a hirer under a h.p. agreement; ss. 20 (2), (4): see below, pp. 402–403.
15. E.g. *W. E. Marshall* v. *Lewis and Peat, Ltd.*, [1963] 1 Lloyd's Rep. 562.
16. E.g. by a contrary trade custom: see above, p. 112.

and gives rise to an unfortunate rigidity in the law. The most notorious example was that the seller of specific goods rarely had any right to reject at all, despite ingenious academic arguments to the contrary[17]; but this particular defect has been avoided by s. 4 (1) of the Misrepresentation Act 1967, which has deleted the italicised words from s. 11 (1) (c). The effect of s. 11 (1) (c), as amended, must now be considered.

The basic notion is that the buyer will lose his rights of rejection and rescission where he accepts the goods tendered in performance of the contract, and that acceptance of part of the goods is to be treated as acceptance of the whole unless the contract is severable. The three possible interpretations of a contract providing for delivery by instalments have already been outlined[18]: where each instalment is a separate contract, clearly acceptance of one instalment cannot bar rejection of the others[19]; and s. 11 (1) (c) states that the position is to be the same where there is a single severable contract. Thus, it is only where there is a single non-severable contract that acceptance of part can bar rejection of the whole under s. 11 (1) (c). As the courts seem reluctant to treat such transactions as a series of contracts, the dispute normally concerns whether the single contract is severable or entire[20]. Assuming that the contract is entire, can the buyer who has accepted part of the goods escape from s. 11 (1) (c) by relying on s. 30 (which deals with delivery of the wrong quantity)[1]? No conflict arises where the seller delivers more than the contract quantity, as the buyer cannot be made to accept the greater amount (s. 30(2)); but there is an apparent conflict where the seller delivers less than the contract quantity (s. 30 (1)), or where he delivers the contract goods mixed with other goods (s. 30 (3)). The matter was considered in *Barker, Ltd.* v. *Agius, Ltd.*[2].

> There was a contract for the sale f.o.b. Hamburg of a quantity of coal briquettes, "size 2 in.". The coal was shipped to Liverpool, being loaded partly as deck cargo, which prevented access to the balance which was below deck. The deck cargo complied with the contract description and was accepted by the buyer, who subsequently discovered that the portion below deck did not conform with the contract, and thereupon gave notice to reject the whole cargo. SALTER J. held that:
>
> (1) the description "size 2 in." was a condition of the contract[3], but that the below-deck cargo did not comply with it;
>
> (2) despite s. 11 (1) (c), the buyer had a *prima facie* right to reject the balance under s. 30 (3) because the contract goods were mixed with other goods within the meaning of s. 30 (3)[4];

---

17. See above, p. 162.   18. See above, p. 277.
19. E.g. *Jackson* v. *Rotax Cycle Co.*, [1910] 2 K.B. 937, C.A.: set out above, p. 82.
20. E.g. *J. Rosenthal & Sons, Ltd.* v. *Esmail*, [1965] 2 All E.R. 860, H.L.
1. See above, pp. 76–79.   2. (1927), 33 Com. Cas. 120.
3. See above, pp. 71–74.   4. See above, pp. 78–79.

(3) the buyer had not exercised that right because he had claimed to reject the whole cargo[5];

(4) therefore all the buyer could now do was to claim damages, and that he was entitled to damages notwithstanding the exclusion clause, as that clause merely excluded liability for breach of warranty[6].

However, this decision must be compared with *E. Hardy & Co.* v. *Hillerns and Fowler*[7].

There was a contract for the sale of 2365 tons of wheat c.i.f. Hull. When the wheat arrived at Hull, the buyer immediately resold part of the cargo, and dispatched it to sub-buyers. Subsequently, the buyer ascertained that none of the wheat complied with the contract description and sought to reject it all. Despite the fact that the buyer examined the wheat as soon as he reasonably could, the Court of Appeal unanimously held that:

(1) by reselling part of the goods the buyer had accepted that part under s. 35[8];

(2) by accepting part the buyer had lost his right to reject any of the wheat, and must be content with damages.

It is true that s. 30 was not mentioned in this case[9]; but the effect of the two cases would appear to be as follows: if none of the goods which are delivered comply with the contract description, acceptance of part will bring the case within s. 11 (1) (c); but if part of the goods delivered comply with the contract description, the buyer may accept that part and reject the rest under s. 30[10]. This result may appear to be illogical. But it is submitted that it follows from his acceptance of goods which do not conform with the contract that the buyer is making his election not to rescind[11]. Suppose a contract for the sale of peas to be delivered in three cases; but only one of the cases delivered contains peas, and the other two contain beans. If the first case accepted contains peas, the effect of s. 30 (3) is that the buyer still has the option to reject the other two. However, if the first case accepted contains runner beans, the

---

5. Even under s. 30 (3) he cannot first accept and then reject: *contra London Plywood and Timber Co., Ltd.* v. *Nasic Oak Extract Factory, Ltd.*, [1939] 2 K.B. 343. Whilst this was the expressed grounds of the latter case, it is submitted that the position should be as follows: the buyer cannot reject the goods which he has accepted; but that does not prevent him rejecting other goods later sent in substitution.

6. See above, p. 139.

7. [1923] 2 K.B. 490, C.A.

8. But see now s. 4 (2) of the Misrepresentation Act 1967: below, p. 401.

9. Because one cannot speak of the delivery of an incorrect quantity where no goods of the contract description are delivered: Atiyah, *Sale of Goods* (3rd Edn.) 219.

10. See *Chalmers' Sale of Goods* (15th Edn.) 134: cited with approval by ROSKILL J. in *Esmail & Sons* v. *Rosenthal, Ltd.*, [1964] 2 Lloyd's Rep. 447, at p. 454.

11. This right of election is considered above, p. 361.

effect of s. 11 (1) (c) is that acceptance of that will bar rejection of the case of peas and of another case of runner beans[12].

Section 11 (1) (c) is expressed to operate where the buyer has accepted the whole or part of the goods; and acceptance is dealt with by s. 35 of the S.G.A., which provides (as amended):

> "The buyer is deemed to have accepted the goods when he intimates to the seller that he has accepted them, or (*except where section 34 otherwise provides*) when the goods have been delivered to him, and he does any act in relation to them which is inconsistent with the ownership of the seller, or when after the lapse of a reasonable time, he retains the goods without intimating to the seller that he has rejected them".

This section deems the seller to have accepted the goods in the following three situations[13].

(1) "When he intimates to the seller that he has accepted them".

As the buyer has a statutory right of inspection under s. 34[14], it follows that mere receipt of the goods by the buyer will not *per se* amount to an acceptance under s. 35[15]. What is required is an intimation by the buyer to the seller that he has elected to accept the goods delivered as conforming with the contract[16]. Moreover, the parties may agree that the buyer's acceptance is to be conditional, as where it is conditional on acceptance by his sub-buyer; and in this case the right to reject and rescind is not lost until the condition materialises[17].

(2) "When . . . (the buyer) . . . does any act in relation to (the goods) which is inconsistent with the ownership of the seller".

The position at common law would appear to be that the buyer was deemed to have accepted if he did any act which clearly showed an intention to affirm; but the statutory formula would appear to introduce two unnecessary difficulties.

(a) What is the interest of the seller with which the buyer must act inconsistently? Clearly, this cannot mean simply the general property in the goods, because this will normally pass at latest at the moment of delivery, so that the buyer cannot subsequently do any acts "inconsistent with the ownership of the seller". In *Kwei Tek Chao* v. *British Traders, Ltd.*[18], DEVLIN J. suggested *obiter* that the seller retained a

---

12. *Contra*, if the third case contained baked beans.
13. Does s. 35 apply where the seller is fraudulent?
14. Set out above, p. 269.
15. *Libau Wood Co.* v. *H. Smith & Sons, Ltd.* (1930), 37 Ll.L. Rep., 296.
16. E.g. *Rosenthal & Sons, Ltd.* v. *Esmail*, [1965] 2 All E.R. 860, C.A.; *Long* v. *Lloyd*, [1958] 2 All E.R. 402, C.A.: set out below, p. 402; the '*Kwei Tek Chao Case*,' [1954] 2 Q.B. 459: set out below, pp. 419–420.
17. See *Heilbutt* v. *Hickson* (1872), L.R. 7 C.P. 438.
18. [1954] 2 Q.B. 459, at pp. 485–488.

conditional right to the goods if the sale is rescinded, and that it is this conditional property in the goods with which the buyer must not act inconsistently. As it would appear difficult to reconcile this view with s. 18[19], it may be that s. 35 should be interpreted to read any act "inconsistent with the *retention or reversion* of ownership *in* the seller".

(b) What acts by the buyer will be inconsistent with the rights of the seller? The pre-1893 cases went no further than to say that a resale by the buyer after he had had an opportunity of inspecting the goods showed an intention to accept. Unfortunately, the Court of Appeal in *E. Hardy & Co.* v. *Hillerns and Fowler*[20] took the view that a resale must necessarily be inconsistent with the ownership of the seller; and the logical outcome of this was that a buyer who "resold" the goods before he purchased, or before the goods were delivered to him, or who ordered delivery direct to his sub-purchaser, never had a right to inspect and reject[1]. With the object of remedying this situation, the italicised words were added to s. 35 by s. 4 (2) of the Misrepresentation Act 1967. Their effect is that the buyer will no longer lose the right to inspect and reject merely because he has done an act inconsistent with the ownership of the seller before he has had a chance to examine the goods[2]; but that he will still lose that right if he cannot place the goods at the seller's disposal, as where the sub-buyer refuses to return the goods delivered to him[3].

(3) "When after the lapse of a reasonable time, he retains the goods without intimating to the seller that he has rejected them".

The mere fact that the goods remain in the buyer's possession cannot, without more, amount to an acceptance, because s. 36 provides that he is under no duty to return the goods[4]. However, assuming that the buyer has not rejected the goods, s. 35 deems him to have accepted if he retains them beyond a reasonable time, which is a question of fact[5]. Thus, in *Leaf* v. *International Galleries*[6], it was held that, even if there was a breach of condition that the painting was a Constable, it was too

---

19. See above, Chapter 13.
20. [1923] 2 K.B. 490, C.A. It has been said that a transfer of c.i.f. documents is not such an act: *per* DEVLIN J. in the *Kwei Tek Chao Case*, above, at p. 488. Cf. *Barrow Lane & Ballard, Ltd.* v. *Phillip Phillips, Ltd.*, [1929]1 K.B. 575: set out above, pp. 252–253.
 1. *E. and S. Ruben, Ltd.* v. *Faire Brothers & Co., Ltd.*, [1949] 1 K.B. 254; [1949] 1 All E.R. 215. But see *Rowland* v. *Divall*, [1923] 2 K.B. 500, C.A.: set out above, p. 58.
 2. E.g. *Tiffin* v. *Pitcher*, [1969] C.L.Y. 3234.
 3. Atiyah & Treitel (1967), 30 M.L.R. 369, 386. And see below, p. 406 note 7.
 4. Set out above, p. 268.
 5. Section 56. See *Sanders* v. *Jameson* (1848), 2 Car. & Kir. 557 (trade custom).
 6. [1950] 2 Q.B. 86; [1950] 1 All E.R. 693 ;C.A.: see above, p. 359, and below, p. 403 . Also the *Kwei Tek Chao Case*, (above).

late to rescind after five years. It is submitted that for this provision to be consistent with s. 34[7], the ordinary rule that time runs from execution of the contract[8] is displaced, and time cannot begin to run until the buyer has had a chance to exercise his right of inspection. Certainly, the seller may by his conduct extend the period of reasonable time, for example, by inducing the buyer to prolong the trial. In *Long* v. *Lloyd*[9],

> The seller of a lorry innocently misrepresented to the buyer that it was in "exceptional condition", and capable of 40 m.p.h. and 11 m.p.g. The buyer paid part of the price, took delivery, and used the lorry in the course of his business for three days. Having discovered several defects after the first day's outing, the buyer complained to the seller, who offered to pay half the cost of some of the repairs. The buyer accepted this; but, after two further days use, he purported to reject on grounds of misrepresentation[10]. The Court of Appeal unanimously held that, from the nature of the representation, it must have been intended that the buyer be allowed a reasonable trial after delivery; but that one day's trial was reasonable, so that sending the lorry on a further journey amounted to a "final acceptance"[11]; and that in any event he had lost the right to rescind by accepting the offer to pay half the cost of repairs[12].

Whilst in the ordinary case the buyer will lose the right to reject and rescind by accepting the documents which represent the goods, he will not do so in the exceptional case of c.i.f. contracts[13]. In a c.i.f. contract, acceptance of these documents will not prevent the buyer from subsequently rejecting the goods on the grounds that they do not conform with the contract description[14]: in this case, there are two separate rights of rejection, one to reject the documents when tendered, and the other to reject the goods when delivered; and acceptance and resale or pledge of the documents will not bar subsequent rejection of the goods[15].

(b) Rescission by the hirer.

Whilst it is probable that a hirer under a h.p. agreement has a duty to accept delivery which is similar to that of a buyer[16], it would seem that,

---

7. And it must be: Atiyah & Treitel (1967), 30 M.L.R. 369, 386. See also *Tiffin* v. *Pitcher* (above).
8. See above, p. 359.
9. [1958] 2 All E.R. 402, C.A.   10. See further below, p. 404.
11. This must be because of a lapse of a reasonable time, not because it constituted an affirmation, as there does not appear to be the intimation to the seller necessary for an affirmation. Cf. *Butterworth* v. *Kingsway Motors, Ltd.*, [1954] 2 All E.R. 694, discussed below, p. 406, note 9.
12. See above, p. 358.
13. C.i.f. contracts are described above, p. 247.
14. But see *Panchand Frères S.A. Co.* v. *Établissements General Grain Co.*, [1970] 1 Lloyd's Rep. 53, C.A.
15. Per DEVLIN J. in the *Kwei Tek Chao Case*, [1954] 2 Q.B. 459, at p. 481: see below, p. 410.
16. See above, p. 270.

unlike a buyer, a hirer does not lose his right to reject and rescind by that acceptance. In *Yeoman Credit Ltd.* v. *Apps*[17] the hirer paid three instalments and retained the defective car for a total of five months. Nevertheless the Court of Appeal unanimously agreed that the hirer was entitled to reject for breach of condition at the end of that five months. HOLROYD PEARCE L.J. explained[18]:

> "Had this been a sale of goods on instalment payments, he could not, of course, have done so after payment of instalments and acceptance of the goods. Had this been a simple hiring . . . he would have been entitled to reject [the goods] and end the hiring, since the owner's breach was a continuing one. The owner's conduct would constitute a continuing repudiation. This hire purchase agreement was, at the material time, more analogous to a simple hiring than to a purchase".

The decision has been rationalised on the basis that "a continuing refusal by the owner to remedy the defects in the goods hired constitutes a continuing breach of the agreement"[19]. Clearly, the Court was determined if it could to find that the hirer had lawfully rejected the goods; and it may be that today a court would, if it were more advantageous to the hirer, decide that he had repudiated the agreement[20], or exercised a statutory right of cancellation[1] or termination[2]. However, the oddity of the doctrine becomes apparent when the measure of damage is considered[3].

2 Rescission for misrepresentation

The principles on which a contract may be rescinded on the grounds that it was induced by misrepresentation have already been outlined. The effect of that misrepresentation subsequently becoming a term of the contract must now be considered. The incorporation will not *per se* bar the right to rescind for misrepresentation[4]. But will that right be lost where there is no right to rescind for breach of contract? This problem may arise (1) where there was never any right to rescind for that breach, or (2) the right to rescind has been lost by acceptance. In *Leaf* v. *International Galleries*[5], where the misrepresentation was incorporated in the contract, DENNING L.J. assumed in the buyer's

---

17. [1962] 2 Q.B. 508, C.A.: set out above, pp. 141–142.
18. At p. 522.
19. Guest, *Law of H.P.* 281. But see Goode, *H.P. Law & Practice* (2nd Edn.) 457–458.   20. See above, pp. 393–394.
1. See above, pp. 42–45.
2. See above, pp. 354–355.
3. See below, pp. 414, 423–425.
4. Section 1 (a) of the Misrepresentation Act 1967: see above, p. 359.
5. [1950] 2 Q.B. 86; [1950] 1 All E.R. 693, C.A.: see above, pp. 359, 401.

favour that it was a condition, pointed out that the right to reject for
breach of condition had been lost by lapse of time[6], and continued[7]:

> "if a claim to reject for breach of condition is barred, it seems to me
> *a fortiori* that a claim to rescission on the grounds of innocent mis-
> representation is also barred".

His Lordship was careful to confine his remarks to innocent misrepresentations which became conditions of the contract[8]; but in *Long
v. Lloyd*[9], PEARCE L.J., in delivering the judgment of the Court of
Appeal, said[10]:

> "A strict application to the facts of the present case of DENNING L.J.'s
> view to the effect that the right (if any) to rescind after completion
> on ground of innocent misrepresentation is barred by acceptance of
> the goods must necessarily prove fatal to the plaintiff's case".

It has been pointed out that no breach of condition was alleged in *Long
v. Lloyd*, and that the Court of Appeal were therefore applying the same
restrictions to the right to rescind for misrepresentation as would be
applied by the S.G.A. to the right to rescind for breach of contract[11].
Even accepting this, certain problems arise. First, does the rule apply
to fraudulent misrepresentations or to innominate terms? Second, does
it follow that at common law, if the misrepresentation becomes a
warranty the right to rescind for misrepresentation is lost[12]? Third,
does the rule apply to h.p. transactions?

2 RESTITUTION IN QUASI-CONTRACT[13]

Where a contracting party has obtained no part of that for which he
bargained, he may be able to recover any money paid on grounds of
total failure of consideration[14]. In relation to such claims by a buyer[15]
or hirer of goods, two questions arise: first, as to the relationship of this
remedy to rescission; and secondly, what amounts to a total failure of
consideration.

---

6. See above, p. 401.
7. At p. 695.
8. The other members of the C.A. do not appear to have gone any further
   than to say that it was too late to rescind for misrepresentation.
9. [1958] 2 All E.R. 402, C.A.: set out above, p. 402.
10. At p. 407.
11. Grunfeld (1958), 21 M.L.R. 550, 555.
12. If so, s. 1 of the Misrepresentation Act 1967 appears to grant the representee
    a new right of rescission: see above, p. 359.
13. This must be distinguished from the process of restitution on conviction:
    see above, p. 332.
14. See generally Stoljar, *Law of Quasi Contract* (1959), 75 L.Q.R. 53; Goff &
    Jones, *Law of Restitution* 340–346.
15. The S.G.A. preserves the common law in this respect: s. 54.

1 The relationship to rescission

Clearly, a claim will lie for total failure of consideration where the parties never reached agreement[16], or where their agreement was rendered void *ab initio* on grounds of mistake or misrepresentation[17]. But what if the contract was valid when made, but was subsequently terminated before it was fully executed? It is settled that the quasi-contractual remedy is generally not available where the contract is illegal[18]; and at one time it was thought that it only lay where the contract was avoided *ab initio*[19]. However, in the *Fibrosa Spolka Akcyjna* v. *Fairbairn Lawson Combe Barbour*[20] the House of Lords said that the test was not whether there had ever been a contract, but whether it had ever been performed, so that a claim on grounds of total failure of consideration might be brought not just where the contract was void *ab initio,* but also where it was subsequently avoided either because the contract was frustrated[1] or because the other party was in breach of it[2]. Indeed, in the *Kwei Tek Chao Case*[3] DEVLIN J. said that,

> "If the goods have been properly rejected, and the price has already been paid in advance, the proper way of recovering the money back is by an action for money paid for a consideration which has wholly failed . . .; but that form of action is governed by exactly the same rules with regard to affirming or avoiding the transaction as in any other case".

It is, of course, logical that the innocent party must elect to rescind before he can recover the price paid on grounds of total failure of consideration; and that the quasi-contractual claim is not open to him if he affirms, or if he cannot rescind[4]. As such a view would entail making the availability of the quasi-contractual remedy dependent on the right to rescind[5], it is difficult to reconcile with the cases where the transferor has no title to the goods: in *Rowland* v. *Divall*[6] the plaintiff had resold

---

16. E.g. *Branwhite* v. *Worcester Finance, Ltd.,* [1969] 1 A.C. 552; [1968] 3 All E.R. 104, H.L.: see above, p. 287.

17. This would seem to follow from *Bell* v. *Lever Brothers, Ltd.,* [1932] A.C. 161, H.L.   18. See above, pp. 38–39.

19. See *Chandler* v. *Webster,* [1904] 1 K.B. 493, C.A.

20. [1943] A.C. 32, H.L.

 1. The decision in the *Fibrosa Case,* [1943] A.C. 32, H.L.

 2. Similarly where a wholly executory contract is rescinded by mutual agreement.

 3. [1954] 2 Q.B. 459, at p. 475.

 4. The *Kwei Tek Chao Case,* [1954] 2 Q.B. 459: set out below, pp. 419–420. This is accepted by most of the authorities as being the position: see Goff & Jones, *Law of Restitution* 21, 343.

 5. The limitations on the right to rescind are considered above, pp. 358–359, 396–404.

 6. [1923] 2 K.B. 500, C.A.: set out above, p. 58.   But compare *Linz* v. *Electric Wire Co., Ltd.,* [1948] A.C. 371; [1948] 1 All E.R. 604, P.C.

the car to X., who had been in possession for two months[7]; and in *Butterworth* v. *Kingsway Motors, Ltd.*[8] PEARSON J. held that the intermediate buyers had lost the right to rescind, but that Butterworth was entitled to rescind notwithstanding his eleven months use of the car[9]. It is submitted that on principle the quasi-contractual remedy should depend on the ability to rescind, and that the two cases should be interpreted in this light.

So far, we have been considering the right of the innocent buyer to rescind for breach and then recover the price paid on grounds of total failure of consideration. Suppose the buyer were the guilty party. Assuming that the contract must be rescinded before a quasi-contractual claim will lie, that claim is probably dependent on the seller electing to rescind[10]. If the seller does so elect, can the buyer recover any sums paid on grounds of total failure of consideration? The early authorities refused to countenance such a claim; but we have seen that STABLE J. subsequently drew a distinction between a deposit and a part-payment, holding that the sum was recoverable in the latter case[11]. His Lordship explained[12]:

> "The real foundation of the right . . . is not total failure of consideration but the right of the purchaser, derived from the terms of the contract and the principle of law applicable, to recover back his money".

It would therefore seem that the guilty buyer cannot recover the price paid on grounds of total failure of consideration, though he may be able to do so on other grounds.

2 The failure of consideration must be total.

The courts have always stressed that money paid under a contract can only be recovered if the failure of consideration is total; and in the *Fibrosa Case*[13] Viscount SIMON L.C. said:

> "When one is considering the law of failure of consideration . . ., it is, generally speaking, not the promise which is referred to as the consideration, but the performance of the promise".

In other words, the correct test is whether one party *in performance of the contract* has conferred any benefit on the other: the vital thing is not

---

7. It is arguable that the resale should not bar rescission because it was cancelled by mutual agreement: see also above, p. 401, note 3.
8. [1954] 2 All E.R. 694: set out above, p. 59.
9. It is a little difficult to accept this in the light of other authorities, though the issue is essentially one of fact: see above, pp. 401–403.
10. See above, p. 361.
11. *Dies* v. *British and International Mining and Finance Corporation, Ltd.*, [1939] 1 K.B. 724: see above, p. 373.   12. At p. 744.
13. [1943] A.C. 32, H.L., at p. 48. But see Treitel, *Law of Contract* (3rd Edn.) 858–859.

whether that other has received *any* benefit, but whether he has received any part of *that* benefit which he was entitled to expect by way of performance of the contract[14]. Thus, it has been held that a hirer under a h.p. agreement cannot recover sums paid under the agreement where that agreement is subsequently determined but he has in the meantime enjoyed both possession of the goods under the bailment[15] and a valid option to purchase[16]. He may, however, do so where there has never been any agreement, notwithstanding his use of the goods for three months[17].

The insistence of the courts that the contract should be rescinded for breach before the innocent party can recover any money paid on grounds of total failure of consideration is essentially just an aspect of this rule that the failure of consideration must be total. But it has been pointed out that the granting of the quasi-contractual remedy on this condition leads to an anomaly: the innocent party can elect either to rescind and sue in quasi-contract, or he can affirm and sue on the contract for damages[18]. However, even this would appear to be an oversimplification. It is clear that, merely because the innocent party rescinds, he does not necessarily have the right to recover any money paid in quasi-contract, though he probably will not have the latter right unless he can and does rescind. Moreover, even where he does rescind and recover any money paid on grounds of total failure of consideration, on principle he should also be able to sue for damages; and conversely, if he affirms, he may be able to recover all the sums paid by way of damages[19].

Notwithstanding the rule that the failure of consideration must be total[1], the scope of the quasi-contractual remedy has been extended to several situations where the claimant has received part of the benefit for which he has bargained. First, where the contract is divisible, in the sense that there is either (1) a series of contracts or (2) a single divisible contract[2], the courts have applied the doctrine to each part individually, so that there might be a total failure in respect of one or more parts notwithstanding that other parts may have been performed[3]. Secondly,

---

14. See Samek (1959), 33 A.L.J. 392, 397. In the case of frustration, this rule has been modified by the Law Reform (Frustrated Contracts) Act 1943: see above, pp. 258-259.
15. *Yeoman Credit, Ltd.* v. *Apps,* [1962] 2 Q.B. 508; [1961] 2 All E.R. 281, C.A.: set out above, pp. 141-142.
16. *Kelly* v. *Lombard Banking, Ltd.* [1958] 3 All E.R. 713, C.A.
17. *Branwhite* v. *Worcester Finance, Ltd.,* [1969] 1 A.C. 552; [1968] 3 All E.R. 104, H.L.: see above, p. 287.
18. See Cheshire & Fifoot, *Law of Contract* (7th Edn.) 596.
19. See below, p. 416.
1. Presumably subject to the *de minimis* rule.
2. See the analysis above, p. 277.
3. *Rugg* v. *Minett* (1809), 11 East 210: set out above, p. 164.

where under a single indivisible contract an obligation is entire[4], there is a total failure of consideration although that obligation has been partially performed because the other party has bargained exclusively for a complete performance[5]. Thirdly, the parties can always agree that the partial failure of the whole consideration is to be treated as a total failure of part of the consideration[6]; and, where the partial performance of the seller shows an intention to repudiate[7], the buyer will have an option to do so[8]. Fourthly, even where the case cannot be brought within any of the above rules, the law does not say that the receipt of part of the benefit for which he has bargained by the buyer or hirer must be fatal to his quasi-contractual claim. It merely requires the claimant to make *restitutio* as a condition precedent to his claim[9]; and it is therefore only where it is impossible to restore the benefit that the quasi-contractual claim may be barred. However, a rigid insistence on restitution by a buyer or hirer would usually avoid this rule, because of the element of intermediate enjoyment of possession. It is easy to see that the enjoyment should be ignored where it was induced by fraud on the part of the seller or owner; but the courts have also adopted this approach where the seller or owner is innocently in breach of the implied condition as to title[10]. It has been suggested above that the latter development was a mistake[11].

3 AN ACTION FOR DAMAGES

A buyer or hirer may have at his disposal an action for damages against the seller or owner or some third party as follows: first, against the seller or owner for breach of the contract of sale or h.p., or some collateral contract, or in tort, or under the Misrepresentation Act 1967; and secondly, as against a third party for breach of a collateral contract, or in tort, or under the 1967 Act. Whilst the general principles for the measurement of damages have been outlined in the previous Chapter[12], it is proposed to concentrate here on the right to damages for breach of the contract of sale or h.p.

The right to damages may be barred or limited by an exclusion or liquidated damages or arbitration clause in the contract of sale or

---

4. See above, p. 352.
5. *Giles* v. *Edwards* (1797), 7 Term Rep. 181: explained by Goff & Jones, *Law of Restitution* 340. *Contra* where the obligation broken is not an entire one.
6. See *Benjamin on Sale* (8th Edn.) 459.
7. See above, pp. 277–279.
8. *Behrend & Co.* v. *Produce Brokers, Ltd.*, [1920] 3 K.B. 530: set out above, p. 77.
9. *Towers* v. *Barrett* (1786), 1 Term Rep. 133.
10. *Rowland* v. *Divall*, [1923] 2 K.B. 500, C.A.; *Butterworth* v. *Kingsway Motors, Ltd.*, [1954] 2 All E.R. 694.
11. See above, p. 64.   12. See above, pp. 378–379.

h.p.; but, where it is not so barred or limited, the rules for the measure of damages will differ according to whether or not the breach is a failure to deliver the goods.

1 Damages for non-delivery

Prima facie, the buyer or hirer will have a right of action for damages for non-delivery where no goods are delivered at all[13], or where the goods tendered by the seller or owner are lawfully rejected and the contract rescinded on the grounds that they do not conform with the contract in quantity[14], quality[15], or any other matter: and he will also be able to recover any part of the price paid on grounds of total failure of consideration[16]. However, whereas the seller or owner has an action in contract for the price or rent[17], an action to recover the goods is seldom available to the buyer or hirer[18].

(a) Sale

The counterpart to the seller's action for damages for non-acceptance under s. 50[19] is the buyer's action for non-delivery under s. 51. Section 51 (1) provides:

> "Where the seller wrongfully neglects or refuses to deliver the goods to the buyer, the buyer may maintain an action against the seller for damages for non-delivery".

This provision does not apply to a mere delay in tendering delivery, where damages will necessarily be assessed on different lines[20]; and it may be a nice question whether the delay is so great as to amount to a non-delivery. However, where there is a "neglect or refusal to deliver" within the meaning of s. 51 (1), the types of damage in respect of which the buyer may recover will depend on the rules of remoteness laid down in *Hadley* v. *Baxendale*[1].

First rule. This receives statutory formulation in s. 51 (2) as follows[2]:

> "The measure of damage is the estimated loss directly and naturally resulting, in the ordinary course of events, from the seller's breach of contract".

Second rule. Where the seller has special knowledge which would

---

13. For the duty to deliver, see above, p. 265, *et seq.*
14. See above, p. 76.
15. See above, pp. 70, 94.
16. *Comptoir D'Achat* v. *Luis de Ridder*, [1949] A.C. 293; [1949] 1 All E.R. 269, H.L.: see generally above, p. 405.
17. See above, pp. 370–376.
18. Whether framed as an action for the specific performance of the contract or in the tort of detinue: see below, p. 414.
19. See above, p. 376.
20. See below, pp. 417–421
1. (1854), 9 Exch. 341: see above, p. 388.
2. Cf. s. 50 (2).

increase the loss naturally arising from his breach, the seller will also be liable under s. 54 for that "special damage".

Prima facie rule. The law assumes that the buyer will mitigate his loss if he can by going out into the market and buying a substitute; so that, leaving aside the possibility of an express provision as to the amount payable by the seller[3], the loss will, *prima facie*, be quantified by reference to whether there is at the place of delivery an available market in which the buyer may purchase substitute goods[4].

1. *Where there is an available market.* Section 51 (3) provides:

> "Where there is an available market for the goods in question the measure of damages is prima facie to be ascertained by the difference between the contract price and the market or current price of the goods at the time or times when they ought to be delivered, or, if no time was fixed, then at the time of the refusal to deliver".

The onus of proving the buying price is on the buyer[5], and the amount recoverable is as follows:

(1) If the market price is above the contract price, the buyer is *prima facie* entitled under s. 51 (3) to the difference between the two; and any subsales by the buyer must be ignored, so that it is irrelevant that he has resold at an intermediate[6] or even a higher[7] price. If the buyer buys on the market at above the market price, he cannot recover that extra expenditure because he has not mitigated his loss[8]; but, if he buys below the market price, he will only recover his actual loss.

(2) If the market price is equal to or below the contract price, the intention of s. 51 (3) is presumably that the buyer will only receive nominal damages because he would suffer no loss by buying in the market[8a]. Unlike the predicament of the seller[9], this result will usually be fair and is therefore normally adopted by the courts.

Thus, the *prima facie* measure of damages is the amount by which the market price exceeds the contract price at the stipulated date[10] and place[11] for delivery of the goods[12], or of the documents of title in the

---

3. This may offend the rule against penalties: see above, pp. 391–395.
4. In practice, the courts have been fairly generous in deciding whether (a) the market is available and (b) what is a substitute: see generally Lawson (1969), 43 A.L.J. 52, 59–61.
5. This is the converse to s. 50 (3): see above, p. 383. Compare the rule on late delivery: below, p. 417.
6. *Williams Brothers* v. *Agius, Ltd.,* [1914] A.C. 510, H.L.
7. *Williams* v. *Reynolds* (1865), 6 B. & S. 495.
8. *Gainsford* v. *Carroll* (1824), 2 B. & C. 624.
8a. See *Pagnon & Fratelli* v. *Corbira Industrial Agropaenaria Ltd.,* [1970] 1 W.L.R. 1306, C.A.   9. See above, p. 383.
10. This may be extended at the request of the seller: *Ogle* v. *Earl of Vane* (1868), L.R. 3 Q.B. 272, Ex. Ch.
11. If this is a foreign country, there will be a foreign currency element involved: see above, p. 378.
12. *Melachrino* v. *Nickoll and Knight,* [1920] 1 K.B. 693; *A.B.D.* (*Metals and Waste*), *Ltd.* v. *Anglo Chemical Co.,* [1955] 2 Lloyd's Rep. 456.

case of a c.i.f. contract[13]. If the contract provides for delivery within a specified period, the last possible moment at which the seller is entitled to tender delivery is taken[14]; and, if delivery is to be by instalments, the market price is fixed separately for each instalment at the time when it is due[15]. The provision, that if no time is fixed for delivery the time of refusal to deliver is to be taken, is clearly relevant where delivery is to be made as required by the buyer[16]; but it is inapplicable where there is an anticipatory breach. In the latter case, the buyer is still, *prima facie*, entitled under s. 51 (3) to damages calculated by reference to the market price at the time fixed for delivery[17], with the following qualifications[18]: first, if the market is rising and the buyer elects to rescind, either immediately on repudiation or at a later date prior to the time of performance, he is under a duty to mitigate his loss from the date of his election by purchasing substitute goods in the market at that date[19]; and secondly, if the market is falling and the buyer similarly elects to rescind either immediately or at an intermediate date, he is only entitled to the amount by which that price then exceeds the contract price as that is his actual loss[20]. Finally, there is the question whether the buyer who has paid the price can be expected to go into the market and buy against the contract[1]: if so, the above rules presumably apply; but otherwise damages are presumably assessed on the basis that there is no market available to him[2].

2. *Where there is no available market.* There may be no available market, perhaps because the buyer has specifically resold the same goods, or demand exceeds supply, or no reasonable substitute was available. In such cases, s. 51 (3) is inapplicable, and the court must make the best estimate it can of the loss. *Prima facie*, this will be the amount by which the value at the date of breach exceeds the contract price; and, if the buyer has resold the goods, the resale price is evidence of their value[3], but not conclusive of their value[4].

---

13. *Sharpe & Co., Ltd.* v. *Nosawa & Co.*, [1917] 2 K.B. 814.
14. See *Leigh* v. *Paterson* (1818), 8 Taunt 540.
15. See *Brown* v. *Muller* (1872), L.R. 7 Exch. 319; *Roper* v. *Johnson* (1873), L.R. 8 C.P. 167.
16. What if delivery is to be made within a reasonable time? See *Millett* v. *Van Heek & Co.*, [1921] 2 K.B. 369, C.A.
17. *Contra* if he affirms, where there is no duty to mitigate by buying in before the delivery date: *Brown* v. *Muller* (1872), L.R. 7 Exch. 319, D.C.
18. These qualifications apply conversely where the buyer is in anticipatory breach: see *Mayne & McGregor on Damages* (12th Edn.) 430.
19. *Melachrino* v. *Nickoll and Knight*, [1920] 1 K.B. 693, at p. 697.
20. *Melachrino* v. *Nickoll and Knight* (above). Cf. *Roth* v. *Taysen* (1896), 12 T.L.R. 211, C.A.
1. This raises questions of remoteness and mitigation: see above, pp. 387, 390.
2. But see *Mayne & McGregor, op. cit.*, 368; *Street on Damages* 217–218.
3. *France* v. *Gaudet* (1871), L.R. 6 Q.B. 199, Ex. Ch.
4. *The Arpad*, [1934] P. 189, C.A.; *Heskell* v. *Continental Express, Ltd.*, [1950] 1 All E.R. 1033.

Consequential loss. Where the buyer could not have made any profit even if the seller had complied with his duty to deliver, the buyer can only recover money expended in reliance on the seller's promise, such as freight[5] and administrative expenses[6]. However, where the buyer could have made a profit, he is entitled at his option to recover under *either* his "reliance" *or* his "expectancy" interest[7]. The *prima facie* rule for measuring the buyer's loss of profit under his "expectancy" interest has already been examined[8]; and the present discussion is concerned with the question of whether that amount can be increased by reason of any consequential loss suffered by the buyer.

Perhaps the most common type of consequential loss suffered by a buyer in these circumstances is the loss of the profit he expected to make on a sub-sale. The major difficulty here is whether the sub-sale is too remote[9]. Whilst it is not sufficient that the seller merely knows that the buyer is a merchant buying generally for resale[10], a resale will not be too remote where the seller knew that the buyer would resell[11], or that he would probably resell[12]. The leading case where the buyer has recovered damages based on the loss of profit on resale is *Re, Hall Ltd. and W. H. Pim & Co.*[13].

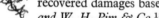

> There was a contract for the sale of a cargo of wheat at 51/9d per quarter, the contract clearly contemplating the possibility of sub-sale by the buyer. The buyer resold the cargo as such at 56/9d per quarter. When the seller refused to deliver, the market price was 53/9d per quarter. The seller argued that he should only be liable for the difference between the contract and market prices (2/- per quarter); but the House of Lords held him liable for the difference between the contract and resale prices (5/- per quarter).

Clearly, the buyer in this case was awarded 5/- per quarter only because of the non-remote resale of that very cargo: if the sub-sale had been too remote, it would have been ignored; and, even if it were non-remote, the seller is normally entitled to expect the buyer to mitigate his loss by buying a substitute[14]. Thus, the decision turns on the finding that the resale of the particular cargo as such was non-remote, and that there was

---

5. *Braude (London), Ltd.* v. *Porter*, [1959] 2 Lloyd's Rep. 161.
6. *Robert Stewart & Sons, Ltd.* v. *Carapanayoti, Ltd.*, [1962] 1 All E.R. 418.
7. These terms are explained above, p. 378.
8. See above, pp. 409–411.
9. The rules of remoteness are considered above, pp. 387–390.
10. *Per* MAUGHAM L.J. in *The Arpad*, [1934] P. 189, C.A., at p. 230.
11. *Household Machines, Ltd.* v. *Cosmos Exporters, Ltd.*, [1947] K.B. 217; [1946] 2 All E.R. 622.
12. *Patrick* v. *Russo-British Grain Export Co.*, [1927] 2 K.B. 535; *Re R. & H. Hall, Ltd. and W. H. Pim & Co. Arbitration* (1928), 139 L.T. 50, H.L.
13. (1928), 139 L.T. 50; H.L. Cf. *Hydraulic Engineering Co.* v. *McHaffie* (1878), 4 Q.B.D. 670, C.A.: see below, p. 421.
14. *Per* DEVLIN J. in the *Kwei Tek Chao Case*, [1954] 2 Q.B. 459, 489–490.

no available market because the resale contract would not allow the buyer to buy a substitute; and it seems likely that, if the sub-sale had been below the market price, this would have reduced the damages[15]. Everything therefore turns on what the seller could have foreseen under the rules of remoteness: if a sub-sale was foreseeable in general terms, he is *prima facie* only liable for an ordinary loss of profit[16]; and the buyer can only recover the greater amount lost on a specially lucrative contract if the seller was aware of that fact[17]. Where the sub-sale is non-remote, the seller should also be liable for any compensation which the buyer has to pay[18] his sub-buyer by way of damages and costs for breach of the sub-contract[19]; and, where there is a string of contracts contemplated, for the buyer to recover in respect of compensation to the further buyers[20]. However, it seems unlikely that the buyer will ever receive any compensation for injury to his business connexions[1].

Besides amounting to a breach of contract, non-delivery by the seller may also enable the buyer to maintain an action in tort for conversion or detinue on the grounds that he has an immediate right to possession[2]. Where the buyer is suing a third party in tort, the measure of his damages is *prima facie* the value of the goods[3]; but, where he is suing the unpaid seller, the damages will be reduced by the price. Thus in *Chinery* v. *Viall*[4],

> The defendant sold some sheep on credit to the plaintiff, but before delivery wrongfully resold and delivered them to X. The plaintiff sued in contract and tort; and the court held—
> (1) in contract, the buyer was entitled to damages for non-delivery calculated on the excess of the market value over the contract price (£5);
> (2) in tort, the buyer was not entitled to the whole value of the sheep without deducting the unpaid price, but only the actual loss sustained (£5).

Since this case, it has become a well-established rule that a buyer suing for non-delivery cannot recover more in compensatory damages[5] by suing in tort than in contract[6]. Thus, whilst it is clear that the buyer

---

15. Treitel, *Law of Contract* (3rd Edn.) 790. Atiyah, *Sale of Goods* (3rd Edn.) 232 *dubitante*.
16. *Household Machines, Ltd.* v. *Cosmos Exporters, Ltd.*, [1947] K.B. 217.
17. Cf. *Victoria Laundry, Ltd.* v. *Newman Industries, Coulson & Co., Ltd.*, [1949] 2 K.B. 528; [1949] 1 All E.R. 997, C.A.: set out below, p. 420.
18. Or an indemnity where he has not yet been sued by his sub-buyer: *Household Machines, Ltd.* v. *Cosmos Exporters, Ltd.* (above).
19. *Grébert-Borgnis* v. *Nugent* (1885), 15 Q.B.D. 85, C.A.
20. Cf. *Kasler and Cohen* v. *Slovouski*, [1928] 1 K.B. 78: set out below, p. 427.
1. *Mayne & McGregor on Damages* (12th Edn.) 381. Cf. below, p. 421.
2. See above, p. 377.   3. See above, pp. 379–380.
4. (1860), 5 H. & N. 288.
5. What of exemplary damages, which are only available in tort?
6. See the authorities collected in *Benjamin on Sale* (8th Edn.) 942, note (u).

should by suing in tort *prima facie* be able to recover a non-remote loss of profit on a sub-sale[7], it may be that the heads of damage in respect of which recovery may be made in a tort action are limited to the types of loss which would be non-remote in a contractual action[8], so that to this extent it is irrelevant that the rules of remoteness may differ as between contract and tort[9]. Nor can the buyer suing in detinue obtain an order for specific restitution[10] where he could not obtain a decree of specific performance of the contract[11].

(b) Hire purchase

If the contract was one of simple hiring, the hirer would *prima facie* be entitled by way of damages to the amount by which the contract rate of hire is exceeded by the market rate at which the hirer could hire similar goods under similar terms. However, this is to ignore the element of option; and presumably the *prima facie* measure of damages should be the amount by which the market h.p. price exceeds the contract h.p. price[12]. Whilst there has been no reported case where the measure of damages for physical non-delivery to a hirer under a h.p. agreement has been discussed[13], the matter has been considered in relation to continuous breaches by the owner[14]. Clearly, a hirer who lawfully rejects the goods tendered and rescinds the contract, is entitled to sue on the basis of a non-delivery[14a]. But is a hirer who has accepted delivery and has subsequently lawfully rejected on grounds of continuous breach entitled to do so? In *Yeoman Credit, Ltd.* v. *Apps*[15], the very case where the doctrine of continuous breach was enunciated[14], the Court of Appeal unanimously[16] decided that, after rescinding the contract, the hirer was entitled to recover by way of damages the estimated sum that would be necessary to put the car into repair. This appears closer to the measure of damages applicable to breach of warranty[17] than to non-delivery; and the decision has been criticised on the grounds that the hirer could have no possible interest in repairing the goods after rescinding the contract[18]. Of course, this very dilemma spotlights the oddity of the doctrine of continuous breach[14]; and the measure of damages where the hirer affirms is discussed below[17].

---

7. See *France* v. *Gaudet* (1871), L.R. 6 Q.B. 199, Ex. Ch.
8. *The Arpad*, [1934] P. 189, C.A. See Goodhart (1937), 2 U.Tor.L.J. 1; *Mayne & McGregor on Damages* (12th Edn.) 105a, 708.
9. See above, p. 389. Is the same true if contract damages would exceed tort damages?
10. See above, pp. 333–334.   11. *Cohen* v. *Roche*, [1927] 1 K.B. 169.
12. Goode, *H.P. Law & Practice* (2nd Edn.) 451–452.
13. The issue arose in *Tommey* v. *Finextra, Ltd.* (1962), 106 Sol. Jo. 1012.
14. See above, p. 403.
14a. But see *Farnworth Finance Facilities* v. *Attryde*, [1970] 2 All E.R. 774, C.A.
15. [1962] 2 Q.B. 508; [1961] 2 All E.R. 281, C.A.: set out above, pp. 141–142.
16. HARMAN and DAVIES L.JJ. had some doubts about the matter (at pp. 524, 526).   17. See below, pp. 423–425.
18. Goode, *op. cit.*, 456, 458; Guest, *Law of H.P.* 283.

2 Damages for other breaches of contract

In respect of sales, the rules governing actions by the buyer for damages for breaches of contract other than non-delivery have partially been given statutory form in s. 53 of the S.G.A.; and, in so far as s. 53 reflects the common law, it is also applicable in h.p. Section 53 (1) provides:

> "Where there is a breach of warranty by the seller, or where the buyer elects, or is compelled, to treat any breach of a condition on the part of the seller as a breach of warranty[19], the buyer is not by reason only[20] of such breach of warranty entitled to reject the goods; but he may (a) set up against the seller the breach of warranty in diminution or extinction of the price; or (b) maintain an action against the seller for damages for the breach of warranty".

Section 53 (1) envisages that the buyer may wish to do one of two things:

(1) Set up the seller's breach by way of a defence to the seller's action for the price. Technically, this is not a set-off, but a counter-claim[1], and therefore must arise in respect of the same contract[2].

(2) Maintain an action against the seller for breach of contract or tort[3], in which case the mere existence of a potential counter-claim by the unpaid seller for the price will not *per se* justify reducing the damages by the price[4].

These two are alternative, in the sense that the buyer cannot recover compensation in respect of the seller's breach and then set up that breach when sued for the price; and a decision that there was no warranty or no breach operates as *res judicata*. However, in case the buyer's loss should exceed the price, s. 53 (4) provides that:

> "The fact that the buyer has set up the breach of warranty in diminution or extinction of the price does not prevent him from maintaining an action for the same breach of warranty if he has suffered further damage".

The S.G.A. also deals with the question of remoteness of damage in contract in terms similar to those used in other sections[5]. Section

---

19. This suggests that the draftsman thought that a condition became a warranty if the buyer only claimed damages; but this is not so: *Wallis, Son and Wells* v. *Pratt and Haynes*, [1911] A.C. 394, H.L.
20. He may be able to reject for some other cause: see *Chalmers, Sale of Goods* (15th Edn.) 174.
1. *Bright* v. *Rogers*, [1917] 1 K.B. 917, D.C.
2. See *Bow McLachlan & Co.* v. *Ship Camosun*, [1909] A.C. 597, P.C.
3. See *Benjamin on Sale* (8th Edn.) 984, note (d).
4. *Gillard* v. *Brittan* (1841), 8 M. & W. 575; *Healing (Sales), Pty., Ltd.* v. *Inglis Electrix, Pty.,Ltd.*, [1969] A.L.J.R. 533, H.C. Compare non-delivery: above, p. 409.
5. Cf. ss. 50 (2), 51 (2): set out above, pp. 388, 409.

53 (2) sets out the first rule in *Hadley* v. *Baxendale*[6] in the following terms:

> "The measure of damages for breach of warranty is the estimated loss directly and naturally resulting, in the ordinary course of events, from the breach of warranty".

It must be borne in mind that there may also be a claim under the second rule in *Hadley* v. *Baxendale* by reason of s. 54; that in some cases the breach of contract may give rise to the possibility of an action in tort, in which case the principles of remoteness in tort are relevant[7]; and that, where the buyer has a cause of action against the same person in contract and tort, he probably cannot recover more by suing that person in tort than if he had sued him in contract[8].

It is convenient to distinguish between the claims of the buyer or hirer in respect of the following: (a) defective title; (b) late delivery; and (c) defective quality.

(a) *Actions in respect of a defective title*

Where the seller or owner is in breach of the implied undertaking that he has a right to sell the goods[9], the buyer or hirer who is evicted from possession by a person with a superior title[10] has a right of election as to the remedy he pursues[11]: he may rescind the contract, and recover the price on grounds of total failure of consideration[12] and have his damages assessed on the basis of non-delivery[13]; or he may affirm the contract and recover by way of damages under his "reliance" interest the purchase or h.p. price[14] and any expenses[15]. Even where the seller or owner is merely in breach of the warranty as to quiet possession or as to freedom from encumbrances, if the buyer or hirer is rightfully evicted from possession by a third person, he is similarly entitled to recover under his "reliance" interest the purchase or h.p. price[16] and any expenditure thrown away[17]. On the other hand, if the breach of warranty did not result in the eviction of the buyer or hirer, presumably he ought not to be able to recover the purchase or h.p. price[18].

---

6. (1854), 9 Exch. 341, at p. 354: see above, p. 388.
7. See above, pp. 387–388.   8. See above, p. 413.
9. See above, p. 56, *et seq.*
10. What if he is not evicted?   See above, p. 64, note 2.
11. See above, p. 58.
12. See above, p. 404.   13. See above, p. 408.
14. *Warman* v. *Southern Counties Finance Corporation, Ltd.*, [1949] 2 K.B. 576; [1949] 1 All E.R. 711: set out above, p. 60.
15. *Warman's Case* (above,; and *per* SINGLETON L.J. in *Mason* v. *Burningham*, [1949] 2 K.B. 545, C.A., at p. 560.   And see Treitel, *Law of Contract* (3rd Edn.) 861–862.
16. *Lloyds and Scottish Finance, Ltd.* v. *Modern Cars, Ltd.*, [1966] 1 Q.B. 764; [1964] 2 All E.R. 732: set out above, p. 65.
17. The *Lloyds & Scottish Case* (above); *Mason* v. *Burningham*, (above).
18. Cf. above, p. 64, note 2.

Where the buyer or hirer might have made a profit from the goods, he may alternatively claim under his "expectancy" interest[19]. If he can and does rescind, then the damages are measured on the basis of non-delivery[1]; but the other cases must now be considered. It would appear that damages are assessed on the same basis as where the goods are defective in quality in respect of both the *prima facie* rule[2] and consequential loss[3] flowing from breach of an undertaking as to title.

(b) Actions in respect of a late delivery

If the late delivery of goods sold amounts to a repudiation[4], the buyer may elect to rescind, in which case damages will be assessed on the basis of non-delivery[1]. However, where the buyer cannot or does not rescind, the action for damages is something of a hybrid: the *prima facie* measure of damages has much in common with claims for breach of warranty because there has been a delivery[5], whereas the measure of damages for consequential loss has much in common with that for non-delivery[6]. Presumably, the rules are similar in the case of the late delivery of goods let under a h.p. agreement.

Prima facie rule. Whilst there is no statutory formulation in the S.G.A. which specifically refers to the measure of damages recoverable for late delivery of goods sold, it would appear that once again the *prima facie* measure of damages depends on whether there is an available market[7], though this time the assumption is that the seller will sell the goods in such a market. Where a h.p. agreement contains the usual prohibition of sale by the hirer, presumably there is no available market in which the hirer can sell the goods during the continuance of the agreement.

1. *Where there is an available market.* The normal *prima facie* measure of damages is the amount by which the market value at the contractual time for delivery exceeds the market value at the actual time of delivery, the relevant price being the selling price[8]. It is the market value at the contractual time of delivery which is to be taken, not the contract price[9]; but the contract price is *prima facie* evidence of that value, just

---

19. The relationship of claims under the "reliance" and "expectancy" interest is explained above, p. 412.
1. See above, p. 408 *et seq.*
2. The issue was avoided in the following case, where it was admitted that the goods were equal in value and price: *Healing (Sales), Pty., Ltd.* v. *Inglis Electrix, Pty., Ltd.,* [1969] A.L.J.R. 533, H.C. The *prima facie* rule for defective quality is considered below, pp. 421–425.
3. See below, pp. 425–428.
4. See above, p. 360.
5. *Per* Lord DUNEDIN in *Williams Brothers* v. *E. T. Agius, Ltd.,* [1914] A.C. 510, H.L., at p. 522.
6. See *Mayne & McGregor on Damages* (12th Edn.) 383.
7. This concept is discussed above, pp. 382–383.
8. *Per* DEVLIN J. in the *Kwei Tek Chao Case,* [1954] 2 Q.B. 459 at p. 495. Compare the rule in the case of non-delivery: above, p. 410.
9. Compare non-delivery, where the contract price is taken.

as any sub-sale price might be[10]. Similarly, a contemporaneous resale price should be no more than evidence of the market value at the date of actual delivery[11], though this view might appear difficult to reconcile with *Wertheim* v. *Chicoutimi Pulp Co.*[12].

> There was a sale of 3,000 tons of wood-pulp at 25/- per ton for delivery September/November. At the time fixed for delivery, the market price was 70/- per ton; but when the pulp was eventually delivered the following June it was 42/6d per ton. Whilst the buyers had *prima facie* lost 27/6d per ton, they had in fact resold[13] the pulp at 65/- per ton. The Privy Council held that the sellers could rely on the sub-sale to reduce damages to 5/- per ton.

This case has been the subject of much adverse criticism: if the sub-sale had been of the same goods *as such*, it is argued that there would have been no market available to the buyer, so that he would have made no loss[14]; and, if the sub-sale had merely been of equivalent goods, it would have been irrelevant, because the buyer need not have committed the goods to that contract but could have sold them on the market[15]. In fact, the sub-sale was merely of an equivalent quantity; and the reason given by Lord ATKINSON for his decision was that the buyer should not "be permitted to make a profit by the breach"[16]. However, it has been pointed out that the buyer would have made a profit not out of the breach, but out of the advantageous sub-sale[17]. Possibly, the case is explicable on the grounds that, whilst the buyer was *prima facie* entitled to the difference between the two market prices, he was under a duty to mitigate his loss[18]; but, even if the sub-sale by the seller goes beyond his duty to mitigate, this may be seen as a policy decision that the buyer is not to recover more than his loss[19].

2. *Where there is no available market.* In this case, the measure of damages is *prima facie* the amount by which the contract price exceeds the actual value at the contractual time for delivery. In *Kwei Tek Chao* v. *British Traders, Ltd.*[20]

---

10. *Mayne & McGregor on Damages* (12th Edn.) 385.
11. Compare the rule in non-delivery and breach of warranty of quality: above, p. 410, and below, pp. 421–422.
12. [1911] A.C. 301, P.C.
13. The buyer in fact used the goods to perform a contract made prior to the one presently litigated.
14. *Contra* if the sub-sale had been non-remote: compare above, p. 412.
15. *Per* SCRUTTON, L.J. in *Slater* v. *Hoyle and Smith*, [1920] 2 K.B. 11, C.A., at pp. 23–24. Accepted by *Mayne & McGregor on Damages* (12th Edn.) 386; Treitel, *Law of Contract* (3rd Edn.) 791.
16. At p. 308.   17. Treitel, *op. cit.*, 652.
18. See generally above, pp. 390–391.
19. Compare *British Westinghouse Electric and Manufacturing Co., Ltd.* v. *Underground Electric Rail. Co., Ltd.*, [1912] A.C. 673, H.L.: see above p. 379, note 10. But see below, p. 422.
20. [1954] 2 Q.B. 459; [1954] 3 All E.R. 165.

There was a contract for the sale of 20 tons of Rongalite C c.i.f. Hongkong at £590 per ton, shipment from Antwerp not later than 31.10.51. The goods were actually shipped on 3.11.51; but the bills of lading were forged by a third party to show 31.10.51 as the date of shipment; and they were consequently accepted by the buyer, who paid the price. Owing to the late shipment, the buyer lost his contract for resale in Hongkong; but he accepted late delivery with knowledge of the breach. The buyer was unable to resell the goods, as a Chinese embargo had destroyed the market. Accordingly, the buyer claimed either the return of the price on grounds of total failure of consideration, or alternatively, damages for breach of contract and loss of profit. Having decided that the sellers were not liable for the fraud of the third party, DEVLIN J. held as follows:

(1) *Prima facie* the buyer has two rights of rejection, (1) to reject the documents and (2) to reject the goods[1]; but, he had accepted the goods with knowledge of the breach[2], and was therefore not entitled to recover the price on grounds of total failure of consideration[3].

(2) There were two separate breaches of contract in respect of which the buyer might therefore claim damages, each with its own measure of damages[4].

(3) *Prima facie*, the measure of damages for late delivery of goods is the difference between the market values at the contractual and actual time of delivery[5]; and that for late delivery of shipping documents is the difference between the contract price and market price at the time of delivery[6]. In both cases, it is assumed that the buyer will resell the goods on delivery to mitigate his loss, so that the relevant price is the selling price then[7]; but, if he is unaware of the breach, the relevant date is postponed until he could with due diligence have discovered the fault and resold[8].

(4) However, because of the Chinese embargo, there was no real market in which the goods could be sold, so that the value of the goods must be taken instead; and, as their salvage value was £70 per ton, the buyer was entitled to £520 per ton (£590 − 70).

(5) His Lordship rejected the buyer's claim for loss of profit on the sub-sale on the following grounds: whilst the sellers might contemplate sub-sales generally, they did not know that the goods had been resold *as such*[9]; and it was therefore to be expected that the

---

1. At pp. 480–481: see above, p. 402.
2. At p. 475: see above, p. 400.
3. At p. 477: see above, p. 405.
4. At p. 483, following *Finlay & Co., Ltd.* v. *Kwik Hoo Tong*, [1929] 1 K.B. 400, C.A.: see below, p. 423. Presumably this is subject to the rule against double recovery: see above, p. 386.
5. At p. 478: see above, p. 417.
6. At p. 479. Compare non-delivery: above, p. 410.
7. At pp. 495, 497.
8. At p. 497.
9. His Lordship was not even convinced that the goods had been resold *per se*: at. p. 490.

buyer would go out into the falling market and buy substitute goods, in which event he would suffer no damage[10].

Consequential loss.   Naturally, the buyer may recover any money expended in reliance on the seller's promise, such as extra freight charges[11], or losses resulting from currency changes[12].   However, where he would have made a profit, the buyer may, alternatively, claim in respect of his expectancy interest[13]; and the major issue here is whether he may recover anything beyond the *prima facie* measure in respect of his intended use or resale of the goods, subject always to the duty to mitigate[14].

1. *Loss of use.*   Obviously, the buyer may recover in respect of any expenses incurred as a result of the loss of use[15]; but he may also recover in respect of loss of profit he would have made from use of the goods.   In *Victoria Laundry, Ltd.* v. *Newman Industries, Ltd.*[16],

> The plaintiff launderers dyers decided to obtain a larger boiler to expand their business in view of the prevailing shortage of laundry facilities.   They contracted to buy one from the defendant, who agreed to deliver and install it on the plaintiff's premises. The seller knew that the buyers needed the boiler in connection with their laundry business, though not the exact use to which it was to be put. When the boiler was delivered some five months late, the buyers claimed damages for loss of profit as follows: (1) £16 per week for the new customers they would have taken on; and (2) £262 per week which they would have earned on a dyeing contract with the Ministry of Supply.

The Court of Appeal unanimously held that the seller could have foreseen that loss of business profits would have been liable to result from the delay[17], but did not know of the contract with the Ministry of Supply; and they therefore held that the buyers could not recover under the specially lucrative Ministry contract, but that that did not prevent them[18]

> "from recovering some general (and perhaps conjectural) sum for loss of business in respect of dyeing contracts to be reasonably expected, any more than in respect of laundering contracts to be reasonably expected".

---

10. At pp. 489–490: cf. above, p. 411.
11. *Borries* v. *Hutchinson* (1865), 18 C.B.N.S. 445.
12. *Aruna Mills, Ltd.* v. *Dhanrajmal Gobindram*, [1968] 1 All E.R. 113.
13. The relationsihp of claims under the "reliance" and "expectancy" interest is explained above, p. 412.
14. See generally above, pp. 390–391.
15. *Henderson* v. *Meyer* (1941), 46 Com. Cas. 209.
16. [1949] 2 K.B. 528; [1949] 1 All E.R. 997, C.A.
17. For criticism of this test of remoteness, see above, p. 389.
18. At p. 543.

2. *Loss on a sub-sale.* Where the seller knew of the sub-sale of the goods *per se* and the sub-contract delivery date, he has been held liable for the loss of profit on the sub-sale[19]. However, such precise knowledge on the part of the seller is clearly unusual; and anyway, such a claim will usually fail on the grounds that the buyer should have mitigated his loss by buying a substitute[20]. Where the loss on the sub-sale is non-remote and there is no chance of mitigation, the buyer is entitled not only to his loss of profit, but also to a reasonable amount in respect of compensation that he has had to pay to his sub-buyer[1]. He has, however, been refused damages arising because of loss of business connexion with his sub-buyer[2].

(c) Actions in respect of a defect in quality

The present discussion is concerned with the situation where the goods delivered by the seller or owner do not comply with the contract description as to quality or undertakings as to quality, but the buyer or hirer elects to accept the goods and claim damages. This situation must be distinguished from the following cases: first, where the buyer accepts the goods delivered in full satisfaction of his rights under the contract, in which case those rights are thereby extinguished[3]; and secondly, where the buyer or hirer properly rejects the goods, in which case there is a non-delivery[4]. Of all the situations falling within the present discussion, the S.G.A. singles out one only: s. 53 (3) provides that

> "In the case of breach of warranty of quality such loss is prima facie the difference between the value of the goods at the time of delivery to the buyer and the value they would have had if they had answered to the warranty";

and even in this context, there may be a claim for "special damage" within s. 54[5]. Clearly, many of the claims for damages by a buyer, and all of those by a hirer under a h.p. agreement, will fall under the ordinary common law rules of remoteness[5].

Prima facie rule. (1) *In Sale.* Where in a contract of sale the price has been paid, the *prima facie* measure of damages is the amount by which the warranted value of the goods exceeds the actual value of the goods delivered and accepted[6], both values being taken at the contractual time

---

19. *Hydraulic Engineering Co.* v. *McHaffie* (1878), 4 Q.B.D. 670, C.A.
20. See above, p. 412, note 14.
1. *Elbinger Aktiengesellschaft* v. *Armstrong* (1874), L.R. 9 Q.B. 473: cf. non-delivery, above, p. 413.
2. *Simon* v. *Pawson and Leafs, Ltd.* (1933), 148 L.T. 154, C.A.: cf. below, p. 427.
3. See above, p. 362.
4. See above, p. 409.   5. See above, p. 388.
6. *Aryeh* v. *Lawrence, Ltd.*, [1967] 1 Lloyd's Rep. 63, C.A.

and place of delivery. Moreover, where there is an available market[7], it is assumed that the buyer will resell in that market within a reasonable time of delivery, so that the relevant price is the market selling price then[8]: the contract price[9] and any sub-sale price[10] are merely evidence of the market price of the goods as warranted; and any resale of the defective goods is only evidence of their actual market price[11]. Nor are the buyer's damages to be reduced because the market price subsequently rises[12], or because his sub-buyer under the original contract specification takes the defective goods without counter-claim[13]. Clearly, it is more likely that there will be a market for the sale of the goods in their warranted condition than in their defective condition, so that there may be an available market in respect of the former, but not in respect of the latter; and, if the actual value of the goods is nil, the *prima facie* measure of damages is the market value of the goods as warranted[14].

It will now be clear that the *prima facie* measure of damages available to a buyer with a right to rescind may differ according to whether he elects to rescind or affirm the contract: if he rescinds, it is the amount by which the market price exceeds the contract price at the contract delivery date[15]; but, if he affirms, it is the amount by which the warranted value of the goods exceeds the actual value at the contract delivery date. A significant difference between these two formulae appears where the market price falls after the contract delivery date. Normally, it does not lie in the mouth of the buyer to complain that he has made a bad bargain; but where he takes the opportunity to rescind he can effectively throw the risk of a price fall back on the seller. What is to happen where the buyer has lost the right to reject through no fault of his own; or, *a fortiori*, where it is the act of the seller which has deprived him of this right? The dilemma has arisen in three cases where the seller shipped goods late, but the buyer only discovered that the shipping documents were misdated after he had accepted them. In *Taylor & Sons, Ltd.* v. *Bank of Athens*[16], McCARDIE J. only awarded nominal damages; but in *Finlay & Co., Ltd.* v. *Kwik Hoo Tong*[17] the Court of Appeal awarded the buyer the contract price less the *fallen*

---

7. This concept is discussed above, pp. 382–383.
8. *Loder* v. *Kekule* (1857), 3 C.B.N.S. 128.
9. *Loder* v. *Kekule* (above).
10. *Clare* v. *Maynard* (1835), 6 Ad. & El. 519.
11. Per WARRINGTON L.J. in *Slater* v. *Hoyle and Smith, Ltd.*, [1920] 2 K.B. 11, C.A., at p. 17.
12. *Jones* v. *Just* (1868), L.R. 3 Q.B. 197.
13. *Slater* v. *Hoyle and Smith, Ltd.*, (above). Perhaps this was because of his potential liability to his sub-buyer: but compare above, p. 418.
14. *Bridge* v. *Wain* (1816), 1 Stark 504.   15. See above, p. 410.
16. (1922), 91 L.J.K.B. 776.   17. [1929] 1 K.B. 400, C.A.

market price, on the grounds that the action was not in respect of the late delivery of the goods but for tendering a wrongly dated bill of lading. The latter decision was applied by DEVLIN J. in the *Kwei Tek Chao Case*[18], where the buyer knew of the inaccuracy of the documents by the time the goods were delivered[19]. In *Finlay's Case*, GREER L.J. said that the buyer would only have been entitled to nominal damages if there had been no "distinct breach of contract by tendering a wrongly dated bill of lading"[20]; and it may be that the better view is that, where there is no breach in respect of the shipping documents, the damages are to be assessed on the basis of a breach of warranty[1].

(2) *In hire purchase.* In the case of a simple hiring, the law assumes that the hirer will let out the goods, and so the *prima facie* measure of damages is the amount of hire that the goods as warranted could command less the amount they could command as they are[2]. However, in the case of h.p., allowance has to be made for the option to purchase; and, at first sight, it might appear that the *prima facie* measure should be the amount by which the h.p. price of the goods in the warranted condition exceeds the h.p. price obtainable in their actual condition. But this is to ignore the possibility that the hirer may determine the hiring, and thus retain damages for a loss he has not suffered. On the other hand, to ignore the option element may be unfair to the hirer who opts to purchase. Logically, this dilemma should not arise where the hirer elects to determine the hiring[3], but only where he affirms after the breach and the agreement continues in force. In the latter case, the ideal solution may be some form of apportionment[4]; but in practice the Courts appear to ignore the possibility that the hirer may determine the hiring.

Where the hirer has been suing the dealer in a directly financed h.p. transaction under a collateral contract of warranty, he has been awarded the amount by which the warranted value exceeds the actual value[5]. A similar approach may, perhaps, be detected where the hirer is suing the owner under the h.p. agreement, though here the courts seem to hanker after an award on the same basis as if the hirer had elected to rescind[6]. In *Charterhouse Credit, Ltd.* v. *Tolly*[7],

---

18. [1954] 2 Q.B. 459: set out above, pp. 419–420.
19. If the buyer had rejected, he would have been left to recover the price as an unsecured creditor: *per* DEVLIN J. at p. 483.
20. At p. 414.
1. *Contra* Atiyah, *Sale of Goods* (3rd Edn.)236. See also *Mayne & McGregor on Damages* (12th Edn.) 421.
2. *Mayne & McGregor*, *op. cit.*, 435.   3. But see above, p. 414.
4. See Goode, *H.P. Law & Practice* (2nd edn.) 459–460.
5. *Brown* v. *Sheen and Richmond Car Sales, Ltd.*, [1950] 1 All E.R. 1102: see above, p. 283; *Yeoman Credit, Ltd.* v. *Odgers*, [1962] 1 All E.R. 789, C.A.
6. See *per* ORMEROD L.J., below, note 15.
7. [1963] 2 Q.B. 683; [1963] 2 All E.R. 432, C.A.: see also above, p. 143.

The hirer elected to affirm the agreement after discovering the owner's breach (in providing an unroadworthy vehicle). He paid £50 in repairs, but failed to pay any instalments. The owner therefore terminated the agreement, and claimed damages for breach; and the hirer counterclaimed for damages in respect of the defective state of the vehicle. The Court of Appeal unanimously held:

(1) As the owner had terminated, the hirer was only liable for arrears of instalments under the rule in *Financings, Ltd.* v. *Baldock*[8];

(2) The appropriate measure of damages was not the cost of repairs[9], but, on the principle *restitutio in integram*, the cost of hiring a similar car on similar terms[10];

(3) Therefore, the hirer was entitled to recover (a) all money paid under the h.p. agreement, (b) all money paid to the owner under (1) above, and (c) the repair bill, less an allowance for use.

In this case, UPJOHN L.J. suggested that, if the owner had not terminated, the hirer would only have been entitled to the amount required to put the vehicle in a proper state of repair, plus damages for loss of use[11]. However, in *Doobay* v. *Mohabeer*[12], where the machine was useless in its defective condition, the Privy Council held that, after affirming the h.p. agreement, the hirer was entitled to recover by way of damages all the sums paid or payable under the agreement. In neither case did the court express much enthusiasm for *Yeoman Credit, Ltd.* v. *Apps*[13], where the Court of Appeal held that the hirer could, after he had rescinded, recover the estimated cost of repairs.

At first sight, it looks as though *Charterhouse Credit, Ltd.* v. *Tolly* should be treated on the same footing as *Yeoman Credit, Ltd.* v. *Apps*, on the grounds that in both cases the hirer, at the time of claiming had no option to purchase[14]. Yet it may be possible to draw a distinction between the two cases as follows: if the agreement is terminated for non-payment of rentals and that default arises from impecuniosity due to the need to meet repair bills, it is arguable that this is a non-remote loss arising from the owner's breach and should be ignored[15]; and damages should therefore be assessed on the basis that the option is still

---

8. See above, p. 385.
9. This might be the appropriate measure where the hirer retained possession and had the repairs done: Atiyah, *Sale of Goods* (3rd Edn.) 272.
10. The present agreement may be a good guide: *per* DONOVAN L.J. at pp. 705–706.
11. At pp. 711–712. His Lordship also suggested that each case should be judged on its own facts, and no general rule laid down (at p. 711).
12. [1967] 2 A.C. 278 ; [1967] 2 All E.R. 760, P.C.
13. [1962] 2 Q.B. 508; [1961] 2 All E.R. 281, C.A.: see above, p. 142.
14. Did UPJOHN L.J. in *Tolly's Case* think the loss of the option to purchase significant? Cf. pp. 710 and 712.
15. It was said that the hirer should not be in any worse position with regard to his claim for damages where he affirmed than where he rescinded: *per* ORMEROD L.J. in *Tolly's Case*, at p. 715. See also *per* Lord WILBERFORCE in *Doobay* v. *Mohabeer*, at p. 289.

alive, thus putting *Tolly's Case* on the same side of the line as *Doobay* v. *Mohabeer*. If this is correct, then the *prima facie* measure of damages where the hirer affirms is basically the amount by which the warranted h.p. value exceeds the h.p. value of the goods in their actual state, less an allowance for use[16]; but where the goods delivered have no actual h.p. value, the warranted h.p. value at the time of contracting is taken[10].

Consequential loss. Naturally, the buyer or hirer may recover any money thrown away in reliance on the promise of the seller or owner[17]. However, where he would have made a profit, the buyer or hirer may, alternatively, claim the value of performance[18]. Whilst the buyer or hirer is under a duty to mitigate his loss once he discovers the breach[19], he may have less opportunity to do so than in the case of a non-delivery or late delivery as the breach may be less obvious; and to this extent there may be greater scope here for recovery beyond the *prima facie* measure of damages in respect of consequential loss. Two difficulties have arisen here: first, whether the buyer or hirer is under any duty to examine the goods with a view to discovering any patent or latent defects[20]; and secondly, whether the buyer or hirer who takes steps to protect himself which go beyond the duty to mitigate is to have his damages diminished by any benefit accruing to him from such further steps[1].

There are several types of consequential loss commonly caused by the defective quality of the goods delivered.

1. *Loss of use.* First, the defect may deprive the buyer or hirer of the enjoyment of using the goods for which he must be compensated[2]. Secondly, he may recover any non-remote loss of profit he would have made by utilising the goods to make some product for re-sale. Thus, in *Holden Ltd.* v. *Bostock Ltd.*[3]

> The defendants sold to the plaintiff brewer sugar for brewing. The plaintiff subsequently discovered that the sugar was contaminated with arsenic, and had to destroy the beer made with it. The defendants argued that they were only liable for the cost of production of

---

16. The repair cost may be a guide to this.
17. E.g. *Doobay* v. *Mohabeer*, [1967] 2 A.C. 278; [1967] 2 All E.R. 760, P.C. (cost of installing engine); *Molling* v. *Dean* (1902), 18 T.L.R. 216 (cost of delivery).
18. The relationship of claims under the "reliance" and "expectancy" interest is explained above, p. 412.
19. For the duty to mitigate, see above, pp. 390–391.
20. See *Mayne & McGregor on Damages* (12th Edn.) 404.
1. See above, p. 379, note 10.
2. *Per* UPJOHN L.J. in *Tolly's Case*, [1963] 2 Q.B. 683, at pp. 710–711. C.A.
3. (1902), 18 T.L.R. 317, C.A. See also *Ashworth* v. *Wells* (1898), 78 L.T. 136, C.A.; *Centra Meat Products, Ltd.* v. *McDaniel, Ltd.*, [1952] 1 Lloyd's Rep. 562.

beer to replace that which had been destroyed; but the Court of Appeal held them liable for the market value of the beer destroyed[4].

Thirdly, the buyer or hirer may recover in respect of loss of profit where the goods were known to be intended to be utilised to make a profitable product. In *Cullinane* v. *British "Rema" Manufacturing Co., Ltd.*[5],

> There was a sale of a clay pulverising machine warranted to pulverise clay at 6 tons an hour. The machine delivered only proved capable of handling 2 tons per hour. The Court of Appeal took it for granted that the buyer was entitled to compensation for loss of profit.

However, in calculating the damages recoverable, the Court of Appeal seem to have put themselves in a completely indefensible position[6]: first, there would not have been any profit in the period covered by the claim; and secondly, they erroneously thought that the buyer's claim (before amendment by the official referee) conflicted with the rule against double recovery[7]. The principles which ought to be applied in calculating damages in these circumstances have been set out elsewhere[8].

2. *Loss on a resale of the goods.* Before the seller can be made liable for any loss suffered by the buyer in connection with any sub-sales, two things must be shown: first, that the sub-sales are not too remote[9]; and secondly, that the loss arising from the sub-sale was caused by the seller's breach of contract[10]. Whilst liability in respect of a non-remote sub-sale on identical terms is not in question[11], the second requirement may give rise to difficulty where the terms of the sub-sale are not identical. Clearly, the buyer cannot recover in respect of liability to his sub-buyer arising out of substantially more onerous terms; but it would seem that he may do so where he would have been liable had the terms been identical[12], or where the difference in terms was verbal rather than substantial[13]. Assuming that these criteria are satisfied, the buyer is entitled to recover from the seller not just any loss of profit[14] and cost of

---

4. For the defendant's claim against his seller, see *Bostock & Co., Ltd.* v. *Nicholson & Sons, Ltd.*, [1904] 1 K.B. 725. Cf. *Wren* v. *Holt*, [1903] 1 K.B. 610, C.A.
5. [1954] 1 Q.B. 292; [1953] 2 All E.R. 1257, C.A. And see *Astley Industrial Trust, Ltd.* v. *Grimley*, [1963] 2 All E.R. 33, C.A. (liability of a dealer in a directly financed h.p. transaction): see above, p. 142.
6. See Macleod, [1970] J.B.L. 19.
7. See above, p. 386.
8. Macleod, *op. cit.*, p. 28.
9. *Clare* v. *Maynard* (1835), 6 Ad. & El. 519.
10. *G. C. Dobell & Co., Ltd.* v. *Barber and Garratt*, [1931] 1 K.B. 219, C.A.
11. See *per* SCRUTTON L.J. in *Dexters, Ltd.* v. *Hill Crest Oil Co., Ltd.*, [1926] 1 K.B. 348, C.A., at p. 359.
12. *Per* DEVLIN J. in *Biggin & Co., Ltd.* v. *Permanite, Ltd.*, [1951] 1 K.B. 422, at p. 434. Rev. on other grounds: [1951] 2 K.B. 314; [1951] 2 All E.R. 191, C.A.
13. *British Oil and Cake Co. Ltd.* v. *Burstall*, (1923), 39 T.L.R. 406, *obiter*.
14. Compare the seller's claim for loss of profit: above, p. 381, *et seq.*

recovering the goods[15], but also in respect of any compensation reasonably paid to his sub-buyer[15a]. In *Kasler and Cohen* v. *Slovouski*[16]

> The defendant sold some dyed rabbit skins to the plaintiff wholesale furrier, knowing that he intended to make them into fur collars for women's coats. The plaintiff made up the skins and sold them to B. B. resold to C. and C. resold to a draper. The draper attached one of the skins to a coat and sold it to E., who contracted dermatitis from the collar. The draper defended E.s' action and lost, having to pay £67 damages and £248 costs. None of the other claims further back the chain of distribution was defended; and the plaintiff successfully sued the defendant for the £67 and over £650 cumulative costs which he had paid to B.

It is to be observed that in this case there was only one defended action; and it is clear that if each of the claims in the chain is reasonably defended the damages could easily increase astronomically[17]. Only at the prospect of a claim in respect of loss of business connection do the courts appear to have called a halt[18]. Whilst it is unlikely that the parties to a contract of h.p. will contemplate a resale of the subject-matter by the hirer[19], similar principles have been applied in relation to claims by the hirer in a directly financed h.p. transaction against the dealer for breach of a collateral contract of warranty[20].

3. *Loss caused by the defect.* Normally, damage which the defect does to the goods themselves will be included in the *prima facie* measure of damages because it will reduce the value of the goods; but it is otherwise where the defective goods damage persons or other property. If loss is caused to the buyer or hirer, it is possible that an action will lie for the tort of negligence[1]; but it is more likely that he will sue for breach of contract, where liability is strict[2]. Where the goods have been put to their contemplated use and the defect amounts to a breach of the

---

15. *Molling & Co.* v. *Dean & Son, Ltd.* (1902), 18 T.L.R. 217, D.C. But the cost of delivering the goods to the sub-buyer is only claimable as an alternative to recovery for loss of profit: see *Mayne & McGregor on Damages* (12th Edn.) 419.
15a. *Biggin, Ltd.* v. *Permanite, Ltd.*, [1951] 2 K.B. 314; [1951] 2 All E.R. 191, C.A.
16. [1928] 1 K.B. 78.
17. E.g. *Butterworth* v. *Kingsway Motors, Ltd.* (above, p. 60), as reported in [1954] 1 W.L.R. 1297–1307; *Bowmaker (Commercial), Ltd.* v. *Day*, [1965] 2 All E.R. 856.
18. E.g. *Bostock & Co., Ltd.* v. *Nicholson & Sons, Ltd.*, [1904] 1 K.B. 725. Similarly late delivery: see above, p. 421.
19. Except where the h.p. agreement is used as a stocking device: see above, p. 289.
20. *Yeoman Credit, Ltd.* v. *Odgers*, [1962] 1 All E.R. 789, C.A. (cost of reasonably defending owner's action).
1. But see above, p. 124. Does the restriction on the amount of damages recoverable considered above (at p. 413) apply here?
2. For the different tests of remoteness, see above, pp. 389–390.

contract of sale, it has been held that the buyer may recover in respect of personal injury[3], death of his wife[4] and injury to his other property[5]. Presumably, the position is the same with regard to actions by the hirer under a h.p. agreement against the owner[6]; and it has been held that a dealer in a directly financed h.p. transaction is liable to the hirer both for breach of a collateral contract of warranty and the tort of negligence[7]. Finally, it is necessary to consider the liability of the seller or owner for loss caused to any other person. It may be that that person can sue the seller or owner directly under a collateral contract[8], or in the tort of negligence[9]. Alternatively, that person may successfully sue the buyer or hirer, either for breach of contract or the tort of negligence; and, in either case, the buyer or hirer may be able to pass that loss back to the seller or owner. Leaving aside the possibility that the buyer (or hirer) and seller (or owner) are joint tortfeasors[10], it may be that such a claim is a non-remote loss flowing from the breach of contract by the seller or owner[2]; and in this event, the seller or owner will be liable for the damages and costs paid by the buyer or hirer to the other person under a judgment[11] or a reasonable settlement[12], or for any costs reasonably incurred in successfully defending such an action[13].

4 SPECIFIC PERFORMANCE[14]

Whilst detailed discussion of the principles on which a decree of specific performance is granted or refused are beyond the scope of this work, it will be recalled that the remedy is discretionary, and that it is only granted where damages are not an adequate remedy[15]. Thus, in relation to contracts for the disposition of goods, the transferee will

---

3. E.g. *Geddling* v. *Marsh*, [1920] 1 K.B. 668, D.C.: set out above, p. 81; *Griffiths* v. *Peter Conway, Ltd.*, [1939] 1 All E.R. 685, C.A.: set out above p. 85.
4. E.g. *Jackson* v. *Watson & Sons*, [1919] 2 K.B. 193, C.A.
5. E.g. *Bostock & Co., Ltd.* v. *Nicholson & Sons, Ltd.*, [1904] 1 K.B. 725; *Wilson* v. *Rickett Cockerell & Co., Ltd.*, [1954] 1 Q.B. 598; [1954] 1 All E.R. 868, C.A.: set out above, p. 81.
6. Cf. *White* v. *John Warrick & Co., Ltd.*, [1953] 2 All E.R. 1021, C.A. (simple hire).
7. *Andrews* v. *Hopkinson*, [1957] 1 Q.B. 229; [1956] 3 All E.R. 422: set out above, p. 283.   8. See above, p. 120.
9. See above, p. 124.   10. See above, p. 127.
11. *Vogan & Co.* v. *Oulton* (1899), 81 L.T. 435, C.A. (simple hire). Cf. *Hadley* v. *Droitwich Construction, Ltd.*, [1967] 3 All E.R. 911, C.A. (simple hire).
12. *Henry Kendall & Sons Ltd.* v. *William Lillico & Sons, Ltd.*, [1969] 2 A.C. 31; [1968] 2 All E.R. 444, H.L.: set out above, p. 88.
13. *Britannia Hygienic Laundry, Ltd.* v. *Thornycroft, Ltd.* (1925), 41 T.L.R. 667. Rev. on facts: (1926), 42 T.L.R. 198, C.A.
14. See generally Treitel, [1966] J.B.L. 211.
15. See Cheshire & Fifoot, *Law of Contract* (7th Edn.) 565–571; Treitel, *Law of Contract* (3rd Edn.) 834–850.

usually only be able to obtain specific performance of the contract where the subject-matter is unique in some way[16]. Nor can he avoid this restriction by suing in the tort of detinue[17].

In the case of sales, the remedy of specific performance has now been regulated[18] by s. 52 of the S.G.A., which provides as follows:

> "In any action for breach of contract to deliver specific or ascertained goods the court may, if it thinks fit, on the application of the plaintiff[19], by its judgment . . . direct that the contract shall be performed specifically, without giving the defendant the option of retaining the goods on payment of damages. The judgment . . . may be unconditional, or upon such terms and conditions as to damages, payment of the price, and otherwise, as to the court may seem just, and the application by the plaintiff may be made at any time before judgment[1] . . ."

In the unlikely event of unique goods being let on h.p., this provision would presumably apply by analogy. At any event, s. 52 only applies where the contract goods are identified and agreed upon either at the time of contracting (specific goods) or subsequently (ascertained goods)[2]; and it does not apply to an unascertained part of a specific whole[3]. On the other hand, it is unnecessary to prove that the property in the goods has passed in order to obtain specific performance; and, in this respect, the buyer is better off than a seller suing for the price[4]. Where appropriate, the buyer may have the contract rectified[5], and then obtain specific performance of the contract as rectified[6].

---

16. E.g. *Behnke* v. *Bede Shipbuilding Co., Ltd.*, [1927] 1 K.B. 649.
17. See above, p. 414.
18. It may have been intended that s. 52 should widen the scope of the remedy; but the post-Act cases do not appear to have so regarded it.
19. This means the buyer: *per* WRIGHT J. in *Shell Mex, Ltd.* v. *Elton Cop Dying Co., Ltd.* (1928), 34 Com. Cas. 39, at p. 46.
1. Compare the powers of the court in an action of detinue: above, p. 333.
2. *Per* ATKIN L.J. in *Re Wait*, [1927] 1 Ch. 606, C.A., at p. 630.
3. *Re Wait*, [1927] (above): set out above, p. 173.
4. Cf. above, pp. 370–372.
5. But see *Rose, Ltd.* v. *Pim, Ltd.*, [1953] 2 Q.B. 450; [1953] 2 All E.R. 739, C.A.
6. *U.S.A.* v. *Motor Trucks, Ltd.*, [1924] A.C. 196, P.C. (realty).

Index

A

ACCEPTANCE
buyer, by, 400
ACTS OR OMISSIONS
liability for, 124
ADOPTION
passing of property, 178
ADVERTISEMENTS
consumer protection, 27, 29
AFFIRMATION
agreement, of, 60
contract, of, 358
AGENT
dealer, as, 285
for finance company, 39
mercantile, 187, 202 *et seq.*
necessity, of, 185
nemo dat quod non habet, 184
notices, for purposes of receiving, 39
repossession, 330
sale or return, goods on, 180
AGREEMENT
affirmation of, 60
conditional sale. *See* CONDITIONAL SALE AGREEMENT
credit sale. *See* CREDIT SALE AGREEMENT
formalities. *See* FORMALITIES
linked-on, 337
master, 310
off-trade-premises, 41
on-trade-premises, 41
rights and duties under, 113
security for price. *See* SECURITY FOR PRICE
termination of, 353, 357
valuation, to sell at, 21
AGREEMENTS, HIRE PURCHASE. *See also* HIRE PURCHASE, CONTRACTS OF

Agreements, Hire Purchase—
contd.
affirmation of, 60
alterations in terms of, 342
barter, compared with, 23
cancellation of, 42. *See also* CANCELLATION
copies of, 40
delivery, 270, 273. *See also* DELIVERY
enforceability, 33
essence of, 7
exchange, compared with, 23
formation. *See* FORMATION OF AGREEMENT
gift, compared with, 22
goods, identification of, 34
legibility, 34
minimum payments clauses, 392
perpetual, 15
price, statements of, 34. *See also* PRICE
risk, 241 *et seq.*
security for price. *See* SECURITY FOR PRICE
signature, 33
boxes, 34
statutory notices, 34
sureties, 347. *See also* SURETY
title. *See* TITLE
trade premises, on or off, 41
transferee, termination by, 353
writing, to be in, 33
APPROPRIATE TRADE PREMISES
meaning, 40
APPROPRIATION
ascertainment and, 174
assent, 175
delivery, actual or constructive, 170
mail order business, 172

431

Appropriation—*contd.*
  unascertained goods, passing of
    property in, 169
APPROVAL
  passing of property, 176
  similar terms, 177
ASCERTAINMENT
  appropriation and, 174
  goods, of, 157
ASSENT
  unascertained goods, passing of
    property in, 175
ASSIGNMENT
  chose in action, 18
  indirectly financed transactions,
    in, 311
  interest of hirer, 12
  legal mortgage, 308
ATTORNMENT
  meaning, 264
  transit. *See* TRANSIT
AVAILABLE MARKET
  actions in respect of late delivery,
    417
  damages for non-delivery, 409
AVOIDANCE. *See also* TERMS
  contract void or voidable, 198

B

BAILMENT
  characteristic of, 7
  hire purchase, statutory definition
    of, and, 15
  risk, 248
BANKS
  moneylenders, distinction be-
    tween, 301
BANKRUPTCY
  goods of bankrupt, right to, 10
BARTER
  nature of, 23
BILL OF LADING
  arrival or ex-ship contracts, 247
  bailment, 248
  characteristics of, 182
BILLS OF SALE ACT 1882
  purpose of, 10

BLOCK-DISCOUNTING
  meaning, 26
BODY CORPORATE
  agreements by, 30
BOOK-DEBTS
  transfer of rights, 307
BREACH OF CONTRACT
  damages for, 415
    action for, 376. *See also*
      DAMAGES
  delivery, delay in, 242
  fundamental, 141
  remedies for, 51. *See also*
    REMEDIES
  rescission, 396
    buyer, by, 397
      inconsistent acts of, 400
    contract treated as discharged,
      361
    defective performance, 360
    repudiation, 360
  series of contracts, 277
BUSINESS
  ordinary course of, 211
BUSINESS PREMISES
  appropriate trade premises, 41
BUYER
  acceptance by, 400
  inconsistent acts of, 400
  possession, in, 220 *et seq.*
  remedies of. *See* REMEDIES

C

CANCELLATION
  effect of, 44
  notice, service of, 43
  part-exchange, effect upon, 44
  right of, 42, 375
  writing, in, 44
CASE LAW
  significance of, 4
CAVEAT EMPTOR
  common law, 115
  scope of maxim, 80
CHANCE
  sale of, 20

CHARGE
  transfer of rights, 309
CHATTELS
  mortgaging, 291
CHATTELS PERSONAL
  meaning, 18
CHEQUES
  payment by, 271
CHOSE IN ACTION
  assignment of, 18
CIRCULAR TRANSACTIONS
  nature of, 293
CLAUSES
  common law, void at, 136
  excluding. *See* EXCLUDING
    CLAUSES
  Law Commission, proposals of,
    135
  minimum payments, 392
  misrepresentation, 134
  penalty, 391
  prohibited, 133
COMMON LAW
  estoppel, 190, 191
  frustration, 257
  hire purchase, in, 115
  liability, 124
  misstatements, negligent, 129
  ownership, absolute, 154
  performance by instalments, 278
  provisions rendered void at, 136
  sale, in, 115
    powers of, 238
  sureties at, 346
  terms and obligations derived
    from, 114
COMPENSATION
  elements of, 14
CONDITIONAL SALE
    AGREEMENT
  meaning, 15
CONDITIONAL SALES
  rules as to, 280
CONDITIONS
  common law and, 115
  meaning, 50
  sample, contracts by, 107
  title, implied as to, 56
  warranty, distinguished from, 75

CONSENT
  meaning, 209
CONSTRUCTION
  contra proferentem rule, 139
  exclusion clauses, 139
CONSUMER PROTECTION
  advertisements, 27, 29
  cautionary wording, 30
  contracts of purchase, 26
  cooling-off time, 31
  door-to-door selling, 31
  financial limits, 30
  instalment credit contracts, 28
  standards, 27
  trade description legislation, 27
  weights and measures, 27
CONSUMER PROTECTION
    ACT 1961
  generally, 4
CONTRACT OF SALE
  absolute, 6
  affirmation of, 358
  agreement, hire purchase, dis-
    tinguished from, 7
  alterations to, 145
  appropriation to, 169
  arrival, 247
  bailee, third-party, 249
  bailment, distinguished from, 7
  breach. *See* BREACH OF CONTRACT
  chain of, 119
  c.i.f., 247
  collateral, 52, 120
  conditional, 7, 161, 164
  conditions. *See* CONDITIONS
  contractual rights, 306
  conveyance, element of, 8,
    153
  definition, 5
  effects of, 153 *et seq.*
  entire, 352
  exclusion clauses. *See* EXCLUSION
    CLAUSES
  ex-ship, 247
  ex-works or ex-store, 246
  formalities. *See* FORMALITIES
  free on board, 246
  frustration of, 254
  generally, 3

Contract of Sale—*contd.*
 hire purchase. *See* HIRE PUR-
  CHASE, CONTRACT OF
 illegality, 38, 122
 impossibility. *See* IMPOSSIBILITY
 liability. *See* LIABILITY
 mortgage, distinguished from, 7
 nature of, 8
 object of, 6
 obligations. *See* DISCHARGE OF
  CONTRACTUAL OBLIGATIONS
 pledge, distinguished from, 7
 price, 8
 property, transfer of, 8
 provisions rendered void by
  statute, 132
 quasi-, 63
  restitution in, 404
 remoteness, 388, 389. *See also*
  REMOTENESS
 rescission, 58
  intention of, 200. *See also*
   RESCISSION
 sample, by, 107
 series of, 277
 spot, 274
 standard-form, 53
 surety, of, 348. *See also* SURETY
 terms. *See* TERMS
 title. *See* TITLE
 tort, action in, 130
  distinguished from, 131
 unconditional, 161, 162 *et seq.*
 unenforceability, 122
 void and voidable, 198
 void, provisions rendered by
  statute, 132
 waiver, doctrine of, 146
CONTRA PROFERENTEM
 rule, 139
CONVEYANCE
 contract and, 153
 element of, 8
 ownership, 153
 property, 153
 title, 153
COPIES
 agreement, of, 40
  trade-premises, on or off, 41

Copies—*contd.*
 relevant document, of, 41
CO-PRINCIPAL
 surety, as, 345
COURT
 orders by,
  postponed, 340
  specific delivery, 340
  split, 340
 repossession through, 332
 sale, powers of, 240
CREDIT BUREAUX
 credit ratings, 35
 records of, 34
CREDIT SALES
 meaning, 14
 rules, statutory, 279
CREDITORS
 sale, power of, 239
CUSTOMER
 dealer, relation with, 282
 deposit given by, 286
 finance company, relation with,
  284

D

DAMAGES
 action for,
  hirer or buyer, by, 408
   breaches of contract, various,
    415
   consequential loss, 420, 425
   defect, loss caused by, 427
   delivery, late, 417
   non-delivery, 409
   quality, defect in, 421
   sub-sale, loss on, 421, 426
   title, defective, 416
   use, loss of, 420, 425
  seller or owner, by,
   breach of contract, 376
   contract of hire purchase,
    breach of, 384
   contributory negligence, 386
   double recovery, 386
   market, available, 382
   misrepresentation, 378

Damages—*contd.*
    mitigation of damage, 390
    penal sum, 394
    penalties, rule against, 391
    profit, loss of, 381
    quantification of damages, 378
    remoteness of damage, 387
    restitutio in integrum, 380
    tort, in, 376
    value of goods, 379
  non-acceptance, for, 374
  non-delivery, for, 409
  quantification of, 378
  rescission, in lieu of, 359
  title, defective, 416
  warranty, breach of, 415
DE MINIMIS
  fitness and merchantability, 81
DEALER
  agency of, 285
  agent of finance company, as, 39
  customer, relation with, 282
  finance company, relationship with, 289
  insolvency of, 307
  misrepresentations by, 288
  recourse provisions, 290
  sales by, 86
    merchantability, 101
  sold note of, 295
  stocking plans of, 289
DEATH
  hirer, of, 342, 356
DEBTS
  book, 307
  harassment for, 331
DECEIT
  tort of, 129
DELAY
  breach of contract, amounting to, 242
    not, 243
  delivery, in, 242, 274
DELIVERY
  acceptance of, 267
  agent of buyer, to, 264
  attornment, 264
  bailee, position of, 270

Delivery—*contd.*
  delay in, 242, 274
  deliverable state, 165
  documents of title, 264
  duty of, 265
  generally, 263
  hiring commences on, 116
  instalments, by, 276
  meaning, 263
  mode of, 265
  non-delivery, damages for, 409
  part, 259, 328
  payment, concurrent condition of, 273
    terms not concurrent, 276
  place of, 265
  refusal of, 268, 327
  rejection, right of, 269
  rules of, 264
  specific, order of court, 340
  spot contracts, 274
  symbolic, 264
  tender of, 266
  time of, 265, 272
  time of the essence, 273
  time, reasonable, 274
  waiver of, 267
DEPOSIT
  customer, given by, 286
  return of, claims for, 287
DESCRIPTION
  exclusion clauses, 76
  goods, correspondence of, 71
  identification of goods, 71
  misdescription, 69
  sales by, 67
    merchantability, 101
    sample, 101
  sample, and, 108
  undertakings as to, 70
DETERIORATION
  transit, in, 244
DISCHARGE OF CONTRAC-
  TUAL OBLIGATIONS
  contracts, entire, 352
  obligations, divisible, 352
    enforcement of, 351
  performance, by, 351
    exact, 351

Discharge of Contractual Obligations—*contd.*
  obligations, enforcement of, 351
  rescission, by,
    affirmation, 358
    breach of contract, 360
      contract treated as discharged, 361
      defective performance, 360
      repudiation, 360
    damages in lieu of, 359
    misrepresentation, for, 357
      innocent, 359
    restitutio in integrum impossible, 358
    time, lapse of, 358
  stipulated event, by,
    agreement, termination of, 357
    events terminating, 355
    hirer, death of, 356
    transferee, termination by, 353
  subsequent act or event, by,
    agreement, subsequent, 362
    judgment, 363
    remedies, election of, 362
    repossession, 363
    total or partial discharge, 362
DISPOSAL
  reservation of right of, 181
DISPOSITION
  buyer, by, affecting lien of unpaid seller, 324
  meaning, 211, 232
  mercantile agent, powers of, 203
  motor vehicles. *See* MOTOR VEHICLES, SALE OF
DISTRESS
  Law of Distress Amendment Act 1908, 11
DISTRIBUTION
  chain of, 125 *et seq.*
DOCUMENT
  title, of, meaning, 207
DOOR-TO-DOOR SELLING
  consumer protection, 31
DOUBLE RECOVERY
  avoidance of, 375
  rule against, 386

E

EMBLEMENTS
  meaning, 18
ENCUMBRANCE
  freedom from, 64
ENFORCEMENT
  generally, 364
ENTIRE CONTRACTS
  exact performance, 352
EQUITABLE MORTGAGE
  transfer of rights, 309
ESTOPPEL
  common law, 190, 191
  negligence, 196
  passing of property, 180
  representations, 192 *et seq.*
  requirements to raise, 195
  title acquired by, 189
EXACT PERFORMANCE
  rule of, 352
EXAMINATION. *See* FITNESS; MERCHANTABILITY
  intermediate, 126
EXCHANGE
  nature of, 23
EXCLUSION CLAUSES
  construction, 139
  contra proferentem rule, 139
  contractual, 136
  courts, attitude of, 138
  description, and, 76
  document, incorporation by signed, 138
  effect of, 136
  fitness of goods, undertakings as to, 93
  fundamental breach, 141
  ineffective, 138
  merchantability, 104
  nature of, 136
  non-contractual, 136
  notice, incorporation by, 137
  transaction, incorporation in, 137
EXECUTION
  stages of, 239
EXEMPTION CERTIFICATES
  finance company, of, 303

F

FALSE STATEMENTS
liability for, 128
FAULT
meaning, 21
FINANCE COMPANY
bankers, as, 301
customer, relationship with, 284
dealer, as agent of, 39
relationship with, 289
exemption certificates, 303
moneylender, as, 301
requirements imposed upon, 302
FINANCING
block-discounting, 26
direct, 25, 35
finance companies, functions of, 24. *See also* FINANCE COMPANY
financial limits, 30
indirect, 25
price. *See* PRICE
FITNESS
continuance of, 82
contract severable, 81
de minimis rule, 81
dealer, sales by, 86
generally, 80
liability, 85
merchantability and, 101, 111
patent or trade name, under, 90
purpose, knowledge of particular, 87
reasonably, 84
reliance, 90
seller, duty of, 84
undertakings as to, 80, 83
content of, 84
exclusion of, 93
qualifications of, 86
use, more than one ordinary, 89
FORMALITIES
Bills of Sale Acts, 32
consumer sales, 33
sales, 32
transfers, absolute, 32
non-absolute, 33

FORMATION OF AGREEMENT
cancellation, 42
copies, 40
illegality, 38
invalidity, 37
mistake, 37
offer and acceptance, 35
pre-contract stage, 34
principles of, 35
statutory provisions, 39
terms controls, 45
FRAUD
dealer, by, 37
false statements, 128
FRUSTRATION
advance payment, 258
contract, of, 254
effect of, 257
part delivery, 259
risk and, 256
FUNDAMENTAL BREACH
doctrine of, 141

G

GIFT
nature of, 22
GOODS
ascertainment of, 157
chance, 20
chattels personal, 18
crops, industrial growing, 18
deliverable state, 165
description of. *See* DESCRIPTION
sales by, 67
destruction of. *See* IMPOSSIBILITY
emblements, 18
existing, 19
fitness of. *See* FITNESS
future, 19, 159
grown, to be, 171
manufactured, to be, 171
identification of, 34, 71, 157
land, things attached to forming part of, 18
meaning, 18, 207

Goods—*contd.*
  merchantability. *See* MERCHANT-
    ABILITY
  mistake as to, 123
  money, 18
  protected, 336, 337
    repossession of, 375
  repossession of, 308, 375
  samples, 70. *See also* SAMPLE
  second-hand, 105
  skill and labour, 23
  specific, 20, 158
    meaning, 159
  types of, 19
  unascertained, 20, 157, 167 *et
    seq.*
  unprotected, 337
GOOD FAITH
  meaning, 199
GUARANTOR
  surety, as, 345

H

HARASSMENT
  debt, for, 331
HIRE PURCHASE. *See also* HIRE
  PURCHASE, CONTRACT OF.
  agency, 39
  agreement, formalities of, 34
  common law, 115
  contract of, 9
  damages, 384, 414
  death of hirer or buyer, 342
  default, 334
  definition of, statutory, 14
  delivery, 263, 273
  description, sales by, 70
  discharge, 354
  financing, 287
  fitness, 83
  implied terms, 53
  inspection, 109
  invalidity, 37
  legal form of, difficulties arising
    from, 16
  merchantability, 94
  mistake, 37

Hire Purchase—*contd.*
  motor vehicles, sale of, 230
  obligations, 112
  offer and acceptance, 35
  part-exchanges, 271
  payment, 271
    by instalments, 279
  penalties, 391
  postponed orders, 340
  price, 22
  proprietary rights, residuary,
    305
  quality, defect in, 423
  quantity, 79
  remedies, 370
  repossession, 330, 336
  rescission, 402
  right to sell, 56
  samples, 106
  security without possession, 329
  sureties, 347
  terms, 51, 112
  title, 55
    implied warranties as to, 64
  transactions, 30
  variation, 145
  void provisions, 133
  waiver, 146
HIRE PURCHASE ACT 1965
  generally, 4
HIRE PURCHASE, CONTRACT
  OF. *See also* AGREEMENTS,
  HIRE PURCHASE
  Bankruptcy Act 1914, 10
  Bills of Sale Act 1882, 10
  breach. *See* BREACH OF CON-
    TRACT
  clauses, prohibited, 133
  common law form, 9
  definition, statutory, 14
  difficulties of legal form, 16
  dual nature of, 16
  exclusion clauses. *See* EXCLU-
    SION CLAUSES
  illegality in, 38
  impossiblity. *See* IMPOSSIBILITY
  inconsistencies, 16
  Law of Distress Amendment Act
    1908, 11

Hire Purchase Contract Of—*contd.*
  motor vehicles. *See* MOTOR
    VEHICLES, SALE OF
  obligations imposed on parties,
    54
  price, meaning, 22. *See also*
    PRICE
  prohibited clauses, 133
  representations, 49 *et seq.*
  rescission, 58. *See also* RECISSION
  security for price. *See* SECURITY
    FOR PRICE
  standard-form, 53
  terms, contractual, 49 *et seq. See
    also* TERMS
  title. *See* TITLE
  void, where, 34
  waiver, doctrine of, 146
HIRER
  death of, 342, 356
  interest of, 12
  obligations of, 116
  remedies of. *See* REMEDIES
  rights and duties of, 113
HIRING
  delivery, commences on, 116
  perpetual, 15
  termination of, 356

I

ILLEGALITY
  formation of contract, 38
  liability for, 122
IMPOSSIBILITY
  causes of, 249
  contract, interpretation of, 250
  initial, 250
    perished, 253
    specific goods, 253
  subsequent, 254
    advance payment, 258
    contract, frustration of, 254
    frustration, effect of, 257
    part delivery, 259
INDORSEE
  surety, as, 345

INSOLVENCY
  insolvent, meaning, 320
  sale, powers of, 239
  transfer of rights, 307
INSTALMENTS
  conditional sales, 280
  credit sales, 279
  default as to, 334
  delivery by, 276
  hire purchase, under, 281
  hirer in arrears, 374
  payment by, 279
  subsequent, 281
INVALIDITY
  offences causing, 37

J

JUDGMENT
  final, 363

L

LABOUR. *See* SKILL AND LABOUR
LAND
  things attached to forming part
    of, 18
LAW OF DISTRESS AMEND-
    MENT ACT 1908
  provisions of, 11
LEGIBILITY
  requirement of, 34
LIABILITY
  acts or omissions, 124
  bailee, of, 248
  common law, 124
  contract, under,
    chain of contracts, 119
    collateral, 120
    illegality, 122
    misrepresentation, 121
    mistake, 122
    promise, 118
    single contract, 118
    unenforceability, 122
  dealer, of, 282
  deceit, 129

Liability—*contd.*
 examination, intermediate, 126
 exclusion clauses. *See* EXCLU-
  SION CLAUSES
 fitness of goods, 85
 illegality, 122
 misrepresentation, 121, 134. *See*
  also MISREPRESENTATION
 mistake, 122
 negligence, 124
 packaged goods, 137
 provisions void at common law,
  136
 relationship, special, 130
 risk. *See* RISK
 statements, for, 128
 strict, 127
 surety, of, 346
 tort, in, 131
 unenforceability, 122
 variation by contract, 145
LIEN
 nature of, 13
 possession, dependence upon, 320
 seller, remedy of, 366
 unpaid seller, of, 318
  right of, 314
  buyer obtaining possession, 322
  ceasing to be, 321
  conditions where exercisable,
   319
  delivery to carrier, 322
  dispositions by buyer, 324
  nature of, 318
  termination of lien, 321
  waiver, 323
LINKED-ON AGREEMENT
 goods under hire purchase, 337
LOANS
 directly financed transactions
  and, 302
LOG-BOOK
 document of title, as, 195, 207

M

MAIL ORDER BUSINESS
 appropriation and, 172

MARKET
 available, 382
  actions in respect of late
   delivery, 417
  damages for non-delivery, 409
MARKET OVERT
 sales in, 236 *et seq.*
MASTER AGREEMENT
 indirect financing, 310
MERCANTILE AGENCY
 agent, meaning, 204
 disposition, in ordinary course of
  business, 211
 powers of, 203
 document of title, meaning,
  207
 possession of, 206
 generally, 202
 goods, possession of, 206
 owner, 210
  consent of, 209
 pledging of goods, 211
 power of, 203
 transferee to take *bona fide* and
  without notice, 214
MERCHANDISE MARKS ACT
 1862
 generally, 4
MERCHANTABILITY
 continuance of, 82
 contract severable, 81
 de minimis rule, 81
 dealer, sales by, 101
 defects, specified, 105
 description, sales by, 101
 examination of goods, 95, 102
 fitness and, 101, 111
 fitness as to, 80
 generally, 80
 meaning, 95, 97
 quality, meaning, 95
 saleability, test of, 97
 second-hand goods, 105
 specified defects, 105
 transferee, examination by, 102
 undertakings as to, 94
  content of, 95
  exclusions of, 104
  qualifications of, 101

MISREPRESENTATION
"any misrepresentation made", 134
clauses, 134
damages, action for, 378
dealer, by, 288
innocent, 121, 359
liability for, 49, 121
Misrepresentation Act 1967, 134
negligent, 121
rescission for, 357, 403
MISTAKE
fraud by dealer, 37
goods, defective, 123
liability, 122
MITIGATION
damage, of, 390
MIXED WITH
meaning, 78
MONEY
meaning, 18
MONEYLENDING
banking, compared with, 302
finance company and, 301
generally, 300
moneylender, meaning, 301
MORTGAGE
chattel mortgaging, 291
equitable, 309
legal, 308
nature of, 7
MOTOR VEHICLES, SALE OF
generally, 230
presumptions, rebuttable, 235
private purchasers, dispositions to, 232
trade or finance purchasers, dispositions to, 234

N

NEGLIGENCE
contributory, 386
estoppel, 196
good faith and, 199
liability for, 125
misstatements, 252

NEMO DAT QUOD NON HABET
exceptions to rule, 184
principle of, 183
NON-DELIVERY
hire-purchase, 414
remedies of hirer or buyer, 409 et seq.
NOTICES
agent for purposes of receiving, 39
statutory, 34

O

OBLIGATIONS
common law, derived from, 114
contractual. See DISCHARGE OF CONTRACTUAL OBLIGATIONS
hirer, of, 116
repudiation of, 360
rights and duties under agreement, 113
statute, derived from, 112
trade, usage of, 112
variation of, 145 et seq.
waiver of, 145 et seq.
OFFER AND ACCEPTANCE
communication of acceptance, 36
conditional, 36
formation of agreement, 35
revocation of offer, 36
OPEN-ENDED TRANSACTIONS
nature of, 297
OWNER
remedies of. See REMEDIES
selling with consent of, 185
OWNERSHIP
concept of, 154

P

PART-EXCHANGE
cancellation, effect of, 44
price, 22
payment of part of, 271

PASSING OF PROPERTY. *See*
PROPERTY
PATENT OR OTHER TRADE
NAME
fitness of goods sold under, 90
PAYMENT. *See also* PRICE
advance, 258
cheques, by, 271
conversion, 272
credit sales and, 279
delivery,
concurrent condition of, 273
terms not concurrent, 276
detinue, 272
generally, 271
instalments, by, 279
part-exchange, 271
post, by, 272
time of, 272, 274
PENALTIES
rule against, 391
PERFORMANCE
discharge of contractual obligations by, 351
meaning, 77
PLEDGE
characteristics of, 7
documents of title, of, 224
mercantile agent, by, 211
POSSESSION
lien dependent upon, 320
property and, permutations of,
316
quiet, 64
POST
cash on delivery service, 325
payment by, 272
PRICE. *See also* PAYMENT
action for, 370
delivery. *See* DELIVERY
determination of, 21
element of, 8
financial limits, 30
financing of,
dealer and customer, relationship between, 282
dealer, misrepresentations by,
288
dealer recourse, 290

Price—*contd.*
deposit, 286
direct,
chattel mortgaging, 291
circular transactions, 293
financing company, requirements imposed upon,
302
moneylending, 300
open-ended transactions,
297
finance company and customer,
relationship between, 284
finance company and dealer,
relationship between, 289
generally, 282
indirect,
charge, 309
contractual rights, 306
transfer of, 306
equitable mortgage, 309
form of, 310
legal mortgage, 308
master agreement, 310
proprietary rights, residuary,
305
transfer of, 306
transfers, absolute, 306
non-absolute, 308
trust, declaration of, 309
stocking plans, 289
hire-purchase, meaning, 22
part-exchanges, 22
security for. *See* SECURITY FOR
PRICE
total purchase, meaning, 22
valuation, agreement to sell at, 21
PRODUCT LIABILITY. *See*
LIABILITY
PROFIT
action for damages for loss of,
381
PROMISE
contractual, 118
PROPERTY
conveyance, 153
definition, 154
meaning, 6
passing of,

Property—*contd.*
  ascertainment, 157
  bill of lading, 182
  disposal, reservation of right of, 181
  generally, 157
  intention of parties, 158
  sale or return transactions,
    adoption, 178
    agency, 180
    approval or acceptance, 178
    bailment, 176
    buyer in possession, 181
    estoppel, 180
    property/title borderline, 180
    rejection, 177
    re-sale, 177
    retention, 179
    risk, 176
    seller unaware of property passing, 180
    time of passing, 177
    time-limit, 179
  specific goods, 159, 161 *et seq.*
    conditional contracts, 164
    deliverable state, 165
    intention of parties, 163
    unconditional contracts, 162
  unascertained goods, 167 *et seq.*
    appropriation, 169
    assent, 175
    delivery, 170
    future goods, 171
    generic goods, 172
    rule, 167
  personal, 154
  possession and, permutations of, 316
  rights relating to, 155
  title, distinguished from, 6
    passing, with, 155
    relationship with, 154
PROPRIETARY RIGHTS
  residuary, 305
  transfer of, 306
PROVISIONS. *See* TERMS
PURPOSE
  particular, meaning, 87

Q

QUALITY
  actions in respect of defect in, 421
  hire purchase, defect in cases of, 423
  meaning, 95
  sample, contracts by, 107
QUANTITY
  intermixed, meaning of term, 78
  mixed with, meaning of term, 78
  performance, meaning, 77
  undertakings as to, 76

R

RECOURSE PROVISIONS
  finance company, of, 290
RECOVERY
  double, 375, 386
RELIANCE
  fitness of goods, 90
REMEDIES
  election of, 147, 362
  enforcement, 364
  generally, 364
  hirer or buyer, of,
    buyer, inconsistent acts of, 400
    damages, action for, 408
      breaches of contract, various, 415
      consequential loss, 420, 425
      defect, loss caused by, 427
      delivery, late, 417
      non-delivery, 409
      quality, defect in, 421
      resale of goods, loss on, 426
      sub-sale, loss on, 421, 426
      title, defective, 416
      use, loss of, 420, 425
    rescission, 396, 402
      misrepresentation, for, 403
    restitution in quasi-contract, 404
      consideration, failure of to be total, 406
      rescission, relationship to, 405

Remedies—*contd.*
  specific performance, 428
  owner letting goods on hire purchase, 370
  quasi-contractual, 404
  seller or owner,
    damages, action for,
      breach of contract, 376
      contract of hire purchase, breach of, 384
      contributory negligence, 386
      double recovery, 386
      market, available, 382
      misrepresentation, 378
      mitigation of damage, 390
      penal sum, 394
      penalties, rule against, 391
      profit, loss of, 381
      quantification of damages, 378
      remoteness of damage, 387
      restitutio in integrum, 380
      tort, in, 376
      value of goods, 379
    lien, 366
    price or rent, action for,
      cancellation, right of, 375
      double recovery, 375
      price of goods sold, 370
      protected goods, repossession of, 375
      rentals, arrears of, 374
    resale, 365, 367
      statutory right of, 366
      title to goods, 368
    seller, discharge of, 365
    stoppage, 366
REMOTENESS
  contract, in, 388, 389
  damage, of, 387
  rules in, 388
  tort, in, 387, 389
RENT
  action for, 374
REPOSSESSION
  action for, rules governing, 339
  agents, use of, 330
  court action, through, 332
    orders of, 340

Repossession—*contd.*
  death of hirer or buyer, 342
  harassment, 331
  hire purchase, goods on, 336
  licence for, 308
  protected goods, 336, 337, 375
  self-help, through, 330
  specific delivery, order for, 340
  termination of agreement, 363
  unprotected goods, 337
REPRESENTATION
  detriment in consequence of, 193
  estoppel, 192
  fraudulent, 49
REPUDIATION
  contractual obligation, of, 360
RESCISSION
  breach of contract, for, 360, 396
    buyer, by, 397
    inconsistent acts of, 400
  breach of undertaking, for, 58
  damages in lieu of, 359
  discharge by,
    affirmation, 358
    breach of contract,
      contract treated as discharged, 361
      defective performance, 360
      repudiation, 360
    misrepresentation, for, 357
      innocent, 359
    restitutio in integrum impossible, 358
    time, lapse of, 358
  hirer, by, 402
    misrepresentation, for, 403
  intention of, 200
  misrepresentation, for, 403
RESALE
  remedy of seller, 365, 367
  title to goods, 368
  unpaid seller, right of, 315
RESTITUTION
  quasi-contract, in, 404
    failure of consideration to be total, 406
    relationship to rescission, 405
    rescission, relationship to, 405

RESTITUTIO IN INTEGRUM
  damages, action for, 380
  impossible, where, 358
RIGHTS
  transfers of. *See* TRANSFERS OF
    RIGHTS
RISK
  arrival contracts, 247
  bailment, 248
  c.i.f. contracts, 247
  delivery, delay in, 242
  ex-ship contracts, 247
  ex-works or ex-store contracts,
    246
  f.o.b. contracts, 246
  frustration, doctrine of, 256
  generally, 241
  property, follows, 241
  transit, 244

S

SALE OF GOODS
  agreement, formalities of, 32
  bailment, 248
  buyer in possession, 220
  common law, 115
  contract of sale, 6
  damages, 409
    action for, 376
  delay, 242
  delivery, 263
    time of, 273
  description, sales by, 67
  disposal, right of, 181
  estoppel, 189
  fitness, 83
  generally, 3
  implied terms, 53
  impossibility, 250
  inspection, 109
  invalidity, 37
  lien, right of, 314
  market overt, 236
  merchantability, 94
  mistake, 37
  obligations, 112
  offer and acceptance, 35

Sale of Goods—*cont.*
  payment, 271
  payment by instalments, 279
  performance by instalments, 276
  price, 21
  property, passing of, 157
  quality, defect in, 421
  quantity, 76
  remedies, 365
  rescission, 397
  right to sell, 56
  risk, 241
  sale, powers of, 238
  samples, 106
  seller, unpaid, 313
  specific goods, 161
  specific performance, 429
  stoppage, right of, 315, 325
  terms, 50, 112
  title, 55
    implied warranties as to,
      64
    property and, 154
    transfer of, 183
  transit, 244
  unascertained goods, 174
  variation, 145
  void provisions, 132
  waiver, 147
  warranty, 50
SALE OR RETURN
  adoption, 178
  agency, 180
  approval or acceptance, 178
  bailment, 176
  buyer in possession, 181
  estoppel, 180
  passing of property, 176
  property/title borderline, 180
  rejection, 177
  re-sale, 177
  retention, 179
  risk, 176
  seller unaware of property pass-
    ing, 180
  similar terms, 177
  time-limit, 179
  time of passing of property,
    177

SALE, POWERS OF
  common law, 238
  court orders, 240
  creditors, of, 239
  execution, 239
  insolvency, 239
  statutory, 239
SALEABILITY
  test of, 97
SAMPLE
  contracts by, 106
  correspondence with, 107
  description and, 108
    sales by, 101
  examination of, 102
  function of, 106
  inspection, opportunity for, 109
  quality, 107
  reasonable opportunity, meaning,
    110
  reference to, sale by, 107
  rejection, rights of, 110
  significance of, 106 *et seq.*
  title, 107
  undertakings in contracts by, 107
SECOND-HAND GOODS
  merchantability, 105
SECURITY FOR PRICE
  generally, 313
  possession, through,
    unpaid seller, 313
      buyer obtaining possession,
        322
      ceasing to be, 321
      delivery to carrier, 322
      dispositions by buyer, 324
      goods, rights against, 314
      lien by, 314
        conditions where exercis-
          able, 319
        of, 318
        termination of, 321
      possession and property,
        permutations of, 316
      resale, right of, 315
      stoppage, right of, 315
      transit, right of stoppage in,
        325, 328
      waiver, 323

Security For Price—*contd.*
  possession, without,
    agreements on hire purchase,
      court, orders of, 340
      death of hirer or buyer,
        342
      default, notice of, 334
      generally, 334
      repossession, 336
    agreements outside hire pur-
      chase,
      harassment, 331
      repossession through court
        action, 332
      repossession through self-
        help, 330
    generally, 329
  surety, provided by,
    common law, 346
    contract of surety, 348
    co-principals, 345
    discharge of, 347
    generally, 344
    guarantors, 345
    hire purchase agreements and,
      347
    indorsees, 345
    liability of, 346
    rights of, 346
    subrogation, right of, 347
SELL
  right to, 57
SELLER
  meaning, 313
  possession, in, 215 *et seq.*
  remedies of. *See* REMEDIES
  unpaid, 313
    goods, rights against, 314
    lien, right of, 314
      buyer obtaining possession,
        322
      ceasing to be unpaid seller,
        321
      conditions where exercis-
        able, 319
      delivery to carrier, 322
      dispositions by buyer, 324
      nature of, 318
      termination of, 321

Seller—*contd.*
    waiver, 323
    meaning, 314
    possession and property, per-
        mutations of, 316
    remedies of. *See* REMEDIES
    resale, right of, 315
    stoppage, right of, 315
    transit, right of stoppage in,
        325
        method of, 328
SIGNATURE
    boxes, 34
    requirement of, 33
SKILL AND LABOUR
    sale of, 23
SOLD NOTE
    significance of, 295
SPECIFIC DELIVERY
    order of court for, 340
SPECIFIC GOODS
    meaning, 159. *See also* GOODS
    passing of property in. *See*
        PROPERTY
SPECIFIC PERFORMANCE
    action by hirer or buyer, 428
SPECIFIED CONSEQUENCES
    default in hire purchase instal-
        ments, 334
SPOT CONTRACT
    meaning, 274*n.*
STANDARD FORM
    contracts, 53
STANDARDS
    consumer protection, 27
STATEMENTS
    false, 128
    liability for, 128
STATUTE
    provisions rendered void by, 132
        et seq.
STATUTE LAW
    background of, 3
    interpretation, 4
STOCKING
    dealer, plans of, 289
STOPPAGE
    remedy of seller, 366
    unpaid seller, right of, 315

SUBROGATION
    right of surety, 347
SUB-SALE
    loss on, 421
SURETIES
    categories of, 345
    common law, at, 346
    contract of surety, 348
    co-principals, 345
    discharge of, 347
    generally, 344
    guarantors, 345
    hire purchase agreements and,
        347
    indorsees, 345
    liability of, 346
    rights of, 346
    subrogation, right of, 347

T

TERMINATION
    hire purchase agreements, 354
    hiring, of, 356
TERMS
    avoidance of, 132 *et seq.*
    common law, derived from,
        114
        provisions rendered void at,
            136
    conditions, 50
    controls, 45
    express, 52
    fundamental breach, 141
    hire purchase, clauses prohibited,
        133
    implied, 53, 112 *et seq.*
    Law Commission, proposals of,
        135
    misrepresentation, 134. *See also*
        MISREPRESENTATION
    nature of, 50
    rights and duties under agree-
        ment, 113
    statute, derived from, 112
    stipulations, 51
    trade, usage of, 112
    variation of, 145

Terms—*contd.*
void at common law, provisions, 136
void, provisions rendered by statute, 132
waiver of, 132 *et seq.*
warranties, 50
THIRD-PARTY
bailee, 248
goods in transit, 326
TITLE
affirmation of agreement, 60
conveyance, 153
defective, actions in respect of, 416
document of, meaning, 207
encumbrance, freedom from, 64
implied condition as to, 56
implied undertakings as to, 55
innocent parties, rights of,
buyer or hirer, ultimate, 62
intermediate parties, 62
owner, original, 61
property, distinguished from, 6
passing with, 155
relationship with, 154
quasi-contract, rule in, 63
quiet possession, 64
resale of goods, 368
rescission, 58
sample, contracts by, 107
sell, right to, 57
transfer of,
agency, 184
bankruptcy, trustee in, 239
buyer in possession, 187
agreed to buy, meaning, 221
bona fide transferee, meaning, 226
buyer, who is, 221
delivery and disposition, meaning, 225
generally, 220
seller's consent to, 223
court orders, 240
estoppel, 187, 189
execution, 239

Title—*contd.*
hirer under hire purchase agreement, 187
liquidator, 239
market overt, sales in, 187
law, 236
meaning, 236
proposals for reform, 238
usage of, 237
mercantile agency, 187, 202
agent, meaning, 204
dispositions in ordinary course of business, 211
powers of, 203
document of title, meaning, 207
possession of, 206
generally, 202
goods, possession of, 206
owner, 210
consent of, 209
pledging of goods, 211
power of, 203
transferee to take *bona fide* and without notice, 214
motor vehicles, sale of,
generally, 230
presumptions, rebuttable, 235
private purchasers, dispositions to, 232
trade or finance purchasers, dispositions to, 234
nemo dat quod non habet, 183
exceptions to rule, 184
owner, consent of, 185
rule, 183
exceptions, 184
sale, powers of, 238
seller in possession, 187
bona fide transferee, delivery and disposition to, 218
generally, 215
possession, meaning, 216
voidable title, 187
undertakings as to, 55 *et seq.*
breach of, 58
voidable, 198 *et seq.*
warranties as to, implied, 64

TORT
 action for damages in, 376
 bailee, third-party, 248
 misstatement, negligent, 252
 remoteness in, 387, 389
 waiver, 146
TRADE
 usage of, 112
TRADE DESCRIPTION
 consumer protection, 27
TRADE DESCRIPTIONS ACT
 generally, 4
TRADE NAME
 fitness of goods sold under, 90
TRADE PREMISES
 appropriate, meaning, 40
TRANSFERS
 absolute, 32
 non-absolute, 33
TRANSFERS OF RIGHTS
 absolute, 306
 book debts, 307
 charge, 309
 contractual, 307
 equitable mortgage, 309
 legal mortgage, 308
 non-absolute, 308
 proprietary, 306
TRANSIT
 arrival contracts, 247
 buyer, carrier or bailee attorning
  to, 327
  rejection by, 327
 c.i.f. contracts, 247
 deliver, wrongful refusal to, 327
 deterioration, 244
 end of, 327
 ex-ship contracts, 247
 ex-works or ex-store contracts,
  246
 f.o.b. contracts, 246
 goods deemed to be in, 325
 interception of goods, 327
 part delivery, 328

Transit—*contd.*
 risk, 244
 stoppage in, method of, 328
  right of unpaid seller, 325
TRUST
 declaration of, 309

U

UNDERTAKINGS. *See* FITNESS;
 MERCHANTABILITY
UNPAID SELLER. *See* SELLER

V

VALUATION
 agreement to sell at, 21
VARIATION
 liability by contract, of, 145
 obligation, of, 145

W

WAIVER. *See also* TERMS
 contractual rights, 146
 delivery, of, 267
  acceptance refused, 148
 doctrine of, 146
 obligations, of, 145
 remedies, election of, 147
 tort, of, 146
 unpaid seller, lien of, 323
WARRANTY
 breach of, 415
 common law and, 115
 condition, distinguished from, 75
 definition, 50
 implied, breach of, 284
 title, as to. *See* TITLE
WEIGHTS AND MEASURES
 consumer protection, 27